Countries, Peoples & Cultures

Eastern & Southern Africa

First Edition

Volume 6

Editor

Michael Shally-Jensen, PhD

SALEM PRESS
A Division of EBSCO Information Services, Inc.
Ipswich, Massachusetts

Grey House
Publishing

Publisher's Cataloging-In-Publication Data
(Prepared by The Donohue Group, Inc.)

Eastern & Southern Africa / editor, Michael Shally-Jensen, PhD. – First edition.

    pages : illustrations ; cm. – (Countries, peoples & cultures ; v. 6)

    Includes bibliographical references and index.
    ISBN: 978-1-61925-782-5 (v. 6)
    ISBN: 978-1-61925-800-6 (set)

    1. Africa, Eastern – History. 2. Africa, Southern – History. 3. Africa, Eastern – Economic conditions. 4. Africa, Southern – Economic conditions. 5. Africa, Eastern – Social life and customs. 6. Africa, Southern – Social life and customs. 7. Africa, Eastern – Religion. 8. Africa, Southern – Religion. I. Shally-Jensen, Michael. II. Title: Eastern and Southern Africa

DT365.5 .E37 2015
967.6

First Printing
PRINTED IN CANADA

Contents

Publisher's Note

Countries, Peoples & Cultures: Eastern & Southern Africa is the sixth volume of a new 9-volume series from Salem Press. *Countries, Peoples & Cultures* offers valuable insight into the social, cultural, economic, historical and religious practices and beliefs of nearly every country around the globe.

Following the extensive introduction that summarizes this part of the world, this volume provides 20-page profiles of the 23 countries that make up the eastern and southern areas of Africa. Each includes colorful maps—one highlighting the country's location in the world, and one with its major cities and natural landmarks—and a country flag, plus 10 categories of information: General Information; Environment & Geography; Customs & Courtesies; Lifestyle; Cultural History; Culture; Society; Social Development; Government; and Economy.

Most profiles also include full color photographs, valuable tables of information including fun "Do You Know?" facts, and a comprehensive Bibliography. Each country profile combines must-have statistics, such as population, language, size, climate, and currency, with the flavor and feel of the land. You'll read about favorite foods, arts & entertainment, youth culture, women's rights, health care, and tourism, for a comprehensive picture of the country, its people, and their culture.

Appendix One: World Governments, focuses on 21 types of governments found around the world today, from Commonwealth and Communism to Treaty System and Failed State. Each government profile includes its Guiding Premise, Structure, Citizen's Role, and modern day examples.

Appendix Two: World Religions, focuses on 10 of the world's major religions from African religious traditions to Sikhism. Each religion profile includes a number of adherents, basic tenets, major figures and holy sites, and major rites and celebrations. The nine volumes of *Countries, Peoples & Cultures* are: *Central & South America; Central, South & Southeast Asia; Western Europe; Eastern Europe; Middle East & North Africa; Eastern & Southern Africa; West & Central Africa; North America & the Caribbean;* and *East Asia & the Pacific.*

Introduction

The continent of Africa is traditionally divided into five, or sometimes six, major regions. The five-region model consists of Northern (or North) Africa, Western (or West) Africa, Central Africa, Eastern (or East) Africa, and Southern Africa. Under the six-region model, Eastern Africa is further divided into East Africa (with Lake Victoria at its center) and the Horn and Middle Nile region (encompassing the Horn of Africa and inland areas). In the present series, we keep it simple and follow the five-region scheme. North Africa is, for cultural and historical reasons, included in the volume entitled *Middle East & North Africa*. Western and Central Africa are likewise dealt with in a separate volume. In the present volume we focus on Eastern and Southern Africa.

The former of these two regions, the eastern part, is made up of the following countries: Djibouti, Eritrea, Ethiopia, Somalia, and South Sudan (all of the Horn area and inland), along with, below the Horn, Burundi, Comoros, Kenya, Madagascar, Mauritius, Mozambique, Rwanda, Seychelles, Tanzania, and Uganda. Some models shift the southeastern nations of Comoros, Madagascar, Mauritius, Mozambique, and Seychelles to the southern region of Africa, but here we include them under Eastern Africa. In Southern Africa, therefore, we have Botswana, Lesotho, Malawi, Namibia, South Africa, Swaziland, Zambia, and Zimbabwe. All told, 23 nations are examined in this volume.

Geography and Environment

One feature of the African continent as a whole is the vast plateau that makes up most of it. The continent is essentially a single plateau covered with flat terrain and gently rolling hills, along with a few high peaks and rift valleys. The plateau is lower in the north and west than in the east and south, and it falls more sharply to the coast in the latter area, forming a rock face known as the Great Escarpment. The northern and western portion of the plateau has elevations of 500 to 2,000 feet, whereas the southern and eastern half generally stands above 3,000 feet. Few areas rise above 7,500 feet, however. Mount Kilimanjaro, the highest peak, reaches over 19,000 feet. Other high peaks, most of them associated with volcanic activity (as is Kilimanjaro), include mounts Meru, Kenya, and Elgon.

Although the tropical rainforest is one prominent feature of Africa's makeup, it is by no means the only or even the most prominent feature. Much of Eastern and Southern Africa, for example, consists of tropical and temperate grassland, and most of the Horn region is characterized by a steppe and desert environment. The rainforest areas are limited largely to the equatorial zone and a long coastal strip on the east extending from southern Kenya to southern Mozambique. Eastern Madagascar, too, features such a tropical strip. Inland from the coast, in the case of both Madagascar and mainland Africa, one encounters savanna grasslands and what is called tropical thorn forest, an area of mixed vegetation falling between rainforest and savanna conditions. Desert and steppes are again encountered in the Kalahari region of the south, which shades into a more temperate zone along the southern coast of South Africa.

Much of the environment is unfavorable to agriculture. Moreover, because of population growth, drought, environmental degradation, and political corruption, food shortages and outright famine have occurred frequently. The worst famines in recent times, however, have been associated not simply with drought or any one of these other conditions, but rather with wars in addition to one or more of these other conditions. Civil unrest has created millions of refugees over the decades and has disrupted the lives of millions more, exacerbating existing environmental problems—which include the depletion of animal and plant resources, the destruction of forests, the denuding and spoliation of the land, and the spreading of pollutants—and putting a strain on economies. Government neglect, and policies that actually discourage agricultural production, add further to the problem.

The obstacles to overcoming Africa's food production and environmental problems are considerable, but some leaders have begun linking economic difficulties with environmental abuse and civil conflict. Such linkage is an important first step toward improved management of agricultural commodities and other resources including the region's flora, fauna, oil, and minerals.

People

There are no fewer than 1,000 different and mutually unintelligible languages spoken in Africa, perhaps as many as half of them spoken in the eastern and southern regions, the focus of this volume. This situation has, to a degree, hindered communication between the various African peoples, since people living relatively close to one another may speak entirely separate languages. Before French, English, and, to a lesser extent, Portuguese came to be spoken as second languages by colonized African populations, certain African languages gained usage outside their native areas, thus serving as "lingua francas." One such language was Swahili, centered in the Great Lakes region (lakes Victoria and Tanganyika) of East Africa. Over time, Swahili acquired a large number of loan words from Arabic, brought by Arab traders. Even today, one or another dialect of Swahili is current as a lingua franca in many parts of East Africa.

Traditional Africa is composed primarily of rural dwellers situated in small villages or dispersed hamlets and of semi-nomadic peoples. This picture has begun to change in recent years, however, as urbanization has become an increasingly dominant trend.

The Horn region, which is separated from the Arabian Peninsula by the Red Sea, has closer cultural affinities with Egypt and the Middle East than with sub-Saharan Africa. A semi-nomadic mode of life is followed by some of the peoples (e.g., Beja, Oromo, Somali) in this region. The area is also characterized by significant internal heterogeneity in terms of peoples and languages, although Islam serves as something of a unifying force. Still, in various areas—notably, in Somalia—religious factions continue to fight among themselves.

Moving inland from the Horn, into South Sudan, the most common characteristic of the Nilotic peoples (Nuer and Dinka) is a lifestyle based on cattle raising—at least, traditionally. In recent years, warfare too has, unfortunately, become a major activity. There are other peoples in the Sudan region who are more dependent on agriculture, or, to the west, who make use of camels rather than cattle and who practice Islam rather than a traditional, or animist, religion as is practiced among the Dinka and Nuer. South Sudan is the newest nation in the world, established only in 2011 after a protracted civil war inside Sudan; yet it has still to find internal peace and begin the process of nation building.

Within the core region of East Africa, centered on the Great Lakes and vast stretches of Kenya and Tanzania, there is another cattle-raising area populated by the Masai, Kikuyu, and other ethnic groups. The area immediately surrounding the Great Lakes region, where Uganda, Rwanda, and Burundi are situated, is relatively densely populated, and is occupied by the Hutu, Tutsi, and other peoples.

Farther south, toward Lake Nyasa (in Malawi, Tanzania, and Mozambique) and westward into Zambia and Zimbabwe, one encounters a great band of Bantu-speaking peoples such as the Bemba, Shona, Thonga and, in southeastern South Africa, the Zulu, Sotho, and Xhosa. Madagascar, an island nation, has its own language and dominant ethnic group, Malagasy.

Finally, the Khoisan area of southwestern Africa is inhabited by the Khoikhoi (Khoekhoe) and San peoples, along with such groups as the Tswana, Kalanga, Kavango, and Herero. The San have traditionally made their livelihood by hunting and gathering, and the Khoikhoi primarily by raising cattle. The other groups generally practice farming, ranching, or other occupations.

History

Prior to the 19th century, most of the Europeans conducting business in sub-Saharan Africa were content to operate on the coasts and have slaves, gold, and ivory brought to them from the interior for shipment abroad. In the early 1800s, however, a more systematic exploration of the continent by European interests got underway. The so-called "scramble for Africa" was a massive effort by British, French, German, Belgian, Portuguese, and other powers to expand their control of selected areas and exploit whatever resources were present there. The colonial history of the continent is too complex to summarize here. Suffice it to say that colonialism brought repression and exploitation along with the introduction of Christianity, literacy, Western education, the beginning of modern cities, a shift toward market economies, the introduction of Western medicine and public health, and the emergence of transportation and communication networks. It also brought, especially in later decades, a desire for independence along with a new class of African politicians who sought to share in or seize the perquisites of power. Thus, even as traditional ways remained strong in the countryside, with its village-based or semi-nomadic lifestyle, its social life based on the family, the lineage, and the clan, major changes were introduced as a result of European hegemony.

After World War I the colonial era began to draw to a close, or at least to change. The British emphasized a strategy of "indirect rule," which promoted chosen local chiefs at the expense of others. The chiefs in office typically exploited their status and created rifts in traditional society. France, in contrast, pursued a policy of assimilation by the populace and direct rule by French colonial leaders. Most Africans, however, were not prepared to assume a French way of life or bow forever to French ministers. They eventually revolted. Portuguese and Belgian systems of colonial rule likewise underwent dramatic change, while German and Italian interests largely disappeared from the region between the first and second world wars. Indeed, World War II served to accelerate the rise of African nationalism. By the early 1950s, the political transformation of Africa was complete. The postwar era brought into existence some 50 new nations, with nearly as many distinct forms of government and unique, albeit often controversial, heads of state.

After a promising start, however, the years since the 1960s have been characterized by economic stasis or decline, and political instability. Many African leaders have eliminated or weakened parliamentary structures and oppositional groups in order to maintain authoritarian rule. Democratic institutions such as political parties, trade unions, and the press have suffered as a result. Since independence, most African states have experienced at least one coup d'état, and many of them more than one. Ethnic and religious conflicts have also arisen, reaching, in some cases, genocidal proportions. Yet, there is room for optimism, as African and international leaders begin to deal more realistically with the region's socioeconomic and political problems. It is notable in this regard that a Ghanaian, Kofi Annan, headed the United Nations recently, and Annan and a number of other contemporary Africans, including Wangari Maathai of Kenya, Albert Luthuli and Nelson Mandela of South Africa, and Ellen Johnson Sirleaf and Leymah Gbowee of Liberia, have won the Nobel Peace Prize.

Michael Shally-Jensen, PhD

Bibliography

Gordon, April A. and Donald L. Gordon, eds. *Understanding Contemporary Africa.* Boulder, CO, Lynne Rienner, 2012.

Grinker, Roy Richard, et al., eds. *Perspectives on Africa: A Reader in Culture, History and Representation.* Malden, MA: Wiley-Blackwell, 2010.

Maxon, Robert M. *East Africa: An Introductory History.* Morgantown, WV: West Virginia University Press, 2009.

Pakenham, Thomas. *The Scramble for Africa: White Man's Conquest of the Dark Continent from 1876 to 1912.* New York: Random House, 1991.

Straus, Scott. *Making and Unmaking Nations: War, Leadership, and Genocide in Modern Africa.* Ithaca, NY: Cornell University Press, 2015.

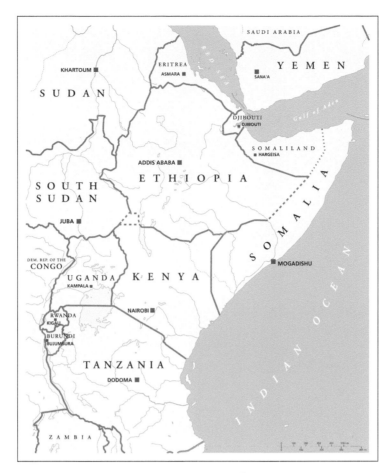

EASTERN AFRICA

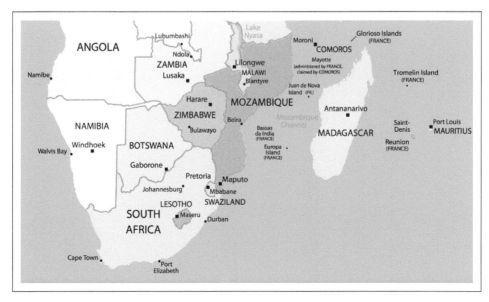

SOUTHERN AFRICA

Herero woman in traditional clothing.

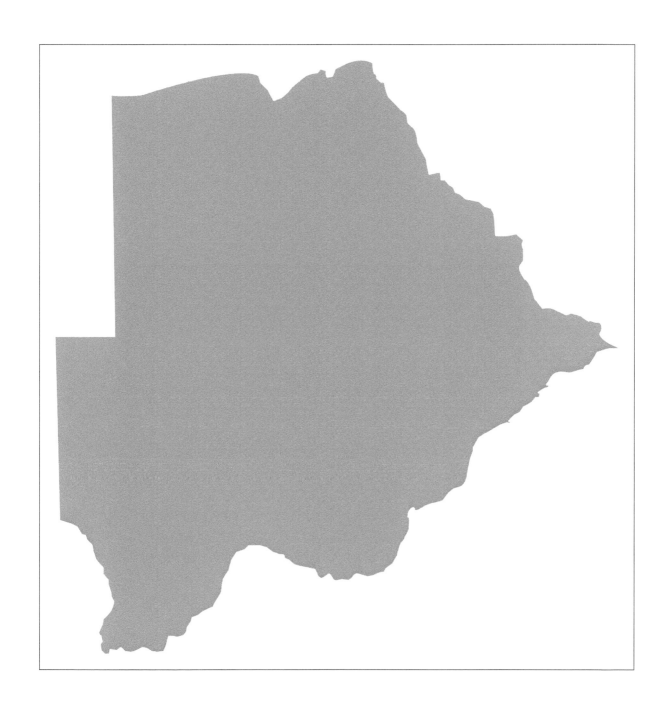

BOTSWANA

Introduction

Botswana is a landlocked country in southern Africa, bordered by Namibia on the north and west, Zimbabwe to the east, and South Africa to the south. Until 1966, Botswana was the British protectorate of Bechuanaland. Botswana's history as a British protectorate has resulted in a culture that is a blend of Tswana and English traditions. Since independence, Botswana has been a success story when compared to other African countries. The country has a stable multiparty democratic government and elections have been held every five years without interruption since 1966.

The Republic of Botswana has one of the world's fastest-growing economies even though it was once one of the poorest countries in Africa. This growth has been driven by the country's diamond mining industry. Botswana is also home to some of the last great wilderness areas in Africa, including the Kalahari Desert and the Okavango Swamps.

Botswana has the highest rate of AIDS/HIV in the world. Thankfully, this is also the country with the most developed programs designed to deal with the disease in Africa.

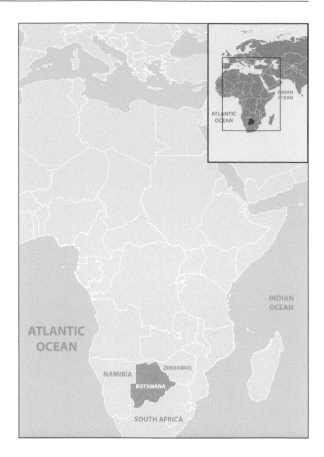

GENERAL INFORMATION

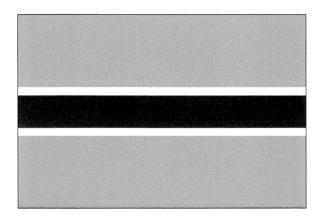

Official Language: English
Population: 2,182,719 (2015 estimate)
Currency: Pula

Coins: The pula is available in coin denominations known as thebe. One pula is equal to 100 thebe. The most commonly used coin is the 50-thebe coin but 5, 10, and 25-thebe coins are available.
Land Area: 566,730 square kilometers (218,815 square miles)
Water Area: 15,000 square kilometers (5,791 square miles)
National Motto: "Let there be rain"
National Anthem: "Fatshe leno la rona" ("Blessed Be This Noble Land")
Capital: Gaborone
Time Zone: GMT +2
Flag Description: The flag of Botswana is light blue with a vertical black and white band running across it. The blue represents rainwater and the black and white represents both the country's zebras and the concept of racial harmony.

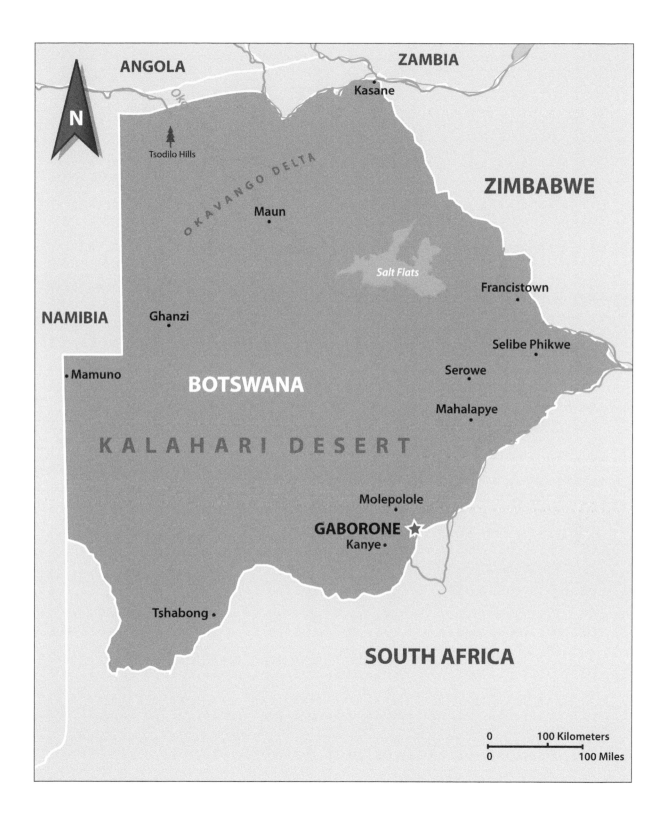

Principal Cities by Population (2012 estimate):

- Gaborone (231,598)
- Serowe (48,040)
- Francistown (101,714)
- Molepolole (69,083)
- Maun (57,067)
- Selibe Phikwe (49,777)
- Mogoditshane (60,871)
- Kanye (45,683)
- Mahalapye (41,582)
- Mochudi (45,162)

Population

Most Batswana live in large agricultural settlements or urban areas in the eastern part of the country, near the main railroad line. The rest live in smaller settlements in the western part of the country.

With about a quarter million (247,000) residents, Gaborone, along with Francistown in the northeast, is one of the most densely populated cities in Botswana. Its population is expected to more than double by 2020, reaching nearly 500,000. Much of this growth can be attributed to the influx of migrants from other areas of the country.

The indigenous peoples of Botswana, known as the San, number approximately 10,000. This population continues to live as traditional hunter-gatherers. However, in recent decades, much of this population has been forcibly moved from their lands as the population of the country continues to increase.

Languages

Although the official language of Botswana is English, a majority of the population—an estimated 79 percent—speak the Tswana language, or Setswana. It is estimated that only about two percent of the population speaks English. Numerous tribal languages are also spoken. Two other major languages are Kalanga,

spoken by about 11 percent of the people, and Kgalagadi, spoken by approximately seven percent of Batswana.

Native People & Ethnic Groups

During the Middle Stone Age, the San (also known as the Basarwa), arrived in what is now Botswana. Today, the San are the second largest hunter-gatherer group on the continent of Africa, next to the Pygmies. The San speak a "click" language in which clicks represent consonants.

The San were followed about 2,000 years ago by the Bakgothu (or Khoekhoe), a pastoral group. The Dutch called them "Hottentots." Like the San, they spoke a click language. They raised large herds of cattle and flocks of sheep, and smelted iron and made pottery. Today, small groups of both the San and Khoekhoe continue to live a nomadic lifestyle. Concurrently, the Bantu were moving into what is now Botswana. They were an agricultural people, with settled villages and large herds of livestock. In time, the Bantu conquered the San and the Khoekhoe.

Around 1300 CE, three groups formed in what is now Botswana: the Batswana, Basotho, and Bakgalagadi. During the next several centuries, groups split off, migrated and formed new communities, and merged with and subjugated other groups. As a result, by the 19th century, numerous Batswana and Bakgalagadi tribes lived in the area.

During the early 19th century, tribal wars decimated the population. In the latter half of the century, the Boers from Transvaal made incursions into what was then known as Bechuanaland. Local chiefs appealed to Britain, and in 1885, the British declared Bechuanaland a British protectorate.

Almost 80 percent of the people are Tswana in the early 21st century. The Kalanga, who constitute eight percent of the population, are the next largest group. Minority groups include the Ndebele, the Herero, the San, and Afrikaners (White African), each accounting for less than two percent of the population.

Because of its many immigrant residents, the population of the capital of Botswana, Gaborone, represents a diverse mixture of Botswana's various ethnic groups. The largest of these is the Tswana, traditionally a village people whose societies are built around the importance of the chief. Other African ethnic groups living in Gaborone include the Kalanga, the Khalagari, the Tswapong, and the Birwa. The city is also home to a small number of white Botswana citizens and, to a much lesser extent, Chinese immigrants. The various ethnic groups are proud of their peaceful, cooperative society.

Religions

There is no established church in Botswana, and freedom of religion is guaranteed in the constitution. Estimates of the percentage of people who adhere to different religions vary widely; according to the CIA World Factbook, an estimated 71 percent of the population is Christian. Several religions are followed, including some Christian denominations and Badimo (six percent), a system of traditional animist beliefs. According to a 2001 census, slightly more than 20 percent of the people claim no religion at all.

Climate

The climate of Botswana is semi-arid. Rain is so precious that the Setswana word for rain, "pula," is the name of the nation's currency. The rainy season comes during the summer months, between November and March. The average annual rainfall varies across the country. In the northeast, along the Chobe, precipitation may measure more than 650 millimeters (26 inches), while the Kalahari Desert may get less than 250 millimeters (10 inches).

In spite of the rain, summer is hot, with an average temperature of 38° Celsius (100° Fahrenheit), sometimes climbing to 44° Celsius (111° Fahrenheit). Summer is also very humid. Winter is dry, with sunny, cool days. At night, temperatures can drop to freezing, particularly in the southwest.

Natural hazards include frequent droughts. In August, sandstorms and dust storms often blow from the west. The storms obscure visibility, contribute to respiratory, and eye diseases.

ENVIRONMENT & GEOGRAPHY

Topography

Botswana is a small, landlocked country in southern Africa. It is bounded on a short section of the north by Zambia, on the northeast by Zimbabwe, on the south and southeast by South Africa, and on the west and north by Namibia.

The Kalahari Desert covers about 84 percent of the country's area and extends into South Africa, Angola, and Namibia. About two-thirds of Botswana (in the north) is in the tropics. The Tsodilo Hills in the northwest are the site of the country's highest point at 1,489 meters (4,885 feet) above sea level. The lowest point, 513 meters (1,683 feet) lies at the junction of the Limpopo and Shashe rivers.

Most of the terrain is flat or gently rolling. The east is rocky and dry. The southeast is higher, a little wetter, and slightly more fertile. The Kalahari is infertile and very dry.

Botswana is watered by four main rivers: the Chobe, Cubango, Cuando, and Limpopo. The Cubango or Kuvango (formerly Okavango) is the longest river in Botswana at 1,609 kilometers (1,000 miles). It rises in Angola, forms part of the Angola-Namibia border, and meanders through northern Botswana. It eventually forms the Okavango Delta, a huge inland swamp.

The Okavango Delta, one of the largest drainage deltas in Africa, is a 12,590-square kilometer (5,000-square mile) depression that once held a prehistoric lake. The northern part of the swamp is wet all year and supports papyrus growth. The southern part is wet only in the rainy season. The delta supports an abundance of wildlife, especially birds and crocodiles.

Plants & Animals

Botswana is home to about 200 edible wild plant species. These are particularly important for hunter-gatherer groups such as the San. Tsamma melons and wild cucumbers, in particular, are useful to both humans and wildlife.

Though most of country is savannah (covered with shrubs, thornbush, trees or grass), Botswana is home to more than 3,000 species

Zebras are highly social, undomesticated creatures that roam the semi-arid land of Botswana.

of plants. Small areas of forest survive, consisting of several species of acacia and mopane (ironwood), with some mogonono (silver leaf), marula and baobab trees.

Animals are numerous, including 550 species of birds, more than 150 species of mammals, 150 species of reptiles, and eighty species of fish. A total of 17 percent of the land area is set aside in national parks and game reserves. Controlled hunting is allowed in the reserves, and there is little poaching in Botswana.

Typical wildlife includes lions, leopards and cheetahs, giraffes, elephants and hippos, aardvarks, jackals and foxes, monkeys, bushbabies and baboons. The zebra is considered by many to be the official animal of Botswana. The local name for the zebra is makgabisa naga, meaning, "to make the bush beautiful."

Most bird species live in the Okavango Delta or along the Chobe River. Species include vultures, ostriches, darters, eagles (such as the African fish eagle), doves (including the Cape Turtle dove and Namaqua dove), bee-eaters, bustards, oxpeckers, weaverbirds, whydahs, and the forktailed drongo. The lilac-breasted roller is the unofficial national bird.

Crocodiles sun themselves on rocks alongside rivers. Other reptiles include pythons, black mambas, several species of cobras (including the spitting cobra), the puff adder and horned adder, and the boomslang. Botswana is also home to numerous lizards, including gekkos and chameleons.

CUSTOMS & COURTESIES

Greetings

In Botswana, recognition of others is often of supreme importance. This may include recognition of a job well done, congratulations for a particular milestone or reward, or compliments on an achievement. There is no better opportunity to recognize others, however, than with an introductory greeting. Indeed, to ignore another's greeting is considered a serious offense and insult.

Batswana typically shake hands upon greeting and departing. There are two distinct ways that most Batswana will shake hands, and the method used in any situation is dictated by relationship. When shaking hands with a stranger or superior (professional or familial), Batswana will shake with their right hand and customarily use the left hand to hold, or support, the right elbow. When shaking hands with close friends, Batswana will shake with their right hand and customarily hold the right arm above the wrist with the left hand. The actual grasp of the handshake is often gentle, sometimes little more than a tender touching of fingers and palms.

People will always greet each other as they approach and ask how the other is doing. Again, due to the widely held belief that recognition is paramount, not greeting another would be a serious insult. The universal greeting is "dumela," followed by the polite forms of address "rra" for men and "mma" for women. Some specific customs surrounding greetings vary according to culture. For example, among the Tswana, elders greet, and are greeted in return, before anyone else. Among the Kalanga, the younger person displays his or her respect by first recognizing and greeting the elder.

Gestures & Etiquette

Like many African and Middle Eastern cultures, customs regarding physical proximity and contact in Botswana are considerably different than they are in Western cultures. For example, it is normal for strangers, just after being introduced, to stand in very close proximity to each other. Good friends of the same sex will often hold hands in public. It is common to see two men or two women openly walking hand in hand down the street. In addition, public displays of affection between men and women are not normal or accepted in Botswana.

When exchanging items or gifts with another person, Batswana will use both hands to give and receive. Sometimes, they will give or receive with the right hand; the left hand is typically used to support the elbow of the right arm. It is impolite to only use the left hand when exchanging an object with another person. Some people may press their palms and fingers together in front of their chest as a sign of thanks before accepting a gift.

Eating/Meals

Mealtime is generally time for families to sit down and enjoy each other's company. Urban families tend to eat a mostly Western-style diet, while families in villages usually eat a larger proportion of traditional dishes. Tea or coffee with a sorghum or maize meal porridge is a particularly popular breakfast. This porridge is a staple of the Botswana diet and is eaten at all times of day. For breakfast, it is often thinned with soured milk, sugar, or tea.

Lunch often consists of bogobe (a thicker version of the staple porridge), samosas, sandwiches, steak, or chicken. For dinner, steak is a popular choice (given that it is plentiful and relatively cheap in Botswana). However, most Batswana will eat leftovers from lunch or a simple meal of tea and bread. Beverages are consumed after the meal, rather than during. Many larger cities and towns now have more options for international dining, and though many families still buy fresh ingredients at markets to cook at home, young Batswana are increasingly choosing to dine out.

Visiting

Among Batswana, unannounced visits are traditionally common, especially in rural areas where technology is scarce. Often an unlocked door is all the invitation one needs to enter. Today, even though cell phone use has proliferated widely, this custom continues.

Batswana typically will only extend formal invitations to their homes for special occasions, such as weddings or religious events. The Western customs of inviting friends over or entertaining at home are very rarely followed. Most Batswana assume that if you want to visit, then you will choose a convenient day and time to drop by of your own accord.

LIFESTYLE

Family

In Botswana, different ethnic groups maintain unique traditions regarding the family, its structure and its significance. Despite any differences that may exist, however, there are still many common features to most of these cultural groups. These include respect for elders and the importance of the extended family. Traditionally, the family, rather than the individual, is viewed as the basic unit of social organization. Children are expected to respect and obey their parents and grandparents, often without question or hesitation. There is also an understanding that they will provide support for the older generations as they age.

Among the Tswana and other cultures, families typically include several households with ancestral ties to a single grandfather or great-grandfather. Historically, they are patriarchal, with the husband considered to be the absolute head of each household. Age certainly plays a factor in family relationships. Older brothers generally take precedence over their younger siblings and can wield considerable control over them. Uncles and male cousins also play important roles. This male-dominated structure has steadily changed to allow for more equality between husbands and wives.

Marriage was traditionally arranged by parents, and today can be either civil or customary. Marriage occurs in villages and is recognized when parents make an agreement (patlo), usually inclusive of a bride price, and celebrate the union at a patlo ceremony. Among most cultural groups in Botswana, the practice of paying a bride price has traditionally finalized the bonding of two individuals. The payment, called bogadi, is paid to the bride's parents by the groom's parents. Symbolically, the payment is given in thanksgiving and respect for raising a suitable woman and in honor of the new marriage. Different cultural groups have different "rates," but payment is usually in live cattle. Like many aspects of traditional life, the practice of paying a bogadi is disappearing in modern Botswana, and many modern weddings now resemble their Western counterparts.

Housing

Traditionally, Batswana families maintained three separate homes: one in the village, one on the farm, and one further afield at the cattle post. Though people in larger cities today tend to live in manufactured concrete apartment buildings or homes, many still maintain these multiple homes.

Houses in villages tend to conform to the traditional roundhouse style known as rondavels. They are made of clay (traditionally, a mixture of mud and cow dung) and have thatched, conical straw roofs supported by a series of wooden poles. This is the primary household and where families spend much of their time. Villages are designed with the kgosi, or tribal chief, and his family at the center. The location of one's house, relative to the kgosi, is mostly determined by familial or other relationships. Relatives are closest to the center, and those with no relation to the kgosi (and non-Batswana) line the outermost periphery of the village.

Farm and cattle post homes are generally smaller, simpler structures. Traditionally, only men stay at the cattle post, which is where livestock is kept and is often part of a compound consisting of several households' cattle and agricultural fields. The San people are nomadic and their homes are typically temporary, circular huts made from a combination of branches and grass.

Food

The semi-arid climate of Botswana considerably limits the agricultural potential of the soil. Staple crops include cereal grain–corn, sorghum, and millet–and a number of vegetables. Meat is supplied (often in abundance) by widespread cattle ranching. Today, more and more people are eating maize (cornmeal), rather than sorghum, as it is widely available in stores and markets. Chicken, lamb, mutton, and goat are other common meats. Subsistence farming and ranching, however, remains a way of life for many cultural groups in Botswana, and nearly half of the entire population.

Many typical and traditional dishes in Botswana utilize the staple crops of corn and sorghum, and focus on beef. Flour is usually pounded manually from the grains and then made into a type of porridge–varieties of which are likely to appear at any meal. Ting, a typical breakfast dish, is a thinned version of this porridge with soured milk, sugar, and/or tea added. A thicker version of this porridge, often mixed with beef and vegetables and called bogobe, is a common lunch or dinner dish. Ting and bogobe are both highly nutritious and inexpensive, part of the reason for their popularity and profusion throughout the country.

Two other dishes unique to Botswana are seswaa and serobe. Seswaa is a dish often served at special occasions, and consists of beef or goat meat boiled in a special three-legged pot, pounded until it is soft and flaky, and then seasoned only with salt. Serobe is a boiled mixture of intestines, tripe, and other internal organs (usually of a goat, sheep, or cow). The meat is served in small pieces with seasoning. Other popular, and unique, ingredients to Botswana cuisine include bitlong (cured strips of meat) and ditloo, a groundnut similar to the peanut that is eaten fresh or grilled. Among the San, the mopane worm, a grub, is considered a delicacy.

The grub is dried in the sun and eaten raw, boiled, roasted, or fried.

Strong palm wine is a traditional drink. Another drink is Kgadi, which is made from distilled sugar or fungi. Ginger beer is a favorite homemade non-alcoholic beverage. Coca-Cola and Fanta soft drinks are also manufactured in Botswana.

Life's Milestones

For most Batswana, the major milestones include birth, puberty, marriage, and death. The most significant rite of passage is the initiation ceremony known as bogwera for boys and bojale for girls. Children, around the age of puberty, would enter special "schools" away from their families that, traditionally, lasted for three months. During this time, children would learn the traditions and customs of their village and culture from tribal elders. Boys would learn how to hunt for food, the duties and responsibilities of men, and the importance of honoring and obeying elders, particularly the chief. The bogwera would culminate with circumcision for all boys – the symbolic final step from boyhood to manhood. At the bojale, girls learned about the traditional female duties of household maintenance, cooking, and rearing and raising children.

After the groups of boys and girls returned to their homes and villages, they were considered adults and ready for marriage. Traditionally, males who didn't attend the bogwera were not considered real men; they couldn't sit on the village council or marry. Today, the ceremonies are much altered. At the bogwera, hunting and the responsibilities of men are still emphasized, but the ritual circumcision has been abandoned and the entire event is no longer considered an essential rite. The bojale is also much altered and, in fact, rarely performed.

CULTURAL HISTORY

Art

Despite the prevalence of art from surrounding southern African countries, Botswana has comparatively little in the way of traditional and unique art or architecture. There are some elements of folk art, however. Important handicrafts in modern Botswana include basket weaving, pottery, woodcarving, and leatherwork.

The oldest evidence of art is found in the Tsodilo Hills, located in northwestern Botswana in the Kalahari Desert. This area contains the highest concentration of rock art in the world. Attributed to the San people, the rock art dates from between 1,000 and 2,000 years ago and is considered sacred by the San minority culture. Today, the San are known for continuing the ancient arts of decorating ostrich eggshells for jewelry and creating ostrich eggshell beads. In their view, these objects represent good luck and fortune. Archaeologists believe this type of bead to be the oldest known manmade bead. The beads have been recovered at archaeological sites in eastern and southern Africa that date back 28,000 to 45,000 years.

Architecture

Traditional architecture is distinguished by the use of natural materials such as mud walls, wooden supports, and thatched roofs. Houses are typically round and the walls are usually decorated with murals. Known as lekgapho, the murals depict a variety of cultural and natural scenes. These murals were generally very detailed and vibrant, but are in danger of disappearing entirely as more people choose to build modern homes out of concrete.

Drama & Dance

Song and dance performances are traditionally part of every public holiday celebration, and every significant religious and spiritual event. Dances, like music, vary according to region and culture. Examples of such dances include the setapa, a celebratory dance performed at weddings and by youths as they return to their villages and families from initiation schools. The kalanga is a dance to bring rain to the mostly desert environment of the Kalahari.

Just as much of the music in Botswana has a call-and-response between a solo vocalist and a chorus of singers, the dances follow a similar pattern. Female dancers typically use exaggerated hip movements and facial expressions to mimic the intensity and beauty of the music. Most rhythmic dances also end with an exuberant and high-pitched wail by one of the female participants.

Clothing is an important aspect of any dance in Botswana. While most modern Batswana wear Western-style clothing, appropriate clothing is still worn when performing traditional dances. Men usually wear short loincloths (or their equivalent), and women wear leather skirts and elaborately decorated headdresses. Leg rattles, worn for both their fashionable and musical attributes, are also an essential part of the wardrobe required for traditional dancing.

Music

For many Batswana, music is intimately connected with the natural world in which they live. Traditional music (among many cultural groups) focuses on the human voice and stringed instruments. In a general sense, music has historically been linked to specific events, ceremonies, or special occasions. Vocal music has also been historically linked to dance. Traditional dances are usually accompanied by energetic music that features drums, leg rattles, whistles, and hand clapping. Songs are often cyclical and repetitive, with a precise meter, and follow a call-and-response pattern, both musically and lyrically.

Traditional instruments are often made from elements found in Botswana's desert and semi-arid climate. Common instruments among Botswana's many cultures include the segaba, setinkane, moropa, and lengope. The segaba is a one-stringed instrument played with a short bow made of animal skin; it has a resonator typically made with a tin can. The setinkane, or hand piano, is made with metal tongues of different lengths attached to a piece of wood. It is sometimes mounted inside a gourd, and notes are produced by plucking the metal tongues with the thumbs. The moropa, or drum, is often made by stretching animal skin over a bucket, plastic jug, or other similar object. The lengope, or mouth bow, is made with a single string attached to a bowed piece of wood. One end of the instrument is placed in front of an open mouth; different notes are made by altering the shape and size of the opening as the string is plucked.

Literature

Botswana has a long oral tradition of storytelling and praise poetry. Folktales, known as mainane, were retold and passed down through the generations by grandparents. These stories often included giants and other mythical creatures, and they typically dealt with such familiar concepts as the weak defeating the mighty and the trouble caused by trickster animals. Praise poetry, usually written in honor of and dedicated to tribal chiefs, are usually recognized as some of the most refined and sophisticated forms of the art. Proverbs also form an integral part of Botswana's cultural heritage. These stories typically have moral lessons. Like folktales, they begin not with the conventional "Once upon a time…," but with the more pragmatic "It is said that…"

A national literature that developed through the most widely used languages—Setswana, English, or San—was never established. Despite this, there have been several remarkable writers whose work was influenced by and rooted in the native Botswana culture. These include Bessie Head (1937–1986), who is widely regarded as the country's most important author. She arrived in Botswana in 1964 as a refugee. Her novels subsequently focused on the difficulties and challenges faced by individuals living within a foreign and unfamiliar culture. Specifically, her work details her racially mixed identity and struggle—she was the offspring of a wealthy Scottish woman and a black servant—as well as African poverty and history.

CULTURE

Arts & Entertainment

Completely landlocked in southern Africa, Botswana is particularly susceptible to cultural trends and influences from surrounding countries, chiefly South Africa. Though there is a burgeoning arts scene native to Botswana, there is not a widespread arts culture that has defined the country with real significance.

The National Museum and Art Gallery in Gaborone is the centerpiece of modern art in the country. It is widely regarded as one of the best art galleries in the region and holds regular exhibitions highlighting the work of local artists. The museum also sponsors an annual celebration for local art and artists. Twentieth- and 21st century Batswana painters include Coex'ae Qgam (1934–2008), Ann Gollifer (1960–), Neo Matome (1967–), and the San painter Thamae Setshogo (c. 1970–2004). The annual Maitisong Festival, held in spring, is the country's largest celebration of the performing arts. The festival includes free outdoor performances at city arenas as well as ticketed indoor events at Gaborone's theaters and arts venues.

Local handcrafts, supported in large part by the tourist trade, are generally utilitarian. Handwoven baskets, one of the specialties associated with Botswana, are of extremely high quality. Made almost exclusively in the Okavango region, they are woven with the leaves of the mokolwane palm. They utilize various roots and barks in order to give the baskets their unique colors and designs (typically associated with the nation's traditional lifestyle). Due to the abundance of cattle livestock, leatherwork has also developed as an important handicraft. Traditionally used to make clothing, blankets, and sleeping mats, leather is today more often used to make designer bags, belts, and accessories. In addition, the town of Oodi is known for their skilled weavers, and the country is home to several traditional potteries.

Historically, many of the writers who have written about Botswana have done so from an anthropological perspective, focusing on the San or one of the other pastoral cultures that live in and around the Kalahari Desert. Writers of fiction have tended to be individuals distinguished by prominent cross-cultural characteristics. Unity Dow (1959–) is one of the best-known contemporary female writers in Botswana. She combines her rural, traditional upbringing with the modern realities of an increasingly urban Botswana in novels such as *Far and Beyon'* (2000) and *The Screaming of the Innocent* (2002). Perhaps no other author, however, has brought Botswana into the Western mass consciousness like Alexander McCall Smith (1948–). Born in what is now Zimbabwe and educated in Scotland, McCall Smith spent many years in southern Africa and has brought the traditions and cultures of Botswana to the pages of his *The No. 1 Ladies' Detective Agency* series of novels.

Cultural Sites & Landmarks

Botswana is home to a wealth of traditional communities and natural sites, but the country's cultural capital is the city of Gaborone. Considered one of the fastest expanding cities on the continent, the capital is home to numerous cultural sites and landmarks, including the National Museum and Art Gallery, the University of Botswana (the country's only such institution of higher learning), and the National Sports Museum. The city also contains several monuments such as the Pula Arch, which commemorates the country's independence, the War Memorial, which honors Batswana who fought in World War II, and a statue of Seretse Khama, the first president of Botswana.

Botswana is also home to various significant archaeological sites, namely the Tsodilo Hills, a United Nations Educational, Scientific, and Cultural Organization (UNESCO) World Heritage Site. The site boasts the world's largest concentration of prehistoric rock paintings. An archeological site known as the Matsieng Footprints is home to footprints attributed to a legendary, ancestral giant. The site was declared a national monument in 1971.

Botswana is primarily known for its unparalleled wildlife tourism. Over 17 percent of Botswana's land has been set aside for national parks and game preserves, namely the Moremi Game Reserve and Chobe National Park. The Okavango Delta and Kalahari Desert are also popular for their natural resources. These vast stretches of wilderness are home to some of the most spectacular natural scenery and wildlife in the world. The Okavango Delta is one of the world's largest inland water systems and supports a staggering diversity of wildlife in the heart of the Kalahari Desert.

Chobe National Park is often cited as one of the best wildlife-viewing locations in Africa. It is home to one of the largest concentrations of wildlife on the continent, including what is arguably the largest surviving continuous population of elephants. Some of the species that are prevalent in the parks and preserves of Botswana include giraffes, elephants, hippopotamuses, zebras, rhinoceroses, impalas, wildebeests, kudus, buffaloes, waterbucks, warthogs, lions, hyenas, jackals, leopards, and cheetahs.

The Okavango Delta was the 1000th site added to the World Heritage list in 2014.

Libraries & Museums

In the center of Gaborone, the National Museum and Art Gallery serves as a showcase for artifacts, crafts, and artwork that reflect Botswana's history and culture. One of its main exhibits is a replica of a traditional hut and a display of different modes of transportation. Headquartered in Gaborone, the Botswana National Library Services serves as both the national library and the national public library service.

Holidays

Independence Day, also called Botswana Day, is celebrated on September 30. Other official holidays include Labour Day (May 1), President's Day (date varies), and Christmas, which is celebrated on both December 25 and 26.

Sir Seretse Khama Day (July 1) honors the first president of Botswana. He was elected four times, beginning in 1966, and died in office in 1980.

Youth Culture

Botswana has one of the highest rates of HIV/AIDS infection in the world, a pandemic that has significantly affected Batswana youth. As a result, the spread and treatment of HIV/AIDS is one of the most important issues facing youth

in Botswana in the early twenty-first century. In recent years, non-governmental organizations (NGOs) and youth agencies have made HIV/AIDS awareness and education a priority. According to a 2008 report on the global AIDS epidemic prepared by the Joint United Nations Programme on HIV/AIDS (UNAIDS), 23.9 percent of all Batswana between the ages of 15 and 49, and 61 percent of women in the same age range, are living with HIV/AIDS. The report also estimated that 15,000 Batswana children under the age of fifteen are living with HIV/AIDS.

Batswana youth also struggle with securing high level or white-collar employment, while an influx of migrant workers (specifically from Zimbabwe) have secured a large percentage of low wage jobs. It is also estimated that less than 10 percent of youth achieve a postsecondary education. Despite these challenges, Batswana youth still strive for more inclusion in their government and actively work for causes in which they believe. They also enjoy pastimes typical of youth in many countries, such as shopping, dancing, socializing, and frequenting bars and clubs that are common in urban areas. Football (soccer) is the most popular youth sport, with cricket and rugby also gaining in popularity.

SOCIETY

Transportation

Gaborone, the capital, has an established public transportation system of minibuses (known as taxis or combos) that follow set routes throughout the city. Passenger's share the minibuses with others, paying a small fee for a ride. Private taxies are also available, but are significantly more expensive. Most of Botswana's major roadways are paved. Vehicles travel on the left hand side of the road.

Botswana Railways operates regular service throughout the country. Service is air-conditioned and dining facilities are available. Air Botswana offers domestic service to Gaborone, Francistown, Maun, and Kasane.

Transportation Infrastructure

Botswana is a sparsely populated country with an unforgiving climate and terrain. Connecting the people within this landlocked country with a viable transportation infrastructure has always been a challenge. The nation has a relatively extensive network of roadways, and major towns and district capitals are now connected by paved highways. Botswana Railways, mainly used to transport freight, has passenger lines that connect Gaborone to Francistown and Lobaste to Bulawayo in Zimbabwe.

Internationally, the Trans-Kalahari Highway connects Botswana to the port of Walvis Bay in Namibia. The main airport in Botswana is the Sir Seretse Khama International Airport in Gaborone, and another international airport is located in Francistown. As of 2015, there are 74 total airports throughout Botswana, 10 paved and 64 unpaved. Air Botswana connects and serves all major cities.

Media & Communications

The Botswana constitution guarantees the freedom of speech and expression to its people. These rights extend to (and are generally respected for) public and private media agencies. As such, Botswana has a very active and independent press. There are seven weekly newspapers (government-owned and private, in both Setswana and English), several radio stations, and the government-owned national Botswana Television. Radio is the most pervasive and important medium of communication. The state-run monopoly, Radio Botswana, has since been replaced by two stations—RB1 (broadcast entirely in Setswana) and RB2 (broadcast in a roughly even mix of Setswana and English). Private radio stations are steadily increasing their presence outside of Gaborone.

Botswana has one of the most modern and extensive telecommunications infrastructures in Africa. All major cities and population centers are connected via fiber-optic networks. There are approximately 170,000 telephone lines connected to this network, translating to about eight lines per 100 people in 2014. There are also 3.4 million total mobile cellular phones in use. Access to the Internet, as in many countries, has experienced unprecedented growth and influence among the current generation. According to the World Factbook, there were a total of 283,500 internet users in 2014. This number only accounts for about 13 percent of the total population.

SOCIAL DEVELOPMENT

Standard of Living

Botswana ranked 109th on the United Nations 2013 Human Development Index, which measures quality of life indicators.

Water Consumption

The availability of fresh drinking water in Botswana is severely limited. The country experiences low levels of rainfall and drought conditions are common. Botswana's increasing population has begun to test water supply levels and water infrastructure. The government has teamed with private contractors to improve storage and pipeline facilities. Seven dams throughout Botswana provide both water and electricity to surrounding regions. The water from dams and rivers make up roughly one-third of the country's total water consumption.

Education

Education is not compulsory in Botswana. As of 2014, Botswana has about 512,000 students enrolled in schools. The primary schools consist of 65 percent of school-aged children. Only 35 percent are enrolled in secondary school. Girls outnumber boys at both levels. Primary education, for children between the ages of seven and thirteen, was free until 2006, when the government reintroduced a fee system. Secondary education is offered in two cycles, of three years (lower secondary), consisting of 120,000 students, and two years (upper secondary), consisting of 61,000 students.

The University of Botswana was established in 1982 in Gaborone. Botswana also has a number of technical schools and colleges. Many students who attend college do so under a government sponsorship.

The average literacy rate in 2015 is 88.5 percent (88 percent among men and 88.9 percent among women). In 2014, the pupil/teacher ratio for Botswana's primary education was an estimated 25.4-to-1. The ratio for secondary education was estimated at 15-to-1.

Women's Rights

Traditionally, women in Botswana were regarded as second-class citizens, both culturally and legally. However, in the years since independence – and particularly in the two decades around the turn of the 21st century – the government has made considerable steps toward gender equality. Women continue to face discrimination from traditional practices, but they are steadily securing legal rights and gaining a foothold in both local and national politics.

Customary law is still practiced in certain regions of the country, particularly in places where the concept of male dominance is prevalent. Under traditional customary law, a woman has no direct right to property and cannot enter into legal contracts without her husband's consent. Additionally, traditional society expects men to marry younger women, which creates an unequal power hierarchy based on age. Domestic violence and rape also continue to be serious problems in Botswana. The county has been suspected as a source, transit, and destination country for human trafficking for the purposes of labor and sexual exploitation. Lastly, gender inequality has significantly affected the spread of HIV/AIDS. Botswana has one of the highest rates of infection in the world, and entrenched cultural practices and discrimination has lead to a disproportionate number of affected women.

Despite these challenges, many significant steps have been made in the direction of equality. The Criminal Procedures and Evidence Act of 1996 mandated the hearing of sexual offenses. The Deed Registration Act of 1996 allowed women to execute deeds and enter into legal contracts without spousal consent, the Abolition of Marital Powers Act of 2004 granted women equal property rights and guardianship over children, and the Domestic Violence Act of 2008 instituted additional protection for victims of violence and abuse. In addition, women have achieved better representation in the federal government and are now allowed to sit on local kgotla, or traditional tribal councils. The emergence of female kgosi, or tribal chiefs, is also testament to the development and acceptance of widespread women's rights in Botswana.

In 2012, a ruling in Botswana brought a big improvement in women's rights. A five-year battle between Molefi Ramantele and his aunts, Edith Mmusi and her sisters, finally ended in the favor of equality. Ramantele felt that, due to Botswana's customs, he should inherit his aunts' property. The judge, Key Dingake, ruled in favor of the sisters, and made the point that women should be allowed to inherit property.

Health Care

In 2003, the World Health Organization (WHO) estimated life expectancy in Botswana as only 36 years for men and 35 years for women. Later estimates are even lower. The figures reflect the high death rate from AIDS. Botswana has one of the highest known rates of HIV/AIDS infection in the world. On the other hand, the country also has one of the best programs in Africa for dealing with AIDS.

Other high-risk diseases in Botswana include bacterial diarrhea, hepatitis A, typhoid fever, and malaria. With roughly one doctor for every 2,500 people, it is difficult to combat such illnesses.

GOVERNMENT

Structure

Botswana is a multiparty republic with a unicameral legislature and a strong presidential system. Suffrage is universal at age eighteen.

The president is head of state and head of government. The president is elected to a five-year term, and may serve only two terms. The president appoints the members of the cabinet, which is responsible to the National Assembly.

The president and the 61-member National Assembly constitute the legislature. Fifty-seven of the assembly members are directly elected to five-year terms, and the other four are elected from a list drawn up by the president. The president can dissolve the National Assembly. The 15-member House of Chiefs must approve some legislation, but the House has no veto. The most recent elections for the National Assembly were held on October 24, 2014.

The judiciary branch is independent of the executive and legislative branches. The High Court is the highest court in the land.

Political Parties

The most well-known and influential political party in Botswana is the Botswana Political Party (BDP). Other parties include the Botswana Movement for Democracy, the Botswana Congress Party, the Botswana People's Party, and the International Socialist Organization. Botswana has held free and fair elections since 1966. On April 1 2008, President Seretse Khama Ian became chief of state.

Local Government

Botswana is divided into 10 districts, which are overseen by district councils. Each council has a commissioner, which is appointed by the central government. In addition, the Ministry of Local Government oversees community projects related to water and education infrastructure in each district. The ministry also oversees the work of district councils and district council commissioners.

Judicial System

Law is based on Roman-Dutch law and customary law. Botswana's judiciary consists of the High Court, Court of Appeal, and Magistrates Courts. Each of Botswana's nine districts has its own Magistrate Court. English law, by way of South Africa, also influenced the development of the country's judicial system. Botswana's criminal laws and contract laws are based on English law. All judges who are appointed are allowed to serve until they are 70 years of age.

Taxation

Corporations operating in Botswana are responsible for a value-added tax (VAT), which replaced a general sales tax in 2002. In Botswana, charitable and religious donations are not taxed. In recent years, the government has moved to simplify the country's tax code in order to stimulate foreign investment in the economy. Citizens pay an annual income tax. Botswana is a member of the Common Custom's Area (CCU), which includes South Africa, Lesotho, Swaziland, and Namibia. Taxes in Botswana account for 33.4 percent of the country's GDP in 2014.

Armed Forces

Botswana's military is known as the Botswana Defence Force (BDF). The president serves as commander in chief of the BDF. The BDF was formed in 1977 and consists of the Botswana Air Force and the Botswana Ground Force. The country apportions approximately 3.5 percent of GDP to military expenditures. There are approximately 12,000 soldiers enrolled in the BDF. Much of the BDF's work is focused on anti-poaching missions and foreign peacekeeping.

Foreign Policy

As a landlocked nation in the heart of southern Africa, Botswana has always had a significant interest in maintaining a peaceful and stable region. The government is the oldest democracy in Africa. As such, it continually seeks to maintain positive relations with its direct neighbors, Namibia, South Africa, and Zimbabwe. The capital of Gaborone is also one of the primary centers for trade and diplomacy in the region, and the host city of the 15-nation Southern African Development Community (SADC). Botswana is also a member of the African Union (AU), and has particular interest in a healthy and prosperous South Africa. Since the end of apartheid, Botswana has welcomed South Africa as a vital partner in the effort to not only stabilize and integrate the region, but also create a more independent community of nations in southern Africa.

Internationally, Botswana is a member of the United Nations (UN) and subscribes to all standard treaties. As a former British protectorate, it is also a member of the Commonwealth of Nations. Botswana maintains friendly relationships with most other African nations, and is generally an advocate for Africa and African issues in the international community. Since independence in 1966, relations with the United States have been productive and amicable. The US generally views Botswana as a positive force for regional stability and security. In 2002, the US and Botswana established the International Law Enforcement Academy in Gaborone. The academy serves all of sub-Saharan Africa and provides law enforcement training for professionals from all member countries of the SADC.

Botswana's economy is one of the fastest developing in Africa, thanks in large part to the country's position as the world's largest producer of diamonds. With a proven record of accomplishment of good governance and the ability to maintain a healthy economy, the country has benefited from recognition by influential international organizations. Examples include ranks as Africa's least corrupt country (Transparency International) and among the most economically competitive nations in Africa (World Economic Forum). As a result, despite the seemingly disadvantageous small market size and landlocked geography, international investment continues to grow.

Human Rights Profile

International human rights law insists that states respect civil and political rights, and promote an individual's economic, social, and cultural rights. The United Nations Universal Declaration on Human Rights (UDHR) is recognized as the standard for international human rights. Its authors sought the counsel of the world's great thinkers, philosophers, and religious leaders, and were careful to create a document that reflects the core values shared by every world culture. (To read this document or view the articles relating to cultural human rights, visit http://www.udhr.org/UDHR/default.htm.)

The multi-party, democratic government of Botswana has a fair human rights record and has strived to maintain broad respect for the individual freedoms of its citizens. However, several issues attract criticism and the concern of international human rights organizations. These include poor prison conditions, occasional mistreatment of prisoners and detainees by the police, relatively limited freedom of the press, child abuse, and domestic violence against women.

Prisons in Botswana are often cited for their disturbingly poor conditions, generally due to overcrowding. In many instances, the overpopulation and lack of basic essentials unduly threatens the lives of prisoners and creates a serious health threat. This results in a high incidence of HIV/AIDS and tuberculosis infection. Overcrowding is an ongoing problem. Occasionally, juveniles younger than 18 are housed in the same population as adults. Though the government does not inhibit the work and monitoring of international non-governmental organizations (NGOs), there has been little improvement in conditions.

Article 19 of the UDHR outlines freedom of expression and the press. Botswana's constitution and laws provide freedom of speech and of the press and, in general, these rights are respected. While several private media organizations exist, the government continues to dominate domestic broadcasting. In addition, some laws effectively work to restrict independent journalism, such as the National Security Act of 1986, which grants government control over press activities. The Media Practitioners' Act of 2008 has also been widely criticized as restricting press freedoms.

The rights of children are set forth in Article 25. Botswana law provides for the rights and welfare of all children and the government generally respects and enforces these rights. Because of the HIV/AIDS pandemic in Botswana, there are a relatively high percentage of orphans. There is no law that specifically prohibits child abuse, and reported cases of abuse, rape, and sexual assault by teachers and extended family have been on the rise. Child prostitution and child labor (defined as children younger than 14, the legal minimum age for employment) are both prohibited by law. However, there have been sporadic cases reported to the authorities.

ECONOMY

Overview of the Economy

Before the development of the diamond industry, Botswana's economy was based on subsistence agriculture. Since 1971, the diamond trade has increased the wealth of the nation several times over; in 2008, Botswana provided nearly 30 percent of the world's diamonds, and is the largest producer of diamonds, by value, in the world. The per capita gross domestic product (GDP) was an estimated $14,906 (USD) in 2008. By 2014, this figure had increased to $16,600 (USD).

Industry

Diamonds account for nearly one-third of the government's revenue. Roughly, 70–80 percent of the country's exports are diamonds. In addition to diamonds, Botswana exports nickel, copper, meat, textiles and soda ash, for revenues of nearly $7.4 billion (USD) in 2014.

The country's other main industries include mining of salt, potash, soda ash, nickel and copper; livestock processing; textiles manufacturing; tourism; and financial services.

Labor

In 2009, the official unemployment rate was an estimated 17.8 percent. However, experts believe that the actual rate may be as high as 30 percent. In 2003, approximately 30.3 percent of the population still lives below the poverty line. The country's total labor force was roughly 1.017 million people in 2014.

Energy/Power/Natural Resources

Botswana's natural resources are primarily mineral. In addition to extensive deposits of diamonds, Botswana has copper, coal, iron ore, silver, nickel, soda ash, salt, and potash. Its wildlife is another rich resource. In 2011, an estimated 3.18 billion kWh of the country's electricity supply was imported.

Environmental concerns include limited sources of fresh water. Overgrazing is also a problem and is one of the causes of desertification.

Fishing

Commercial fishing in Botswana is restricted to citizens. The country's Department of Wildlife & National Parks sets catch limits and regulations for minimum mesh sizes. Natural supplies of fish in Botswana are decreasing and fish farming operations are becoming more common, although development is slow because many fishmongers are unfamiliar with the technology involved. The Okavango Delta is the primary and most important fishery in Botswana.

Forestry

Approximately 20 percent of Botswana's land is forested. However, much of the country's land is rainforest and continued forestry operations have threatened regional wildlife and plant life. Various non-government organizations continue to work to make Botswana's forests a sustainable source of income for indigenous populations.

Mining/Metals

Botswana's mining industry is the engine of the national economy. For over twenty years, the country has been one of the world's largest diamond producers. In addition, the country has large supplies of copper, gold, and nickel. Botswana's mining industry represented approximately 40 percent of GDP in 2005. Economists confirm that the country's mineral supplies will continue to sustain its economy for decades to come.

Agriculture

Less than one percent of the land in Botswana is arable. Farming is almost all at the subsistence level. Common crops include millet and sorghum, corn, beans, sunflowers and groundnuts (peanuts).

Animal Husbandry

Beef production represents the largest portion of Botswana's agricultural sector. However, much of its 2.3 million cattle are raised in communal areas and not bred and produced by modern means. In addition, overgrazing has begun to present challenges to the country's cattle farmers. The vast majority of animal skins from Botswana's livestock is exported to China and Namibia. Botswana imports most of its dairy products and small stock animals from South Africa. The country's poultry industry has seen growth in recent years. Other livestock include pigs, sheep, and goat.

Tourism

The developing tourist industry is becoming important to Botswana's economy. In 2012, the country welcomed nearly 250,000 visitors, generating about $400 million (USD) in revenue.

Eco-tourism is growing as communities cooperate to provide handicrafts and cultural demonstrations for visitors. The San, for instance, perform dances, tell stories, and guide tourists on hunting and gathering expeditions. Popular tourist sites include the Savuti Marsh, the Okavango Delta, and the Kalahari Sand Dunes.

The numerous and varied wildlife draws both hunters and eco-tourists. Game reserves and national parks provide opportunities for hunting and fishing, birdwatching, horseback safaris, and photography.

Jamie Greene, Ellen Bailey, M. Lee

DO YOU KNOW?

- Botswana, Zimbabwe, Zambia, and Namibia meet at a point in the middle of the Zambesi (Zambezi) River at Kazungula, Botswana.

- Gaborone was not officially declared a city until 1986, 20 years after it had become the capital of Botswana.

Bibliography

Alan Murphy, et al. "Botswana and Namibia." *Lonely Planet*, 2013.

Alexander Karin and Gape Kaboyakgosi. "A Fine Balance: Assessing the Quality of Governance in Bostwana." *Idasa*, 2012.

Alexander McCall Smith. "The No. 1 Ladies' Detective Agency." *Anchor Books*, 2003.

Bessie Head. "A Question of Power." *Heinemann*, 1995.

Bessie Head. "When Rain Clouds Gather." *Heinemann*, 1987.

Frederick Klaits. "Death in a Church of Life: Moral Passion during Botswana's Time of AIDS." *University of California Press*, 2010.

Laurens van der Post. "The Lost World of the Kalahari." *Harvest Books*, 1986.

Rupert Isaacson, Rupert. "The Healing Land: The Bushmen and the Kalahari Desert." *Grove Press*, 2004.

Unity Dow. "Far and Beyon'." *Aunt Lute Books*, 2002.

Works Cited

Elizabeth Devine and Nancy L. Braganti. 1995. "The Traveler's Guide to African Customs and Manners." New York: *St. Martin's Press*.

http://allafrica.com/stories/200811270298.html

http://botswana.usembassy.gov/od-ilea.html

http://physiciansforhumanrights.org/library/report-2007-05-25.html

http://www.botswanaembassy.or.jp/culture/body4.html

http://www.everyculture.com/Bo-Co/Botswana.html

http://www.state.gov/g/drl/rls/hrrpt/2008/af/118987.htm

http://www.unaids.org/en/KnowledgeCentre/HIVData/GlobalReport/2008/2008_Global_report.asp

http://www.unbotswana.org.bw/aya.html

http://www.womensworkbw.com/osbabout.htm

Mike Main. 2007. "Culture Smart! Botswana." New York: *Kuperard*.

Sara Louise Kras. 2008. "Botswana: Enchantment of the World." New York: *Scholastic Children's Press*.

Suzanne LeVert. 2006. "Cultures of the World: Botswana." New York: *Marshall Cavendish Benchmark*.

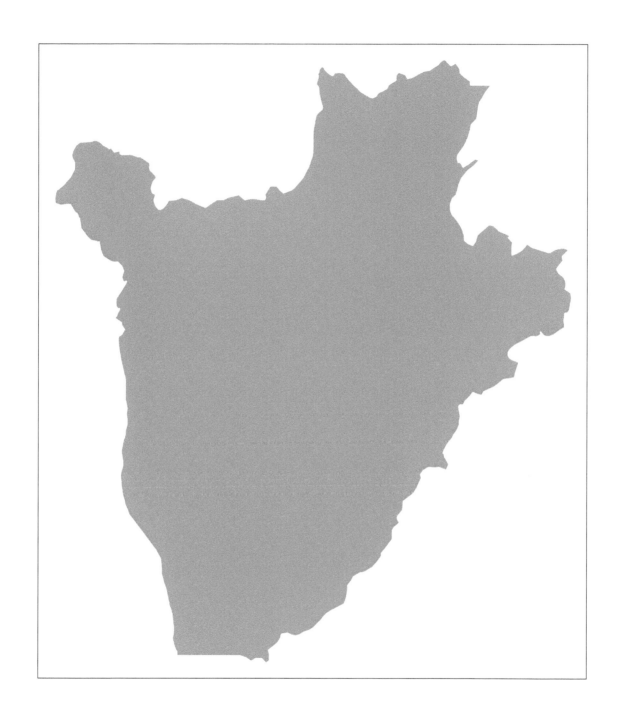

BURUNDI

Introduction

The Republic of Burundi is located in east-central Africa near Lake Tanganyika, the world's second largest and deepest freshwater lake. It is bordered by Rwanda to the north, Tanzania to the east and south, and the Democratic Republic of the Congo to the west. The rest of the western border is formed by Lake Tanganyika.

A Belgian colonial territory from World War I until 1962, Burundi has been divided by ethnic conflict between the Hutu (Bantu) majority and the Tutsi minority since the early 1990s. This sectarian strife has impeded the country's development, and has also involved countries such as Rwanda. Elections held in 2015 only brought more controversy and strife as disputes erupted over the eligibility of President Pierre Nkurunziza.

Burundi's economy is largely agricultural, with coffee as the main cash crop. Burundian culture is strongly based on the oral tradition, and traditional activities such as storytelling, riddling, and poetry recitation remain popular.

GENERAL INFORMATION

Official Language: Kirundi and French
Population: 10,742,276 (2015 estimate)
Currency: Burundi franc
Coins: Coins are available in denominations of 1, 5, and francs.
Land Area: 25,680 square kilometers (9,915 square miles)

Water Area: 2,150 square kilometers (830 square miles)
National Motto: "Unité, Travail, Progrès" (French, "Unity, Work, Progress")
National Anthem: "Burundi Bwacu" ("Beloved Burundi")
Capital: Bujumbura
Time Zone: GMT +3
Flag Description: The flag of Burundi features a white saltire, or Saint Andrew's Cross, which divides the flag into four quarters. The flag's top and bottom color fields are red, representing Burundi's fight for independence. The flag's left and right color fields are green, symbolizing hope. Three red stars in the center of the flag, outlined in green, represent the Hutu, Twa, and Tutsi, Burundi's three main ethnic groups.

Population

Approximately 85 percent of the population is Hutu, while around 14 percent is Tutsi.

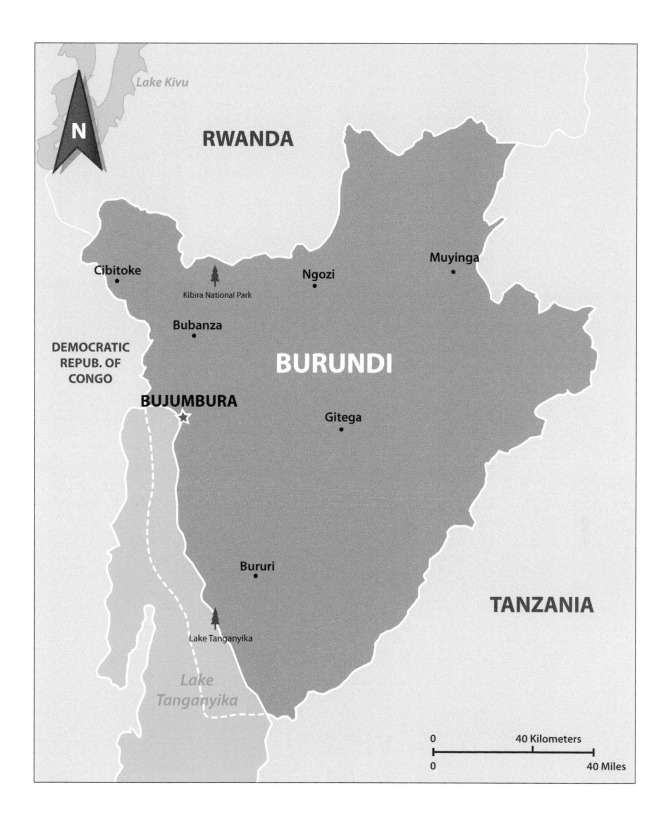

**Principal Cities by Population
(2012 estimate, unless noted):**

- Bujumbura (392,863)
- Gitega (22,989)
- Ngozi (24,932)
- Muyinga (100,715)
- Rutana (23,654)

Historically, the Tutsi have been the dominant group, owning much of the land and cattle, while the Hutu have worked as farmers and herders.

The Twa (or Batwa), one of the Pygmy peoples of the Central African rainforests, comprise around 1 percent of the population. A hunter-gatherer people, they were the original inhabitants of what is now Burundi. The country also has very small populations of Europeans and South Asians, numbering several thousand each, as well as other African ethnicities.

Over 70 percent of the population is rural, in 2015. Population density is among the highest in sub-Saharan Africa, with over 270 people per square kilometer (over 530 people per square mile). The main cities are Bujumbura, the capital, and Gitega. Bujumbura, located on Lake Tanganyika, is the country's port and cultural center.

Decades of warfare in Burundi have resulted from the country's ethnic divisions. The ethnic violence between Hutu and Tutsi, part of a broader African conflict, has uprooted hundreds of thousands of people in central Africa. Approximately 140,000 people within Burundi had become "internally displaced persons," or refugees. Most of these people are located in the northern and western parts of the country. Around 60,000 inhabitants of the Democratic Republic of the Congo have fled to Burundi to escape the violence in their own country.

The population of Burundi is extremely young, with an average age just over sixteen years. This is the result of rampant disease, high infant mortality, and decades of war. In 2005, it was estimated that around 46 percent of the population was under fifteen years of age, with only 2.6 percent over the age of sixty-five.

Languages

Burundi's two official languages are Kirundi (29.7 percent) and French (0.3 percent). Reflecting Burundi's colonial history, French remains the language of government, education, and business. Kirundi (or Rundi), a Bantu language, is the main spoken tongue; it is also spoken in neighboring Rwanda, Tanzania, and Uganda. There are approximately six million speakers in the entire region. Kirundi is closely related to the Bantu languages Kinyarwanda, spoken in Rwanda, and Giha, spoken in Tanzania. Most Kirundi speakers in Burundi are Hutu (85 percent).

A dialect of Swahili is the country's third main language, but does not have official status. It is spoken mainly in western Burundi, in the capital, and near Lake Tanganyika.

Native People & Ethnic Groups

The Twa were the first settlers in what is now Burundi. Hunters and gatherers, they have lived in Central Africa since ancient times. The Hutu arrived later, around 1000, and conquered the Twa.

The Tutsi arrived around 500 years later and in turn conquered the Hutu, who outnumbered the Tutsi. They established a monarchy which lasted until the 19th century. The Tutsi king, or mwami, ruled through a land-owning aristocracy. A ruling system known as ubugabire gradually developed, involving a feudal relationship of obligations between the ruler and his subjects. Although the Tutsi kingdom lost its independence during the European colonial period, the Tutsi remained the dominant ethnic group.

Today, an estimated 85 percent of Burundians are Hutu. Minority ethnic groups include the Tusti (14 percent) and the Twa (one percent). Burundi is also home to a small number of Europeans and South Asians.

Religions

Approximately 62 percent of Burundians are Christians, with 23.9 percent Protestant. Most of the Twa are animists. A certain amount of "syncretism," or mixture of Christian and traditional beliefs, exists in the Burundian churches. There is also a small Muslim minority, around 2.5 percent of the population.

Climate

Burundi's climate is largely equatorial, though the country's varying altitudes mean a wide variation in temperature. Low-lying regions tend to be hot and humid. Higher zones have more temperate weather. The average annual temperature varies between 17° and 23° Celsius (63° and 73° Fahrenheit).

Burundi experiences two seasons: the rainy season lasts from November until May, and the dry seasons lasts from June to October. The country receives around 1,500 millimeters (60 inches) of rain each year.

ENVIRONMENT & GEOGRAPHY

Topography

Located in Central Africa, Burundi is a landlocked nation but is at the head of the Nile-Congo watershed. Burundi is home to Ruvyironza River, a branch of the Kagera River and the farthest headstream of the Nile. The Ruvyironza has its source at Mount Kikizi. The Kagera flows into Lake Victoria, part of the White Nile watershed.

Burundi is divided into three main geographical zones. Most people live in the eastern part of the country, which is covered by plateaus and plains. The central part of the country is characterized by high mountains, including Burundi's highest point, Heha, at 2,670 meters (8,760 feet) above sea level.

Western Burundi is much lower, including part of the north-south Great Rift Valley. Lake Tanganyika, which is the country's lowest point (772 meters/2,533 feet above sea level), forms part of Burundi's western border and is the site of Bujumbura, the capital. Bujumbura also touches Zambia, Tanzania, and the Democratic Republic of the Congo, and is Burundi's main port and export center.

The snipe is one of the most common species of birds in Burundi.

Plants & Animals

Savannah, or lightly wooded grassland, is common in Burundi. Native tree species include acacia and eucalyptus. However, the land has suffered extensive deforestation, partly to clear farmland and partly because wood is a major source of fuel for Burundians.

Burundi has an abundance of wildlife, although over-hunting and poaching have threatened many species. As in many African countries, elephants and antelopes, as well as great cats such as the lion and leopard, are found in Burundi. The country's lakes, including Tanganyika, are home to many species of birds and fish. Among the most common avian species are game birds such as the partridge and the snipe.

CUSTOMS & COURTESIES

Greetings

Greeting customs vary throughout Burundi, but they share similar characteristics. Generally, Burundians shake hands when greeting each other. After shaking hands, they might touch the other's right elbow with their left hand. Burundians might hold hands while talking, and typically stand close to each other. In the large city of Bujumbura, men and women greet each other by embracing and kissing three times on the cheeks. It is typical for women to also greet other women this way.

Cattle are revered and considered sacred to Burundians. Cow's milk is an important part of Burundians' diet, and families who have large herds are viewed as lucky. As such, cattle are referenced in greetings and in regular discussions. When Burundians greet each another, they frequently wish each other the good fortune of having a large herd. This greeting is often first offered from a distance, before they have gotten close enough to shake hands.

Burundians typically speak in Kirundi. Common phrases of greeting include "Bwakeye" ("Good morning") and "Mwiriwe" ("Good afternoon or evening"). When addressing elders, it is customary to add "Amahoro?" ("Is there peace?"). Respect for elders carries into regular greetings in Burundi, with the addition of a person's age or role attached to the end of the greeting. Common additions include adding "Nyokuru" when addressing a mother or old woman, "Mutama" when addressing a father or old man, or "Kibondo" for addressing youth. Burundians address the person with their family name, or surname, before their given name.

Gestures & Etiquette

Social interaction is extremely important in Burundian culture. Burundians place special significance on even casual meetings with friends and family, regarding each as an occasion to share news and updates. They take the time to talk even when running into each other at the market, or conducting other errands and chores. Time for conversing takes precedence, frequently causing Burundians to be late for appointments or other social gatherings. In addition, Burundians treat authority figures or those who hold high social positions, whether in the community or family, with a certain reverence. For example, when greeting an elder or someone in a respectful status, Burundians show respect by bowing slightly and not making eye contact.

Another unique aspect of social etiquette in Burundi culture is the use of proverbs in typical, daily discussions. For example, Burundians use the proverb "Better the glares of a foreigner than those of a mother-in-law" to illustrate the precedence that Burundians give to family and close friends. This shows the importance of building long-lasting relationships with family. It is also important to note that because Burundians give social precedence to close friends and relatives, visitors to the country tend to have a somewhat lower social status.

Burundians value social events at which they share food and drink, such as beer. When invited to a social gathering, especially when offered food or beer, Burundians accept as a matter of tradition and social etiquette. At the typical gathering, visitors are often treated to poetry and folk-story recitations. Burundians also enjoy singing when they gather for all types of occasions.

Eating/Meals

Burundi is an agricultural country whose primary crops include beans, corn, wheat, and cassava (also called manioc), in addition to various cash crops such as coffee. As a result, Burundian cuisine consists mostly of beans and vegetables, such as sweet potatoes, cassava root, and peas. Kidney beans are the staple and most commonly eaten crop, and are usually consumed at least once a day. However, rice is becoming an increasingly more common staple on the Burundian table. Other common foods include ibitoke (plantains), which are similar to the sweet banana. They are grown and eaten, along with bananas, throughout the country.

Burundians do not eat much meat, possibly only once or twice monthly. It is expensive for them, and they value their livestock, such as cattle and cows, for milk and usually prefer not to eat their meat. However, they occasionally eat goat and sheep. They cook their food by roasting, boiling, or stewing it over a fire of wood. Desserts are not usually a part of a meal, but drinking homemade banana wine, called urwarwa, is common. Burundians also use sorghum to make a homemade beer, called impeke, which they traditionally drink with long straws from a large gourd.

Most Burundians eat at home, as it is expensive to eat in restaurants. Restaurants serve Burundian, French, Asian, and Greek food mainly in Bujumbura and in the city's major hotels. South Asian cuisine has influenced contemporary cuisine in Burundi, mainly by the addition of spices and the grilled Indian bread chapatti.

Visiting

Like many African societies, hospitality is an important and traditional facet of Burundian culture. Burundians always offer visitors something to drink, such as coffee, water, or beer, and it is considered impolite to refuse. However, it is not customary to offer food, since such an offering is traditionally reserved for more organized or social occasions, such as ceremonies.

In general, visitors are not expected to bring anything when visiting a Burundian home. It is also not necessary to call ahead before visiting. Burundians warmly welcome drop-in visitors, which is part of their custom. Should a person invite another out to a place for food and drinks, typically called a cabaret, it is customary for the host to pay the entire bill.

LIFESTYLE

Family

The family holds primary importance among all ethnicities in Burundi culture. The family clan lives within its own social unit, maintaining strong family ties. Nuclear families are becoming increasingly common, especially in urban areas, and families continue to reside near the husband's extended family.

Burundi is traditionally a patriarchal society in which the people also continue to practice polygamy. In a polygamous marriage, one man can have several wives at once. When selecting a bride, the groom's family gives such things as goats, cash, or furniture to the bride's family on the day of the wedding. Though a Hutu married couple share a home, Tutsi wives live separately from their husbands. Upon the death of the

father, the oldest son receives all of the father's inheritance.

Children are valued for carrying on family and cultural traditions, which they are taught at home and at school. When Hutu children are five years old, they are given certain tasks and responsibilities in the home, which include learning respect for and obedience to elders. Tutsi males are instructed at a young age in learning their culture's public speaking and storytelling skills, as well as cultural dances.

Housing

Many Burundians in rural areas construct their homes in a traditional manner, with mud and grass in the shape of a dome or beehive. The roof is made from leaves that are woven together. However, due to massive deforestation, leaves are in short supply, and roofs are instead often made from scrap metals such as tin. In more recent times, sticks are substituted for grass for building the home. In urban areas, homes are built from cement block and wood, with tin roofs or tiled roofs. The traditional Tutsi home is called an urugo, around which the family cattle live. Usually, two or three buildings make up the urugo for the nuclear family. In rural areas, where most Burundians live, homes are clustered in small groups and generally surrounded by a wall constructed of mud and other natural building materials.

Food

The cuisine of Burundi is similar to the cuisines of neighboring Central Africa, and includes staple foods such as beans, eaten prominently, and cassava, maize, plantains, and sweet potatoes, as well as exotic fruits. Meat is not commonly eaten (livestock such as cattle are traditionally prized), and the majority of popular and traditional dishes are starch-based and include vegetables. Burundians throughout the country often eat a dish made from cornmeal called ugali. Ugali consists of cornmeal and water that is mixed into porridge. To eat ugali, Burundians roll a small piece of the porridge into a ball that they dip into a vegetable stew or a sauce. The dish is easy to make and affordable for most families, making it one of the most common staples on the table.

Beans are eaten at least once a day in Burundi. A popular Burundi dish for celebrations is plantains with beans. Dried red kidney beans that had been soaked for hours are combined with plantains, palm oil, sliced onion, salt, and hot pepper. The combination is then stir-fried, with water then added to simmer the ingredients. Another dish with beans, called maharggwe, is made by boiling red kidney beans, and then adding tomatoes, cabbage, onions, garlic, allspice, and oregano. The pot simmers until the combination is almost cooked, and potatoes are added to finish the dish. Another dish prepared in Burundi is called boko boko harees, which is chicken with bulgur wheat. It is made by cooking bulgur wheat, chicken, onion, turmeric paste, sugar, ghee (clarified butter), and salt in a large pot of water and simmering. It is traditionally served with fried onion on top.

Life's Milestones

Christianity is the dominant religion in Burundi, and the Christian population (mostly Roman Catholics) is estimated at 80 percent of the entire populous. As such, many milestones and cultural observances are rooted in the Christian faith. Nonetheless, Burundians continue to adhere to many traditional practices and milestones. For example, Burundians drink impeke (homemade beer made with sorghum) through long straws at celebrations, an act which symbolizes unity among those present.

A Burundian's birth is a revered occasion. A ceremony called ujusohor is held on the sixth day after a child's birth. During the ceremony, the infant is shown to the family and is named by the paternal grandfather. This often includes a nickname as well as a formal and clan name. When seeking a marriage partner, Burundians' parents usually get involved to discuss the bride price, especially for a husband's first wife. Although polygamy is legally forbidden, many Burundians still practice the tradition. The groom's family gives the bride's family either cash or furniture,

whereas traditional gifts were goats and cattle. Traditional Burundi wedding ceremonies, which occur at the groom's home, exclude the bride's parents. Because of the patrilineal tradition, inheritance passes to the eldest son.

CULTURAL HISTORY

Art

For centuries, Burundians have created a wide range of traditional arts that were both functional and decorative, including basketry, pottery, beadwork, sculpture, and metalwork. In particular, the Twa people (pygmies), which now account for 1 percent of the population, are renowned for their skillful pottery making. Many of these traditional art forms are characterized by geometric and decorative motifs. For example, geometric designs were used to decorate papyrus panels depicting Burundian folk stories.

Two important items that reveal the utilitarian yet aesthetic nature of Burundi's traditional arts are baskets and weapons. Baskets are traditionally woven using papyrus root and banana leaves. Before weaving the baskets, Burundians color and decorate the leaves with special mud dyes that they then weave in numerous patterns. The decorated baskets serve many daily functions; Burundians, especially women, balance baskets on their head to carry food and water, and use them to store food and spices. Decorated swords reveal the importance of weaponry in Burundian culture. These swords are decorated and passed from father to son, maintaining a traditional custom.

Traditional arts also continue to be widely practiced, including some new art forms introduced by foreign cultures. During the last half of the 20th century, when Italian missionaries traveled to Burundi, Burundians developed an Italian process for making ceramics, beginning with the École céramique de Giheta (Giheta Ceramic School) in 1952. Burundians continue to create pottery they decorate with traditional folk themes and designs. Abstract designs are somewhat less common than figurative designs. They also continue to practice traditional basket weaving and bead making, both of which continue to hold functional and aesthetic value in Burundian culture.

Architecture

Traditional Burundian dwellings are huts made of mud and straw. The country is also home to examples of colonial architecture, such as the National Museum of Gitega. There are also several cathedrals that were built in colonial times. The best example of modern design and construction in Burundi is the Bujumbura National Airport. Urban areas also feature homes made of cement and red clay tiled roofs.

Music & Dance

Dance and song have long been an integral part of Burundi's culture. Dance songs are performed at many traditional milestones, including weddings, the birth of a child, and to accompany work or trades such as hunting, fishing, and even beekeeping. Each region had its own special dance songs. Traditional Burundian folk songs and dances also described reverence for kings and their thrones. One celebration in which Burundians showed such reverence was the umuganuro, an annual sorghum festival. At the festival, folk songs and dances were accompanied by drumming.

Drumming on the karyenda, one of many sacred drums, was an especially important aspect of the sorghum celebration. Other sacred drums include the rukinzo, which accompanied the king; the ruciteme ("for whom one clears brush"), which brought royal protection to livestock; and the murimirwa ("for whom one ploughs"), which protected the crops. Before Burundi was colonized, the tradition was more powerful and drums were kept in guarded sanctuaries. The king allowed only certain Hutu families to create and guard the royal or sacred drums. Within these families were the abatimbo ("those who hit hard"), who played the drums at rituals and ceremonies.

Traditional-style drumming remained popular. The performing group known as the Master (or Royal) Drummers of Burundi has achieved an

The karyenda drum is a traditional instrument of Burundi music often used in sacred rituals and other special occasions.

international reputation; the group helped usher in the "world music" trend in the early 1980s, and has released three albums. Other traditional instruments include the umwironge (flute), the indonongo (fiddle), the idono (musical bow), and the inanga (a sitar-like zither), as well as various rattles (made from gourds), calling horns, and bells.

Literature

The literature of Burundi, like that of many other African nations, is rooted in the culture's oral traditions. Stories, fables, legends, poems, proverbs, and songs have served to transfer history from generation to generation. In their stories and fables, Burundians share life lessons and impart values and morals. For example, animals often represent moral lessons in traditional Burundian stories, such as the arrogance in the behavior of a leopard. Villagers and herders would also exchange stories and poems at night around a fire, often drinking urwagwa, which is banana beer. Pastoral themes were an important part of these oral traditions. In the kivivuga amazina, a form of improvisational poetry, cattle herders competed by describing their herds and their many accomplishments.

Burundian literature started to focus on local customs and belief systems in the 20th century. Poet Michael Kayoya (1934–1972) attempted to reconcile modern life with the traditional Burundian lifestyle. His works include *Sur les traces de mon père* (*In My Father's Footsteps*, 1973) and *Entre deux mondes* (*Between Two Worlds*). More recent Burundian writers include Antoine Kaburahe (1965–), and Esther Kamatari (1951–). After her father was overthrown following independence in 1962 and then assassinated in 1964, Kamatari fled Burundi to Paris. She has been interested in restoring the monarchy and wrote a memoir in 2001 called *Princesse des rugo, mon histoire*.

CULTURE

Arts & Entertainment

Traditional Burundian arts continue to be influential in modern society. For example, the oral recitation of poetry remains commonplace, and pastoral themes remain prominent. Burundians continue to recite poems that celebrate livestock (such as cattle and cows), particularly discussing their provisions, including milk, which is still used for payment at a wedding. With the introduction of organized education, these oral traditions were transcribed and further committed to the nation's collective culture and memory.

Dance in Burundi remains important to the culture and has helped carry the Burundian culture to other countries. Burundi is particularly renowned for its ancient drumming traditions, and the Intore Dancers, who have popularized these traditions worldwide, have won international dance competitions. Their drummers use the karyenda drums, as do other well-known groups. Descendants of families who guarded the sacred karyenda drums have also performed their cultural dances in other countries. The dance group Les Maîtres-Tambours du Burundi (Master Drummers of Burundi), which includes up to thirty dancers and percussionists, travels around the world showcasing traditional dances that include rhythmic sounds and movement. The amashako and ibishikiso drums are included in their performances that have become very popular in recordings as well. In fact, the singer Khadja Nin (1959–) has become famous for singing in Swahili, French, and her native language, Kirundi.

Popular sports include football (soccer), traditional ball games, and track-and-field. The country competes against other African nations in soccer tournaments, and at the international level in track-and-field events.

Cultural Sites & Landmarks

Burundi is home to dramatic geographical landmarks, including several national parks and reserves. Kibira National Park, in northwestern Burundi at the border with Rwanda, has dense evergreen forest and sits at the top of the Zaire-Nile Rivers. It is the largest area of untouched forest in the country, with wildlife that includes monkeys, chimpanzees, baboons, and many species of birds. Rusizi Natural Reserve is a wetland located near Bujumbura, the capital, in the river delta where visitors often encounter crocodiles, hippopotamuses, migrating birds, and aquatic antelope. The Bururi National Reserve, in Bururi, features a wide variety of bird species, as does the Rwihinda Lake Natural Reserve.

Another important natural attraction is Lake Tanganyika, considered the second largest by volume in the world. Lake Tanganyika is also the deepest lake on the African continent. On its shores sits Saga Beach, renowned for its characteristic white-powder sands and ample waves. Burundi is also home to some picturesque waterfalls, including the Chutes de la Kagera (Kagera Falls), near Rutana in southeastern Burundi. The site includes numerous falls that drop into the valley below. Hikers make the trek to the top for valley vistas. Another famous natural attraction is the Kibabi Hot Springs, where visitors choose among numerous spring-fed pools, each of which has a different temperature, ranging up to 100° Celsius (212° Fahrenheit).

Bujumbura's downtown district has a number of buildings left from the nation's German colonial period, and within the city center is the Roman Catholic cathedral and a Muslim mosque that are among the oldest and most significant religious monuments in the city. The National Stadium in Bujumbura is the site of many of the city's major sports contests and is also sometimes used for state celebrations and other events.

Libraries & Museums

Burundi is home to numerous museums. The Burundi Musée Vivant (Museum of Life, Living Museum), located near Lake Tanganyika, is dedicated to educating visitors about traditional life in Burundi, and also houses living reptiles, an aquarium, and botanical gardens. Among the museum's displays is a reconstruction of a colonial village. Exhibits in the village include many traditional Burundian crafts and arts, such as drums, baskets, and pottery. The museum's most famous exhibit is a full-scale reconstruction of an African royal house.

In Gitega, the National Museum exhibits traditional Burundian musical instruments, including drums. Along with a library, the National Museum showcases traditional Burundian weapons, which include spears and shields. Bujumbura's Burundi Geologic Museum contains examples of the mineralogical diversity of the region.

Holidays

Burundi's national holiday is Independence Day (July 1), which commemorates the country's independence from United Nations trusteeship under Belgian administration in 1962. Unity Day (February 5) reflects the desire for national unity.

Several political holidays commemorate the country's struggle for independence. September 18 commemorates the victory of the National Unity and Progress Party (UPRONA) in the 1961 election. Two holidays in October commemorate the deaths of two assassinated heroes: Prince Louis Rwagasore (killed October 13, 1961) and President Ndadaye (killed October 21, 1993).

Youth Culture

As Burundi transitions from a war-torn nation towards peace and democracy, youth in Burundi face a challenging future. Most live in poverty and estimates of unemployed youth in the early 21st century in Burundi have been as high as 90 percent. The country has made some strides in terms of education. As of 2009, net enrollment for children between the ages of six and 12 was 85 percent, up from 53 percent in 2005. The government also increased educational spending by 50 percent for the 2009 national budget, while building 7,000 new classes since 2006.

While civil war and violence over the last few decades have created serious challenges for Burundian youth, the government has tried to unite the country through sports. Football (soccer), as in most African nations, is the national sport and very popular among young people—though the national team has yet to qualify for the finals of the African Nations Cup or the World Cup. Burundi is also the second African nation to have a woman in charge of its national football federation (Liberia is the first). Other popular sports include basketball, track and field, tennis and table tennis, and volleyball.

Burundian youth are perhaps one of the more isolated youth cultures in Africa in the early 21st century. The majority of the population resides in rural areas, where Western influence and culture is often nonexistent. Like the rest of society, Burundian youth are also accustomed to a culture of modesty. Traditional clothing is common, and most clothes are second-hand. Young girls wear colorful, patterned wraparound skirts with t-shirts or the traditional igigambara, which is a woven cloth that is wrapped around the head. One notable event that signaled change in the country's culture was the 2008 Miss Burundi beauty pageant, the first event of its kind to be organized and sponsored through official channels. Organizers hoped to make the event, which many considered groundbreaking, an annual occurrence.

SOCIETY

Transportation

Minibuses are the primary mode of public transportation in Burundi. The national road network reaches the majority of the country, though many roads are unpaved. The landlocked nation has no rail system. Burundi has one of the lowest rates of car ownership in the world; in fact, its 2010 rate of car ownership is one car per 1,000 people. Traffic moves on the right-hand side of the road.

Transportation Infrastructure

Foreign aid and development have improved the infrastructure in recent years, including the construction of a 97-kilometer (60-mile) paved road between Rwanda and Burundi to promote intra-regional trade that was inaugurated in April 2009. The country lacks a national railway, but waterways, such as Lake Tanganyika, are used to facilitate the transportation of goods and passengers.

As of 2013, there are seven airports in the country, and one heliport from 2012. Domestic flights as well as international flights to Tanzania, Rwanda, and the Democratic Republic of the Congo (DRC) occur through the Bujumbura International Airport.

Media & Communications

Burundian media is not afforded the freedom to cover political and other issues objectively. After the long period of civil war, government censorship and manipulation of media remains common and self-censorship widely practiced. Generally, views in the media are limited to those of the ruling political party.

Radio remains the dominant medium in Burundi. There are two government-owned papers, *Le Renouveau* and the weekly *Ubumwe* (Unity). There is also a private French-language paper, as well as a newspaper operated by the Catholic Church. There are about 10 radio stations, as of 2007, that operate in Burundi, two of which are government-run. The only television station, La Radiodiffusion et Television Nationale de Burundi (RTNB), is government-controlled. It broadcasts in four languages: Swahili, Kirundi, French, and English.

Burundi has one of the lowest densities of telephone use in the world. However, mobile cell-phone use has increased rapidly, with 3.2 million people using cell phones and only 21,700 fixed-line telephone subscriptions, as of 2014. There were an estimated 144,500 internet users, representing just 1.4 percent of the population.

SOCIAL DEVELOPMENT

Standard of Living

Burundi ranked 180th out of 187 countries on the 2009 United Nations Human Development Index, which measures quality of life and standard of living indicators.

Water Consumption

Water is readily available to approximately 75 percent of Burundians, due to the country's close proximity to the African Great Lakes, which include Lake Tanganyika in the west and Lake Rweru and Lake Cohoha Sud in the north. The state utility company, Regideso Water, provides water to the urban areas of the country. However, Burundi's water infrastructure is need of repair and development and much water is wasted. Water availability is scarce in some of the country's rural areas, away from the water infrastructure that exists in Burundi's cities.

Education

In 2015, 85.6 percent of Burundi's population is literate. This is partly due to the country's strong oral traditions, but also to the ongoing violence and poverty. In 2015, literacy rate estimates are slightly higher among men (88.2 percent) than among women (83.1 percent). International organizations such as the United Nations Educational, Scientific, and Cultural Organization (UNESCO) and the United States Peace Corps provide agricultural education.

Many of Burundi's educational problems are inherited from the colonial era. The Belgian government did not develop a comprehensive system of public education. What formal education existed was not compulsory, and generally did not extend beyond primary school. At the time of independence, Burundi generally lacked an educated class to provide leadership.

Today, primary education is compulsory for children between the ages of seven and twelve. At the primary level, Kirundi is the language of instruction. Secondary school, taught in both official languages, is not compulsory. As of the 1990s, only around 10 percent of the population received secondary education.

Burundi's first university, founded in 1964 as the Official University of Bujumbura, was the result of a merger of an agricultural school, a Jesuit college, and a scientific institute. It was replaced in the early 1970s by a new University of Burundi, which merged the Official University, the national teacher-training college, and the institute for civil-service training.

Women's Rights

Women are guaranteed equal rights under constitutional law and the Convention on the Elimination of All Forms of Discrimination against Women (CEDAW) was ratified by Burundi in 1992. Nonetheless, Burundi, like many African nations, remains a strongly patriarchal society where women are essentially unrepresented in government and business. A woman's primary responsibilities also remain traditionally domestic in nature, and they are expected to care for the family, especially child rearing. Women also continue to wield little to no power within the family or society to make decisions. Thus, despite constitutional law and the ratification of international treaties on human rights, women hold a subordinate societal role.

Legally, Burundian women continue to face certain degrees of discrimination. For example, penalties for adultery favor men and inheritance continues to be based upon custom. In rural areas, women are commonly prohibited from inheriting land. Women also face discrimination in terms of the legal age for marriage (18 for women and 21 for men). In addition, a Burundian women

married to a non-Burundian cannot transmit her nationality to her children. Burundi has also abolished polygamy, but continues to honor the polygamous marriages still in existence.

Violence against women continues to be a major concern in Burundi. Based on a report in 2006, violence against women remains common, with incidents of domestic violence largely unreported. Although women in Burundi have the right to report spousal abuse, many refrain from doing so due to social stigma and inadequate protection. In addition, though rape is punishable by up to 20 years in prison and spousal rape is not even considered a crime. In fact, about one in three women who are raped are believed to be reporting the crime. Women and young girls who report being raped are frequently abandoned or ostracized by the men in their family, and in many cases, women had to feed and pay for jailing those they accused of rape. Investigations and prosecutions of rapists were rare. Child rape also accounted for about 14 percent of the total reported cases of sexual violence in 2006.

Burundian refugee women returning from Tanzania have also faced various forms of human rights violations. Women who were suspected of belonging to the once-government rebel group, the FNL, were often arrested, harshly treated, and often detained in illegal facilities or raped. Schoolchildren have likewise been unlawfully detained on a regular basis in Burundi. As recently as 2006, Burundian security forces have been blamed for raping young girls and women. Lastly, though prostitution is illegal in Burundi, the practice is considered common.

In 2008, Amnesty International recommended that the Burundian government increase its surveillance and enforcement of violence against women. The organization specifically addressed the need for accurate documentation of cases of rape and sexual violence, for law enforcement personnel to treat such cases as criminal, and for timely and impartial investigations of such cases. Burundi's new constitution also mandates that women represent 30 percent of government positions. As of 2006, 37 women were serving in the National Assembly, which seats 118 people. A woman had also been elected to the position of speaker. Women have also increased their representation in the senate and as ministerial leaders in recent years.

Health Care

Health care in Burundi is extremely poor, and infectious diseases are widespread. There are very few hospitals and medical personnel. The best medical care is available in Bujumbura and Gitega, though even in the cities medical care is inadequate. Free universal health care was abolished in 2002 due to a lack of funds. Many Burundians seek traditional remedies, including herbal cures from traditional practitioners.

Around one-third of the population is infected with HIV/AIDS. Safe drinking water is unavailable to more than half the population. Emerging infectious diseases include malaria and the so-called "Blackwater fever" (BWF), a severe clinical syndrome that is characterized by acute kidney failure.

Life expectancy in Burundi is low, but has improved. As of 2015, average life expectancy at birth was 60 years (58.45 for men; 61.78 for women). Infant mortality has decreased in recent decades. In 2015, there were about 10 deaths per 1,000 live births.

GOVERNMENT

Structure

An independent Tutsi kingdom ruled the territory of present-day Burundi for several centuries before Europeans arrived in the late 19th century. In 1890, the German Empire annexed the region as part of German East Africa. During World War I, Belgian forces captured the region. After the war, the League of Nations created the territory of Ruanda-Urundi as a Belgian mandate territory. The Belgians exercised rule through the Tutsi aristocracy. In 1946, Ruanda-Urundi became a United Nations trust territory, still under Belgian rule. The Belgian government granted territorial autonomy in January 1961.

On July 1, 1962, the territory gained its independence as the Kingdom of Burundi, a constitutional monarchy. In 1966, the monarchy was abolished and the country was renamed the Republic of Burundi. From the 1960s through 1980s, the country suffered extended periods of instability, punctuated by military coups and dictatorships. In the early 1990s, Burundi became caught up in the ethnic war between Tutsi and Hutu, and political conditions declined even more. A 1996 coup established another dictatorship, termed a "transitional republic." As violence increased, the United Nations sent peacekeepers to the area.

In August 2000, the government signed the Arusha Accords with the National Assembly and representatives of the main Hutu and Tutsi parties; this established a process for restoring constitutional government. In October and November 2001, a transitional constitution and government were set in place. A formal constitution was approved by national referendum in February 2005. As of August 2005, parliamentary and local elections had been held, and a new president had been elected.

Under the February 2005 constitution, the president serves as chief of state and head of government, and is elected by Parliament. The president appoints the 26-member cabinet, known as the Council of Ministers.

The 2005 constitution called for a bicameral legislature. The National Assembly (Assemblee Nationale) has 220 members, of whom 85 are elected and 134 are appointed by the signers of the Arusha Accords. The 54 member Senate is balanced between Hutu and Tutsi. The Twa are also represented in the Senate.

The most recent elections held in July 21 2015 resulted in the reelection of Pierre Nkurunziza. However, the opposition boycotted the election to protest Nkurunziza's alteration of the constitution to allow him to run for a third term. The first vice president, Prosper Bazombaza, was elected in February 2014. The second vice president, Gervais Rufyikiri was elected in August 2010.

Political Parties

Political parties in Burundi are organized along ethnic lines. Major Hutu parties include the National Council for the Defense of Democracy (CNDD) and the National Council for the Defense of Democracy-Forces for the Defense of Democracy (CNDD-FDD). Tusti parties include the Movement for the Rehabilitation of Citizens-Rurenzangemero and the Union for National Progress. Minority parties include the Burundo-African Alliance for Salvation, the Green Party-Intwari, the Liberal Party, and the Party for a Non-Violent Society.

Local Government

Burundi is divided into fifteen provinces, which are subdivided into arrondissements (administrative divisions), and communes. Municipal administrators and members of the Burundian Association of Local Representatives (BALR) are appointed by the central government.

Judicial System

The Supreme Court (Cour Supreme) is Burundi's highest court, and consists of nine judges. Other judicial bodies include the Constitutional Court and Courts of Appeals. Local courts are known as tribunals. Burundi's legal system is a mixture of traditional law and the civil codes of its former colonial rulers, Germany and Belgium. There are three subordinate courts: the Courts of Appeal, the County Courts, and the Courts of Residence.

Taxation

Corporations in Burundi are required to pay a flat income tax of 35 percent. In addition, include vehicle taxes, a capital gains tax, and a building tax. Taxes contribute to 27.9 percent of the country's GDP.

Armed Forces

The Burundian armed forces, known as the National Defense Force (Forces de Defense Nationale, or FDN), consist of the army, including naval and air units, and the national gendarmerie (policing force). Service is voluntary and the minimum military age for enlistment is sixteen. Burundi, along with Rwanda, has the smallest military budget in the East Africa Community; however, the military budget is the highest in the region in terms of percentage of gross domestic product.

Foreign Policy

Following the Burundi Civil War (1993–2005), the country has focused on regional stability and improving foreign relations on the international stage, particularly for the purposes of securing foreign aid and assistance. As a member of the African Union (AU), Burundi has engaged in peacekeeping efforts beyond the immediate region, including in Somalia. The AU was established in 2001 to promote democracy, human rights, and conflict resolution in African countries. Burundi also belongs to the World Trade Organization (WTO), the African Development Bank (ADB), the Common Market of East and Southern Africa (COMESA), and the East Africa Community (EAC), among other international bodies and institutions. Burundi has held membership in the UN since 1962.

Burundi's current lack of solid national stability stems from its long civil war and relations with neighboring Rwanda, Tanzania, and the DRC—a region called the Great Lakes—where hundreds of thousands of Burundian refugees have fled. However, the majority of Burundian refugees are in Tanzania. Some reports say that up to 470,000 Burundians have returned to Burundi since 2003. In 2009, numerous armed groups, including the National Liberation Forces (FNL), were still in existence. The Burundian government and the rebel FNL signed a ceasefire in early 2008, signaling peaceful negotiations; in early 2009, the UN accepted the accreditation of the FNL as a viable democratic, political party in Burundi. Burundi's good relations with other Great Lakes countries remain steady as the country moves further toward internal peaceful political processes.

Nonetheless, a border dispute since the 1960s between Burundi and Rwanda on the Kagera/

Nyabarongo and the Akanyaru/Kanyaru rivers continues. Tutsi, Hutu, other ethnic groups, armed gangs, political rebels, and government forces continued to engage in cross-border conflicts in early 2009. About 100,000 internationally displaced persons (IDPs) remain in western and northern Burundi, as well as nearly 10,000 refugees from the DRC.

The United States maintains a supportive relationship with Burundi. The US was involved in supporting the UN peacekeeping force in Burundi in 2004, called the Arusha Peace Process. The Peace and Reconciliation Accord ended the civil war, which occurred between the minority Tutsis and majority Hutus. The US has also assisted Burundi's move towards a democratic system of government by helping to strengthen the country's internal political processes, including openness, respect for human rights, economic development, and democratic reforms. Likewise, the US government is working to help stabilize democratic and economic processes in the African Great Lakes states, which will further increase prospects for long-term democratic processes throughout the region.

Human Rights Profile

International human rights law insists that states respect civil and political rights, and promote an individual's economic, social, and cultural rights. The United Nations Universal Declaration on Human Rights (UDHR) is recognized as the standard for international human rights. Its authors sought the counsel of the world's great thinkers, philosophers, and religious leaders, and were careful to create a document that reflects the core values shared by every world culture. (To read this document or view the articles relating to cultural human rights, visit http://www.udhr.org/UDHR/default.htm.)

Burundi is a constitutional republic whose population has the power to elect its government. In 2005, Burundians voted to approve a new constitution, brought about by the Peace and Reconciliation Accord signed in Arusha, Tanzania in 2000. Burundi remains one of the poorest nations in the world, and about 80 percent of the population lives in poverty. The people have little access to education, with the overall literacy rate at an estimated 59 percent. Children attend school until about the age of eight and less than 10 percent of the population attends secondary school. Though schooling is compulsory to the age of twelve, it is not enforced. As such, Burundi has not made Article 26 of the UDHR a priority.

As of 2006, both Amnesty International (AI) and the U.S. Department of State have criticized Burundi for political terror, which includes the use of torture and murder, as well as the prevalence of political disappearances. Overall, the human rights record in Burundi is poor, with the government's security forces behind many human rights abuses in the country. Arbitrary arrest was common, and the condition of detention centers and prisons was very poor. AI has strongly recommended that Burundi abolish the practice of torture and provide for methods to make such perpetrators accountable to their crimes, including law-enforcement officials accused of such crimes. Further, the international organization encourages the country to train properly law-enforcement officials to protect the human rights of Burundians. In April 2009, Burundi's government passed legislation to abolish the death penalty. However, the legislation simultaneously outlaws consensual same-sex relations.

Burundians are guaranteed the freedom to practice their religion, which is also stipulated under Articles 2 and 18 in the UDHR. However, the Burundi government has violated numerous human rights in the country. For example, Burundians are imprisoned for expressing criticism of the government, which blatantly disregards Articles 2 and 19. Amnesty International and other international monitoring agencies have additionally raised the concern that though Burundi declared its intention to establish an independent national human rights commission, the law includes limits on the powers of inquiry into human rights abuses. The law additionally would limit the commission's independence from Burundi's government.

As of 2009, one of the worst human rights violations remaining in Burundi was human trafficking. Burundi is considered a country of origin for the trafficking of humans, particularly for the purposes of sexual exploitation or forced labor. In fact, the United Nations Children's Fund (UNICEF) has listed Burundi as one of the top ten African nations for the trafficking of children. Burundi also has a poor record regarding child soldiers, and has been listed as a destination country for children trafficked from Tanzania for military purposes. Furthermore, the government has failed to provide protection to children when they have been accused of child soldiering or have been forced into armed conflict.

ECONOMY

Overview of the Economy

Burundi's gross domestic product (GDP) ranks it as one of the world's poorest countries, though the economy is no longer shrinking. In 2008, the GDP was estimated at $3.1 billion (USD), with a per capita GDP of $389 (USD). Most of the population is engaged in subsistence agriculture, and approximately 68 percent of the population lives below the poverty line. Coffee and tea are the nation's chief exports and constitute more than 90 percent of export revenues.

Since 2007, the UN has remained active in helping Bujumbura to institute economic initiatives, though ethnic warfare in and around the capital continues to hinder infrastructural improvements. Progress has been made in improving conditions in Bujumbura, including new roads and repairs on prominent buildings. The UN contributed approximately $35 million in aid to Burundi in 2007. Burundi remains heavily dependent on foreign aid. In 2009, Burundi became part of the East African Community. This is expected to help decrease transportation costs and make the country's travel connections better.

Industry

There is relatively little industry in Burundi, except for light consumer goods, as the economy is heavily agricultural. As of 2008, industry represented about 19 percent of the gross domestic product, while services represented around 21 percent. The production of consumer goods focuses on locally used items such as cigarettes and clothing, as well as tourist items such as baskets. Public works projects are another important sector.

In addition to coffee and tea, cotton, tin ore, and animal hides are also chiefly exported in Bujumbura, the capital. The city also has several light manufacturing industries, including the manufacture of soap, textiles, and foodstuffs. Other industries include the processing and refinement of sugar and coffee. Bujumbura is the country's commercial and financial center, as well as the transportation hub.

Burundi's chief export partners are Switzerland, the United Kingdom, and Pakistan, while many of the nation's imports are purchased from Saudi Arabia, Kenya, and Japan. Belgium, Burundi's former colonial ruler, also remains a major trading partner. Other important markets include the other "Benelux" countries of the Netherlands and Luxembourg, and Germany, Great Britain, and Switzerland.

Labor

Burundi's unemployment rate was estimated at 14 percent in 2003. In 2002, 68 percent of Burundians were impoverished. Agriculture, including forestry and fishing, represents the country's largest employment sector; an estimated 90 percent of Burundi's workforce is involved in agriculture, including subsistence farming. The country's largest exports product is coffee, and a large number of Burundians are involved in coffee production.

Energy/Power/Natural Resources

Although it is one of the poorest countries in the world, Burundi is rich in natural mineral resources. Precious metals such as platinum and gold, as well as industrial minerals such as nickel, cobalt, copper, and tungsten are found in the country. These resources are largely unexploited, however.

About 35 percent of the land is arable, but agriculture is poor because of deforestation and erosion (due in part to overgrazing.) These environmental problems have in turn led to floods and landslides.

Fishing
Freshwater fishing, particularly on Lake Tanganyika, represents an important part of the Burundian economy. However, the lake faces increasing issues related to overfishing and over development. The country's freshwater fish catch was an estimated 14,000 tons in 2004. Species include torpedo robber, catfish, and sardines.

Forestry
Wood is a major fuel source in Burundi and this has led to extensive deforestation. In 2005, it was estimated that Burundi had the highest deforestation rate in Africa, losing over five percent of its overall forest cover each year. The loss of forest area in Burundi has negatively affected the country's elephant and gorilla population, in addition to hundreds of other native animal species.

Mining/Metals
Burundi is a significant exporter of gold. Gold mining in the country is administered by the Burundi Mining Corporation. In addition to gold,

Burundi has reserves of copper, cobalt, nickel, and uranium and produces limestone, sand, and gravel for domestic use. In 2005, mining and metals represented one percent of the country's total GDP.

Agriculture
Burundi's economy is largely agricultural. In 2008, agriculture represented approximately 33 percent of the country's GDP and employed around 33 percent of the population. Agriculture has suffered in recent decades, due to war and environmental problems such as drought. Coffee, tea, and sugar are the country's major cash crops. Coffee represents more than three-quarters of Burundi's exports.

Most agricultural production is at the subsistence level. Major food crops include corn, sorghum, cassava, beans, sweet potatoes, and bananas. Fishing is important on Lake Tanganyika.

Animal Husbandry
Burundians have traditionally been cattle-herders, but also raise sheep and goats. As cattle are a sign of wealth, they are generally not killed for meat.

Tourism
Tourism is in Burundi is minimal, because of the country's poverty and ethnic violence.

Kathryn Bundy, Eric Badertscher, Micah Issitt

DO YOU KNOW?

- Vénuste Niyongabo became Burundi's first Olympic medalist in 1996, by winning the gold medal for the 5,000-meter race.

- Lake Tanganyika, which is estimated to be more than 3 million years old, is the world's second largest and deepest freshwater lake. The lake contains more than 300 species of fish. The lake is of interest to scientists who believe it has the potential to help them learn about the process of speciation in relatively closed ecosystems.

Bibliography

Francis Bebey. "African Music: A People's Art." Chicago, IL: *Lawrence Hill Books*, 1999.

Jean-Pierre Chrétien. "The Great Lakes of Africa: Two Thousand Years of History." Brooklyn, NY: *Zone Books*, 2006.

Simon Gikandi. "Encyclopedia of African Literature." New York, NY: *Routledge*, 2002.

Robert Kruger, et al. "From Bloodshed to Hope in Burundi." Austin: *University of Texas Press*, 2007.

Peter Uvin. "Life After Violence: A People's Story of Burundi." London: *Zed Books*, 2008.

Nigel Watt. "Burundi: Biography of a Small Country." London: *Hurst*, 2015.

Works Cited

"Africa on a Shoestring." Oakland, CA: *Lonely Planet*, 2004.

"Arms Control and Disarmament Agreements: Burundi." http://first.sipri.org/search?country=BDI&dataset=agreements&dataset=international-organizations&dataset=political-terror-scale&dataset=press-freedom-index&dataset=conflict-barometer&dataset=global-peace-index&dataset=internally-displaced-person&dataset=major-conflicts&dataset=peace-missions.

"Background Note: Burundi." *U.S. Department of State.* http://www.state.gov/r/pa/ei/bgn/2821.htm.

"Burundi." https://www.cia.gov/library/publications/the-world-factbook/geos/by.html.

"Burundi Rebels in Ceasefire Pact." *BBC News.* http://news.bbc.co.uk/2/hi/africa/7420067.stm.

"Burundi: Statistics." *UNICEF.* http://www.unicef.org/infobycountry/burundi_statistics.html.

"Burundi: Bureau of Democracy, Human Rights, and Labor." *U.S. Department of State.* http://www.state.gov/g/drl/rls/hrrpt/2006/78722.htm.

"Country Profile: Burundi." http://news.bbc.co.uk/2/hi/africa/country_profiles/1068873.stm. *BBC News.*

Donn Bobb. "Ban Welcomes Burundi's FNL Renunciation of Armed Conflict." *United Nations Radio.* http://www.unmultimedia.org/radio/english/detail/73380.html.

"Document—Burundi: Human Rights Council Adopts Universal Periodic Review Outcome on Burundi: Amnesty International Outlines Key Human Rights Concerns in Burundi." http://www.amnesty.org/en/library/asset/AFR16/002/2009/en/2aa6d422-00fc-47aa-afcc-b6947b6f388a/afr160022009en.html. *Amnesty International*, March 19, 2009.

"Modern African Art: A Basic Reading List." http://www.sil.si.edu/silpublications/modernafricanart/maaprint.cfm?subcategory=Burundi. *Smithsonian Institute Libraries.*

Nigel Watt and Michael J. Dwyer. "Burundi: The Biography of a Small African Country." West Sussex, England: *Columbia University Press*, 2008.

Old Friday Mosque in Moroni, Comoros.

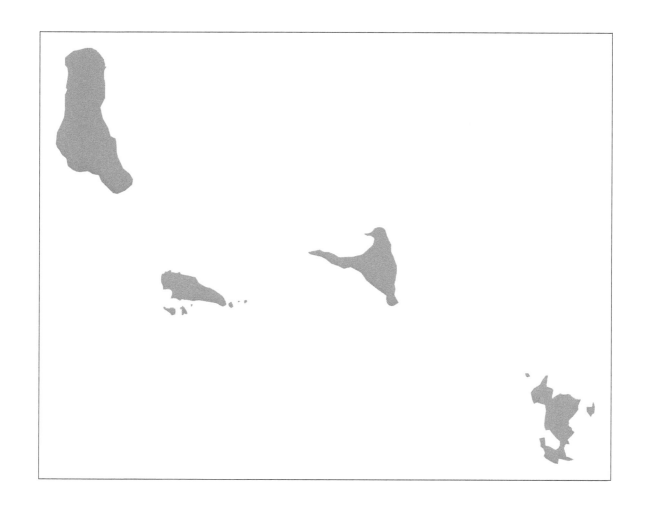

COMOROS

Introduction

The Union of the Comoros is an island nation located off the southeastern coast of Africa. The three largest islands in Comoros are Grande Comore (Njazidja), Moheli (Mwali), and Anjouan (Nzwani).

Known as the Perfume Islands, the Comoros islands are the world's largest producer of ylang-ylang flower, a main ingredient in perfumes, and the world's second largest producer of vanilla. Major tourist attractions include the islands' beautiful beaches and landscapes, as well as the islands' unique mix of Arab, African, Southeast Asian, and European cultural influences.

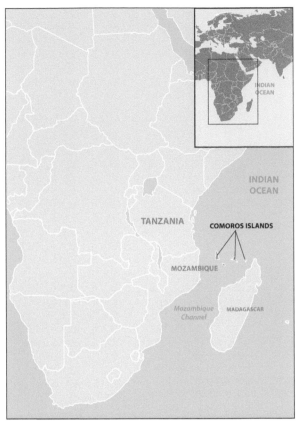

GENERAL INFORMATION

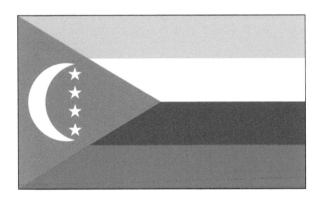

Official Language: Arabic and French
Population: 780,971 (2015 estimate)
Currency: Comorian franc (KMF), with banknotes issued in the form of 500, 1,000, 2,000, 5,000, and 10,000 francs.
Coins: The Comorian franc is available in coin denominations of 1, 2, 5, 10, 25, 50, and 100. The lower denominations of 1, 2, 5, and 10 francs are rarely seen.
Area: 2,235 square kilometers (863 square miles)
National Motto: "Unité, Justice, Progrès" (French, "Unity, Justice, Progress")
National Anthem: "Udzima wa ya Masiwa" ("The Union of the Great Islands")
Capital: Moroni
Time Zone: GMT +3

Flag Description: Displaying the traditional symbols of Islam (the color green and a crescent and stars), the flag of Comoros features a green triangle on the hoist side of the flag within which is a white crescent with four white stars forming a line between the crescent's tips. The green triangle is superimposed on four horizontal and equal stripes of yellow (representing Moheli), red (Anjouan), Mayotte (white), and blue (Grande Comore). Each individual island has its own flag, in addition to the national banner.

Population

The Comorian population represents a mix of many ethnic groups from the Middle East, mainland Africa, and the islands of Malaysia and Indonesia. However, 2015 estimates place the population at over 780,900, the 2003 population and housing census put the number at approximately 576,000 inhabitants on Moheli, Anjouan, and Grande Comore.

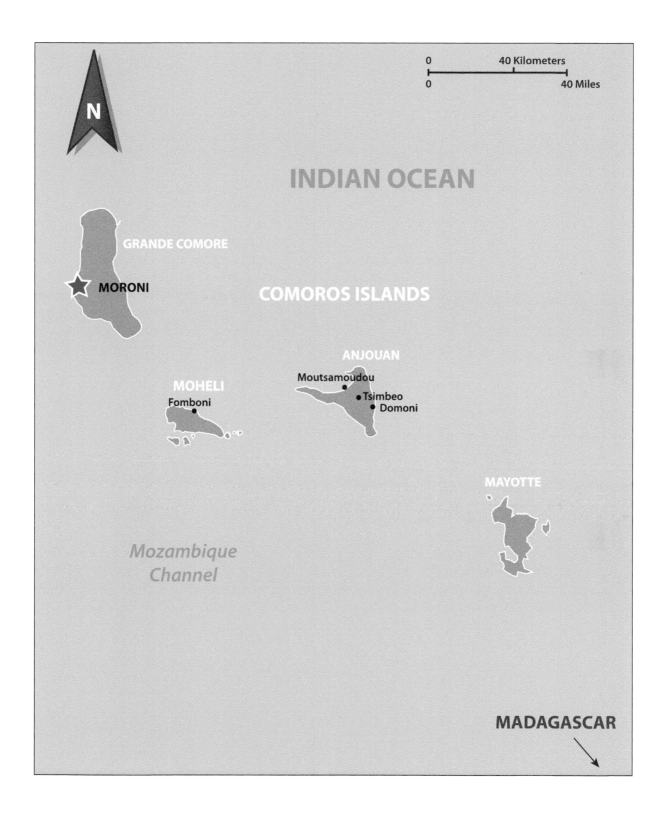

Principal Cities by Population (2012):

- Mutsamudu (26,469)
- Domoni (16,2799)
- Fomboni (18,277)
- Tsémbéhou (12,962)

Emigration has risen since the country's independence, in part because of political and economic instability. By the early 1990s, as many as 100,000 Comorians were living in other countries, mostly in East Africa and France. As of the early twenty-first century, this number had risen to over 150,000.

The islands' traditionally rural nature is also changing as more people move to cities. The largest cities are the capital Moroni, on Grand Comore, and Mutsamudu, on the island of Nzwani. As of the 2003 general population and housing census, however, Moheli was the only island where the majority of the population—and estimated 54.8 percent—lived in urban areas. Estimates in 2015, show that the total urban population was at 28.3 percent.

Languages

Though Arabic and French are often cited as the official languages—French is the language of government—the predominant local language is Comorian, or Shikomor, a Swahili-related language with many Arabic influences. Different dialects of Shikomor are spoken on the various islands: Shingazidja on Grand Comore, Shindzwani on Anjouan, Shimwali on Moheli, and Shimaore on Mayotte. Malagasy, a language of Madagascar, is also spoken. Both the Arabic and Latin alphabets are in common use.

Native People & Ethnic Groups

The Comorian population represents a mix of many ethnic groups from the Middle East, mainland Africa, and the islands of Malaysia and Indonesia. The mainland African peoples include the Cafres and Makoa; the Cafres were

early settlers, while the Makoa descend from the Arabs' slaves. Other groups include Malagasy, Oimatsaha, Sakalava, and Europeans. The islands' Creole population is of mixed French and local ancestry.

The islands were settled by the sixth century CE. Although the identity of the first settlers is not clear, it is believed they were from Arabia, the East African mainland, or Indonesia. The Shirazi, a group of Sunni Muslim traders from the Iranian city of Shiraz, began arriving in the tenth century. They established themselves as the dominant group, and developed the islands into a major trading center, connecting East Africa with the Middle East.

The Europeans, beginning with the Portuguese, arrived in the sixteenth century and helped to promote both the growth of the slave trade and the local use of slave labor, which led to arrival of new African groups on the islands. The French, who had had a presence in the Indian Ocean since the 1600s, annexed Mayotte in the 1840s and the other islands in the 1880s.

A Comorian peasant woman.

Religions

Most Comorians (an estimated 98 percent) are Sunni Muslim, and Islam is the country's official religion. Until 2002, the nation's official name was the Islamic Federal Republic of the Comoros. The 2001 constitution protects religious freedom, but missionary activity is prohibited and the government disapproves of the public practice of non-Islamic religions. The public is strongly opposed to other religions, and has at times persecuted the country's small Christian minority (two percent of the population). Mayotte, which officially remains part of France, has a larger Christian minority, most of whom are Roman Catholics.

Climate

Comoros has a tropical maritime climate, with two main seasons (dry and wet). Climate varies dramatically between islands. Each individual island also displays distinct variations from one point to another, because of changes in elevation.

The dry season runs from October/November to April, and is characterized by monsoon winds from the north, as well as the possibility of cyclones. The season is hot and humid, with average temperatures rising to 25° Celsius (77° Fahrenheit).

Each year, Comoros receives around 2,000 millimeters (79 inches) of rain. The wet season runs from May to September, bringing winds from the south.

ENVIRONMENT & GEOGRAPHY

Topography

The Comoros are located off the southeastern coast of Africa, at the northern end of the Mozambique Channel. Its closest neighbors are Madagascar (another island nation) and the mainland African state of Mozambique. The three largest islands in Comoros are Grande Comore (Njazidja), Moheli (Mwali), and Anjouan (Nzwani). The capital, Moroni, is located on the western coast of Grand Comore Island.

All four large islands in the Comoros chain (including Mayotte) are volcanic and mountainous, and the soil cover is generally thin. Grande Comore (Njazidja) is the largest island, with an area of 1,148 square kilometers (443 square miles). There are two volcanoes on the island, including Le Karthala, the country's highest point at 2,360 meters (7,743 feet) above sea level. The volcanoes' slopes are covered in places with lava flows.

The islands' terrain is generally rugged. Soil cover is thin, and only about 35 percent of the land is arable. There are stretches of rainforest on Moheli, and mangrove swamps along the islands' coastal areas.

Plants & Animals

Despite their small size, the Comoros islands are home to many species of plants and wildlife, some of which are also found on Madagascar and on the East African mainland.

The slopes of the volcanic peaks are heavily forested, often with evergreens. Erosion is common, because of the relative lack of soil cover. There are few large animal species, but many species are unique to the Comoros; these include two kinds of fruit bats. Several species are unique to Anjouan, including the Anjouan sunbird.

Conservationists are concerned about the degradation of natural habitats due to the encroachment of human settlements, cyclonic activity, and volcanism.

CUSTOMS & COURTESIES

Greetings

The Comoros is an Islamic nation, and most customs and courtesies are dictated by the Muslim faith. Shaking hands is the common gesture of greeting between Comorian men, but they will only greet women verbally—touching a woman in public is considered improper. Women customarily greet each other with a kiss on the cheek, and men and women may kiss one another on the cheek if they are in a private setting or if they are relatives. Proper greetings also depend on traditional gender roles and age. Elders are treated with great reverence, and children are expected to greet elders with respect. The traditional greeting for the child is to cup both hands while approaching the older person and saying "Kwezi," to which the older person will say "Mbona" in response. On the island of Mwali (Mohéli), the elder will traditionally raise the child's cupped hands to the child's forehead before responding.

Common greeting phrases include the informal "Edje" ("Hello"), in Shingazidja, a Bantu language popularly spoken in the Comoros islands. With superiors, elders, and strangers, Comorians will likely employ the more formal "Bariza husha" ("Good morning") or "Bariza masihu" ("Good evening"). In Mwali (Mohéli), it is common for friends to greet each other with "Djedje?" ("How how?"), followed by "Habari?" ("News?"). Muslim Arabic is also widespread in the Comoros, and one will often hear the traditional greeting of "Asalaam alaikum" ("Peace be unto you"). Other common expressions, such as "Insha'Allah" ("Allah willing") or "Alhamdul'illah" ("Thanks be to Allah"), are also frequently used.

When calling someone's name, Comorians on Ngazidja (Grande Comore) will usually say "Bo" before the name. Titles commonly used in the Comoros to express respect or affection include "mzé" for an older man, "mwana hangu" (my child/my brother) for close friends, "coco" for a grandmother and "fundi" for a teacher or artist.

Gestures & Etiquette

Islamic customs are generally practiced in the Comoros. It is inappropriate to wear very revealing clothing, and women are expected to dress conservatively, keeping their shoulders and ankles covered. It is also improper to drink in public. It is especially important not to eat, drink, or smoke during the daylight hours of the holy month of Ramadan. In addition, as the left hand is considered unclean and associated with personal hygiene, Comorians refrain from using it to eat or pass anything.

Comorians have a great deal of respect for elders, and age always precedes social class. The

town elders lead religious and ceremonial traditions and are often seen as counselors in political decision-making.

Lastly, speaking French is respected and signifies a good educational background, but it may be considered pretentious in everyday social interaction.

Eating/Meals

Comorians usually eat with their hands or with a spoon, and they usually wash their hands in a bowl of water before and after eating. Traditionally, people eat sitting on mats on the floor, and the food is prepared outside the house in open courtyards. In urban areas or in wealthier homes, families will eat sitting at a table. In rural areas and in traditional homes, women eat separately from the men, especially if they are hosting guests. Guests who are very close to the family may eat with the family. Otherwise, men and guests will eat at the dinner table or living room, and women will eat in the kitchen. Meals are traditionally served family-style, and a blessing is usually bestowed before eating begins.

A typical breakfast in the Comoros consists of tea with cold leftovers or a hearty meat broth. One popular breakfast broth is called supu, which has shredded meat and a few leftover bones or pieces of cartilage, and is generally bought from a market vendor and taken home in a plastic bag. Lunch, usually served in the afternoon, often consists of meat served with cassava or green bananas prepared with a savory sauce. Dinner is the main meal of the day and usually involves a rice dish, served with meat and sauce.

Dining out has traditionally held different connotations in Comorian society. For example, if a Comorian man eats out, especially in rural areas, the locals will wonder if he has no family, or is poorly fed at home.

Visiting

Comorians visit each other frequently, and it is considered rude to let too many days go by without connecting with friends and family. Extended families are often large, so many Comorians lead very full social lives. Visiting traditionally occurs in the late afternoon or early evening, and visiting is typically a casual affair. When visiting from out of town, however, it is polite to give the host oulaha (advance notice) for adequate preparations Visits on weekdays tend to be short, lasting an hour or less, but visits during the weekend may last an entire afternoon and might include at least one meal.

Guests are customarily expected to remove their shoes before entering a Comorian household. A host is typically expected to offer food and drink, which a guest is expected to accept graciously. While Comorians love to entertain, and are known for being friendly and passionate, those living on Mahoré (Mayotte) are known for being more reserved.

LIFESTYLE

Family

Comorian families are traditionally large and family needs generally take precedence over an individual's needs. When one shares wealth with the local community, it raises that person's esteem within that social group. Adult children are customarily responsible for caring for their parents. The Comoros are also a matriarchal society in the sense that women are considered the head of the household. Men are responsible for finances and property, and women maintain responsibility for domestic duties. In rural areas, many women seldom leave home. In urban areas, women are increasingly taking jobs that involve work outside the home.

In the Comoros, the father's given name becomes his child's surname. Daughters live at home and help with household chores until they marry and leave home. If there are younger siblings, daughters will help to raise her younger siblings. Sons typically move out of their childhood home at age 18 and traditionally build themselves a paillotte (thatched hut) nearby. They continue to eat at home and take part in family activities, but they will sleep and entertain in their own home.

Housing

Homes in the Comoros were traditionally constructed from natural resources, namely braided coconut leaves, mud mixed with straw, volcanic rock, and coral lime. Over time, cement has replaced stone, and metal sheeting has replaced coconut fronds. In 1975, a social housing project urged builders to use earthen bricks and paint homes in bright colors.

A typical home will be comprised of two rooms, one for receiving visitors, and one for private living; larger homes will also include a living room. Many homes still have a central courtyard that is traditionally used for domestic activity. Homes tend to be vibrant and colorful, and one will often see colorful fabrics and black and gold plastic furniture. On Mahoré (Mayotte), banga (bachelors) build their own homes, which are similar to the paillotte of the other islands, and allow local youths (usually teenagers) to paint brightly colored murals on them.

Food

Traditional Comorian cuisine combines East African traditions, such as root-based stews, with South Asian and Indonesian influences, notably rice-based curry dishes. Seafood and mutton are the most common protein options, followed by chicken and imported beef. Lobster, prawns, fish, and squid can be found almost everywhere, and they are usually inexpensive; tuna, barracuda, wahoo, and red snapper are the most commonly served fish. Pork is prohibited by Islam and thus rarely seen in the Comoros.

The most common starches served are breadfruit, cassava, green bananas, potatoes, and taro. Fruits such as bananas, litchi (lychee), mangoes, oranges, papayas, passion fruit, and pineapples are abundant. The only vegetables usually found in the markets are cucumbers, green beans, onions, and tomatoes. Locally grown spices, including vanilla, cloves, coriander, cardamom, cinnamon, saffron, and nutmeg, are used in many dishes. Comorian cuisine is often characterizes as spicy, and a hot pepper sauce, known locally as putu, is popular across all of the islands.

French cuisine and imported beverages are becoming increasingly popular, and bread and pastries have become more prevalent over the years. However, Comorian cuisine remains traditionally comprised of the staples of rice, cassava, plantains, coconut milk, and seafood. Some popular local dishes include poulet au coco (a rice dish with chicken and mixed vegetables), langouste à la vanille (a lobster dish steeped in vanilla), and kebabs (chunks of meat grilled on skewers). Porridge is also common and often served with dried fruit. Meals are usually taken with water, tea, or fruit juice. Comorian tea is spiced with lemongrass and ginger, and Comorian coffee is served black with sweet syrup.

In Mahoré (Mayotte), imported products from France and South Africa are commonly seen in both supermarkets and home-cooked meals. Restaurants in Mahoré (Mayotte) are often French, and all wine, beer, and spirits on the island are mostly imported from France. For festivals and special occasions in the Comoros, beef and goat meat are served with rice and curdled milk, and cake is often served for dessert.

Life's Milestones

The Comoros is an Islamic nation—nearly 98 percent of the population adheres to Sunni Islam—and milestones are generally observed in accordance with the Muslim faith. Births are considered divine blessings and children are treated exceptionally well. Polygamy is an accepted practice, though becoming less common, and it is normal for many Comorians to marry more than once. However, women who have previously married cannot participate in the Grand Mariage again, which is considered the most important event in Comorian society.

The Grand Mariage (Great Wedding) is often between an older, wealthy man and a young bride. These lavish celebrations can take three years to plan, and are a source of debt for many Comorian men. The tradition requires a two- to nine-day toirab, which is a celebration with copious amounts of food, dancing, and music to which an entire village is invited. In addition, the

groom is expected to offer a large dowry of gold jewelry, and women afterward wear the bwibwi, a black garment that displays their now elevated status. Additionally, once a man has completed a Grande Mariage, he is considered a wandru wadzima (a grand notable), and he is allowed to wear a special m'ruma (sash). This indicates his new elevated status and signals his participation in village councils that are traditionally held in the bangwes (town squares). Her family also traditionally gives each bride a house, and the size of the home is considered a status symbol.

CULTURAL HISTORY

Art

Comorians are known for their traditional arts, including basketry, folk pottery, woodcarving, embroidery, doll making, and jewelry making. Wooden carvings are most often seen in furniture and doors, but can also be found in functional objects such as carved coconut graters and children's toys. Coral is also used to make intricate carvings, often for use as accent pieces in doorways and furniture. Embroidery is typically designed for attire, but it can also be found in curtains and other home accents. Comorian jewelry is usually crafted from gold or silver.

Different regions produce different crafts, as well. For example, Nswani (Anjouan) is known for crafting dolls and long swaths of chiromani cloth, worn draped over the shoulder in a manner similar to the Indian sari dress. Mbéni produces traditional kofias (embroidered round Muslim hats), and Itsandra has a reputation for fine crafting Comorian djohos (traditional dress for men). Production of traditional pottery has declined, but Foumbouni on Ngazidja (Grande Comore) is still known as the pottery center of the Comoros. Ngazidja (Grande Comore) and Mahoré (Mayotte) are both known for the traditional art of basketry.

Architecture

The architecture of the Comoros islands reflects the culture's diverse heritage, incorporating traditions from Africa, France, and the Middle East. On the French island of Mahoré (Mayotte), the architecture has a distinctly Arabic feel, while on the other islands of Ngazidja (Grande Comore), Mwali (Mohéli), and Nswani (Anjouan), Swahili and Arabic influences are evident. Many cities and villages in the Comoros are fortified, and contain numerous buildings that feature artfully designed doors with intricate carvings. These carvings include Islamic text, artwork, and symbols, or inlaid brass studs. Traditional Comorian townhouses are typically built around a courtyard, with an internal balcony lining the upper floors. An open kitchen is usually situated in the back of the home.

Popular building materials in traditional Comorian architecture include stone, wood, and coral. Stone is often used in monuments, such as tombs, or in structures that Comorians refer to as "Doors of Peace." These can include mosques, palaces, public spaces, and arched doorways. Elaborate tombs include domes and pillars made of stone. Wood and coral are also used in decorative ways, often with carvings of calligraphy from the Koran (Islam's holy book) or arabesque patterns, which are generally geometric or floral.

Moroni and Mutsamudu, cities on the islands of Ngazidja (Grande Comore) and Nswani (Anjouan), respectively, have impressive Arab quarters with winding medinas (walled Arabic quarters) of narrow and maze-like stone streets. In Tsingoni, the sultan capital of Mahoré (Mayotte), a mosque and several royal tombs dating back to the sixteenth century have been restored. Restoration and preservation efforts have also saved nineteenth-century sugar factory chimney remnants from the colonial era.

Dance

Traditional dancing in the Comoros is often gender-specific. Women customarily dance the deba, wadaha, bora, and lelemama, while men dance the shigoma, diridji, mshogoro, sambe, and zifafa. The deba has its origins in a Muslim prayer that is usually performed by young girls, with an emphasis on movement of the head and hands. For special occasions, the young girls will be adorned with flowers and gold. A more intricate dance is the wadaha, a seductive and rhythmic dance that is sometimes considered a prenuptial dance. The wadaha is often called the dance of the pestles, and women and girls will dance around a mortar filled with rice while gesturing as if using a mortar and pestle to crush the rice. The men's diridji dance often involves dancing around a table.

The one dance in which women, men, and children all participate is the mougodro, a circle dance of Malagasy and African origin. Over the years, the mougodro has become a central part of Muslim festivals.

Music

Music is an important part of life in the Comoros, and combines elements from Arabic, African, Indian, and European traditions. Taarab music from Zanzibar is especially popular, and the Comorians have created their own version, which is known as twarab. Rap and reggae have also been incorporated into popular Comorian music. Several Comorian musicians have moved to France, where they have collaborated with European producers to cultivate a loyal following. The most common musical instruments in the Comoros include accordions, guitars, violins, drums, gongs, and rattles. Instruments unique to the Comoros include the gabusi and the 'ud, both stringed instruments similar to a lute; the ndzendze, a box-shaped stringed instrument; and the mkayamba, a percussion instrument made of reeds sewn together and filled with seeds.

Literature

Comorian literature is rooted in the ancient oral traditions of storytelling, particularly folktales, or hali. These are often moral and didactic fables passed down through the generations. Common themes and subjects include creation stories and the history of different villages, as well as the tales of valiant war heroes. Philosophical poetry, proverbs, and riddles are also popular. Many popular folk stories are performed as plays, and native Comorian dialects are still the norm in these theater pieces. Humor is employed to make social commentary more palatable, and productions will often be accompanied by village orchestras. Comedies and tragedies are equally popular, and works continue to deal with everyday issues, such as marriage, polygamy, and intergenerational relations.

While many Comorian folktales revolve around male heroes, there is also a tradition of stories that honor the mother-daughter relationship. In several different tales, an orphaned girl will be mistreated by another woman, only to later triumph, similar to the classic story of Cinderella. Interestingly, just as females are often merely props in stories with male protagonists, men often do not figure prominently in stories with women protagonists. The Office of Cultural Affairs has been working to preserve, transcribe, and organize Comorian oral literature into a coherent body of work.

The folklore also reflects the island nation's diverse roots. The story of Sabour, which is of Indian origin, is told in both Mauritius and on the island of Mahoré (Mayotte). The father asks his daughter what she would like him to bring back from his travels, and she says "sobur" (wait). Only when he finally meets Prince Sobur does the father realize that the daughter had something different in mind. The story traditionally starts with a riddle and is solved with a play on words, an example of how Indian Ocean folklore often combines several cultural traditions and employs linguistic confusion for both humor and meaningful puns.

The oldest Comorian literature was written by royalty and intellectuals, particularly princes, sultans, and aristocrats. They recorded traditional folk tales and historical events, usually in Arabic. Much of modern Comorian literature is unpublished or in Comorian dialects, but the number of Comorian novels and poetry collections available in French is increasing. Notable writers in the Comoros include Aboubacar Said Salim (1949–) and Abdou Salam Baco (1965–).

The two dominant contemporary writers from the Comoros are Mohamed Toihiri (1955–) and Nassur Attoumani (1954–). Toihiri's two novels, *La République des Imberbes* and *Le Kéfir*

du Karthala, are two of the first internationally recognized Comorian works of fiction. The first novel is an unforgiving satire of Comorian socialist Ali Soilih (1937–1978) and his government, in which both conservative Muslims and radical revolutionaries are scrutinized. Toihiri's second novel is another satire that focuses on the apartheid rule in South Africa that helped overthrow Soilih's regime.

Attoumani is a novelist and playwright who uses a great deal of satire in his work. In his plays, *La Fille du polygame* (*The daughter of a polygamist*, 1992), *Le Turban et la capote* (*The turban and cape*, 1997), and *Interview d'un macchabé* (*Interview with a stiff*, 2000), Attoumani examines the uneasy intersection between traditional Muslim values, French culture, and Western materialism. He addresses the practice of polygamy, the silence around HIV/AIDS, misconceptions about contraception, and government corruption. In *Interview d'un Macchabé,* Attoumani's national pride comes through as the devil disguised in a sash with the three colors of the French flag causes the protagonist's downfall. Attoumani is even more critical in his novels: *a Le Calvaire des baobab (The plight of the baobabs, 2000) features* a doctor unable to cure with Western medicine. *Nerf de boeuf* (*Nerf beef*, 2000) shows the brutality of the slave trade on the Comoros islands; and *Mon Mari est plus qu'un fou: c'est un homme* (*My husband is a fool is a man,* 2006) critiques both materialism and domestic violence.

CULTURE

Arts & Entertainment

Comorian art and culture reflects the diversity of the islands' Arab, East African, and Southeast Asian populations, and also undeveloped mass media.

Radio is the primary means of media dissemination in the Comoros, and musical events are often broadcast over national radio stations. Television is steadily growing, but most families do not own a television set.

Modern art forms such as painting are also increasing in popularity, especially among the youth in Mahoré (Mayotte). The island is home to the Mahoran Center for Cultural Action, a publicly funded organization that supports artists and encourages the incorporation of both Comorian and French cultures. In Itsandra, on the island of Ngazidja (Grande Comore), the Centre National de l'Artisanat Comorien (the National Center for Comorian Crafts) was founded in 1995 to train and support local artisans.

The Volo Volo Market, located outside Moroni's downtown area is a major community center. A variety of products can be obtained at the Volo Volo Market, including native art and handicrafts, clothing and food. The market and surrounding areas are also a prime location for cultural ceremonies, music, and food.

Cultural Sites & Landmarks

In 2007, the Comoros islands submitted four sites for consideration of World Heritage status by the United Nations Educational Scientific and Cultural Organization (UNESCO). These include the marine ecosystem of the archipelago of the Comoros, the terrestrial ecosystems, and cultural landscape of the archipelago of the Comoros, the historic sultanates of the Comoros, and the cultural landscape of the perfume plantations of the Îles de la Lune.

The marine ecosystem southwest of Ngazidja (Grande Comore) is home to the coelacanth. This 400-million-year-old "living fossil" was believed to have gone extinct 80 million years ago, only to be rediscovered in 1938. The first coelacanth was discovered off the coast of South Africa, but the Comoros islands appear to be one of the only regions on earth where colonies of coelacanth have been found. Scientists estimate the population of coelacanth to be around 500 worldwide, and they are considered critically endangered by the International Union for the Conservation of Nature (IUCN). Included in the Comorian terrestrial ecosystems is Mount Karthala, one of the world's largest active volcanoes. It is also home to many endemic bird species, four of which are only found in the Comoros: the Comoro drongo,

the Comoro scops Owl, the Comoro white-eye, and the Humblot's flycatcher.

The UNESCO World Heritage proposal also highlights the old medinas of Mutsamudu from the 14th century: Domoni from the 12th century, Itsandra from the 14th century, Iconi from the 12th century, and Moroni from the 14th century. While these towns are different in both size and history, they share beautiful palaces that span seven centuries, as well as religious buildings, defense fortifications, and bangwes (open spaces).

Another natural environment of note in the Comoros is Îlot Bouzi, a large island in the Mahoré (Mayotte) lagoon, with its own species of lemur. Over 300 makis (Comorian for lemur) live on this conservation area and have grown accustomed to humans, but remain endangered. The other manmade landmarks of note in the Comoros are the two "Friday Mosques" found on Ngazidja (Grande Comore): the Ancienne Mosquée du Vendredi, dating back to 1427, and the Nouvelle Mosquée du Vendredi, the main mosque Comorians attend on Fridays. To enter, one has to be male and properly dressed in pants with properly cleaned feet.

Libraries & Museums

Cultural institutions in the Comoros include the National Library and the National Museum.

Holidays

Comoros' national holiday is Independence, or National, Day (July 6), which celebrates the country's independence from France in 1975. Islamic holidays, particularly Ramadan, are also widely observed. Other observed holiday include New Year's Day (January 1) and Labor Day (May 1).

Youth Culture

Malagasy (the culture of Madagascar) and Islamic influences remain strong in the Comoros, particularly in terms of education (Koranic teaching, for example). Unlike many forms of Western education, which values individualism, Comorian education emphasizes loyalty to a group and obedience to elders and the proper way to live. Growing Islamic fundamentalism among the younger generations, particularly those studying abroad, has become a concern for some monitoring agencies. As of 2004, the youth literacy rate was an estimated 59 percent.

Nonetheless, the youth of Comoros are becoming increasingly more westernized and enjoy similar fashions, music, and recreational sports as youth in Western countries. European music trends, afropop, and reggae are all popular styles of music, and traditional music has remained influential. Popular recreational activities for youth include the staging of village dances and beach picnicking. Older youth enjoy congregating in restaurants, clubs, and discotheques. In July 2008, amid fears of "loosening morals" among the youth population, the government, specifically the Islamic affairs ministry, launched a crackdown that targeted immodest clothing, alcohol consumption, and teenage parties. Since the turn of the twenty-first century, there is also a prevailing sentiment among the older generations that interest in preserving the traditional bangwe culture is waning among Comorian youth.

Football (soccer), basketball, and volleyball are all popular, and Comoros has a national football team. The squad officially joined FIFA (Fédération Internationale de Football Association) in 2005, but as of 2009, the squad has yet to qualify for a World Cup or African Nations Cup berth. Regardless, each town has a soccer team that competes at the national level, and there is a great deal of team spirit. In 2015, Comoros was 190 in the FIFA world ranking.

SOCIETY

Transportation

Because short distances are the norm, popular modes of transportation are walking or bicycling. Taxis-brousses (bush taxis) and charettes (cattle-drawn wooden carts), the latter more common in rural areas, are used for longer distances. Taxis-brousses can vary in size between a car, a mini-van, and a small bus, and they are often crowded.

When traveling between the islands, travel by boat is the norm, in either larger cargo boats or smaller galawas, which are similar to dugout canoes. Because most of the boats do not have motors, departures depend on the outgoing tide. Domestic flight service between islands, provided by the domestic carriers Comores Air Service and Comores Aviation, is also available. There are no direct flights to the Comoros from most areas of the world.

Drivers in Comoros travel on the right-hand side of the road. Seatbelts are mandatory for those operating the vehicle. Rural roads can be in poor condition.

Transportation Infrastructure

The Comoros islands has four main airports, the international airport of Moroni International Prince Said Ibrahim (HAH), and the secondary airports at Ouani (Anjouan) and Baderessalam (Moheli), all of which are paved. There are two main ports—one on the French island of Mahoré (Mayotte) and one on the island of Nzwani (Anjouan) in Mutsamudu. As of the early twenty-first century, the island of Grand Comore accounts for an about 80 percent of the archipelagic nation's trade activities, despite lacking a deep-water port.

As of the early 21st century, the road network in the Comoros, both nationally and regionally, included an estimated 849 kilometers (527 miles) of roadways, approximately 665 kilometers (413 miles) of which are paved. Over half—nearly 60 percent—of the road network is on Grand Comore.

Media & Communications

The government often limits the media in Comoros and self-censorship is commonly practiced. The major newspaper is the state-operated *Al Watwan,* which is published weekly in both French and Shingazidja (the dialect of Comorian spoken on Grande Comore). *KashKazi* is an independently owned newspaper that is printed weekly, and *L'Archipel* is a magazine issued monthly. *La Gazette des Comores* is another weekly newspaper available in French and the main newspaper of Mahoré (Mayotte) is *Kwezi*, which is also published weekly.

Television service is very limited, and radio remains the island nation's dominant medium. The Comorian government owns Office de la Radio et de la Television des Comores (ORTC), which runs Television Nationale Comorienne (TNC), the main network, and Radio Comoros, the national radio network. Regional radio stations are state-run, and there are several private radio stations, as well. There is one AM station, four FM stations and one shortwave station. In Moroni, there is an educational and cultural channel, Mtsangani Television (MTV), and Nswani (Anjouan) runs its own Radio-Television Anjouanaise (RTA). The one private television station is TV Ulezi.

Communication technology is sparse on the Comoros and only about 23,500 Comorians, as of 2014—uses a landline telephone. Roughly 383,000 Comorians, as of 2014—use a cellular phone. In fact, Comoros is often considered the last country to have a mobile phone network. In 2006, teledensity was estimated at 2.3 percent. As of 2008, there were eight Internet hosts, and in 2014, there were an estimated 50,200 Internet users.

SOCIAL DEVELOPMENT

Standard of Living
Comoros is one of the world's least-developed nations. As of 2013, the country was ranked 159th on the United Nations Human Development Index (HDI), which measures quality of life indicators.

Water Consumption
Depending on the island, surface waters, subterranean waters, and rainfall are the three principle sources of water supply in the Comoros. Foreign aid, namely non-governmental organizations (NGO), has helped to construct piped water networks in the latter half of the twentieth century. According to a 2004 household survey, less than 31 percent of the population relies on public

faucets and fire hydrants for their drinking water supply, while nearly 25 percent rely on collected rainfall in cisterns. In 2006, The European Commission stated that it was time to address the country's water conditions. A clean up was funded with roughly $1.3 million in European aid. This led to over 1,500 water supplies being treated and protected.

A lack of a universal sanitation system and a waste management system has become a growing health concern in both the urban and rural populations.

Education
Public education in Comoros is a mixture of secular French and Islamic (Sunni) models. Islam is studied in the public schools at the lower secondary level. Prior to entering public school, between the ages of five and seven, many children attend Koranic school, where they learn the basics of the Qur'an (Islam's holy book) and classical Arabic.

At the elementary level, schooling is free and compulsory between the ages of six and twelve, and organized into three states of instruction. There were approximately 295 public elementary schools in the early 21st century, 173 of which were located on Grand Comore, as well as 85 private schools. Secondary education lasts up to age 19, and is offered at public or private schools (public schools are known as rural colleges.) It consists of a lower secondary education and a higher secondary education (high school). Most secondary schools, public or private, were on Grand Comore.

Higher education is relatively undeveloped. As of the early 21st century, technical and vocational education comprised post-secondary education, and was handled at four centers: the National School of Technology Versatile Ouani (ENTP); the National School of Fisheries in Anjouan; the Ecole Nationale d'Agriculture (ENA) on Moheli; and the National Horticultural Center (CNH) on Grand Comore.

The overall literacy rate in 2015 is at 77.8 percent (81.8 percent among men and 73.7 percent among women).

Women's Rights

While the Comorian constitution guarantees equal rights for women, in practice, these rights are not always enforced. Comorian society has also historically maintained matriarchal traditions, such as the female ownership of land. Still, women remain marginalized in society and are expected to focus on domestic responsibilities. Overall, Comorian women experience a lesser social status, and very few women hold positions of power, in both business and the political arena. These gender attitudes are also rooted at an early age. For example, many poor families are forced to commit their young daughters to domestic servitude while sons are prioritized. Often, these young female servants work for wealthier families in exchange for only room and board.

The lack of professional opportunities for women in the Comoros stems from a lack of educational opportunities. As of 2003, 64 percent of men were literate, while less than half—an estimated 49 percent—of Comorian women could read and write. In addition, as of 2004, men attended school for nine years, while women attended school for an average of seven years. In rural areas, this gender division is more apparent, as women are more often confined to farming and childrearing, with few other options. In urban areas, the numbers of women in the workforce are increasing. However, even though more women are earning comparable salaries to male counterparts, few women held positions of leadership.

Women also remain marginalized politically. Women won the right to vote in 1959, but continue to have little political representation. As of 2015, only one seat of the 33-member Comorian national assembly was held by a woman, Djoueria Abdallah. In fact, in 2004, Abdallah, a former village midwife, became the first woman to become a member of the Assembly of the Union of the Comoros. Overall, women's groups are not political and less established, and tend to revolve around community development and education. However, while women are not allowed in mosques, they are respected as instructors of the Koran, and elder women are often treated with great respect.

Rape and domestic violence are illegal, but are not properly enforced or monitored. These are often considered familial matters, and village elders or family members typically intervene in these cases. Prostitution is illegal but arrests for prostitution are rare. Sexual harassment is also illegal and considered a common problem, but is usually unreported. Lastly, while women are not required by law to wear head coverings, it is generally expected in Comorian society.

Health Care

Comoros has poor health care, and disease is widespread; malaria is an especially serious problem, which affects a large majority of the population. Tuberculosis and leprosy are also widespread.

There are few trained physicians in Comoros, although conditions have improved since independence. International organizations have provided some medical assistance, although this remains limited.

Infant mortality is high, at 63.55 deaths per 1,000 live births (2015 estimate). As of 2015, average life expectancy was 63.85 years—61.57 years for men and 66.19 years for women.

GOVERNMENT

Structure

Under the constitution adopted in 2001, Comoros has a national president and three regional island presidents. The national president is chief of state, and governs with the assistance of Council of Ministers and a prime minister, all of whom are appointed by the president. The constitution specifies that the presidency rotate among the three regional presidents every four years.

The unicameral legislature is known as the National Assembly. Its 33 members, or deputies, serve five-year terms. Eighteen deputies are popularly elected, and the island assemblies elect the others. Suffrage is universal.

In general, the Comoros has been a politically fragile nation. Recently, Comoros has experienced much political and institutional conflict, hampering both administrative and financial management, as well as data collection and monitoring.

Political Parties

Generally, the Comoros does not have an organized system of political parties. Groups tend to rally around certain leaders and ideologies, such as autonomous island governance or centralized government. During the legislative elections of 2004, there were two primary parties—the Convention for the Renewal of the Comoros (CRC) and the Camp of the Autonomous Islands, which won the majority of seats.

As of 2009, the U.S. Department of State lists seventeen political parties. During the 2009 parliamentary elections, supporters of President Ahmed Abdallah Mohamed Sambi (unofficially, a personality-driven presidential party) won the majority of seats in the National Assembly.

Local Government

When the island nation implemented a new constitution in December 2001, three levels of government were established: central government (the Union of the Comoros), regional government (island government), and local government (Commune). Each island can maintain its own constitution, and has the right to financial autonomy. Generally, outside of foreign relations, national defense, nationality, higher education (the nation maintains one university) and religion, islands can administer their own affairs.

In 2010, the last election, Ikililou Dhoinine was elected president with a 61.1 percent vote.

Judicial System

Comoros' judicial branch is headed by the Supreme Court (Cour Supreme). The national president and former presidents, the National Assembly, and the island governments select judges. The legal system is based on a mixture of French and Islamic (Sharia) law consolidated into a single code. Operational and structural difficulties continue to hamper the judicial system. In the Supreme Court, the president, two by the Assembly of the Union, and one from each of the three island councils appoints two judges. All appointed judges serve for life.

Taxation

Since 2006, Comoros has expanded indirect taxation and decreased customs tariffs, effectively exchanging them for excise taxes as a main source of revenue. Customs taxes and sales taxes also increased. In addition, income tax was redesigned as a tax on salaries. In 2014, taxes amounted to 24.3 percent of the country's GDP.

Armed Forces

The armed forces are made up of a small army and police force, the latter numbering about 500 police officers. The Comoros also maintains a 500-member security force. The island nation has a treaty with France in which the latter country provides naval protection, air surveillance, and training.

Foreign Policy

The Comoros have been plagued by instability since achieving independence in 1975—the country has endured 20 coups—and it remains one of the poorest nations in the world. The country still struggles for sovereignty and held its first peaceful elections in 2006. The country also has a history of human rights abuses, particularly on the autonomous island of Nswani (Anjouan). In 2008, price hikes and food and fuel shortages resulted in increased social unrest. As a result, economic and social aid and regional relations define the foreign relations of the archipelagic nation.

Comoros has historically remained close with France, which holds a claim over the island of Mayotte the Glorioso Islands. French sovereignty of these territories has been questioned, and both countries are signatories to a mutual security treaty. (The other unresolved dispute is the Comorian claim to Banc du Geyser, a reef in the Mozambique Channel that is also claimed by France and Madagascar.) Frustrated by perceived equalities between their people and those on the main island of Ngazidja (Grande Comore), the islands of Mwali (Mohéli) and Nswani (Anjouan) declared independence from the Comoros in 1997. The Comoros islands have since found a peaceful solution by creating a rotating presidency in which each island rules the archipelago in four-year terms. Comoros remains dependent on French aid, both economically and politically.

The Comoros islands currently enjoy a generally positive relationship with their immediate neighbors and the global community at large. The island nation became a member of the United Nations (UN) in 1975, and is a member state of numerous other international organizations, including the African Union (AU), the Arab League, the Group of 77, the European Development Fund (EDF), the World Bank, the International Monetary Fund (IMF), the African Development Bank (ADB), and the Indian Ocean Commission (IOC). The country also maintains observer status in the World Trade Organization (WTO). The Comoros has also signed on to many environmental pacts, including the Kyoto Protocol.

In addition, Comoros served as the chair of the Eastern African Standby Brigade (EASBRIG) from 2008 through 2010. The EASBRIG, established by the African Union, is the reserve brigade of the states of East Africa.

Human Rights Profile

International human rights law insists that states respect civil and political rights, and promote an individual's economic, social, and cultural rights. The United Nations Universal Declaration on Human Rights (UDHR) is recognized as the standard for international human rights. Its authors sought the counsel of the world's great thinkers, philosophers, and religious leaders, and were careful to create a document that reflects the core values shared by every world culture. To read this document or view the articles relating to cultural human rights, visit http://www.udhr.org/UDHR/default.htm.

While the Comorian government generally respects the human rights of its citizens, monitoring agencies have branded the archipelagic nation with a poor human rights record. Problem areas include gender discrimination, child labor, and abuse, a lack of government transparency, and poor prison conditions. Islamic law inspires the Comorian constitution, but the nation does not claim Islam as the official religion. Nonetheless, religious freedom remains an issue, and Christians and other religious minorities are often discriminated against. In 2008, a country report on human rights abuses by the U.S. Department of State also focused on similar areas of concern.

Official corruption remains a concern in the Comoros. In Transparency International's (TI) 2007 Corruption Perceptions Index (CPI), the Comoros was ranked 123 of 180 countries, and both government officials and police officers were reported to have taken bribes in exchange for miscellaneous favors and to have paid for promotions. Prison conditions also remain deplorable, and are largely criticized as being overcrowded and having inadequate sanitation and medical facilities. In some cases, families have to provide proper meals for prisoners in order to combat poor nutrition.

The government has kept a tight rein on the media, and many journalists reported extensive self-censorship. While citizens are guaranteed free speech, criticism of the government is often punished. For example, Colonel Mohamed Bacar (1962–), who reigned as president of one of the autonomous islands of the Comoros from 2001 to 2008, punished political prisoners by locking them in shipping containers after prisons became overcrowded. In fact, the worst human rights violations in the Comoros, including torture, rape, illegal detention, and forced exile, occurred under Bacar's regime on the island of Nswani (Anjouan). Since his forced removal in March 2008, such extreme violations in the archipelago have been rare.

ECONOMY

Overview of the Economy

Comoros has one of the world's weakest economies, and relies heavily on foreign aid and wages earned by citizens working overseas. As of 2014, the country's gross domestic product (GDP) was estimated at $ 717 million (USD), with a per capita GDP of $1,000 (USD). The economy is growing at 3.3 percent in 2014.

Industry

Industry in Comoros is largely undeveloped, represents 13.7 percent of GDP. Major industries are vanilla production and the distillation of perfume essences, such as that of the ylang-ylang flower.

The United States is Comoros' largest export market, but France is an important trading partner for both exports and imports. Tourism is an important industry, although this continues to be hindered by poor transportation links to the outside world.

Despite the importance of ocean-borne freight, there are few ports in Comoros, and large vessels are generally unable to enter the harbors.

Labor

The Comoros labor force was estimated at 239,000 in 2012. Agriculture accounted for approximately 80 percent of the national workforce, with the industry and services sector rounding out the remaining 20 percent. Unemployment remains high; the last broadcasted rate was 20 percent in 1996.

Energy/Power/Natural Resources

Comoros has negligible natural resources. The soil cover is generally thin, and has eroded in places due to improper agricultural techniques. The nation cannot feed itself, and must import most of its food. As recently as 2004, the primary source of energy was wood.

Fishing

Fishing in Comoros remains mostly traditional (non-industrialized) and for subsistence purposes, and occurs in nearshore waters. In 2002, the fishing fleet of Comoros numbered 4,500 boats, 1,500 of which were motorized. That year, fish production was estimated at 15,300 tonnes. Under an agreement with the European Union, foreign vessels, mainly French and Spanish, are permitted to fish for tuna. Unsustainable and illegal fishing methods remain a concern.

In recent years, the government has focused on increasing fishery production; in 2009, the government took out a loan from an Indian bank to improve the fishing industry, which included the procurement of better vessels.

Forestry

The islands have no intact natural forests.

Agriculture

Known as the Perfume Islands, the Comoros islands are the world's largest producer of ylang-ylang, the main ingredient in most high-quality perfumes, and the world's second-largest producer of vanilla. Ylang-ylang flowers can be harvested three times per month all year long without depleting the environment, making it a sustainable crop for the Comoros and a steady source of income for the farmers.

Comoros' agricultural sector accounts for around 40 percent of GDP, but engages the majority (80 percent) of the workforce. Only around 35 percent of the land is arable, and the soil is generally thin. As of the early 21st century, it is estimated that 80 percent of agricultural production is for domestic and home consumption.

Most commercial production goes into cash crops such as vanilla, cloves, copra, and ylang-ylang flowers. The bulk of agricultural products are exported rather than consumed internally. Export crops are generally grown on plantations, a remnant of the French colonial period. Roughly, one-third of the country's food supply must be imported.

Animal Husbandry

Comorian farmers raise small numbers of cattle and goats, and then sheep, and poultry to a lesser extent. Donkeys are bred on the island of Moheli, and milk cows are breed on Anjouan.

Tourism

Tourism has become an important part of Comoros' economy, but the islands' isolation and political instability has made it difficult for tourists to travel there. In addition, the industry, particularly the tourism infrastructure, still has yet to be sufficiently developed. Services, including tourism, represent more than half of Comoros' GDP.

The tourism industry experienced an increase of nearly 5 percent in tourist arrivals in 2008, a large percentage of which were French.

Jennifer Kan Martinez,
Eric Badertscher, Micah Issitt

DO YOU KNOW?

- Wealthy Comorian Arabs practice a wedding custom known as the "grand marriage," which involves elaborate and expensive gift giving. The custom is seen as a person's entry into formal society, and as a prerequisite to holding high political office.

- The islands of Comoros appear as a destination in the medieval Arab legends of Sinbad, which make up part of the tales known as *One Thousand and One Nights*, or *Arabian Nights*.

- In 1938, Comorian anglers caught a coelacanth, a fish previously thought to have become extinct millions of years ago. The fish became known as a "living fossil."

- The Comoros is home to the Livingstone's flying fruit bat, which is a large—its wingspan can stretch over 4 feet—and rare species of bat that is found nowhere else in the world.

Bibliography

Aaron Anderson, et al. "Madagascar & Comoros." Hawthorn, Australia: *Lonely Planet*, 2008.

Donald Haase. "The Greenwood Encyclopedia of Folktales and Fairy Tales." Westport, CT: *Greenwood Publishing Group*, 2007.

Edward A. Alpers. "A complex relationship: Mozambique and the Comoro Islands in the 19th and 20th centuries." Paris: *Cahiers d'études africaines,* no. 161, 2001.

Fiona MacDonald, et al. "Peoples of Africa." Oregon City, OR: *Marshall Cavendish*, 2000.

Helen Chapin Metz, ed. "Comoros: A Country Study." Washington, DC: *GPO for the Library of Congress*, 1994.

Lee Haring. "Indian Ocean Folktales: Madagascar, Comoros, Mauritius, Réunion, Seychelles." Chennai, India: *National Folklore Support Centre*, 2002.

Peter Hawkins. "The other hybrid archipelago: introduction to the literatures and cultures of the francophone Indian Ocean." Lanham, MD: *Lexington Books*, 2007.

Samantha Weinberg. "Last of the Pirates: The Search for Bob Denard." New York: *Pantheon Books*, 1994.

Simon Broughton, et al. *"World Music."* London, England: *Rough Guides*, 1999.

Works Cited

"Background Note: Comoros." *U.S. Department of State,* Mar. 2009. http://www.state.gov/r/pa/ei/bgn/5236.htm.

"Comoros." *Central Intelligence Agency World Factbook.* https://www.cia.gov/library/publications/the-world-factbook/geos/cn.html.

"Comoros." *Encarta Online Encyclopedia.* http://encarta.msn.com/encyclopedia_761566120_2/Comoros.html.

"Comoros." *Encyclopædia Britannica Online.* http://www.britannica.com/EBchecked/topic/129467/Comoros.

"Comoros." *European Institute for Research on Mediterranean and Euro-Arab Cooperation.* http://www.medea.be/index.html?page=2&lang=en&doc=34.

"Comoros." *Lonely Planet.* http://www.lonelyplanet.com/comoros.

"Comoros." The Index on Africa. *The Norwegian Council on Africa.* http://afrika.no/index/Countries/Comoros/index.html.

"Comoros." The Weather Channel Comoros Travel Guide, *Atevo,* 2007. http://www.weather.com/outlook/travel/vacationplanner/destination/guide-comoros?from=vac_amelist.

"Comoros." *The World Bank.* http://web.worldbank.org/WBSITE/EXTERNAL/COUNTRIES/AFRICAEXT/CO

MOROSEXTN/0,,menuPK:349947~pagePK:141132~pi
PK:141107~theSitePK:349937,00.html.

"Comoros." *U.S. Department of State*. http://www.state.
gov/g/drl/rls/hrrpt/2007/100474.htm.

"Comoros." *UNESCO Country Profile*. http://portal.
unesco.org/ci/en/ev.phpURL_ID=1340&URL_DO=DO_
TOPIC&URL SECTION=201.html.

"Comoros." *UNESCO World Heritage*. http://whc.unesco.
org/en/statesparties/km/.

"Comoros." *Freedom House*. http://freedomhouse.org/
template.cfm?page=22&country=7374&year=2008.

"Comoros and the EU." Delegation of the European
Commission to the Republic of Mauritius, Comoros,
and the Republic of the Seychelles, 2000. http://www.
delmus.ec.europa.eu/en/coop_comoros_overview_
p2.aspx.

"Comoros Business." *I-Explore*. http://www.iexplore.com/
world_travel/Comoros/Business.

"Comoros: Cautious optimism after calm Anjouan
elections." IRIN (Integrated Regional Information
Networks), *UN Office for the Coordination of
Humanitarian Affairs*, 2 Jul. 2008. http://www.irinnews.
org/Report.aspx?ReportId=79057.

"Comoros: Concerns over possible social unrest." IRIN
(Integrated Regional Information Networks), *UN
Office for the Coordination of Humanitarian Affairs*,
22 Aug. 2008. http://www.irinnews.org/Report.
aspx?ReportId=79944.

"Comoros Islands." *International Crisis Group Crisis
Watch*, 1 Sept. 2008. http://www.crisisgroup.org/
home/index.cfm?action=cw_search&l=1&t=1&cw_
country=30&cw_date=.

"Country Profile: Comoros." *BBC News*, 7 Nov.
2008. http://news.bbc.co.uk/2/hi/africa/country_
profiles/1070727.stm.

"Customs of Comoros." *Encarta Online Encyclopedia*,
2008. http://encarta.msn.com/encnet/refpages/
RefAuxArt.aspx?refid=631524668.

"The Fish Out of Time." *Coelacanth Information*, 2009.
http://www.dinofish.com/.

"The Union of the Comoros: Humanitarian Country
Profile." IRIN (Integrated Regional Information
Networks), *UN Office for the Coordination of
Humanitarian Affairs*, Jul. 2007. http://www.irinnews.
org/country.aspx?CountryCode=CO&RegionCode=SAF.

"Timeline: Comoros." *BBC News*. http://news.bbc.co.uk/2/
hi/africa/1070770.stm.

"Trade in Goods (Imports, Exports and Trade Balance)
with Comoros." *U.S. Census Bureau, Foreign Trade
Statistics*, 2009. http://www.census.gov/foreign-trade/
balance/c7890.html.

"Travel Alert." *U.S. Department of State*, 16 Mar. 2009.
http://travel.state.gov/travel/cis_pa_tw/pa/pa_4203.html.

"Union des Comores." *Présidence de l'Union des Comores*
[site official], http://www.beit-salam.km/index.php.

"Universal Declaration of Human Rights." http://www.
udhr.org/UDHR/default.htm.

Abouhariat S. Abdallah and Elie-Dine Djouma. "Portrait:
M'ma Amina ou la couturière du luxe traditionelle."
Al-watwan, 6 Mar. 2009. http://www.alwatwan.net/
pdf/06032009.pdf.

Anna Gilibert and Milena Maccaferri. "Public Places in
the Comoros." Africa Revisited, *UNESCO*, 11 Jun.
2007 http://whc.unesco.org/uploads/events/documents/
event-442-1.pdf.

Mahmood Keldi. "Social Housing and Architecture in the
Comoros Islands." *BATICOM (the First International
Forum on Housing in the Comoros Islands)*, 16 Feb.
2009. http://baticom.org/contenu%20forum/archives/
KELDI_-_English_-_social_housing_and_architecture_
Comoros-_Final.pdf.

Michael McCarthy. "Why Canada is the best haven
from climate change." *The Independent*, 4 July 2008.
http://www.independent.co.uk/environment/climate-
change/why-canada-is-the-best-haven-from-climate-
change-860001.html.

"Mohéli, l'île nature." *Mohéli Tourisme*, 2006. http://www.
moheli-tourisme.com/.

"Omni Country Guide for Comoros." *Overseas Moving
Network International*, 2006. http://www.asiantigers-
china.com/country_guides/Comoros.doc.

Peter Hawkins. "Until when shall we remain postcolonial? Globalisation, nationalism and cultural self-
determination in the literatures of the Indian Ocean."
*University of Bristol, 'L'ici et l'ailleurs': Postcolonial
Literatures of the Francophone Indian Ocean*, special
issue of e-france: a Journal of French Studies, Volume 2
(2008), www.reading.ac.uk/e-france.

Raymond G. Gordon, Jr., (Ed.). "Languages of Comoros."
Ethnologue: Languages of the World, Fifteenth edition.
Dallas, Tex.: *SIL International*, 2005. http://www.
ethnologue.com/.

Sarah Grainger. "Comoros seeks sweet smell of success."
BBC News, 14 Sept. 2004. http://news.bbc.co.uk/2/hi/
africa/3652780.stm.

Susan L. Jewett. "On the Trail of the Coelacanth, a Living
Fossil." *The Washington Post*, 11 Nov. 1998. http://www.
washingtonpost.com/wp-srv/national/horizon/nov98/
fishstory.htm.

Suzanne Daley. "Mutsamudu Journal; Indian Ocean Island
Yearns to Retie Colonial Bond." *New York Times*, 29
Sept. 1997 http://www.nytimes.com/1997/09/29/world/
mutsamudu-journal-indian-ocean-island-yearns-to-retie-
colonial-bond.html?.

Afar woman in traditional clothing.

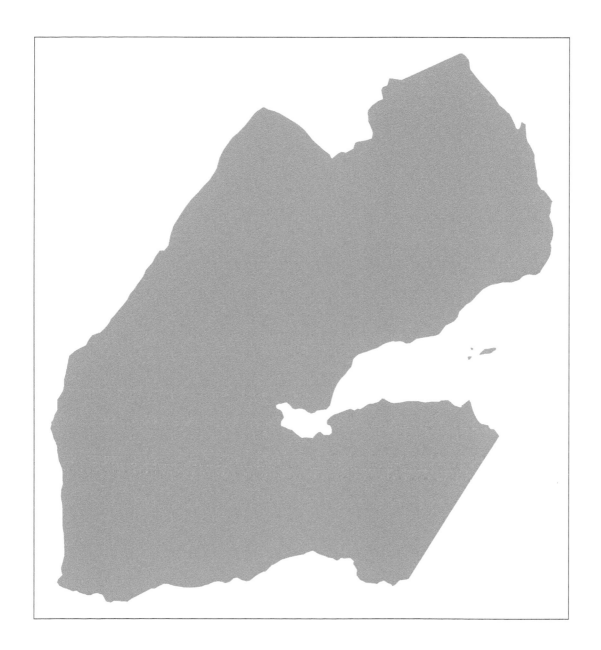

DJIBOUTI

Introduction

Djibouti, formerly known as French Somaliland and the French Territory of the Afars and Issas, is a small nation in northeast Africa. It is located on the western shore of the Red Sea at the Gulf of Aden, and is bordered by Eritrea to the north, Ethiopia to the west and south, and Somalia to the southeast. The nation, famous as a seaport and trade route, was colonized by Italy, Great Britain, and France before gaining independence in 1977.

In the 1990s, a civil war broke out that lasted until 2001. It ended in with a peace agreement between the Afar rebels and the Somali Issa (clan) government. The accord brought in the first multiparty government and the newly elected Ismail Omar Guelleh. Guelleh was reelected in 2005, and in 2011 instituted an amendment that granted him eligibility for a third term, which he won.

Dance, oral literature, and poetry are prevalent art forms in Djibouti. Most of Djiboutian music and poetry is used to narrate the history of the country's people, particularly the Afar. Traditional Djiboutian crafts include the knives of the Afar and Issa and woven straw mats called fiddima.

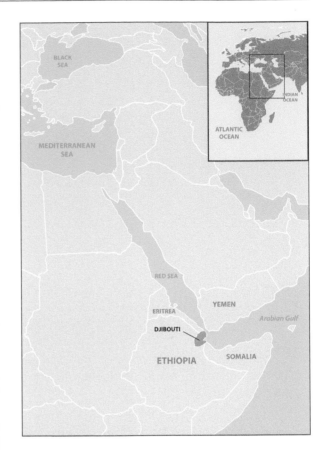

GENERAL INFORMATION

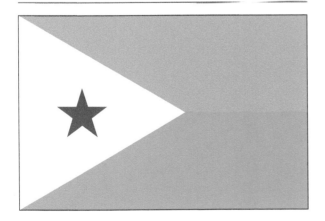

Official Language: Arabic, French
Population: 828,324 (2015 estimate)
Currency: Djiboutian franc
Coins: Coins are available in denominations of 1, 2, 5, 10, 20, 50, 100, and 500 francs.

Land Area: 23,180 square kilometers (8,949 square miles)
Water Area: 20 square kilometers (8 square miles)
National Motto: "Unité, Égalité, Paix" ("Unity, Equality, Peace")
National Anthem: "Djibouti"
Capital: Djibouti (City)
Time Zone: GMT +3
Flag Description: The flag of Djibouti features a triangle design, with the base of the white isosceles triangle extending along the entire width of the hoist (left) side. A horizontal band of blue (top) represents sea and sky, while an equal horizontal band of green (bottom) symbolizes the earth. A five-pointed red star is centered within the white triangle, symbolizing unity. The colors have also been interpreted as representing ethnicity, most specifically green for the Afar and blue for the Issa.

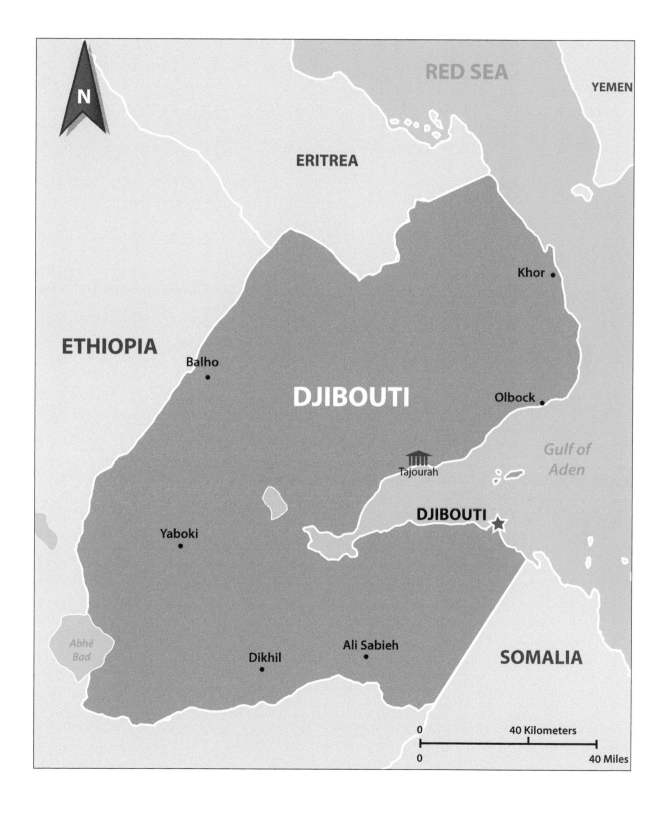

Principal Cities by Population (2012):

- Djibouti (513,669)
- Ali Sabieh (24,456)
- Dikhil (20,908)
- Tadjorah (13,138)
- Arta (11,934)
- Obock (10,734)

Population

Djibouti's population is divided into two main ethnic groups: the Issa and the Afar. The Issa are a group of ethnic Somalis living in the southern and eastern areas of Djibouti, near the capital. The Afar, a group of nomadic herders, lives in the northern part of the country.

Roughly, 60 percent of all Djiboutians are Somali, while 35 percent are Afar. Minorities account for the remaining 5 percent of the population, and include people of French, Arab, Ethiopian, and Italian descent.

It is estimated that more than 80 percent of Djiboutians live in or around Djibouti City, the capital and by far the largest city in the country, with a population of more than 529,000 (2015 estimate). The capital is known for its blend of African, French, and Arabic culture. Djibouti City features a marché central ("central market"), the nation's largest Islamic mosque (Hamoudi Mosque), and an important seaport that conducts the majority of East Africa's trade.

Other population centers in Djibouti include Ali Sabieh, located in the Great Barra Plains; Tadjoura, the oldest city in the nation; Obock, the area first colonized by the French; and Dikhil, where Afar land divides into Issa land.

Languages

Although French and Arabic are the nation's two official languages, most Djiboutians speak Afar or Somali. Afar belongs to the Cushitic language family, while Somali is largely influenced by Arabic.

Native People & Ethnic Groups

The Afar people are considered the first ethnic group to inhabit Djibouti. In the ninth century, Arab traders brought Islam to East Africa. The herders living in Ethiopia and Eritrea converted to Islam and developed into the nomadic Afar society. The group then migrated to the area now known as Djibouti. Arabs controlled Djibouti for roughly 700 years before the arrival of Europeans.

As nomadic herders, many of the Afar people live in self-governed clans and settle in temporary camps called burra. The typical dwellings of the Afar are portable huts called ari, which are made of sticks.

Due to harsh heat and droughts in the desert, many Afar have moved to Djibouti City to adopt urban jobs, Western-style clothing, and permanent dwellings. In the 20th century, the Afar felt oppressed by the Issa-dominated government, and instigated rebellions and conflict. During the 20th century, civil war broke out several times, over issues of colonialism and political representation. The two groups are now at peace as the result of a 2001 agreement.

Religions

Nearly 95 percent of Djibouti's population is Muslim. The remaining 6 percent is Christian. The form of Islam practiced by Djiboutians is relatively liberal. Most Djiboutian Muslims drink alcohol, which is sold throughout the nation. Both the Issa and the Afar were among the first Africans to adopt Islam.

Climate

Djibouti has a dry, hot climate typical of the sub-Saharan region. Djibouti City is the hottest city on the African content, with an average temperature of 30° Celsius (86° Fahrenheit). Most rainfall is received between November and April, when the temperature cools to an average of 25° Celsius (77° Fahrenheit). During the dry season, temperatures often reach 45° Celsius (113° Fahrenheit).

Djibouti experiences numerous natural hazards, including earthquakes, droughts, cyclones, and flash floods from the Indian Ocean.

ENVIRONMENT & GEOGRAPHY

Topography

Djibouti's three geographical regions are the coastal plains in the east at Ghoubbet El Kharab (the Bay of Ghoubbet), the volcanic plateaus in the south surrounding the Ardoukoba volcano, and the mountain ranges in the north. There are some forests in the northern region, but for the most part Djibouti's land is dry and bare.

There are several mountain ranges in Djibouti, including the Dalha Mountains, the Mabla Mountains, and the Goda Mountains. The highest point in Djibouti is at the peak of Mount Moussa Ali, 2,028 meters (6,654 feet) above sea level.

Djibouti is one of the only nations in East Africa that is primarily covered with desert. The desert plains consist of the Petit Barra Depression and the Grand Barra Depression, which neighbor each other in the south, the Alol Depressions in the west, and the Gammaré and Hanlé Plains in the southwest.

Lac (Lake) Assal, which lies at the bottom of a crater 155 meters (509 feet) below sea level, is the lowest point on the African continent. Lac Abbé in the southwest is the nation's other major lake. Moucha Island, Maskali Island, and the Sawabi Islands are the major islands off the coast of Djibouti.

Djibouti, the capital, is located on a coral reef isthmus, a narrow strip of land connecting two large landmasses, on the southern shore of the Gulf of Tadjoura. The city is in the south end of the country, near the Somali border, and is home to a number of dormant volcanoes.

Plants & Animals

Due to long droughts and low average annual rainfall, vegetation in Djibouti is mostly limited to drought-resistant trees and shrubs. These include acacia trees, doum palms, and date palms. The euphorbia, a plant that resembles the cactus, is also common. Several varieties of boswellia trees, which produce frankincense, are also found in Djibouti.

There are several dense forests in the northern regions of the country, particularly in the Forêt de Day National Park (Day Forest National Park). However, these forests are in danger of being cleared to provide more grazing land for the country's many herds of cattle, sheep, goats, and camels.

Djibouti is home to numerous endangered animal species, including elephants, giraffes, zebras, wildebeests, dik diks, cheetahs, hyenas, lions, and vultures. The encroachment of the desert threatens the existence of many of these wild species.

In the waters off the country's coast, marine animals such as sea slugs, clown fish, and green sea turtles are commonly found. Birds such as curlew and sanderling live in the Red Sea habitat, while numerous flamingoes inhabit the area surrounding Lac Abbé.

A dik-dik is a small antelope that lives in the bushlands of eastern and southern Africa.

CUSTOMS & COURTESIES

Greetings

The shaking of hands is a common greeting in Djibouti, though people seldom shake hands with members of the opposite sex. The right hand is used exclusively, as the left hand is associated with personal hygiene. Among friends and family, Djiboutians may clasp hands for a longer period than is common in other cultures. Issa men may also place their hands over their hearts.

French and Arabic are the official languages of Djibouti, and the languages most often used in an official or business setting. Most people speak either Afar or Somali, depending on their ethnicity. Greetings may be made in any of these languages, depending on who is speaking and in what context. Generally, however, the most common greeting among Muslims of all ethnicities is "Salaam alaikum" ("Peace be with you"), to which the proper response is "Malaikum salaam" ("And also with you"). A similar greeting in the Somali language is "Ma nabad bna" ("Is it peace?"), to which the reply is "Waa nabad" ("It is peace"). Other common greetings in Djibouti include "Marhaba" ("Hello") in Arabic and "Bonjour" ("Good day") in French. It is considered polite to ask after the other person's health following the initial greeting.

Gestures & Etiquette

Almost 95 percent of Djibouti's population is Sunni Muslim. Although many nomads are not strictly orthodox in their religious practices, the country shares a code of polite behavior with other Islamic countries. It is considered polite to use formal modes of address, including honorific titles, unless invited to use first names. For example, the Muslim honorific titles of sheikh and hajji are used for learned men and people who have made the pilgrimage to Mecca respectively. Worshippers remove their shoes when entering a mosque and women must cover their hair. It is also customary to remove one's shoes when entering someone's home.

A number of gestures are considered rude, such as beckoning to someone with your index finger or pointing. It is also considered offensive to use the left hand to gesture or hand objects between people, as it is traditionally associated with the cleansing of the body, and therefore perceived as impure. Thus, pointing at someone with the left hand is particularly insulting. In addition, sitting in a way that shows the soles of the feet or shoes to someone is generally perceived as disrespectful.

Traditional Islamic ideas concerning the modest behavior of women are prevalent in Djibouti. Adult members of the opposite sex typically do not touch one another, with the exception of close family members. However, it is common for members of the same sex to hold hands in public or walk arm in arm. Women do not wear a veil, as is common in some Islamic countries, but generally refrain from wearing revealing clothing. Many women drape themselves in a sheer, brightly colored length of fabric called a shalma. Married Afar women typically wear a black scarf that covers their head and shoulders.

Eating/Meals

Islamic dietary restrictions are largely followed in Djibouti. For example, Muslim Djiboutians refrain from consuming pork and alcohol and observe Ramadan, the Muslim holy month of fasting. During this period, Muslims do not eat or drink from sunrise to sunset.

The majority of Djiboutians typically eat two meals per day. Meals are generally organized around the workday, with the main meal eaten in the middle of the day. A second, smaller meal is then eaten in the evening. A typical meal will consist of a soup or stew served with a starch, usually rice, or durra, a flatbread made from sorghum. While meals are generally eaten at home, families traditionally do not eat together. Typically, the adult males eat first, in the main room, served by the women of the family; women and children eat later in the kitchen.

It is customary for Djiboutians to eat sitting on the floor. In this manner, the meal is served in a common bowl or platter set on a mat in the center of the group. Djiboutians use the right hand to eat, breaking off a piece of bread or scooping up a portion of rice, and then using the starch as a utensil for eating the main dish. Hands are washed at the table before and after eating.

Visiting
Much of the social life in Djibouti is segregated by gender. A large portion of male social life in Djibouti centers on chewing the narcotic leaf qat, which is imported from Ethiopia. Many men spend their leisure time at their local mabraz, or public qat café, where they can chew qat. Women generally meet together in their homes in the late afternoon or evening, often doing basketwork or other handiwork.

Guests to a Djiboutian home are generally treated with honor. Traditionally, milk was served to guests, as this made the host responsible for protecting the guest from harm. The arrival of a guest at the tribal encampment was often a cause for a feast consisting of a butchered animal from the tribe's herds. In contemporary Djibouti, this hospitality extends to even a casual visitor, who is generally offered tea or coffee.

When someone is invited for a meal, the host will wait for a guest to begin eating. Even though family meals are segregated, a couple that is invited to dinner will typically eat together, though the hostess will probably not eat with her guests. Guests are not expected to contribute food or drink to a meal, but it is considered polite to bring a gift for an initial visit to a Djiboutian home. Common gifts include small amounts of household staples such as sugar, rice, millet, or flour. Gifts that are more extravagant include perfume, cloth, or gold rings. Overeating is generally perceived as disrespectful.

LIFESTYLE

Family
The traditional lifestyle of the nomadic peoples of Djibouti depends on seasonal grazing patterns and the necessities of herding. As such, they are often grouped as three or four extended families, led by the senior male of the most important family. The extended family is made up of the nuclear family (husband and wife and their unmarried children), their married sons, and their wives. Daughters that are married off join their husband's extended family.

The nuclear family model remains the norm in Djibouti, but the extended family remains ideal. With unemployment rates as high as 40–60 percent in the early 21st century, food, and other resources may be customarily shared among extended family and tribe members. Polygamy (the practice of multiple wives) is allowed—a man may take up to four wives—among the Issa, with each wife responsible for specific tasks and raising her own children.

The prevalence of the nuclear family unit can be attributed to the fact that the majority of Djiboutians reside in the city of Djibouti. Nonetheless, it remains common for one family to have six to eight children, and for elders to remain with an adult son. It is also common for students to live with relatives while studying in the city. In addition, the combination of extreme poverty, civil war (1991–1994), emigration and urban migration, and an increase in the divorce rate has created a large number of households headed by a single woman.

Housing
Because of their lifestyle, the nomadic peoples of Djibouti traditionally live in modest and temporary housing. This generally consists of dome-shaped huts built of a framework of branches that are covered with a layer of cured hides and several layers of coarse mats made from the fibers of palm leaves or acacia tree bark. The huts for the entire tribe are grouped into a temporary village. Often, a circular fence of thornbush is erected for protection. These huts are easily disassembled and transported when it is time to move the herds.

Houses in urban Djibouti are typically made from cut coral blocks and cement (which may also be made from coral). For the most part, houses are Arabic in style and built to stay cool in the extreme heat of summer. Walls are thick and whitewashed to reflect the sun, and window screens are perforated with elaborate designs to help circulate the air and block out direct sunlight. It is estimated that two-thirds of Djibouti's population lives in the capital, many of them in shantytowns (informal settlements) and squatters' camps on the city's outskirts

Food

Because Djibouti is mostly volcanic desert, arable land is very limited. The country also suffers from periodic droughts and food shortages. As a result, Djibouti produces only three percent of the food it requires, and most food is imported. The main staples of Afar and Issa nomads are grains, such as rice and sorghum, and dairy products produced by their herds, such as ghee (clarified butter), milk, and yogurt. Because their herds are seen as wealth rather than food, animals are butchered only when they became too old or for special occasions. A dish often served at celebrations is muqmad, which is made from dried meat cooked in clarified butter and served with dates. Durra (sorghum) is most often eaten in the form of griddle breads similar to pancakes, often with a sauce of ghee and red pepper.

Residents of the city of Djibouti, where meat, vegetables, and fruit are imported daily, enjoy a more varied diet than the country's nomadic population. In fact, Djibouti City is considered to have some of the finest food in Africa, combining French and Arab influence with traditional African ingredients. Popular dishes include roast lamb with yogurt sauce, lentil stews, cucumber salad, and a spicy oven-baked fish dish known as poisson yemenite. Both croissants and Middle Eastern-style flatbreads are commonly served with meals.

Even though Djibouti has a long coastline and access to a wide variety of fresh seafood, only the inhabitants of the coastal cities of Obock and Tadjourah include fish in their daily diet. Similarly, sweet dishes are also rare in Djibouti cooking. An exception is moksaba, a mixture of honey and dates. Typical drinks in Djibouti include sweet spicy hot tea, coffee flavored with cardamom or lemongrass, fruit juices, and locally produced soft drinks.

Life's Milestones

Islam is the predominant religion in Djibouti, and many milestones are accordingly observed in the Muslim faith. This includes the circumcision of Muslim boys, generally before the age of five, and the Muslim requirement—it is, in fact, Djibouti law—that marriages involve a religious ceremony. In addition, as is common in Islamic culture, there are both male and female undertakers for funerals, and only a member of the same sex prepares bodies for burial.

Many Djiboutian women give birth at home. Among the Issa, a mother and child are confined to the house for 40 days after birth. During this period, both wear bracelets and earrings made from garlic and herbs to protect them from the "evil eye."

The family may also light incense twice a day to protect the baby from the smells of everyday life, which are considered dangerous. Traditionally, the baby is not named until the end of the 40 days. Most marriages are arranged, and men traditionally pay a bride price, now mostly money, to the bride's family. In the case of divorce, a woman keeps her bride price. Premarriage rituals vary from tribe to tribe.

CULTURAL HISTORY

Art

Like many nomadic peoples, the Issa and Afar of Djibouti traditionally created portable art designed for utilitarian purposes. Afar women are known for their textiles, and weave colorful mats known as fiddima from palm tree leaves. These mats are woven in many different patterns and their complexity of design has been compared to Persian rugs. Depending on the size or design, fiddima are used as prayer rugs, sleeping mats, or in burial preparations. There are also traditionally used as a dowry item. Issa women weave less complex mats for use as carpets and mattresses, sometimes using colored cloth rags to create decorative patterns. The most common craft is basketry, which includes plates, containers, and the coarse mats used under loads

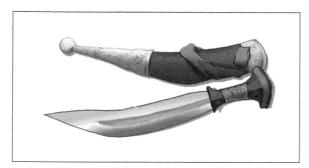

The jile, or "gile" is a short sword specifically associated with Djibouti and Ethiopia.

on a camel's back, made by both Afar and Issa women. The skill of basketry is also applied in the construction of huts.

Djibouti nomads also create jewelry from amber and malachite and household objects from wood and metal. Single pieces of wood are carved into elaborately decorated wooden headrests, finely carved combs, spoons and ladles, and drinking cups. Smiths make jewelry and weapons from old railroad spikes. The city of Tadjoura is known for making beautiful examples of the jile, the three-foot long curved dagger that Afar tribesmen traditionally wore at their waists.

Architecture

Djibouti is known for its unique architecture, which blends the styles of the Arabs, Moors, and French, and this intriguing blend of cultures can be seen in the capital. The city of Djibouti was planned by the French during the 19th century as a deepwater port in order to bypass the established caravan trade routes. The architecture and layout reflect France's wealth and dominance in Djibouti—the streets are arranged in a grid with numerous arched walkways, government buildings are clustered at the city center, and the houses are built in a French style.

The city's French colonial heritage is particularly evident in the European Quarter, which blends Arabian and European architecture. As a result, Mediterranean-style whitewashed houses and Moorish arcades are juxtaposed next to Parisian-style cafés and shops, and buildings decorated with art deco plasterwork stand

adjacent to structures decorated with Islamic vinework designs and calligraphy. (Similarly, the African Quarter of the city mixes traditional African and Moorish architectural elements.) Indigenous architecture is more likely to be found in the surrounding towns and villages of the capital.

Drama

Belwo is a popular urban art form that can be described as the dramatic meeting of song and poetry. Belwo are very short poems—generally only two to four lines—about love and passion. It was believed to have been invented in the 1940s by Abdi Deeqsi (c. 1920s–1967), popularly known as Abdi Sinimo, a Somali truck driver. Deeqsi adapted the elaborate imagery of classical Somali-language poetry to a condensed form that sang of erotic love, creating linguistic puzzles to be decoded by the audience. He also introduced lively tunes to which the poems were sung, often accompanied by tambourine and lute.

Belwo rapidly became a popular item at qat parties, where they were sung in a format called "string of pearls," in which a number of the short poems are sung one after another. When Djibouti's first radio station, Radio France d'Outremer, began broadcasting in 1955, belwo were used as a popular way of filling time between programs.

Music & Dance

Traditionally, music in Djibouti was interwoven into the daily life of the nomadic Afar and Issa Somali tribesmen who make up the country's two major ethnic groups. Songs were performed as part of a group activity, which included religious rites and celebrations of birth, marriage, or circumcisions. There were functional songs such as war and praise songs; songs meant to preserve history, such as genealogical songs; and communal work songs. Music involved the whole community, or tribe, and there was no distinct class or caste of musicians. Most traditional music was performed in a call and response style and songs were often accompanied by rhythmic clapping or stomping.

Musical instruments also traditionally served a functional purpose. Both the Afar and Issa use wooden flutes to accompany the movement of animals. The tanbura, a six-stringed bowl-shaped lyre decorated with small mirrors, is used in pagan possession rituals known as zar. In addition, copper kettledrums with a head of steer skin symbolize the power of the sultan of Tadjoura, Djibouti's oldest town. A new drum is made when a sultan is enthroned—when he dies, the head of the drum is torn, and the instrument is buried.

With the advent of local television programming in the 1980s, Djibouti began to produce professional musicians for the first time, many of whom perform traditional songs. The development of a national music scene was helped by the introduction of an annual music festival in the capital in 1982, hosted by the French Cultural Center. At the same time, younger musicians in urban Djibouti, particularly the capital, began to form Western-style musical groups, borrowing musical styles from the pan-African diaspora and Western instruments such as the electric guitar, saxophone, and electronic keyboards. By the 1990s, some musicians were describing themselves as distinctly Djiboutian, rather than Afar, Issa, or Arab.

Both the Afar and Issa traditionally perform rhythmic dancing, accompanied by drumming and clapping, to mark special events and rites of passage. Some dances are intended to encourage warriors, such as the barri horra, an Afar war dance, and the hari mondé, a Somali dance in which male and female dancers are divided into opposing lines. Some are tied to events, such as the barimo, which is danced at weddings by men and women in pairs, or the dinkara, which is danced at the enthronement of the sultan of Tadjorah. The hogwayn is a Somali courtship dance.

Some dances have a ritual or magical function, such as the hirwo, which is a rain dance, or the dance used to inspire the Afar poet-prophets known as ginnili. Other dances are linked to specific locations such as the zayla'i, a Somali dance from the town of Zela'I, and the hafat

malabo, an Afar dance from the city of Tadjoura. As Djibouti's population becomes increasingly urbanized, its traditional dances have been preserved through wedding ceremonies or cultural shows.

Literature

Djibouti does not have an indigenous tradition of written literature. However, both the Afar and the Issa have extensive traditions of oral poetry. Afar poetry, known as gad, is traditionally recited or sung at evening gatherings or ceremonies. One of the most common themes of Afar poetry is praising camels. Camels are the most valuable animals in the nomadic Afar economy. They are symbolic of values that are important in nomadic culture, such as virility, endurance, and self-reliance.

The poetry of the Issa, like that of other Somali tribes, is highly alliterative. Alliteration of a single consonant appears in every line of a poem. There are four traditional types of Issa poetry. Gabay and jiifto both run between thirty and 150 lines and deal with serious political, philosophical, and religious issues. Geerar are shorter, and were traditionally used to rouse warriors to go to war and to taunt the enemy (and now take a derogatory form). Burambor are written and recited by and to women, and are often accompanied by rhythmic clapping, stomping, or a sung chorus.

With no indigenous tradition of written stories and a very limited educational system, Djibouti was slow to create a national body of literature. William J. F. Syad (1930–) is generally considered the first Djiboutian writer in the Western sense. Educated in Saudi Arabia and Paris, Syad published his first volume of poetry, *Khamsine,* in 1959. Later works include *Cantiques* (1976), *Harmoniques* (1976*), Naufragés du destin* (1978), and *Symphoniques* (1991). His poetry is written in French, but uses the coded imagery and short line structure of belwo to create lyrical poetry dealing with love and political aspirations.

Since achieving independence in 1977, Djibouti has seen the emergence of a new generation of writers, many of whom now live in France or the United States. They use the French language and Western literary forms to write about Djiboutian life and issues. The best known of these is novelist and short story writer Abdourahman A. Waberi (1965–). He gained international attention for "Le Galerie des fous" (Gallery of fools), a story published in 1991. His novels and short stories have won a number of international prizes, including the Grand Prix Littéraire d'Afrique Noir in 1996. Daher Ahmed Farah (1962–) published the first Djiboutian novel in 1993, titled *Splendeur éphemère* (*Ephemeral splendor*), and other contemporary Djiboutian writers such as Idris Youssouf Elmi (1961–) and Ali Coubba (1961–) have combined Western-style fiction and indigenous poetry traditions in innovative ways.

CULTURE

Arts & Entertainment

An herbal drug called qat is the focus of Djiboutian leisure and culture. Nearly all Djiboutian men and some Djiboutian women partake in the chewing of qat leaves, which can have mild mood- and perception-altering properties when chewed. Each day, people congregate in a mabraz (qat den) to take the drug and meet with friends. Many Djiboutians spend up to five hours daily in a mabraz, and it is estimated that many working men spend up to 50 percent of their income on the drug. The colloquialism "brouter la salade," which is French for "graze the salad" refers to the activity of chewing qat.

A popular sport among the Afar is kwosso, a ball game that resembles soccer. Other popular sports throughout Djibouti include football (soccer), track and field, and basketball. The national football team, nicknamed Riverains de la Mer Rouge (Shoremen of the Red Sea), won its first FIFA-sanctioned international match in 2010. The Djibouti Premier League, formed in 1987, represents the highest level of football played in the country.

Cultural Sites & Landmarks

Located at the gateway between the Red Sea and the Indian Ocean, Djibouti has been a crossroads for trade routes between the Mediterranean and the Middle East since the time of ancient Egypt. For much of its history, the area was part of larger empires, from the early African empire of Aksum in the first century BCE to the French empire in the late 19th and 20th centuries. Because of this rich historical heritage, Djibouti has been the site of many important archaeological finds, particularly in the geological region known as the "Afar Triangle," which straddles Djibouti, Ethiopia, and Eritrea. Most notable are the remains of early hominids that lived between 3.2 and 5 million years ago, and the remains of Neolithic settlements that include hand tools made of volcanic glass and gigantic basalt millstones.

Tadjorah (or Tajourah) is the oldest city in Djibouti, and was founded as the seat of an early Afar sultanate. Muslim traveler and geographer Ibn Batuta (1304–c. 1368) reported that the city was already a strong center of Islamic culture in the 13th century. Tadjorah was also the major port for the Horn of Africa and anchored the caravan trade between the Arab states and Addis Ababa, the capital of Ethiopia, until the completion of a railway to Ethiopia in 1917. At its height, the city was an important trade center, exporting slaves, ivory, and salt to the Middle East and importing tobacco, cloth, knives, dates, and rice into the African interior. The city remains home to numerous traditional Islamic mosques.

Because of its coastal location, the capital of Djibouti is well known for its marinas. L'Escale (The Stopover) runs the length of the coast, giving visitors a full view of the water and the popular Doralé beach. The coastal city is also home to the Aquarium Tropical de Djibouti, which has on display much of the diverse marine life unique to the Red Sea. One of the most popular attractions in the capital is the central market, a bustling bazaar in the middle of the city. The market is perhaps best known for its Ethiopian qat leaves. Djibouti's salt-water lake, Lac Abbé, is also a popular landmark.

Libraries & Museums

There is no national museum in Djibouti, and most of the artifacts unearthed from the country are exhibited in museums in France. The country also has no national library or legal deposit law.

Holidays

Djibouti's national holiday is Independence Day (June 27), which celebrates the country's independence from France in 1977. Because of the large Muslim population, religious observations such as Ramadan, Eid Al Adha, and the birthday of the prophet Mohammed are also widely celebrated in Djibouti.

Youth Culture

Because of the extreme poverty in which many Djiboutians live, children are expected to contribute to the family income from an early age, resulting in widespread child labor. While it remains illegal to hire anyone younger than 14, the law is seldom enforced. Many children find employment as domestic servants and in family businesses. However, child prostitution is also commonplace. A high rate of HIV/AIDS infection among youth has become a major concern. In addition, although education is free and mandatory between the ages of six and 12, many children are unable to attend due to costs such as books and transportation. Secondary education is available only in the capital of Djibouti, and students wishing to attend a university must go abroad, generally to France or Arab states.

SOCIETY

Transportation

Djibouti is linked by bus and rail to the major towns and cities in Ethiopia, with only a few domestic stops. Much of the railway, however, has become inoperable. Minibuses travel daily between the capital and Ali Sabieh, Dikhil, Tadjourah, Yoboki, and the Ethiopian border. There is no fixed schedule for arrivals and departures—buses leave when they are full. Speedboats and dhows carry passengers and commodities along the coast, and there are a small number of domestic flights between the capital, Obock, and Tadjourah. As of 2013, there are 13 airports in the country. Many areas outside of Djibouti City are not accessible by any form of public transportation. Traffic moves on the right-hand side of the road.

Transportation Infrastructure

Because of its strategic location on the Strait of Mendeb, where the Red Sea meets the Indian Ocean, Djibouti is a major transit port for the region and an international transshipment and refueling center. Much of its economy depends on its modern deepwater port and the railway that connects Djibouti to Addis Ababa, which is jointly owned by Djibouti and Ethiopia. Dubai Ports World operates both the port and Djibouti-Ambouli Airport. In 2009, a South African firm, Comazer, took over management of the railway.

Media & Communications

Access to media is limited in Djibouti and there is no private broadcasting. The state broadcaster, Radiodiffusion-Television de Djibouti (RTD), broadcasts in French, Somali, Afar, and Arabic. There are three major newspapers, all published in French: *Le Nation* is a daily paper owned by the Djiboutian government, and *Le Renouveau* and *Le Republique* are weekly papers owned by opposition political parties. Small private newspapers, such as the *Carrefour Africaine*, which is published fortnightly by the Roman Catholic mission, are allowed to circulate without restrictions. Due to a high illiteracy rate—more than half the population is illiterate—newspapers reach a limited audience. Self-censorship is commonly practiced.

Although Djibouti has one of the best telecommunications infrastructures in Africa, less than 10 percent of the population has telephone service. Mobile phone use is more common than landlines and is increasing, but limited to the capital. In 2014, there were an estimated 73,500 Internet users, representing just over nine percent of the population.

SOCIAL DEVELOPMENT

Standard of Living

Djibouti ranked 170th out of 187 countries on the 2013 United Nations Human Development Index, which measures quality of life and standard of living indicators.

Water Consumption

Drinking water supply and sanitation coverage remain dire issues for Djibouti. Water consumption in Djibouti is largely sourced from underground water. In rural areas, less than 50 percent of the population has access to an improved drinking water source, and an estimated 70 percent of all consumption goes to agriculture. Water coverage is higher in urban areas, but in the case of Djibouti city, estimates from the early 21st century suggest that approximately 48 percent of those households with water access are simply connected to the pipes of other households. A majority of the population also lacks access to improved sanitation.

As with health and education, accurate or reliable statistics for water and sanitation coverage are lacking.

Education

Djibouti's education system is largely based on the French educational system; the most common language of instruction is French, although Arabic is sometimes used in schools. A nine-year education is compulsory, consisting of five years of primary education (the second stage of basic education) and four years of middle education. This can be followed by secondary education, which generally lasts three years, and then tertiary education, though gross enrollment rates dating back to 2008 in each level are severely low. The University of Djibouti, the country's only formal institute of higher learning, was founded in 2006.

According to reports, the education system in Djibouti comes at a high cost, limiting reforms due to the lack of teachers, materials, and school construction. Attendance is limited due to the associated costs of attending school. Adequately trained teachers, teacher attrition, the integration of information technology in the classroom, and the education of nomadic peoples also remain pressing challenges.

As with health care statistics and water coverage data, recent data concerning the literacy rate in Djibouti is lacking, and many estimates are made based on outdated statistics. Nonetheless, the country is ranked low globally in terms of its national literary rate, with some estimates dating back to the early 21st century suggesting that only between one-quarter and one-half of the population is literate. A 2003 USAID statistic on adult literacy in the country places the rate at 65 percent, while the UNDP, in its 2009 Human Development Report (which is based on 2007 data) lists the adult literacy rate at 70.1 percent, though noting that the figure is based on earlier data. Currently, the literacy rate for men is 75.6 percent while for women it stands at 54.4 percent.

Women's Rights

Legally, women in Djibouti possess the same rights as men and the constitution of Djibouti prohibits discrimination based on gender. Women received the right to vote in 1946 and the right to run for office in 1986. In 2002, the secular Family Code replaced Muslim law (sharia) and traditional tribal law (xeer) in matters of divorce, inheritance, and other family and personal issues.

In practice, discrimination in terms of access to education and employment are almost universal, and customary law prevails in matters of family law. For example, sons inherit a great share of property, and fewer than 50 percent of girls attend even the primary level of schooling. The literacy rate for women is an estimated 32 percent in the early twenty-first century, compared to 60 percent for men. Women consistently earn less money than me do and are not even allowed to travel without a male relative.

The values of traditional nomadic cultures and Islam both contribute to Djibouti's patriarchal culture. Girls are often married between the ages of eleven and fifteen to men several years their senior. A woman's status is then tied to the number of children she bears, and there is a strong preference for male children. Often, a woman is not considered to be a full member of her husband's family until she gives birth to a son. Generally, women also maintain a subordinate position in the household. Women among the nomadic tribes of Djibouti traditionally managed the day-to-day affairs of the family, leaving men to graze the camel herds. Women were also responsible for setting up and taking down the huts at every move, managing the herds, weaving, cooking, and child rearing.

Due to a strong cultural bias and a high employment rate, only a third of Djiboutian women work outside the home. Those who do work outside the home often stop with the birth of their first child. This is because there is little public or private day care, and women who continue to work outside the home typically depend on their extended family for childcare support. For the most part, women in the urban workforce hold clerical and administrative positions or run small-scale retail or service businesses. Many work in the informal economy as domestic servants. Few women hold management positions, at best rising to the level of a department head or assistant director. One major exception to this is in the judiciary, where women hold a third of the positions and have held seats on the Supreme Court.

Domestic violence exists in Djibouti, but there are few cases reported, limiting the knowledge of its extent. There are no laws prohibiting spousal rape, and violence against women is generally settled out of the courts and among family and clans. Sexual discrimination has also been reported to be a problem. One notable abuse against women is female genital mutilation (FGM), at one time estimated to affect over 95 percent of the population. Despite anti-FGM campaigns and laws that impose prison sentences, the practice is still widespread, particularly in rural areas.

The Djiboutian government has made some efforts to improve the status of women. The Ministry of Women, Family, and Social Affairs was established in 2002 as part of the new Family Law. A woman was then appointed head of the new ministry, effectively becoming the first woman to serve as a government minister. In 2007, the government established a network of counseling offices to help women understand and protect their rights.

Health Care

Djibouti has a substandard health care system. In general, residents do not receive adequate medical attention and do not have health insurance coverage. Malaria, bacterial and protozoal diarrhea, hepatitis A, hepatitis E, dengue fever, meningitis, and typhoid fever are common diseases and infections.

Frequent droughts pose serious health risks for the Afar population. The lack of potable water in Djibouti is a significant threat to the population. In 2015, the average life expectancy was estimated to be almost 63 years: 60.3 for males and 65.4 for females.

GOVERNMENT

Structure

Djibouti is a democratic republic. The president, elected by popular vote to a six-year term, is the chief executive and head of state. The president appoints a prime minister, who is the head of government. The executive branch is rounded out by the Council of Ministers, the president's cabinet that is headed by the prime minister.

The National Assembly, a unicameral parliament of 65 elected members, is Djibouti's legislative branch. Members of parliament serve five-year terms. The Supreme Court is the country's highest judicial authority. In Djibouti, 18 is the age of suffrage.

As a colony of France since the late 19th century, Djibouti began to experience political uprisings in 1949, when the Issa Somalis rebelled against the French colonists. The Afar people supported French rule, and fought back against the Issa in civil war.

In 1967, many Somalis were expelled from the nation, Issa leaders were arrested, and a referendum was passed ensuring that Djibouti would remain a French territory. Extensive rioting broke out, and after ten more years of civil warfare, the nation was declared independent on June 27, 1977, with the Issa in power.

In 1991, the Afar felt underrepresented in the Issa government, and started another civil war. Fighting ceased after peace accords in 1994 and 2001, and the People's Progress Assembly (RPP) was formed as a moderate party representing both ethnic groups.

In an effort to increase foreign aid, Djibouti allowed France, Italy, and the United States to deploy troops in Djibouti during the Persian Gulf War in 1991. The nation was seen as a strategic location during the war, and France has maintained an overseas military base in Djibouti since that time.

Beginning in 2000, France was encouraged to reduce its military presence in Djibouti. Since 2003, the United States' invasion of Iraq and the broader "war on terror" have led to an increased United States military presence in Djibouti, which is again considered a frontline location.

The head of the government, since April 1, 2013, is Prime Minister Abdoulkader Kamil Mohamed. In the executive branch, the cabinet consists of a Council of Ministers who are appointed by the prime minister.

Political Parties

The People's Rally for Progress is considered the dominant political party in Djiboutian politics. It is part of the Union for the Presidential Majority (UMP) coalition, which won the majority of seats in both the 2003 and 2008 parliamentary elections. Other parties in the coalition include the Front for Restoration of Unity and Democracy (or FRUD, aligned with the Afar), the National Democratic Party, the center-left Social Democratic People's Party, and the Union of Reform Partisans, which broke off from FRUD. (In terms of voting, a political party that wins a majority of the vote in a certain district then wins each seat in that particular district—a winner-take-all system).

Local Government

Djibouti is subdivided into six administrative or regional districts. Due to decentralization, government has more representation locally.

Judicial System

The judicial system in Djibouti is influenced by both the Islamic and French traditions of law. Courts of First Instance represent the lower level of the judicial hierarchy, while Superior Appeals Courts preside over criminal matters. Religious courts address Muslim laws and traditions. The Supreme Court is the highest court of law. The Constitutional Council is made up of six magistrates.

Taxation

Tax rates are considered moderate; the highest income tax rate is 32 percent, while the highest corporate rate is 25 percent. Other taxes levied include an excise tax, property tax, and a value-added tax (VAT, similar to a consumption tax). Taxes represent 35.6 percent of the country's GDP in 2014.

Armed Forces

Djibouti's armed forces (Djibouti National Army) are small, and consist of land forces and a navy and air force. Prior to 1991, the military was generally made up of volunteer soldiers. As of 2008, active personnel number 11,000. France maintains a military base in Djibouti, and the Djiboutian government has a formal security accord with the European nation. As of 2012, voluntary military training is available to people ages 16 to 25.

Foreign Policy

Formerly known as French Somaliland (1896–1967) and the French Territory of the Afars and the Issas (1967–1977), the Republic of Djibouti became an independent state on June 27, 1977. Since independence, Djibouti has maintained strong ties with France, including cooperative treaties guaranteeing military and economic assistance. The capital of Djibouti is home to a French naval base, which is the largest French military installation in Africa.

Regional stability is a major issue for Djibouti since its economy is based on providing transportation-related services to the surrounding region. As a result, the government attempts to maintain a neutral position in regional politics. Conflicts in the surrounding countries of Ethiopia, Eritrea, and Somalia have periodically disrupted the international shipping on which Djibouti's economy depends. This has resulted in thousands of refugees fleeing into Djibouti, placing additional burdens on an already distressed economy. Since 1986, Djibouti has worked actively with the Intergovernmental Authority on Development (IGAD), an organization of East African states, to promote peace and stability in the region.

The U.S. is an important source of humanitarian aid, famine relief, and economic assistance for Djibouti. In September 2008, the U.S. Agency for International Development (USAID) provided $2.7 million for health and educational programs. In December 2008, USAID donated computer equipment to assist the Djibouti government's 2009 census. Djibouti also provided strategic support to the U.S. during both Gulf Wars and in the search for al-Qaeda following the terrorist attacks of September 11, 2001. In addition to providing a base of operations for coalition forces, Djibouti became home to the only US military base in Africa in 2002. Additionally, Djibouti enjoys strong diplomatic relationships with the Arab States, China and Japan. Saudi Arabia and Kuwait provided important financial support for the Doraleh Project, a three-stage plan for the development of a new port facility in Djibouti City. Kuwait was also a primary investor in a major upgrade to Djibouti's railway system in 2008. Like many of its Arab allies, Djibouti does not recognize Israel as an official country.

Djibouti is a member of the United Nations (UN), the World Bank, the International Monetary Fund (IMF), the World Trade Organization (WTO), and other international organizations. Djibouti is an African, Caribbean and Pacific (ACP) member state of the ACP-European Union (EU) relationship.

Human Rights Profile

International human rights law insists that states respect civil and political rights, and also promote an individual's economic, social, and cultural rights. The United Nations Universal Declaration on Human Rights (UDHR) is recognized as the standard for international human rights. Its authors sought the counsel of the world's great thinkers, philosophers, and religious leaders, and were careful to create a document that reflects the core values shared by every world culture. (To read this document or view the articles relating to cultural human rights, visit http://www.udhr.org/UDHR/default.htm.)

Djibouti has a strong presidency and a weak legislative branch, putting the effective control of the government in the hands of one man. In 2005, Guelleh was re-elected to a second six-year term with 100 percent of the votes cast and no alternative candidate.

Djibouti's constitution prohibits discrimination based on language, race, or gender, as provided for in Article 2 of the UDHR. Nonetheless, discrimination occurs based on ethnicity, nationality, and clan background at both the personal and the governmental level. In addition, the regime of President Ismail Omar Guelleh (1947–), who succeeded his uncle in 1999—and who was reelected uncontested in 2005—has been criticized as repressive, and accused of corruption and restricting the privacy rights of citizens, including freedom of press and assembly. Other human rights abuses involve arbitrary arrest and detention, poor prison conditions, and the treatment of refugees.

Roughly, 60 percent of the Djibouti population is made up of members of various Somali tribes, notably Issa, Gadaboursi, and Issaf, while 35 percent of the population is Afar. (The remainder is made up of Europeans, mostly French, and Arabs.) The southern part of the country is predominately Issa, the northern part is predominately Afar, and the capital is effectively segregated along ethnic lines. Historically, the country's borders of were established without reference to the demographic patterns of the Afar and Issa peoples that lived in the region. In the early 20th century, the French encouraged rivalries between the two ethnic groups in order to discourage indigenous independence movements. The resulting ethnic problems have troubled Djibouti since independence.

The first president of Djibouti, Hassan Gouled Aptidan (1916–2006), installed a one-party government dominated by his own Issa community. Long-standing ethnic tensions between the Issa and Afar came to a head in 1991 when the Afar rebel group known as the Front for the Restoration of Unity and Democracy (FRUD) launched a civil war in the north. Over the course of three years, thousands were killed in the fighting and more were displaced. FRUD signed a Peace and National Reconciliation Agreement with the government in December 1994, but a radical splinter faction of FRUD continued to fight. The war officially ended in 2001.

The Djiboutian constitution guarantees religious freedom to all, and this right is generally upheld. Islam is the state religion and roughly 95 percent of the population is Sunni Muslim. The government exercises no control over the practice of other religions, but foreign religious groups are required to register with the Ministry of the Interior. The constitution of Djibouti also provides for freedom of speech, association, and assembly, but these rights not generally upheld. The government maintains tight control over media and does not tolerate public protest. Since Guelleh's election in 2005, journalists have been arrested and newspapers have been banned on charges of spreading false news likely to demoralize the state. Dissidents who participate in public protests are threatened with excessive force.

ECONOMY

Overview of the Economy

Almost all of Djibouti's economic activity is in the service sector. With virtually no natural resources and little agricultural activity, the nation depends on its status as a free trade zone, and maintains good foreign relations with countries providing economic aid. Likewise, the capital's economy is largely transportation- and service-based due to the city's scarce natural resources and its role as a port city and storage and refueling center.

In 2014, the gross domestic product (GDP) was estimated at almost $1.6 million (USD), with a per capita GDP of $3,100 (USD).

Industry

Industrial activity in Djibouti is limited to the service sector, which generates 80 percent of the country's revenues. This sector includes construction, processing of agricultural goods, and transportation. France and Ethiopia built the Addis Ababa-Djibouti City railway to ship Ethiopian goods from Djibouti.

The country's two soft drink plants provide the only manufacturing. Food is the nation's main import, followed by beverages, chemicals, transport equipment, and petroleum products. With the exception of animal hides, goods exported from Djibouti's port are in transit from other nations. Salt production is also an important industry in the capital. Djibouti's largest trade partners include Saudi Arabia, Ethiopia, India, China, the United States, France, Yemen, and Somalia.

Labor

Unemployment is an epidemic in Djibouti, and has been estimated at 60 percent of a labor force of just 294,600 (2014). Nearly half of the population lives below the poverty line. Besides the shipping and port industries, the government is the main employer in the capital.

Energy/Power/Natural Resources

There are no significant natural resources in Djibouti. The nation's most significant resource is its seaport, which accounts for most of the country economic activity. The dry land is devoid of minerals, oil, and natural gas. With very few areas of vegetation, there are no exploitable timber resources, either.

Fishing

Djibouti's fishing industry is underexploited and underdeveloped, and the development of fishing ports, including cold storage, has been a primary focus in the early 21st century. Trawlers have been banned from the country's coastline and more traditional fishing methods still predominate. Fish such as tuna, grouper, and swordfish represent the targeted commercial species of the burgeoning but small fishing industry.

Forestry

Due to the inhospitable climate and non-arable land, forestry is not a viable economic activity. Forests only cover an estimated one percent of the country's territory.

Mining/Metals

The production of mineral commodities in Djibouti is limited to basalt and other construction materials and salt (primarily mined at Lake Assal), and, to a lesser extent, other commodities such as pumice, gold, gypsum, and diatomite (though none are exploited to reach a sustainable level of economic interest).

Agriculture

Djibouti receives little rain, and has sparse vegetation and a lack of arable land. Because of these factors, agriculture is limited to livestock such as camels, goats, and cattle, and few fruits and vegetables can be planted.

Most of the nation's agricultural activity occurs among the nomadic Afar clans. This form of agriculture is largely at the subsistence level, and therefore does not affect the nation's economy. The only exported agricultural goods are animal hides, and revenues from agriculture are therefore negligible.

Animal Husbandry

Livestock is mostly limited to camels, goats, sheep, donkeys, and cattle, and most livestock holdings are nomadic in nature. Livestock and agriculture play a small part in the economy of the capital, but the outlying land of Djibouti City is mostly barren. Nevertheless, livestock is a part of Djibouti's identity; the city and surrounding areas are home to many nomadic traders, most notably camel caravans.

Tourism

Djibouti City is not known for cultural attractions. The city has no museums and few historical sites, and most colonial buildings lay in ruin. Therefore, most of Djibouti's tourism is based on wildlife, scenery, and outdoor activities. Most tourists in Djibouti visit the city's central market and the Hamoudi Mosque, but the majority of tourist attractions are outside of the city.

Tourists visit Lac Abbé to see flocks of flamingoes. Lac Assal is another tourist favorite, because of its landscape of dormant volcanoes surrounding the lake. Other attractions include snorkeling and diving around the coral reef of the Maskali and Musha Islands, windsurfing on wheeled boards in the Grand Barra plains, and hiking in the Forêt du Day National Park. Revenues from tourism are negligible, as the country receives a low number of visitors.

Pamela D. Toler, Richard Means, Alex K. Rich

DO YOU KNOW?

- Due to its size and lack of natural resources, Djibouti is often referred to as the Dubai of the Red Sea, a reference to the tiny Middle Eastern city of Dubai.
- Dubai City, a port city located on the Persian Gulf, has invested heavily in rebuilding the port infrastructure of Djibouti in recent years.

Bibliography

Carol Beckwith and Angela Fisher. "African Ark: People and Ancient cultures of Ethiopia and the Horn of Africa." New York: *H. N. Abrams*, 1990.

Daoud A. Alwan and Yohanis Mibrathus. "Historical Dictionary of Djibouti." Lanham, MD. *Scarecrow Press*: 2000.

I. M. Lewis. "Peoples of the Horn of Africa: Somali, Afar, and Saho." Lawrenceville, NJ. *The Red Sea Press, Inc.* 1998.

Jean-Bernard Carillet. "Ethiopia, Djibouti, and Somaliland." Oakland, CA: *Lonely Planet*, 2013.

Nigel Pavitt. "Africa's Great Rift Valley." New York: *Harry N. Abrams, Inc. Publishers*. 2001.

Robert Tholomier. "Djibouti: Pawn of the Horn of Africa." Tr. Virginia Thompson and Richard Adolff. Metuchen, NJ: *The Scarecrow Press*. 1981.

Suzanne Lilius. "Djibouti Connections". The Road Less Traveled: Reflections on the Literatures of the Horn of Africa. Ed. Ali Jimale Ahmed and Taddesse Adera. Trenton, NJ: *The Red Sea Press, Inc.* 2008

Virginia Thompson and Richard Adolff. "Djibouti and the Horn of Africa." Stanford: *Stanford University Press*. 1968.

Works Cited

"Africa." Oakland, Ca. *Lonely Planet Publications*. 2007

"Africana: The Encyclopedia of the African and African-American Experience." Kwame Anthony Appia, and Henry Lewis Gates, Jr. Eds. New York. *Basic Civitas Books*. 1999.

"Association Djibouti Espace Nomade." (http://www.tourismesolidaire.org/f/nosvoyages/lesvoyagistes/associationdjiboutiespacenomade.html)

"Background Notes, Djibouti." *United States State Department*. (http://www.state.gov/r/pa/ei/bgn/5482.htm)

"Country Profile: Djibouti." *BBC News* (http://news.bbc.co.uk/2/hi/africa/country_profiles/1070579.stm) https://www.cia.gov/library/publications/the-world-factbook/) CIA. *World Fact Book*.

"Country Report on Human Rights Practices in Djibouti." United States State Department. (http://www.state.gov/g/drl/rls/hrrpt/2008/af/118998.htm)

"Djibouti Country Review." Houston. *Country Watch, Inc.* 2008.

"Djibouti." *Encyclopædia Britannica Online*. (http://search.eb.com/eb/article-37645).

"Djibouti—Society and Culture." Petaluma, California. *World Trade Press*. 2008.

"Statesman's Yearbook Online." Barry Turner, Ed. *Palgrave*. 2008 (www.statesmansyearbook.com)

"The Africa Book: A Journey through Every Country in the Continent." Oakland, Ca. *Lonely Planet Publications*. 2007

B. W. Andrzejewski and S. Pilaszewicz and W. Tyloch, Eds. "Literatures in African Languages: Theoretical Issues and Sample Surveys." Cambridge and Warsaw. *Cambridge University Press with Wiedza Powszechna*. 1985

B. W. Andrzejewski and I. M. Lewis. "Somali Poetry: An Introduction." Oxford. *Clarendon Press*. 1964.

Christian Poché. "Djibouti." Grove Music Online. *Oxford Music Online*. (http://www.oxfordmusiconline.com/subscriber/article/grovemusic/47072)

Didier Morin. "Afar Praise Poetry." African Languages and Cultures. Suppl. No. 3. Voice and Power: The Culture of Language in North East Africa. Essays in Honor of B.W. Andrzejewski, 1996.

Gladson I. Nwanna. "Do's and Don'ts around the World: A Country Guide to Cultural and Social Taboos and Etiquette. Africa." Baltimore. *World Travel Institute*. 1998.

Harold Woods and Geraldine. "The Horn of Africa: Ethiopia, Sudan, Somalia, and Djibouti." New York. *Franklin Watts*. 1981.

James Morrow. "Djibouti." Philadelphia. *Mason Crest Publishers*. 2004.

Michael Hood. "East African Handbook." Bath, England. *Footprint Handbooks*. 1998.

Ottó Károlyi. "Traditional African and Oriental Music." London. *Penguin*. 1998.

Peter Cooke. "East Africa: An Introduction." The Garland Handbook of African Music. Ruth M. Stone, Ed. New York and London. *Garland Publishing, Inc.* 2006.

Philippe Oberlé and Pierre Hugot. "Histoire de Djibouti, des origins à la République." Paris and Dakar. *Présence Africaine*. 1985.

Degghi Selam Chapel, Asmara, Eritrea.

ERITREA

Introduction

The State of Eritrea, a small country on the Horn of Africa, is bordered by Sudan, Ethiopia, Djibouti, and the Red Sea. Some of the oldest human fossils have been unearthed in Eritrea, and the country's culture is steeped in ancient traditions derived from an array of peoples.

Eritrea's traditional folk culture remains vibrant today. It includes the performance of energetic dances and songs on various social occasions. Music is also important during religious rituals, and drums and several stringed instruments, such as the krar, are commonly played. Icons, illuminated manuscripts, and religious literature in the ancient Ge'ez language are other important aspects of the culture. There is also a strong oral tradition of both sacred and secular stories.

For much of the 20th century, Eritrea was dominated by foreign powers. It won its independence from Ethiopia in 1991 after a long war, and began struggling with challenges related to widespread poverty and economic stagnation, only to become involved in a bloody border war with Ethiopia once again. Years of continuous war and an oppressive political regime have taken a serious toll on the country.

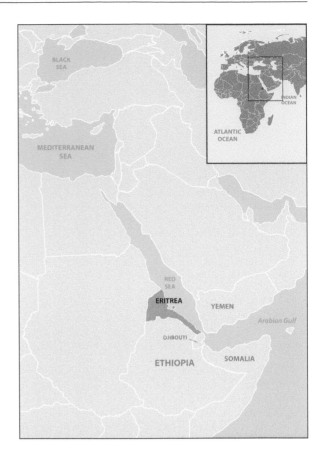

GENERAL INFORMATION

Official Language(s): Tigrinya, Arabic, and English
Population: 6,527,689 (2015 estimate)
Currency: Eritrean nakfa

Coins: The Eritrean nakfa is divided into 100 cents, and is minted in coin denominations of 1, 5, 10, 25, and 50 cents, and 1 nakfa.
Land Area: 101,000 square kilometers (38,996 square miles)
Water Area: 16,600 square kilometers (6,409 square miles)
National Anthem: "Ertra, Ertra, Ertra" ("Eritrea, Eritrea, Eritrea")
Capital: Asmara
Time Zone: GMT +3
Flag Description: The flag of Eritrea features three horizontal triangles: one green, one red, and one blue. The green represents the land, the blue represents the ocean, and the red represents the country's fight for independence. The red triangle features a golden wreath and olive branch.

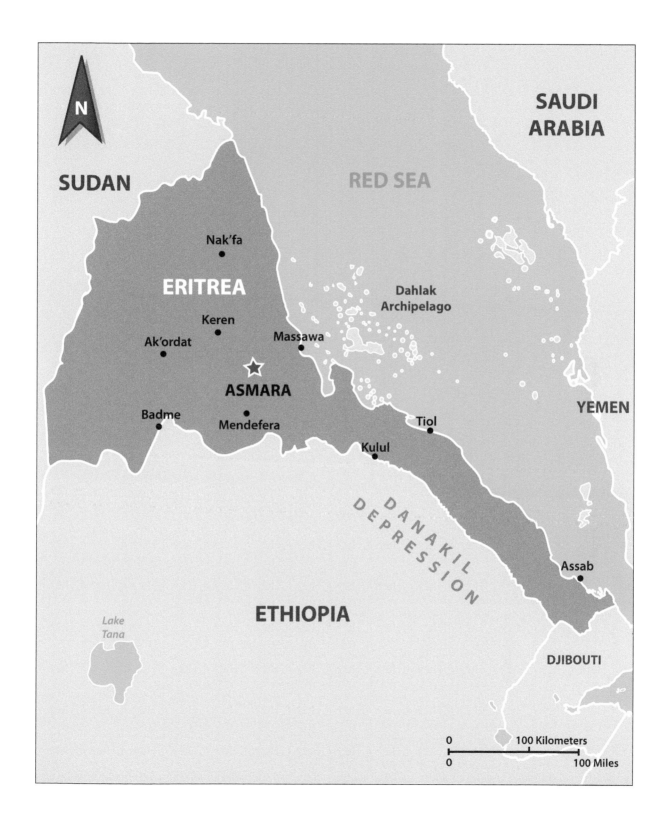

Principal Cities by Population (2012):

- Asmara (697,013)
- Asseb (101,284)
- Keren (82,198)
- Massawa (53,090)
- Addi Ugri (25,332)

Population

Eritrea has a young, growing population, with each woman bearing an average of more than four children. Life expectancy at birth is 61 years for males and 66 years for females (2015 estimate). Population density is 43 persons per square kilometer (112 persons per square mile); the central highlands are the most densely populated area. The population growth rate was estimated at 2.25 percent in 2015.

The Eritrean population is predominantly rural, with only 22 percent living in urban areas. Asmara, the largest city, has a population of 697,013. (The population of Asmara was last measured in 2015 at over 804,000 for the entire metropolitan area, with 697,013 unofficially living in the central urban area.) Other urban centers are Keren, Nakfa, and the coastal cities of Massawa and Assab.

The Eritrean population is a complex ethnic composite. Roughly, half of the people belong to the Tigrinya ethnic group and 40 percent to the Tigre and Kunama ethnic groups. Minorities include the Afar, the Saho, the Bilen, the Baria, and the Hedareb. Each group tends to live in distinct regions: the Tigrinya in the highlands, the Tigre in the northeast and on the western plain, the Kunama in the southwest, and the Afar in the Danakil region and on the Dahlak Archipelago.

Languages

In Asmara, Tigrinya is the dominant language and is spoken by over 80 percent of the population. Because of the nation's colonial heritage, Italian is still spoken by many residents in Asmara and nearby cities. Arabic is also commonly spoken and one of the most popular languages for business and commerce. English is taught in many Eritrean schools.

Each ethnic group speaks its own language, and all but a few of these belong to the Afro-Asiatic super-family, which includes the Semitic languages. Tigrinya, Tigre, and Arabic are the most widely spoken. Only the ethnic groups living near the Sudanese border speak languages that derive from the Nilotic family.

Native People & Ethnic Groups

The major and minor ethnic groups and the major religions have been long established in Eritrea, and have coexisted peacefully for centuries. During the war for independence, the emphasis on a common identity united the various groups in a common cause. This identity remains strong today, but each group's unique traits are also recognized.

The primary ethnic group in Eritrea is the Tigrinya, which constitutes 50 percent of the national population and over 70 percent of the population of Asmara. The Tigre and Kunama people, comprising roughly 40 percent of the national population, are also common in the major cities. A number of small ethnic groups contribute to the remaining 10 percent of the population. Minority ethnic groups include Italian Eritreans and the Rashaida.

Religions

Orthodox Christianity and Islam both have long histories in Eritrea. Approximately half of the population is Christian, and half is Sunni Muslim. There are small denominations of Roman Catholics and Protestants, but the majority of Christians adhere to the Orthodox faith. These are the only four religions, which the government recognizes; a growing number of Pentecostals have claimed that they are persecuted by the authorities.

Climate

Eritrea's three regions have distinct climates. The cool central highlands have an average annual temperature of 18° Celsius (65° Fahrenheit) and receive the most precipitation. During the rainy season, heaviest in July and August, an average of 40 to 60 centimeters (16 to 24 inches) rain falls. The western hills and lowlands are semi-arid. They are hotter than the highlands, with average temperatures ranging between 30° and 41° Celsius (86° and 106° Fahrenheit), and receive less rainfall.

The eastern lowlands along the Red Sea are extremely hot and dry. Temperatures in the southeastern Danakil Depression, one of the hottest and lowest places on earth, can exceed 50° Celsius (122° Fahrenheit). The port city of Massawa, however, which has the advantage of breezes from the Red Sea, has an annual temperature of 30° Celsius (86° Fahrenheit) and receives rainfall measuring 205 millimeters (8 inches) annually.

Eritrea suffers from frequent droughts, especially in the western plain and the eastern lowlands. They vary in length and intensity and can induce widespread famine. Periodic locust swarms are also a problem, and can damage crops.

While much of Eritrea is located in an arid climatic zone, Asmara's higher elevation gives the city cooler average temperatures. The city also receives more rainfall than the rest of the country. Asmara has relatively stable year-round temperatures, divided into wet and dry seasons. The average temperature is 16° Celsius (60° Fahrenheit) with a range between 8° and 23° Celsius (46° to 73° Fahrenheit). The hottest months are from May to August. Asmara receives approximately 50 centimeters (20 inches) of rain annually, most of which falls between April and August.

ENVIRONMENT & GEOGRAPHY

Topography

Eritrea's terrain consists of a western plain, the central highlands, the coastal lowlands and numerous small islands in the Red Sea. The western plain is characterized by rolling hills and decreases in elevation as it runs towards the border with Sudan; it ranges from 1,370 to 760 meters (4,500 to 2,500 feet). The Baraka River divides the western plain from the central highlands, a long, narrow core region that covers one-quarter of the country's total area and has an average elevation of 1,980 meters (6,496 feet). Amba Soira is the country's highest mountain at 3,018 meters (9,880 feet).

The terrain drops sharply from the central highlands to the long coastal lowlands. This region covers one-third of Eritrea's area and includes a coastline that measures 1,151 kilometers (715 miles) along the Red Sea. Narrow in the north, the lowlands broaden in the south into the Danakil Plains, part of the Great Rift Valley. The Danakil Depression (113 meters/371 feet below sea level) and the Kobar Sink (116 meters/380 feet below sea level) are both found there. Volcanic activity and minor earthquakes are common in this area.

Several hundred islands in the Red Sea are part of Eritrean territory. Most prominent are those in the Dahlak Archipelago.

Eritrea's few rivers flow only during the rainy season. The Baraka, Setit, Anseba, and Mereb Rivers flow from the central highlands and into Sudan. The Falkat, Alighede, and Laba Rivers leave the highlands and flow towards the Red Sea, where they generally disappear into the arid terrain.

Asmara is located at the eastern edge of the Ethiopian Plateau, a mountain range covering portions of Ethiopia, Eritrea, and Somalia and surrounding Africa's Great Rift Valley. The highest point in Asmara rises to over 2,300 meters (7,600 feet) above sea level and declines over the 65 kilometers (40 miles) between the center of Asmara and the city's port on the Red Sea. Mountain scrubland surrounds the city and is punctuated by arid patches of desert plain. Eritrea is divided into six administrative divisions, or provinces. Asmara is located in the Maakel Province.

Plants & Animals

The hotter, drier regions of Eritrea have little significant vegetation. Shrubs, grasses, and an occasional stand of trees dot the arid landscape.

One of the few trees that can withstand the harsh environment is the acacia. Palm trees and mangroves are found along the coast wherever oasis-like conditions exist. Vegetation in the central highlands is limited by the intense cultivation of the area and deforestation; less than three percent is forested. Junipers, the African olive, and the imported eucalyptus are the most common trees.

Eritrea is home to 112 mammal species, 12 percent of which are listed as endangered. The lion and elephant populations are listed as vulnerable, and the wild African ass is critically endangered. Other common animals include jackals, gazelles, warthogs, and wild cats. In addition, several-hundred bird species are found in the country, and the Red Sea supports a wide range of marine life, including sea cows and turtles.

CUSTOMS & COURTESIES

Greetings

There are a variety of greetings appropriate in Eritrea, depending on the level of intimacy, but the most common greeting is to say "Salaam" ("Peace") and shake hands. The typical response is to say "Salaam" back. The expression "Salaam" is also used when taking leave of someone. In Arabic-speaking parts of the country, it is common to shake and kiss right hands while saying either "Kefelhal?" ("How are you") or simply "Keff" for short. The common response is "Hamdellah" or "Marhaba," both conveying the message "I'm fine." "Marhaba" is also used to express welcome when someone comes to visit.

If men are greeting each other and are close, they will often hug or tap each other's right shoulder. Women who are close will often hug or exchange kisses on each other's cheeks. Between a man and a woman, it is considered good manners to wait for the woman to extend her hand for a handshake first. If the man and woman are close friends or family, hugging or exchanging kisses is also common. However, it is common for friends and family to look each other in the eye, too much direct eye contact can be considered disrespectful when first meeting someone.

Furthermore, averting one's gaze or looking down while someone is speaking conveys admiration and respect for the person speaking.

Another Eritrean greeting is the shoulder bump, usually between men or people who fought during the war. The two people greeting will shake hands and bump their right shoulders together three times. This custom started on the battlefield, and when women were fighting alongside the men, they were often greeted in the same way.

Gestures & Etiquette

In Eritrea, proper etiquette dictates that, when greeting someone, one must first inquire as to the well-being of the person and other general matters. If people are meeting for the first time, it is common to inquire which town each person is from, as well. After these inquiries, conversation in Eritrea tends to be very direct. Controversial topics such as politics, war, or religious beliefs are typically avoided unless a rapport has been established. If someone fought in the war, however, it is acceptable to discuss how they participated in the struggle since fighters, men and women alike are highly respected in Eritrea.

Professionally, Eritreans address each other by their formal titles, but socially, they often address each other with nicknames. Elders are treated with respect and addressed by both their title and name. The Tigrinya word for "thank you" is formal and seldom used for small favors, as Eritreans feel it is their duty to help others.

In terms of gestures and personal space, Eritreans are generally comfortable with less than an arm's distance between them and another person when speaking. Even less personal space is required if addressing someone of his or her own gender. Holding hands is seen as a gesture of friendship, and it is common to see men holding hands. In addition, it is common to see people touching while talking if they are of the same sex, but it is rare to see men and women touching while speaking. To show agreement, one can snap their fingers or raise their eyebrows during conversation.

When beckoning for someone to approach, Eritreans gesture with the palm facing down, curling the fingers in rapidly. When waving at someone, the correct way is to raise one's hand high into the air, but not wave it; to raise one's hand very little or to wave one's hand is considered impolite. One taboo in Eritrea is to show another individual the bottom of the feet, whether covered or not. Additionally, one should never touch something with their feet when interacting with Muslim Eritreans. It is acceptable to point at a place or thing, but pointing at a person is considered rude. In addition, among Muslim Eritreans, the right hand is usually used because the left hand is associated with the cleansing of the body in Muslim culture, and thus considered impure.

Eating/Meals

Typically, Eritreans eat three times per day, and meals are communal. Traditionally, everyone gathers around a low table and shares food served in a large, shallow tray; however, one should only eat the food directly in front of them. Traditional Eritrean food is eaten with one's right hand, but other foods are eaten with utensils. It is considered impolite to lick one's fingers, but it is a sign of affection for someone to scoop up food and feed it to a loved one.

One particular Eritrean custom requires that the oldest man present bless the food (usually symbolized by a piece of bread) before the meal. He will then offer bread to each person. Meals tend to be jovial or relaxed occasions where guests are always welcome. While, it is common to enjoy tea or coffee outdoors in cafés, meals are usually taken indoors.

Proper eating etiquette is stressed in Christian homes because they believe God is observing their behavior. Christian Eritreans will fast for Lent, and Muslim Eritreans will fast for Ramadan. In addition, Copts (which traditionally refers to Eritrean Christians) will abstain from meat and dairy on Wednesdays and Fridays. Muslims avoid pork and alcohol, and Christians will usually avoid dairy altogether during Lent.

Adults and children from the highland areas usually eat separately. Families from the other areas of Eritrea usually eat together, except when guests are present, in which case the adults will eat with the guests before the children. Women usually prepare food, and if a guest comes to eat, the hostess will usually serve the guests and then eat with the children after the adults have finished eating.

Visiting

Eritreans are known for being open and welcoming, and a warm sense of family permeates the culture. Friends and family often visit each other unannounced and uninvited, and guests are usually always welcome, with the host typically serving coffee or tea. The Eritrean coffee ceremony is a long process whereby coffee beans are roasted and pounded; the coffee is then boiled and sweetened, and served in small cups. Often, three rounds of coffee are served, and fresh popcorn may be offered with each round of coffee. This coffee ceremony can last for two hours, allowing time for leisurely conversation, and it is considered impolite not to stay for the full three rounds.

Though the coffee ceremony has become a part of Eritrean hospitality, coffee is not grown domestically. As a result, it is considered a special treat in areas outside of the larger cities.

Additionally, though gifts are not necessarily expected, guests will commonly arrive with a small gift of either local produce or firewood (if they are from a smaller village), or coffee or sugar (if they are from a larger town).

LIFESTYLE

Family

The concepts of kinship, clanship, and blood lineage are important aspects of Eritrean culture, particularly in terms of identity, social structure, and community. The family as a whole takes priority over its individual members, and relatives will often sacrifice some personal benefit for the greater good of the group. One of the greatest casualties of the prolonged conflict that has plagued Eritrea is that many families have been separated.

It is typical for grandparents to live in the same home as a nuclear family (commonly, a father, mother, and their children), and the elderly, respected for their wisdom, often help raise the grandchildren and are cared for by their children as they age. Children are expected to contribute to household tasks from an early age; in rural areas, boys will help herd the livestock, and girls will help their mothers with domestic duties.

Traditionally, Eritreans are known by their first name and their father's first name. Most Eritreans defer to the men in their families, but the Kunama are a matrilineal society. This means that the woman is the head of the household, and only maternal relatives are considered family.

Housing

Many of the Afar, Hedareb, Rashaida, and Tigre peoples are either nomadic or semi-nomadic, meaning they move from place to place in search of food, water, and/or grazing land, often according to the seasons. Thus, their homes are built with native and local materials and are often easy to assemble and disassemble. No matter what style they are, however, these temporary homes are known for being orderly and clean. This nomadic group was estimated to constitute roughly 35 percent of the total Eritrean population in 2010.

In the villages, homes are usually made of stone. The roof will be either metal or thatched, and the floor will be either concrete or dirt. In urban areas, homes are made of either stone or brick. The roof will be metal, and the floor will be tile. Urban homes usually have electricity, running water, and other modern amenities. In the lowlands, homes are generally round to ward off heat. In the highlands, where the temperatures are cooler, homes are rectangular and are known as hidmo.

Food

While Eritrean cuisine varies regionally, it is generally similar to the cuisine of Ethiopia, and has been influenced by African and southern European culinary traditions, most notably Italian. Specifically, Eritreans are known for their love of spicy food and bread. Due to Eritrea's close proximity to the Red Sea, fish is a traditional staple (meat is often considered a luxury), and traditional cereal crops feature prominently.

A typical lunch or dinner in Eritrea consists of zigini, a stewed chicken, beef, or lamb dish that is prepared with spices, garlic, onions, red peppers, and butter. In the highlands, the zigini is usually eaten with injera, a spongy bread made of wheat, teff, or sorghum. Injera looks similar to a crêpe or pancake, but tastes quite different. The grains are ground, mixed with water, and allowed to ferment for several days, giving it a characteristic slightly sour taste, somewhat like sourdough bread. Injera is usually baked on a mogogo, a special clay stove about 30 inches in diameter, which used to be heated by wood fires (but now is often electric). When eating traditional Eritrean food, people typically use the injera to pick up the meat and/or sauce. In the lowlands, akelet or asida, a wheat-based porridge-like dish, is more commonly eaten during lunch and dinner, served with a berbere (many spices) and butter sauce and milk or yogurt.

An Eritrean woman preparing a traditional meal.

Breakfast is usually light and served with sweetened tea. Typical breakfast foods include yogurt, fit (sauce-covered injera), basha (a cake-like bread), honey, and an unleavened bread called k'itcha, fool (a chickpea purée), or ga'at, a thick porridge made from barley. In some areas, the Italian frittata (scrambled eggs with onions and peppers) is eaten for breakfast. In urban areas, the Italian influence is more obvious, with pasta being served in many restaurants.

In Eritrea, drinks are usually served at room temperature. Two popular locally-made alcoholic drinks are sowa, a bitter barley-based drink, often drunk from a particular cup called a millileek, and mez, a sweet honey wine, usually reserved for special occasions.

Life's Milestones

Births are cause for celebration in Eritrea. Usually, Tigrinya women ululate (or make a high-pitched trilling sound with their tongue) when their child is born—seven times for a boy, and three to four times for a girl. While natural homebirths are common and traditional medicine is used, more and more women are encouraged to deliver their babies in hospitals to counteract the high infant mortality rate. The birth of twins is traditionally considered incredibly unfortunate. Twins are such an ill omen that they and the mother are usually exiled from the tribe or village altogether. Tradition says that a woman must be circumcised in order to marry, so even though female circumcision has been outlawed, circumcision for both boys and girls is still common.

Marriage is the other major milestone in Eritrea. While marriages are often arranged (based on class and wealth or to solve political disputes) among the Tigrinya, it is becoming more common, especially among the younger populations in urban centers, for an individual to select their own partner. Virginity is not considered a necessary or desirable trait in a young woman, and a woman who has already given birth is traditionally more sought-after because she has demonstrated her fertility.

CULTURAL HISTORY

Art

Eritrea's cultural heritage is diverse, beginning with the Aksumite Empire that developed in the fourth century BCE. This empire extended into much of present-day Eritrea and neighboring northern Ethiopia. Considered the first significant empire to convert to Christianity, the Aksumite Empire peaked around the first century CE. Along with Rome, China, and Persia, it was one of the four greatest civilizations of the ancient world. The empire's cultural influences ranged from Egyptian, Arabic, and Indian to Buddhism, Judaism, and Christianity. The empire's most significant cultural achievements included its coinage, the development of its own alphabet, and temple and monument architecture.

After the decline of the Aksumite Empire and the spread of Islam in the seventh century CE, the region of Eritrea fell under the control of various other cultures and countries, most notably Egypt, Ethiopia, the Ottoman Empire, and Italy. During this long period, Christianity and Islam both remained influential, and Islamic and Coptic art (art developed in the early Christian period with roots in the art of ancient Egypt and Greece) was popular. This is evidenced in artistic artisanship such as metalwork and textiles, manuscript illustrations, and architecture (Eritrea has numerous medieval Coptic churches and Islamic mosques). Eritrea is also known for its traditional and tribal handicrafts including ceramics, jewelry making, metalwork, woodcarving, and leather goods. For example, the Nara tribe was known for fashioning saddles, while the Beni-Amer tribe was known for making an ornate, curved dagger with an ebony hilt.

Architecture

Eritrea's architectural heritage is a product of its colonial past, blending Egyptian, Ottoman, and Arabic styles. However, one of the most profound influences on Eritrean architecture was Italy. Eritrea historically represented Italy's lone colonial venture (during the late 19th and early 21st centuries), and the country served as a training ground for Italian architects throughout the 1920s and 1930s. The capital, Asmara, highlights many pastel-hued art deco buildings and other avant-garde modernist styles. The downtown area of Asmara is a blend of Italian colonial and modern architecture organized into an irregular grid, and streets in Asmara were designed to be aesthetically pleasing, with wide avenues lined by trees, numerous piazzas, and urban parks. The city has even been dubbed the "Miami of Africa" for its wide walkways, palm trees, and passeggiata (evening stroll) culture.

Perhaps the most famous building in Asmara is the Fiat Tagliero Building, a gas station that resembles a plane or a bird and features concrete "wings" that span roughly 30 meters (98 feet). The building is an example of futurist architecture and was completed in 1938. The designer, Italian architect Giuseppe Pettazzi, was forced to keep wooden beams under the wings while it was under construction, and people assumed the wings would fall once the beams were removed. The building remains structurally sound, and was restored in 2003.

Drama

Eritrean drama has its roots in religious festivals. In addition, Eritrean playwrights have also used the stage to discuss the social and political issues related to the country's liberation from Ethiopia. Dramatic works continue to be performed on national holidays. However, artistic works considered inappropriate by the government are censored in Eritrea. In 2007, it was reported that political dissident and playwright, actor, and director Fessehaye "Joshua" Yohannes died while in detention. He was arrested in 2001 with other members of Eritrea's political opposition.

Music & Dance

Music has always been a significant part of Eritrean culture. Much of Eritrean music is based on the pentatonic scale, which is a five-note scale rather than a seven-note scale. (In C-major, for example, the pentatonic scale would be the five black keys on a piano, rather than the white

The krar is a traditional stringed instrument of Eritrea and Ethiopia often tuned to the pentatonic scale.

keys.) Pentatonic music is often associated with East Asia, but it can be found in folk music from all over the world and in modern genres such as blues and jazz.

Several traditional musical instruments in Eritrea are unique to the region. The three most common stringed instruments are the krar, wata (or cira-wata), and the abangala. The krar has either five or six strings, and is shaped like a triangular lyre with a bowl-shaped body in the middle and two wooden arms on either side. Some modern krars are rectangular and resemble a guitar with two necks.

The wata has one string and is played with a bow, similar to the violin, and the banjo-like abangala can be found among the Kunama people (who make up two percent of the population). Drums are also an integral part of Eritrean music, and the most popular is the kebero, a cylindrical hand drum that is wider on top than on the bottom (like a cone with two flat ends).

Eritreans enjoy singing and dancing, and have historically used performance art as a way to celebrate religious festivals, births, marriages, and holidays, among other events. One particular traditional dance is the circle dance, performed at joyous events, and which includes the formation of a slowly moving circle. In the lowlands, men dance the someeya, in which they leap and wave sticks. Women dance the sheleel, in which they shake their long braids from side to side.

Women often ululate, or make a high-pitched trilling sound with their tongue, while they dance to express joy. (The singing technique of ululation is also a worship feature of the Eritrean Orthodox Church.) On occasion, drummers stand in the middle of the circle and increase the tempo of the music to build energy. Dancing is usually a festive and happy event, and Eritreans laugh and joke with each other while they dance. However, dancing is more subdued for religious events. "Church dancing," or "zayma," usually consists of standing in place and clapping and moving the body to the music. Only men are allowed to dance in the church, and must do so in certain designated areas. For certain religious holidays, men will walk in a circle around the church three times, but not dance outside.

Literature

Eritrea has a rich history of oral tradition, in which poetry and folklore was memorized and then sung or recited. The poems were usually in couplets (two rhyming lines with the same meter) and would often be about the loss of a loved one, the suffering of poverty or of feeling homesick.

Early written literature in Eritrea was mostly religious in nature, and written in the Ge'ez language used by the Aksumite Empire. The first published literary text written in Tigrinya (the most spoken language in modern Eritrea) is believed to be from 1895, when Fesseha Giyorgis wrote about his voyage from East Africa to Italy, entitled *About the Author's Journey from Ethiopia to Italy and about the Impressions Made on Him by His Stay in That Country in Tigrinya*. From then on, Eritreans began to print their famous fables, folktales, and poems.

Eritreans are also well known for their proverbs, and many volumes have been published over the years. Three of the most popular Eritrean proverbs are "If you are patient, you will get butter" (Zurugay sava luchae yo-u-se); "Little by little an egg will walk" (Kwakolo kus bekus bougru yehahid); and "You do not have a donkey, but you sneer at my horse" (Adgi zeybulu bakeali yenekeah).

Arts & Entertainment

Because the Eritreans fought for their independence for so long, it is no surprise that their contemporary art is often a tribute to their struggle. A great majority of Eritrean art pays tribute to the courage of the many that fought for the nation's independence. Many artists made it their goal to use their art to inspire and uplift the people, or to pay respect to those who had fallen in battle. For example, artist Michael Adonai (1962–)—along with his brother, Berhane—is known for his "liberation art." The two have been heralded as examples of African artists taking the suffering of slavery and racism and transforming it into something beautiful in the form of music, art, or literature.

In Asmara, there is a monument of tanks, and one can see images of soldiers all over. What is unexpected, however, is a statue of a pair of shida (Arabic for "sandals") in the capital. This inexpensive plastic black shoe has gradually become an empowering symbol of the war for independence. Beginning in the 1960s, when the Eritrean soldiers fighting for their country had no uniforms, these sandals were adopted as such. They were practical in the desert heat, allowing air to circulate around weary feet, and when a strap broke, all one needed was a match to melt the plastic and make repairs. In the 1980s, when an underground shida machine remained unharmed through every attack, the sandals became a nationally recognized symbol of Eritrean pride.

Even music in Eritrea became a declaration of national interest. One of the most famous songs in Eritrea is "Shigey Habuni" (literally "Give me my torch," but also translated as "Give me my freedom"), first sung in the mid-1960s by Tewolde Redda (considered to be one of the first to have played an electric guitar in all of Africa). Some claim that music and its powerful messages were what often kept the resistance fighters motivated during their long struggle. In contrast to Tigrinya lyrics, which are often about independence, war, and national pride, Amharic music, usually from Ethiopia, focuses more on love. Amharic music had been popular in Eritrea, despite its being banned from the radio. In 2003, in a "morality movement," Ethiopian music was banned from being played in public in Eritrea. Music also plays a large role in religious life in Eritrea. Festivals are filled with singing and chanting, and songs can be sung for hours, with festivities continuing into the families' homes after the larger ceremonies have finished. Women will often ululate during religious events or other momentous events, such as births or funerals, to express great joy or grief.

Eritrean literature also pays homage to their fight for freedom and self-sovereignty. Tigrinya novels came to light after 1949, and most fiction and poetry since then has either focused on or incorporated themes of national pride and fighting off external oppression. Some are more direct, and others are more symbolic, but it is rare to find a work of Eritrean literature with no reference to their struggle.

After Eritrea declared its independence in the 1990s, the government encouraged artists to branch out from solely representing images of war and to embrace images of the land and the people, as well. Since then, artists like Seare Fessahaye have started creating art that emphasizes the diversity of Eritrea rather than just its struggle. Co-sponsored by the United States embassy, Fessahaye's art exhibit entitled "Eritreans from all walks of life" was showcased in June 2008 in Asmara. Tirhas Iyassu is another Eritrean artist who has taken slice-of-life images and added her feminist twist to it, such as creating images of men attending children.

Cultural Sites & Landmarks

With its modernist architecture, ranging from art deco to neoclassical, and storied colonial past and atmosphere, the capital of Asmara is perhaps the most important cultural destination in Eritrea. Significant landmarks include the Cinema Impero, a cinema built in the art deco style that resembles an old radio, and the Roman Catholic Cathedral, considered one of the finest Romanesque-style churches built outside of Italy.

Another popular destination in Asmara is the Central Market. Early Saturday morning is the best time to visit, when people come to the market from all over Eritrea. The city is also home to the Eritrean National Museum. Due to Asmara's architectural heritage and urban planning, the city is a proposed World Heritage Site, as designated by the United Nations Educational, Scientific, and Cultural Organization (UNESCO). The non-profit World Monuments Fund (WMF) also lists it as an endangered site.

One of the most recognizable structures in Asmara is the Fiat Tagliero Building, which currently serves as a gasoline station for the Shell Oil Company. The building was built in 1938 by Italian architect Giuseppe Pattazzi and was constructed in an early 20th-century design fad known as futurism, wherein buildings were constructed to defy historical architectural traditions. The Fiat Tagliero Building consists of a central tower with two broad, wing-like structures attached to form a roof over the building's parking areas. Although the building is unimportant in terms of function, it has become a popular spot for tourists and is a symbol of the nation's modernist architectural traditions.

Architecture is also an important cultural heritage of the port city of Massawa, and reflects Turkish and Egyptian rule between the 16th and 19th centuries. The white Banco d'Italia from the 1920s displays gothic windows, towers, and balconies with arched frames. The 15th-century Sheikh Hanafi Mosque is representative of early Islamic architecture. For hundreds of years, coral was the main building material, and there are several famous coral-block houses. However, much of the city's famed architecture is now in disrepair from the Eritrean War of Independence (1961–1991), and rebuilding has been slow due to insufficient funding.

Eritrea is also home to several important natural sites, most notably the Dahlak Archipelago in the Red Sea (which borders Eritrea on the north and northeast). There, the water sometimes turns from blue-green to a maroon color due to the algae present. The Red Sea itself is a popular destination for scuba divers and snorkelers because the volcanic activity under the water's surface keeps the water warm, and 15 percent of its marine life can only be seen in this region. In addition, because no rivers flow to the Red Sea, its higher salinity keeps swimmers especially buoyant. While some areas of the Red Sea are heavily visited, the Dahlak Archipelago is a group of over 200 mostly untouched islands and is considered one of the best and most unspoiled scuba diving and snorkeling spots in the region.

Libraries & Museums

Many of the buildings in Asmara that were built during the Italian occupation have been converted to serve as cultural centers. The former residence of the colonial governors, for example, has been converted into the Eritrean National Museum, which contains artifacts from the nation's archaeological and cultural history. Asmara also has a number of small art museums, which generally showcase native artists. A network of regional museums is being established under the National Museum, including one already in Massawa, which focuses on ethnicity and the country's struggle for independence.

Without a formal national library, the country's Research and Documentation Center serves as the legal depository of Eritrea and houses the country's archives. As of 2008, the country was home to approximately 156 school libraries (of nearly 870 schools), 33 community libraries, and 166 specially designated libraries, such as academic, governmental, or religious libraries.

Holidays

Religious holidays celebrated in Eritrea reflect the country's dual religious heritage. In addition to Christmas and Easter, Orthodox Christians celebrate Meskel (September 27 and 28), marking the discovery of the True Cross, and Timkat, which commemorates the baptism of Christ. Meskel entails a procession followed by a bonfire, singing and dancing, and the harvesting of the fields. Timkat entails a procession in which each church's representation of the Ark of the Covenant is transported to a river and then returned to its repository in the church. These

events also draw families together for large feasts.

Muslims celebrate Ramadan, Eid al Fatr at the end of the month-long fast, and Eid al Ahda, which commemorates Abraham's willingness to sacrifice his son to God as well as the annual pilgrimage to Mecca. These holidays are marked by feasts, prayers, and visits to family and friends.

Independence from Ethiopia is marked on May 24, Martyr's Day is observed on June 20, and the beginning of the struggle for independence is observed on September 1.

Youth Culture

For generations, Eritrean youth have been confronted with war. As a semblance of normalcy is slowly being established, youth in Eritrea are generally faced with little educational or career prospects. Further hampering the development of a cohesive youth culture is the presence of a strict military culture within the country. In fact, national service in the armed forces is mandatory in Eritrea, and many youth are subjected to service that extends beyond the obligatory twelve to eighteen months.

Though the quality of education has deteriorated in Eritrea due to war, the educational system is well organized, and considered a privileged environment. For example, Eritrean students dress up for college (men wear dress pants or nice jeans with collared shirts or the equivalent, and women wear nice pants or dresses), and despite the warm climate, shorts, worn t-shirts, and flip-flops are considered unacceptable for class. Outside of the classroom, young Eritreans tend to congregate in cafés, go to the movie theater, or visit each other's homes for either casual visits or parties. Football (soccer) is the most popular sport in Eritrea, as in most of Africa, and is played in public parks and on school grounds.

It is rare to see couples holding hands in public, as public displays of affection are not socially acceptable, and visitors will seldom see young Eritreans drinking or smoking in public. Smoking is costly and not well regarded among young people. Though some Eritrean students do drink in public, it is culturally frowned upon.

SOCIETY

Transportation

Generally, bus service is the most extensive and cheapest mode of public transportation in the country, with taxi service constituting a secondary and more expensive means of travel. Private car ownership remains low, and cycling is a popular mode of local transportation. Vehicle traffic moves on the right-hand side of the road in Eritrea.

Additionally, railroads built by the Italian colonists fell into disuse and were nearly destroyed during the war. By 2003, they were able to rebuild the scenic section that connected Asmara to Massawa, but continued westbound construction towards Sudan has been delayed by strained relations.

Transportation Infrastructure

Eritrea's transportation system suffered during the country's thirty-year struggle for independence from Ethiopia, and the rebuilding process has been slow due to limited funds. Once Eritrean-Ethiopian trade ceased, Ethiopia attacked the coveted coastline, and Assab, on the southern coast and once the largest port in Eritrea, never fully recovered. Massawa, on the northern coast and repaired in 2005, became the country's most active port. All roads leading into Ethiopia were closed during the conflict, and the two paved roads from Assab and Massawa into Ethiopia were damaged during the war.

Asmara is the primary transportation hub in Eritrea. The international airport is located approximately three kilometers (1.8 miles) from the downtown area. Most of the roads in Asmara are paved, though dirt roads cover the city's periphery. Asmara is serviced by a public bus system and is connected by regional rail to many of the nation's other cities and ports. Despite years of economic hardship, partially due to the conflict with Ethiopia, Asmara's infrastructure has shown steady improvements and the city currently has one of the best irrigation and sewage systems in Africa.

As of 2012, Eritrea has fourteen airports with unpaved runways and four airports with paved runways: the international airport in Asmara; one in each of the ports of Assab and Massawa; and one inland in Tessawa (also known as Tessenai) in the western part of the country. There are few airlines servicing the country.

Media & Communications

The government closed down eight privately owned newspapers and arrested several journalists in 2001. Since then, Eritrea has become the only country in Africa to control all of its press, television, radio, and news outlets. The main newspaper, *Hadas Eritrea,* is published three times per week, and the English newspaper, *Eritrea Profile,* and youth newspapers *Tirigta* and *Geled* are published once per week. The government's television station is Eri TV, and Erina is the news agency of Eritrea. Radio Zara is the FM station run by the government, and Dimtsi Hafash (Voice of the Broad Masses of Eritrea) offers two radio stations with programs in 11 languages.

Censorship remains a key issue in Eritrea, and journalists who criticize the country or its presidency risk imprisonment (it was reported that four journalists died while imprisoned in 2008). In fact, in 2007 and 2008, Reporters Without Borders, a non-governmental organization (NGO) committed to freedom of the press, ranked Eritrea last–out of 169 countries—in its annual Worldwide Press Freedom index. The Committee to Protect Journalists (CPJ) also cited Eritrea in 2012 as the most censored nation on Earth.

In 2000, Eritrea became the last African nation to establish local Internet connectivity. As of 2014, there were an estimated 58,100 Internet users, representing under 1 percent of the population. The country's telecommunications infrastructure also needs to be developed, and Eritrea, in recent years, has made efforts to privatize its telecommunication services; the Eritrean Telecommunications Corporation (EriTel) remains the sole national provider.

SOCIAL DEVELOPMENT

Standard of Living

Eritrea ranked 182nd out of 187 countries on the 2014 United Nations Human Development Index, which measures quality of life and standard of living indicators.

Water Consumption

According to recent statistics from the World Health Organization (WHO), approximately 57 percent of the population had access to improved sources of drinking water, while an estimated 15 percent had access to improved sanitation (one of the lowest in the world). Droughts, poor sewage facilities, and poor infrastructure all contribute greatly to the lack of water and sanitation coverage in the country, particularly in rural areas.

The UN Development Programme continues to work to improve Eritrea's water infrastructure and establish renewable energy sources for the pumping out of wells. Eritrea currently has no desalination facilities. In 2009, the country's Department of Environment had plans to construct 200 small dams throughout the country in order to improve water access to farmers.

Education

Education in Eritrea's urban areas is limited by the lack of funding, facilities, qualified educators, and materials. The situation for the rural population is even more limited. Moreover, a greater number of males are educated, since it is commonly believed that females should learn to take care of the home. The average literacy rate is 73 percent.

Elementary and middle school are free and compulsory in Eritrea and comprise seven years of education. Enrollment, however, is not strictly enforced, and the number of students quickly tapers off in the higher grades. After middle school, students can attend four years of secondary school. They have the option of attending technical school following the tenth grade. The language of instruction depends on the region until the seventh grade, when courses are taught in English.

Eritrea has one university, the University of Asmara. Also located in the capital is the Teacher Training Institute. Students must pass a rigorous national exam in order to secure placement at the university level.

In 2015, the literacy rate among Eritrean males and females was 82.4 percent and 65.5 percent, respectively.

Women's Rights

Eritrean women traditionally have less power and a lower status than their male counterparts do, but there is slow progress toward gender equality. In 1979, the National Union of Eritrean Women (NUEW) was created to level the disparity, and its motto was "Emancipation through equal participation." In the 1990s, the NUEW launched a literacy campaign to help women enter the workforce. Traditional "feminine" training, such as secretarial skills, was offered along with traditionally "masculine" skills, such as electrical or plumbing work.

Education continues to be an area of concern for women, however. As recently as 1999, 85 to 90 percent of Eritrean women were illiterate. In 2001, the number dropped to 80 percent, and by 2015, more than half of the women in Eritrea were literate. A 2006 survey of primary and secondary school enrollment estimates 39 percent of the students were girls, and 54 percent were boys; in higher education, 13 percent of the students were women, and the remaining 87 percent were men.

A third of the soldiers fighting in the thirty-year liberation struggle were women, and they were treated as equals on the battlefield. Many expected gender equality to improve after the war was over, but traditional expectations have held strong. In rural areas, only men can plow or sow in the fields. Women are expected to attend to all domestic responsibilities, including child rearing. This division of labor according to gender begins at a young age: boys are directed to herd animals, while girls are asked to fetch water and firewood. Furthermore, women are expected to be home at night, and women who are seen out at night, especially in rural areas, are assumed to be either working in a restaurant or bar, or as a prostitute.

It has also been hard for women to start their own businesses, as women usually have lower education levels and difficulty accessing adequate funding to start up entrepreneurial projects. Often, they receive little community support for their efforts as well. Additionally, the UN International Fund for Agricultural Development (IFAD) has tried to offer women hectares of land to farm on their own to empower them and give them ownership. However, women are conflicted by generations of elders telling them that women were not to plow the fields.

Another area of concern for women in Eritrea is female genital mutilation (FGM). Though outlawed by the government, the practice is said to be prevalent. As of 2002, it was estimated that 89 percent of women have been circumcised, and that number is believed to have increased in recent years.

Officially, progress has been made in the realm of women's rights. Generally, women's rights are protected by law in Eritrea, and women are guaranteed equal rights in family and citizenship. In addition, women are represented politically, and the Eritrean National Assembly now reserves 30 percent of its seats for women. However, the Eritrean government canceled scheduled 2001 elections, and has not made plans to hold new elections. Thus, the constitution ratified in 1997 was never implemented.

Health Care

Eritrea's long war with Ethiopia, its poor economic situation, and the number of refugees who returned to the country after the war have slowed the development of an already inadequate health care system. Medical care is centered in the capital, but even Asmara's hospitals are short of trained personnel, equipment, and supplies. Only the wealthy can afford private health care services, and many Eritreans depend on traditional medicine to alleviate their illnesses.

Dengue fever, malaria, HIV infection, hepatitis, and meningitis are a few of the serious illnesses that threaten the health of the population, and perhaps as much of half suffer from varying degrees of chronic malnutrition. Despite these problems, some improvements have been made since independence, particularly in the areas of pre- and post-natal care and HIV/AIDS education.

GOVERNMENT

Structure

From 1890 until the Second World War, Eritrea was part of an Italian colony in East Africa. Administered by Britain until 1952, it enjoyed 10 years of independence before it was annexed by Ethiopia. This led to a 30-year war that claimed 70,000 Eritrean lives and displaced many more. Eritrea defeated Ethiopia in 1991 and voted for independence two years later. The relationship with Ethiopia remains strained and erupted into a border war from 1998 to 2000. Though fighting has ended, the border remains closed, and the line of demarcation has yet to be resolved.

Eritrea's government is still considered to be in transition, since it has not implemented the constitution approved in 1997. The post-independence government has postponed elections indefinitely. In 2014, President Isaias Afworki promised that a new constitution would be drafted. As of 2015, this has yet to happen.

Currently, executive power is vested in the State Council, which is headed by a president. The president is the head of the government, the state, and the National Assembly. He is also responsible for appointing the State Council.

The legislative branch is under the control of the unicameral National Assembly. Its 150 members are theoretically responsible for electing the president to a five-year term, with a limit of two-terms. The constitution states that the National Assembly is elected by popular vote, but as of 2015, an election has yet to be held.

Political Parties

Only one party has legal standing in Eritrea, the People's Front for Democracy and Justice (PFDJ). Political opposition is considered treasonous by the government, and has resulted in state-controlled violence and detainment without trial. Among the parties that are considered illegal in the country are the Eritrean People's Party, the Eritrean Liberation Front, and the Eritrean National Alliance.

Local Government

Eritrea has six regions that are headed by administrators appointed by the president. Regions are subdivided into districts. Because the country is an authoritarian state, political power is highly centralized and little power is entrusted with the local government. Although local government elections were held in 2004, they were not considered fair or legitimate.

Judicial System

Eritrea's system of law is based on traditional culture and Ethiopian law, which is influenced by Napoleonic law. The country's judicial system is organized into civilian, military, and special courts. The civilian judicial system is headed by the High Court, which adjudicate above regional, sub-regional, and village courts. Regional courts hear cases regarding the most serious criminal matters. Military courts have two levels: higher courts and lower courts. The official role of special courts is to hear cases regarding corruption. However, Eritrea's legal system and judicial system are widely considered corrupt. Allegations that the government uses the judicial system to help enact its political authority are widespread.

Taxation

Eritrea has a top corporate and income tax rate of 30 percent.

Armed Forces

The armed forces of Eritrea, officially the Eritrean Defence Forces, consist of an army, navy, and air force. Conscription exists, and has been the source of human rights complaints, ranging from forced conscription and compulsory service up until the age of fifty. Conscription consists of a six-month training period and one year of service, but indefinite obligation periods have also been alleged.

Foreign Policy

When Eritrea emerged from 30 years of fighting and became an independent nation recognized by the world in 1993, it was heralded as a modern success story and an example for all other developing nations. Since, then, however, the country has dealt with political instability and economic unraveling. Generally, its foreign relations have been defined by foreign aid and territorial disputes, including conflicts with neighboring Ethiopia, Sudan, Djibouti, and Yemen, located across the Red Sea.

Eritrea's foreign relations are perhaps best characterized by its ongoing conflict with Ethiopia, a tense situation that culminated in the Eritrean-Ethiopian War (1998–2000). The UN Peacekeeping Mission to Ethiopia and Eritrea (UNMEE) was stationed in the disputed border area between Ethiopia and Eritrea in 2000. In 2002, the Ethiopia-Eritrea Boundary Commission (EEBC) proposed a border upon which Eritrea and Ethiopia agreed. However, by November 2006, neither country had complied fully with the Demarcation Statement. The EEBC granted Badme, the contested territory, to Eritrea, but Ethiopia did not accept this ruling and continued to occupy the area, along with UNMEE troops.

Furious that the ruling in its favor was not recognized or supported by the international community, Eritrea tried to expel UNMEE troops, accusing them of occupying Eritrean land. After seven years of trying to stabilize the region, the EEBC finally disbanded on November 30, 2007. However, the hostilities continued, and in January 2008, Eritrean troops entered the Temporary Security Zone (TSZ) and blocked the UNMEE's fuel supply. In March 2008, without adequate fuel, the UNMEE was forced to withdraw from the area. As of 2015, the situation between Ethiopia and Eritrea continues to be dangerous, and experts agree that war is very possible, unless the international community steps in to mediate.

Eritrea's relations with Djibouti are equally unstable and tense. The U.S. formally condemned Eritrea's military aggression in June 2008 after nine Djibouti soldiers were killed and 60 were injured. In October 2008, Djibouti expressed concern over Eritrea's continued military expansion into Djibouti territory and refusal to participate in international mediation. Djibouti threatened war if the confrontational behavior continued.

Despite evident need, Eritrea has decided that self-reliance is its priority. In 2005, the government asked the United States Agency for International Development (USAID) and other humanitarian aid agencies to cease their activity. The U.S., which had donated $65 million (USD) in mostly food aid to Eritrea in 2004, complied and stopped providing assistance to Eritrea. The relations between the U.S. and Eritrea continued to deteriorate, and in 2007, the US closed the Eritrean consulate in Oakland, California, and considered adding Eritrea to the list of states that sponsor terrorism. (A UN monitoring group said Eritrea was sending large numbers of weapons and arms to Somalia in support of insurgents fighting against the Ethiopian-backed government.) The Eritrean government denied such claims, and has decided not to inform the U.S. embassy if Americans are detained or allow embassy officials to visit American citizens who have been imprisoned.

The rest of the Western world started distancing itself from Eritrea when the government abolished its freedom of the press in 2001. However, while much of the West has pulled away from Eritrea for its human rights violations, China, South Korea, Italy, South Africa, and Germany were reportedly still pursuing trade opportunities with Eritrea. In 2007, Eritrea's main import partners were Saudi Arabia, Italy, China, Turkey, Germany, and Ukraine. Its main export partners were Italy, China, Sudan, France, Saudi Arabia, and Australia. Regionally, Eritrea maintains membership in the African Union (AU) and the Common Market of Eastern and Southern Africa

(COMESA), and is an observant member of the Arab League.

Human Rights Profile

International human rights law insists that states respect civil and political rights, and promote an individual's economic, social, and cultural rights. The United Nations Universal Declaration on Human Rights (UDHR) is recognized as the standard for international human rights. Its authors sought the counsel of the world's great thinkers, philosophers, and religious leaders, and were careful to create a document that reflects the core values shared by every world culture. (To read this document or view the articles relating to cultural human rights, visit http://www.udhr.org/UDHR/default.htm.)

According to the 2008 World Report by NGO Human Rights Watch, Eritrea is one of 17 nations requiring immediate attention. President Isaias Afeworki, elected in 1993, has not held a single presidential election since he was instated and no political party other than his People's Front for Democracy and Justice (PFDJ) party is allowed to participate in politics. During Afeworki's administration, many privately owned businesses have been taken over by the government.

Using the current border dispute with Ethiopia as an excuse, the government does not allow for any dissent from the people. Articles 19 and 20 of the UDHR have been blatantly ignored, as the government controls all media sources. Reporters have been in jail for years without proper access to legal counsel, and the government has rejected all international claims of any wrongdoing. People are unlawfully arrested, tortured, and kept in solitary confinement for years in underground cells.

The Eritrean constitution, adopted in 1997, is in line with Articles 2 and 18 of the UDHR in protecting religious freedom, but the constitution has never been implemented. A new promised constitution has yet to be drafted. For religions to be considered legal in Eritrea, they must register with the government. No new religions have been legalized since 2002, and the only four religions sanctioned in Eritrea are the Eritrean

Orthodox Church, the Evangelical (Lutheran) Church of Eritrea, Islam, and the Roman Catholic Church. People who follow other faiths have been harassed and persecuted. For example, weddings, baptisms, prayer groups, and church services have been raided, and often, all of the participants are imprisoned. The three main targets have been Jehovah's Witnesses, for refusing to enlist in the military, and followers of the Evangelical and Pentecostal churches, because of alleged ties to the U.S. government.

In 2004, Eritrea was declared a U.S. Department of State "Country of Particular Concern" (CPC), along with seven other nations, for its religious discrimination. There have been numerous reports of harassment, arrest and detainment, as well as forcing people to recant their faith or torturing them if they refuse. One example was a man whose arms and legs were tied together while he balanced on his stomach on the ground for almost six days straight. He was told that he would be released as soon as he signed the paper, which said he was formally giving up his faith.

As recently as 2007, people were being beaten, forced into grueling manual labor, crowded into metal shipping containers, and starved because of their religious beliefs.

ECONOMY

Overview of the Economy

Eritrea's current economic situation is dire; the northeastern African country is an economically impoverished nation and over 50 percent of Eritreans live below the poverty line. The long fight for independence and, more recently, the border war with Ethiopia, was costly, damaged much of the infrastructure, and caused a serious refugee crisis. Moreover, droughts frequently threaten the country's crops and increase the population's reliance on food aid. In 2014, the gross domestic product (GDP) per capita was estimated to be $1,200. The country's main exports are salt, meat, hide, textiles, sorghum, and processed food.

Italy is Eritrea's primary trade partner and accepts over 30 percent of Eritrea's goods. The United States, France, Belarus, and the United Kingdom also accept exports from Eritrea. Though agriculture is the chief form of employment, agricultural exports contribute less than 10 percent to the nation's GDP.

Industry

The Italians left some light industrial infrastructure in Eritrea. Today, industry engages less than 20 percent of the labor force and generates 26 percent of the GDP. Eritrea has factories for food, beverage, and salt processing as well as an oil refinery and a cement-making plant. Commercial ship repair is offered at the country's two major ports, Massawa and Assab.

In Asmara, agriculture, industry, and services are the most common forms of employment. The services industry, which includes tourism, contributes over 60 percent to the nation's annual GDP. Cities such as Asmara have become popular destinations for African tourists. Industrial manufacturing plants in and around Asmara produce a variety of products including clothing and textiles, cement, and other stone products.

Labor

Unemployment is widespread in Eritrea. Many Eritreans are employed in the country's informal economy, either on the trade of black market goods or in subsistence farming. In 2004, the percentage of the population living below the poverty line was estimated at 50 percent.

Energy/Power/Natural Resources

Eritrea's proven natural resources include gold, zinc, copper, and potash, but these have not been exploited; the country is also thought to have oil and natural gas reserves. Salt is found in the lowlands and is mined extensively. The most important natural resource for a large portion of the population is the arable land of the central highlands.

Since Eritreans use firewood for fuel, the forests of the highlands have been largely depleted. Deforestation and overgrazing has in turn led to soil erosion and, at lower elevations, desertification. Along the border with Ethiopia, the threat of landmines exists.

Fishing

Fishing and the harvest of ocean commodities are more common in communities along the Red Sea, but do not contribute significantly to Eritrea's national revenues. However, fishing exports are increasing and the economic potential of fishing in the Red Sea is beginning to be realized on a wider scale. According to the International Fund for Agricultural Development (IFAD), Eritrea anglers have not overfished or exploited the country's marine resources. The development of fishing docks and fishing processing sites continues, with financial aid from the European Union and the African Development Bank. In addition, efforts to improve the viability and quality of Eritrea's fishing fleet continue. Most anglers continue to use traditional vessels known as "houris."

Mining/Metals

Numerous foreign mining companies are active in Eritrea, including companies from Australia, China, Canada, Libya, and the United Kingdom. Eritrea is thought to have a significant amount of mineral resources, but mining is not currently a contributor to its gross domestic product. Ongoing violence in the country has prevented proper exploration of its supplies of gold, copper, potash (a type of salt), and petroleum. Ongoing developments in the UN trade sanctions brought against Eritrea will affect the development of its mining industry.

Agriculture

Subsistence agriculture is the primary occupation and employs over 80 percent of the population. Despite this, agriculture only generates less than 10 percent of the GDP. Crops include cereals, fruits, vegetables, peanuts, tobacco, corn, and coffee.

Animal Husbandry

Herding is the largest agricultural activity and meat products are one of Eritrea's principal exports. Many nomadic herders live in the lowlands. Goats, cattle, sheep, chickens, and camels are the most commonly raised animals, the majority of which are used for subsistence farming purposes. Eritrea exports an estimated $50 million worth of animal skins, meat, and live animals annually.

Tourism

The tourism industry is growing in Eritrea as the country begins to lose its image of famine, drought, and conflict, and to improve its infrastructure. The number of visitors peaked in the mid-1990s, only to fall again during the recent border war. Currently, around 80,000 foreign tourists visit Eritrea each year, generating $35 million (USD) annually.

Eritrea is not short of attractions, which range from the scenic beauty of the Red Sea and its colorful marine life, to the art nouveau architecture of Asmara and the restored Ottoman-era buildings of Massawa. Camel treks, safaris, deep-sea diving, snorkeling, and fishing are a few popular activities enjoyed by visitors.

Jennifer Kan Martinez,
Michael Aliprandini, Micah Issitt

DO YOU KNOW?

- The camel has been designated the national symbol of Eritrea for its significance as a beast of burden, especially during the war.

- The Eritrean currency, the Nafka, is named for the town in which a decisive battle for independence was fought.

Bibliography

Ghirmai Negash. "A history of Tigrinya literature in Eritrea: the oral and the written, 1890–1991." Leiden: Research School of Asian, African and Amerindian Studies (CNWS), *Universiteit Leiden*, 1999.

Ghirmai Negash and Charles Cantalupo. "Who Needs a Story? Contemporary Eritrean Poetry in Tigrinya, Tigre and Arabic." Asmara, Eritrea: *Hdri Publishers*, 2006.

Mawi Asgedom and Dave Berger. "Of Beetles & Angels: A Boy's Remarkable Journey from a Refugee Camp to Harvard." Boston: *Little, Brown and Company*, 2002.

NgCheong-Lum. *Eritrea*. Tarrytown, NY: Marshall Cavendish, 2001.

Robert G. Kaplan. "Surrender or Starve: Travels in Ethiopia, Sudan, Somalia, and Eritrea." New York: *Vintage Books*, 2003.

Ruth Iyob. "The Eritrean struggle for independence: Domination, resistance, nationalism, 1941–1993." Cambridge [England]; New York, NY: *Cambridge University Press,* 1995.

Works Cited

"Annual Report: Africa." *Reporters Without Borders.* http://www.rsf.org/IMG/pdf/rapport_en_afrique.pdf.

"A Tried and Tested Path towards Nation Building." *The State of Eritrea Ministry of Information*, 05 Dec. 2007. http://www.shabait.com/cgi-bin/staging/exec/view.cgi?archive=16&num=7562.

"Africa on your street: Glossary." *BBC*. http://www.bbc.co.uk/africabeyond/africaonyourstreet/glossary/.

"Airports in Eritrea." *Aircraft Charter World*. http://www.aircraft-charter-world.com/airports/africa/eritrea.htm.

"Alliance of Eritrean National Force." *Federation of American Scientists*, 03 Oct. 1998. http://www.fas.org/irp/world/para/aenf.htm.

"Annual Worldwide Press Freedom Index." *Reporters Without Borders*. 05 Nov. 2008 http://www.rsf.org/article.php3?id_article=24025.

"Art Exhibition – by Seare Fessahaye 'Eritreans from all walks of life'." *United States Embassy in Asmara, Eritrea, News*, June 2008. http://eritrea.usembassy.gov/seares_art_exh.html.

"Background Note: Eritrea." *The U.S. Department of State*. http://www.state.gov/r/pa/ei/bgn/2854.htm.

"Badme: Village in no man's land." *BBC News*, 22 April 2002. http://news.bbc.co.uk/2/hi/africa/1943527.stm.

"Beyond the Fragile Peace between Ethiopia and Eritrea: Averting New War." *International Crisis Group*, 17 June 2008. http://www.crisisgroup.org/home/index.cfm?id=5490&l=1.

"Black History Month with Eritrean Artists." *United States Embassy in Asmara, Eritrea, News*, March 2007. http://eritrea.usembassy.gov/eritrean_art.html.

"Countries of Particular Concern under the International Religious Freedom Act Fact Sheet." *U.S. Department of State Bureau of Democracy, Human Rights and Labor,* 9 May 2007. http://www.state.gov/g/drl/rls/84565.htm.

"Country Profile: Eritrea." *BBC News*, 17 June 2008. http://news.bbc.co.uk/2/hi/africa/country_profiles/1070813.stm.

"Country Profile: Eritrea." *Library of Congress – Federal Research Division*. http://lcweb2.loc.gov/frd/cs/profiles/Eritrea.pdf.

"Culture." *Eriview*. http://www.eriview.com/culture.htm.

"Culture and Society." *Embassy of the state of Eritrea in South Africa, 2006*. http://www.eritreaembassy.co.za/Culture%20Society/Culture%20and%20Society.htm.

"Dahlak Archipelago." The Columbia Encyclopedia, Sixth Edition. New York: *Columbia University Press*, 2008.

"Djibouti says Eritrea risking war." *BBC News*, 24 October 2008. http://news.bbc.co.uk/2/hi/africa/7687503.stm.

"Eritrea." *Culture Crossing*. http://www.culturecrossing.net/basics_business_student.php?id=64.

"Eritrea." *Encyclopædia Britannica Online*. 05 Nov. 2008. http://www.britannica.com/EBchecked/topic/191577/Eritrea.

"Eritrea." *Infoplease*. http://www.infoplease.com/ipa/A0107497.html.

"Eritrea." *Lonely Planet*, 10 Sept. 2008. http://www.lonelyplanet.com/eritrea.

"Eritrea." *Nations Online*. http://www.nationsonline.org/oneworld/eritrea.htm.

"Eritrea." *United Nations Data*. http://data.un.org/CountryProfile.aspx?crName=Eritrea.

"Eritrea." *University of Military Intelligence*. http://www.universityofmilitaryintelligence.us/tcc/cultural/HornAfrica/Eritrea/ERITREA%20LESSON%20PLAN.doc

"Eritrea: Arts and Literature." *Cultural Profiles Project*. http://www.cp-pc.ca/english/eritrea/arts.html.

"Eritrea: Country Specific Information." *U.S. Department of State Bureau of Consular Affairs*. http://travel.state.gov/travel/cis_pa_tw/cis/cis_1111.html.

"Eritrea – Intercultural Issues." *Centre for Intercultural Learning Foreign Affairs and International Trade Canada*. http://www.intercultures.ca/cil-cai/intercultural_issues_print-en.asp?lvl=8&ISO=ER.

"Eritrea bans Ethiopian songs." *BBC News*, 6 Jan. 2003. http://news.bbc.co.uk/2/hi/africa/2632399.stm.

"Eritrea denies new Horn talks." *BBC News*, 5 March 2004. http://news.bbc.co.uk/2/hi/africa/3531923.stm.

"Eritrean Artists to Discuss African-American and Eritrean Art." United States Embassy in Asmara, Eritrea, *News*, Feb. 2007. http://eritrea.usembassy.gov/bhm_with_eritrean_artists.html.

"Ethiopia/Eritrea." *International Crisis Group*. http://www.crisisgroup.org/home/index.cfm?id=1229&l=1.

"How Eritrea fell out with the west." *BBC News*, 11 September 2007. http://news.bbc.co.uk/2/hi/africa/6987916.stm.

"International Religious Freedom Report 2008: Eritrea." *U.S. Department of State Bureau of Democracy, Human Rights, and Labor*, 19 Sept. 2008. http://www.state.gov/g/drl/rls/irf/2008/108367.htm.

"It's coffee time." *Network Africa*, April 2008. http://www.networkafricaonline.com/eritrea-coffee-cere.htm.

"Listening to Diverse Voices: Multicultural Mental Health Promotion Research – Eritrean, Ethiopian, Somali & Sudanese Communities in Western Australia." *Centre for Social and Community Research*, 2004.

"Statement issued by the international relations office of the ELF_RC in response to the report by the U.S. Department. of State on human rights in Eritrea on January 30, s1997." *Federation of American Scientists*, 10 Mar. 1997. http://www.fas.org/irp/world/para/docs/humanr~2.htm.

"Sub-Saharan Africa: Eritrea." *USAID*, 13 Aug. 2007. http://www.usaid.gov/locations/sub-

"The World Factbook: Eritrea." *The Central Intelligence Agency*. https://www.cia.gov/library/publications/the-world-factbook/geos/er.html.

"Tigre Music." Awkir. http://awkir.com/tigre_music.htm.

"Travel Warning: November 15, 2008." *U.S. Department of State Bureau of Consular Affairs,* http://travel.state.gov/travel/cis_pa_tw/tw/tw_2939.html.

"U.S. considers putting Eritrea on terrorism list." *Reuters News*, 17 Aug. 2007. http://www.reuters.com/article/politicsNews/idUSN1744634320070817.

"U.S. condemns Eritrea 'aggression'." *BBC News*, 12 June 2008. http://news.bbc.co.uk/2/hi/africa/7450075.stm.

"U.S. warns Eritrea over 'terrorism'." *Aljazeera News*, 09 Sept. 2007. http://english.aljazeera.net/news/africa/2007/09/2008525141651310569.html.

"Who needs a story?" *African Books Collective* (review), http://www.africanbookscollective.com/books/who-needs-a-story.

"World Report." *Human Rights Watch*. http://www.hrw.org/en/reports/2008/01/30/world-report-2008.

"World Report: Eritrea." *Human Rights Watch*, http://www.hrw.org/legacy/englishwr2k8/docs/2008/01/31/eritre17746.htm.

Andrew Cawthorne. "Africa's "Miami" boasts Art Deco trove." *Reuters*, 18 May 2008. http://www.reuters.com/article/lifestyleMolt/idUSL1596553200080519.

Andrew Cawthorne. "Tiny Eritrea Makes Big Footprint in Africa." *Reuters*, 30 May 2008. http://www.reuters.com/article/reutersEdge/idUSL3058212620080530.

Andrew Cawthorne and Jack Kimball. "Travel Postcard: 48 Hours in Asmara." *Reuters*, 22 Aug. 2008. 21 Nov. 2008. http://in.reuters.com/article/lifestyleMolt/idINLD399036620080822?sp=true.

Binyavanga Wainaina. "Memories of the Future." *The New York Times*, 19 March 2006. http://travel.nytimes.com/2006/03/19/travel/tmagazine/19ts-memories.html.

Elsa Gebreyesus. "Native Stranger." *New Internationalist*, December 1992. http://www.newint.org/issue238/native.htm.

Jeffrey Gettleman. "Battle scars and Art Deco mingle in Eritrea." *International Herald Tribune*, 07 Oct. 2008. http://www.iht.com/articles/2008/10/08/travel/treritrea.php.

Jonah Fisher. "Religious persecution in Eritrea." *BBC News*, 17 Sept. 2004. http://news.bbc.co.uk/2/hi/africa/3663654.stm.

Marc Lacey. "For Eritrean Guerrillas, War was Hell (and Calluses)." *The New York Times*, 02 May 2002. http://query.nytimes.com/gst/fullpage.html?res=9C04E7DD1231F931A35756C0A9649C8B63 http://www.cscr.murdoch.edu.au/african.pdf.

Nkrumah, Gamal. "Giving Voice to the Voiceless." Al-Ahram, 31 July-6 Aug. 2003. http://weekly.ahram.org.eg/2003/649/profile.htm.

Paddy Magrane. "The Art Deco Gem Baking in the African Sun." *The Guardian*, 26 Feb. 2006. http://www.guardian.co.uk/travel/2006/feb/26/hotels.eritrea.observerescape.

"Partnership for Eritrea." *Physicians for Peace*. https://secure2.convio.net/pfp/site/SPageServer?pagename=Parternship_for_Eritrea_ABOUT_ERITREA.

"Pentatonic." *Nation Master Encyclopedia*. http://www.nationmaster.com/encyclopedia/Pentatonic.

Plaut, Martin. "New Unity in Eritrean opposition." BBC News, 15 Aug. 2004. 07 Dec. 2008. http://news.bbc.co.uk/2/hi/africa/3567190.stm.

Ryu, Alisha. "UN Move on Eritrea-Ethiopia Border Issue Raises Fears of Stalemate Collapse." Voice of America, 26 Oct. 2007. http://www.voanews.com/english/archive/2007-10/2007-10-26-voa42.cfm?CFID=281309909&CFTOKEN=16315579.

Steve Bradshaw. "Tough Choices for Eritrea's Three Sisters." *BBC News*, 18 Sept. 2008. http://news.bbc.co.uk/2/hi/africa/7618405.stm. saharan_africa/countries/eritrea/index.html.

Tanya Datta. "Eritrean Christians tell of torture." BBC News, 27 Sept. 2007. http://news.bbc.co.uk/2/hi/africa/7015033.stm.

Tesfa-alem Tekle. "Eritrean opposition radio starts broadcasting from Ethiopia." *Sudan Tribune*, 08 Mar. 2008. http://www.sudantribune.com/spip.php?article26287.

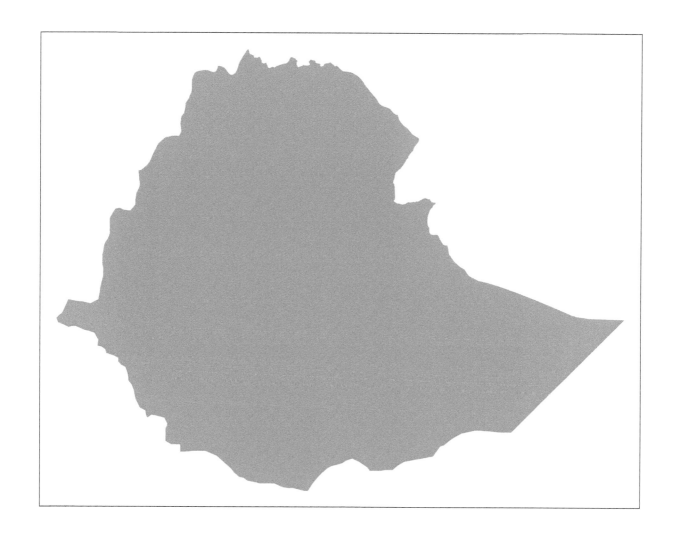

ETHIOPIA

Introduction

The Federal Democratic Republic of Ethiopia is a landlocked country located in East Africa, occupying most of what is known as the Horn of Africa. One of the most populous countries in Africa, Ethiopia is home to ancient and unique culture, and some of the oldest discovered hominid fossils. It is also one of the world's oldest Christian nations, as well as the source of the Blue Nile River. Ethiopia is one of the only African nations that was not colonized by a European power during the early modern era.

GENERAL INFORMATION

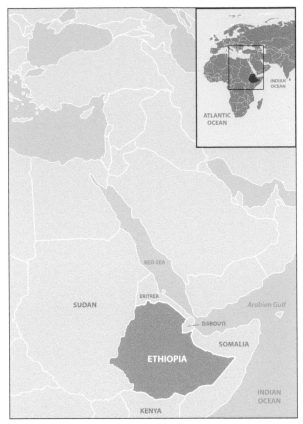

Official Language: Amharic
Population: 99,465,819 (2015 estimate)
Currency: Birr
Coins: The birr is available in a 1-birr coin and in coin denominations known as santim. There is a 1, 5, 10, 25, and 50 santim piece.
Land Area: 1,104,300 square kilometers (426,371 square miles)
Water Area: 7,444 square kilometers (2,874 square miles)
National Motto: "Unity in Diversity"
National Anthem: "Ethiopia, Land of Our Fathers"
Time Zone: GMT +3
Flag Description: The flag of Ethiopia features three horizontal bands of color— red, yellow and green. The red symbolizes strength, the yellow represents hope, and the green represents the land. In the center of the flag is a light blue circle, inside of which sits a yellow star. The star

stands for unity and diversity while the blue represents peace.

Population

The majority of Ethiopia's population is concentrated in the central highlands. The hot, dry lowlands are less hospitable and do not support the agricultural production in which most Ethiopians are engaged. Eighty-four percent of the population lives in rural areas. Addis Ababa is the country's largest city, with over 3.5 million people. Other large cities include Dire Dawa and Nazret.

There is a close ratio of male to females in Ethiopia and nearly half the population is 14 or younger. However, the country continues to have a low life expectancy; 48 years for males and 50 years for females. In addition, Ethiopia's infant mortality rate remains high, at 77 deaths for every one thousand births. Approximately 35 percent of children five years-old or younger are underweight.

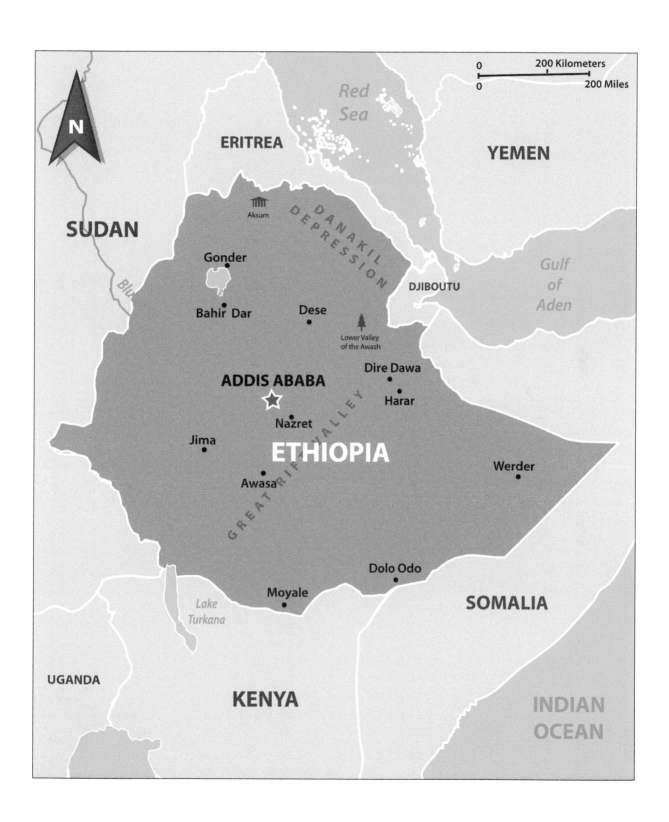

Principal Cities by Population (2012):

- Addis Ababa (3,500,000)
- Dire Dawa (355,641)
- Nazret (299,621)
- Gonder (252,537)
- Mek'ele (219,818)
- Dese (219,423)
- Bahir Dar (218,429)
- Jimma (207,573)
- Debre Zeyit (171,115)

Languages

There are over 80 languages are spoken in Ethiopia, over fifty of which belong to three families of the Afro-Asiatic language family. English is also widely spoken. Amharic and Tigrinya are both Semitic languages and written in a unique script. More than half of the population speaks Amharic, in part because it was imposed on heterogeneous peoples during imperial rule. Orominya, a Cushitic language, uses the Latin alphabet with some variations. Both Arabic and English are taught in schools.

Native People & Ethnic Groups

The ethnic diversity of Ethiopia is one of its most complex features. The largest groups are the Amhara, Tigray, and Oromo. The first two peoples are ethnically related and together make up about 32 percent of the population, while the Oromo account for approximately 40 percent. In general, the Amhara occupy the central highlands and the Tigray occupy the northern highlands. The Oromo live in the central and southwestern regions. Minority ethnic groups include the Somali and Afar, both lowland peoples.

Historically, the ruling class came from the Amhara, but their domination ended in 1974 when Emperor Haile Selassie was overthrown. Thereafter, ethnic groups attempted to gain more power for themselves, but this period was marked by civil strife. The implementation of a constitutional democracy in 1991 brought greater self-determination to majority and minority groups.

There are over eighty smaller ethnic groups in Ethiopia.

Religions

The majority of Ethiopians are either Muslim or Christian. Muslims make up between 45 and 50 percent of the population, while Christians make up about 45 percent. Most Ethiopian Christians belong to the Ethiopian Orthodox Church, which was designated as the state religion in the fourth century. Amhara and Tigray peoples generally adhere to the Orthodox faith, whereas the Oromo are equally divided between Islam and Christianity. About 12 percent of the population, many living in the south, practices some form of animism.

Climate

Given its great topographical variances in elevation, Ethiopia encompasses three climatic zones. The cool and temperate zones which prevail across the highlands yield warm and sunny days and cool nights outside of the rainy seasons.

The cool zone occurs above 2,400 meters (7,874 feet), with general temperatures ranging between 26° and 4° Celsius (80° and 40° Fahrenheit), though mountain heights can reach freezing. The temperate zone occurs on the lower parts of the plateau between 1,500 meters (4921 feet) and 2,400 meters. Average temperatures in this zone fall between 16° and 30° Celsius (61° and 86° Fahrenheit).

The lowlands, below 1,500 meters, constitute the hot zone. Average temperatures range from 27° to 50° Celsius (81° to 122° Fahrenheit), but the climate varies. In the west, a tropical climate prevails, whereas in the east and portions of the south, there is desert.

There are two rainy seasons on the Ethiopian plateau; the rains are heavier in the central and southern areas than in the north. The long rainy season, during which it rains torrentially nearly every day, lasts from the middle of June to the middle of September; 30 centimeters (12 inches) usually falls during each month of this season. The shorter, less intense rainy reason generally occurs from February to April, yielding just under 13 centimeters (five inches) of rain each month. Droughts generally occur every seven years in the highlands, more frequently in the eastern lowlands.

ENVIRONMENT & GEOGRAPHY

Topography

The Ethiopian highlands consist of a mountainous central plateau divided by the Great Rift Valley; this plateau comprises over half of Ethiopian territory. The peripheral lowlands are desert, which become hotter and drier towards the borders with Djibouti, Somalia and Kenya. The Great Rift Valley opens into a basin in the north called the Danakil Depression. At 115 meters (377 feet) below sea level, it is one of the lowest and hottest places on earth.

Among the important mountain ranges are the Simien, Chercher, and Bale Mountains. Ras Deshen, rising in the Simien Mountains, is the highest peak in Ethiopia and the fourth highest in Africa, at 4,620 meters (15,157 feet).

Near the source of the Blue Nile, in the north of the country, is Lake Tana. It is the largest lake in Ethiopia. In the south, a string of lakes is found along the Rift Valley, including Lake Awasa and Lake Langano.

The principal rivers are the Blue Nile, the Tekaze, and the Baro, all tributaries of the Nile; and the Awash and Omo. Ethiopian rivers flow from the highlands into the lowlands along deep valleys.

Plants & Animals

One of the most commonly seen trees on the central plateau is the non-indigenous eucalyptus, introduced as a fast-growing source of lumber and firewood. There are also modest evergreen forests, particularly in national parks.

Indigenous trees such as the acacia dominate the lowlands, along with a variety of savannah grasses and desert shrubs. Grasses and shrubs cover 41 percent of the total area of Ethiopia. It is thought that the coffee plant, which is now heavily cultivated, originated in the Ethiopian highlands.

The Ethiopian wolf, similar to the coyote in size and build, is differentiated by its long, narrow skull and red and white fur.

There are 255 animal species, 31 of them endemic, living in Ethiopia. Large animals such as the lion, elephant, zebra, hippopotamus, and rhinoceros are found, though in small numbers, and small primates abound. The mountain nyala, Menelik's bushbuck, the gelada baboon, and the hartebeest are all endemic animals. About 15 percent of the species found in Ethiopia is listed as threatened; some of the critically endangered species include the African Wild Ass and the Ethiopian wolf.

Over 800 bird species inhabit the country. Some of the unique species are the golden-backed woodpecker, the Abyssinian catbird, and the yellow-fronted parrot.

CUSTOMS & COURTESIES

Greetings

When approaching an individual or group, it is considered polite to extend a handshake and to give one's first name. While this may seem informal, first names have significant meaning to Ethiopians, and convey much about an individual. Honorific titles such as "Ato" ("Mr."), "Weizero" ("Mrs."), and "Weizerit" ("Miss") may also be used.

In addition, many Ethiopians will bow their heads or offer a simple nod to show deference. Common greeting phrases include "Teanastellen"

("Hello") and "Dehna neh?" ("How are you?"), for a male, or "Dehna nehs" for a female.

Gestures & Etiquette

Ethiopian culture is traditionally stoic and conservative. Actions and interactions are always friendly but usually not overly expressive. For example, pointing or excessive noises, such as shouting, are generally considered disrespectful. This also applies to attire, and women customarily refrain from wearing revealing clothing. Public affection is also generally considered inappropriate. However, members of the same sex are frequently seen holding hands and embracing. Ethiopians also value self-control and equality, and meals are traditionally shared evenly among family members and friends.

There is also certain etiquette relating to attending church or mosque, two of the most important and sacred places for many Ethiopians. When individuals arrive at a church or a mosque, they remove their shoes before entering. In addition, regardless of financial status, Ethiopians will offer a monetary contribution each week as a show of faith.

An Ethiopian family respectfully dining together.

Eating/Meals

At dinnertime, families customarily gather around a seating area, either a table or a mat on the ground, and wash their hands in a communal water basin. Food is laid out in communal dishes from which all diners eat. However, it is considered rude for someone to reach beyond the food set immediately in front of him or her. Ethiopians traditionally eat with their hands, often wrapping their food in injera, a pancake-like bread. However, as in most Muslim cultures, they refrain from using the left hand, which is reserved for bathroom hygiene and thus considered unsanitary. As a family eats, those who prepared the meal, most likely women, are responsible for breaking up the food if necessary. For example, meats and large vegetables are served whole, and need to be broken up and distributed evenly. Traditionally, elders and guests are served first.

One distinct Ethiopian eating tradition is gursha, or Ethiopian hand feeding. This is the art of arranging and placing food in the mouth of fellow diners. (Gursha translates as "mouthful" in Amharic.) It is considered an honorable and affectionate act. However, allowing someone's fingers to touch the mouth is seen as unsanitary and impolite.

Visiting

Visiting friends and family is a common custom in Ethiopia and there is rarely a designated time for visits. However, women commonly visit each other during the day and help prepare the evening meals. Men usually visit during meals or for a coffee ceremony, which traditionally follows dinner.

The coffee ceremony has been a part of Ethiopian society for centuries and is a celebrated and time-consuming tradition. Generally, a charcoal-burning mini-stove is brought into an area reserved for sitting and socializing. As guests take a seat, the hostess scatters freshly cut grass in the sitting area to awaken the senses. The coffee beans are ceremoniously roasted in an open pan until the steam fills the air, and guests may be expected to waft the steam toward them. The roasted beans are hand ground with a pestle and mortar, and then brewed in scalding water. The thick, dark roast is then served in tiny cups reminiscent of Italian espresso cups, with sugar used to cut the bitterness. The coffee is brewed thrice in one sitting, and missing any of the rounds, particularly the third round, is considered bad luck.

LIFESTYLE

Family

Ethiopian families are large and include extended family, generally from the father's side. Most families are based around a nucleus that includes a husband, a wife, and their children. These families customarily all inhabit the same home or compound, and strict gender guidelines determine familial roles. In general, women are responsible for the work of household tasks and child rearing while men work to earn money and teach their sons the family trade. Other family members are expected to contribute in exchange for the shelter and food provided.

The Ethiopian constitution references the sanctity of family and states that special attention should be paid to its preservation. It is believed that this, by extension, will help preserve Ethiopian values. The disruption of traditional cultural trends and changes in traditional family has become more commonplace in the early twenty-first century, as many young Ethiopians opt for schooling over traditional trades and chose to live more non-traditional lifestyles. The spread of HIV/AIDS is also impacting many families and leaving orphans to fend for themselves when their extended families abandon them.

Housing

During Ethiopia's imperial history, and later during Italian occupation (1936–1941), housing was more diverse. Early architecture included castles and royal court dwellings, some of which still stand in Gondar's royal enclosure where they were first built in the 1600s. These structures are reminiscent of Indian and Muslim designs. During Italian rule, many military bases and barracks were erected in Gondar. The Italians also established housing units segregated for various trades. For example, public housing for artists and artisans was built near the imperial ruins so that workers could make their crafts and sell them to tourists.

Most Ethiopians live in rural areas where the housing is generally uniform. The most common housing unit is a traditional hut known as a tukul, which is cylindrical, single-room building with conical roofs. Walls are generally made from a mud mixture, while the roofs are made from thatch or a straw and grass weave. This helps keep out the rain and ventilates the crowded rooms. For most families, several of these buildings are built on one plot of land as a compound. It is estimated that 85 percent of all houses in Ethiopia are constructed from mud and thatch. It is also estimated that most of the population—approximately 75 percent—lacks access to proper sanitation.

Food

Ethiopian cuisine is characterized as a spicy blend of meats, lentil stews, and vegetables. One of the best-known dishes is berberé, a red pepper spice mixture, or paste, which is used in most sauces and stews. Due to its spiciness, it is sometimes referred to as "red gunpowder." Another national specialty is wat (translated as "sauce"); a stew that commonly includes meat or fish, vegetables, berberé, and niter kibbeh, or clarified butter. Butter is widely available in Ethiopia because of the large cattle industry. There are numerous variations of wat. In the northern highlands of Ethiopia, the Tigrayan peoples eat a daily wat with lamb as the central ingredient. Beef wat is common in larger cities where there are more butchers. Doro wat is a chicken stew and the most widely available of the national wat dishes.

Injera, a spongy flat bread, is the national staple and, outside of coffee beans, one of the most famous Ethiopian culinary contributions. It is traditionally served on a large flat plate with wat poured on top. The best injera has tiny air bubbles cooked into it that allow excess sauce to gather and soak into the spongy dough. When Ethiopians eat injera, they tear pieces off from the edges first and use them to lift larger pieces of the stew. As the food diminishes, and only sauce and the center of the injera remain, the diners then use the soaking pancake to sop up the rest of the sauce. The soaked-through last bites are packed with flavor.

The Orthodox Church requires its adherents to fast on certain days throughout the year; during these fasts, animal products must not be eaten. Coffee and tej, a honey mead, are both popular drinks.

Life's Milestones

The most popular religions practiced in Ethiopia are Christianity, Islam and to a lesser extent, Animism. Many of life's milestones, such as birth, transition into adulthood, and marriage, are commemorated in accordance with these faiths. For example, the Ethiopian Orthodox Church claims that half the population are members of the church. Generally, music and feasting are essential elements in most milestone events in Ethiopia.

The Oromo people, the largest ethnicity in Ethiopia, celebrate milestones every eight years in accord with the Gada system they employ to stratify society by age. Society is divided into age groups that transition from one stage of life to the next every eight years. With each succession, an individual's role in the home and greater community changes usually becoming larger and more involved.

CULTURAL HISTORY

Art

Art in Ethiopia has been dominated by traditional design and a Coptic Christian influence. Early Ethiopian art was both functional and aesthetic, and consisted of woodcarving, textile arts, basketry, ceramics, and leatherwork. Early Ethiopians were particularly known for their skilled carving of items such as wooden headrests. These headrests were carved from single pieces of wood, generally sections of whole tree trunks that were shaped and smoothed to a shiny finish. They are also referred to as "wooden pillows" and keep the head level with the body during sleep, while protecting elaborate hairstyles. Other functional items carved from wood included furniture and weaponry, such as shields. The shields were covered with an animal hide, such as the skin of a rhinoceros, to help protect against weapons.

The arts flourished in Ethiopia following the introduction of Christianity in the sixth century. Christian Ethiopian art is particularly notable for its religious icons and metalwork crosses, as well as manuscript art and paintings. What makes the crosses and paintings of Christian Ethiopian art distinct is the use of lace-like loops in crosses, believed to be taken from Islamic art, and the depiction of the eyes, or pupils, in paintings. Generally, the eyes were painted as large and black, and it is believed that villainous or evil characters were painted in profile, with only one eye visible. The visual arts were also used to beautify churches and palaces, and frescoes portraying biblical scenes are still extant in Ethiopia's oldest churches. Sculpture was also introduced by Muslim and European traders who came to the region. Much of Ethiopia's visual arts are still dominated by religious themes.

Ethiopia's most famous and celebrated artist is Afewerk Tekle (1932–2012). Tekle showed artistic talent from a very young age and became the first African to enroll in London's prestigious art school, the Slade School of the Arts. There his artistic skills flourished as he majored in painting, sculpting, and architecture. He returned to Ethiopia in the 1950s with the ultimate goal of seeing his entire country and finding inspiration in its everyday livelihood. His first exhibition came in 1954 when he displayed paintings inspired by his travels. The money he earned from his first show allowed him to return to Europe where he learned the art of making stained glass windows. He also conducted a formal study of illuminated scrolls.

Upon returning to Ethiopia for a second time, Tekle opened his own gallery in the National Library. He was commissioned by the national government to paint murals and design windows for Ethiopia's most famous cathedral, St. George's Cathedral in the capital of Addis Ababa (sometimes spelled Addis Abeba). He was also commissioned in 1958 to design his largest work, the stained glass panels installed in Africa Hall, the headquarters of the United Nations Economic Commission for Africa (UNECA). After these major works, his popularity grew overseas. His style, characterized by bright, vibrant colors, geometric human forms, and shard-like shaping in his stained glass windows, is unique, and continues to influence Ethiopian artists.

Architecture
The Orthodox religion has inspired several unique architectural and artistic styles. Church interiors are often painted with elaborate narratives telling scriptural history. Some churches have been hewn out of rock and painted with similar iconic frescoes.

Drama
The Ethiopian National Theater is located in Addis Ababa. In addition to housing performances of traditional dance and music groups, the theater also features performances of Shakespeare and Ethiopian playwrights Mengistu Lemma and Kebede Michael.

Music
Ethiopian music, while influenced by the region's traditional music, is diverse and generally more reflective of a worldly influence. Traditional instruments, such as harps, lutes, and reed flutes, and traditional sounds, such as light percussion mixed with chanting, are more reminiscent of Gregorian chant than African tribal styles. Other traditional instruments include the kabaro (or kebero); a handheld drum made from wood and stretched animal hide, and the tsinatseil, which resembles a rattle. In fact, Ethiopian music

has been largely influenced by the Ethiopian Orthodox Church since the sixth century, when church music was first developed in conjunction with the spread of Christianity. Secular and folk music was influenced by the surrounding Horn of Africa, which includes Eritrea, Somalia, and Djibouti.

Another Ethiopian musical tradition is that of the azmari, a singer-musician similar to the European minstrel or bard. Centuries ago, the azmari performed at liturgies (public worship) and ceremonies at Ethiopia's royal courts. Their traditional instrument was the masenqo, a one-stringed fiddle. Azmari also sang about the glory of the emperors, who most Ethiopians believe to be descendants of biblical King Solomon and the Queen of Sheba. With the arrival of the Italians, azmari were famed for singing about Ethiopian culture. So influential was their music that many of them were exiled or executed for their insults to the Italians. Thus, the meaning of the word "azmaris" changed from "praise-singers" to "those who criticize."

Literature
Ethiopia's early literature was mainly written in an antiquated language known as Ge'ez. Referred to as a liturgical language, Ge'ez belongs to the Semitic family and can be traced to the third and fourth century, and it became the official language of the Ethiopian imperial court. The period from 1270 CE to the early 1500s is known as the golden age of Ge'ez literature. Work from this period includes mostly theological writing, as well as historical narratives and poetics. One of the most important literary works is the 14th century *Kebra Negast* (Book of the Glory of the Kings), which detailed the origins of the Solomonic dynasty, which was founded in 1270 CE. As time passed, the Ge'ez language was relegated to the Ethiopian clergy and the translating of ancient literature. The Amharic peoples soon came to dominate Ethiopian politics and culture, and most literary work from the seventeenth century onward was written in the Amharic language, with the exception of English literature following World War II.

CULTURE

Arts & Entertainment

Ethiopian art has become more visible abroad as more contemporary artists are settling outside of the country. Thus, contemporary Ethiopian art has become more associated with the Ethiopian diaspora, and often lacks activist themes or social statements because of this disconnect. Contemporary art in Ethiopia has also established itself as separate from religious or tradition church art and painting, and has become more commercialized. Notable modern Ethiopian artists include Julie Mehretu (1970–), best known for her abstract paintings, and the artist duo Meseret and Mekbib (Meseret Desta and Mekbib Gebertsadik). Alexander "Skunder" Boghossian (1937–2003) is considered the "father of Ethiopian modernism" and was the first African artist to have work bought by the Museum of Modern Art (MoMA) in New York.

Ethiopia also has many active folk ways, including indigenous dances, music, and an oral tradition that encompasses proverbs, poems, and tales, sometimes recited by wandering minstrels. One very popular dance is the isikista, in which only the dancers' shoulders gyrate rhythmically. The krar and the masinko are common stringed instruments. Among a host of popular singers, Aster Awoke, Gigi, and Tilahun are perennial favorites. Long distance running is one of the most popular sports in Ethiopia, with several athletes having garnered international stature. Haile GebreSellassie (1973–), a national hero, is the most widely known outside of the country.

Cultural Sites & Landmarks

Ethiopia is home to a wealth of cultural sites and landmarks, many of which are ancient. In fact, Ethiopia's rich archeological heritage is well documented, including the discovery of "Lucy," a hominid (human ancestor) skeleton estimated at 3.2 million years old.

The legendary Ark of the Covenant (a biblical artifact that is said to house the tablets inscribed with the Ten Commandments, among other items) is said to be housed in an ancient Ethiopian church in the town of Axum. The Obelisk of Axum, a granite monument originally constructed in the fourth century, was looted by Italian forces in 1937, only to be wholly returned in 2005, more than 50 years after Italy was asked to do so by the United Nations (UN) in 1947.

Ethiopia is also home to eight World Heritage Sites, as designated by the United Nations Educational, Scientific, and Cultural Organization (UNESCO). They include the archeological sites of Aksum; the Fortified Historic Town of Harar Jugol; the fortress city of Fasil Ghebbi (royal enclosure), known as Africa's Camelot; the Lower Valleys of both the Awash and Omo Rivers, which have contributed to the study of human evolution; the Rock-hewn Churches of Lalibela; the archeological site of Tiya, which contains thirty-two ancient erected stones; and Semien National Park, which is home to numerous rare species. In 1996, the park was added to the list of World Heritage Sites in danger, where it remains until this day.

Two of the most notable World Heritage Sites are located in the historic cities of Aksum and Lalibela. At the height of its power in the first six centuries CE, the Aksumite Empire was the most important and powerful state linking Eastern Rome and the Persian Empire. The remnants of this powerful kingdom are still extant in the city of Aksum (or Axum), and include tall standing stones, palatial ruins, underground tombs, and mysterious carvings. It is a long-held belief that ancient Aksum was the seat of power when the legendary Queen of Sheba ruled. During the 13th century CE, at the onset of Ethiopia's golden age of Christianity and literature, nearly a dozen monolithic churches (made from a single stone) were carved from the bedrock at sites around modern-day Lalibela in central Ethiopia. Because of the rock-cut architecture, the churches can only be entered at the subterranean level. The churches have a distinct Coptic Christian influence, and are believed to mostly date from the 12th and 13th centuries. Aksum and Lalibela are considered Ethiopia's holiest cities.

Libraries & Museums

The National Museum, in Addis Ababa, houses one of the oldest hominid fossils ever discovered, nicknamed "Lucy." A plaster cast of the fossil is on permanent view. The museum also houses a large collection of traditional and modern paintings. Other museums of note include the Ethnographic Museum at the Institute of Ethiopian Studies, the Addis Alem Museum, housed in a former palace, and the Zoological Natural History Museum. The National Archives and Library of Ethiopia is situated in Addis Ababa; established in 1944, it is home to manuscripts that date back to the 14th and 15th centuries. The library's total collection numbers over 64,000 items, including nearly 30,000 volumes of books.

As recently as 2009, in rural Ethiopia, donkey carts carrying books have been used to reach rural children, in part to promote literacy, as well as to promote respect for animals.

Holidays

Ethiopians celebrate a mixture of secular and religious holidays. Important secular holidays include New Years, which falls on September 11 according to the Julian calendar, and the Downfall of the Dergue (the regime that lost power in 1991) on May 28.

The Ethiopian Orthodox church designates several unique holy days, in addition to the traditional Christmas and Easter. Meskel (September 27 and 28), a celebration of the finding of the True Cross, involves parades, bonfires, and singing. Timkat (January 19), commemorating Christ's baptism, is marked by processions bearing each church's representation of the Ark of the Covenant, called a tabot, to water and then back to its sacred repository in the church. Muslims celebrate Ramadan, Eid Al Fatr at the end of the month-long fast, and Eid al Ahda, which commemorates Abraham's sacrifice.

Youth Culture

Young people in Ethiopia are raised with a reverence for family and their elders. In traditional cultures, young boys are trained in the cattle herding or agrarian industries, while young girls are trained to undertake domestic duties.

However, more and more young Ethiopians are rebelling against traditional mores, particularly as rising youth unemployment and limited freedom of expression have become concerns in the early twenty-first century. On university campuses, youth have been known to stage protests against what they view to be oppressive school regulations. In 2001, an unprecedented 10,000 students rioted at the University of Addis Ababa, in the capital, to protest for freedom of speech, particularly against rules prohibiting school newspapers and the presence of a strict police guard. The rules were later overturned. In recent decades, Ethiopian has become increasingly urbanized and many are brought up without a traditional family structure to due the high prevalence of HIV/AIDS.

Similarly, jobless young people in the capital have rioted in response to Ethiopia's staggeringly high youth unemployment rate. Ethiopia has one of the largest youth populations in sub-Saharan Africa, and two thirds of the country's population was estimated to be twenty-five years or younger in 2015.

However, youth unemployment in urban Ethiopia is estimated at over 50 percent. The absence of educational opportunities for young people exacerbates challenges related to employment. In 2004, according to the World Bank, only 40 percent of Ethiopian youth completed their primary education and enrollment in secondary school was at 13 percent.

SOCIETY

Transportation

The most popular modes of public transportation in Ethiopia are buses, minibuses, and the shared taxis. Motor vehicles travel on the right hand side of the road in Ethiopia, similar to the United States and Canada.

Mini-buses are refurbished vans and minivans that are characteristically overcrowded but offer affordable rides on established routes.

Shared taxis, or contracted taxis, are also common. Drivers often call out a route in order to pick up additional passengers in mini-buses or taxes. Cheaper and more rural transportation consists of horse-drawn flat bed wagons. Although they are more expensive, private taxis are also available.

Transportation Infrastructure

Ethiopian Airlines is the national air carrier. The government has begun improving the country's rail network through the newly established Ethiopian Railway Corporation (ERC). The corporation, formed in 2007, brought in consultants to help design rail routes in 2009. A railway installation project was launched in 2011 and is expected to be completed by 2015. Additional rail projects have been planned.

Media & Communications

When Mengistu Haile Mariam (1937–), a prominent figure of the Derg (a military junta which came to power in 1974), was ousted in 1991, many of the strict constraints on print and broadcast media in Ethiopia loosened. This lead to an increase in privately owned print media, and many papers now offer critical reporting that is in contrast to the state-owned publications. Nonetheless, self-censorship is still widely practiced, and the government still reserves the right to charge anyone with inciting civil unrest or defamation of character. In addition, Ethiopia has one of the highest illiteracy rates in the world, and print readership is usually concentrated among the urban upper classes.

Radio is the most popular medium, reaching rural areas where the majority of the population lives. Most radio stations and the singular national television network, Ethiopian Television (ETV), are operated by the state. In addition, the Ethiopian Telecommunications Corporation (ETC) is the national telecommunications provider. Starting in 2006, ETC has worked with several Chinese firms to improve the nation's telecommunications infrastructure, including securing a $1.5 billion (USD) loan. There were an estimated 1.6 million Internet users in Ethiopia, representing less than 2 percent of the population in 2009.

SOCIAL DEVELOPMENT

Standard of Living

Ethiopia's 2014 UN Human Development Index (HDI) rank was 173 out of 187 countries. The index measures qualify of life indicators. An estimated 64 percent of the Ethiopian population lives below the poverty line. Life expectancy at birth is 63 years for women and 59 years for men (2015 estimate).

Water Consumption

Ethiopia faces challenges related to the availability of clean drinking water. In addition, the effective distribution and quality maintenance of available water remains problematic. Although water infrastructure in urban areas is old, access is better than in rural areas. In some rural communities, drought is common and drinking water remains scarce throughout the year. The Addis Ababa Water and Sewage Authority have taken steps in recent years to improve water quality and availability.

Education

Education in Ethiopia has improved dramatically since the 1950s. It is free but not compulsory from primary school through the college or university level. Students must pass a national examination in order to leave the eighth grade and to win a place at the university level. About 49 percent of the adult population is now literate.

Public elementary schools are only able to handle 64 percent of school-age children, with many schools operating on a split-shift system. The number of students attending secondary schools drops dramatically, from approximately 6.5 million elementary students to 1.5 million secondary students.

There are six universities in Ethiopia. Addis Ababa University, the largest, has branches in several cities. Various colleges and institutes offering instruction in agriculture and teaching training, for example, also operate. Approximately 90,000 students are enrolled at the post-secondary level each year.

In 2008, 16.1 million children were enrolled in primary school in Ethiopia. Approximately 8.7 million of these were male students, while approximately 7.4 million were female. The country continues to face major challenges related to higher education, as very few of those who receive a higher education continue to live and work in Ethiopia.

Women's Rights

By international human rights standards, women in Ethiopia suffer great inequalities in their traditionally male-dominated culture. While the constitution provides equal protection for men and women, in the reality of everyday practice, such laws are often outweighed by ingrained cultural biases.

Violence against women is prohibited by law. Despite this legal provision, rape, assault, domestic violence, and abduction are all common. Spousal rape is not legally addressed, and domestic abuse is traditionally considered the right of the husband. In fact, it was estimated in 2005 that 81 percent of Ethiopian women still believe that husbands should use violence to discipline their wives when needed. Female genital mutilation (FGM) also continues to be a pressing issue. The 2005 Ethiopian Demographic and Health Survey (EDHS) reported that 74 percent of females were still subjected to FGM. The government has since claimed that they are taking action to curb the practice, and established the National Commission for Children's and Women's Affairs that same year. The commission is responsible for investigating human rights violations against both women and children.

Women's rights seem to diminish with marriage or are not upheld by law enforcement officials. Under Ethiopian law, married men are the legal heads of household. This ensures them property rights and sole custody over all children over the age of five. As a result, men are able to remain on their property and may also choose to raise their older children completely independent

of their former wives after a divorce. Men are also free of any obligation to support their children should they decide to give up custody, and women may not give up custody of their children if the husband does. In addition, 18 is the legal age of marriage in Ethiopia; however, this written law is overlooked in favor of custom in some regions. In Amhara Region for example, it is estimated that nearly 50 percent of the female population is married before 15 years of age.

Furthermore, when a wife becomes a widow, she technically becomes the owner of her husband's land. However, in most rural areas, this constitutional provision is not upheld and women are forced to turn their lands over to their eldest sons. If those sons are not of legal age to own land, many widows resort to marrying male members of their deceased husband's family in order to stay in their homes. It is also still a taboo for women to live without a male head of household, although the constitution allows for it.

Health Care

Ethiopia's urban-centered health care system lacks both resources and adequately trained health care providers. Both illiteracy and the remoteness of many rural settlements prevent the spread of modern ideas about health and hygiene. A plethora of illnesses, many of which are preventable or curable, thus afflicts or potentially afflicts significant portions of the population. Among them are malaria, AIDS, schistosomiasis, leprosy, and meningitis.

GOVERNMENT

Structure

Ethiopians have changed their government three times in the 20th century. Historically, a dynasty tracing its heritage to King Solomon of Israel ruled the country. This rule came to an end in 1974, when the last emperor was overthrown.

Until 1991, a Marxist-inspired junta controlled the country and power was concentrated in a dictatorship. Many Ethiopians resisted the regime, and many of its opponents were killed.

Throughout the first half of the 1990s, the government worked to make Ethiopia a full-fledged federal democratic republic. Today, citizens have much more recourse to the political process.

The executive branch is headed by a president and a prime minister, in whom power is concentrated. Both the president and the prime minister are nominated and elected by representatives in the legislative branch. The representatives are chosen by direct vote, and minority ethnic groups are guaranteed a set number of seats.

Ethnic identity determines most of Ethiopia's nine regions; Addis Ababa and Dire Dawa have been designated as multiethnic-chartered cities. The regions, over which local governments exercise jurisdiction, are further divided into administrative districts. Judicial power is similarly divided between the Federal Supreme Court and regional supreme courts.

Political Parties
Since the advent of democracy in Ethiopia, many political parties have been formed, most of which have been organized based on ethnicity. Major parliamentary groups include the Ethiopian People's Revolutionary Democratic Front (EPRDF), the Coalition for Unity and Democracy (CUD), and the United Ethiopian Democratic Forces. The EPRDF is a democratic socialist coalition, while the CUD promotes a platform of social liberalism.

Local Government
Ethiopia is divided into nine regional states or kililoch, which are organized by ethnic groups. These regions are further divided into 68 zones, which are subdivided into smaller districts known as woreda. Regional governments provide woredas with funding for infrastructure improvement projects and education initiatives.

Judicial System
The Ethiopian government established the Justice System Reform Program (JSRP) in 2002 in an effort to put a stop to rampant corruption within its judicial system. Ethiopia's upper house of parliament handles the appointments of judges and prosecutors. However, critics have said that unqualified individuals have been made judges, which has led to inconsistencies in the application of federal law throughout the country. Nonetheless, the law affords that individuals accused of a crime be given a fair public trial by a court. There are both federal and regional criminal courts, which have jurisdiction below that of high courts. The Ethiopian Supreme Court has supreme judicial authority.

Taxation
As part of a great effort to improve its standing as one of the poorest countries in the world, the government of Ethiopia has worked to reform and modernize its tax policy in recent years. In 2003, Ethiopia replaced its sales tax with a value-added tax (VAT). The VAT does not apply to exports but does apply to services and productions, with few exemptions. Other taxes in Ethiopia include a personal income tax and excise tax. Taxes are overseen by the Ethiopian Revenues and Customs Authority.

Armed Forces
The armed forces of Ethiopia are known as the Ethiopian National Defense Force (EDNF). It consists of the Ethiopian Army, Air Force, and Navy and is one of the largest military forces in Africa. The EDNF's annual budget is approximately 0.91 percent of Ethiopia's GDP. The EDNF has played a significant role in peacekeeping missions in Rwanda, Burundi, Liberia, the Ivory Coast, and the Darfur region of western Sudan.

Foreign Policy
Ethiopia's foreign policy objectives include national security, democratization, and international economic diplomacy, as well as the establishment of strong economic links throughout Africa. Ethiopia is an active participant in regional affairs and Pan-Africanism, and is a founding member of the African Union (AU). Ethiopia is a charter member of the UN, a founding member of the Non-Aligned Movement (NAM), and a

member of the Common Market for Eastern and Southern Africa (COMESA). Ethiopia is also a member of the seven-country Intergovernmental Authority on Development (IGAD), a developmental organization in East Africa.

Ethiopia is one of the world's poorest countries, and it is a leading recipient of international aid. Due to famine and severe droughts, a large majority of international assistance has been food aid. Ethiopia is also a leading beneficiary of the World Bank, the International Monetary Fund (IMF)—Ethiopia qualified for debt relief under the Heavily Indebted Poor Countries (HIPC) initiative—and the European Union (EU). In fact, the EU is considered Ethiopia's main trading partner. The country's relations with the West, and the United States in particular, have strengthened due to economic aid and involvement. Ethiopia became a vital partner in the U.S.-led "war on terror," and is one of the largest recipients of aid from the U.S. The majority of financial assistance is used to combat HIV/AIDS and hunger.

Ethiopia's relations in the Horn of Africa have often been contentious, and the country has had several disputes with neighboring Somalia and Eritrea, most notably the Eritrean-Ethiopian War (1998–2000). The war began over disputed territory, and once officially resolved in 2002, resulted in minor boundary changes. Conflicts with Somalia include a territorial dispute over Ogaden, also known as the Somali Regional State, which is in Ethiopia. Ethiopia also supports Somalia's Transitional Federal Government (TFG), which has been engaged in conflict with the Islamic Courts Union (ICU) for control over Somalia in the early 21st century. Relations with Djibouti remain good due to Djibouti's ports, which are significant to Ethiopian exporting and importing.

Human Rights Profile

International human rights law insists that states respect civil and political rights, and promote an individual's economic, social, and cultural rights. The United Nations (UN) Universal Declaration of Human Rights (UDHR) is recognized as the standard for international human rights. Its authors sought the counsel of the world's great thinkers, philosophers, and religious leaders, and were careful to create a document that reflects the core values shared by every world culture. To read this document or view the articles relating to cultural human rights, visit http://www.udhr.org/UDHR/default.htm.

Generally, Ethiopia has a poor human rights record, and the country is still struggling to establish itself democratically. Many basic human rights are not respected, and international monitoring agencies such as Human Rights Watch (HRW) and Amnesty International (AI) have reported incidents of murder, torture, and rape by the Ethiopian army. Media watchdog organizations such as Reporters Without Borders have also reported repressive tactics against the private media. Ethiopia was also criticized for its adopting of the Charities and Societies Proclamation (or the CSO Law) in January 2009, which restricts non-governmental organizations (NGO), both foreign and domestic. To aid with the democratization process and to monitor human rights abuses, the Ethiopian Human Rights Council (EHRCO) was established in 1991.

Government corruption remains an issue, and the Ethiopian government has been accused of scare tactics preceding elections, arbitrary arrest and killings, and coercing votes. In Ethiopian region of Ogaden, a Somali stronghold, the major opposition party, Ogaden National Liberation Front (ONLF), has accused the government of suppressing opposition views and actions through arbitrary arrest, lengthy detention without criminal charge, torture, and murder. The government claims this crackdown is due to the 2007 murder of two international oil workers at the hands of members of the opposition. Whether or not members of the opposition were responsible for the murders, the Ethiopian government has cut the region off from international workers. Human rights groups claim this is to hide the government's human rights violations in the region, while the government claims it is trying to protect people. In an effort to quell calls for more open access to the region, the government launched its own investigation into human rights violations there.

Suicide bombing throughout the nation and remaining landmines on the border with Eritrea, left over from the 1998–2000 conflict, continue to resonate in Ethiopia's daily life. Public transportation and markets were the main targets of bombers, while overlooked landmines killed innocent civilians. In an effort to stave off these terrible deaths, the government established the Ethiopian Mine Action Office, which recovered and disarmed 5,274 landmines in 2008. The organization is making significant headway in the safety of the border region.

Ethiopia is also strong on religious freedom. However, the freedom of academia is limited and most students have to profess allegiance to the government. Further, professors and even public school teachers are forbidden from deviating from structured lesson plans and talking about political views. To protest these strict academic measures, students rioted in 2001.

Other reported human rights abuses include restrictions on the freedom of assembly; infringements on privacy, including illegal searches; human trafficking (Ethiopia is considered a source country) for the purposes of forced labor and sexual exploitation; and limitations of the freedom of association. Prison conditions are also reported as harsh. According to a report by AI, the torture and ill-treatment of prisoners is common, and medical facilities or provisions are inadequate. In 2007, Ethiopia launched a campaign to counter the reported harsh conditions and treatments of its prisons and prisoners, most notably focusing on al-Qaeda suspects. However, as recently as 2013, Amnesty International reported that harsh treatment and even torture of prisoners continues.

Migration

Increasing numbers of Ethiopians are moving from rural to urban areas of the country, particularly to Addis Ababa, in search of employment and education opportunities. In addition, seasonal migration occurs in Ethiopia, related to weather conditions, drought conditions and food insecurity.

ECONOMY

Overview of the Economy

In 2008, the estimated Ethiopian GDP was $52.34 billion (USD); its per capita GDP was $1,600 (USD). The country receives over $308 million (USD) in economic aid annually. Its primary exports are agricultural and earn $442 million (USD) each year. One reason the Ethiopian economy underperforms is that it must periodically rely on imports to satisfy the basic needs of its population.

Industry

Industry accounts for 10 percent of Ethiopia's gross domestic product (GDP). Food processing, textile manufacturing, construction, cement production, and petroleum refinement are the most significant industries in a largely agrarian society. What little manufacturing occurs in Ethiopia is usually dependent on agricultural production.

Labor

Unemployment is serious problem in Ethiopia. Agriculture makes up nearly half of the countries GDP and employs an estimated eighty-five percent of Ethiopians. Although the country has no major mining or industrial sector, there is a fledgling tourism sector. The government controls telecommunications and banking. Youth unemployment has been estimated to be as high as seventy percent.

Energy/Power/Natural Resources

Ethiopia's most prominent natural resources are agricultural. Soil erosion is increasingly problematic, and large areas are not cultivated, since they are low enough for malaria to be widespread.

Of enormous potential are the rivers of Ethiopia, which could generate billions of kilowatts of hydroelectric power. Yet only a few of the rivers, like the Awash, are exploited for energy. Both the lack of funds and geopolitical tensions with other countries which need the waters of the Nile might continue to prevent Ethiopia from further development in this area.

Fishing

Although some fishing occurs in Ethiopia's lakes and rivers, the domestic market for fish is minimal and fishing is not a significant contributor to the country's GDP.

Forestry

The forests of Ethiopia have been seriously reduced over the last one hundred years and now occupy only 20 percent of the total land. Wood is exploited by the populace for use as a fuel source and as construction material, so it is a challenge to protect the land from deforestation and, in more extreme cases, desertification.

Mining/Metals

A variety of minerals are mined in Ethiopia, but the operations are generally small. Metals include copper, iron, gold and platinum. There are also deposits of potash, clay, salt, and limestone.

Agriculture

Approximately 85 percent of the working population is engaged in agriculture and animal husbandry. Agricultural products account for over half of Ethiopia's GDP and 85 percent of its exports.

Coffee sometimes referred to as "black gold" in Ethiopia for the money it earns, is the most important cash crop, and engages one-quarter of the working population. It is cultivated for the most part in the western and southern regions. Coffee prices on the international market can fluctuate, but it generally accounts for 60 percent of annual export earnings.

Other important crops are pulses (legumes) and cereals, which are central to the Ethiopian diet, as well as oilseeds, sugarcane, and chat. The latter crop is a green-leafed shrub that is chewed for mildly stimulating effects. It is important to the domestic economy and as an export to Djibouti and Somalia. Ethiopia was also the largest producer of honey on the African continent at the turn of the 21st century.

Animal Husbandry

It is estimated that Ethiopia has the largest livestock population in all of Africa, with 95.5 million animals. Poultry is the most common, followed by cattle, which serve as important beasts of burden and sources of meat. Sheep and goat, important for their meat and hides, are also raised in large numbers.

Tourism

Ethiopia has grown as a tourist destination since 1991, and the potential for further growth is considered promising. The infrastructure is limited, however, particularly outside of the capital. Roughly, 180,000 tourists visit Ethiopia annually, bringing in $80 million in revenue.

Kristen Pappas, Michael Aliprandini

DO YOU KNOW?

- Some believe that the Ark of the Covenant is kept in the Church of St. Mary of Zion, in Northern Ethiopia.

- The hominid fossil "Lucy" received its nickname from a Beatles' song. When the fossil was discovered by archaeologists in 1974, "Lucy in the Sky with Diamonds" was playing.

- Ethiopia uses the Julian calendar, which divides the year into 13 months. Despite its two rainy seasons, Ethiopia is nicknamed the Land of 13 Months of Sunshine.

Bibliography

Asafa Jalata. "Oromia and Ethiopia: State Formation and Ethnonational Conflict 1868–2004." *Red Sea Press*, 2005.

Bahru Zewde and Siegfried Pausewang. "Ethiopia: The Challenge of Democracy from Below." *Nordic Africa Institute*, 2002.

Donald N. Levine. *Greater Ethiopia: The Evolution of a Multiethnic Society*. The University of Chicago Press, Chicago, 2000.

Hans Silvester. "Ethiopia: Peoples of the Omo Valley." *Harry N. Abrams*, 2007.

Jean-Bernard Carillet. "Ethiopia, Djibouti, and Somaliland." Oakland, CA: *Lonely Planet*, 2013.

Mario Di Salvo, "Crosses of Ethiopia: The Sign of Faith. Evolution and Form." 1st Edition. *Skir*, 2006.

Sarah Howard. "Ethiopia—Culture Smart! The Essential Guide to Customs and Culture." London: *Kuperard*, 2009.

Sellassie, Haile I. "The Autobiography of Emperor Haile Sellassie I: King of Kings of All Ethiopia and Lord of All Lords (My Life and Ethiopia's Progress)." *Research Associates School Times Publications and Frontline Distribution International, Inc.* Chicago, 1999.

Works Cited

"Afewerk Tekle." Alpha, the Son of Thunder. http://www.maitreafewerktekle.com/Biography.html

"Discovering our most famous ancestor. Lucy's Legacy: The Hidden Treasure of Ethiopia." *Houston Museum of Natural Science. h*ttp://www.lucyexhibition.com/lucys-discovery.aspx

"Ethiopia." *City Population.* http://www.citypopulation.de/Ethiopia.html

"Ethiopian Highlands: Music." *PBS Online: Africa Explore the Regions.* http://www.pbs.org/wnet/africa/explore/ethiopia/ethiopia_music_lo.html

"Ethiopia." 2009. *Encyclopedia Britannica Online.* http://www.britannica.com/EBchecked/topic/194084/Ethiopia

"Ethiopia." UNESCO World Heritage. http://whc.unesco.org/en/statesparties/et

"Ethiopian Art, Ethiopia." *Hamill Gallery of Tribal Art.* http://www.hamillgallery.com/ETHIOPIAN/Ethiopian.html

"Ethiopian Literature." *Encyclopedia Britannica Online.* 2009. http://www.britannica.com/EBchecked/topic/194186/Ethiopian-literature

"Family Life: How does family Affect Ethiopian Children?" *Tulane University.* http://www.tulane.edu/~rouxbee/kids98/ethiopia3.html

"Oromo." *National African Language Research Center.* http://lang.nalrc.wisc.edu/nalrc/resources/press/brochures/oromo.pdf

"Youth cultures – generation gaps in Ethiopia." *Radio Netherlands Worldwide.* http://www.radionetherlands.nl/africa/programmes/africainprogress/youthcultures/youthsethiopiawondimu

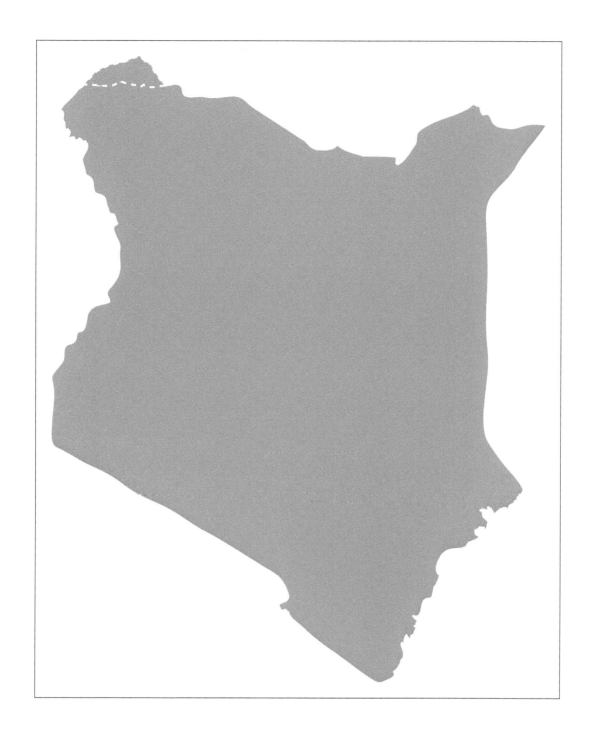

KENYA

Introduction

Located on Africa's eastern coast, Kenya has long been regarded as one of Africa's favorite tourist destinations. Nairobi, the capital of Kenya, plays an important role in connecting East Africa with the rest of the modern world. A noted stop for tourists on safari, the capital is also one of Africa's largest cities. However, the country suffers from many of the same economic challenges that beset its neighbors, and has struggled with civil strife in recent years.

Kenyans are renowned for their artistry. For centuries, the East African country has exported makonde (carvings done in ebony wood), soapstone carvings, beaded and shell covered jewelry, batik fabrics, and sisal rugs and baskets. Music also remains an important part of Kenyan life. Traditional instruments include guitar-like stringed instruments, such as the nyatiti, and homemade rattles attached to the ankle for percussion.

GENERAL INFORMATION

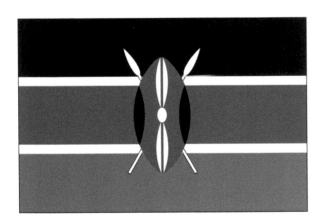

Official Language: English and Kiswahili
Population: 45,925,301 (2015 estimate)
Currency: Kenyan shilling
Coins: The Kenyan shilling is divided into 100 cents. Coins are available 5, 10, and 20 shillings, which are frequently used, and 1, 40, 50 shillings, and 50 cents, which are rarely used.
Land Area: 569,140 square kilometers (219,746 square miles)

Water Area: 11,227 square kilometers (4,334 square miles)
National Motto: "Harambee" ("Let's work together")
National Anthem: "Ee Mungu nguvu yetu" ("O God of all creation")
Capital: Nairobi
Time Zone: GMT +3
Flag Description: The flag of Kenya is a tricolor design that features three equal and horizontal bands of black (top), red (middle), and green (bottom), with white fimbriations (small stripes of color) between the black and red bands, and the red and green bands. Centered in the flag is a red Masai shield over two crossing white spears. (The Masai are an ethnic group centered in Kenya.) The colors associated with the flag symbolize the blood shed for independence (red), the fertility of the land (green), and the black majority, while white represents peace.

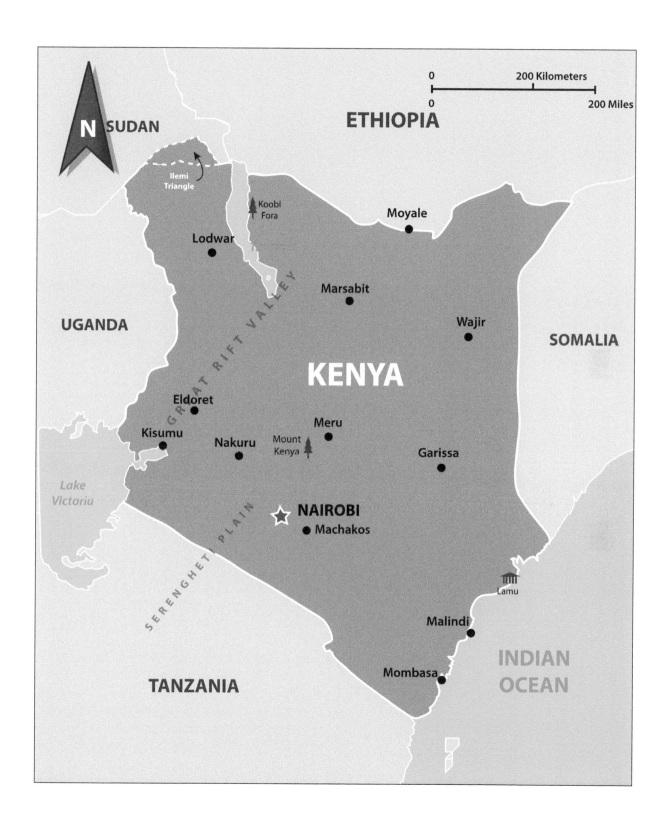

Population

Kenya's population includes about 70 African tribes. The most significant groups are the Kikuyu (22 percent of the population), the Luhya (14 percent), the Luo (13 percent), the Kalenjin (12 percent), the Kamba (11 percent), the Kisii (six percent), and the Meru (six percent). Other African peoples and non-Africans (mostly of Asian, European, and Arab descent) account for the remainder of Kenya's people.

An estimated 25.6 percent of the population resides in urban areas. With a population of approximately 3.5 million people, Nairobi is one of the most populous cities in East Africa. The city's population growth rate is nearly seven percent, about three percent higher than the national average in Kenya. It is estimated that nearly 60 percent of the population of Nairobi live in informal settlements, or urban slums.

Kenya's high birth rate (26 births per 1,000 people in 2015) and an influx of refugees from neighboring countries have resulted in a steadily growing population. However, economic growth has been significantly lower, leaving about half of Kenya's population living below the poverty line. As a result, Kenya's infant mortality rate stands at roughly forty deaths per 1,000 births of the population (2015 estimate). As of 2015, the population growth rate was an estimated 1.93 percent.

Languages

English and Swahili, or Kiswahili as it is formally known, are both official languages of Kenya. Most Kenyans also speak a third, tribal language. This language takes on the name of the tribe in the same form as Kiswahili. For instance, members of the Kamba tribe speak Kikamba.

Native People & Ethnic Groups

Kenya's African tribes migrated to the area from all over the continent. The Cushitic tribes from Ethiopia were probably first to arrive in the second and first centuries BCE. Over the next 2,000 years, Bantu speakers like the Gusii, Kikuyu, Akamba, and Meru from West Africa joined the Cushitic tribes. Nilotic speakers like the Maasai, Luo, Samburu, and Turkana arrived from the Nile Valley in southern Sudan.

Muslim and Persian (Shirazi) tribes from the Middle East settled along Kenya's eastern coastline as early as the eighth century.

Religions

Kenya's population is mostly Christian. It is estimated that about 45 percent of Kenyans belong to Protestant denominations and 33 percent to the Roman Catholic Church. However, all estimates of Kenya's religious landscape note the difficulty of determining how many Kenyans are now Muslim or are following tribal belief systems. The coastal and eastern portions of Kenya are predominantly Muslim.

Climate

Kenya lies on the Indian Ocean coast of East Africa. Straddling the equator, the country has a warm, tropical climate year-round with minimal variation in temperature from season to season, but great variation from region to region and from low altitudes to high altitudes.

Breezes off the Indian Ocean keep the coastline humid, with temperatures ranging from 21° to 28° Celsius (70° to 82° Fahrenheit) throughout the year. The coast is prone to storms and heavy rainfall during the rainy season. Annual rainfall is 1,100 millimeters (43 inches) per year.

The Nyika highlands are arid, with only 350 millimeters (14 inches) of annual rainfall. Temperatures are extreme, ranging from 37° Celsius (99° Fahrenheit) during the hottest days to 21° Celsius (70° Fahrenheit) on cool nights. Temperatures fall to 20° to 30° Celsius (68° to

86° Fahrenheit) in the southeastern area of this region around Mount Kilimanjaro.

The Rift Valley and highlands contain Kenya's most diverse climates. Around Mount Kenya, the land is covered in large pockets of rainforest, changing to bamboo forest in altitudes above 2,000 meters (6,562 feet). The savannah, which creates a buffer between the rainforests and the semi-desert ecosystems of the north and northeast, receives regular, adequate rainfall. The Lake Victoria Basin also receives substantial rainfall, allowing for an area of tropical rainforest at the base of Mount Elgin.

Temperatures range according to altitude: Nairobi, at 1,700 meters (5,577 feet) above sea level, has an average temperature of 25° Celsius (77° Fahrenheit), although nighttime temperatures can drop to 12° Celsius (54° Fahrenheit). In Mount Kenya's higher elevations, temperatures drop below 10° Celsius (50° Fahrenheit) at night.

ENVIRONMENT & GEOGRAPHY

Topography

Kenya is bounded by the Indian Ocean on its eastern side, and by the countries of Sudan, Ethiopia, Somalia, Tanzania, and Uganda around the periphery.

The country has four primary geographic regions, although there is surprising variety even within these zones. The coastal plain region runs for about 400 kilometers (250 miles) along the shoreline from the southern border with Tanzania to the northern border with Somalia. The land to the south is formed by corals, and features white sandy beaches broken by bays, inlets, and creeks. A long barrier reef extends along the coast, protecting the coastal areas. In the northern part of the coastal plain, the Lamu Archipelago juts out into the Indian Ocean.

North of this coastline, the eastern highlands, or Nyika, are situated on a smooth, but largely barren plateau that extends southward toward the coastline. Broken only by small groups of hills, the eastern highlands host two large, ocean-bound streams, the Tana and Galana.

Kenya's most dramatic and most photographed landscapes are found in the central interior, where Africa's Rift Valley helped form the Kenyan Highlands. The Rift Valley is an enormous tectonic fault that runs across eastern Africa and into the Middle East. Tectonic plate movements beginning about 35 million years ago split Kenya's central plateau down the center, forming the Mau Escarpment and Cherangani Hills to the west, and the Aberdare Range, Ngong Hills, and Laikipia Escarpment to the east.

In this eastern section of the highlands, Mount Kenya rises to the highest elevation in the country and the second highest elevation on the continent of Africa. The tallest of Mount Kenya's snow-covered peaks is Batian, at 5,199 meters (17,057 feet) above sea level. At the foot of the mountains, fertile valleys extend across the highlands.

Kenya's Lake Victoria Basin lies in the country's central western region, near where Uganda borders Tanzania. The basin lies on an elevated plateau adjacent to the Rift Valley. At 68,000 square kilometers (42,253 square miles) in area, Lake Victoria is actually an inland sea with shores in Kenya, Uganda, and Tanzania. On its eastern side by the Mau Escarpment, the lake lies at 1,200 meters (3,937 feet) above sea level.

Nairobi is located in the middle of a large region of grasslands, farmland, and mountains. The city is situated along the Great Rift Valley with Ngong Hills to the west of the city, Mount Kenya to the north, and Mount Kilimanjaro to the southeast. The Nairobi River runs along the north side of the city's center.

Plants & Animals

Kenya has ample numbers of the large mammals and exotic species for which Africa is famous. Elephants, lions, rhinoceroses, zebras, buffaloes, and giraffes roam Kenya's wide, grassy plains in the shadow of sugarbush and beechwood trees.

Kenya's mountains are home to their own rare species. At lower altitudes, forests of bamboo and moss-covered trees hide leopards, waterbuck, monkeys, bush pigs, hyenas, and bongos (a rare type of antelope). At higher altitudes, the vegetation thins out to occasional African and Helichrysum bushes. Few large mammals can survive at these altitudes, but elands and a unique species of high-altitude zebra make their way across the northern moorlands of Mount Kenya. The humid, sandy beaches of the coast are home to coconut palms, seabirds, and lizards.

In order to protect its many endangered species, Kenya's government has set aside protected land in areas like Amobseli National Park, Serengeti National Park, Losai National Reserve, and Masai Mara National Reserve.

CUSTOMS & COURTESIES

Greetings

Kenya is home to many ethnic groups with diverse customs. Though English is the official language and Swahili is the national language, 40 other languages are spoken in the nation. Kenya's population is largely Christian, but there is also a sizable Muslim population and small groups of Sikh, Baha'i, Hindu, and Jewish people. Indigenous African tribal groups include the Kikuyu, Luyia, Luo, Kalenjin, Kamba, Kisii, Meru, and Masai, each with their own specific traditions.

Generally, Kenyans are conservative but open people who extend and expect simple courtesies. Handshakes, done with the right hand, are the most typical form of greeting, and are usually less firm than handshakes in Western cultures. People often say "Jambo?" (Swahili for "How are you?") prior to shaking hands. Friends or people with a close connection may hold a handshake longer than new acquaintances, sometimes for the length of an exchange or conversation. Close female friends often embrace and kiss each other on both cheeks instead of shaking hands. Eye contact is also brief in an initial introduction, but maintained and direct between acquaintances.

A person shows respect when greeting someone who is older or higher in station by grasping his or her own right wrist with his or her left hand while shaking the other person's hand. Similarly, a child shows respect to an elder by bowing slightly, and the adult responds by touching his or her palm to the child's head. Specific ethnic groups in Kenya may have their own special ways of greeting each other. For example, the Masai (or Maasai) often greet one another by asking, "And how are the children?" and responding, "All the children are well." This exchange demonstrates the central importance of children in Masai society.

Gestures & Etiquette

People in Kenya exchange greetings by shaking hands with their right hands. Offering one's left hand is considered inappropriate and disrespectful. This is similar to Muslim culture in which the left hand is associated with the cleansing of the body, and is thus considered impure. Kenyans also present gifts or offer items with their right hand or with both hands. Gifts are given to mark special events in a person's life or in honor of certain religious holidays. Generally, lavish and expensive gifts are not expected, and most people prefer practical gifts.

Kenyans often avoid making prolonged direct eye contact with people that they do not know well. Keeping eye contact brief is considered courteous and respectful, rather than evasive when two people are not familiar with each other. When people know each other, however, lengthier eye contact, especially when accompanied by a smile, is considered friendly, open, and sincere. Similarly, personal space is often respected when people do not know each other. After shaking hands, people may move back to arm's length. However, people who know each other well may hold hands longer while they talk, and will be less concerned about maintaining a certain space.

In general, Kenyans are friendly but polite. They attempt to show one another respect and courtesy, and appreciate respectful behavior in others. They tend to be non-confrontational and may avoid expressing a direction opinion or emotion. Though Kenyans often gesture expressively when talking, they consider raised voices or angry outbursts rude or disrespectful. Pointing with one's finger is also considered rude, and most people simply nod or jut their chin at something to draw attention to it.

Eating/Meals

Though certain eating and meal rituals vary across ethnic groups in Kenya, a few basic courtesies apply to most of Kenyan society. People are expected to wash their hands before eating, and a basin of water is often brought to the table. Guests hold their hands over the basin while water is poured over them. It is considered rude to eat and drink at the same time, so Kenyans often serve drinks at the end of a meal. In addition, it is considered polite to eat all of the food on one's plate.

In more traditional settings, males and elders are served first, and some ethnicities separate male and female family members during mealtimes. Additionally, due to Kenya's colonial past, certain eating customs are European in nature. For example, the daily custom of afternoon tea—borrowed from the British—became popular in urban areas.

Visiting

When visiting someone's home for a dinner or party, guests may bring flowers, pastries, sweets, or similar small gifts. (Gifts should be given with the right hand, or both, but not with the left hand only.) In rural communities, people often give gifts of tea or sugar, or of similar practical use, when visiting another's home. In return, Kenyans often offer their guests refreshment, such as tea, and it is considered polite to accept.

LIFESTYLE

Family

Family life is central to Kenyan society. Kenyans customarily value the group over the individual, and the family, including extended family, is the core group. This grouping extends to one's biological family, family through marriage, and close friends.

Though family structures and responsibilities vary across ethnic groups in Kenya, most Kenyan families are male-dominated. In rural areas, women assume not only domestic and child-rearing responsibilities, but account for up to 80 percent of agricultural work as well, including planting and harvesting. This is largely a result of urban migration, as males often travel from rural areas to find wage-paying jobs. Children typically remain with their mother and help with household chores and farm work. In urban areas, women may work in small businesses and industries such as the hospitality sector. However, they are still responsible for maintaining their home and looking after the children.

Housing

Housing varies according to one's socioeconomic status and location. In most rural areas of Kenya, housing is small and modest, and often made from earthen or native materials. Many rural homes have wood siding, a roof made from sheet iron, and two rooms. Masai huts are made from wood branches bound together with clay and have roofs made with thatch, or straw. Many other tribal groups, including the Mbere in the east and the Borana in the north, also build homes with wood and thatch. Access to electricity and plumbing is also limited in rural Kenya.

In urban areas, the average middle class family has a home with two bedrooms, a kitchen, a living room, and electricity and indoor plumbing. Homes in cities may be built from a variety of materials, including wood, stone, brick, and mud or clay. Shantytowns (informal settlements) comprised of tents and shacks surround the larger cities due to an increasing influx of people searching for employment and better opportunities. Thus, overcrowding has become a common characteristic of many urban centers in Kenya. Along the coast, structures reflect the people's Arabic heritage; unlike the largely wood and mud homes in the interior, these houses are often made from coral rag and coral stone with slate roofs.

Food

Along with the various culinary traditions of Kenya's indigenous ethnicities, the national cuisine has also been influenced by foreign settlement and colonialism, most notably British, Arabic, and Indian cuisine. Traditionally, Kenyans maintain a relatively basic diet of meat, greens and other vegetables, fruit, milk, and the national food, ugali. Ugali is a porridge-like dish made by grinding corn into flour and mixing it with water. Though bland by itself, Kenyans often use ugali as a base for other dishes, mixing it in stews with meat and vegetables or thinning it with milk for breakfast.

Kenyans eat a great deal of leafy green vegetables, including kale and collard greens. Other staple foods include rice and bread. Generally, Kenyans flavor stews and other dishes with spices, chilies, and coconut. Most Kenyans also eat small amounts of roasted meat, including beef, chicken, and goat, as well as seafood and freshwater fish from the country's many lakes and rivers. One of the most popular Kenyan dishes is sukuma wiki (which means, "stretch the week"), made from collards or kale sautéed with other vegetables, spices, and flour. The dish is often served with ugali. Other traditional and popular dishes include nyama choma, a roasted meat dish; karanga, a stew made with potatoes and meat; and maandazi, which is a deep fried dough dish typically served with breakfast or as an accompaniment to tea or coffee.

Lastly, different ethnic groups have specific preferences and taboos regarding food. The Masai prefer to eat the meat of goats and sheep, and raise their cattle for milk. They often mix the milk with blood obtained by making a non-lethal cut in a cow or bull's neck.

Life's Milestones

In general, the majority of Kenyans identifies as Christian, and adheres to milestones and rites that are rooted in the Christian church. However, Kenyan society comprises dozens of tribal ethnic groups with their own unique cultural milestones. In traditional Kikuyu villages, girls go through ceremonial rites between the ages of ten and fifteen, signaling their transition into womanhood. Often, they may not be married before they have completed the rites. Among the Masai, children are born into age groups comprising all the youth within a specific couple of years. After turning fifteen, young men go through a rite of passage with their age group to become warriors. Later, they retire from their life as warriors, again with their age group, and become the village elders who serve as the governing body of the Masai.

Among the Kalenjin, boys may not sleep in the house of their mothers beyond the age of five. Many Kenyan groups, including the Masai, Kisii, and Luhya, practice male circumcision as a means of marking the transition from boyhood to adulthood (often between the ages of 10 and 15). Girls in many tribal groups have also undergone a process of circumcision to pass into adulthood, but the process of female circumcision, or female genital mutilation, is now widely criticized. The Luo mark the transition to adulthood by removing a child's six lower front teeth.

CULTURAL HISTORY

Art

Kenya's artistic heritage places little emphasis on the two-dimensional painting styles of Europe and the Americas. The nation's arts are instead more functional and organic, and centered on traditional crafts and ritualistic and personal decoration. Thus, the fine arts in Kenya were not particularly developed, and were relegated to European artists during the country's colonial period.

Most of Kenya's indigenous groups came from nomadic traditions and built small, often temporary homes. Their artistic expression thus took shape in personal adornments, such as masks, headdresses, weaving, metal, and bead jewelry, and dyed fabrics for clothing. Other common art forms included pottery and small sculptures made from metal, wood, and stone that could be easily carried. Jewelry, masks, and headdresses often showed a person's wealth or status within society, or marked special events such as religious ceremonies, marriages, or hunting. Such items were also traded for other goods and have become a key component of the modern tourist industry.

Architecture

Kenya's architecture is a reflection of the nation's diverse blend of traditional cultures, its important location along ancient trade routes, and its colonial history. A range of architectural styles is evident, from indigenous earthen and timber-framed architecture to Arabic and European styles. Often, the style of architecture was based on the availability of native materials. For example, coastal structures were often constructed from coral rag and stone, while rural buildings were made of plastered mud, grass, and wood.

In the capital of Nairobi, historic homes and gardens are examples of early colonial architecture. In the historic city of Mombasa and other coastal communities, mosques and minarets show the region's Islamic heritage. Kenya's coast is also home to the Swahili culture, whose architecture has historically combined African, Arabic, and European traditions. Swahili architecture, like their art, is also known for its ornate geometric designs, and for borrowing the Muslim custom of avoiding human depictions, instead presenting intricate patterns of color and form. Buildings, especially in towns, were often two stories tall and narrow, with interior patios or courtyards and terraces or balconies.

Further inland, the nation's architecture shows more of Kenya's distinctly African and colonial heritage, as well as its more recent modern European influences. In recent years, interior urban centers such as Nairobi have combined modern materials such as metal, vinyl, cement, and glass with traditional materials such as wood, stone, and mud. These cityscapes are often adorned with skyscrapers, plantations, and traditional homes. In rural areas, tribal groups such as the Masai, Kikuyu, and Luo largely rely on simple earthen building techniques. Small huts and similar structures, often with only a few rooms, are built from mud, thatch, and straw, or wooden sticks woven and bundled together.

Drama

Kenya's theatrical tradition was in large part defined by the nation's political environment. Like the country's musical and literary traditions, indigenous drama was largely communal, ceremonial, and celebratory. During the British colonial period, however, drama was suppressed. When Kenya gained independence, after decades of exposure to European literature and drama, Kenyan playwrights began producing scripts in English with plots that portrayed a benign or subdued picture of colonialism. However, most Kenyans could not connect to or did not approve of the plays.

Beginning in the 1970s, playwrights began writing scripts in indigenous African languages, and local community and school groups began putting on new kinds of plays. Performed in community centers, schools, markets, and other communal settings, these plays addressed economic, political, and social issues, as well as historical events and cultural mythologies. Plays became more experimental, incorporating music and dance. One notable Kenyan playwright is Francis Imbuga (1947-2012), considered the leading figure in Kenyan theater.

Music & Dance

Like most African nations, music and dance play an integral part in Kenya's culture. Early peoples in Kenya developed the use of voice, percussion, and simple stringed instruments. Drums, such as the Bantu ngoma and other percussion instruments, were made from wood, soapstone, animal skins, and gourds. The Luo people developed two unique stringed instruments—the nyatiti, a small wooden instrument with several strings similar to a lyre, and the orutu, a fiddle made from the soft wood of a certain cactus with one string. Taarab (or tarabu) music emerged along the coast and incorporated the region's Arabic heritage. Swahili for "enchantment," taarab music is largely sung by women, incorporates a variety of instruments, and is poetic in its lyrics and harmonies.

Music was mostly a communal event, and Kenya's various ethnic groups used both music and dance to tell stories and pass down histories, to mark rites of passage and other special events, and to celebrate religious beliefs. Traditional music also dealt with communal interests, such as family, harvest, hunting, and war, and served to relieve the tedium of daily activity and work. Thus, people sang and made music while planting, harvesting, weaving, building, and performing other tasks. Consequently, much of Kenyan music developed in a call-and-response form, wherein one singer leads with a set of lyrics and other singers echo the lyrics or add new lyrics. Modern musical performances in Kenya are generally still communal and performed in open areas where the musicians and audiences can still interact, rather than in concert halls on stages.

Literature

Kenya's literary tradition is rooted in the oral traditions of its ethnic peoples. Indigenous groups in Kenya have long passed on stories and histories through the spoken word. The earliest such tales of Kenya's various tribal groups are largely creation stories and fables meant to teach lessons about living. Traditional fables in Kenya and other parts of Africa most often feature animal tricksters, such as hares, hyenas, and spiders. Such tales emphasize the virtues of determination and perseverance as well as cleverness.

Like its art and architecture, Kenyan literature reveals many cultural influences. Kenya's written literary tradition begins with Swahili poetry and the recordings of Arabic and European traders, merchants, and explorers. Though written down, often in Arabic script, Swahili poetry was generally meant to be read aloud or sung. The long, formal verses told stories and offered advice reflecting Islamic beliefs and ideas.

During the British colonial period, scholars recorded much of Kenya's original oral traditions. Travel and exploration also became a central theme of writing associated with Kenya. Explorers such as Britain's Sir Richard Francis Burton (1821–1890), who traveled across southern Kenya in the 19th century in search of the source of the Nile River, often published their experiences. Other notable European authors writing fiction or nonfiction set in Kenya include Henry Rider Haggard (1856–1925), who wrote adventure novels, and Isak Dinesen—the pen name of Danish author Karen Blixen (1885–1962)—who wrote what is perhaps the best known literary tale from Kenya, *Out of Africa* (1937).

Like its music, Kenyan literature often served as a vehicle for social commentary and protest. Kenya's most respected native author, Ngugi wa Thiong'o (1938–), earned international acclaim for his novels *Weep Not, Child* (1964) and *Petals of Blood* (1977) written in the decades following Kenya's independence in 1963. Written in English, these novels called attention to the poverty, corruption, and violence in Kenyan society. In 1977, Thiong'o decided to stop writing in English and to start writing in Kikuyu and Swahili to reach a larger audience. His play, "I Will Marry When I Want," first performed in Kikuyu at a local community center, led to his arrest. For decades, any of Thiong'o's works written in Kikuyu were banned.

CULTURAL HISTORY

Arts & Entertainment

The contemporary arts in Kenya are strongly rooted in cultural traditions and reflect the nation's combined African, Arabic, and European heritage. Modern Kenyans practice many of the same arts and crafts as their ancestors once did. Traditional arts such as ceramics, textiles, beadwork, and metalwork, once crafted to show status or for trade are still made for much the same purpose. In particular, the Luo are known for their pottery and woodcarving, the Masai and the Kamba are also known for woodcarving, and the Kisii are known for their soapstone sculptures.

Traditional Kenyan crafts not only help people maintain cultural ties and express themselves artistically, they also help communities support themselves by making up a large part of the modern tourist industry. Silver and gold jewelry, woodcarvings, baskets, soapstone sculptures, and tribal masks are particularly popular among tourists, as are women's wraparound skirts and headscarves made from kanga cloth.

Kanga cloth is cotton fabric dyed in brightly colored and unique patterns. Similarly, many modern Kenyans inherited the skill of making batiks. An art brought by Asian colonists, batik involves dyeing fabric that has been stained with wax. The dye only takes on the parts of the fabric not marked with wax.

Modern Kenyan music also reflects the influence of indigenous tradition on Kenya. During the colonial period of the 19th century, missionaries and British officials suppressed many traditional music and dance forms. By the late 20th century, a revival of these forms occurred. International radio stations and the mass production of albums, tapes, and CDs began to encourage this revival, while also introducing new musical forms such as benga to Kenya. Benga, developed by the Luo people, mixes traditional music with modern instruments and pop rhythms. However, it retains African music's distinctly polyrhythmic nature, in which each voice or instrument follows its own beat. Like most African musical styles, benga still relies heavily on a large and diverse percussion section.

Modern Kenyan music largely addresses political and social concerns, as well as matters of personal choice and responsibility. Epic songs, particularly in the taarab tradition, teach lessons and offer advice on living. Popular modern artists include Garbiel Omolo, a Luo artist, and Maliki. In addition, the Muungano National Choir of Kenya made famous the "Missa Luba," an African adaptation of a Roman Catholic mass that incorporates music, dance, and traditional costume.

Like music, literature and drama suffered during Kenya's colonial period. Under British control from the 1880s through 1963, most literary attention went to European authors. Following independence, Kenyan authors slowly reclaimed their national literature and voice. Though they initially wrote in English, many Kenyans soon began returning to their native languages. Kenyan authors who produced notable works about the Kenyan experience in the 20th and early 21st centuries include Ngugi wa Thiong'o, Grace Ogot (1930-2015), renowned

for her short stories and insight into the Luo people, and novelist Meja Mwangi (1948–).

In 2002, writer Binyavanga Wainaina (1971–) started *Kwani?* which is Swahili for "What's up?" This independent literary journal publishes short stories, poems, cartoons, nonfiction, and other material written in a mix of English, Swahili, and sheng, a local slang. This magazine remains popular today, and now has its own website that provides content ranging from creative fiction to critical commentary on current events.

The capital of Nairobi is often considered the cultural center of modern-day Kenya. In 1968, the National Theatre School was founded to help train a new generation of Kenyan playwrights and performers, and helped launch the tide of experimental theater that took performances into local communities. Today, the Kenya National Theatre is the primary venue for the dramatic arts, while independent art organizations like the GoDown Arts Centre and the Kenya Performing Arts Group offer alternative venues for performers and artists.

Football (soccer) is the country's national sport, but cricket, field hockey, netball, volleyball, and track and field events are popular. Kenya's runners dominate marathons around the world.

Cultural Sites & Landmarks

Known as a cradle of civilization, Kenya has become key in providing evidence of early human life and evolution. Koobi Fora, in northern Kenya, has provided more human remains, particularly Hominini (humans and their ancestors) fossils, than any other site in the world. The shape of skulls and other fossils found throughout the various sites provide clues about how humans evolved. Stone artifacts also excavated in Koobi Fora have provided insight into how early humans and their ancestors lived. While some contention exists as to the exact age of the various cultural deposits, most of the remains date back one to two million years.

The United Nations Educational, Scientific, and Cultural Organization (UNESCO) recognizes four sites in Kenya as requiring international recognition and preservation efforts. They include the Lake Turkana National Parks, the Mount Kenya National Park, the historic town of Lamu, and the Sacred Mijikenda Kaya Forests. The Lake Turkana National Parks, a series of three national parks, is known for its outstanding flora and fauna communities, as well as the home of the fossil remains and cultural deposits of Koobi Fora. Mount Kenya National Park, in central Kenya, is one of the nation's most well-known destinations. Mount Kenya is the highest mountain in Kenya and the second highest in Africa. Many plants and animals, including elephants, leopards, and zebras, make their home in the national park, which was also designated as an UNESCO Biosphere Reserve.

Kenya's location along the Indian Ocean has led many peoples to the country. Coastal cities and islands boast the ruins of settlements built hundreds of years ago, the most famous being the Lamu Old Town. Designated a World Heritage Site in 2001, the old town retains original stone and timber structures built by Swahili inhabitants in the 14th century. Arabic peoples later built Lamu Fort in 1813. The fort's expansive walls and towers now shelter the public library and other civic offices. The Sacred Mijikenda Kaya Forests became Kenya's fourth World Heritage Site in 2008. Comprising eleven forests sites, the collective World Heritage Site was recognized for the cultural history and remains of the Mijikenda people.

Other notable cultural and natural sites in Kenya include the Siyu Fort on Pate Island and the ruins at Gede, as well as the Great Rift Valley. The Siyu Fort, built in the 15th century, is the only fort in Kenya built by African inhabitants, and is now considered a national monument. The ruins at Gede, first built by Swahili peoples in the 12th century, blend African and Arabic culture. Both sites contain the remains of tombs and mosques, and a palace at Gede stands amid encroaching forest. Kenya's Great Rift Valley is a large system of faults that extends from Syria in Southwest Asia to Tanzania, south of Kenya. Notable features of the Great Rift Valley include Mount Kenya and the Masai Mara

Game Reserve, whose rivers and grasslands are home to the nomadic Masai people and countless animals. Each year, millions of wildebeests converge on Masai Mara as they migrate from Tanzania's Serengeti plains to Kenya's Mara River.

Libraries & Museums

Popular museums in Nairobi include the Nairobi Railway Museum and the Karen Blixen Museum, named for Danish author and former Kenyan plantation owner Karen Blixen (who wrote under the pen name Isak Dinesen). The Nairobi National Museum, also in Nairobi, displays traditional and modern Kenyan arts, and numerous other local museums and galleries afford artists the opportunity to share their work.

The leading public library network, the National Library Service of Kenya, serves as Kenya's national library and legal depository. It was established in the mid-20th century, and houses a collection of nearly one million books. The library service has set up the "Camel Mobile Library," a mobile library transported on camel, to reach rural residents and to improve the country's literacy rate.

Holidays

In addition to Christian holidays, Kenya also recognizes a series of national holidays, including anniversary of Kenya's self-government on Madaraka Day (June 1), Labour Day (May 1), the anniversary of Kenyan independence on Jamhuri Day (December 12). Kenyatta Day (October 20) commemorates the birthday of Jomo Kenyatta, the first president of an independent Kenya.

Kenya's Muslims celebrate Ramadan, a holy month of fasting between sunup and sundown; Eid-al-Fitr, the three-day celebration of giving, feasting, and festivals that marks the end of Ramadan; and other days central to the Islamic calendar.

Kenya has a significant number of Hindus who celebrate their own holidays. The largest of these celebrations is Diwali, the festival of lights, in which Hindus hang lamps outside homes and businesses.

Youth Culture

Children in Kenya are both highly valued and sorely undervalued. Poverty, environmental conditions, and a strict adherence to tradition have resulted in many children performing work within and outside the home. Cases of forced labor have also been documented. More significantly, many children have fallen prey to human trafficking and child prostitution. The swift spread of AIDS within Kenya has also resulted in the orphaning of hundreds of thousands of children, many of whom end up as homeless street youth. In 2004 alone, Nairobi was home to an estimated 50,000 street youth.

Conditions for children have been steadily improving, however. In 2003, the country introduced free and compulsory primary education, and by 2006, the United Nations Children's Fund (UNICEF) estimated that nearly 80 percent of all youth were enrolled in primary schools. The International Programme on the Elimination of Child Labor (IPEC), a subsidiary organization of the International Labour Organization (ILO), has also been working to reduce child labor in the nation. In June 2004, the government enacted a national plan to eliminate the worst forms of child labor, as stated in the ILO's Worst Forms of Child Labour Convention. International aid organizations and government agencies are also working to address the growing numbers of homeless youth.

With the exception of orphaned street children, youth in urban Kenya generally enjoy more amenities and less hardship than rural youth. Urban life offers a wider range of youth activities, ranging from dance and pool halls and community centers, to cinemas, parks, and other facilities. Urban and suburban youth also have greater access to athletic and recreation programs. Youth in rural ethnic groups are typically raised in the traditions of their tribes. They are expected to help their families with domestic and agricultural chores, as well as other tasks, while learning the skills and arts of their ancestors. During leisure time, they play games and participate in the music and dance of their communities.

SOCIETY

Transportation

The primary modes of transportation in Kenya are its extensive network of roads, as well as its railroads (though many are used for tourist purposes). Bus transport, particularly minibuses, is the primary mode of public transportation. Share taxis are common in urban areas, as well. Within the capital, Nairobi, the most common form of transportation is the matatu, or minibus. Matatus are plentiful through the city and generally quicker and cheaper than taxis. Traffic travels on the left side of the road.

Transportation Infrastructure

Kenya's roads are its most important ways of connecting rural and urban areas, and it has one of the better road systems in eastern Africa. However, a large majority of the nation's roads are unpaved and in need of repair. The railroads are operated by Kenya Railways, and connect major urban centers. The main line of the railroad runs from Mombasa in the southeast to Nairobi, in central Kenya, and westward to Nanyuki.

International airports are located in Nairobi and Mombasa, while numerous regional and national airports throughout the country support local air traffic; supported by Jomo Kenyatta International Airport, Nairobi is easily accessible for travel and business. For more than 1,000 years, Mombasa, located along the Indian Ocean, has been a center of trade and shipping, and it remains so today. Other port cities have grown along the eastern coast, but they largely service coast trade and fisheries. Most international shipping traffic goes through Mombasa.

Media & Communications

Kenya has a liberal policy toward its mass media. With dozens of radio and television stations and numerous print publications, Kenyan citizens have access to wide range of news, opinions, and entertainment. Kenya's constitution protects the freedoms of speech and the press, though the government has not always upheld that protection. Today, most journalists practice self-censorship to defend against harassment, but reports of media corruption have decreased since the end of the repressive regime of Daniel arap Moi (1924–) in 2002.

Kenya has numerous privately owned print and broadcasting groups, in addition to the state-run Kenya Broadcasting Corporation (KBC). Several international radio groups, including the British Broadcasting Corporation (BBC), Voice of America, and Radio France Internationale, also broadcast in Kenya, and Kenyans having increasing access to international newspapers, magazines, websites, and television networks.

The number of telephones in Kenya more than doubled in the last 20 years of the 20th century. However, a large number of people remain without access to local telephone lines in the early 21st century. At the turn of the century, cellular phone use was on the rise as was the use of most electronic communications tools. Radio remains the primary means of obtaining news and information, but television and Internet usage has increased dramatically. As of 2014, an estimated 36 percent of the population—roughly representing 16.5 million citizens—used the Internet.

SOCIAL DEVELOPMENT

Standard of Living

Kenya ranked 147th out of 187 countries on the 2014 United Nations Human Development Index, which measures quality of life and standard of living indicators.

Average life expectancy in Kenya is 63 years—65 for women and 62 for men (2015 estimate). HIV/AIDS epidemic claimed about 33,000 lives in 2014 alone. The UNAIDS report from 2014 estimated that about 1.36 million Kenyans are living with HIV/AIDS.

Water Consumption

According to 2015 statistics from the World Health Organization, approximately 63 percent of the Kenyan population has access to an improved source of drinking water, which is below the regional average for Africa, while an estimated 30 percent have access to improved sanitation. Limited access to basic services is widespread throughout the country, with the exception of the Nairobi province, the smallest province (and mostly urban). Lack of clean drinking water and sanitation continues to be a chronic issue in Kenya's informal settlements, or urban slums; a 2009 census also found that approximately one in five Kenyans uses the African bush, or rural areas, as a toilet.

Education

Kenya's Ministry of Education oversees a system based on eight years of primary school ("standards"), four years of secondary school ("forms"), and four years of college. In addition to its academic secondary schools, Kenya also has technical high schools and technical and vocational secondary schools. All schools give instruction in English, although some schools will provide instruction in local tribal languages during the first three years of primary school.

Kenya's five public and 12 private universities include the University of Nairobi, Jomao Kenyatta University, United States International University (USIU) Nairobi, Moi University, and Strathmore College.

The Kenyan government's effort to improve the country's educational system since independence has raised the average literacy rate to just over 78 percent, although literacy is only about 74 percent among women.

Women's Rights

Under the Kenyan constitution, women are guaranteed full equality and protection. In 1997, the constitution was amended to prohibit specifically discrimination against persons based on their gender. Tradition and daily practice, however, results in a variety of discriminatory practices and abuses against women that violate both the constitution and the United Nations Universal Declaration on Human Rights (UDHR).

Kenyan women lead a life of "second-class citizenship." Though women perform nearly 80 percent of the agricultural labor in the nation and work in other businesses and industries, they often do not earn wages for their work. If they do receive pay, it is generally less than half the pay of their male counterparts. In terms of education, girls typically receive fewer years of schooling in comparison to boys, and 70 percent of those found to be illiterate in Kenya are women. Women are also under-represented in government itself, holding fewer than 10 percent of the seats in the national legislature.

Women are also considered secondary within the family structure, both traditionally and legally. For example, they are not allowed to own or inherit property without the consent of male relatives or their children. A wife must also have the consent of her husband to obtain a national identification card or a passport. Violence against women by their husbands is largely condoned or ignored, as tradition has long supported a husband's right to "discipline" his wife by physical means. There is also no law prohibiting spousal rape, and instances of non-spousal rape are largely underreported and under-prosecuted due to social stigma and reluctance on the part of officials to prosecute the crime. Violence against women is particularly rampant within and around refugee camps; women are often attacked when they leave the camps to collect resources such as water or firewood. In recent years, international aid groups have begun delivering these resources in order to reduce the possibility of such violence. In 2014, gender equality was further crippled when Kenya's Parliament passed a law allowing polygamy.

The practice of female genital mutilation (FGM) continues to be practiced in Kenya, despite international calls to end the practice. Often practiced as part of a rite of passage, the procedure can cause permanent harm to girls and women, and is fatal in the most extreme cases. The World Health Organization (WHO) and other agencies have decried the procedure and urged nations to stop the practice. However, studies in 2004 found that 38 of the nation's 42 ethnic groups still practice FGM.

According to the U.S. Department of State, Kenya has made strides in recent years in addressing the status of women, particularly

by reducing incidents of violence. In 2004, the Kenyan Parliament created a national commission on gender and gender development, and a growing number of organizations addressing women's needs have begun operating in the nation. Women are also gaining a greater voice in the political sphere through organizations such as the League of Kenyan Women Voters (LKWV) and the Women's Political Caucus. In April 2008, thirteen women—seven cabinet ministers and six assistant ministers—were appointed to Kenya's coalition government, representing the largest number of women representatives to date. These steps forward, however, were compromised by an increasingly anti-woman governmental agenda.

Health Care

Kenya's current health system is inadequate to meet the basic needs of the population. As of a 2002 study, only one percent of Kenya's wealthiest citizens had adequate private health insurance. Expensive private insurance plans are not generally available to people outside of Kenya's urban areas or to high-risk patients.

The government established the National Hospital Insurance Fund in 1996 to alleviate health care costs for poorer citizens. Under the corresponding plan, Kenyans can purchase partial health insurance coverage at a rate that is set according to the patient's income level. As of 2002, only about 2 million of Kenya's 33 million people were covered under the plan.

The Kenyan government and a number of international non-governmental organizations provide free or low-cost basic care in Kenya with the help of charitable funds or government aid grants. At present, most health care services are focused on improving prenatal, infant, and family care, preventing communicable diseases (particularly HIV/AIDS), and educating the populace about preventative care.

In addition to HIV/AIDS, Kenya struggles with outbreaks of malaria, typhoid, Hepatitis A, and a variety of other air- and water-borne diseases. High rates of vitamin deficiencies and malnutrition complicate treatment of these diseases. In part because of the lack of access to Western health care and in part because of traditional belief systems, many Kenyans use indigenous spiritual or physical health care providers.

GOVERNMENT

Structure

Once a centerpiece of the British Empire's East African colonies, Kenya earned its independence on December 12, 1963, under the leadership of national icon Jomo Kenyatta. Since that time, the African republic has been run by a Bunge (national assembly) and a president.

Under the former current constitution, the president was elected by popular vote to a five-year term. Of the Bunge's 224 members, 210 were elected by popular vote to five-year terms, 12 were appointed by the president based on party representation, and two were ex-officio members. Judges of Kenya's High Court and Court of Appeals were appointed by the president. A new constitution was adopted in August 2010. Under this constitution, the office of prime minister was eliminated and a series of new checks and balances were introduced.

Political Parties

While Kenya has a multi-party system, the government essentially operates under a two-party system. As of the 2013 parliamentary elections, the Orange Democratic Movement came to control the parliament with 96 seats, followed by the National Alliance with 89 seats. Other political parties include the United Republican Party of Kenya (75 seats), the Wiper Democratic Movement (26 seats), and the United Democratic Forum Party with 12 seats. Several other parties held 10 seats or fewer.

Local Government

For administrative purposes, Kenya is divided into seven provinces (or mkoa) and one special area (Nairobi). There are 69 rural districts within the provinces. A presidentially appointed commissioner heads each district.

Judicial System

Kenya's judiciary branch consists of a High Court, with judges appointed by the president, and a Court of Appeals. Beneath these courts are the two-tiered magistrate courts, where both civil and criminal cases are heard. Kenya's legal system is similar to the British legal system.

Taxation

Kenya has a top personal and corporate income tax rate of 30 percent. Other taxes levied include a value-added tax (or VAT, similar to a consumption tax), and an interest tax.

Armed Forces

The armed forces of Kenya consist of three service branches: the army, navy, and air force. The driving philosophy behind the country's military is national defense, and, as of 2012, the military budget accounts for less than two percent of Kenya's gross domestic product (GDP). Kenya has focused on upgrading its armed forces in the 21st century—it ranked fourth in weapons purchases out of twenty-three other African countries in 2008—and the Kenyan military is considered the most professional army in East Africa. Following the unrest building in neighboring Somalia, Kenyan troops were dispatched along the Kenya-Somalia border beginning in 2009. There is no conscription, and 18 is the minimum age for service.

Foreign Policy

Located in east-central Africa along the Indian Ocean, Kenya has long held a unique position in connecting Africa to the rest of the world. Its location and resources have made it a key trading partner with nations in Europe and Asia, and have made it a major point of interest for nations hoping to gain access to the African interior. Since attaining its independence in 1963, the Kenyan government has struggled to define Kenya's place in Africa and on the world stage, while trying to address national economic, social, and political challenges. For decades, first under the restrictive control of Jomo Kenyatta (1894–1978) and then under the heavy-handed authority of Daniel arap Moi, who ruled from 1978 until 2002, Kenya remained largely disengaged from world politics. In order to secure much needed aid, Moi and his successor, Mwai Kibaki (1931–), introduced political reforms.

Kenya's foreign policy in the early 21st century is focused on several key areas, including pursuing cooperative and beneficial trade relations, maintaining peace through diplomacy, respecting the sovereignty of other nations while maintaining national security, and supporting the principles of the charters of the United Nations (UN) and the African Union (AU). Overall, Kenya's foreign policy is geared more toward economic development than political diplomacy, though Kenyan official actively cultivate close ties with other nations—it still maintains a defensive pact with neighboring Ethiopia—and uphold a "good neighbor" policy in eastern Africa. Kenya has joined many region trade groups meant to foster diplomatic relations through economic exchange, including the East African Community (EAC), the Common Market for Eastern and Southern Africa (COMESA), and the Indian Ocean Rim-Association for Regional Cooperation (IOR-ARC). Kenya's primary trade partners are Uganda, Tanzania, the countries of the European Union (EU), and the United Arab Emirates (UAE).

Though Kenya prefers to distance itself from international events, it also works to maintain stability in the region. Because of conflicts in neighboring Somalia, Ethiopia, Uganda, and the Sudan, thousands of people have been displaced as refugees. Since the 1990s, Kenya has taken in some 421,789 refugees from Somalia, 91,734 from the Sudan, 31,023 from Ethiopia, and a significant number of Ugandans and other African peoples dispossessed by war, ethnic violence, and natural disasters. Kenya also has supplied troops to various UN peacekeeping missions in Africa.

Kenya has also played a significant role in regional mediations. In February 2005, Kenyan officials hosted the peace negotiations between northern and southern forces in the Sudan and helped negotiate a peace in Somalia. Following the 1998 terrorist bombing of the United States embassy in Nairobi, and the 2002 bombing of an Israeli hotel in Mombasa, Kenya has also become an important partner in the U.Ss-led "war on terrorism." The U.S. uses Kenyan territory as a base of operations for its forces in eastern Africa. In return, Kenya has received millions of dollars in aid from the U.S. to combat terrorism.

Human Rights Profile

International human rights law insists that states respect civil and political rights, and promote an individual's economic, social, and cultural rights. The United Nations Universal Declaration on Human Rights (UDHR) is recognized as the standard for international human rights. Its authors sought the counsel of the world's great thinkers, philosophers, and religious leaders, and were careful to create a document that reflects the core values shared by every world culture. (To read this document or view the articles relating to cultural human rights, visit http://www.udhr.org/UDHR/default.htm.)

For decades, as Kenyans suffered under the oppression of Kenyatta and Moi, Kenya's human rights record was often criticized internationally. Since 2002, Kenya has been regaining ground in the area of human rights, but much room is left for improvement. While the Kenyan constitution guarantees many of the rights and freedoms protected by the UDHR, many rights are not successfully protected. However, increasing violence since 2014 has caused the Kenyan government to introduce even stricter security laws, greatly affecting human rights.

Kenya maintains a liberal press that is generally free and fair, though the harassment of journalists has been documented. The Kenyan constitution also protects the freedom of religion, though Muslims have complained of discriminatory practices. Kenyan law provides for free primary and secondary education for all children, and guarantees universal suffrage at the age of eighteen, as well as multiparty elections. Workers also have the right under law to organize into unions, to engage in collective bargaining, and to strike. All of these laws are in accordance with the various articles of the UDHR. In addition, Kenya has also provided refuge for tens of thousands of refugees from neighboring nations and protected them from return to their home country where conflict still rages. This granting of asylum, though Kenyan law does not require it, honors the spirit of Article 14.

Despite this general adherence to the UDHR, certain shortfalls exist. Most notably, ethnic violence has often threatened the life and security of citizens, and evidence suggests that such violence has been tolerated or overlooked by the government. In fact, local violence has been used to enact more stringent laws and regulations. Also equally important, yet also overlooked, is forced prostitution among women, children, and trafficking in human slaves, which continues within Kenya and across its borders. Kenyan police have also been accused of arbitrary arrests and abuse and torture of prisoners, incidents that have been fatal in some cases. Due to what many perceive as a lack of faith or trust in the judicial system and national security or police forces, mob violence and vigilante justice has also been documented. Moreover, prisons remain overcrowded, with conditions routinely described as unsanitary, and human rights abuses have been prevalent in and around refugee camps.

Kenya has taken steps to correct these issues. The Kenya Human Rights Commission (KHRC) has access to prisons, police stations, and information, and regularly investigates and reports on human rights issues. Non-governmental organizations (NGOs) are also active in the country, working to relieve human suffering and to advocate on behalf of groups suffering violence or discrimination. Increasing police attention has also been directed at stopping the traffic in slavery, and other programs have been put in place to help victims of human trafficking recover and to increase awareness about trafficking in Kenya. Nonetheless, terrorism and local violence have increasingly begun to overshadow Kenya's best efforts, as the government has taken on a harsher stance.

ECONOMY

Overview of the Economy

Although Nairobi is a financial, transportation, and trading center for East Africa, Kenya's economic growth has been slow, due in large part to extensive government corruption and foreign debt. The economy relies on agriculture and service industries related to tourism. In 2014, the per capita gross domestic product was estimated at $3,100 (USD).

Industry

Kenya produces an assortment of consumer goods, including plastics, furniture, batteries, textiles, soap, cigarettes, and flour. The country also exports agricultural goods, aluminum, steel, lead, and cement. Other industries include oil refining, commercial ship repair, and tourism. Nairobi's key industries are processed foods, textiles, construction, communications, transportation, banking, and tourism.

Labor

Kenya's labor force was estimated at 17.7 million in 2014, with an unemployment rate of 40 percent in 2013. Three-fourths of the labor force works in agriculture, while industry and the services sector account for the remaining one-fourth.

Energy/Power/Natural Resources

Kenya has large natural reserves of limestone, salt, gemstones, fluorspar, zinc, and gypsum. The massive expanse of Lake Victoria and its tributaries provide significant hydropower resources. Kenya's most famous natural resources are the wildlife and dramatic open landscapes that draw safari-goers from around the world.

Fishing

Kenya began exporting fish in the 1980s, and the fishing industry has moved from domestic consumption to exports. Lake Victoria represents the country's primary fisheries source, followed by the country's coastline. For the most part, fishing remains mostly small-scale in nature, with artisanal methods still in practice. Commercially viable species include perch, tuna, lobsters, and prawns. Nile Perch, from Lake Victoria, is the dominant fish export, though weak market prices and dwindling stocks have hurt the export market heading into 2010. As of 2008, fishing represented less than two percent of Kenya's gross domestic product (GDP), and the government worked on forming a new policy to help improve fisheries revenue and GDP contribution.

Forestry

As of 2010, Kenya's forest cover fell from 12 percent to 1.2 percent, due to encroachment and agriculture expansion. In response, the government enacted logging bans and worked to evict illegal settlements. Kenya's forestry industry produces timber, wood products such as cork, boards, crates, and furniture, and paper, and pulp products. Heading into the early 21st century, the industry contributed approximately three percent to the country's gross domestic product (GDP), which dropped to less than two percent in 2002. Wood also provides for three-fourths of the country's domestic energy needs (including in the form of charcoal). Illegal logging remains a concern.

Mining/Metals

Kenya's mineral industry is dependent on the production of fluorspar, soda ash, and industrial minerals such as cement and stone, sand, and gravel. Other facets of the mineral industry include gemstone production, while gold production in the country has decreased in the early 21st century.

Agriculture

Kenya's strongest agricultural exports are tea, coffee, and horticultural products. Kenya's fertile land also produces corn, wheat, sugarcane, fruit, and vegetables, and sustains beef, dairy, pork, and poultry farms.

Animal Husbandry

Livestock in Kenya include cattle, sheep, goats, pigs, and poultry. Mostly, the livestock industry is composed of small farmers and producers.

Tourism

Kenya's tourist industry has been a feature of the country's economy since American and European big game hunters made the country a destination at the end of the 19th century. Now, tourism brings in about $500 million (USD) dollars every year, although the AIDS epidemic and fear of global terrorism have weakened the industry in recent years. Known as the safari capital of Africa, Nairobi, in particular, attracts a large number of tourists each year.

In 2010, Kenya witnessed the most tourist arrivals in its history, an estimated 2.8 million visitors.

Christina Dendy, Amy Witherbee, Lynn-nore Chittom

DO YOU KNOW?

- Anthropological findings from the Lake Turkana area of show that human beings have been living in the region that is now Kenya for at least 2.6 million years.

- Kenya is one of the world's largest producers of pyrethrum, a natural mosquito repellant that comes from the dried flowers of a chrysanthemum plant native to the area.

- The Carnivore Restaurant, one of the top restaurants of the world, is located in Nairobi and is a popular attraction for tourists on safari. The restaurant is known for its menu of exotic meats including zebra, hartebeest, ostrich, and crocodile. Since wild gaming is illegal in Kenya, all meats sold at the restaurant are farmed.

Bibliography

Anthony Ham, et al. "Kenya." Oakland, CA: *Lonely Planet,* 2015.

Alexandra Polier. "What's Up Kenya?" *Foreign Policy.* September/October 2006. http://www.foreignpolicy.com/story/cms.php?story_id=3549

Daniel Branch. "Kenya: Between Hope and Despair." New Haven, CT: *Yale University Press,* 2013.

Godfrey Mwakikagile. "Kenya: Identity of a Nation." Edinburgh: *New Africa Press,* 2007.

Helena Halperin. "I Laugh So I Won't Cry: Kenya's Women Tell The Story Of Their Lives." Trenton, New Jersey: *Africa World Press,* 2005.

Elspeth Huxley, ed. "Nine Faces of Kenya." New York: *Viking Penguin,* 1991.

Jane Barsby. "Kenya—Culture Smart! The Essential Guide to Customs and Culture." London: *Kuperard,* 2007.

Joseph Lemasolai Lekuton and Herman Viola. "Facing the Lion: Growing Up Maasai on the African Savanna." Washington, D.C.: *National Geographic Children's Books,* 2005.

Nigel Pavitt. "Kenya: A Country in the Making, 1880–1940." New York: W.W. *Norton & Co.,* 2008.

Ngugi wa Thiong'o. "Petals of Blood." New York: *Penguin Classics,* 2005.

Richard Trillo, Daniel Jacobs, and Nana Luckham. "The Rough Guide to Kenya." London: *Rough Guides,* 2006.

William R. O'Chieng, ed. "Themes in Kenyan History." Nairobi, Kenya: *Heinemann Kenya Limited,* 1990.

Works Cited

"2005 population estimates for cities in Kenya." *Tropical Rainforest Conservation.* http://www.mongabay.com/igapo/2005_world_city_populations/Kenya.html

"About the Ministry." *Ministry of Foreign Affairs, Republic of Kenya.* http://www.mfa.go.ke/mfacms/index.php?option=com_content&task=view&id=5&Itemid=6

"AFROL Gender Profiles: Kenya." *Afrol News.* http://www.afrol.com/Categories/Women/profiles/kenya_women.htm

"Background Notes: Kenya." *U.S. Department of State.* June 2008. http://www.state.gov/r/pa/ei/bgn/2962.htm

"Bilateral Agreements." *Ministry of Foreign Affairs, Republic of Kenya.* http://www.mfa.go.ke/mfacms/index.php?option=com_content&task=view&id=50&Itemid=72

"Country Reports on Human Rights Practices—2004, released by the Bureau of Democracy, Human Rights, and Labor—Kenya." *U.S. Department of State.* February 28, 2005. http://www.state.gov/g/drl/rls/hrrpt/2004/41609.htm

"Etiquette in Kenya." *Travel Etiquette.* http://www.traveletiquette.co.uk/EtiquetteKenya.html

"Country Profile: Kenya." *BBC News Channel.* April 18, 2008. http://news.bbc.co.uk/2/hi/africa/country_profiles/1024563.stm

"Foreign Policy." *Ministry of Foreign Affairs, Republic of Kenya.* October 3, 2007. http://www.mfa.go.ke/mfacms/index.php?option=com_content&task=view&id=13&Itemid=31

Joel D. Barkan, "Kenya After Moi." *Foreign Affairs.* January/February 2004. http://www.foreignaffairs.org/20040101faessay83109/joel-d-barkan/kenya-after-moi.html

"Kalenjin Tribe." *enhols.com.* http://www.enhols.com/kenya_safari/people/kalenjin/

"Kenya." *Africa Guide.* http://www.africaguide.com/country/kenya/culture.htm

"Kenya." *The Columbia Encyclopedia.* Sixth Ed. 2007. http://www.bartleby.com/65/ke/Kenya.html

"Kenya." *Culture Crossing.* http://www.culturecrossing.net/basics_business_student_details.php?Id=7&CID=107

"Kenya Cultures." *Kenya Travel Ideas.* http://www.kenyatravelideas.com/kenya-cultures.html

"Kenya." *Encyclopedia Britannica.* 2008. http://search.eb.com/eb/article-9108363

"Kenya Foreign Policy." *Permanent Mission of the Republic of Kenya to the United Nations Office in Geneva.* 2007. http://www.kenyamission-un.ch/?About_Kenya:Kenya_Foreign_Policy

"Kenya's Foreign Policy." 2007. *Embassy of the Republic of Kenya in Rwanda.* http://www.kenemb.org.rw/fpolicy.html

"Kenya in Brief." State House Mwai. http://www.statehousekenya.go.ke/

"Kenya Information." *World Info Zone.* http://www.worldinfozone.com/country.php?country=Kenya#architecture

"Kenya: Language, Culture, Customs, and Etiquette." *Kwintessential.* http://www.kwintessential.co.uk/resources/global-etiquette/kenya.html

"Kenya Missions Abroad." *Ministry of Foreign Affairs, Republic of Kenya.* February 28, 2008. http://www.mfa.go.ke/mfacms/index.php?option=com_content&task=view&id=17&Itemid=29

"Kenya." *The World Factbook.* CIA. October 9, 2008. http://www.cia.gov/library/publications/the-world-factbook/print/Kenya.html

"Kikuyu Tribe of Kenya." *enhols.com.* http://www.enhols.com/kenya_safari/people/kikuyu/

Laurel Corona. "Kenya." San Diego, California: *Lucent Books,* 2000.

Lisa McQuail. "The Masai of Africa." Minneapolis: *Lerner Publications Company,* 2002. http://books.google.com/books?id=cYT_BuP3-qsC&pg=PT31&lpg=PT31&dq=masai+greeting&source=web&ots=uRYkOepEMo&sig=jFwHkdaNAatKU

Ak0-VS8DrfhnMM&hl=en&sa=X&oi=book_
result&resnum=2&ct=result

"Luhya Tribe." *enhols.com.* http://www.enhols.com/kenya_
safari/people/luhya/

"Luo Tribe." *enhols.com.* http://www.enhols.com/kenya_
safari/people/luo/

"Maasai Tribe." *enhols.com.*

"Management Team." *Ministry of Foreign Affairs, Republic
of Kenya.* http://www.mfa.go.ke/mfacms/index.
php?option=com_content&task=view&id=32&Item
id=47

Suzanne Girard Eberle. "Eat Like a Kenyan." *Running
Times Magazine.* October 2000. http://runningtimes.
com/Article.aspx?ArticleID=3955

"The Swahili Coast." *PBS.* http://www.pbs.org/wonders/
Episodes/Epi2/2_wondr2.htm

"Treaties." *Ministry of Foreign Affairs, Republic of Kenya.*
October 3, 2007. http://www.mfa.go.ke/mfacms/index.
php?option=com_content&task=view&id=15&Item
id=30

Lesotho man wearing the traditional mokorotlo hat.

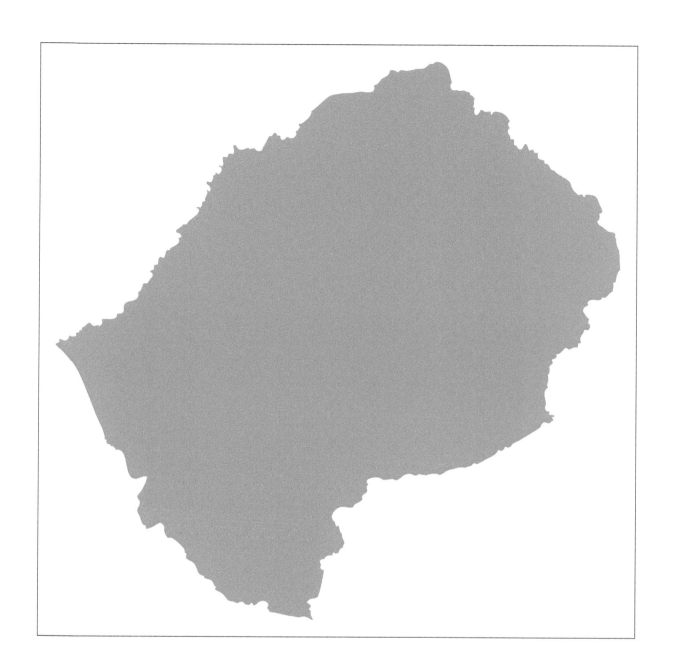

LESOTHO

Introduction

Hidden high among the Drakensberg, Maluti, and Thaba Putsoa Mountains, the Kingdom of Lesotho is surrounded on all sides by South Africa. The country owes its existence to its founding king, Moshoeshoe, who in the early 19th century gathered together several disparate refugee populations—which became known as the Basotho people—and created a small enclave in the mountains. Today, the Basotho are working aggressively to create a new economy, energize educational systems, and control one of the world's worst HIV/AIDS epidemics.

Much of Basotho life revolves around music. Herd boys can be found playing the lekolulu, a type of flute, while the setolo-tolo, a stringed instrument played with the mouth, is generally played by men. The qwadinyana, a single string fiddle, is also prevalent among the herdsmen of Maluti. As in other African nations, Lesotho's musical tastes have become a vibrant blend of traditional and contemporary music. The kingdom is also known for its traditional arts; Basotho artisans create traditional tapestries, tribal wools, and Letlotlo folk art. The Lesotho government has created a market center for all of these items in the town of Teyateyaneng (called "TY" for short). Maseru, the country's capital and only major town, also features a number of weaving centers where traditional Basotho products are made.

GENERAL INFORMATION

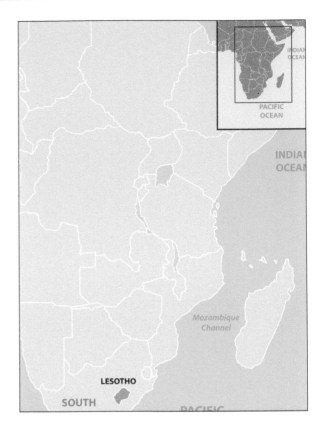

Official Language: English
Population: 1,947,701 (2015 estimate)
Currency: Lesotho loti (the South African rand is also legal tender)
Coins: The Lesotho loti is divided into 100 lisente; coins are available in denominations of 1, 2, 5, 10, 20, and 50 lisente, and 1 loti and 2 and 5 maloti (plural).
Land Area: 30,355 square kilometers (12,727 square miles)
National Motto: "Khotso, pula, nala" ("Peace, rain, wealth")
National Anthem: "Lesotho Fatse La Bontata Rona" ("Lesotho, Land of Our Fathers")
Capital: Maseru
Time Zone: GMT +3
Flag Description: The flag of the Kingdom of Lesotho features a tricolor design of three equal horizontal bands of blue (top), white (middle), and green (bottom). Centered in the white band is a traditional conical black hat associated with the Basotho people, called a mokorotlo (or Basotho hat). Concepts represented by the colors of the flag include Africa, peace, prosperity, and rain.

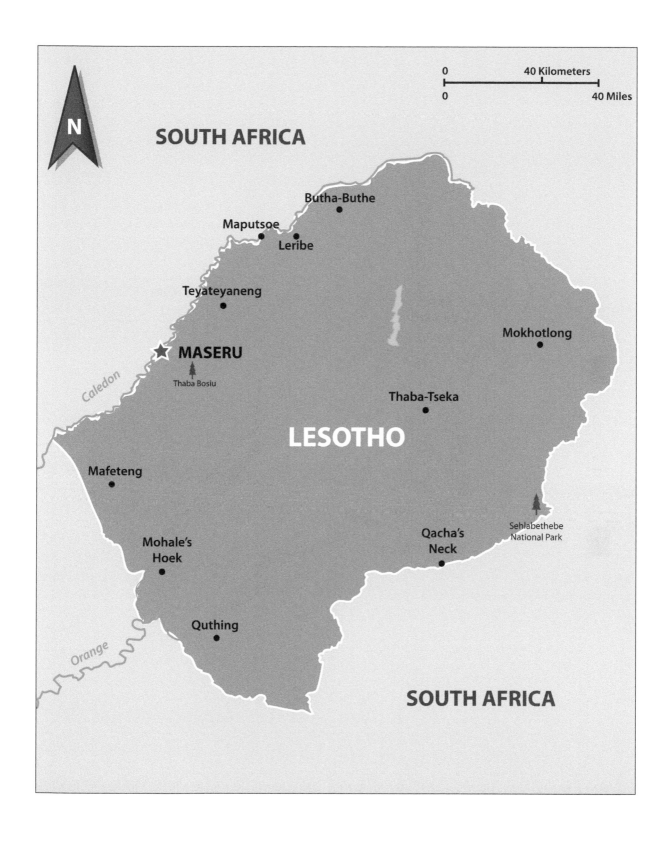

Principal Cities by Population (2012 estimate):

- Maseru (267,559)
- Hlotse (47,894)
- Mafeteng (43,200)
- Teyateyaneng (28,142)
- Molale's Hoek (23,481)
- Maputsoe (23,029)

Population

Almost all of Lesotho's population, over 99 percent, is ethnic Sotho. The remainder of the population is of European or Asian extraction.

Maseru is Lesotho's most populous town and is one of the region's fastest-growing urban centers. Since the mid-1990s, the capital's population has increased around seven percent annually. The boom has been fueled by the capital's growing textile industry.

Most of Lesotho's population lives in small rural villages of fewer than 250 people. Although many Basotho men make their livings from mining in South Africa, life generally revolves around agriculture. Women do much of the farming work in common fields around the village, while young boys grow up herding flocks in the shared herding grounds.

Basotho live in extended family units, although the thousands of orphans left behind by the AIDS pandemic has already changed family structures in the country. Because of illness, political instability, recent drought, and a drop in South African mining jobs, a full 49 percent of Lesotho's people live below the poverty line.

Languages

Although English is Lesotho's official language, Sesotho (southern Sotho), part of the Bantu language family, is the national language. In Maseru, most residents speak Sesotho. English is used in government, business, and educational settings, where it is far more common than in other parts of Lesotho. Xhosa and Zulu is also spoken to a lesser extent, the latter commonly used by migrants to from the northeastern part of Lesotho.

Native People & Ethnic Groups

The San were the earliest known inhabitants of the region that is now Lesotho. Displaced by small groups from the Nguni branch of Africa's Bantu-speaking peoples during the early modern era, the San left traces of their existence in cave paintings and simple weapons.

The Bantu-speaking Mapolane, Maphetla, and Baphuthi, and the Bafokeng, first speakers of Sesotho, eventually displaced the San and collectively became known as the Sotho peoples. In the early 19th century, the Zulu Empire (also Bantu) expanded through raids and warfare, and refugees fled toward the mountains. Between 1815 and 1823, King Moshoeshoe gathered together locals and refugees to make a stand against the African Zulu. Today, all of their descendants are considered Basotho, citizens of the nation founded by Moshoeshoe. Today, minority groups in Lesotho include small numbers of Europeans and Asians.

Religions

About 80 percent of Basotho are practicing Christians, while 20 percent follow traditional religious beliefs. The majority of Maseru's inhabitants are Christian, a reflection of Lesotho's colonial past and the influence of Western missionaries. Roman Catholics make up the largest denomination. Some adherents combine their Christian faith with indigenous spiritual beliefs and practices.

Climate

Lesotho's climate is unusually cool because of the country's high elevation. During the winter months from May to September, temperatures in the highlands fall to $-18°$ Celsius ($0°$ Fahrenheit), and to $-7°$ Celsius ($20°$ Fahrenheit) in the lowlands. Snow in the highlands is a regular occurrence all winter, but rapidly changing conditions in the mountains can bring a sudden hailstorm or snowfall at any time of year.

During the summer months from October to April, lowland temperatures rise to about 30° Celsius (86° Fahrenheit), while the highlands reach a significantly cooler 18° Celsius (64° Fahrenheit). Lesotho's hottest months are January and February. The rainy season lasts from March to May, and then returns in October and November. Average rainfall is a plentiful 760 millimeters (30 inches) per year. Afternoon thunderstorms are common.

Maseru features a temperate subtropical climate, although frost and even snowfall can occur in winter. The rainy season, characterized by intense thunderstorms, lasts from October through April. Daytime temperatures in the summer range between 30° Celsius (86° Fahrenheit) and 35° Celsius (95° Fahrenheit) while in winter they range between 10° Celsius (50° Fahrenheit) and 15° Celsius (59° Fahrenheit).

ENVIRONMENT & GEOGRAPHY

Topography

The entire country of Lesotho sits at a high elevation amidst the Drakensberg, Maluti, and Thaba Putsoa mountains. The country's highest point, at Thabana Ntlenyana, is at an elevation of 3,482 meters (11,424 feet). At its lowest point, where the Orange River meets the Makhaleng River, Lesotho reaches an elevation of 1,400 meters (4,593 feet).

The country's most rugged, mountainous terrain is found in the east, near the city of Mokhotlong. In the interior, the terrain softens into foothills, running toward the lowlands in the west. The Orange (Senqu) River Valley cuts across the country from the northeast to the southwest.

Maseru is located in western Lesotho on the left bank of the Caledon River, near the border of South Africa. Lesotho itself is a tiny enclave completely surrounded by South Africa. Although built on what are considered the lowlands of Lesotho's largely mountainous terrain, the capital sits, nonetheless, at an altitude of more than 1,000 meters (3,280 feet). The town lies along Lesotho's chief highway and is also linked by rail to neighboring South Africa. The capital's main thoroughfare,

Kingsway Road, runs from Maseru's center all the way to the South African border.

Plants & Animals

Most of Lesotho's landscape is treeless, either because of its high elevation, or in the case of certain regions, deforestation created by the population's needs for fuel and building materials. In the remaining forested areas, white stinkwood, wild olive, highland protea, and mountain cabbage trees grow naturally. Fruit trees bearing apples, apricots, pears, and quince have been introduced to the landscape over centuries, and thrive in the mountain climate.

Many of the animals that once roamed across Lesotho are now gone. However, different species of hare, rabbits, and porcupine still live in the grasslands, along with diminished species such as deer, African elephants, and lions. Trout and carp are plentiful in the rivers and streams of Lesotho, and nearly 300 species of birds still inhabit the various regions of the country.

CUSTOMS & COURTESIES

Greetings

Handshakes are the common gesture of greeting in Lesotho. The most common greeting in Sesotho is "Lumela," which literally means, "agree." (The plural is "Lumelang.") Other common greetings include "O kae?" ("How are you?"), "O phela joang?" ("How do you live?"), and "O tsohele joang?" ("How did you get up?"). If one is speaking with friends or family member, it is customary to ask about one's well-being and family. Common phrases of departure include "Sala hantle" ("Stay well") and "Tsamaea hantle" ("Go well").

Gestures & Etiquette

In Lesotho, there is little physical self-consciousness, and it is common for individuals to stand close when conversing and frequently to lay an encouraging hand on one another to fuel the discussion. However, public affection is generally uncommon, and men and women are not typically seen holding hands, though it is very common to see individuals of the same sex showing public affection. Pointing is common, curtsying is polite when trying to show respect, and bowing is occasionally reserved for the same purpose. Drinking is only acceptable in the confines of the home or a public space specifically meant for drinking.

Eating/Meals

When resources are available, the Basotho generally eat three meals daily. Breakfast may be taken late, and typically consists of light fare. Lunch is then taken in the late afternoon and dinner, customarily eaten with family, is in the mid-evening, and may be similar to lunch. It is normal for men to eat first while women serve them; the women will then eat afterward and may distribute the remaining food to neighbors or any less fortunate people. Guests must also be served before any women of the household.

Utensils such as forks or tablespoons may be used to eat dishes that are particularly messy or soupy, but the right hand is traditionally used for eating. For example, starch is balled up by hand and dipped into sauce, so that the starchiness absorbs the sauce. Separate dishes are customarily used for eating. In recent years, there has been a growing trend of migration to urban areas and South Africa for work, particularly in the South African mines. This has led to the development of a strong food industry at these sites, including makeshift cafeterias that offer breakfast sandwiches, snacks, and full lunches.

Visiting

Visiting among the Basotho is common and nearly always unannounced. Many homes have a place reserved for socializing, which may be one of many buildings on a family compound or an outside space. If the guest arrives during dinner, it is expected that there will be enough food to feed him. It is customary for all guests and male household members to eat before the women of the house. Before and after a meal, a guest will also be offered something to drink, such as tea, coffee, soda, alcohol, or water.

In larger towns, the people of Lesotho may socialize and visit in public gathering places such as bars. Public intoxication is frowned upon, and only in these places is it acceptable to drink.

LIFESTYLE

Family

In Basotho culture, the idea of family often extends to include entire villages. Generally, rural villages, where most citizens live, are composed of one or more clans living in a settlement of compounds. These compounds, or motse, include several buildings housing a nuclear family (husband, wife, and children) and their related family members. One or more nuclear families may also inhabit the same motse. However, the family may also include the husband's extended relatives, as he is traditionally expected to provide them shelter. Each occupant of the motse is expected to contribute, whether through domestic and agrarian responsibilities, child rearing, or earning wages.

With a 23 percent infection rate, Lesotho has one of the world's highest rates of HIV/AIDS. This has led to the destruction of the family unit in the early 21st century. The trend is most destructive in major cities and towns, where nuclear families tend to live in single homes. This prevalence of HIV/AIDS has led to an increase in orphaned children.

Housing

Homes in rural Lesotho are relatively uniform in design because of their practical function: to protect against the harsh weather that consists of a hot summer climate and cold winters. Most traditional rural homes are cylindrical in shape, and often built from medium stones cemented together with cow dung and mud. The conical roofs are thatched and layered, and sealed where they meet the walls. There are generally no windows and the doors are small. These houses are typically single-room units built on a motse (compound), which generally features many buildings all used for daily living. They include bedrooms, kitchens, and even a visiting room.

In urban areas, Western building techniques and materials are now common, and modern architecture often incorporates traditional elements. Many homes are built from mud brick with corrugated tin roofs. High-rise apartment buildings are common in the capital of Maseru.

Food

The diet in Lesotho is based on a few key staples, the most important of which is maize. Maize is eaten in several common ways, including as papa, a porridge made from ground maize that is stewed into a sticky paste, or as kernels. Other traditional staples include cassava, rice, plantains, millet, potatoes, peanut, eggplant, tomato, wild spinach, mango, banana, grapes, sugar beans, and papaya. Beef, mutton (sheep), goat, and chicken are generally reserved for special occasions. The Basotho are also famous for their smoked pork, or hams, and shellfish and freshwater fish from the river are also very popular components in dishes. Generally, dishes include a main starch accompanied by a thick stew or sauce. Sauces may mix peanuts, tomatoes, or eggplant bases with mohoro, or cooked greens, and a meat of some sort.

The cuisine of Lesotho has also a multicultural flavor, and includes culinary influences from neighboring African cultures, European cuisines, and the traditions of both Malaysia and India. For example, spicy curry, chutneys, and curried grilled kebabs are popular throughout the country.

Life's Milestones

Important celebrated milestones in Basotho culture include birth, transition into adulthood, and marriage. Coming of age ceremonies are held for young men and women transitioning into adulthood. Though the Basotho are relatively unified, their methods for celebrating this transition differ greatly. Some groups cover the bodies of young men and women in a grey mud and smear off sections exposing the dark skin in wavy patterns. Others parade the youngsters through town, with young men often wearing animal-patterned blankets to portray an image of strength and vitality, and to proclaim that they are of adult age.

Marriage traditionally involves a bride gift, or a gift of money, food, or cattle to the bride's family. This is customary, as the bride's departure from her family or clan deprives them of the work she would be able to contribute, and the gifts are meant to compensate for this loss.

CULTURAL HISTORY

Art

Lesotho is home to a large collection of rock art. The San Bushmen, hunter-gatherers who were the early occupants of southern Africa, decorated the walls of caves throughout the nation's southeastern regions with nuanced carvings. This was thousands of years before the arrival of Bantu-speaking tribes during Bantu migrations (1000 BCE–1100 CE). The petroglyphs (images carved into rock) portray the semi-nomadic existence of the Bushmen, including traditions and hunting methods. Images of men and women hunting, dancing, and inhabiting huts are carved next to detailed depictions of wildlife, notably leopards, lions, eland, blue crane, and guinea fowl. This selection of wildlife seems to focus on both prey and predators important to the San.

In comparison to other African cultures, the artistic heritage of Lesotho is perhaps minimal. There is no legacy of carved wooden masks or modern fine arts. Nonetheless, the region's inhabitants have a strong tradition of artistic crafts. These early arts and crafts include hand-woven textiles, pottery, grass weaving (such as baskets, mats, and other functional items), and beadwork. Many of these traditions are limited, and are now cottage industries for the tourism sector. Crafts that are more contemporary include mohair weaving, introduced in the 20th century, and jewelry. Many crafts, such as wire toys and handbags, are made using scraps.

Textiles

Textiles only recently became an integral part of life in Lesotho. Lesotho is the only African nation where a majority of the population experience

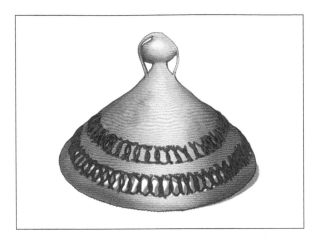

The traditional mokorotlo hat of Lesotho.

snowfall for a lengthy period, and the Basotho traditionally dressed in animal skins to stay warm in the frigid weather. When Europeans were allowed to visit Lesotho's strongholds in the 19th century, they brought with them blankets as gifts for King Moshoeshoe I (c. 1786–1870), whose death marked the advent of Lesotho's colonial era. European weaving was soon integrated into the culture, and contemporary textiles, such as carpets and blankets, are woven from indigenous mohair. It is uncommon, in fact, to see individuals walking about without a blanket draped about them. These blankets feature complex designs, some of which appear similar to Native American prints.

The Basotho are also known for the traditional mokorotlo hat (also called Basotho hat) woven from indigenous reeds from the river marshes. The hat is cone-shaped, a design choice attributed to the very first hat weavers. The hat is believed to be modeled after Qiloane Mountain, which is sacred to the Basotho.

Architecture

The early architecture of the Basotho also dates back to the Bushmen, whose simplistic huts are depicted in their rock art. Composed of mud, cow dung, and thatch, these homes served their functional purposes for thousands of years. The traditional common hut in Lesotho is the cylindrical mokhoro (also called rondavel, the traditional African-style house). It is made from raw materials such as stones and mortar for the walls, soil, and dung for the floors, and grass, wood poles, and thatch for the conical roofs. Though this style is still predominant in many rural areas, homes made of mud brick with corrugated tin roofs are also now common.

Juxtaposed with these simple designs are the more modern buildings in the capital of Maseru, Lesotho's only substantial city. There, high-rise apartment buildings and cement strip malls stand next to traditional and colonial architecture—Lesotho was once a British protectorate—such as the Roman Catholic Cathedral of Our Lady of Victories and the Anglican St. John's Church. In fact, Maseru radiates out from a small but bustling center where scattered remnants of the town's 19th-century British colonial past—modest structures built of locally mined reddish sandstone—are intermingled with modern buildings and informal marketplaces. Much of the center remained under reconstruction in the early part of the 21st century as part of the government's efforts to revitalize areas burned and looted during the civil unrest of 1998, which destroyed around 80 percent of the capital's commercial infrastructure.

A large percentage of the dwellings in Maseru's residential areas, although poor, are not densely packed together. In recent years, more and more migrants have flocked to the capital in search of an escape from rural poverty. Many of the new arrivals live in makeshift housing, without running water, electricity, or sanitation services. These sprawling shantytowns, which are informal settlements, have pushed Maseru's boundaries steadily outward.

Music & Dance

Traditional Basotho music dates back to the first hunter-gatherers who raised and bred cattle on the flatlands around the mountains. The lesiba is the most popular indigenous instrument and is unique for its string and wood elements.

Constructed from a feather, a taut string, and a flexible piece of wood, the instrument is played by adjusting the string's tautness while blowing on the feather, creating a violin-like sound. Early Basotho claimed that the music of this instrument was soothing to their cattle, and led them to produce better milk, hides, and meat.

The Basotho are also famous for a few of their ceremonial and celebratory dances. Traditionally, dances were a part of most festivities, particularly rite of passage ceremonies. One notable dance is the mohobelo, during which males stomp in wild, albeit synchronized, movements, alternating between stomping and high kicking. The mokhibo is a dance that involves women singing and dancing on their knees.

Literature

Like many ethnic cultures in Africa, the Basotho people have a strong oral tradition strengthened by generations of storytellers. Through this oral tradition, early cultures maintained their values, history, and other cultural information from one generation to the next. The ability to memorize and recite such oral tales and proverbs was, and still is, looked upon favorably by most members of society. As Europeans, particularly missionaries, moved further inland toward Lesotho in the late 16th century, they spread Christianity and introduced the written word. This was believed to have had a profound effect on Sotho (or Sesotho), the language indigenous to the region.

The first notable, and perhaps greatest, Basotho author was Thomas Mofolo (1876–1948), whose novel *Chaka* (1925) has been translated into English and is considered one of the pivotal works of 20th-century African literature. The historical novel tells the story of the Zulu emperor-king as he rises to immense power and falls after great tragedy. Other notable authors include Mzamane Nhlapo (1938–) and Mpho Matsepo Nthunya (1930–). These contemporary authors deal with modern issues facing the tiny landlocked kingdom.

CULTURE

Arts & Entertainment

While Lesotho's contemporary arts scene includes modern painters and sculptors and traditional artisans, there is often minimal appreciation for formal art and little government support. In fact, formalized art training and funding is relatively nonexistent. However, the government has recognized the importance of national art in unifying the culture, and has made some effort to promote the arts.

Following the civil unrest during the late 1990s, the government used the Morija Museum as the site for its first national arts endeavor. The Morija Arts & Culture Festival first took place in 1999, and was meant to unify the nation and mend ethnic rivalries through the sharing of arts and crafts. It was also meant to boost tourism, a major source of national revenue, which underwent significant decrease in the years following political instability. The festival has since taken place each October at the museum. It includes a horserace featuring the famous Sotho Ponies and a tournament of moraba-raba, an African board game that resembles chess.

Further initiatives to grow the arts industry in Lesotho include the recent creation of Lesotho Craft Works (LCW), a non-profit organization begun to help local artisans sell their creations abroad. LCW has a wider affiliation with the fair trade social movement, an international initiative meant to insure international artisans' rights are protected and that they receive due wages for their work sold abroad. Through LCW, Lesotho artisans are able to sell their goods abroad at fair prices. Most artisans specialize in weaving, the most significant of Lesotho's crafts. Wall hangings, blankets, and rugs are among the most commonly sold items through the group. These hand-woven tapestries date back centuries and depict strong symbolism with the simplest shapes and images.

Of particular importance is the Lesotho blanket, which dates back to the first contact between King Moshoeshoe and the first Europeans to arrive to his "kingdom in the sky." The Lesotho blankets feature geometric patterns, vibrant colors, or specific images symbolizing important cultural elements to the Basotho. For example, corn has long been a symbol of female fertility among the Basotho, and many young women wear blankets with the image of maize woven into the pattern. Crowns are meant to symbolize both British and Lesotho royalty, and cabbage or other vegetables are meant to symbolize plentiful harvests and good health. Blankets are strictly meant to be worn with the weave running vertically, as superstitious beliefs are associated with the wearing of a blanket with the weave running horizontally.

Cultural Sites & Landmarks

Lesotho was founded through the unification of scattered tribes under the leadership of King Moshoeshoe I. Under the threat of encroaching European and tribal powers, the king gathered the Basotho into one group, settling them in a kingdom in the Maluti and Drakensberg mountain ranges that now form the natural habitat of Lesotho. The steep and flat-topped mountain location proved significant for protection, as the steep inclines leading up to the plateau can only be traversed on foot. The site, now relatively barren, remains sacred to the Basotho people. Its name, Thaba Bosiu, means "Mountain at Night," and may come from the night hour during which Moshoeshoe settled the area. Nearby is Mount Qiloane, another smaller peak held sacred by the Basotho for its perfect shape.

Two of the most historically and culturally significant towns in Lesotho are Roma and Teyateyaneng, both located in the more hospitable northern region. Roma is a former missionary stronghold and is home to the National University of Lesotho. Teyateyaneng is considered the heart of Lesotho's arts and crafts, including the renowned traditional weaving of tapestries and blankets. The other notable city is the capital, Maseru, founded in 1869 as a British outpost. The city has undergone significant modernization in the aftermath of civil unrest in the late 1990s. It is still home to some colonial era buildings, as well as the royal palace and Setsoto

Stadium, the national stadium. The Catholic Cathedral of Our Lady of Victories is situated at the main point of entry to the capital. The church's colossal size and colonial-style architecture make it one of the capital's most imposing structures. Not far from the city center stands the Papal Pavilion, which was built for the 1988 visit of Pope John Paul II.

Lesotho is also known for its paleontological sites. Dinosaur footprints are located in the area of Roma. Outside of Lesotho's southernmost city Quthing, or Moyeni, there is also an extensive track of dinosaur prints. The Masitise Cave House Museum, originally built into a San rock shelter in 1866, houses a vast collection of cultural artifacts and one preserved dinosaur print protected by glass. Bushmen rock art is also considerable throughout Lesotho, particularly at Ha Baroana and the Liphofung Cave Cultural Site, which house some of the most lucid and well-preserved images of humans, wildlife, and hunting throughout ages. Lesotho is also home to Sehlabathebe National Park, the nation's largest national park offering a unique blend of flora and fauna.

Libraries & Museums

The Morija National Museum and Archives, located in the small village of Morija outside of Maseru, is home to a collection that documents the African nation's culture and history, as well as paleontology. It is the chief repository of culture and history for the country, with a collection spanning fossilized dinosaur remains to rare books in its archives, to memorabilia and artifacts from the Boer Wars.

The Lesotho State Library and Archives, in Maseru, serves as the country's national library, and houses Lesotho's published heritage. As of 2010, the country was home to 12 public libraries and 200 school libraries. There is Internet access in between 20 to 40 percent of school libraries.

Holidays

The predominantly Christian Basotho celebrate Christmas, Easter, and Ascension Day (in May).

A national holiday in honor of Lesotho founder, King Moshoeshoe, is observed on March 11. The Basotho also celebrate King Letsie's birthday on July 17, and National Independence Day on October 4.

Youth Culture

With 60 percent of the population under the age of twenty-nine, the majority of Lesotho's population is young by global standards. This is largely due to the prevalence of HIV/AIDS nationwide. Men between the ages of eighteen and twenty-five have a 25 percent infection rate, while women in the same age bracket have an infection rate of 50 percent. As a result, 100,000 children have been left orphaned, and between 100,000 and 200,000 homes nationwide run by children. Children orphaned by AIDS are often ostracized by their communities or abused and abandoned by remaining family members. This children turn to life on the streets, and many become prostitutes or turn to other means to support themselves.

In homes where families remain intact and unaffected by disease and death, youth culture is predominantly influenced by traditional values, most notably respect and deference for elders. Basotho youth are very conscious of age lines and must care for their elders and heed their advice.

SOCIETY

Transportation

One of the many striking cultural features of Lesotho is the preferred transportation mode of many rural Basotho—Lesotho ponies. Bred from Javanese and European horses hundreds of years ago, the Lesotho ponies are distinctive to this mountain-dwelling people. (Lesotho is often referred to as the "Switzerland of Africa"). In fact, the Basotho have long been famed for their excellent horsemanship and strong horse stock, and have used horses for many centuries. It is said that the Basotho were inspired to make the Lesotho pony a central part of their culture when

King Moshoeshoe first rode one into the kingdom's mountain stronghold in 1830.

In urban areas and between the major cities and towns, mini-buses and mini-bus taxis are the most common modes of public transportation. Most can hold anywhere from eight to thirty passengers. Larger buses make longer trips and taxis and scooters are frequently seen in big towns. Traffic moves on the left side of the road in Lesotho.

Transportation Infrastructure

Lesotho is a landlocked nation and its transportation infrastructure is limited to roadways and rail. As of 2004, the road network spanned roughly 8,000 kilometers (4,970 miles), with the roads largely unpaved (consisting of just gravel or earth) in rural areas. A small rail line, operating out of South Africa, handles some freight, while the remainder of Lesotho's imports and exports—an estimated two-thirds—is transported by truck. Lesotho does have a fair number of airports—twenty-eight, according to the CIA World Fact Book—and one international airport, Moshoeshoe I International Airport, which services the capital.

Media & Communications

Lesotho's media is generally considered free and fair and freedom of speech is guaranteed in the constitution. Private press is consistently able to criticize the government with little backlash. However, the government has tried to use the law to punish some private press publications, including filing defamation lawsuits against private papers such as *The Mirror* and *Mololi* for character attacks. The government also runs most of the widest-reaching media. Internet and academic freedom are widely practiced where such services are available.

The radio is the primary means of mass communication in Lesotho. The state-run *Radio Lesotho* is the national radio broadcaster and there are several private stations. Lesotho Television is the national, state-run television broadcaster. Radio and television programming from South Africa is also available. Print news is also available in major cities and is largely run by private interests. *The Public Eye* and *The Mirror* are weekly English papers and *Makatolle, MoAfrica,* and *Mohlanka* are all weekly Sotho papers.

Telecom Lesotho is the national telephone and Internet provider. In 2014, mobile phone use outweighed landline use. In the same year there were an estimated 102,000 Internet users, representing about 5 percent of the population.

SOCIAL DEVELOPMENT

Standard of Living

Lesotho ranked 162nd out of 187 countries on the 2014 United Nations Human Development Index, which measures quality of life and standard of living indicators.

Lesotho has one of the highest rates of HIV/AIDS infection in the world; as of 2014, nearly one-quarter of Lesotho's adult population is estimated to be HIV positive. The impact of HIV/AIDS shows in the country's human index statistics. The average life expectancy in Lesotho is 52 years (2015 estimate).

Water Consumption

According to 2015 statistics from the World Health Organization, approximately 81 percent of the population has access to improved drinking water, while an estimated 18 percent of the population has access to improved sanitation. Lesotho has abundant water resources—consumption is less than total availability—and the company has diverted water from its mountains to South Africa. Inadequate sanitation and clean water facilities remain a concern, and are primary contributors to poverty in the country.

Education

Lesotho has the oldest formal education system in Africa. Founded by French missionaries, the educational system was financially supported by British colonial bureaucrats after 1868, and is still maintained through a tense balance between churches and government administration. Because young boys are sent to watch herds while the girls attend school, Lesotho is also one of the few countries in the world where the literacy rate among women is significantly higher than that among men.

Over the years, the Basotho government and educational department have made generally ineffective efforts to wrest control of the churches that control them. A change in the law in 2000 provided free education for the first seven years of school, starting with first grade. The Ministry of Education has announced plans to extend compulsory primary education from seven to ten years.

Secondary education can be attained through a general course of education, a three-year course to obtain the Junior's Certificate, and then a two-year course to receive the Cambridge Overseas School Certificate, or technical or vocational training.

Students may receive a tertiary level degree at the National University of Lesotho (NUL), or at one of the numerous specialized degree institutions in Lesotho, including one of two National Teacher Training Colleges (NTTC), Lerotholi Polytechnic, the National Health Training College (NHTC), one of several nursing colleges, and the Lesotho Agricultural College (LAC).

As part of the government's aggressive campaign to combat the HIV/AIDS epidemic in Lesotho, primary school curricula now includes instruction in HIV/AIDS awareness and prevention. Lesotho has one of the highest literacy rates in Africa. In 2015, the country's adult literacy rate was estimated at 79 percent.

Women's Rights

Women's rights are still quite limited in some facets of Lesotho life. While the constitution outlaws rape and sexual abuse, occurrences are frequent. The punishment for rape is a minimum sentence of five years in prison, but most tried and convicted cases receive only this minimum sentence, regardless of the severity of the crime. Still, many cases are tried each year and convictions are common. Rape still pervades society, with reported cases on the rise. Many attribute this increase to a rise in unemployment, as increased layoffs often correlate with increased violence against women nationwide. The most common victims of rape are young virgin girls who, according to superstition, can cure a man of AIDS. As a result, younger and younger women are falling prey to both the sexual abuse and infection.

Prostitution also contributes to the high rates of HIV and AIDS among the women of Lesotho. It is a common practice for women of rural Lesotho to leave their homes to migrate to Maseru for work in the textile and garment factories. However, wages at these factories are often non-negotiable and barely enough to sustain the woman alone. Coupled with financial demands from families back home, this dire situation forces many women to find other means of income, the most common of which is prostitution. Often, women make arrangements with several men in Maseru to offer them sex in return for financial support. Common in the poorer neighborhoods around Maseru, this transactional sex has furthered the HIV/AIDS epidemic and has even brought it to rural Lesotho, where unwitting husbands contract the disease during visits to their wives.

In addition Lesotho has increasingly become a hotbed for sex trafficking. Basotho men, women, and children in particular are often exploited for both sex and labor. Although the government has made gestures toward combating the problem, substantial action has yet to be taken. A 2011 anti-trafficking law, for instance, has yet to be enacted.

Between husbands and wives, abuse and sexual assault are also illegal, though they are filed as general assault. Such abuse is commonly left unreported by most women. A man dominates most family affairs and can determine the sexual activities of his wife. Generally, condoms are not used or available, so frequent pregnancy and HIV/AIDS infections occur. Because of these limited freedoms and sexual exploitation, 50 percent of the women between the ages of 15 and 24 are infected with HIV/AIDS in the early 21st century. This has contributed significantly to the number of AIDS orphans in the country and is threatening the traditional family structure.

Furthermore, married women under traditional Lesotho law are considered minors until the death of their husbands. Thus, all constitutional provisions for their property and custody rights are null and void in most households. Most women are aware of their constitutional rights to property and child custody, but still do not protest the commonly practiced cultural rights. The constitution does protect the rights of women to work and earn wages, and women have a strong representation in national politics. Furthermore, the government established the Ministry of Gender, Youth, Sports, and Recreation to educate women on their traditional and formal legal rights, and how to reconcile the two.

Health Care

Lesotho's top health care priority is the prevention, diagnosis, and treatment of HIV/AIDS, which has infected approximately one-quarter of the country's population. In association with this effort, Lesotho focuses its health care on basic family, prenatal, infant, and childcare. Lesotho has also prioritized programs to prevent and treat tuberculosis.

The country has a centralized, government-run network of hospitals, clinics, and health centers available to most of the population. This network includes a flight service to transport doctors to the most remote mountainous areas. With financial support from the government, Christian Health Association provides most of the primary health care services in the country's less-accessible rural areas. Patients requiring the most specialized care are taken to South African hospitals.

Lesotho also has a strong market in traditional medicines, including the use of indigenous medicinal plants like wormwood, bitter aloe, wild sugar bush, and parsnip tree.

GOVERNMENT

Structure

After being established as a kingdom in the early 19th century, Lesotho underwent a long period of foreign rule. Repeated losses to the Boers (South African farmers of Dutch extraction) prompted

Lesotho's founding king to seek protection from the British government in 1868. Only three years later, the British relinquished control of the territory to South Africa, but took it back after the 1880 war with the Boers.

Basotho leaders formed the Basotholand National Council in 1910, petitioning the British government for semi-autonomous status in the aftermath of World War II. Lesotho gained its independence as Basotholand, a parliamentary constitutional monarchy on the British model, in 1966. The government changed the name of the country soon thereafter.

After a 1970 election defeat, Lesotho's first prime minister suspended the constitution and expelled the king. A 1986 coup overthrew the government, possibly with assistance from South Africa, which had imposed sanctions based on Lesotho's criticism of the apartheid system. Another coup in 1991 sent the king into exile. Negotiations brought the king back in 1992, and elections resumed.

After rebel violence in 1994, King Letsie dissolved parliament and attempted to claim absolute authority over the government. Bowing to international pressure a short time later, the king reinstated the constitution and abdicated in favor of Moshoeshoe II. Moshoeshoe's death in a 1996 auto accident put Letsie back on the throne.

Civil violence continued through the end of the 1990s, resulting in the entrance of South African troops to defend Lesotho's ruling party, and a postponement of elections scheduled for 2000. Since that time, Lesotho appears to have recovered from the instability of the 20th century. The 2002 elections went off as planned and both the monarchy and parliamentary branches of government appear to have accepted the terms of the constitution.

Although peaceful parliamentary elections took place in 2002, the National Assembly elections of 2007 generated much controversy, despite their validation by international observers. Disputes over the allocation of parliamentary seats sparked massive protest rallies that disrupted commerce and transportation in the

capital. Maseru also experienced unrest in the aftermath of government efforts to evict unlicensed street vendors from the capital's business district. The 2012 and 2015 election, although tense, took place largely without incident.

The parliament consists of a 33-member Senate, with 22 chiefs and 11 members chosen by the ruling party; and a 120 member Assembly, with 80 members elected by direct popular vote to five-year terms, and 40 members elected by proportional vote. The office of chief of state (the monarchy) is hereditary.

Political Parties

Although numerous political parties exist in Lesotho, for years it was considered a one-party state. The Lesotho Congress for Democracy continues to control power in the country, however in recent years it has been challenged by the All Basotho Convention. Today, the Democratic Congress retains power through a coalition government built with several small parties. Other parties include the Communist Party of Lesotho, the Alliance of Congress Parties, the National Progressive Party, and the Lesotho Workers' Party.

Local Government

Lestho is divided into ten administrative regions. Local government is organized into 128 community councils, ten district councils, and one municipal council. The country held its first elections for local government positions in 2005. Political power and administrative authority in the country remain highly centralized.

Judicial System

Traditional forms of law exist alongside a more Westernized legal system in Lesotho. Non-traditional laws are a combination of Roman, Dutch, and English law, while traditional laws are rooted in the histories of given ethnic groups. Local and central courts adjudicate on a regional level, while the high court oversees issues related to federal laws. Many judges in Lesotho's judicial system are of South African descent. Efforts to further develop the country's laws and courts continue.

Taxation

Lesotho's taxes are high in sum, and consist of a top personal income tax rate of 35 percent, and a more moderate corporate tax rate of 25 percent (excluding agricultural and manufacturing companies, who are subject to a 10 percent tax rate). Other taxes levied include a value-added tax (VAT, a tax on the purchase of goods and services) and a dividends tax.

Armed Forces

Armed forces in Lesotho consist of the Lesotho Defence Force and the national police service. The national defense force consists of several service branches, including an army and air force. There is no conscription, and the age for voluntary military service is between 18 and 24 years of age. The primary functions of the armed forces are national protection and the prevention of crime and illegal weapons movement and trade along the border. In recent years, the armed forces have also focuses on social development within the country.

Foreign Policy

Lesotho is a landlocked nation located amid the only mountain ranges in South Africa. The Drakensberg and Maluti ranges dominate most of Lesotho, and extend into South Africa. The mountains to the east, and the Mohokare (or Caledon) River to the west, form the nation's natural boundaries. Lesotho was originally founded as an entity separate from South Africa in 1843, when the leader of the Basotho people, King Moshoeshoe I, lead his people into the mountain sanctuary. There, he was able to protect his kingdom from the ever-encroaching conflicts among the Boer (Dutch colonists or descendents), British, and other Bantu tribes vying for power over the region. Through strategic geographic location and diplomatic relations with England, Moshoeshoe was able to keep his land free from invasion. On October 4, 1966, Lesotho achieved independence and instituted a constitutional monarchy run by a prime minister, with the king as the symbolic head of state.

Lesotho is completely surrounded by South Africa. Thus, Lesotho has maintained strong political ties and trade relations with the nation heading into the 21st century. As part of this trade relationship, Lesotho exploits is most prized natural resource, water, from the Orange River to supply South Africa with water and electricity. According to the 1986 Lesotho Highlands Water Project (LHWP), Lesotho agreed to a thirty-year contract to extract fresh water from the river and export it to major South African cities. The profits from this project have allowed Lesotho to gain near complete self-sufficiency in supplying its own electricity and food. It exports some power and food to South Africa, as well. Another key export to South Africa is migratory labor based on the farming seasons and mining needs.

Lesotho has strong trade ties with the United States, and became the largest supplier among all sub-Saharan African nations of textiles to the US in the early 21st century. In 2007, the U.S.-run Millennium Challenge Corporation (MCC) also gave Lesotho $362.5 million (USD) in developmental funding. Lesotho is a member state of the United Nations (UN), African Union (AU), the Non-Aligned Movement (NAM), the South African Development Committee (SADC), the Organization of African Unity (OAC), the World Trade Organization (WTO), and the South African Customs Union (SACU), among other organizations. Canada, Libya, Ireland, the US, the European Union (EU), China, and South Africa all have diplomatic missions in Lesotho. The UN also has a strong presence in the nation.

Human Rights Profile

International human rights law insists that states respect civil and political rights, and promote an individual's economic, social, and cultural rights. The United Nations (UN) Universal Declaration of Human Rights (UDHR) is recognized as the standard for international human rights. Its authors sought the counsel of the world's great thinkers, philosophers, and religious leaders, and were careful to create a document that reflects the core values shared by every world culture. (To read this document or view the articles relating to cultural human rights, visit http://www.udhr.org/UDHR/default.htm.)

In general, human rights in Lesotho are guaranteed and protected by the government. Basic freedoms such as freedom of association, religion, movement, property ownership, fair elections, and privacy are protected in the constitution and are generally upheld in practice. The 2002 and 2008 national and local elections were considered free and fair by most of the international community, and opposition groups and minorities are accounted for in the nation's national assembly. This is due to the 1998 Interim Political Authority's decision to add forty seats to the Lesotho National Assembly that can only be filled by opposition and minority groups. As such, the results of each election have been little contested.

Occasional violence committed by national and local police forces, limited freedom of speech, and slow and inefficient legal processes still hamper Lesotho's overall human rights record. Following a surprise attack on government officials and their homes by unknown gunmen in 2008, the government reacted viciously to all suspected perpetrators. Suspects were limited to opposition party members and without much substantial evidence many suspects were arbitrarily arrested, tortured, and killed.

Prison conditions have been criticized by international monitoring agencies for being overcrowded, deteriorating, and lacking proper bedding and nutrition. However, the government has improved the healthcare available for convicted felons, including medical examinations. Overall, the judiciary rights of Lesotho citizens closely resemble those of most Western nations. Right to trial, habeas corpus, and legal representation are all built into the constitution and are generally practiced when resources are available.

Other complaints against the government have come from professors at the National University of Lesotho, who claimed they were punished by the university at the behest of the government for portraying the Lesotho government in a negative light. Government transparency was also criticized as non-existent, and nepotism (favoritism for relatives and friends) was evident in branches of the government in the early 21st century, particularly the prime

ministry. This resulted in many foreign agencies criticizing and doubting the legitimacy of the government to work in the interest of the public.

Finally, as the HIV/AIDS epidemic has grown substantially in Lesotho in the past decades, the government has been forced into taking action on perhaps the nation's most compelling human rights issue. With over a quarter of the adult population suffering from HIV/AIDS, leaders have come to the realization that they are battling an epidemic that has devastated families and increased the orphan population. The National AIDS Secretariat was established as a branch of the government in 2005, and charged with the task of helping infected individuals and those around them better understand the implications of the disease.

ECONOMY

Overview of the Economy

Lesotho's economy relies on exports (mainly water) to South Africa. The country's abundant water resources are also important to the production of electricity; Lesotho generates enough for its own needs, as well as a surplus, which is exported. The Lesotho Highlands Water Project, a large-scale water and hydroelectricity export program, generates significant revenue for a country that has few natural resources other than its mountain streams. The project utilizes the headwaters of the Orange River system to export water to industrial areas concentrated in and around the South African capital of Johannesburg. Ancillary dams generate hydroelectricity, which is also exported.

The textile industry has also played an increasingly significant role in the capital's economy. Many women have migrated to Maseru to find employment at the various Taiwanese-owned garment factories located on the outskirts of the capital. Maseru's modest manufacturing base also consists of processing facilities for wool, hides, grains, footwear, and food and beverage products.

Lesotho is a member of the Southern African Customs Union (SACU), which facilitates trade between African countries in the region. As part of the Rand Monetary Area, Lesotho uses the South African Rand as well as its own currency, the loti. In 2014, Lesotho's GDP was estimated to be $2.1 billion (USD), or $2,800 (USD) per capita.

Industry

Lesotho's largest industries are food and beverage processing (including milling and canning) leather and jute processing, handicrafts, construction, and tourism. In 1998, the Lesotho government completed work on a hydropower facility that allows the country to sell water to South Africa.

A small, but rapidly growing textile industry has also established itself in the country, although changes in the international regulation of garment manufacturers may have a negative impact on textiles in Lesotho.

Labor

In 2014, the labor force totaled 894,400, with the majority engaged in agricultural occupations. In fact, an estimated 86 percent of the population is involved in subsistence agriculture. The unemployment rate was recorded as 28 percent in 2014. That same year, only an estimated 14 percent of the work force was employed in the industrial and services sectors.

Energy/Power/Natural Resources

Lesotho's mountainous landscape hides caches of diamonds, sand, clay, and building stone. During the 20th century, Lesotho's most valuable natural resource was the agricultural and grazing land that sustained the Basotho and the miners who worked in South Africa's diamond mines. In recent years, however, Lesotho has produced revenue by selling portions of its ample water supply to the more developed cities in neighboring South Africa (through the Lesotho Highlands Water Project).

While the project accounts for a significant portion of Lesotho's gross domestic product (GDP), it has had some negative impact on Maseru, where water shortages have become common. Periodic drought conditions have strained a water supply already diminished by exporting, as well as increased demand for water by Maseru's own growing industrial sector.

Forestry

Forestry is not a significant source of income for Lesotho, although efforts to develop further the country's wood products sector continue. Less than two percent of the country is forested.

Mining/Metals

In 2009, diamond production contributed an estimated seven percent of Lesotho's gross domestic product and employed approximately 1,300 people. Diamonds are mined in Lesotho with the assistance of the UK-based Kopane Diamond Development Company. In addition to diamond reserves, the country is thought to have some deposits of minerals in its northern region.

Agriculture

Subsistence agriculture and herds of livestock still form the foundation of economic life in Lesotho. Approximately 86 percent of Basotho rely on some form of agriculture to feed their households, and more than half of the country's income is derived from agricultural products. Farmers traditionally grow corn, wheat, pulses, sorghum, and barley. In recent years, drought and HIV/AIDS have significantly decreased agricultural production throughout the country, adding to poverty and food shortages.

Animal Husbandry

Cattle, goats, and sheep are the primary livestock bred in Lesotho. Sheep and goats, introduced in the 19th century, are kept for their wool and mohair, respectively. Meat from livestock is mostly used for domestic or household consumption.

Tourism

Lesotho has a small tourist industry that has regained its footing since the political situation in the country stabilized in 2002. Tourists are drawn to the country's natural beauty, including its dramatic mountains and valleys, and rich cultural heritage. Nonetheless, the country's health problems and security concerns have limited the development of the tourist sector. Tourism spending in Lesotho increased two percent in 2009 and tourism contributed a record 15 percent of GDP in 2010. The government continues to invest in

roads and improve other infrastructure in order to attract more travelers to the country.

Kristen Pappas, Amy Witherbee, Beverly Ballaro

DO YOU KNOW?

- Many Basotho men and women wear traditional garb including the cone-shaped straw Basotho hat, which features a decorative topknot. The design of the Basotho hat, known locally as a mokorotlo, is said to have been inspired by the appearance of Qiloane, a cone-shaped pinnacle at the natural fortress of Thaba Bosiu, located about 24 kilometers (15 miles) east of Maseru.

- Maseru's most distinctive landmark is a large structure featuring a thatched roof in the shape of a traditional Basotho hat. The building, in which traditional local handicrafts are sold, serves as key point of orientation in the capital. Destroyed in the civil unrest of 1998, it was rebuilt in 2001.

- At the Masitise Cave House near Quthing in southern Lesotho, visitors can see dinosaur footprints dating back 180 million years.

Bibliography

James Bainbridge, et al. "South Africa, Lesotho, & Swaziland." Oakland, CA: *Lonely Planet*, 2012.

David B. Coplan. "In the Time of Cannibals: The World Music of South Africa's Basotho Migrants." London: *University of Chicago Press*, 1994.

Tim Couzens. "Murder at Morija: Faith, Mystery, And Tragedy on an African Mission." *University of Virginia Press*, 2005.

Elizabeth Eldredge. "Power in Colonial Africa: Conflict and Discourse in Lesotho, 1870-1960 (Africa and the Diaspora)." *University of Wisconsin Press*, 2007.

Marc Epprecht and Andrea Nattrass. "This Matter of Women Is Getting Very Bad: Gender, Development and Politics in Colonial Lesotho." *University of Kwazulu Natal Press*, 2000.

K. Limakatso Kendall. "Basali! Stories by and About Women in Lesotho." *University of Kwazulu Natal Press*, 1995.

Robin Meakins. "…And None Were Innocent: Unreliable Memories of Lesotho's Struggle Against Apartheid." Indiana: *AuthorHouse*, 2007.

Mpho Matsepo Nthunya and K. Limakatso Kendall. "Singing Away the Hunger: The Autobiography of an African Woman," Indiana: *Indiana University Press*, 1996.

Works Cited

"Background Note: Lesotho." January 2009. *U.S. Department of State: Bureau of African Affairs.* http://www.state.gov/r/pa/ei/bgn/2831.htm

"Country Profiles: Lesotho." BBC News: *Country Profiles.* http://news.bbc.co.uk/2/hi/africa/country_profiles/1063291.stm#media

"Customs of Lesotho." MSN Encarta: *Sidebar.* http://encarta.msn.com/sidebar_631522223/customs_of_lesotho.html

"HIV/AIDS Health Profile." September 2008. *USAID.* http://www.usaid.gov/our_work/global_health/aids/Countries/africa/lesotho_profile.pdf

"How Our Wares Are Made." *Lesotho Craft Works.* http://www.lesothocraftworks.com/how-our-wares-are-made

"Lesiba." Encyclopedia Britannica. 2009. *Encyclopedia Britannica Online.* http://www.britannica.com/EBchecked/topic/337095/lesiba.

"Lesotho Artist Simon Ralitsebe and others." *Sotho: The Destiny of a People.* http://basotho.wordpress.com/2004/03/03/lesotho-artist-simon-ralitsebe-and-others/

"Lesotho Facts." *National Geographic: Travel & Cultures.* http://travel.nationalgeographic.com/places/countries/country_lesotho.html

"Lesotho gardens relieve food crisis." June 2008. *BBC World News.* http://news.bbc.co.uk/2/hi/africa/7432972.stm

"Lesotho." March 2008. *U.S. Department of State: Bureau of Democracy, Human Rights, and Labor.* http://www.state.gov/g/drl/rls/hrrpt/2007/100488.htm

"Lesotho." *USAID: HIV/AIDS Countries.* http://www.usaid.gov/our_work/global_health/aids/Countries/africa/lesotho.html

"Lesotho: Country Reports on Human Rights Practices." February 2005. *U.S. Department of State.* http://www.state.gov/g/drl/rls/hrrpt/2004/41610.htm

"Lesotho: Districts & Urban Areas." *City Population.* http://www.citypopulation.de/Lesotho.html

"Morija Arts and Cultural Festival." http://www.morijafest.com/index.html

"Morjja Museum and Archives." *Travel Maps of the World.* http://travel.mapsofworld.com/lesotho/tourist-attractions-in-maseru/morija-museum-and-archives.html

"Sehlabathebe National Park." *UNESCO World Heritage Centre.* http://whc.unesco.org/en/tentativelists/5391/

"Thaba-Bosiu National Monument." *UNESCO World Heritage Centre.* http://whc.unesco.org/en/tentativelists/5392/

"The Basotho Blankets." *The Global Travel & Tourism Partnership.* http://www.gttp.org/docs/casestudies/2006/sa.pdf

Peter Magubane and Alan Mountain. "Vanishing Cultures of South Africa." *Struik Publishers,* 1998. http://books.google.com/books?id=eEkafdK0SxcC&pg=PA28&lpg=PA28&dq=basotho+marriage+ceremony&source=bl&ots=97LRIBeRhp&sig=KqWy145jUhPbaPlNuR3qXoA21ro&hl=en&ei=KqPPSY-1H8f-vnQe47K3lCQ&sa=X&oi=book_result&resnum=1&ct=result#PPP1,M1

A young girl wearing the makeup of Nosy Be, Madagascar.

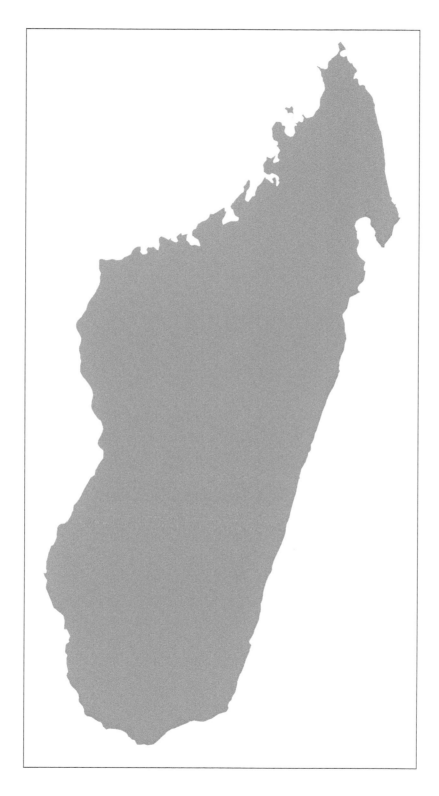

MADAGASCAR

Introduction

Located in the Indian Ocean, just east of Mozambique, Madagascar is the world's fourth largest island and one of the most environmentally complex places on the planet. Madagascar became one of the last places in the world to become colonized when the French government took possession of the island in 1896. Less than 70 years later, Madagascar regained its independence. Since 1970, the citizens of Madagascar have survived the tumultuous early years of independence to form a stable government.

The arts in Madagascar show both African and Indonesian influences. In music, dance rhythms predominate, and melodies and percussion are woven together using the flute, whistles, and the cordophone or lokanga voatavo. Malagasy musicians also use the kabosy, a small, box-shaped guitar, and the valiha, a long, slender harp-like instrument with twenty-eight strings. Another hallmark of Malagasy culture is kabary, a traditional form of oral storytelling and speaking. Begun as a form of political debate, kabary is now an important form of entertainment and a source of inspiration for the Malagasy literary tradition.

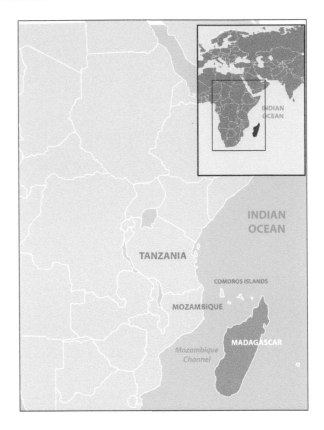

GENERAL INFORMATION

Official Language: French and Malagasy
Population: 23,812,681 (2015 estimate)

Currency: Malagasy ariary
Coins: The Malagasy ariary is divided into five iraimbilanja; coins are available in denominations of 1 and 2 iraimbilanja and 1, 2, 4, 5, 10, 20, and 50 ariary.
Land Area: 581,540 square kilometers (224,533 square miles)
Water Area: 5,501 square kilometers (2,123 square miles)
National Motto: "Tanindrazana, Fahafahana, Fandrosoana" ("Fatherland, Liberty, Progress")
National Anthem: "Ry Tanindraza nay malala ô" ("Oh, Our Beloved Fatherland")
Capital: Antananarivo
Time Zone: GMT +3
Flag Description: The flag of Madagascar is a tricolor design that consists of a white field on the hoist (left) side, and two equal, horizontal bands of red over green in the fly (area furthest from the flagpole). The white field is two-thirds the size of the other field. The origins of the colors have been attributed to historical Malagasy kingdoms.

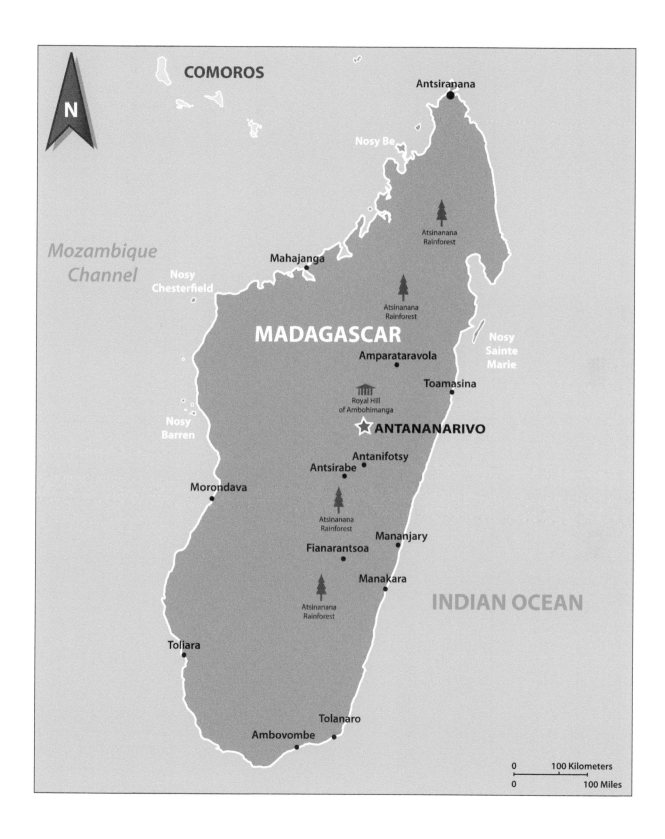

Principal Cities by Population (2012):

- Antananarivo (1,800,000)
- Toamasina (236,784)
- Antsirabe (205,811)
- Fianarantsoa (194,287)
- Mahajanga (174,023)
- Toliara (128,629)

Population

The inhabitants of Madagascar are known as Malagasy. As remote as the island of Madagascar has often seemed to outsiders, its lush forests and ample coastline have been home to more cultures and ethnicities than scholars have been able to trace. Although some earlier culture may have existed on Madagascar, most of the island's first people emigrated from Africa, Southeast Asia, and Indonesia 1,500 to 2,000 years ago. Blending cultural practices from all of these locations with influences from Arab traders, European pirates, and French colonists, Malagasy history blurs the boundaries between old and new, native and newcomer.

Madagascar has eighteen different ethnic groups. The Malagasy, the indigenous people of Madagascar, are of Indonesian, East African and Arab ancestry, and are divided into a number of tribes. Ethnic groups frequently intermarry, and the native culture is becoming more homogeneous as a result. In the central plateau, the most common ethnic groups are the Merina and Betsileo. Antananarivo is also home to a large non-indigenous population, including French, Indonesians, and people of the Comoro Islands.

About 65 percent of its population lives in rural areas, where most major roads are unpaved. Antananarivo is the capital and largest city, and its metropolitan area is home to nearly 1.8 million. As of 2015, the country had a population growth rate of approximately 2.5 percent.

Languages

The official languages of Madagascar are French and Malagasy. The majority of residents speak Malagasy, which is divided into at least 10 regional dialects. The Malagasy dialect of Antankarana is the most commonly spoken language in Antananarivo, followed by French and Indonesian.

Native People & Ethnic Groups

The population is divided into 18 tribes, based on the boundaries of old kingdoms. Within these tribes, ethnicities blend, but some common regional traits may be found. The areas around Merina and Betsileo, for instance, are home to a primarily Malayo-Indonesian based people. In Betsimisaraka, Tsimihety, Antaisaka, and Sakalava, most people are characterized as Cotiers (a blend of African, Malayo-Indonesian, and Arab ancestry). Other Malagasy ancestors hail from France, India, and the islands of Comoros between Madagascar and Mozambique. In addition, Madagascar has a significant Creole population (those born in the country but of African or French ancestry). Other ethnic minorities in Madagascar include people of Chinese and Indian descent.

Religions

About 41 percent of Madagascar's population practices Christianity, and there is a growing population of Muslims (approximately seven percent of the total population). Even among these portions of the population, however, traditional beliefs and practices remain important. Just over half of Malagasy adhere to traditional beliefs exclusively. Ancestor worship plays a large role in these beliefs, and burial tombs are a major feature of the landscape surrounding Antananarivo.

Climate

Except for its southern tip, Madagascar is located in a tropical climate that harbors six microclimates: the North, the Western Dry Forest, the East, the Southern Rainforest, and the Southern Dry Forest. While the island is best known for the rainforests in the east and south, the dry forests in the west are striking for their eroded limestone peaks and the sparse remnants of ancient deciduous forest.

The rainy season lasts from December until April, drenching the island with 355 centimeters (340 inches) of rainfall each year on wetter parts of the island, and as little as 30 centimeters (12 inches) of rain in drier areas. The dry season from May to November brings average midday temperatures of 25 degrees Celsius (77 degrees Fahrenheit) in the mountains and 30 degrees Celsius (86 degrees Fahrenheit) along the coast.

Because of its location in the Indian Ocean, Madagascar is prone to hurricanes from November to March. Despite the tropical climate prevalent on much of the island, Madagascar is also prone to occasional droughts, exacerbated by deforestation on the island. In 2004, the Indian Ocean tsunami also hit Madagascar's eastern shore, wreaking havoc in the towns of Manakara, Sambava, and Vohemar, but taking no lives.

ENVIRONMENT & GEOGRAPHY

Topography

Madagascar is over 1,580 kilometers (1,000 miles) long and 570 kilometers (350 miles) wide. A large mountain chain runs the length of the island, soaring to a height of 2,876 meters (9,435 feet) on Mount Maromokofro on the northern part of the island.

Antananarivo is located in Madagascar's central plateau and is built on the slopes of the Great Cliff of Angavo, a ridge that rises to 1,430 meters (4,692 feet). The central plateau contains rocky volcanic soil blended with low-lying marsh vegetation. Antananarivo sits alongside a rift valley to the east, which contains Lac Alaotra, the largest body of water on the island at 40 kilometers (25 miles) in length.

Isolated by the Tsaratanana mountain chain, the northern region of the country experiences the island's most extreme weather, creating a mixed landscape of barren promontories, sunken lagoons, and high altitude rainforest. To the east and south of the mountains, the land flattens toward coastal plains spotted by rivers, caves, and waterfalls. Part of an ancient

rainforest still thrives in these areas. Dry forests cover the western coast and southernmost point of the island.

Plants & Animals

Madagascar's biodiversity is world-renowned. Isolated off the coast of Africa, many unique plant and animal species have developed and been preserved on the island. Dense, vibrant rainforests once covered large swaths of the country. Today, Madagascar's rainforests provide a unique home for lemurs, geckos, medicinal periwinkles, sifakas, and octopus trees.

Although more than 50 percent of the island's rainforest has been destroyed for human habitation or for short-term farming, the country is still home to 10,000 species of plants, many of which can only be found in Madagascar.

The country also boasts 400 species of reptiles and amphibians, 1,000 species of orchids, and a host of birds and animals that exist only on the island. Unfortunately, Madagascar's pervasive

Lemurs are a species of primates common in Madagascar.

The flowers of the Madagascar rainforest come in an abundant and unique variety.

poverty and huge population growth has provided scant protection for the country's ecology, and many species are on the endangered list.

CUSTOMS & COURTESIES

Greetings

Madagascar has two official languages, French and Malagasy. Since more than 90 percent of Malagasy residents speak French as their primary language, greetings are usually offered in French. Common expressions of greeting include "Bonjour" ("Hello"), typically spoken in the morning or afternoon, or "Bonsoir" ("Good evening") and "Bonne nuit" ("Goodnight"). The Malagasy language is derived from the tribal languages of the Merina people and bears little relation to the other languages used in the country. A basic greeting among Malagasy speakers is "Manahoana" ("Hello"); the word "Veloma" ("Take care") is also used as a common greeting

or farewell. The Malagasy also use the phrase "Comment allez-vous?" ("How are you"), though the phrase is usually used among close friends.

In general, the handshake is the most common form of greeting, though it is not uncommon for close associates to kiss one another on the cheek. When shaking hands, some Malagasy will place their opposite hand on the elbow of the person they are greeting. Family members and close friends may embrace one another as a display of affection.

Gestures & Etiquette

As in many cultures, pointing with the index finger is considered impolite in Madagascar. The Malagasy point toward a person or object with the knuckle of the index finger, which is considered more polite. The concept of personal space, especially during conversation, is lessened in Malagasy culture, and Malagasy stand close to one another when speaking. It is also common for close acquaintances and family members to have physical contact while conversing, such as the touching of the arms, elbows or shoulders. In addition, backing away from a speaker is considered unfriendly, and may be taken as a sign of disrespect.

Eating/Meals

The Malagasy eat three meals a day, roughly corresponding to the European traditions of breakfast, lunch, and dinner. The morning meal is generally light, often consisting of reheated rice and meat with coffee and fresh fruit. The largest meal of the day is typically served at midday and usually consists of roasted meat and vegetable dishes served with rice. The Malagasy prepare light meals in the evening, usually after dark, which in many families consist of leftovers from the afternoon meal.

Food is an important aspect of Malagasy culture and eating meals with friends and family is considered an important part of maintaining social and familial bonds. Feasts and holidays are always marked by a family meal, many of which involve the preparation of special dishes. It is acceptable for both men and women to consume alcohol with meals. Beer and wine are also commonly served in social situations and at business meetings held in the afternoon or evening.

It is customary for the eldest family members to be served first at family meals. When passing drinks or food across the table, it is customary to use both hands, with one hand holding the opposite wrist to avoid spilling. People usually use their right hand to pass food, as some Malagasy are Muslim. It is considered unclean to handle food with one's left hand in Muslim culture because it is associated with the cleansing of the body. Traditionally, Malagasy people sit on a thatched floor mat when eating.

The Malagasy view of time and punctuality differs from that of Western cultures. While urban Malagasy may be more precise in their time management, rural Malagasy often tell time by the relative position of the sun. For this reason, the Malagasy use the expression "Fotoana gasy" ("Sun time") to refer to the perception of time outside urban areas.

Visiting

When visiting a Malagasy home, it is considered customary to bring a small gift such as flowers, candies, or pastries. Small cash gifts may be appropriate if the visit involves a holiday or family event. Most Malagasy are poor and it is considered impolite to call attention to perceived disparities in wealth and/or status. It is also considered polite to refuse any food offered when visiting a Malagasy home, though guests are not required to finish all the food offered.

LIFESTYLE

Family

Malagasy society is based on an extended family system, with two or three generations living in close proximity and sharing domestic duties. Among the Merina tribe, these kin groups, called karazana, involve several families who may be interrelated. Within a karazana, society is divided into families, which include individuals with blood or direct marriage relationships. Often, these families share common land linked by a burial space for shared ancestors. Merina men and women tend to marry distant cousins from within their karazana to ensure that ownership of the land is kept within the same kin group. The next subset of society is the nuclear family, consisting of a couple and their children. Family structure is traditionally patriarchal, and eldest males are typically given preference and treated with respect.

Traditionally, the social structure of the Merina and other Malagasy tribes was hierarchal, with social privilege and authority based on caste and gender. The concept of "hasina," which is a type of life-generating power, also figures prominently because it is used to justify the difference in status between social castes. It is believed that hasina is passed down from parent to offspring, and it is this force that makes life possible. The Merina, for instance, are divided into nobles and common people, according to the belief that certain families and individuals have greater social influence because of uneven distribution of hasina within society. Because of the hasina system, the Malagasy revere their ancestors. The urbanization of Madagascar has begun to deteriorate the karazana and hasina systems as financial dominance has begun to supplant birthright as the determinant of status.

Housing

The traditional Malagasy home is a small one- or two-bedroom rectangular building usually with a thatched roof and earthen floors. In rural areas, families may construct their houses of earthen blocks, while brick and stone are more common in urban areas. In parts of the country vulnerable to flooding, it is common for homes to be constructed on short stilts. Wattle-and-daub housing, in which wooden construction is packed with mud or clay, is still used by some poor Malagasy communities, though many are now shifting to other inexpensive housing materials.

Estate houses in urban Madagascar are often two or more stories, with the kitchen at the roof of the home and the bedrooms on the middle or bottom level. This traditional arrangement is similar to upscale housing in Indonesia and is an artifact of Madagascar's Asian heritage. In Antananarivo, many residents live in one-bedroom apartments or in shared housing complexes, with several families living in adjacent units. Overcrowding is a major problem in Antananarivo and surrounding areas, where the rocky terrain has made it difficult to construct enough housing to accommodate the growing population.

Food

Malagasy cuisine is a unique blend of African and Asian influences. Rice, a principal crop, is the staple of the Malagasy diet and the base for most dishes. The Malagasy cook rice in a pot, purposefully burning some of the rice at the bottom of the pan and then removing the unburned rice from the top. The burned rice at the bottom may be mixed with water and cooked into a beverage called ranonapango.

For the morning and midday meals, Malagasy often serve varenga, which is a simple dish of slow-cooked pork or beef shredded and served with rice. Varenga is generally flavored only with salt, pepper, garlic, and parsley. Some recipes call for a small amount of vanilla used to flavor the meat. For the midday and evening meals, roasted meats are commonly served. Roasted pork with cassava leaves is a popular entrée consisting of pork prepared with garlic, onion, and ginger, and served with mashed cassava leaves over rice. A similar dish is prepared using mashed cassava leaves, tomatoes, and roasted fish.

The national dish of Madagascar is romazava, a stew made from beef, pork and chicken cooked with tomatoes, cloves, garlic, and spinach. As with most dishes, romazava is served with rice and ranonapango. Another popular Malagasy stew, called lasopy, utilizes a meat stock made from boiled bones and includes a variety of vegetables, including carrot, turnip, string beans and tomatoes. Lasopy may also be served in a puréed form. For dessert, many Malagasy simply eat fresh fruit flavored with sugar and/or vanilla. Chocolate desserts are also popular in Madagascar because locally produced cocoa is high quality widely available at affordable prices. The Malagasy also make extensive use of vanilla bean, which is produced locally and shipped worldwide.

Life's Milestones

An estimated 41 percent of Malagasy—divided equally between the Catholic and Protestant faiths—follow Christian rites of passage, including communion, baptism and marriage. Another seven percent of the population is Muslim, and follows Islamic rituals and rites of passage. The remainder of the population, constituting the majority of Malagasy, follows indigenous beliefs mostly centered on ancestor worship.

An engagement party precedes the traditional Malagasy marriage, which marks the transition from childhood to adulthood. Both the bride and groom's families gather to celebrate the engagement with a festive celebration including music, dancing and a feast for friends and family. The groom traditionally brings gifts for the bride's family and presents the engagement ring to his future bride. Circumcision is another major rite of passage in Malagasy culture. Prior to the procedure, the family throws an overnight party and the child is taken to the hospital at dawn to be circumcised. When the child returns, friends and family present the child with gifts and food signifying the end of the celebration.

Reverence for one's ancestors is an important component of native Malagasy culture. Family members are buried in a family tomb and members of the family pay respect to their deceased ancestors regularly. The family tomb, or tombstone, is built by family members and renovated by subsequent generations. The appearance of the family tomb is a matter of family and personal pride. Each year, many Malagasy participate in the "famadiahana," which involves removing deceased family members from the tomb and wrapping the bodies in new shrouding.

CULTURAL HISTORY

Art

The woodcarving traditions of the Zafimaniry people are an important part of Madagascar's cultural heritage. The Zafimaniry live in villages scattered throughout southeast Madagascar, where they decorate any wooden surface in their homes. These ornate and elaborate carvings adorn anything from window trim to kitchen tables and chairs. The designs of the Zafimaniry are associated with the tribe's cultural and social beliefs. The "spider web" motif, for example, symbolizes the ties between family members, while other designs represent community integration and spiritual life.

In recent years, the woodworking traditions of the Zafimaniry have become threatened by deforestation and the loss of the trees traditionally used in Zafimaniry arts. In 2003, the United Nations Educational, Scientific, and Cultural Organization (UNESCO), which endeavors to protect living cultural heritage through inclusion on the Masterpieces of the Oral and Intangible Heritage of Humanity List, designated the woodcrafts of the Zafimaniry as an Intangible Cultural Heritage (ICH). Woodcarving also remains the primary source of income for the Zafimaniry.

Architecture

Malagasy tribes, who are descended from the African and Indonesian natives who originally inhabited the island, are famous for their funerary traditions and architecture, including the construction of elaborate tombs. The Mahafaly and Antandroy tribes, native to southern Madagascar, create stone tombs decorated with detailed paintings and carvings. Entire communities work together to construct a single tomb, which may take more than a year to complete. Mahafaly artists paint their tombs with depictions of the deceased person's life, while the Antandroy use symbolic decorative patterns. Both tribal groups adorn tombs with "alaolo," which are wooden plaques decorated with geometric designs and images of daily life and activities.

The Sakalava and Merina tribes of Madagascar changed their tomb design considerably after the arrival of the Europeans, who introduced advanced masonry to the island. Modern Sakalava and Merina tombs are constructed from brick and/or concrete. These tombs are decorated with geometric designs painted or carved on the exterior and interior. The Malagasy often associate the possession of livestock with wealth, and

it is therefore traditional to include depictions of livestock or bones and skins in burial tombs. As such, many tombs are decorated with the horns and skins of zebus, native cattle prized for their meat and labor.

Drama

There are three basic categories of performance art in Madagascar: works created by the Merina tribe that ruled Madagascar before the arrival of Europeans, works created by Malagasy artists in their native language with European influence, and French language plays created by immigrants or locals. One traditional form of theater, called hira-gasy, which emerged before the arrival of Europeans, involves a blend of song, dancing and improvisational theater. Hira-gasy was invented as a tool for fostering community integration and involvement and consisted of plays in which actors would perform scenes that illuminated local problems. In the 19th century, the hira-gasy enjoyed a renaissance as a popular form of entertainment for the Merina aristocracy.

In the 19th and early 20th centuries, popular theatrical productions were often written in the Malagasy language. This changed with the onset of French colonial control, after which most of the plays produced in Madagascar were written in French. By the late 20th century, Madagascar boasted a relatively large French language theater community working in both traditional and contemporary styles. In modern Madagascar, both Malagasy and French are spoken in theatrical productions.

Music

Madagascar's indigenous music is a reflection of the country's diverse cultural history. The most basic traditional music is polyharmonic singing, similar to that of South Africa. Folk instruments include the lokanga, a three-string fiddle, and a Marovany, a wooden box with strings on each side. A type of flute known as the sodina and a zither-like instrument known as the valiha are also used in traditional Malagasy music.

In Antananarivo, Western dance music, jazz, and R&B are popular. "Watcha watcha," a distinct brand of Malagasy pop music, combines a 6/8 rhythm with British techno, South Africa kwela and Mauritanian and Tanzanian sounds.

Literature

Because most of the earliest Malagasy stories and legends were passed on through oral tradition, few have been committed to paper. In the 19th century, a small number of Malagasy writers began to translate and transcribe these tribal stories and myths. Radama I (c. 1793–1828), the first king of Madagascar, is often credited with introducing written language (with the aid of Christian missionaries) to the Malagasy tribes in the early 19th century.

By the late 19th century, a variety of literature was being produced in Madagascar, ranging from sacred and religious texts to comedy and poetry. The nation's first newspaper appeared in the 1880s, followed by a proliferation of news media. Madagascar's first famous literary figure was Jean-Joseph Rabearivelo (1901–1937), a poet and playwright who wrote in both Malagasy and French. Rabearivelo's works feature elements of traditional mythology woven into modern themes. He is considered the first major French-language poet in Africa, and one of the more important modern African poets.

CULTURAL HISTORY

Arts & Entertainments

Traditional Malagasy culture derives from the artistic traditions of the native Malagasy tribes. While native dancing, music, and visual art are acknowledged as important components of the nation's cultural heritage, there are few resources or funding opportunities available for Malagasy artists. As such, the tourist trade is important for the survival of native artistic traditions. The Zafimaniry woodcarvers, for instance, make their living by selling carvings in local markets and to tourists.

While there are few funding opportunities for local artists, the central government supports the development and expansion of local art through museums and other artistic exhibitions. The Ministry of Sports, Culture, and Leisure is the governmental agency responsible for distributing the nation's limited arts funding. In addition, Antananarivo hosts the nation's premier artistic community, with a number of museums and private galleries highlighting native artwork.

In rural areas, the arts continue to play a traditional and spiritual role. Family and community celebrations, holidays, and spiritual activities are all accompanied by artistic performances. Music and dancing is an important part of the Malagasy rituals. Some songs and dances that have been passed down through generations are now considered a cherished part of Malagasy cultural heritage.

Cultural Sites & Landmarks

Centrally located on the island, the capital of Antananarivo is the cultural center of Madagascar. It is sometimes referred to as the "City of a Thousand Warriors" due to the number of guards historically assigned to guard it. Already a thriving major city prior to the colonial era of southern Africa, it is known for its range of architectural styles, from traditional and French colonial architecture, to modern and urban aesthetics. The city is home to the Rova of Antananarivo, a royal palace that is preparing for reconstruction due to a 1995 fire that destroyed all monuments except for the main structure, known as the "Queen's Palace." Other cultural landmarks include the Prime Minister's Palace, the artisans' market of Androvoahangy, and the Tsimbazaza Zoo and Cultural Museum.

The city of Fianarantsoa is considered the cultural and historical center of the Betsileo tribe, the third largest ethnic group in Madagascar. During the 19th century, the city served as the administrative capital of the Merina kingdom, which had conquered the Betsileo. The "old city" of Fianarantsoa was built during the French colonial period and still contains dozens of buildings from that era. The city is known today as the home of the nation's Protestant and Lutheran population, and as the wine capital of Madagascar.

Madagascar is also home to three World Heritage Sites as designated by UNESCO, which administers these cultural and natural sites through the World Heritage List. They include the Royal Hill of Ambohimanga, the Rainforests of Atsinanana, and Tsingy de Bemaraha Strict Nature Reserve. The Royal Hill of Ambohimanga is an archaeological site that contains a ruined royal city and numerous holy and burial remnants. It is considered the most significant symbol of the cultural identity of the Malagasy, and attracts pilgrims as a place of worship.

The Rainforests of Atsinanana is a collection of six national parks on the eastern side of the island. The area is home to thousands of endemic species, including more than 25 species of lemur, many of which are threatened by habitat loss. Scientists estimate that between 80 and 90 percent of the animals and plants in the Atsinanana forests are endemic to the region. Similar to the Rainforests of Atsinanana, the Tsingy de Bemaraha Strict Nature Reserve is renowned for its wildlife, specifically its wild bird and lemur populations. It is also recognized for its limestone landscapes and preserved mangrove forests.

Libraries & Museums

At the center of Antananarivo, the capital, is the Queen's Rova, a palace originally built by King Andrianjaka in the 1600s. The Rova was destroyed by the French Army in 1895, and suffered a fire in 1995. Despite ongoing reconstruction, it remains a popular tourist attraction, and houses a cultural museum dedicated to the history of Antananarivo and its monarchy. In addition, the zoological park at Tsimbazaza contains a cultural museum that provides visitors with an introduction to the history of the wildlife and native cultures of Madagascar. The University of Antananarivo, founded in 1955, houses the Museum of Art and Archaeology, which is a popular tourist attraction and introduces the unique art and history of the Malagasy.

The capital is also home to the national library, Bibliothèque Nationale de Madagascar, though the Ministry of the Interior serves as the legal depository.

Holidays

Madagascar celebrates a combination of Christian holidays, such as Easter and Christmas; national days such as Insurrection Day (March 29), in celebration of the Malagasy rebellion against the French; and traditionally based events such as the Donia, a music festival held in early summer.

The Malagasy also celebrate Organization of African Unity Day (May 25), Anniversary Day (May 8), Republic Day (December 30), and Alahamady Be (a Malagasy New Year celebration in March). During Fisemana, in June, the indigenous Antakàrana participate in a ritual purification ceremony, and the Famadihana ("turning of the bones") ceremony in which bones of Malagasy ancestors are exhumed, entertained with stories and music, and reburied during the summer months.

Youth Culture

Imported fashions, music, and films from Western cultures such as the U.S. and Europe heavily influence Malagasy youth. However, popular trends and cultural tastes differ between the island's Francophone and Anglophone populations. French chanson and reggae music are especially popular with young people, and many local bands play music inspired by popular foreign artists. There are a number of distinct ethnic groups living in Madagascar and some children are raised in ethnically homogenous groups, socializing primarily with members of the same ethnic group.

Rampant poverty significantly limits the recreational choices of Malagasy youth. Many children begin working in family businesses before age 10, though children are not permitted to engage in official employment until they reach 15 years of age. Children in urban families are often raised in more affluent surroundings, and therefore have greater access to recreational options. In Antananarivo, and other cities, abandoned children sometimes gather into large groups. These street children of Madagascar may engage in petty crime or odd jobs to earn income, and often turn to panhandling.

Transportation

Transportation in Madagascar consists of public buses, private taxi services, passenger rail services, and domestic air travel. The capital of Antananarivo is the hub of the bus system and provides connections to suburban buses and tour buses, which travel to distant parts of the country. Though there are numerous buses on the Malagasy roads, schedules are irregular and most busses are overcrowded. Many buses charge a flat rate for travel, regardless of the distance traveled.

Private taxis, which are widely available in the cities, will take visitors to distant locations for a modest fee, which should be negotiated in advance as few taxis have meters. There are also taxis known as "taxi-brousse" or "bush taxis," which may pick up multiple passengers en route to a location, but are often more affordable than private taxis. Traffic moves on the right-hand side of the road.

Transportation Infrastructure

There are nearly 50,000 kilometers (31,068 miles) of roads in Madagascar, of which a small percentage is paved. Passenger rail services are available to some destinations, especially those along the east coast. However, most railways are dedicated to commercial traffic to and from the capital. There are over 25 paved airports in Madagascar, many of which offer passenger flights within the country. Air Madagascar is the nation's airline, which offers travel within the country and international flights. Madagascar's primary international airport is located near Antananarivo and provides passage to Africa, Europe, and the United States.

Media & Communications

Freedom of the press is enshrined in the constitution of the republic and, in general, the government allows the press to function without interference. There have been reports that some media agencies tend to follow the political viewpoint of the ruling political party, or to report on issues according to the political leanings of the outlet's owners.

As of 2008, Madagascar had twelve privately owned daily newspapers in addition to a number of weekly and monthly publications. Most of the major newspapers were published in Antananarivo including *Le Quotidien*, which is the nation's most widely distributed news publication. *Le Quotidien* is owned by the state and is generally regarded as a tool for state-disseminated information. In addition to local publications, a number of international publications are available in Madagascar's cities, including French-language newspapers imported from Europe.

According to the U.S. Department of State, there are more than 240 radio stations operating in Madagascar, of which 195 have obtained legal licenses. Most radio broadcasts are in French or Malagasy and broadcast a mixture of news, music, and local information. The government owns a radio station that primarily broadcasts news, traffic, and emergency announcements. Madagascar has more than thirty television stations, most of which are based in Antananarivo. As with radio, the government operates television stations presenting news and a variety of educational programs. Satellite television is available in Antananarivo and some other areas and the audience and many European and American television programs are rebroadcast in Madagascar.

Internet coverage is expanding in Madagascar in an arc surrounding Antananarivo. The government places no restrictions on Internet usage, and there were no censorship restrictions. The Malagasy government has developed an Internet presence and has begun to provide government statistics and other information online. The government allows the formation of Internet discussion groups and has made no attempt to prevent criticism of government policy on the Internet.

SOCIAL DEVELOPMENT

Standard of Living

Madagascar ranked 155th out of 187 countries on the 2014 United Nations Human Development Index, which measures quality of life and standard of living indicators.

The country's poverty, transportation issues, and weak health care and education systems have contributed to a high infant mortality rate (almost 44 deaths per 1,000 lives birth), and a low average life expectancy (65 years).

Water Consumption

International observers estimate that 81 percent of Madagascar's urban population and 35 percent of its rural population has access to clean water. Widespread poverty and climate issues continue to hamper efforts to provide water to the country's population. Poor sanitation and water quality continues to be a major cause of illness, particularly diarrhea, in Madagascar.

Supplies of water in the country's urban areas are administered by the state-owned utility company JIRAMA (Jiro Sy Rano Malagasy). The UN continues to work with Malagasy officials to improve the country's water infrastructure and the availability of water for the country's rural population.

Education

Madagascar has been slowly improving its educational system. According to statistics from 1999, approximately 63 percent of the country's school age children attend primary school. Secondary school attendance is significantly less, at only 12 percent of male children and 13 percent of females. Only two percent of the population is enrolled in higher education. The low enrollment rates are reflected in the country's adult literacy rate (about 62.6 percent of adult women and 66.7 percent of adult men as of 2015).

In the past, the government has not been able to provide fee access to the country's educational system. However, after a drawn-out legal dispute over the outcome of 2001 and again the 2009 presidential elections further weakened the country's governmental programs, the government announced a temporary policy of funding primary schools.

Women's Rights

Madagascar's constitution guarantees women and men the same rights, privileges, and protections under the law. However, domestic abuse and spousal rape remain serious problems in Madagascar. According to the penal code, rape is punishable by prison sentences ranging from three years to life in prison. The penal code also provides specific penalties for rape cases involving underage girls or pregnant women. Domestic abuse is a severe problem. According to some internal estimates, between 30 and 50 percent of Malagasy women have been victims of domestic abuse during their lives. The government established clinics in 2006 and 2007 to aid victims of domestic violence and abuse.

While the penal code prohibits sexual harassment, women's rights organizations report that police do not usually consider harassment a serious crime and are reluctant to investigate complaints. NGOs report that few harassment cases are reported, but that the government has displayed willingness to prosecute harassment cases when they occur. In addition, some reports indicate that more than half of Malagasy women have been the victims of sexual harassment in the workplace. Foreign laborers especially have seen a rise in abuse and exploitation. Sex trafficking is also a growing concern.

In terms of ownership and labor, women in Madagascar take an active role in business and industry. Women owners control between 30 and 50 percent of private companies. Women frequently serve in management positions, though not as often as men do, and women often earn less, on average, than men working in similar positions do do. Nonetheless, NGOs have criticized Madagascar for failing to create a governmental office dedicated to women's rights. Some NGOs have proposed that establishing a ministry of women's issues could help to organize the structure and distribution of services.

Health Care

Madagascar's health care system is a patchwork of public health clinics, internationally run programs, and traditional medicine. The government sponsored the creation of 1,500 public health clinics throughout the country during the 1970s. Only about two-thirds of those clinics remain in operation, and essential services can be difficult to obtain.

The government's emergency program has waived temporarily fees for the use of clinics for basic health care and essential medicines. More advanced and reliable care is available from clinics and hospitals run by international non-governmental organizations (NGOs), and through programs funded by other governments.

GOVERNMENT

Structure

Since the 16th century, Madagascar's natural resources and strategic ports have attracted European powers. After the Portuguese and the Dutch failed to establish the island as a colony, the Merina tribe established its domination of the island with official recognition from the British government in 1820. By 1883, however, the British had traded their influence in Madagascar for France's release of Zanzibar. Two years later, the French invaded and declared Madagascar a French colony.

The British seized Madagascar again during World War II, but returned it to the French government at the end of the war. In 1947, the Malagasy began an armed rebellion against French authorities. The French responded brutally, killing as many as 80,000 Malagasy. Madagascar memorializes the rebellion each year on Insurrection Day. In spite of lingering hostilities, the Malagasy voted to become semi-autonomous within the French collective of overseas nations in 1960.

Madagascar gradually disassociated from France, but a series of repressive and often short-lived regimes kept the country in a state of economic and political turmoil until the 1996 reelection of Admiral Didier Ratsiraka. Since that time, Madagascar has worked closely with the International Monetary Fund (IMF), the World Bank, and international authorities to rebuild the country's economy. In spite of a dramatic downturn following the 2001 election crisis, Madagascar shows signs of slow improvements in economic and social conditions. In fact, following an international mediation free democratic elections were held in 2013 leading to a slow, but noticeable improvement.

Madagascar is officially a republic with six provinces, or faritany: Antananarivo, Antsiranana, Fianarantsoa, Mahajanga, Toamasina, and Toliara. The country's president is elected by popular vote to a five-year term. He or she appoints a prime minister, and the prime minister appoints a Council of Ministers.

The legislative branch consists of a National Assembly with 160 members and a Senate with 100 members. National Assembly members are elected by popular vote to four-year terms. Senate members also serve four-year terms. Two-thirds of the Senate seats are filled by popular vote within regional assemblies; the president appoints the remaining third.

Political Parties

Madagascar's National Assembly and Senate are comprised of representatives from numerous political parties. There are approximately 120 active political organizations in the country. Political parties in the country are known by their acronyms. These parties include the Party of Andry Rajoelina, the Ravalomanana Movement, Young Malgasies Determind (TGV), the Party of the Independence Congress of Madagascar (AKFM), Activists for Madagascar Progress (MFM) and Madagascar for the Malagasy (MONIMA).

Local Government

The government of Madagascar introduced a new system of local governance in 1994 that divided the country into Decentralized Territorial Authorities. Under the system, Madagascar is organized into 28 regions, 100 departments, and 1000 communes. Implementation of this system of local government has been slow due to internal political strife.

Judicial System

Madagascar's legal system is based on French civil law and traditional laws. The Supreme Court, comprised of 11 judges, is the country's highest court. Other courts include the High Court of Justice, the Administrative and Financial Constitutional Court and the Appeals Court. Issues related to judicial corruption continue in Madagascar. Bribery continues to permeate each level of the country's judicial infrastructure.

Taxation

Madagascar remains an impoverished country and many Malagasys work within the island's informal economy. Individuals who do pay taxes are responsible for an individual income tax of 23 percent. Employees contribute one percent of their income to social security while employees contribute 13 percent of individual salaries. There is a flat corporate tax rate of 23 percent and a VAT (Value Added Tax) of 20 percent.

Armed Forces

The military of Madagascar, the People's Armed Forces, includes a large army, and small naval and air force contingent, both listed as 500-strong. There is no conscription, and the minimum age for voluntary service is eighteen. The armed forces were involved in the 2009 Malagasy political crisis, an event that was called a coup internationally, when Malagasy soldiers helped to install politician Andry Rajoelina. The military essentially maintained power for several weeks, before handing over power to the High Transitional Authority, headed by Rajoelina. This coup wasn't overturned until the international community intervened which led to free, democratic elections in 2013.

Foreign Policy

Madagascar is an active member of the international community and a member of the African Union (AU) and Southern African Development Community (SADC). Until the early 1990s, the Malagasy government was closely aligned with socialist and communist allies in Cuba, Libya, and Iran. Since 1993, the Malagasy government has attempted to adopt a non-aligned foreign policy and to develop functional diplomatic relationships outside of certain regional or political spheres. Madagascar's diplomatic ties are strongest with francophone (French speaking) countries in Europe and Africa. In the 21st century, the Malagasy government has made it a priority to strengthen the nation's ties with Anglophone (English speaking) countries.

Madagascar has several ongoing territorial disputes with France since gaining independence from the French government in 1960. Madagascar claims ownership over the Glorioso Islands, which are administered by France and claimed as part of the Seychelles and Comoros island groups. Madagascar also claims Bassas da India, Europa Island, and Juan de Nova Island, all of which are controlled by France. Despite ongoing territorial disputes, France is still the nation's leading trading partner in terms of both exports and imports. Madagascar also receives substantial international aid, a majority of it for environmental purposes due to its status as a unique natural wonder.

Human Rights Profile

International human rights law insists that states respect civil and political rights, and promote an individual's economic, social, and cultural rights. The United Nations (UN) Universal Declaration of Human Rights (UDHR) is recognized as the standard for international human rights. Its authors sought the counsel of the world's great thinkers, philosophers, and religious leaders, and were careful to create a document that reflects the core values shared by every world culture. (To read this document or view the articles relating to cultural human rights, visit http://www.udhr.org/UDHR/default.htm.)

While the government of Madagascar generally respects the human rights of its citizens, monitoring human rights organizations have identified several areas of concern. Most pressing were reports that police in some parts of the country engaged in unlawful arrest and killings of suspected criminals without due process in 2007. There have also been reports of police using excessive force to restrain suspects, sometimes resulting in serious injury. Additionally, the prison system in Madagascar is in need of modernization as facilities are inadequate for the current population. Detainees and prisoners suffer from malnutrition and poor sanitation and have inadequate access to medical care. Human rights groups have also objected to the fact that underage offenders are typically incarcerated alongside adult offenders, placing juveniles at risk for violence and rape.

Though the constitution and penal code require due process for all accused, the penal system houses a large population of criminals in pretrial detention, accounting for nearly 60 percent of the total population. There have been reports that of individuals held in pretrial detention for years because of lengthy delays in the trial schedule. The judicial system is also plagued with corruption and some observers allege that there is no presumption of innocence in the Malagasy courts.

The government provides for freedom of the press, assembly, and expression, as dictated by articles 19 and 20 of the UDHR. However, there were some reports, in 2005 and 2006, of government interference with the media. In particular, the dominant political party was accused of using its influence to prohibit the dissemination of information seen as contrary to the party's platform. Most news outlets are seen as favoring certain aligned political groups. The government also provides for, and generally recognizes, freedom of religion, in keeping with Article 18 of UDHR. Some Islamic groups have alleged governmental discrimination. Corruption within the government is an ongoing problem.

Child welfare is a significant problem in Madagascar as both internal agencies and non-governmental organizations (NGOs) have reported that police and social services are inadequate to address children's issues. Abandoned children are common in many cites due to high poverty levels and inadequate state care facilities. The government of Madagascar is committed to addressing the child welfare issue and adopted a new program in 2008 to update children's services. This includes increasing funding and training for law enforcement personnel to address underage victims. In 2013, an anti-trafficking law was enacted in the hope of combatting the exploitation of women and children.

Despite a minimum employment age of 15, monitoring agencies discovered instances of children below the minimum age working in a number of industries. In 2000, the U.S. Department of State reported that over 33 percent of children between the ages of seven and 15n were involved in part- or full-time labor. Combating child labor was a major focus of the government's 2007 action plan for domestic development. The problem was complicated by the fact that most child laborers are working with their families in family-owned or family-operated businesses, including mining, fishing, and manufacturing.

ECONOMY

Overview of the Economy
Madagascar maintains a primarily agricultural economy, with agriculture centers in the fertile and temperate high plateau regions around the country's capital. Because the high plateaus are also home to Madagascar's commercial and intellectual centers (Andasibe, Antananarivo, Antsirabe, and Fianarantsoa), new industries tend to appear in this region.

In recent years, the garment industry has flourished because of tax-free access to the United States retail market. Tourism is also a significant industry for Madagascar, though the long-term future of tourism in the country depends upon finding ways to stop the rampant deforestation of the rainforest areas. The estimated per capita gross domestic product in 2014 was $1,400 (USD).

Industry
Major industries in Madagascar include meat processing, breweries, and tanneries. Soap, sugar, glassware, cement, and paper are also produced on the island. Madagascar has natural petroleum reserves and one automobile assembly plant. The major industries in Madagascar, however, are agriculture, fishing, forestry, and ecotourism. Together these industries account for 80 percent of employment and provide a quarter of the country's gross domestic product.

In Antananarivo, retail markets provide additional economic opportunity including automobile manufacturing, meat processing, and textile industries. As well as being the administrative center of the Malagasy government, Antananarivo is also the economic capital. Most of Madagascar's chief exports (coffee, vanilla, shellfish, cotton, chromites, and petroleum) pass through Antananarivo on their way overseas. The country's largest export partners are France, the United States, Germany, and Mauritius.

Labor

Madagascar's labor force was estimated at approximately 12.15 million in 2014. As of 2009, the majority of the work force—an estimated 57 percent—is employed in the service sector, while nearly 27 percent work in the agricultural sector. Industry accounts for 16 percent of the labor force. Unemployment has been on the rise and has become a pressing issue, particularly since unrest and political turmoil has continued to hamper the tourist industry. About half of the population is thought to be living below the poverty line.

Energy/Power/Natural Resources

Madagascar's natural resources include graphite, chromite, coal, bauxite, salt, quartz, tar sands, semiprecious stones, and mica. In addition, multinational drug companies have been scouring the island's amazing rainforests for medicinal plants.

Fishing

Madagascar's fishing industry is a major contributor to the country's economy. Shrimp is one of the country's major export products. Agriculture, which includes fishing, represents an estimated 34 percent of Madagascar's GDP. Tilapia and crayfish are also harvested in Malagasy waters. In addition to the country's formal fishing industry, much of the fishing that occurs in the country is done by artisanal fishers for domestic consumption.

Forestry

Timber and paper goods are produced in Madagascar. However, forest products are supplied by the country's endangered rainforests. Although the international community and the government of Madagascar continue to work to prevent illegal logging and harvesting of the

country's rainforests, they continue to decrease in size. Timber is still the most common building material in the country, and charcoal and wood are still the most common form of fuel. Efforts to establish plantation forests as sources of renewable forestry products continue.

Mining/Metals

Madagascar, as a source for gemstones, particularly sapphires, was in question at the end of 2008. Prior to 2008, the country was a major producer of sapphires, but a government ban in March 2008 halted production on exports. The global economic crisis that began in the same year added to the industry's decline. The industry is showing potential for development in the areas of cement, ilmenite, rutile, and zircon production.

Agriculture

Agriculture has long been the mainstay of the Malagasy economy and employs four-fifths of the country's workforce. Malagasy farmers grow coffee, sugarcane, cloves, cocoa, rice, cassava (tapioca), beans, bananas, peanuts, and livestock.

Madagascar's most famous crop, however, is the vanilla bean, which it exports to countries around the world. The vanilla (as well as the coffee and cloves) tends to come from Madagascar's lush eastern forests, making the local Betsimisaraka people Madagascar's wealthiest.

Madagascar only uses about five percent of its land for agriculture. Unfortunately, impoverished farmers on the eastern half of the island have been clearing and burning rainforest lands in order to grow short-term crops. The erosion created by this deforestation and the intensive harvesting mean that these lands are fertile for no more than five years worth of farming. Ecologists are looking for ways to improve farming techniques in the country in order to preserve the ancient rainforests while still alleviating poverty.

Animal Husbandry

Zebu, or humped cattle, are an important livestock species in rural Madagascar. The animals are used for meat and dairy production, in addition to be used for labor purposes. Poultry is also raised for domestic consumption.

Tourism

Ecotourism is an important part of Madagascar's economy. The country's coastline is dotted with national reserves designed to preserve the unique plants and animals that draw visitors from all over the world. Montagne d'Ambre is Madagascar's most visited park, complete with at least seventy-three bird species and a unique blue-nosed chameleon.

Since becoming a United Nations Educational, Scientific, and Cultural Organization (UNESCO) World Heritage Site, Parc National des Tsingy de Bemaraha is gaining popularity. Comprised of Grand Tsingy Park and Petit Tsingy Park, Tsingy de Bemaraha lies north of the Manambolo Gorge.

In November 2010, the return of political violence in Madagascar negatively affected the country's tourism industry. Since then the industry has seen some moderate rebound.

Micah L. Issitt, Amy Witherbee

DO YOU KNOW?

- The name "Antananarivo" means "city of a thousand," in reference to a historical episode during which a Malagasy king conquered the local tribes and established garrisons in the central plateau. The king housed 1,000 troops in the city, from which the name was derived.

- The Malagasy people once believed that ancestors were reincarnated as the island's native lemurs, and many tribes had prohibitions against hunting or killing lemurs. Freed from the threat of hunters, some lemurs will approach travelers in remote areas.

Bibliography

Alison Jolly. "Lords and Lemurs: Mad Scientists, Kings with Spears and the Survival of Diversity in Madagascar." Boston, MA: *Houghton Mifflin Publications*, 2004.

Emily Filou, et al. "Madagascar & Comoros." Oakland, CA: *Lonely Planet Publications*, 2012.

Martin Banham, Hill Errol, and George William Woodyard. "The Cambridge Guide to African and Caribbean Theatre." Cambridge, MA: *Cambridge University Press*, 1994.

Peter Tyson. "The Eighth Continent: Life, Death, and Discovery in the Lost World of Madagascar." New York: *Harper Perennial*, 2001.

Solofo Randrianja and Stephen Ellis. "Madagascar: A Short History." Chicago: *University of Chicago Press*, 2009.

Steven M. Goodman, Jonathan P. Benstead, and Harald Schultz. "The Natural History of Madagascar." Chicago, IL: *University of Chicago Press*, 2007.

Virginia Thompson and Richard Adloff. "The Malagasy Republic: Madagascar Today." Palo Alto, CA: *Stanford University Press*, 1965.

Works Cited

"Madagascar: Largest Cities and Towns and Statistics of their Population." *World Gazeteer* http://www.world-gazetteer.com/wg.php?x=&men=gcis&lng=en&des=wg&srt=npan&col=abcdefghinoq&msz=1500&geo=-137

"Madagascar: Country Reports on Human Rights Practices—2007" *Bureau of Democracy, Human Rights, and Labor.* http://www.state.gov/g/drl/rls/hrrpt/2007/100490.htm

"Madagascar." *The World Factbook Online.* https://www.cia.gov/library/publications/the-world-factbook/geos/ma.html.

"Madagascar Travel Information and Travel Guide." *Lonely Planet Online.* http://www.lonelyplanet.com/madagascar.

"Background Information: Madagascar." *United States Department of State.* http://www.state.gov/r/pa/ei/bgn/5460.htm.

"Travel and Cultures: Madagascar." *National Geographic Online.* http://travel.nationalgeographic.com/places/countries/country_madagascar.html.

"Country Profile: Madagascar." *BBC News Online.* http://news.bbc.co.uk/2/hi/africa/country_profiles/1063208.stm.

"Madagascar." *University of Pennsylvania Online.* Madagascar Cookbook. http://www.africa.upenn.edu/Cookbook/Madagascar.html.

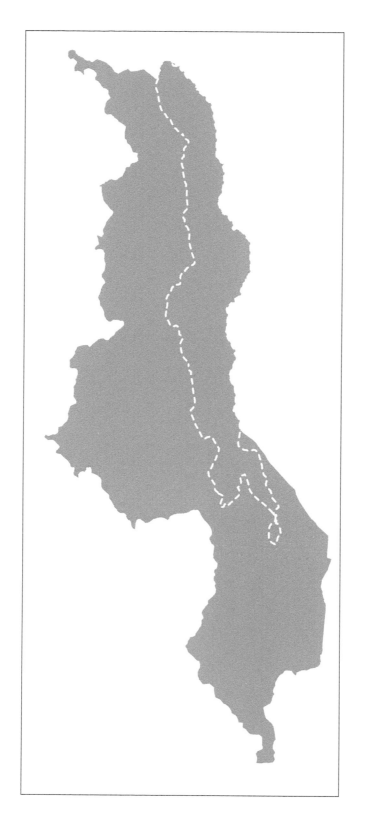

MALAWI

Introduction

Home to some of the world's most spectacular landscapes and rarest plant and animal species, Malawi is a contemporary African country with a violent history and an uncertain future. The citizens of the country, which is sometimes referred to as "the warm heart of Africa," are known for their generosity. Although political reforms in 1994 ushered in Malawi's first multi-party elections, corruption and poverty continue to challenge Malawi's development.

Like other African cultures, Malawi's artistic heritage blends the traditional with the modern. Christian-based songs and hymns hold an important position in any occasion of village life, while Malawian-style reggae blends with music from other parts of Africa, the Caribbean, and North America; traditional carving, furniture-making, and batik appear in stores and stalls all over the country, but so do the works of acrylic, watercolor, and oil painters; itinerant actors still travel from village to village putting on plays, often based on traditional or Christian themes, but Malawi's urban centers also show signs of the growing art of filmmaking in Africa; lastly, while most of Malawi's literary tradition is still in the form of oral storytelling, there is a growing canon of written literary works by Malawian authors.

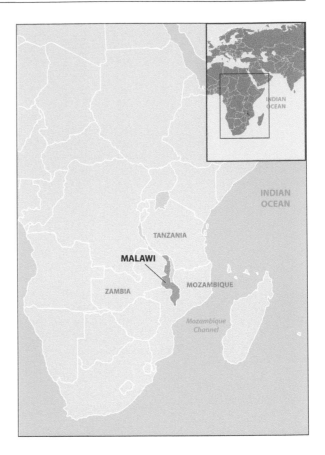

GENERAL INFORMATION

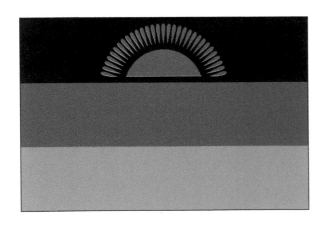

Official Language: English and Chewa (or Chichewa)

Population: 17,964,697 (2015 estimate)

Currency: Malawian kwacha

Coins: The Malawian kwacha is divided into 100 tambala, though its coin denominations, 1, 2, 5, 10, 20, and 50 tambala, are rarely used. Coins more frequently in use are those in denominations of 1, 5, and 10 kwacha.

Land Area: 94,080 square miles (36,324 square miles)

Water Area: 24,404 square miles (9,422 square miles)

National Motto: "Unity and Freedom"

National Anthem: "Mlungu salitsani malawi" ("Oh God Bless Our Land of Malawi")

Capital: Lilongwe

Time Zone: GMT +2

Flag Description: The flag of Malawi features a tricolor design of three equal horizontal bands

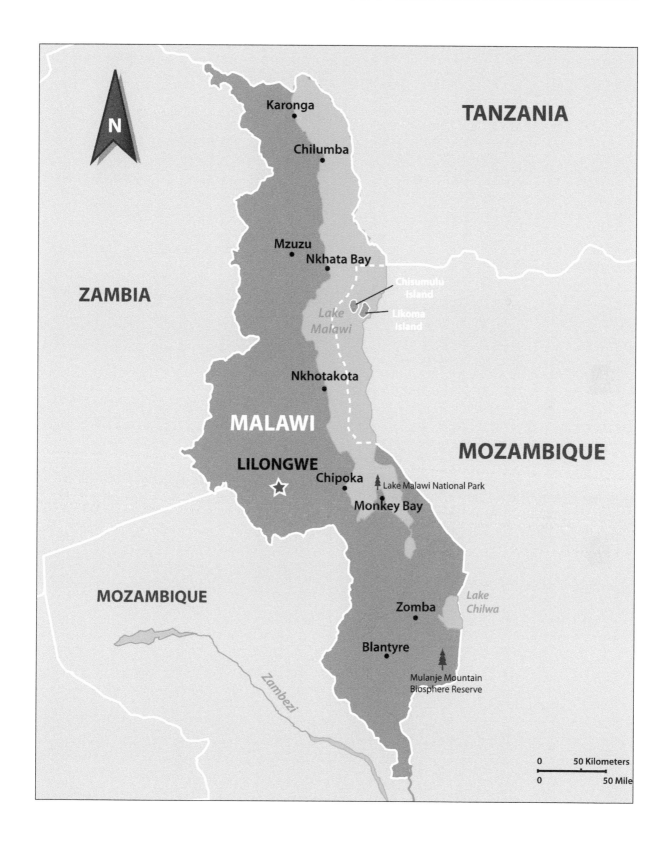

Principal Cities by Population (2012):

- Lilongwe (781,538)
- Blantyre (728,285)
- Mzuzu (148,754)
- Zomba (96,460)
- Kasungu (51,082)

of red (top), black (middle), and green (bottom). The colors represent Pan-Africanism, while a centered white sun represents the country's economic progress.

Population

Malawi's population of over 15 million people includes a number of different ethnic groups, including Chewa, Nyanja, Tumbuka, Yao, Lomwe, Sena, Tonga, Ngoni, Ngonde, Asian, and European. The Chewa is the largest of these groups.

In purely demographic terms, Malawi has four urban centers: Mzuzu in the north, Zomba (the former capital) in the south, Lilongwe (the present capital), and Blantyre in the south. In contrast, large areas of parkland and nature reserve blanket the country, particularly along the borders. Most of the remaining populated areas of Malawi lie in the middle and southern parts of the country, with large rural areas predominantly in the north. About 80 percent of Malawians live in small, rural villages.

With a 2012 population of over 781,000, Lilongwe is Malawi's most populous city. In recent years, Lilongwe has been overwhelmed by massive numbers of migrants from predominantly rural Malawi. The Chichewa people represent the largest ethnic group in the city. There are small communities of Indian, South African, and Western expatriates, most of whom are British. Many of the expatriates work for sub-Saharan African international aid organizations or for international corporations, especially tobacco companies.

Languages

While the country's official languages, Chichewa and English, are widely spoken, many Malawians also speak a regional language. About half a million people in the northern part of the country speak Chitimbuka, for instance, and about 600,000 in the south speak Chiyao. English is used in government, business, and educational settings.

Native People & Ethnic Groups

Evidence of human habitation dating as far back as 8000 BCE has been discovered at archaeological sites throughout Malawi. The much older remains of prehistoric hominids have also been found along the banks of Lake Malawi.

Malawi's national population actually consists of a number of regional identities that trace their histories back to the Bantu tribes of the 16th century. It is believed that the country's name is derived from one of these tribes, the Maravi.

The Chewa are the largest ethnicity in modern Malawi. Other ethnicities include the Nyanja, Tumbuka, Yao, Lomwe, Sena, Tonga, Ngoni, and Ngonde.

Religions

Catholic missionaries arrived in Malawi during the 19th century, and today, most Malawians practice Christianity, usually in association with one of the Protestant churches. A sizable number of Malawians in the north and near Lake Malawi are followers of Islam, the legacy of Arab slave traders who once operated in area. There are also animists, those who believe that some form of soul inhabits everything, scattered throughout the country.

Climate

The southern part of Malawi has a tropical climate, with temperatures ranging between 28° and 37° Celsius (82° to 98° Fahrenheit). Average annual rainfall is 740 millimeters (30 inches).

The central region is more temperate on average, but rainfall ranges from 1,500 to 2,000 millimeters (60 to 80 inches) per year, mostly falling during the rainy season from November to May. Like the central region, Malawi's northern region has a subtropical climate, warm and rainy from November to May, but with cooler temperatures at higher elevations.

Lilongwe features a tropical climate characterized by a dry season, which lasts from April through November, and a rainy season, which generally runs from December through March. Daytime temperatures average roughly 25° Celsius (77° Fahrenheit), but during the hottest part of the year in late November to early December, temperatures are often higher on average.

ENVIRONMENT & GEOGRAPHY

Topography

Malawi is a landlocked country, bordered by Tanzania to the north and east, Zambia to the west and Mozambique to the south. The country is part of the Great Rift Valley. Covering 20 percent of the country, Lake Malawi sits along the eastern border of Malawi from its northern tip to three-quarters of the way down to Mozambique. From the southernmost point of the lake, the Shire River flows south into Lake Malombe and Lake Chirwa before flowing into the Zambezi River in Mozambique.

Malawi is divided into three regions. Most of the northern region is rugged, mountainous, and blanketed with forests. At its highest point, the grass-covered Nyika Plateau soars to over 3,000 meters (9,843 miles) above sea level. Where the peaks meet Lake Malawi, mountain waters cascade down Manchewe and Chembe Falls. Because of its elevation, much of the northern region experiences slightly cooler weather than the rest of Malawi.

Like the north, the southern region of Malawi is extremely mountainous. Mount Mulanje is Malawi's highest peak, while the country's lowest point, in the Shire Valley, is also found in the south. The south is home to the Liwonde National Park and the Zomba Plateau. Malawi's central region is largely flat, with rich soil. It is, however, surrounded by chains of mountains to the east and to the south.

Lilongwe is located on Malawi's Central Region Plateau. The city lies some 80 kilometers (50 miles) west of the southern tip of Lake Malawi. It is built along the banks of the Lilongwe River, at the crossroads of Malawi's main transportation routes.

Plants & Animals

Malawi's plethora of lakes, streams, rivers, ponds, marshes, and temporary pools are home to a wide array of aquatic plants and animals. Lake Malawi alone is home to more species of fish than any other lake on earth.

The highlands of Malawi, particularly the Nyika Plateau in the north, sustain large swaths of evergreen forest and high altitude grasslands. Mount Mulanje has the largest montane (coniferous) forest in the country. Intermingled with its forests and plateaus, Malawi boasts an extraordinary collection of native wild flowers.

Malawi also has five national parks and four wildlife reserves that sustain large mammals such as waterbuck, antelope, zebra, wild dogs, African elephants, cheetahs, lions, leopards, and rhinoceros. In spite of the large tracts of protected land, poaching and climate destruction threaten many of Malawi's plant and animal species.

Malawi is home to diverse and vibrant species of fish.

CUSTOMS & COURTESIES

Greetings

In Malawi, people customarily greet one another with a firm, energetic, and sustained handshake. The right hand is always used for greetings. When greeting a person of high status or importance, people may grasp their right wrist or elbow with their left hand when shaking hands, bow, dip their knees, or kneel down in respect. Female friends and family may embrace when greeting one another.

Verbal greetings most often occur in either English or Chichewa (a Bantu language primarily spoken in Malawi). Common Chichewa greetings and phrases include "Akulandirani" ("Welcome"), "Moni" ("Hello"), "Muli Bwanji" ("How are you?"), and "Kodi Mukupita Kuti" ("Where are you going?"). In Malawi, people covey respect by affixing the prefix "a" before a name or title. Honorific titles are also commonly used, followed by the last name. In casual settings, people may refer to one another by last name, and first names are rarely used in greeting. After a friendly greeting or salutation, Malawians ask one another about the health and well-being of their respective families.

Gestures & Etiquette

In Malawi, hand gestures tend to be energetic. Gestures are also most often used to communicate with peers or across distances. For example, on a crowded street Malawians may gesture to one another to come by facing their outstretched palm forward and making a scratching motion with their fingers. Other gestures include placing an open palm atop a closed fist, which means "often" or "a lot," while the "thumbs up" gesture is commonly understood to convey enthusiasm or agreement. The OK symbol or gesture (finger and thumb touching to form a circle) is taboo and considered rude.

Malawi's social etiquette has developed in response to the physical and space limitations of the country. Malawi is a densely populated country. As such, Malawians may be comfortable with limited space and typically stand very close to one another when engaged in conversation. To cope with the density of the population and the lack of personal or private space, Malawians have developed great respect for personal privacy. Malawians dislike overly intrusive and overly direct people and value humility and politeness. Obfuscation, or concealment of meaning, to spare feelings or avoid confrontation, is common and displays of physical anger are rare.

Social custom allows for people of the same gender to touch in public, but generally discourages people of opposite genders from physical displays of affection. Eye contact is common for people of the same gender, age, or status, but uncommon otherwise. In Malawi, people traditionally do not look directly into the eyes of their boss, teacher, or any other authority figure. In addition, many Malawians follow the movements of the sun rather than a standard clock. As a result, meals, gatherings, meetings, and appointments may not happen at an exact or standardized time.

Eating/Meals

The social aspects of dining in Malawi vary between urban and rural areas. In rural areas, people eat without utensils, while in urban areas, utensils are increasingly common. Similar to Muslim custom, people across Malawi eat exclusively with their right hand, as the left hand is reserved for personal hygiene. Malawians generally eat two main meals a day, including breakfast and supper. Lunch may or may not be eaten depending on occupation, the season, and available food. For example, food is often most abundant after the spring harvest. Breakfast usually includes tea with cornmeal porridge or bread, while suppers may commonly include cornmeal porridge and a meat or vegetable stew.

In rural areas, women cook meals over an open fire outside or in a mud-brick kitchen attached to the home. All members of a household wash their hands in a communal pot of water before eating. Traditionally, men and women eat separately; men will eat first and be served their food by the women in the house. When utensils are not present, people use bite-size balls of nsima (cornmeal mush) to scoop up sauce or stew. Malawians generally leave a small portion of food uneaten to signal to the cook that they are satisfied. In urban areas, such as Lilongwe and Blantyre, restaurants are increasingly common.

Visiting

Malawians have close bonds with friends and family and visit formally and informally throughout the week, with Sundays the most common day for social visits. Households gain status by hosting and welcoming many guests. Households with new babies or suffering a family death can expect a great number of visitors. When visiting someone's home in Malawi, there is special etiquette to keep in mind. Visitors bring small gifts of money, tea, or sugar to their hosts. Large gifts will likely be returned. Visitors from foreign countries should bring small gifts representative of their home country, if possible.

Traditionally, visitors to a private home may call out to announce their presence rather than knock. The head of the household might then reply and invite the guest into the home. The host will customarily serve a visitor food and drink rather than ask the visitor if they are hungry or thirsty. Social custom requires the visitor to accept what food or drink is offered. When visitors leave, a host may typically send them away with a small gift of food to show their appreciation for the visit. This gesture will be made whether or not the household has enough food to eat. Visitors are expected to accept the gift of food with gratitude and respect.

LIFESTYLE

Family

Families in Malawi live close to one another in compounds of loosely connected huts or neighboring villages. Extended families often share farm plots, grain storage huts, water wells, and cooking facilities. Households typically include extended family from the husband's side. Fathers, uncles and grandfathers take the lead in managing the household, disciplining children and arranging marriages, while women are traditionally responsible for cooking, farming, and cleaning.

Marriages tend to be arranged. Dowries, or the payment a bride and her family brings to her new husband, are expected and influence marriage matches. Couples do divorce in Malawi but divorce strips women of all possessions. Divorced women must also return to their birth families and ask to be allowed back into the household. Polygamy is legal in Malawi and practiced by those men who can afford to support more than one bride.

Housing

In Malawi, housing types vary between urban and rural areas. In urban areas, such as Blantyre, Lilongwe, and Mzuzu, housing includes government-built houses, privately built houses and squatter villages (informal settlements). In Malawi, the majority of the population lives in rural areas and maintains an agrarian lifestyle. Rural housing options include the traditional village hut made of mud bricks and thatched roof, or newer housing types made of concrete, stone, and corrugated metal sheets. Floors may consist of dirt or pressed cow dung.

Rural houses or huts are usually grouped into family compounds, generally have two to three rooms (for sleeping, eating, or storage), and lack electricity or plumbing. Typically, cooking facilities include the use of wood or charcoal, and will be housed in a separate building or be set up outside over a fire pit. Rural water sources for drinking and bathing include rainwater, wells, boreholes, and rivers or lakes. Homes are illuminated with wood fires and candles, and all rural households include at least a small plot on which to grow the food staple of corn.

Food

In Malawi, food is grown and consumed locally. Staple foods include cornmeal, beans, and cassava, meats from the chicken, goat, and pig, and fruits such as mangoes, oranges, pineapples, melons, and banana. Rice and vegetables are grown and eaten, but tend not to be favorite foods. Preferred drinks include soda and chibuku (a home-brewed liquor). Common dishes include nsima, mkhwani, mbatata biscuits, zitumbuwa and caterpillars.

Nsima (cornmeal or white maize mush) is the mainstay of the Malawian diet, and most Malawians will eat nsima at least twice a day. Nsima is prepared by heating and stirring ufa (cornmeal), water, and butter or margarine until soft. Nsima may be flavored with hot sauce or a pumpkin relish. Mkhwani (pumpkin leaves) are commonly cooked with groundnut (peanut) flour into a hearty vegetable stew (ndiwo) and eaten with nsima or rice. To prepare mkhwani stew, chopped pumpkin leaves, water, tomato, and groundnut flour and salt are combined and cooked until thickened. Vegetable stews (which may be made with pumpkin leaves, cassava leaves, sweet potato leaves, bean leaves, cabbage, mustard leaves, kale, cabbage, and collard greens) are a common dish in Malawi.

Mbatata biscuits (sweet potato biscuits) are a popular snack for children and field workers. Mbatata biscuit dough is made with mashed sweet potato, milk, margarine, flour, baking powder, and salt. The prepared biscuit dough is baked in a hot pan.

Zitumbuwa (banana fritters) are commonly eaten during celebrations. Zitumbuwa are prepared with ripe banana, sugar, ufa, salt, and oil. The ingredients are mashed together, formed into balls, and fried in hot oil until golden brown.

Malawians also eat fried ants and caterpillars as snacks. In Malawi, caterpillars are a seasonal snack treat. During the month of November, Malawians search out adult caterpillars, remove and discard the insides, and dry the caterpillar skins in the sun. Once the caterpillar skins are dry, they are salted and eaten.

Life's Milestones

Malawi's traditional milestones include birth, initiation ceremonies, marriage, and funerary traditions. Traditions and life milestones are changing in Malawi due to the health and economic impact of the HIV/AIDS pandemic. In particular, the life milestones of adulthood initiation ceremonies and funeral ceremonies are affected by HIV/AIDS.

Traditionally, pre-pubescent boys and girls undergo manhood and womanhood initiation ceremonies involving genital circumcision or cutting, dancing, and instruction on traditions. Initiation rites involving genital circumcision, along with other traditional practices, such as wife inheritance (the practice of marrying a widow to someone in the deceased man's family), have begun to change as a result of spread of HIV/AIDS infection in Africa. Today, genital circumcision and cutting practices are a declining part of the initiation ceremony, while safe sex education is a growing part of the initiation ceremony.

Traditionally, when someone dies in Malawi, all the members of a village attend the funeral. In addition, custom dictates that the family of the deceased serves a feast at the funeral to honor the deceased and the funeral guests. Due to the high number of deaths caused by HIV/AIDS infection, the people of Malawi are finding it increasingly difficult to attend every funeral required by social custom and to afford the cost of funeral feasts for their dead relatives. As a result, funeral customs and culture are changing.

CULTURAL HISTORY

Art

Traditional Malawian arts and crafts are used as artifacts in village ceremonies, serve as functional items, and are produced and sold for the tourist trade. They include basket weaving, woodcarving, mask making, batik (textile dyeing), oil painting, and ceramics. Many of Malawi's arts and crafts traditions are associated with one particular region or group of artists. For example, Malawian pottery is primarily produced in the Dedza region, along the border between Malawi and Mozambique. Malawian pottery is traditionally covered with graphite and rubbed with fabric or grass until the pieces shine. Tourist pottery is usually decorated with painted scenes of well-known areas of the country such as Lake Malawi.

Historically, Malawian artists and craftspeople carved ornamental furniture, pipes, and household tools out of wood. Jewelry such as rings, anklets, headdresses, and bracelets were made out of ivory, brass, copper, and iron. These traditional arts have been replaced by the production of items with more commercial value in the tourist trade, which has influenced artistic production and aesthetics in Malawi. The tourist trade provides income for many local craftspeople and artisans. Wooden carvings of animals and chief chairs (stout wooden chairs) are popular tourist items. Popular types of wood for carving include teak, mahogany, and ebony. Carvings are sold on the street, in galleries, and even in grocery stores.

Drama & Dance

Dance and drama are an integral part of Malawi's social and cultural life. In Malawi, traditional dance tends to be elaborately costumed and dramatic. The Malawi National Dance Troupe (formerly known as the Kwacha Cultural Troupe) was formed in 1987 by the Malawi government (specifically the Ministry of Education and Culture's Art and Craft Department) to preserve and promote Malawi's performing arts heritage and culture. The troupe performs locally and travels to international festivals to showcase Malawi performing arts. The troupe's repertoire of dances includes a wide range of traditional dances.

Traditional Malawi dances are often informed by historical events. For example, the traditional dance called malipenga, also called beni, is a response to or reenactment of 19th-century colonialism in Africa. The malipenga dance imitates the British colonial dress costumes, marching bands, and military pomp. The malipenga is still commonly danced on the island of Likoma and isolated and rural areas of northern Malawi, and is evolving in response to current cultural and political tensions. For instance, in some modern performances, South Africa's upper class has replaced the role of the British colonists.

Amateur theater companies are also active in Malawi. The main amateur theater companies are the Wakhumbata Ensemble Theater, Kwathu Drama Group, the Chancellor College Traveling Theater and the Lonjezo Traveling Theater. They undertake national tours, with most plays performed in the Chichewa language, the prominent native language. Performances in Chichewa have created a national demand for and enjoyment of theater in Malawi.

Music

Traditional music is integrated into all parts of village and tribal life in Malawi. Individual tribes, often living in isolation from one another, have distinct songs and accompanying dances. Rite of passage and healing ceremonies include musical components, and traditional healing ceremonies usually require that both patient and healer sing and dance. In Malawi villages, local bands play traditional instruments in regional festivals and celebrations such as initiation events and marriage ceremonies. Musicians accompany dance troupes and traveling theater groups throughout the country, but rarely perform internationally.

Traditional instruments include the ulimba (a small drum made from a pumpkin), the marimba (similar to a xylophone), and rattles and ceremonial drums (large drums made from tree trunks). In Malawi, traditional dancers usually wear maseche (wooden clappers) to make music as they dance. Traditional Malawian music is also influenced by foreign cultures, including the Zulu culture of South Africa and the Yao culture of Tanzania.

Literature

Malawi's literary tradition is rooted in oral history and storytelling. Contemporary Malawian writers incorporate traditional elements of spoken myths, legends, and folktales, as well as modern issues of corruption and oppression, into their works of poetry, fiction, and history. Well-known Malawian writers include poet Jack Mapanje (1944–), novelist and literary critic Paul Zeleza (1955–), novelist Legson Kayira (1942–2012), poet and playwright Felix Mnthali (1933–), poet and fiction writer Frank Chipasula (1949–), and poet David Rubadiri (1930–).

Malawi's contemporary writers have suffered imprisonment, harassment, and exile for writing about political issues and government conduct under the repressive rule of Hastings Banda (1898–1997), who served as Malawi's leader from 1961–1994. Many of Malawi's writers spent the latter decades of the 20th century living in political exile in foreign countries. Increased literacy in the 20th century has strengthened the literary community in Malawi. However, poverty and low literacy rates (65 percent in 2015) limit the influence and readership of Malawian writers in their home country. Malawi's best-known writers publish their books in English and have international audiences.

CULTURE

Arts & Entertainment

In Malawi, the role of the arts is a reflection of the country's 21st century culture, traditions, collective experience, and social consciousness. Malawi is facing overcrowding from population growth, political challenges as the nation transitions to a multi-party democracy, extreme poverty, and a rising HIV/AIDS infection rate. The arts, while not a solution to these social, economic, and political problems, offer an opportunity for the Malawian people to come together and celebrate their shared cultural heritage and achievements. Traditional arts such as mask making, pottery, and basketry are celebrated with pride as examples of Malawi's unique skills, aesthetics, and traditions.

Malawi, one of Africa's poorest countries, does not provide sufficient government resources to support the arts. In 1987, the Malawi Ministry of Education and Culture's Art and Craft Department did gather the resources to form the Malawi National Dance Troupe (formerly known as the Kwacha Cultural Troupe). Today, the Malawi National Dance Troupe is the Malawi government's only funded (or subsidized) art endeavor.

The Malawi government funds the Malawi National Dance Troupe to preserve the existence and continuity of Malawi's traditional dance and performing arts, and to promote respect for, and appreciation of, Malawi's traditional music and dance abroad. The troupe also serves as a symbol of national unity for Malawi's diverse ethnic groups and performs at government functions.

Ultimately, while the arts in Malawi are subject to social and economic forces created by Malawi's poverty, political climate, and the demands of the tourist trade, the arts are one of Malawi's strongest national assets and resources. They unite Malawi and serve as a point of national pride. Organizations, such as the University of Malawi, French Cultural Centre and The Malawi Ministry of Education and Culture's Art and Craft Department, offer exhibit space for contemporary visual artists. The Malawi Council for the Handicapped promotes disabled artists through the production and sale of artist-created cards and calendars. Perhaps the best-known artist in Malawi is Cuthy Mede. His work has been featured in various international museums and he has been actively engaged in promoting Malawian arts, both home and abroad, throughout his career. He opened up the first art gallery in the country in the late 1970s.

Cultural Sites & Landmarks

The United Nations Educational, Scientific and Cultural Organization (UNESCO) recognizes two sites in Malawi as requiring international recognition and preservation efforts: Lake Malawi National Park and the Chongoni Rock-Art Area. Lake Malawi National Park is a protected habitat of hundreds of endemic fish species and home to Lake Malawi, the third largest lake in Africa. Malawians living along the lakeshore fish the lake and use the water to irrigate their fields and fruit trees. Tourists and Malawians alike visit Lake Malawi for leisure and sightseeing.

The Chongoni Rock-Art Area, located in central Malawi, is a rich concentration of approximately 127 rock art sites. The sites are primarily located within rock shelters or caves and include examples of rock painting made by agrarian peoples from the late Iron Age and Batwa hunter-gatherers from the late Stone Age. Archaeologists believe that the rock art was made for ceremonial and ritual purposes. The regions rock art is painted in red or white pigments. The red paintings tend to be older and include geometric designs and shapes, while the white paintings are naturalistic and include figures of humans and animals.

UNESCO is currently considering adding two other sites in Malawi to the World Heritage List: the Mulanje Mountain Biosphere Reserve and Nyika National Park. The Mulanje Mountain Biosphere Reserve is a mountainous region with enduring specimens of syenite, quartz, and granite rock. The biosphere reserve is recognized and protected due to its unique physical and cultural importance. The area is the highest elevation in all of Malawi and south-central Africa and includes a unique biosphere and numerous important endemic species of plants and animals. The Malawian people consider the area to be sacred and travel to the area for rituals and celebrations.

The Nyika National Park is located in the North of Malawi. It is the country's largest national park. Biologists consider the Nyika National Park to be an important location of plant diversity, including endemic and endangered plant species. The park is also home to over 400 species of birds, many of which are rare and endemic. According to local legends, the area is the home of a half-serpent, half-human being.

Libraries & Museums

The government of Malawi manages four public museums. The Chichiri Museum (in Chichiri) houses the country's natural and cultural artifacts; the Mtengatenga Museum (in Namaka) displays a collection of postal and communication artifacts; the Lake Malawi Museum (in Mangochi) houses a collection related to those who have settled on the lake's shores; and the Mzuzu Regional Museum (in Mzuzu City) has a collection of cultural artifacts related to the people of northern Malawi.

Malawi's National Library service is committed to ensuring that the citizens of the country have access to reading and information materials across the nation. The library service promotes a reading culture through public, school, and rural libraries.

Holidays

Malawi's public holidays include John Chilembwe Day (January 16), Martyr's Day (March 3), Labour Day (May 1), Freedom Day (June 14), Republic Day (July 6), Mother's Day in October, National Tree Planting Day in December, Christmas Day (December 25), and Boxing Day (December 26).

Youth Culture

As of 2015, the median age in Malawi was approximately fifteen. The Malawian childhood is brief and very different from Western childhood. Life expectancy is approximately forty-three years, and Malawians usually marry as teenagers or very young adults. Generally, school attendance for Malawi youth is dependent on costs, such as school fees and uniforms. The majority of Malawi's population lives in rural settings, and many youth leave school early to help with agricultural or household work. For example, boys may learn the agricultural trades of their fathers, while girls work with their mothers and learn about the household chores of gathering firewood, carrying drinking water, and making and serving food. Older siblings are often responsible for the care of younger siblings.

Leisure time for young Malawians is generally filled with impromptu games of football (soccer), the most popular sport, or netball and basketball. Church activities and quiet games such as bao are also popular amongst youth. Bao is a game of strategy involving a carved board and a pebble or seed. Television and movies are rare in most of rural Malawi, and children commonly make their own toys out of scarp metal or other discarded items.

SOCIETY

Transportation

Local travel in Malawi is undertaken by train, taxi, bus, car, or by foot. Walking and hitchhiking are the primary ways that Malawi's poorest people travel between towns. Local train travel in Malawi tends to be slow, unpredictable, and overcrowded, but bus travel is affordable and generally runs on schedule. Few Malawians own reliable cars, as maintaining a car is typically expensive in Malawi. Local roads tend be unpaved and poorly maintained, and Malawi's road system is not generally well marked with signs. Traffic moves on the left-hand side of the road.

Transportation Infrastructure

In 2007, Malawi had an estimated thirty-nine airports, 797 kilometers (495 miles) of railways, 15,451 kilometers (9,656 miles) of roadways, and 700 kilometers (434 miles) of waterways. The majority of airport runways and roadways are unpaved, and the main waterways are on Lake Nyasa (also known as Lake Malawi) and the Shire River. Passenger ferries travel on Malawi's waterways, and Malawi's ports and terminals include Chipoka, Monkey Bay, Nkhata Bay, Nkhotakota and Chilumba. Roads and railways connect Malawi to its neighboring countries of Tanzania, Mozambique and Zambia.

Media & Communications

In Malawi, the media enjoys new constitutional protections regarding censorship and free speech. The contemporary Malawian government generally respects the rights and freedoms of the independent press. Popular daily and weekly newspapers include *The Daily Times*, *Michiru Sun*, the *Enquirer*, *U.D.F.* (United Democratic Front) *News*, the *Malawi News*, the *Independent*, the *Nation* and the *New Express*. Due to the lack of advertising money, magazines and commercial media are rare in Malawi. There is one television broadcast station and numerous FM and AM radio stations. Radio broadcasts in Chichewa, Malawi's main language, educate Malawians about HIV/AIDS prevention and political elections.

Malawi's communications system is considered rudimentary by international standards. In 2014, there were an estimated 387,500 Internet users.

SOCIAL DEVELOPMENT

Standard of Living

Malawi is ranked 174th out of 187 countries on the 2014 United Nations Human Development Index, which measures quality of life and standard of living indicators.

Malawi has been hit hard by the AIDS epidemic. Officials estimate that about 1 million people were infected with HIV or AIDS as of 2014. The disease has killed over 650,000 people. Malawi's high birth rate (more than 41 births per thousand) is offset by a fairly high death rate (8 deaths per thousand). Largely because of the AIDS crisis and increased poverty, infant mortality is also high, averaging about 41 deaths per thousand live births. Life expectancy is about sixty years (2015 estimate).

Water Consumption

According to 2015 statistics reported by the World Health Organization, approximately 90 percent of the Malawian population has access to improved drinking water, while an estimated 41 percent of the population has access to improved sanitation. However, statistics regarding water and sanitation have been characterized as unreliable or overstated. Other estimates place the rural sanitation coverage at 30 percent, if not less, while some estimates state that more than 90 percent of Lilongwe's population lack sewer connections. Malawi has been characterized as a "water stressed" nation, with scant freshwater resources.

Education

Prior to implementing an improvement plan in the 1990s, Malawi had only a 58 percent school attendance rate among primary school children. Since then, the country has eliminated fees for primary school and invested in school infrastructure, teachers, and textbooks, working in partnership with charitable organizations and local districts. As a result, primary school attendance has increased significantly. In 2007, the primary school attendance rate was 75 percent;

in 2006, 86 percent of those who began primary school completed grade five, up from 64 percent in 2000.

Malawi does not provide free schooling beyond primary levels. Secondary schools, vocational schools, and the University of Malawi provide further education to students for a fee. Because of the pervasive poverty in the country and the difficulty of transportation to schools in Malawi's large rural areas, Malawi continues to struggle to provide education beyond primary school.

Women's Rights

Women face disadvantage and adversity in Malawi and the country's culture has deeply ingrained beliefs about gender differences and biases against women. As a result, women are responsible for an inequitable amount of household duties—women's responsibilities include gathering firewood, carrying drinking water, preparing and serving food, and making household items such as baskets or pottery vessels. They do not participate in community or government-level decisions or policy-making. They tend to experience harsh living conditions and, due to societal prejudices, lack education. The gender imbalance in Malawi also favors men in areas of income, credit, jobs, inheritance, and divorce. In addition, men may have more than one wife, and in cases of divorce, women are stripped of all belongings.

Domestic violence continues to be a common problem in Malawian society. Exacerbating the problem is a widespread reluctance of the behalf of victims to report abuse. Because domestic disputes are largely viewed as a familial issue, police rarely intervene. Female genital mutilation (FGM) has also been reported among certain ethnicities. Prostitution remains legal and sexual harassment, though prohibited by law, is also reported to occur commonly.

The Malawi government has developed a national Poverty Alleviation Program (PAP) to significantly reduce the poverty in Malawi, particularly as experienced by women, by 2020. The Malawi Government has recognized the potential of women to contribute to national development and is working, alongside the UN and women's rights organizations, to create opportunities for women to make social, economic, and political contributions. Malawi's initiative for women, which promotes equality and equity for women, is called the Malawi Platform for Action.

Organizations working in Malawi to improve women's rights include the National Commission on Women in Development (NCWD), Project Officers and Entrepreneurs Training, and the Society For the Advancement Of Women. The National Commission on Women in Development is a unit of the Malawi Ministry of Women, Children Affairs & Community Development and Social Welfare (MWCACDSW). The National Commission on Women in Development has the following responsibilities: plans and implements women's rights programs; coordinates women's involvement with non-government organizations and government agencies; improves the management of women's programs; evaluates the role and contribution of women in development; and raises awareness about the Malawi government's commitment to gender equality and equity.

Health Care

Malawi has a socialized system of health care under the direction of the Ministry of Health and Population. A network of rural hospitals and health clinics provide ground level healthcare for no fee to the majority of Malawians. Staffed by nurses and clinicians, these rural health centers must cater to the basic needs of about 50 villages each.

Because of the widespread poverty in Malawi and the difficulty of procuring basic first aid equipment like bandages and aspirin, most of the population turns to the rural health centers for even minor injuries and illnesses, creating long waiting lines for care. The rural clinics and hospitals also provide wellness care for expectant and new mothers and infants. They also provide the base for a system of Health Surveillance Assistants who travel throughout the villages to teach better health practices and to provide outpatient assistance.

For more serious injuries, Malawians are directed to the country's twenty-eight district hospitals. Staffed by physicians, nurses, and clinicians, these hospitals have basic diagnostic equipment, laboratories, and surgical facilities. Like the rural clinic and hospitals, all care provided through district hospitals is free to citizens of Malawi. Three central hospitals in urban areas of the country provide free advanced care for the most serious injuries and illnesses. These central hospitals are better staffed, have more advanced equipment, and a greater capacity for treating complex medical problems.

Outside of the government-run system, Malawi also has private clinics and physicians for which wealthier Malawians can pay, and traditional medicine practitioners ("African doctors") who use a variety of spiritual, herbal, and other traditional remedies. The AIDS epidemic has overstrained Malawi's already minimal health care system and foreign organization have attempted to bridge the gaps.

Government vaccination programs and new family planning programs have begun to show results in the form of fewer problems with pregnancy and childbirth and an 80 percent vaccination rate in children under five years of age.

Nevertheless, Malawi's health care system is still fighting an uphill battle. One in five children die before the age of five, and pregnancy related deaths are still dangerously high. Malaria, cholera, and other epidemics are prevalent, and AIDS has ravaged Malawi's workforce. The Health Ministry cites the prevalence of HIV infections, poor transportation, widespread poverty, poor sanitation, and inadequate education as among the greatest obstacles to Malawi's health care system.

GOVERNMENT

Structure

Malawi was originally the home of the Maravo Confederacy of Bantu peoples from the 14th through 16th centuries. During the 18th century, the area was prey to the growing African slave trade under Arab traders and another Bantu tribe, the Yao. The 19th century explorer David Livingstone first raised British interest in the region with his work to establish commercial trade routes and the University Mission in Central Africa. Many places in the country still bear his name.

The Livingstonia Central Africa Mission Company, a Scottish corporation, arrived in 1878 to establish a river route through the area. The Shire Highlands in the south became a British protectorate in 1891 under the name Nyasaland. The first rebellion came in 1900 under the leadership of Reverend John Chilembwe, whose failed effort is celebrated with a national holiday in his name. Malawi finally took its new name and its independence in 1964, but fell under the dictatorship of Dr. Hastings Kamuzu Banda.

Since Malawi became a multiparty democracy in 1994, the president, who also holds the title of chief of state, is elected by popular vote to a five-year term. He is joined by a first and second vice president and a cabinet of forty-six members, chosen by the president. Voting is open to all citizens over the age of 17. Malawi held its first multi-party national elections in 1994. The legislative branch consists of 193-member National Assembly. A Senate is provided for in the constitution, but it has never been seated. Legislators are chosen by popular vote, and also serve five-year terms.

Political Parties

In Malawi's 2014 general election, numerous political parties participated. The Democratic Progressive Party (DPP), led by Peter Mutharika, prevailed, winning almost 36 percent of the vote in the presidential election and securing 51 seats in the National Assembly. The newly established People's Party took 26 seats. The Malawi Congress Party, a party that is strongly supported by the ethnic Chewa and Nyanja people in the central region, garnered almost 27 percent of the vote in the presidential election and gained forty-eight seats in the assembly. The United Democratic Front, the parent of the DPP and a liberal party with strong support from the Yao people in the north, gained fourteen seats in the assembly. Other participating parties included the Alliance for Democracy, the Maravi People's Party, the Malawi Forum for Unity and Development, the New Rainbow Coalition, and the People's Democratic Movement.

Local Government

Malawi is divided into three divisions or regions: Northern, Central and Southern. It is further divided into twenty-eight districts and numerous autonomous municipalities. Regional administrations and district assemblies govern the development of their respective jurisdictions.

Judicial System

Malawi's legal system is based on English and Welsh common law, with judiciary review of legislation. The Supreme Court of Appeal is the highest appellate court. The High Court may review cases from lower courts, as well as government laws or actions as they pertain to the constitution. High Court judges are appointed by the president. Lower courts include magistrate and industrial relations courts.

Taxation

The government of Malawi levies personal and corporate income, value-added, fringe benefit, import, and export taxes. Tax revenues have increased in the early 21st century, allowing citizens hope for advancing the country's social development issues.

Armed Forces

The government of Malawi has an army with both navy and air divisions.

Foreign Policy

Malawi maintains positive foreign and diplomatic relations with Western and African nations and favors peaceful resolution to conflicts between African nations. To further Malawi's peaceful resolution agenda, the Malawian government received peacekeeping training from the United States' African Crisis Response Force Initiative. Malawi holds an overall pro-West stance regarding policy and, as one of the poorest countries in Africa, receives significant amounts of foreign aid

from the US, Canada, Germany, Iceland, Ireland, Japan, the Netherlands, Norway, Sweden and the United Kingdom (UK). Significant organizations active within Malawi include the European Union (EU), the International Monetary Fund (IMF), the African Development Bank (ADB), and the United Nations (UN) and it subsidiaries. They all help the Malawian government achieve its goals of strengthening the national economy, reducing government corruption, improving social services and improving its human rights record.

Historically, Malawi's support of South Africa during apartheid caused tension between Malawi and other African nations. In 1994, when apartheid ended, Malawi's relationships with African nations became more positive. For instance, Malawi has admitted approximately 1 million political refugees from Mozambique and thousands from Rwanda and the Congo. Today, Malawi maintains supportive diplomatic relations with nearly all African nations. That said, Malawi is party to an international dispute with neighboring Tanzania regarding country boundaries within Lake Malawi.

Since Malawi transitioned to a democratic government with multiple parties, the US has become more actively involved in improving health and living conditions in Malawi. The US Peace Corps, the US Center for Disease Control and Prevention (CDC), and the US Agency for International Development (USAID) maintain active programs in Malawi. The Malawian government works with the USAID on the shared agenda of increasing rural incomes, increasing civic involvement in politics, improving access to health services, and improving access to basic education.

Human Rights Profile

International human rights law insists that states respect civil and political rights, and also promote an individual's economic, social and cultural rights. The United Nations Universal Declaration on Human Rights is recognized as the standard for international human rights. Its authors sought the counsel of the world's great thinkers, philosophers, and religious leaders, and were careful to create a document that reflects the core values shared by every world culture. (To read this document or view the articles relating to cultural human rights, go to: http://www.udhr.org/UDHR/default.htm.)

Malawi has an overall positive human rights record. Article 2 of the UDHR, which states that everyone is entitled to legal rights and freedoms without distinction of race, color, sex, language, religion, political or other opinion, national or social origin, property, birth or other status, is supported by the Malawian constitution, but not always in the actions of the government. International human rights organizations have noted a growing trend in incidents of politically motivated detentions, arrests and prosecutions.

International human rights organizations also cite the need for improvement in the following areas: excessive police force, prison conditions, free speech, human trafficking, child labor, and violence against women.

Article 16 of the UDHR, which states that men and women of any race, nationality, or religion have the right to marry and found a family, is supported by Malawian law. However, Gambian men and women do not have the same rights within the marriage or in the event of divorce. Article 18 of the UDHR, which supports the right to freedom of thought, conscience, and religion (so long as the practice of religion does not violate public morality, decency, or the public order), is supported by Malawian law. The government requires that religious groups register with the government, but does not impose any limitations on religious worship or thought. Article 19 of the UDHR, which guarantees the right to freedom of opinion and expression, is guaranteed by law. However, the Malawian government still struggles with incidents of press censorship and intimidation, but is overall believed to be working to foster a free speech environment for citizens and journalists.

Malawian human rights policy is based on the notion that social, moral, economic, and cultural rights are interrelated and equally impor-

tant. The nation of Malawi values this notion for their citizens, as well as people around the world. Despite the social, moral, economic, and cultural rights guaranteed by Malawi's constitution, Malawi's citizens are ultimately limited by their nation's poverty, underdeveloped infrastructure, and inadequate healthcare.

ECONOMY

Overview of the Economy

Malawi's economy is still overwhelmingly agricultural, with most of the country's inhabitants dependent on small family gardens to provide their food. Farming, in fact, employs 90 percent of the national population, accounts for more than 90 percent of Malawi's export revenue, and more than a third its gross domestic product (GDP). The economy of Lilongwe, the capital, is based heavily on the civil services sector as well as small businesses. Lilongwe's informal economy is also massive in scope. Lacking formal education and professional skills, many of the impoverished rural newcomers who have migrated to Lilongwe in the late 20th and early 21st century have survived by becoming street vendors and manual laborers. In 2007, Malawi's government ordered a crackdown on foreign businesses operating unlawfully in the capital and other urban centers.

In 2007, the United States made Malawi eligible to receive financial support within the Millennium Challenge Corporation (MCC) initiative, which is designed to fund sustainable growth in developing countries. In 2008, government officials in Lilongwe signed off on a new plan aimed at promoting democracy, the rule of law, and justice in Malawi. Officials in the capital hope that such steps will encourage outside investment and economic development in Lilongwe.

Industry

The processing of tobacco, tea, sugar, lumber products, cement, and consumer goods accounts for approximately 20 percent of the country's gross domestic product GDP. Farmers raise maize, millet and rice, bananas, citrus fruit, and vegetables for domestic consumption. In recent years, growers have also begun to export peanuts, macadamia nuts, paprika, and chili peppers. In Lilongwe, the largest city, the industrial base is modest in size, as the national economy is largely based on agriculture.

Labor

The labor force in Malawi was estimated at 5.7 million people in 2007. The government of Malawi reports that the unemployment rate stood at 3.1 percent in that same year.

Energy/Power/Natural Resources

In addition to the country's rich arable land and hydropower capacities, Malawi has limestone, untapped uranium deposits, coal, and bauxite.

Fishing

In Malawi, fish is the primary protein among the country's population. Fish stocks in Lake Chilwa and Lake Milawi, though, are in danger due to environmental degradation and over-fishing. In 2008, the BBC reported that the WorldFish Centre, a member of the Consultative Group on International Agricultural Research (CGIAR), had begun a program to support fish farming or subsistence aquaculture. These small farms create a cycle of agriculture that involves using manure from livestock to feed pond plankton, which is eaten by the fish, which are then harvested and sold, the profits from which are reinvested in the growing of maize, which feeds the livestock. WorldFish calls this an integrated agriculture-aquaculture (IAA) system. At the same time, these small farms are providing much-needed protein to small communities.

Forestry

Malawi's forests are in danger of over-exploitation. Because the cost of electricity is so high and is unreliable, much of the rural population depends on wood for fuel, resulting in massive deforestation. Illegal logging also contributes to the problem. The Forest Governance and Learning Group has warned that the Chikangawa forest is in danger of depletion by 2020 if action is not taken to reverse the course. Forest fires have also contributed to the demise of forest cover.

Mining/Metals

Mining is not a major contributor to the country's GDP. Limestone, cement, coal, crushed and ornamental stone, some gemstones, phosphate, and uranium are the major products in this industry.

Agriculture

Most Malawians depend on family gardens as their primary source of food, even in urban areas where crops are grown in gardens that belong to relatives outside the city. Malawi does export some of its crops, including tobacco, sugarcane, cotton, tea, corn, potatoes, cassava (tapioca), sorghum, groundnuts, and macadamia nuts. The nation's agricultural industry also depends heavily on cattle and goats.

Animal Husbandry

The livestock industry in Malawi is underdeveloped; about 50 percent of dairy products consumed in the country are imported. The Mzimba District has been identified as a region ripe for beef and dairy investment, as cattle are already raised there and the existing infrastructure can support the industry's development.

Tourism

Malawi is working aggressively to increase tourism to the country. Lake Malawi, with its spectacular scenery and opportunities for snorkeling and boating, takes a central role in this campaign, as do the wildlife reserves and parks that provide rare glimpses of endangered species. To date, the tourist industry remains only a small part of the economy.

Simone Flynn, Amy Witherbee,
Beverly Ballaro

DO YOU KNOW?

• Malawi is often referred to as the "warm heart of Africa," a reputation said to have derived from the friendliness of its citizens.

• Malawi is famous for the more than 400 hundred species of orchids that grow in its diverse ecosystems.

Bibliography

Briggs, Phillip. *Malawi*. London: Bradt Travel Guide, 2013.

Fitzpatrick, Mary, et al. *Zambia, Mozambique, and Malawi*. Oakland, CA: Lonely Planet, 2013.

McCracken, John. *A History of Malawi, 1859–1966*. Rochester, NY: James Currey, 2012.

Power, Joey. *Political Culture and Nationalism in Malawi*. Rochester, NY: University of Rochester Press, 2010.

Wilson, Anika. *Folklore, Gender, and AIDS in Malawi: No Secret under the Sun*. New York: Palgrave Macmillan 2013.

Works Cited

"Background Notes: Malawi." U.S. Department of State. http://www.state.gov/r/pa/ei/bgn/7231.htm.

"Culture of Malawi." Countries and Their Cultures. http://www.everyculture.com/Ja-Ma/Malawi.html.

Kiš, Adam. "An Analysis of the Impact of Aids on Funeral Culture in Malawi." NAPA Bulletin 27.1 (March 2008): 129–140.

"Land of Lake and Sunshine." Malawi: The Warm Heart of Africa (n.d.). http://members.tripod.com/~malawi/.

"Malawi." CIA World Fact Book. https://www.cia.gov/library/publications/the-world-factbook/print/mi.html.

"Malawi." Encyclopedia of the Nations. http://www.nationsencyclopedia.com/Africa/Malawi.html.

"Malawi." Malawi Sustainable Development Network Program. http://www.csr.org.mw/.

"Malawi." UNESCO World Heritage List. http://whc.unesco.org/en/tentativelists/state=mw.

"Malawi." Women's Organizations. http://www.distel.ca/womlist/countries/malawi.html.

"Malawi." World Atlas (n.d.). http://www.worldatlas.com/webimage/countrys/africa/mw.htm.

"Malawi." Culture Crossing (n.d.). http://www.culturecrossing.net/basics_business_student.php?id=124.

"Malawi: Country Reports on Human Rights Practices." U.S. Department of State. http://www.state.gov/g/drl/rls/hrrpt/2006/78744.htm.

"Malawi, Africa." Wow Gambia News (2009). http://wow.gm/africa/malawi/news.

"Malawi: People and Culture." The Africa Guide. http://www.africaguide.com/country/malawi/culture.htm.

"Malawi Traditions." Project Malawi (n.d.). http://www.projectmalawi.it/archivio/en/il_malawi/le_tradizioni.html.

"Malipenga Dance."://cwis.usc.edu/dept/elab/oconnell/malipenga.html.

"Population Estimates for Cities in Malawi." Mongabay. http://www.mongabay.com/igapo/Malawi.htm.

"Universal Declaration of Human Rights." United Nations. http://www.udhr.org/UDHR/default.htm.

"Vegetable Ndiwo." Celtnet Recipes. http://www.celtnet.org.uk/recipes/miscellaneous/fetch-recipe.php?rid=misc-vegetable-ndiwo.

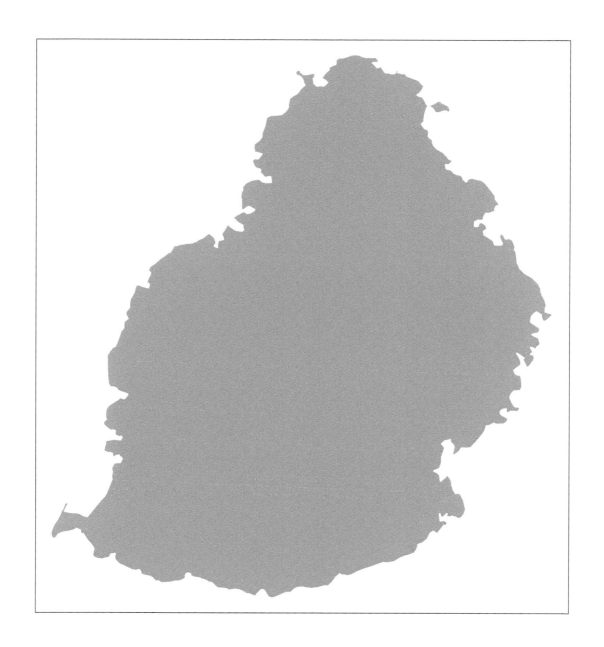

MAURITIUS

Introduction

The Republic of Mauritius is an island nation that lies in the Indian Ocean, east of Madagascar, in the shadow of the African continent. The French and British influences on its culture are unmistakable. Since its discovery in 1505, the Dutch, French, and British have colonized Mauritius. It became an independent nation in 1968. The republic's territory encompasses the island of Mauritius and the islands of Agalega, Rodriguez, and the Saint Brandon Rocks (or Cargados Carajos Shoals).

Port Louis is the national capital of Mauritius and was established by the French colonial government in the 18th century as a waypoint for the French shipping fleet. The city is now the economic hub of the nation. Port Louis has a long history of both colonial and modern immigration, and possesses an ethnically diverse population of Chinese, African, Indian, and European descent.

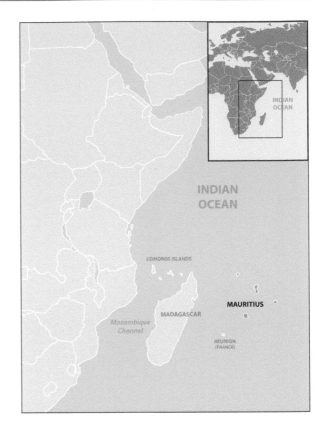

GENERAL INFORMATION

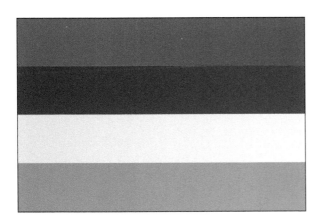

Official Language: English
Population: 1,339,827 (2015 estimate)
Currency: Mauritian rupee
Coins: The Mauritian rupee is divided into 100 cents, and coins were minted in denominations of 1, 5, 20, and 50 cents, and 1, 5, and 10 rupees, with a commemorative 20-rupee coin issued in 2007.

Land Area: 2,030 square kilometers (783 square miles)
Water Area: 10 square kilometers (3 square miles)
National Motto: "Stella Clavisque Maris Indici" (Latin, "Star and Key of the Indian Ocean")
National Anthem: "Motherland"
Capital: Port Luis
Time Zone: GMT + 4
Flag Description: The national flag of Mauritius consists of four equal, horizontal bands of red, blue, yellow, and green—and in that order from top to bottom. The colored stripes are said to represent independence (red), the Indian Ocean (blue), hope for a better future (yellow), and the island nation's abundant flora.

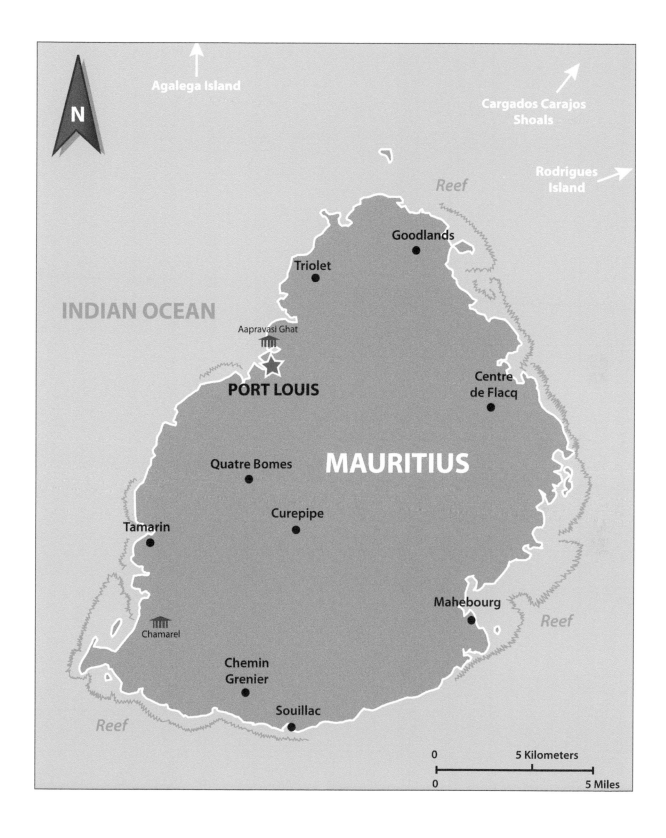

Principal Cities by Population (2012):

- Port Louis (158,965)
- Beau Bassin-Rosehill (112,215)
- Vacoas-Phoenix (108,103)
- Curepipe (85,259)
- Quatre Bornes (81,979)

Population

Few countries are more densely populated than Mauritius; as of 2009, the country ranked eighteenth in the world in population density, with a density figure of 631 per square kilometer (1,634 per square mile). The population is evenly divided between rural and urban areas—an estimated 40 of the population lives in urban areas (2015 estimate). As of 2015, the population growth rate was 0.64 percent.

Port Louis, with approximately 158,965 people, is the country's capital and largest city. The city is more ethnically diverse than the nation as a whole, and there are substantial populations of ethnic Chinese and Europeans living in the city. Other large urban centers include Beau Bassin and Vacoas, each with over 100,000 residents. Approximately 35,000 people (mostly Creole) live on Rodrigues, the only other inhabited island in the country.

The population of Mauritius is comprised of many ethnic groups and cultures. Originally brought from India as indentured servants to work the sugar plantations, Indo-Mauritians comprise the majority (about 68 percent as of the 2011 census) of the population. The Creole population, whose ancestors were slaves, claims a mixed African and European heritage, and accounts for 27 percent of the population.

Minority groups include Sino-Mauritians (roughly 3 percent of the population) and Franco-Mauritians (two percent of the population), who control many of the sugar plantations in Mauritius.

Languages

Although English is the country's official language, and used in government and educational settings, approximately 85 percent of the population speaks Mauritian Creole (or Morisyen). Morisyen is largely based on French, but also contains elements of English and African languages.

Bhojpuri and other Indian dialects are spoken by 12 percent of the population; most Bhojpuri speakers are of Indian heritage. French is also common in major cities, like Port Louis, though less than 5 percent of the population use standard French as their primary language.

Native People & Ethnic Groups

The island of Mauritius was uninhabited until the Dutch began a colony there in 1638. They were followed by the French and the British, all of whom added their own traders, plantation owners, and slaves to the island's population.

By the time the British seized the island from France during the Napoleonic Wars in 1810, slavery had been outlawed in Britain. Large numbers of Indians were brought in to make up for the labor shortage on the sugar plantations. Since that time, the Indo-Mauritian population has been the country's main ethnic group.

Religions

More than half of Mauritians practice the Hindu religion, reflecting the country's large Indian population. Catholicism is also popular in Mauritius, especially among the Afro-Creole population; approximately 24 percent of the population practices Catholicism. Other forms of Christianity are practiced by approximately eight percent of the island population, though more often in other major cities. Small populations of Buddhists and Taoists may be found among the nation's Chinese population. Approximately 17 percent of the population is Muslim.

Climate

Weather in Mauritius can vary greatly depending on elevation and proximity to the coast. The plateau region, including the city of Curepipe, is often slightly cooler than coastal areas. The main island's central and western regions receive more rainfall during January and February than the rest of the island, due to the influence of the mountains and the easterly winds. Cyclones, usually occurring between November and May, bring heavy rains.

The warmest months are between January and April, with an average high temperature of 35° Celsius (95° Fahrenheit). From July to September, the temperature drops to an average of 24° Celsius (75° Fahrenheit) during the day and 16° Celsius (60° Fahrenheit) at night.

ENVIRONMENT & GEOGRAPHY

Topography

Although the Mascarene Islands (Réunion, Mauritius, and Rodrigues) are volcanic in origin, there are no active volcanoes in Mauritius today. Historical evidence of volcanic activity may be found in the Trou aux Cerfs volcanic crater in Curepipe, and lava rocks can be found everywhere throughout the islands.

The southern end of Mauritius is dominated by mountains, which decline gently until they reach the northern coastline. The mountains provide a dramatic backdrop for the capital of Port Louis, which lies in the north central region.

Piton de la Petite Rivière Noire, in the central plateau, is the highest point on the island, at 828 meters (2,717 feet) above sea level. Many lakes and streams flow through the highland region, some stretching from the mountains all the way to the coast.

Mauritius is nearly blockaded by coral reefs, however, there is a large enough break in the reef at Port Louis to provide an excellent harbor for ships. There are other smaller breaks in the reef, and another large break between Souillac and Le Bouchon to the south that is not as commercially exploited as the one at Port Louis.

Port Louis, the capital and largest city, is located on the northwestern coast of Mauritius within the Moka Mountain Range, which forms a semi-circle around the city and rises to more than 800 meters (2,647 feet). Elevations fall swiftly from the mountains to the port harbor and most of the urban area sits at sea level.

Plants & Animals

Wildlife is scarce in Mauritius, due in large part to the fact that only about 1 percent of the island's original rainforests remain. The best chance to spot any wildlife is to try to visit one of the country's small nature preserves. Deep in the interior of the country, wild animals such as mongoose, Java deer, and wild pigs may be found.

Many species of birds fill the trees and skies of Mauritius. The famous flightless dodo bird once inhabited the islands, but has since become extinct, along with other native species. Threatened bird species found in Mauritius include the echo parakeet (or Mauritius Parakeet) and the endemic pink pigeon, both of which are rare. Introduced species of songbirds, including the Madagascar Fody and the Indian Mynah, are common.

While coconut palms and casuarina trees grow along the coast, nearly three-quarters of Mauritius' area is covered with volcanic rock. Acacia, pine, and aloe trees, along with lush grasses, grow at the base of the mountains.

CUSTOMS & COURTESIES

Greetings

While English is the official language of Mauritius, people typically greet each other in French. Common phrases include "Bonjour" ("Good day") or the less formal "Salut" ("Hi"). Among friends or youth, a common greeting is "Ca va?" ("How's it going?"). In Mauritian Creole, which is strongly influenced by French, "Bonzour" ("Hello" or "Good day") is common. A commonly spoken greeting among members of the Indian community is "Namaste" ("I bow to you"). This is traditionally accompanied by a slight bow of the head with the palms pressed together in front of the chest.

Introductions and greetings are typically accompanied by handshaking. Mauritian women typically greet friends with the bisou, which is a light kiss on each cheek. This greeting is slightly less common between men greeting men, but can be common between male and female acquaintances. Elders are treated with a great deal of respect and are generally referred to using honorific titles. It is common to use the "vous" form when speaking to strangers and to switch to the "tu" form only after a relationship has been established. When speaking to children, the "tu" form is used. The younger generation uses the "vous" form far less than was common in the past.

Gestures & Etiquette

Mauritians are warm and friendly, but somewhat conservative in their public behavior. Loud talking or actions are generally looked down upon. In Mauritian Creole, this kind of behavior is called "sauvaze" (meaning "wild" or "uncivilized") and may be met with looks of disapproval. In addition, people tend to be orderly about their approach to sharing space in public. For example, queuing, or waiting in line for public transport or service at a store is the norm. Holding hands is an acceptable practice for couples, but kissing or other public displays of affection are poorly regarded, even by the younger generation.

While Mauritius has a relaxed, informal atmosphere, appearances are important, and most Mauritians wear casual but conservative clothes. When visiting a Hindu temple, it is customary to remove one's shoes, and women are expected to wear modest clothing, which covers their knees and shoulders.

Eating/Meals

In the past, eating habits varied according to ethnic community and religion. People tended to stick with their own ethnic cuisine, and it was rare to see an Indo-Mauritian eating Chinese-Mauritian food and vice-versa. However, as divisions between Mauritius' different ethnic communities have started to dissolve, more Mauritians have adopted customs from other groups.

Breakfast is usually a small meal, and typically includes light fare such as a baguette with cheese, a croissant or other pastry, a piece of fruit, and coffee or just a cup of tea with milk. Lunch generally consists of a hot dish such as a curry with rice or fried fish and has traditionally been eaten at home with family. This has changed in recent years as more women start to work outside the home. Mauritians follow the British tradition of tea time, a late afternoon snack that consists of tea and a sweet treat such as biscuits (cookies).

Dinner is the main meal of the day, and can stretch over the course of hours. Lunch and dinner are social times for Mauritians, and the conversation and company are just as important as the food.

In Indian culture, many foods are eaten by hand rather than with utensils, and this custom carries over to Indo-Mauritian foods. Chinese Mauritian food is customarily eaten with chopsticks. Because of a cultural taboo against the left hand—it is associated with personal cleansing, and is thus considered impure—food may only be touched or eaten with the right hand. It should also be noted that members of the Muslim community refrain from consuming alcohol and pork.

Visiting

Mauritians are warm and welcoming to their guests and it is not necessary to arrange a time before stopping by for a visit. On the weekends, Mauritians often entertain a steady steam of kompanye (Mauritian Creole for "company") all day long. When the weather is nice, visitors often sit outside if the home has a garden or a verandah. A visit is a relaxed affair, and it is customary for the host to offer the guest something to eat and drink, typically soda or tea (often vanilla tea) with milk and biscuits. In a Sino-Mauritian home, the tea might be black or green tea served without milk. The guest is expected to accept the offer, even if only a small portion of it is eventually consumed.

It is not necessary to bring a gift to a host, but guests often bring something from their garden or something sweet for the children of the house. When the visit is over, the host may offer the guest something from the garden, such as flowers or fruit. Mauritians are known for lingering goodbyes: while a guest may be out the door already, the conversation may continue for quite some time.

LIFESTYLE

Family

It is still common for several generations to reside in one household, although this practice is starting to wane with the younger generation. This includes grandparents, particularly since retirement homes are nonexistent in Mauritius. Extended family members typically live in the same neighborhood also. Twenty-five is the average age for marriage and children. Family roles continue to be defined by tradition—women stay home and care for children while the men provide financial support. Grandparents often help out with childcare when a mother works outside the home.

In Hindu families, arranged marriages are still the norm, but both parties are given a say in the arrangement and it is never forced. Dating has traditionally been frowned upon in the Hindu population, but this is starting to change with the younger generation. Once forbidden, intermarriage between different ethnic groups on the island is becoming more common, as is marriage between members of different castes in the Indo-Mauritian community. Divorce is also on the rise.

Housing

Houses in Mauritius range from typical flat-roofed, two-room structures made of concrete, brick, or corrugated iron, often painted in bright colors, to colonial or Mauritian Creole-style houses with balconies and gardens in front. The former is common in rural areas, while the latter two styles are common among the middle class. In the urban areas, it is common for to people expand their homes by building additional stories to the top of the house as their financial situation improves. European-style villas, often featuring amenities such as a swimming pool, are common among the upper class. Because of the island's heavy reliance on tourism, there are many vacation homes in the coastal towns, but these are occupied mostly by short-term tourists or used as second homes by part-time foreign residents.

In the past, neighborhoods in urban areas tended to be segregated by ethnicity, but now class divides them. In the rural areas, different ethnic groups still tend to live in separate communities.

Food

Thanks to immigration, Mauritian cuisine is a unique blend of influences from India, France, China, England, and cultures all over Africa. The staples of the Mauritian diet are baryonic (an Indian spicy rice dish often served with meat), dhooll puri (a flat chickpea bread filled with curried vegetables), roti (a flat bread), mine frite (fried noodles), and rougaille (a tomato sauce that is used on fish, meat or vegetables). Commonly, rice and curry form the basis of most dishes, and are complemented by vegetables, fish, chicken, or goat.

Because of the proximity to the sea, fish is plentiful and relatively inexpensive. Consequently, nearly all Mauritians, regardless of ethnicity, incorporate seafood into their diet. Snapper, tuna, swordfish, marlin, and octopus are common, and are served fried, cooked in rougaille, or covered in masala (a curry sauce). Octopus stew is a popular dish.

Food stalls or parlors have become popular in Mauritius. There are certain inexpensive dishes that are often served there, such as samoussas (a fried pastry filled with spicy vegetables), bredes (a spinach-like mixed with onion, garlic, and hot chilies), and gateaux piment (spicy chili cakes). A uniquely Mauritian beverage called alouda (made from milk, sugar, basil seeds, rose syrup, vanilla, and other local ingredients) can also be found at markets. It is sold chilled or accompanied by snacks called gadjacks, which is typically a chicken croquette or octopus in tomato sauce.

Tea is a very popular beverage in Mauritius, and customarily served in the British style, with milk and sugar. Vanilla tea (which is grown on the island) is considered a special treat. Lassi is a traditional Indian drink that combines yogurt and ice water; as is alouda, which is a thick blend of agar, milk, and a variety of flavorings. Rum making was one of the first industries on Mauritius and rum remains a big part of Mauritian culture. It is common to drink wine with dinner and rum afterward with dessert. Mauritians like sweets, and some of the most popular ones are gateau batate (a thin wafer made from sweet potato and coconut) and pineapple mousse.

Life's Milestones

Among Hindu families, a naming ceremony is held when a baby is nine days old. Within the first year of life, the child's head is shaved in order to remove impurities from past lives, but a small tuft of hair is left on the head to preserve memories. In the Chinese-Mauritian community, the baby's first birthday is a widely observed celebration, customarily accompanied by a huge party.

Indian and Chinese weddings in Mauritius are grand, multi-day events with music, dancing, and feasting. In Indian tradition, the bride and groom circle a fire together seven times as part of their nuptials. This practice has been adopted by many tourists who come to the island for their weddings, regardless of whether or not they are of Indian descent.

CULTURAL HISTORY

Art & Architecture

The earliest permanent architecture on Mauritius is attributed to the colonizing efforts of the Dutch and the French. A Dutch wooden fort overlooking Mahebourg Bay, built in 1638, is believed to be the first durable fabricated structure on Mauritius. When the Dutch abandoned their settlement in 1710, they destroyed the stone fort. The French, who arrived in 1722, rebuilt on top of its foundations. Early French buildings on Mauritius more or less replicated the style of architecture common in France at the time. They include architectural elements such as stone foundations, timber frames, and shingled roofs.

With the second generation of settlers, a Mauritian style had developed. Houses featured wide verandahs and double French doors that could be opened to allow for better air circulation. The doors had full-length shutters that could be closed to block out heat in the middle of the day or for protection during storms. Larger houses or government buildings had second-floor balconies and dormer windows. When the British took over

in 1810, they brought their own style, including houses with ornamental woodwork called lambrequins. In the 20th century, concrete or corrugated iron, often painted in bright colors, became the materials of choice for modest houses.

Early Mauritian art imitated European traditions and trends. Romantic landscape paintings were common in the early 1800s. Later, the same artistic experimentation that was going on in France, including impressionism, symbolism, and art nouveau, came to the island. The most celebrated Mauritian artist of the 20th century was Hervé Masson (1919–1950), an expressionist painter whose work is represented in the Museum of Modern Art in Paris.

Additionally, in the world of correspondence, Mauritius was one of the first countries in the world to adopt the usage of postage stamps, and has since become well known among international stamp collectors. The country's Red Penny and Blue Penny stamps, issued in 1847, are among the rarest and most sought-after stamps among collectors.

Drama

The first theater on Mauritius was erected in 1754 and featured French plays performed by actors brought in from Paris. The British took over the island in 1810, but most of the middle class spoke only French, so performances in English were infrequent. The first Mauritian theater company was formed in 1932. In the 1950s, Indian dance-dramas that were performed in Hindi became a popular form of entertainment on the island. Since independence, Mauritian producers and playwrights have begun writing plays in Mauritian Creole and translating plays from English into Creole. This is challenging for writers and translators as Mauritian Creole was never a written language and has no standardized spelling. It does, however, make theater more accessible to the Creole-speaking majority.

Music & Dance

The early settlers of Mauritius included freed Africans from the Dutch West Indies and slaves

Music and dance are still a means of communication and unification among the Mauritians.

from different parts of Africa and Europeans. For these early Mauritians, music was a way to communicate since they lacked a common language. Music was also a means of preserving cultural heritage and staying optimistic in the face of harsh living and working conditions. Over the course of the 18th century, a new form of music known as sega developed on Mauritius and the neighboring islands of Rèunion and the Seychelles. This style of music combined European dance music with the traditional music of the island culture.

Sega generally relies on three main instruments: the ravanne, which is goatskin stretched over a wooden frame in a manner similar to a tambourine; the maravanne, a rectangular instrument that is filled with dried nuts or seeds that sounds similar to a maraca; and the triangle. Sega lyrics are sung in Mauritian Creole, a blend of French and African languages. Because sega started out as the music of slaves and former slaves, it was played only by the poor people of the island. Because of this association, sega was looked down upon for years and was not truly embraced as the national music of Mauritius until the 1950s.

Historically, sega music was played on the beach and accompanied by spontaneous dancing. Eventually, steps became more formalized and sega dancing became characterized by a rhythmic swaying of the hips by both male and female dancers. Female sega dancers wear colorful long flowing skirts and swish their skirts to the beat, while the men have traditionally worn loose cotton tops and cropped pants.

Literature

Although the author, Bernadin de Saint-Pierre (1737–1814), only lived on Mauritius for two years, *Paul et Virginie* (1787) is generally accepted as the first example of Mauritian literature. Published on the eve of the French Revolution, the story follows two Mauritians who eventually die in a shipwreck. The novel depicts Mauritius as an egalitarian society where everyone owns land and has rights, a stark contrast to France at the time. Viewed as a strong political statement against the French monarchy, the book became very popular and helped to shape European views about the island.

Few significant developments in Mauritian literature took place until the 20th century. While achieving little fame outside of Mauritius, author Malcolm de Chazal (1902–1981) is considered one of the most influential figures in Mauritian literature. Also a painter, he is best known for his *Sens-Plastique* (1948) which was a collection of several thousand aphorisms (philosophical observations).

CULTURE

Arts & Entertainment

One of the most popular art forms in Mauritius is the traditional Creole dance known as the sega. Inspired by European polka and quadrilles combined with African rhythms brought to the islands by slaves, the dance is performed to the accompaniment of drums and other percussion instruments. After being disregarded as the music of the island's poor Creole population, sega made a national comeback in the 1950s thanks in large part to Ti Frere (1900–1992), a musician who became something of a national hero. Once a new generation of Mauritians had embraced the music, they started to experiment with it, and in the 1970s, seggae music (blend of traditional sega and reggae) was born. Popularized by Kaya (1958–1999), seggae music gained audiences in Africa and Europe.

From sega and seggae, an Indian-influenced urban form of music called ragga has developed. Ragga lyrics are in Hindi or Bhopjuri rather than Creole, and the musical style borrows from Bollywood film soundtracks. (Bollywood is India's Hindi-language film industry.) The Bhopjuri Boys are one of the best-known ragga bands. Groups such as the Otentikk Street Brothers, who are popular on Mauritius but also play in Europe, blend forms even further, adding hip-hop beats to seggae-ragga styled music. Mauritius is best-known for sega dancing and local dancers perform sega routines at hotels and resorts on Mauritius almost nightly. However, Indian dance, typically performed during religious ceremonies is also gaining popularity outside of the Indian community. This is largely due to the popularity of Bollywood movies, which typically feature elaborate dance numbers. The influx of American and European hip-hop music has also increased interest in hip-hop dance.

Mauritius has an active visual arts scene. There are many galleries in the bigger cities, most of which cater to the tourist market. The National Art Gallery in Port Louis hosts frequent exhibitions of local artists, as well as workshops and discussions on art. Several of the universities in Mauritius offer visual arts programs so that Mauritians can receive training without having to leave the island. Mauritius was also one of the first countries in the world to issue postage stamps. Known for their striking designs, Mauritian stamps are among the most sought-after in the world for stamp collectors. The Mauritius Postal Museum displays the evolution of the country's postal art through the years.

Since independence, Mauritian writers and playwrights have been largely focused on issues of language and cultural identity. There is an annual theater festival in Port Louis, which allows groups from around the country to stage their productions at the Municipal Theater. The best-known Mauritian playwright is Dev Virahsawmy (1942–), a former politician who is noted for his efforts to promote the Mauritian Creole language in theater and literature. His play *Li* (1981) was the first play written in Mauritian Creole (which is called Morisen in Mauritius). He won the top award in a Radio France Internationale (RFI) competition that same year. Virahsawmy has also translated Shakespearean plays into Mauritian Creole. For example, *Toufann* (1994) retells Shakespeare's *The Tempest* in a Mauritian context.

While not many Mauritian writers are known outside the country, a few have gained international recognition. Ananda Devi (1950–), a writer of Indo-Mauritian descent who writes in French, is known for her portrayal of the gritty side of Mauritian life. Carl de Souza (1949–) writes about the relationship between Mauritians and the countries of their ancestors. He won the international francophone literature prize, Prix de l'ACCT, in 1993 for his novel *Le Sang de l'Anglais*. He was awarded the French government's prestigious Chevalier de l'Ordre des Arts et des Lettres award in 1996. Nathacha Appanah (1973–), who is also of Indian descent and writes in French, is an up-and-coming Mauritian writer who writes about issues of cultural identity in Mauritius. The government has co-sponsored an International Writers Conference in Mauritius in recent years in order to promote literature on the island and expose Mauritians to other kinds of writing. Other notable writers are Malcolm de Chazal, poet Edouard Maunick, and humorist Yvan Lagesse. Modern Creole writers include René Asgarally and Ramesh Ramdoyal.

Football (soccer) and tennis are among the most popular sports on the island and are often played in public venues. As Port Louis is located near a number of popular beaches, ocean activities such as boating, scuba diving, snorkeling, and parasailing are also common recreational activities for many Mauritians.

Cultural Sites & Landmarks

Mauritius is renowned for its blend of cultures and natural beauty. The island nation is home to a number of unique natural attractions, including the Sir Seewoosagur Ramgoolam Botanic Garden, and the "colored earth" of Chamarel. Ile aux Cerfs (Island of the Deer) is a tiny island off the eastern coast famous for its calm, turquoise waters and sugar-white sand.

Sir Seewoosagur Ramgoolam Botanic Garden (formerly Pamplemousse Garden) is named for the country's first Prime Minister, Seewoosagur Ramgoolam (1900–1985). The garden was originally developed by a French botanist, Pierre Poivre (1719–1786), who came to the island in the mid-18th century with the aim of challenging the Dutch monopoly on the spice trade. Poivre brought seeds from exotic species such as nutmeg, camphor, clove, and pepper to the island and later introduced laws to protect the species. The garden was tended and expanded by other botanists through the centuries and is now known for its incredible diversity. One highlight is a pond featuring giant Victoria Amazonica water lilies, the largest species of water lily in the world. The garden is also home to a herd of Javanese deer (introduced to the island by the Dutch), giant tortoises, and several different species of lizard. There is also a replica of a 19th-century sugar mill on the grounds and a recreation of Poivre's original home.

Another unique natural attraction in Mauritius is the "colored earth" at Chamarel. A volcanic eruption thousands of years ago left an area of lava flow which cooled at different temperatures. As the lava eroded through the years, the sandy earth below took on different hues, resulting in an area where the color varies between red, orange, blue, and yellow. The effect is a rainbow-colored landscape of undulating sand hills that contrast with the vivid green of the tropical forest behind it.

Port Louis is also known for its bustling Chinatown area, an ethnic neighborhood that contains a variety of Chinese shops and restaurants and is home to many of the nation's 30,000 Chinese residents. Royal Road, the main street in the city's Chinese district, is lined with dozens of small stores selling crafts, food products, and other items. Chinese holidays, including the New Moon Festival and the Chinese New Year, are celebrated in Chinatown with parades and other festivities.

The Jummah Mosque, which is located in the center of urban Port Louis, is one of the largest religious institutions in the nation. The mosque was constructed in the 19th century and was expanded in the 20th century. The mosque is a popular site for tourists and holds a significant place in the lives of the Islamic population of Port Louis, many of whom visit the mosque for religious services. As a majority of the Mauritian and Port Louis population is Hindu, the city is also home to numerous Hindu structures.

Libraries & Museums

Among the most popular attractions in Port Louis is the Natural History Museum of Port Louis, which contains a variety of exhibits about the island's ecological history. The museum's collection includes the only remaining skeleton of the extinct dodo, a flightless bird that once populated the island until the 18th century, when it was hunted to extinction. In addition, Port Louis has the Blue Penny Museum, founded in 2001, which presents the history and art of the Mauritius Commercial Bank Limited.

La Maison Creole (also known as the Euréka Plantation) at Moka is considered the finest surviving example of colonial architecture on Mauritius. With its long verandah and sloped roof featuring dormer windows on the second floor, its style evokes the early days of sugar cane plantations on the island. Built in 1830 for a British executive, the house later became home to a succession of wealthy French families. Today, it is a museum of colonial life and is surrounded by extensive gardens that feature a waterfall and a restaurant. The interior is full of period furniture and artifacts, as well as early photographs taken on the island.

The National Library of the Republic of Mauritius, located in the capital of Port Louis, was established in 1996 and officially opened in 2000. The library serves as the island nation's legal depository. Important artifacts in its collection include newspapers dating back to the 1700s. The University of Mauritius helped launched the first digital library in the country in June 2010.

Holidays

National holidays in Mauritius include Independence Day (March 12) and Labour Day (May 1). Father Laval Day (September 9) commemorates the work of Father Jacques-Désiré Laval (1803–1864), a French missionary who came to Mauritius in the 19th century. On the anniversary of his death, Mauritians of all faiths visit his shrine in Port Louis. Hindu festivals such as Diwali and Holi are celebrated by most of the population; Muslim and Christian holidays are also observed in Mauritius.

Youth Culture

The youth in Mauritius are exposed to many different cultures living within the country, and the island hosts a great many international tourists. Consequently, the youth tend to be open and accepting of new ideas and adopt music and fashion trends from different groups, blending them together to create their own style. Education from the pre-primary to the post-secondary level is free and the country enjoys a relatively high literacy rate for the region. Most young people finish secondary school and are reasonably fluent in three languages (English, French, and Creole), but others also speak Hindi, Bhopjuri, or Chinese.

Football (soccer) is the most popular sport, and even the smallest towns have a local youth club and a field. Many young people follow English or French football teams. French television programming and Indian or American cinema are common forms of entertainment, and older youth in cities frequently socialize at bars and clubs. Going to the beach or going bowling on the weekend are also popular recreational activities.

SOCIETY

Transportation

Private cars and public buses are the primary means of transportation. Public buses run on a regular schedule and are generally well maintained. Within the cities, people get around by car, bus, bicycle, and motorbike. Mauritius has a "taxi train" service that is similar to the bush taxi service available on the African continent. Taxi trains are large vans that will pick up individuals along their way, and do not operate on a fixed route or schedule. Although regular taxis are also available, their fares are not well regulated, so they tend to be very expensive. Traffic moves on the left side of the road in Mauritius.

Transportation Infrastructure

Mauritius has a network of paved roads connecting the larger towns and cities on the island, especially around the coast.

Sir Seewoosgur Ramgoolam is the international airport, and serves the national airline Air Mauritius, as well as Air France, British Airways, and South African Airways. There are two other small airports on the island, for use by private and charter planes.

The islands of Rodriges, Agelega, and St. Brandon's are part of the republic of Mauritius, and can be reached by airplane or ferry. Ferry and charter service is also available to the neighboring island nations of Rèunion, Seychelles, and Madagascar.

Media & Communications

Television is the most popular medium in Mauritius. There are two government-run channels that air programs in English, French, and Chinese, as well as news reports in Mauritian Creole. In addition, there are five government-run radio stations broadcasting in English, French, Chinese, and several Indian languages. Periodic news updates are also offered in Mauritian Creole. Three private stations on the island offer music and news. The British Broadcasting Corporation (BBC), World Service, Voice of America (VOA), and RFI all have regularly scheduled programs on the public radio stations. There are two daily independent newspapers published in French and two in Chinese. Despite the fact that English is the country's official language, there is no daily newspaper in English (the English newspaper is a weekly).

Mauritius has invested a substantial amount of money in its communications infrastructure. Telephone service is widely available and cell phone usage is widespread and reliable. Private Internet access is becoming more common and the government recently introduced a program to bring public Internet access to local post offices in each town. There are also Internet cafés in larger towns or tourist areas. According to 2014 statistics, Internet usage was measured in an estimated 6.1 percent of the population. In order to attract foreign businesses to the island, the government is also developing a "cyber city" with fiber-optic cable networks connected to Europe.

SOCIAL DEVELOPMENT

Standard of Living

Mauritius ranked 63rd out of 187 countries on the 2014 United Nations Human Development Index, which measures quality of life and standard of living indicators.

Water Consumption

According to 2015 statistics released by the World Health Organization, the population of Mauritius enjoys relatively universal coverage in regards to improved or clean drinking water, while an estimated 93 percent have access to improved sanitation. The largest source of water on the islands is rainwater, and a system of four aquifers supplies approximately 40 percent of the nation's potable water supply. Most groundwater sources will be largely depleted by the close of the first decade of the 21st century.

Education

Education in Mauritius has been free through the post-secondary level since 1988, and is patterned after the British system. Elementary school (through grade six) is compulsory.

The University of Mauritius, established in 1967, is the country's main institute for higher education. Other higher education options include the Mauritius Institute of Education for teacher training, the Mauritius College of the Air, and the Mahatma Gandhi Institute. Mauritius also offers several vocational training centers as well as technical institutions.

In recent years, the country has been making strides in improving overall literacy. In 2003, the average literacy rate was 86 percent (89 percent among males and 83 percent among females). Improvements in the education system have led to shortages in the agricultural work force, as more young people leave rural areas for the cities.

According to the 2014 Gender Gap Index, which is published by the World Economic Forum, Mauritius ranks 106th out of 142 countries in terms of gender equity regarding economic, political, and educational opportunities.

Women's Rights

Mauritius is a signatory to the Convention on the Elimination of All Forms of Discrimination against Women (CEDAW) and the additional optional protocol to the convention. In addition, the National Women's Council coordinates the work of non-governmental organizations (NGOs). The government gender bureau is assigned with overseeing the implementation of the agreements made by all the Commonwealth nations. Despite these commitments, women lag far behind men in rights in many areas and generally hold a subordinate role in society due to traditional attitudes and beliefs.

While girls have equal access to education in Mauritius, this has not translated to equal economic opportunities. Traditionally, women were expected to stay home and take care of domestic duties while men were expected to provide financial support. This has changed in recent years as the economy in Mauritius has shifted from sugar production and other agricultural activities to textile manufacturing and tourism; women now make up nearly a quarter of the workforce. However, women earn less than their male counterparts in the business sector, particularly in agricultural jobs, despite the fact that the government passed legislation requiring equal pay for equal work. In addition, women continue to hold mostly low-level positions and are typically encouraged or trained to go into low-paying jobs such as tailoring, handcrafts, and food preparation. In fact, only five percent of the top jobs in commerce are held by women. Sexual harassment is also common in the workplace and is largely unreported.

In terms of political representation, women have gained some power in the Mauritian parliament; as of the 2005 elections, women held 17 percent of the seats. Several women have also been appointed to head government ministries, including the Ministry of Women, Family Welfare, and Child Development. At the local level, however, few women hold positions of power. The government recently committed resources to promoting awareness of gender inequality and stereotyping in the country. Part of this commitment includes leadership training for women at the local levels and encouraging government agencies to award contracts to women-led businesses.

The increase in women entering the work force has created new issues in Mauritian society, including the need for childcare and eldercare. There are few systems in place to help working women handle family responsibilities in addition to their paid work. The government has started to work on creating these systems, but has not yet been able to keep up with the demand. As a result, female family members often continue to provide childcare or eldercare without pay.

Although there are specific laws against domestic violence and rape, these crimes have generally gone unreported in Mauritius because of strong social taboos and fear of retaliation. There has been no support system in place for victims in terms of immediate and ongoing counseling. There are few shelters where women and their children can go to escape abusers. Police have not had training in dealing with the specific issues of these crimes. As a result, women who

report abuse have been treated with suspicion, which further discourages victims from reporting the crime.

Health Care

The government of Mauritius funds a variety of health care services throughout the country, although the majority of the treatment facilities are located in urban areas. Government centers provide training for maternal and childcare, as well as nutrition education programs. Food and lodging for the sick and elderly are provided at government expense.

Life expectancy at birth is roughly 79 years for women and 71 years for men (2015 estimate). In 2015, the infant mortality rate was an estimated at nearly 11 deaths per 1,000 live births.

GOVERNMENT

Structure

Mauritius gained its independence from Great Britain in 1968. The country's current constitution was adopted on March 12, 1968. The republic is a parliamentary democracy, with a legal system based on French and British law.

The executive branch consists of the president, who is chief of state, and the prime minister, who acts as the head of government. The executive branch also includes a vice president and a Council of Ministers. The president and vice president are elected by the legislature to five-year terms. The prime minister and deputy prime minister are appointed by the president, who also appoints the Council of Ministers.

The legislative branch consists of the unicameral National Assembly. Of the body's 70 seats, 62 are elected by popular vote, while the remaining seats are appointed by the Supreme Court to ensure that all ethnicities are represented. National Assembly seats are held for five-year terms.

Political Parties

Mauritius has a multi-party system, traditionally, the Mauritian Labour Party, modeled after the

British Labour party, was the ruling party, while the socialist Mauritian Militant Movement was the opposition party. In the 2014 parliamentary elections, an alliance consisting of the Militant Social Movement, Mauritian Social Democrat Party, and Muvman Liberater took 49 percent of the vote and the majority of seats in the parliament, while the Mauritian Labour Party and Mauritian Militant Movement took 38 percent of the vote and became the opposition. Other parties represented in parliament include the Rodrigues People's Organisation and the Front Solidarite Mauricien.

Local Government

For administrative purposes, Mauritius is divided into nine districts and three dependencies. Local governance consists of five municipal councils and four district councils. There are 124 village councils that make up a lower tier of local government, while Rodrigues enjoys a semiautonomous status.

Judicial System

The legal system of Mauritius is based on a blend of British and French law. The Supreme Court is the highest court, while the Judicial Committee of the Privy Council (in the United Kingdom) can hear direct appeals, and maintain local representation.

Taxation

Personal income and corporations in Mauritius are both taxed at a flat rate of 15 percent. Other taxes levied include a value-added tax (VAT, similar to a sales or consumption tax, and which applies to applicable goods and services) and property tax.

Armed Forces

With no active standing army, Mauritius relies upon a National Police Force for law enforcement and paramilitary units, the Special Mobile Force and the National Coast Guard, for matters of national defense (and which consist of police officers). The Special Mobile Force is the main security force of the island nation, and assists in disaster relief efforts if needed.

Foreign Policy

Mauritius gained independence from Great Britain in 1968. Since then it has been a member of the Commonwealth, a group of former British colonies that works with the United Kingdom (UK) to created mutually beneficial international policies. Since becoming a republic in 1992, Mauritius no longer recognizes the British monarchy as head of state, but the UK remains strong ally in trade and one of the island nation's closest diplomatic relationships. As a member of the Commonwealth, Mauritius also has close ties to Australia, Malaysia, Singapore, and other French and English-speaking African nations.

Post-independence, France has been one of Mauritius' top sources of foreign investment, bilateral aid, and trade. France has even provided training for the island nation's security forces, which are a division of the police department (Mauritius has no national military). France retains its control over Mauritius' neighboring island Rèunion, as well as a small island called Tromelin where France maintains a weather station. Mauritius also claims Tromelin as part of its territory and this dispute has been the only source of tension between the two nations; the issue remains unresolved.

Over 60 percent of Mauritians are of Indian descent, and Mauritius has close diplomatic ties with India. Among African nations, Mauritius is close to South Africa. In the twenty-first century, many South Africans have immigrated to Mauritius or bought second homes there, and trade between the countries is strong. The governments of the two nations have a health cooperation agreement that allows Mauritian citizens to access advanced South African health care that is not available on the island. Mauritius also has friendly relations with its Indian Ocean neighbors Madagascar, Comoros, Seychelles, and Rèunion.

While trade between the United States and Mauritius is growing and the relationship is strong and friendly, there is a territorial dispute between the two countries that remains unresolved. Before granting independence to Mauritius, the British government granted the U.S. military a 50-year lease to Diego Garcia, an island that is part of the nearby Chagos Archipelago. The people who lived on the island were displaced and ended up as refugees in Mauritius. In the 1990s, Mauritius lodged an objection to the lease and the return of the Chagossians to their homeland. A British court ruled in 2007 that they should be allowed to return, but provisions have yet to be made.

In addition to being part of the Commonwealth, Mauritius is a member of the Indian Ocean Commission (a group of countries in located in the Indian Ocean), the United Nations (UN), the African Union (AU), the Organization of African Unity (OAU), World Trade Organization (WTO), and La Francophonie, a group of countries with strong ties to France.

Human Rights Profile

International human rights law insists that states respect civil and political rights, and promote an individual's economic, social, and cultural rights. The United Nations Universal Declaration on Human Rights (UDHR) is recognized as the standard for international human rights. Its authors sought the counsel of the world's great thinkers, philosophers, and religious leaders, and were careful to create a document that reflects the core values shared by every world culture. (To read this document or view the articles relating to cultural human rights, visit http://www.udhr.org/UDHR/default.htm.)

Internationally, Mauritius is frequently cited as an example of how different religions, ethnicities, races, and cultures can harmoniously blend. This success is frequently attributed to respect for human rights on the part of individuals and the government. Nonetheless, certain challenges still remain, including the discrimination against people of Creole descent by the Hindu majority—specifically discriminatory hiring in the civil service sector—police brutality, and corruption at the government level.

The constitution of Mauritius protects numerous individual and group rights. Mauritius has signed on to many international human right treaties, including the International Convention on the Elimination of All Forms of Racial Discrimination, the International Covenant on Economic, Social, and Cultural Rights, and the International Covenant on Civil and Political Rights. Mauritian citizens are free to practice their respective religions without persecution and groups such as labor organizations are permitted freedom of assembly. Elections have been judged by international observers to be free and fair.

While the judicial system is generally considered to be fair and those accused of crimes have access to fair trials, there have been complains in Mauritius about police brutality. The most famous case involved well-known seggae musician Joseph Reginald Topize, otherwise known as Kaya. While attending a rally in support of the legalization of marijuana, he was arrested and died under mysterious circumstances while in police custody. While the police were cleared of wrongdoing, the case strengthened the perception that police in Mauritius use excessive force. (Another musician, Berger Agathe, was shot dead by police while protesting Kaya's death.) Prison conditions and overcrowding also continue to be concerns.

In recent years, there have been corruption charges brought against government officials, generally in cases involving misappropriation of development and investment funds. There is a fair degree of transparency when it comes to government accountability in Mauritius. In addition, Mauritius has a human rights commission, which is charged with responding to human rights complaints and ensuring that all branches and offices of the government comply with the laws. The government continues to make human rights a priority through legislation and commitment of resources.

ECONOMY

Overview of the Economy

Mauritius lacks extensive natural resources, and in recent years has developed a diversified industrial economy, while moving away from its dependence on sugarcane crops. The majority of the work force is employed in services and industry.

The primary industry on Mauritius is the refinement of sugar. A number of sugar refineries are located around Port Louis and employ a large portion of the population. In addition to sugar refinement, other industries include textile and chemical production, mining, and the tourism industry, which has grown in the 21st century to become one of the city's fastest growing industries.

Since the country gained independence in 1968, the Mauritians have been successful in diversifying their economy and have achieved economic growth; on average, the Mauritian economy has grown by approximately seven percent per year. Mauritius has one of the highest standards of living among African nations and has consistently invested its economic surplus into the infrastructure and services sector. Though Mauritians still suffer from relatively high levels of poverty (eight percent) and unemployment (7.8 percent), government initiates have fostered a high level of income equality, which has helped to stabilize the economy. As the nation's principal port, Port Louis is the first city on the island to benefit from economic growth.

Mauritius' chief trading partners are in Europe. The United Kingdom purchases over 30 percent of the nation's export products, while France accepts a further 15 percent. France is the nation's largest import partner, and provides approximately 15 percent of the nation's imported materials. Other important trade partners include India, China, South Africa, and the United Arab Emirates.

Industry

Sugarcane was once the sole export of Mauritius. A number of sugar refineries are located around Port Louis and employ a large portion of the population. In addition to sugar refinement, other industries include textile and chemical production, mining, and the tourism industry, which has grown in the early 21st century to become one of the country's fastest growing industries. A strong textile industry has also developed. The clothing industry has flourished in the manufacturing sector. Recently, the government has been successful in its attempts to diversify the economy by expanding in the areas of finance and telecommunications. However, major industry still revolves around food processing, with a heavy emphasis on sugar mills. The country also produces equipment and machinery.

Industrial production employs over 30 percent of the population and contributes approximately 25 percent to the nation's gross domestic product (GDP). The services industry, which includes tourism and eco-tourism, constitutes over 60 percent of the nation's GDP and employs over 39 percent of the population. In 2014, the gross domestic product (GDP) per capita was estimated at $18,600 (USD).

Labor

Unemployment is estimated at roughly 7.8 percent of a workforce numbering 600,000 (2014 estimates). By occupation, the services sector accounts for the largest percentage of the workforce, at nearly 47 percent, followed closely by industry, including finance, transportation, communications, and construction. As of 2014, an estimated nine percent of the workforce was employed in agriculture.

Energy/Power/Natural Resources

Mauritius has few natural resources. With only a small percentage of its forests still standing, the country's most significant resource is its fertile soil, known for producing large amounts of sugarcane.

Fishing

The fish in the waters surrounding the islands are considered a natural resource, and fishing is an important part of the country's economy. As of 2005, Mauritius was responsible for the handling of approximately 100,000 tons of fish, with tuna being a primary commercial species. That same year, the government reported the issuing of approximately 215 fishing licenses to foreign fishing vessels. Artisanal fishing remains a strong contributor, particularly in terms of meeting local demand, and the fishing industry contributes about one percent to the country's gross domestic product (GDP). In 2010, to boost the economic vitality of the fishing industry, the government announced plans to join the South West Indian Ocean Fisheries Commission (SWIOFC).

The country enjoys an enormous exclusive economic zone (EEZ), estimated at 1.2 million square kilometers (463,222 square miles), and the industry reportedly employs nearly 12,000 people.

Mining/Metals

Due to few limited natural resources in the way of minerals, mining is not a substantial or economically viable sector in Mauritius. Commodities produced included limited amounts of salt and fertilizers, and cement, sand, and reinforcement steel.

Agriculture

Nearly 90 percent of cultivated land in Mauritius is used for growing sugarcane, which accounts for one-quarter of the country's export earnings. Molasses is second to sugarcane in crop production, and cut flowers are an important export. Other important crops include tea, bananas, potatoes, and corn.

Fish and goats are significant parts of Mauritius agriculture. About 14 percent of the labor force works in agriculture and fishing. Combined, these account for nearly eight percent of the GDP.

Animal Husbandry

Poultry and pork represent the primary livestock bred in Mauritius, while beef is largely imported, as is some dairy products. There is small population of raised Creole cattle.

Tourism

The majority of the island nation's labor force works in service industries, many of which involve the island's tourist trade. In 2005, the government announced plans to make Mauritius a duty-free island, in order to lure more tourists. In the first half of 2010, the government announced that tourism revenue had increased; earlier, the government gave the tourism sector a boost through a government-issued stimulus package, aimed at increasing arrivals from Russia, China, and India. In 2013, tourism revenue accounted for approximately 25.3 percent of the country's gross domestic product (GDP).

A tropical paradise, Mauritius attracts visitors with its dramatic mountain views and beautiful beaches. A modern city, Port Louis is known for its casinos, cinemas, shops, bars, and restaurants. The Sir Seewoosagur Ramgoolam Botanical Gardens is one of the country's most popular tourist attractions. Founded in 1735, the gardens and are home to many plants and animals that cannot bee seen anywhere else on the island.

Joanne O'Sullivan, Christopher Stetter,
Micah Issitt

DO YOU KNOW?

- Mauritius has established itself as a global leader in the conservation of endangered species. The country hosts conferences where scientists from around the world meet to discuss strategies to prevent the extinction of threatened species and to rebuild endangered populations. Among the threatened animals on Mauritius are the pink pigeon, the Mauritius kestrel and the Rodriguez Island fruit bat.

- The Portuguese explorers who discovered Mauritius named the large, flightless bird they encountered there "dodo," meaning "simpleton." Less than 200 years later, the bird was extinct; it is still featured on Mauritius' coat of arms.

- At one time, Mauritius was renamed Île de France, after French captain Guillaume Dufresne d'Arsal claimed the island for his native country.

- Port Louis was an important military base during World War II and was developed into a major naval port.

Bibliography

Alexandra Richards, et al. "Mauritius" (Bradt Travel Guide). Guilford, CT: *Globe Pequot*, 2012.

Jean-Bernard Carillet, et al. "Mauritius, Rèunion, and Seychelles." Oakland, CA: *Lonely Planet*, 2013.

Tim Cleary. "Mauritius—Culture Smart! The Essential Guide to Customs and Culture." London: *Kuperard*, 2011.

The Official Site of the Government of Mauritius. http://www.gov.mu

The Official Web Site of Mauritius. http://www.mauritius.net

The Official Web Site of Mauritius Tourism Promotion. http://www.tourism-mauritius.com

Works Cited

"Ananda Devi." *Alliance Française USA* http://www.alliance-us.org

"Art and Taste in the Mauritian Context." *Visual Art and Culture in Mauritius* http:// artmauritius.wordpress.com

"Country Insights: Mauritius." *Center for Intercultural Learning.* www.intercultures.ca.

"Country Profile: Mauritius." *BBC* http://news.bbc.co.uk.

"Country Studies: Mauritius." *Library of Congress* http://ww.loc.gov.

"Cultural Heritage Structures and Sites in Mauritius." National Heritage Sites, Government of Mauritius http://www.gov.mu

"Mauritius: Country Specific Information." *United States State Department* http://travel.state.gov.

"Mauritius." *Division of Democracy, Human Rights, and Labor United States Department of State* http://www.state.gov 11 March 2008.

"Mauritius." *Foreign and Commonwealth Office of the Government of the UK.* February 2008. http://www.fco.uk.gov

"Mauritius." Tageo http://www.tageo.com

"Mauritius Fact File: International Relations." *Institute for Security Studies* http://www.issafrica.org.

"Mauritius: High Literacy Rate Due to Country's Size and Vision, Says Education Minister." *Irin News,* 4 December 2003. http://www.irinnews.org

"Mauritius to Canada." *The Country Profile Project, Citizenship, and Immigration Canada.* www.cp-pc.ca

Alain Jeannot. "Mauritius: Broken Families Can Lead To Poor School Performance." *L'Express* 25 March 2008.

Alistair Leithead. "Cyber City in Mauritius." *BBC News* http://news.bbc.co.uk. 4 February 2003.

Martin Banham, Errol Hill and George Woodyard, Eds. "The Cambridge Guide to African and Caribbean Theater." Cambridge: *Cambridge University Press,* 1994.

Martin Banham. "The Cambridge Guide to Theater," 2nd ed. Cambridge: *Cambridge University Press,* 1995.

Nita Bhalia. "Speaking Out Against Rape in Mauritius." *BBC News.* <http://news.bbc.co.uk 26 September 2005.

Saskia Virahsawmy-Naidoo. "Mauritius Launches Woman Friendly Budget." *Afrol News* 26 June 2007.

The Web Site of the U.S. Embassy, Port Louis, Mauritius http://mauritus.usembassy.gov

"The World Factbook: Mauritius." *Central Intelligence Agency.* http://www.cia.gov.

Cassava, a root vegetable, is a staple of Mozambican cuisine.

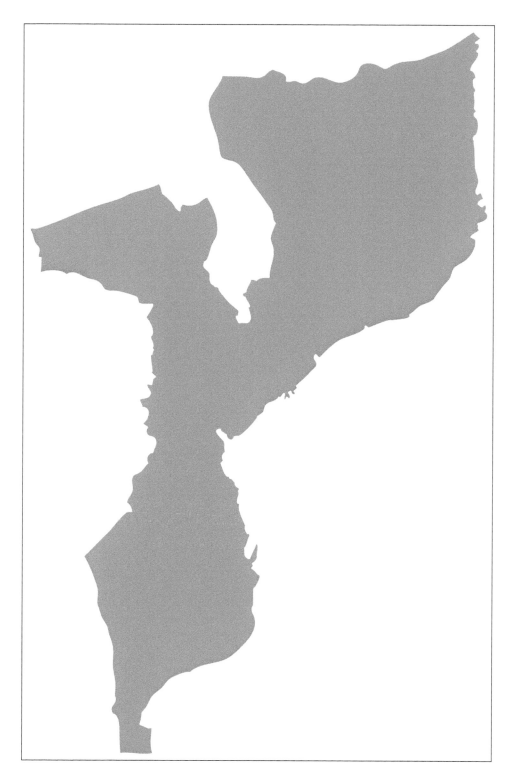

MOZAMBIQUE

Introduction

Mozambique, formerly known as Portuguese East Africa, is a nation in southeast Africa. It borders the countries of Tanzania, Malawi, Zambia, South Africa, and Swaziland to the south, and the Indian Ocean to the east. Its people are known as Mozambicans.

Once a colony of Portugal, it gained independence in 1975. Maputo is the capital of Mozambique and that nation's political, economic, and cultural center. Originally, a modest development that grew around a fortress, Maputo eventually became the jewel in the crown of Portuguese imperial claims in East Africa.

Mozambicans are known for their traditional African arts and crafts. The Makonde produce carvings and sculptures that are regarded as some of the finest in Africa. Cultural centers promote indigenous arts and crafts, while government-established radio programs broadcast traditional music.

The nation ended a period of civil war that lasted throughout the 1980s. Though Mozambique has been at peace since 1992, many of its current environmental, economic, and social problems stem from that period of unrest.

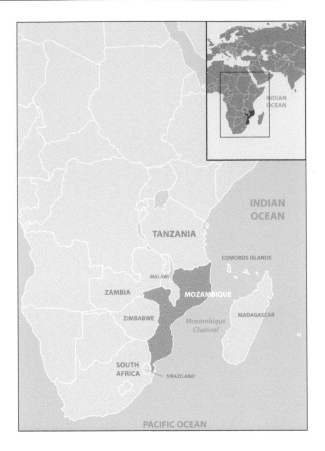

GENERAL INFORMATION

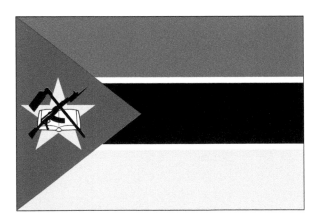

Official Language: Portuguese
Population: 25,303,113 (2015 estimate)
Currency: Mozambican metical

Coins: The metical (plural: meticais) is subdivided into 100 centavos. Coins are available in denominations of 1, 5, 10, 20, and 50 centavos, and 1, 2, 5, and 10 meticais.

Land Area: 786,380 square kilometers (303,623 square miles)

Water Area: 13,000 square kilometers (5,019 square miles)

National Anthem: "Patria Amada"

Capital: Maputo

Time Zone: GMT +2

Flag Description: Mozambique's flag features a triangle design, with a red triangle extending the length of the hoist (left) side. Three equal, horizontal bands of green (top), black (middle), and yellow (bottom), separated by white fimbriations (small stripes), represent the colors of the African National Congress. Centered in the red triangle is a five-pointed gold star, upon which is superimposed an open white book, and then a crossed gun and hoe, representing, respectively, study, defense, and production.

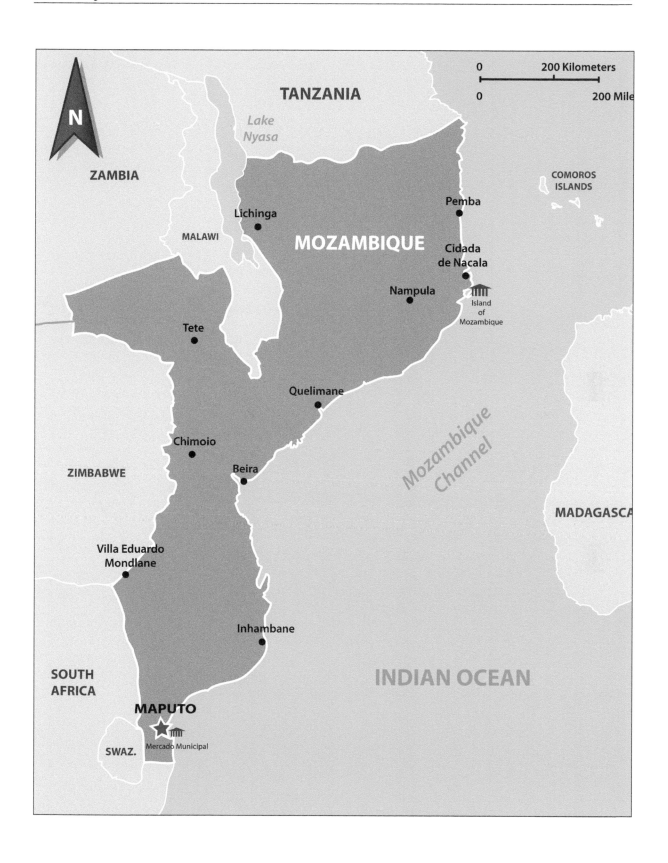

Principal Cities by Population (2012):

- Maputo (1,100,000)
- Matola (817,008)
- Nampula (575,587)
- Beira (441,723)
- Chimoio (272,875)
- Nacala (230,229)
- Quelimane (212,519)
- Mocuba (168,736) (2007 estimate)
- Tete (155,870) (2007 estimate)
- Gurué (145,466) (2007 estimate)

Population

Mozambicans are black Africans belonging to various ethnic groups. Most are farmers who live in the country's rural areas. The largest ethnic group is the Makhuwa-Lomwe, which accounts for about 40 percent of the total population. The Makhuwa-Lomwe people are divided into many different tribes, and primarily inhabit the northern region of Mozambique. The second largest ethnic group is the Tsonga people, who live in the country's southern region. Other prominent groups are the northern Makonde people, known for their woodcarvings, the Sena people in the central region, and the Shanagaan in the south. Mozambique's minorities account for less than 1 percent of the population. Foreign minorities include people of Arab, European, and Indian descent.

Urban centers are concentrated in the south, and include Maputo, the capital and largest city. Famous as an ancient Arab merchant kingdom during the ninth century, Maputo is now the only city on the African continent with an overwhelmingly Latin culture.

Beira is also one of Mozambique's largest cities and, like Maputo, is a seaport. Other notable cities are Nampula, known as an agricultural trade center; and Tofo, a popular beach resort; and Maxixe, known for its restaurants. An estimated 28 percent of the population lives in urban areas.

With roughly two million inhabitants (unofficially), Maputo is Mozambique's largest city, as well as the national capital. The vast majority of the population is made up of more than a dozen indigenous ethnic groups, primarily Bantu that also comprise the whole of Mozambique's population. The largest group consists of the Makua people, while the Ronga and Shaangan peoples are the other key ethnicities in the greater Maputo region.

Maputo also has small communities of people with racially mixed backgrounds as well as those of Portuguese, Arab, Indian, and East Asian descent, with most of the latter the descendents of colonial-era settlers. Their numbers, however, are much smaller than they were during the pre-independence era.

Languages

Most Mozambicans speak Bantu languages, even though Portuguese is the country's official language. In fact, less than 8 percent of the population can speak or read Portuguese. The most prominent linguistic dialects are Emakhuwa, Xichangana, Elomwe, Cisena, and Echuwabo. Swahili is also spoken in some parts of the country, and English is used for business.

Native People & Ethnic Groups

Black Africans have inhabited the area occupied by Mozambique since 4000 BCE. Bantu-speaking Africans, including the Swahili and Makonde, came to Mozambique in the ninth century. There are over 200 Bantu tribes in southern Africa. Most of these are autonomous chiefdoms comprised of farmers.

Much of Mozambique's native population was victimized and decimated by the European colonial slave trade. Portugal, the Netherlands, and Great Britain participated in slave trading in Mozambique for centuries, and in the process relocated or killed many native Mozambicans.

Religions

Indigenous religions are practiced by 55 percent of the population. Most of Mozambique's indigenous population adheres to some form of animism, the belief that all things have a soul. Roughly, 25 percent of the population is Christian, and 18 percent is Muslim.

Climate

Mozambique has a tropical climate. The average summer temperature is 27° Celsius (80° Fahrenheit), while the average winter temperature is 20° Celsius (68° Fahrenheit).

The wet season is between November and March. Mozambique receives an annual average rainfall of 41 centimeters (16 inches) on the grasslands and up to 122 centimeters (48 inches) in the rainforest regions. The upper plains are victim to long droughts, while the coast is often devastated by floods.

In 2000, Cyclone Eline hit Mozambique. The storm caused massive flooding, killing 700 people, and displacing another 500,000. In 2001, coastal flooding occurred again, killing 100 and displacing 200,000.

ENVIRONMENT & GEOGRAPHY

Topography

Mozambique borders Tanzania on the north, Malawi and Zambia to the northwest, Zimbabwe to the west, South Africa and Swaziland to the south, and the Indian Ocean to the east.

Most of Mozambique is either grassland or tropical forest. The coastal region features many swamps and sand dunes, as well as many natural harbors. Plains along the coast become mountains along the western borders of the country. The highest point in Mozambique is Monte Binga, at 2,436 meters (7,992 feet) above sea level.

Roughly, 25 rivers run through Mozambique, including three of the longest rivers in Africa: the Zambezi, the Limpopo, and the Rovuma. The country's longest river is the section of the Zambezi that runs through Mozambique for 820 kilometers (509 miles). The Cahora Bassa Dam on the Zambezi forms the Lago de Cahora Bassa, a lake measuring 270 kilometers (170 miles) across.

As the nation's capital, Maputo is located in the southwestern corner of Mozambique. It is an Indian Ocean port city, situated on the western side of Maputo Bay, at the mouth of the Tembe River. Although the surrounding province bears the same name, Maputo is administered as a separate political entity.

The capital's grid of broad avenues and squares is reminiscent of European port cities such as Lisbon, upon which Maputo was modeled. The capital's spacious and orderly design and colonial-style buildings have earned the city a reputation as a place where Mediterranean and African atmospheres are melded together.

The port of Maputo, around which the capital's economy revolves, plays a critical role in the region. The port has been functioning as far back as the late 18th century, although it did not become a major trading center until the arrival of Portuguese settlers in the mid-19th century.

The Bazaruto Archipelago lies off the shore of Mozambique. The chain of small islands comprises one of the country's national parks, and contains much of the country's marine wildlife.

Plants & Animals

Animals native to Mozambique include elephants, buffalo, rhinos, giraffes, lions, zebras, monkeys, crocodiles, and tropical birds such as the parrot. Environmental factors such as flooding and droughts are significant threats to these species.

Civil warfare and poaching have destroyed much of Mozambique's wildlife. Ivory poaching is an ongoing problem, and endangers the country's elephant population. During the civil war, soldiers often shot animals for target practice. Leftover landmines pose an additional threat to wildlife.

Trees such as mangroves, palm groves, and flame trees are common throughout the coastal region and in the nation's swamps. Deforestation has destroyed the Zambezi delta region's tropical rainforest, which once contained many species of valuable hardwoods.

Four national parks have been established in Mozambique. These are the Gorongosa, the Zinave, the Banhine, and the Bazaruto. Much of the wildlife in these parks was devastated by the civil war. The Bazaruto Park, located on the archipelago, has successfully protected its marine wildlife. The Maputo Elephant Reserve is one of many parks dedicated to protecting the endangered African elephant.

The Great Limpop Transfrontier Park, connected to South Africa's and Zimbabwe's national parks, has been designed as a "peace park" to protect habitats in the neighboring countries.

CUSTOMS & COURTESIES

Greetings

Mozambican greeting styles differ somewhat between the northern and southern regions of the country. The north retains more native traditions common throughout East Africa, while the south exhibits more signs of Portuguese influence. Northern greetings are often accompanied by soft handclaps and may be spoken in a local dialect or in Swahili. Typical Swahili greetings include "Jambo" ("Hello") and "Habari gain" ("What's new"), as well as the more formal "Shikamoo" ("Hello, how are you"). The traditional response to this formal greeting is "Marahaba" ("I am well").

In the south, a handshake, or quick kiss on the cheek are common ways of greeting others. Often, one lightly holds the right elbow with the left hand while shaking with the right hand. African handshakes are not typically as firm as Western handshakes. Many people in the south speak Xitsonga, a Bantu language that stretches from the coastal area around Maputo into South Africa. A common Xitsonga greeting is "Avuxeni" ("Hello").

Portuguese greetings can also be heard throughout the country, particularly such phrases as the formal "Bom dia" ("Good day") and "Boa noite" ("Good evening"), and the informal "Olá" ("Hello"). Mozambicans customarily greet and bid farewell to each person present when entering or leaving a room. Some common leave-taking phrases include the Swahili "Kwaheri" ("Goodbye") and the Portuguese "Até a vista" ("See you soon").

Gestures & Etiquette

As in the rest of East Africa, the underlying concept of Mozambican etiquette is respect, which is displayed through both words and actions. Honorific titles are commonly used along with surnames, and close friends and family typically use first names or nicknames. Younger people show respect for their elders by addressing them as tio (uncle) or tia (aunt), regardless of whether an actual familial relationship exists. Additionally, young people may bow or curtsey in the presence of elders.

Gift giving is an important part of Mozambican culture, and refusing a gift can be perceived as disrespectful to the gift giver. It is also important to receive a gift with both hands. Additionally, similar to Muslim culture, the right hand is used exclusively for handshakes and passing items, as the left hand is associated with personal hygiene, and thus considered impure. Displaying the sole of one's shoe is also considered offensive, as the bottoms of shoes collect dirt from walking. One acceptable physical gesture in Mozambique is the thumbs-up, which is used to signify approval. Placing one's hands on one's hips, however, is considered an aggressive gesture.

Certain customs are specific to Mozambique's Muslim population. For example, Islam considers the head to be the most sacred part of the body. As a result, Mozambican Muslims avoid touching the heads of others, even young children. Because Muslims fast during the day in the holy month of Ramadan, it is considered impolite to eat in front them during the daylight hours. All Mozambicans, regardless of religion, frown on public displays of affection. Although sleeveless tops and shorts are seen in resort areas catering to foreigners, Mozambicans prefer to dress modestly, with long pants or skirts and sleeves covering the arms.

Eating/Meals

Mozambican meal customs combine native traditions with those imported from Portugal. Although people in some rural regions dine while seated on mats or stools around a low table, many urban and southern Mozambicans instead sit on upright chairs around a Western-style dining table. Table settings can be quite formal, with decorative table linens made of lace and floral centerpieces. Utensils are typically European in style, although both utensils and the hands may be used to eat, showing the Mozambican fusion of African and European culture. The right hand is used exclusively when eating, whether the diner is holding a utensil or eating with his or her hands.

Mozambicans traditionally eat three meals a day, with the evening meal generally the most substantial. Liqueurs, port wine, and homemade beer may be served at evening meals. Although those in countryside have few opportunities to dine away from home, urban Mozambicans regularly enjoy eating meals at restaurants. Restaurants tend to keep irregular hours and may construct their daily menus based on the changing availability of ingredients. Some dishes are available only by special request and may need to be ordered several hours before a diner plans to arrive at a restaurant.

Visiting

Guests are practically always welcomed in Mozambique culture. Visits between friends and family are often informal and unannounced, particularly in rural areas where communications systems may be lacking. When arriving at an East African home, guests often remove their shoes so as not to bring dirt into a host's home. For the same reason, visitors also should not allow their food to come near or point directly at food or other people. A small gift such as tea, flowers, or fruit is always appreciated.

A visitor arriving around a mealtime will typically be offered food or drink. Guests dining in a Mozambican home are usually served first and receive the best parts of the dish, such as the meat. When sharing a meal, guests should neither eat too quickly nor take the last portion of food, as this implies that the host has provided insufficient food. Instead, a visitor should leave a little bit of food on his or her plate to indicate that he or she is full. Otherwise, the host typically assumes that that person is still hungry and offers another helping. After a meal, a polite guest offers a compliment on the quality of the food, but refrains from excessive praise.

LIFESTYLE

Family

Traditionally, the extended Mozambican family has been a vital and vibrant part of the culture. Family members lived close together and relied on one another for support and the good of the family and community trumped individual desire. However, the dual factors of war and migration have negatively affected these traditional ties. Years of fighting claimed the lives of many Mozambicans and left many families broken. The many southern Mozambican who have migrated to South Africa, often to take mining jobs, live a great distance from their relatives. Nevertheless, Mozambicans continue to reach out to remaining family members, and a sense of community informs daily life in the nation.

Men retain the superior role in family relations, and family elders are perhaps even more greatly respected. In the north, however, family ties have traditionally been traced through the mother in a matrilineal system. Polygamy, or having several wives, is practiced in some parts of rural Mozambique. Mozambicans also have close, family-like ties to others in their particular regional ethnic group.

Housing

Mozambican houses vary based on location, surrounding levels of development, and personal wealth. Rural homes are usually simple structures with mud walls built on wooden frames and thatched roofs. They may be either circular or rectangular, but are usually small structures with only one room. Typically, these houses are built with few or no amenities, such as electricity or running water. Urban homes are more likely to be made of cement blocks and topped with metal roofs. The shape of the cement blocks dictates the square and rectangular forms that dominate the urban landscape. Both rural and urban houses may be built in small compounds, with a shared courtyard acting as the kitchen.

The homes of Mozambique's wealthy are large and comfortable. Many of these homes date from the Portuguese colonial period and lie in less-heavily developed urban areas. Stone and brick replace cement as the common building material, and the structures may rise two stories above ground.

Food

Mozambique is famous for its seafood. In particular, the country's prawns (a crustacean similar to the shrimp) are among the largest in the world. Many of Mozambique's chief agricultural crops, such as cashews, cassava, and tropical fruits, are used in the local cuisine.

Mozambican cuisine typically reflects the nation's historic cultural and commercial interaction with neighboring cultures and the country's colonial heritage. In addition to the Portuguese influence evident in many national dishes, Mediterranean, American, and Asian foods and culinary traditions play important roles in Mozambican cooking. Crops such as Indonesian sugar cane and Indian ginger thrive alongside European citrus fruits and American cassava and peanuts.

Cassava, a root vegetable that can be used like a potato or ground into flour, is a staple of the Mozambican diet, particularly in rural regions. Millet, the sole native grain commonly consumed in Mozambique, is often used to brew homemade beer. Other common beverages include tea, coffee, and Portuguese wines.

Stews and soups made with cassava or other ingredients are also mainstays of Mozambican cooking. Matapa is a stew made with peanuts and spinach. Another common soup is sopa de feijao verde (green bean soup), made by simmering together green beans, potatoes, onions, tomatoes, salt, pepper, and water. In rural areas, corn porridge is prepared by finely pounding corn and cooking it over an open fire.

Some common Mozambican dishes are xima, which is made from cassava and corn, and frango, or barbequed chicken. Meats such as chicken, goat, and beef are expensive and eaten only occasionally. Chicken is more widely consumed than red meat. Spices such as hot peppers are used in the preparation of many meals.

Mozambican woman preparing cassava over an open fire.

For example, chicken is frequently served with a condiment called piri-piri. This spicy, hot sauce is made by combining red chili peppers with garlic, salt, and olive oil. Many of these dishes are adapted from traditional Portuguese cuisine.

The ties to Portugal can also be recognized in a popular dessert, ananas con vinho de porto (pineapple in port wine). This simple preparation calls for fresh pineapple slices to be soaked in sweet port wine for several hours. Sometimes, cashews are sprinkled over the marinated pineapple for added flavor and crunch.

Life's Milestones

In north and central Mozambique, boys and girls of the Makhua ethnic group participate in traditional coming of age ceremonies. Girls between the ages of ten and twelve take part in a period of initiation called cipitu. During this time, an adult female teaches the girls about their duties and roles as wives and mothers in Mozambican society. For boys, the jando ceremony provides instruction in how men are expected to behave and contribute to community life. At the close of the ceremonial period, boys are circumcised to mark their status as adult men. After these ceremonies, boys and girls are considered ready to marry. All Mozambican marriages require the payment of lobola, a bride price, to be finalized.

Southern, urban, and coastal Mozambicans are more likely to follow Western or Muslim customs. Weddings often take place in a religious tradition, and ceremonial rites of passage are rare. The birth of a healthy child is an event of great celebration throughout the country. All Mozambicans also recognize the important and solemnity of death and mourning. In rural areas, death typically results in the suspension of all regular activity for three days while community members mourn the loss.

CULTURAL HISTORY

Art

For centuries, decorative body art such as tattoos, lip plugs, and lip stretching were popular among many tribal Mozambicans. Tattooing was considered a form of self-beautification, and women were typically more extensively tattooed than men were. To create the tattoos, a series of small cuts was made in the desired pattern, usually in a geometric form. Charcoal ash was then rubbed into the cuts. As the cuts healed, a small amount of scar tissue formed with the pigmentation of the ash. To make these designs more distinct or complex, the process could be repeated.

The northern Makonde people also engaged in traditional lip plugging. This plug was worn almost exclusively by women as a sign of beauty. A small hole was made in a young girl's upper lip, which was then slowly stretched over time through the insertion of progressively larger twigs. In adulthood, women placed small ebony discs called ndonas into the lip holes. The Makonde also ritually chipped their teeth as part of coming of age ceremonies. The practice of body art has significantly faded since the 1970s for a variety of reasons. The government has worked to deter the practice, while the modern, Western-influenced generation has displayed little interest in traditional body art.

Woodcarving, including sculpture, is perhaps the best known of Mozambique's traditional arts. One of the most notable forms of traditional Mozambique wood art is the carving of masks, which dates back to early Bantu tribal traditions. Masks have served significant cultural, ritual, and political functions and a person wearing a mask traditionally takes on the characteristics of whom that mask depicts. This assumption of personality lends masks great importance during funerary and memorial ceremonies and coming of age ceremonies, in which Mozambican boys effectively take on new identities in the community. Mozambicans also used masks to mock their Portuguese rulers during the colonial era. Skilled craft workers continue to produce ceremonial and traditional masks, particularly in the northern and central areas of the nation. The carving of wooden sculptures also dates back centuries. Northern sculptors traditionally used ebony, while southern artisans preferred sandalwood. The Makonde have traditionally been the best-known Mozambican figure carvers, producing both realistic and abstract figures depicting daily life, human emotion, and animistic spirits.

Architecture

Located off the northern coast, Ilha de Moçambique (Mozambique Island) is the site of the ancient city of Moçambique. This city served as Mozambique's first colonial capital and became an important Portuguese trading port during the 16th and 17th centuries. The historic section of the city, now known as Stone Town, reflects both an architectural unity and diversity, in that there is a range of architectural styles, but a consistent use of materials. Portuguese architecture elements, visible in the city's church façades, meld with Muslim terraced roofs and courtyards, and remnants of the city's trading history are extant in the decorative elements imported from India. In the modern portion of the city, called Makuti Town, scores of residences use a typical Swahili rectangular layout. Despite this cosmopolitan blend, the continuous use of native coral limestone and wood as construction materials throughout a 500-year period, and in both historical and modern buildings, gives the island a distinctly cohesive appearance.

In 1991, the United Nations Educational, Scientific, and Cultural Organization (UNESCO) recognized the unique architectural heritage of Ilha de Moçambique by declaring the fortified city island a World Heritage Site. Since that time, renovations have begun on some of the city's most significant buildings, such as the Portuguese Fort de São Sebastião and the late Gothic Chapel de Nossa Senhona de Baluarte, considered the oldest European building in the Southern Hemisphere.

Music & Dance

Two traditional Mozambican art forms have also earned cultural distinction from UNESCO as intangible cultural heritages (ICH): the Chopi Timbila and the Gule Wamkulu. In southern Mozambique, the ethnic Chopi communities are renowned for their orchestral music, which is traditionally played by a group of xylophones, called the timbila. These instruments are finely manufactured and tuned, and produce a rich, resonant sound. The Gule Wamkulu is a secret male cult and ritualistic dance practiced among the ethnic Chewa. The cult is a form of solidarity for male tribal members, and the accompanying ritual dance is performed at various ceremonies, including weddings, funerals, and initiations. In 2005, both cultural practices were proclaimed Masterpieces of the Oral and Intangible Heritage of Humanity. However, youth are increasingly disengaging themselves from these traditional practices, and the Gule Wamkulu in particular is often performed only as entertainment for tourists.

Literature

Mozambican poets and writers played an instrumental role in the independence movement that began in the 1940s. Typically written in Portuguese, Mozambican poetry explored themes relating to liberation, longing, and, later, the devastating effects of war. Poets such as Noemia de Sousa (1926–2003) and José Craveirinha (1922–2003) expressed the need for a national

identity and spoke out against colonial oppression. Craveirinha rose to prominence during the mid-20th century with poetry that called for African self-rule and national solidarity, and was eventually arrested and imprisoned for his work. His later works gained international acclaim, and Craveirinha has been considered numerous times for the Nobel Prize in Literature.

Poet Jorge Rebelo (1940–) also supported the Mozambican independence movement. In addition to penning rousing poetry during the rebellion against Portuguese rule, he also edited publications for the Liberation Front of Mozambique (FRELIMO) guerilla movement that later rose to prominence as Mozambique's governing political party. He and other writers of the revolution, including Marcelino dos Santos (1929–) and Luis Bernardo Honwana (1942–), depicted the harsh racism of the colonial regime, the intense guerrilla fighting of the rebellion, and the deep-seated nationalism. Their work continues to be strongly associated with the fight for colonial liberation.

CULTURE

Arts & Entertainment

Mozambique is home to what is perhaps southeast Africa's most vibrant and diverse arts community. In addition to the continuing practice of traditional arts and crafts, modern-day Mozambique is recognized for its thriving culture of literature, visual arts, music, and dance.

Contemporary Mozambican authors have translated the difficult experiences of colonial-era conflict and civil war into wrenching novels. In addition to the internationally recognized short stories of Mia Couto (1955–), stories and novels by writers such as Lina Magaia (c. 1940s–2011), Eduardo White (1963–), and Lidia Jorge (1946–) have captured the pulse of a country shifting from colonial rule to independence. Many stories are critical of the human rights violations common in the nation both before and after independence.

In Mozambique, music is a vital part of everyday life. In rural areas, songs accompany daily agricultural chores and are used to tell stories of the nation's history. After the end of colonial rule, traditional music surged in popularity as part of a movement to embrace a fully African culture. In 1979, the National Song and Dance Company formed to encourage the performance of native arts. This group of musicians, dancers, storytellers, and actors has traveled the globe to bring Mozambican arts and culture to new audiences. The late-20th-century return to traditional forms also led to the popularity of marrabenta music made famous by the Orchestra Marrabenta during the 1980s.

Some modern Mozambican music reflects themes vital to the country. Singer and musician Feliciano dos Santos (1964–), front man of the band Massukos, has become one of Africa's best-known performers. A native of the Mozambican province of Niassa, dos Santos contracted polio as a child. After becoming known for his music combining Western and African music, dos Santos embarked on a personal mission to help the people of his homeland learn about improved sanitation to prevent others from suffering from diseases such as polio. Since 1996, dos Santos has headed a charity dedicated to bringing clean water and sanitation to Niassa. In 2007, Massukos' second album reached the top of the RTP Portugal charts, and in 2008, he won the Goldman Environmental Prize for his humanitarian work.

Traditional dance also experienced a similar rebirth as traditional music in Mozambique. In some regions of the country, dances reminiscent of military maneuvers, complete with wooden replicas of weapons, are used to commemorate Mozambican history. The n'ganda dance of the Niassa Province derives from the military displays of soldiers after World War I. Other dances hearken back to colonial rule and the fight for liberation. One of these is the Zambezia Province's niquetxe dance, traditionally used to honor those who died under the difficult conditions of colonial rule. Modern Mozambican dance also has important ceremonial functions. Originally, from the provinces of Manica and Sofola, the makwaya dance is performed at weddings to celebrate the union of two families. A similar dance, the semba, has spread from Sofola to the rest of the country.

In the late 20th and early 21st centuries, Mozambican sculptors helped transform instruments of war into a vision of peace through the Transformation of Arms into Tools program. Volunteers traveled throughout the country to buy guns and other weapons used during the years of civil violence, and in 1998, fourteen Mozambican artists began turning the weapons, which ranged from rifles to grenades to land mines, into works of contemporary sculpture with peaceful themes. The project culminated with the creation of the *Tree of Life* in 2003 and 2004. This half-ton sculpture repurposed weapons into a metal tree filled with wildlife to represent Mozambique's transformation from a war-torn to peaceful, growing modern nation. The *Tree of Life* and other sculptures have since been exhibited internationally.

Mozambique's most respected contemporary drama troupe is Mutumbela Gogo, based in Maputo. Founded in 1986, the troupe has staged performances not only in Mozambique, but also around southern Africa and Europe. Its productions often combine Western and African literary and performance techniques to form a uniquely Mozambican form. Amateur troupes based at schools, social organizations, and community centers throughout the country allow those outside of Maputo to enjoy dramatic productions. Some of the best known of these amateur groups are Quelimane's Falados de Zambézia and Xenhê in the Zambezia Province.

Cultural Sites & Landmarks

As Mozambique's capital, Maputo is home to a variety of historic and cultural sites. Maputo's famed Mercado Municipal (Municipal Market), with a wide selection of fresh seafood and produce, offers visitors a close-up view of the capital's lively daily life. Other popular markets selling foodstuff and traditional crafts include the Janeta Market and the Xipamanine Market. Maputo is also home to Estádio da Machava, Mozambique's national stadium.

Located near the popular beach resorts at Tofo and Barra, the town of Inhambane was settled by the Portuguese during the 18th century. Although the modern town does not have the economic prominence that it held during the 18th and 19th centuries, it remains a pleasant tourist destination known for its relaxed atmosphere and attractive colonial buildings. Historic buildings include the 18th-century Cathedral de Nossa Senhora de Conceição, the 19th-century Old Mosque, and the Portuguese governor's mansion. The southern town of Vilankulo is also known for its relaxed atmosphere and as a gateway to explore the Bazaruto Archipelago. Composed of six islands, the archipelago was designated a national park in 1971.

Gorongosa National Park, located in the southern province of Solofa, offers particularly impressive bird-watching opportunities, with over 100 different species reported. In 2006, significant efforts to restore wildlife damaged during the decades of conflict began. The northern Niassa Wildlife Reserve, at about 42,000 square kilometers (26,100 miles), is one of Africa's largest protected areas. The reserve is located near Lake Niassa, the continent's third-largest lake and itself an important ecological area.

Although less developed than the relatively comfortable southern provinces, the rural northern regions of Mozambique offer unparalleled cultural opportunities. The historically and architecturally significant Ilha de Moçambique lies off the northeastern coast, and other colonial Portuguese settlements can be visited on the islands of the Quirimba Archipelago. Two historic Portuguese forts, the Fort of São João and the Fort of São José, are located on the archipelago's island of Ibo. Many small villages in rural north also maintain the traditional agrarian way of life that has sustained Mozambique for centuries.

Libraries & Museums

In Maputo, the Chissano Museum displays works from Mozambique's best-known 20th-century artist, Makonda sculptor Alberto Chissano (1935–1994). The Natural History Museum is best known for its exhibitions on native insects and the development of elephants, and features a mural painted by respected Mozambican artist Valente Malangantana (1936–2011). Other museums in Maputo include the National Museum of Art, the Museu da Revolução, which focuses on Mozambique's struggle for independence, and the National Museum of the Currency. The National Ethnology Museum is located in Nampula, the largest northern city.

After an extensive rehabilitation period, which included the construction of a new two-story building, the National Library of Mozambique reopened in 2010. The library houses a collection of 150,000 books. As of 2007, the country was home to eleven public libraries, including one library for each district.

Holidays

Mozambique's national holiday is Independence Day, and is celebrated on June 25. Other public holidays include Heroes' Day (February 3), Women's Day (April 7), Victory Day (September 7), and Revolution Day (September 25). Christian and Muslim observations are the most common religious holidays in Mozambique.

Youth Culture

The arrival of television and mass media brought the next generation of young Mozambicans into a globalized world foreign to former generations. Western-influenced clothing styles such as t-shirts, jeans, and short skirts have replaced traditional Mozambican clothing among the young, and Western-influenced music, such as hip-hop and reggae music, have grown increasingly popular. Increased education has also separated youth, both culturally and opportunistically, from the influence of their families.

Young Mozambicans, both urban and rural, enjoy many of the same recreational activities as other young cultures, including watching television and participating in sports, particularly football (soccer). Discotheques and bars are popular nightlife destinations for older youth, as are video clubs where movies and music videos are shown. Although discotheques are popular with all, bars and video clubs are primarily frequented by young men.

SOCIETY

Transportation

Public transportation in Mozambique is limited. Buses (machibombos) are the main mode of public transportation, and travel all main routes. Minibuses (chapas) and trucks (called camions) travel to smaller urban centers, but are frequently overcrowded. Train service connects to neighboring countries, but service is limited. Ferry service is in operation along the coast. Generally, provincial roads are in fair condition. Traffic moves on the left-hand side of the road.

Transportation Infrastructure

Because of Mozambique's long-standing commercial relationships with countries lying to its west, the wide majority of the nation's overland transportation routes run in that direction. Early rail lines stretched from Maputo to South Africa, and later road and rail development centered on the nation's southern commercial and industrial centers.

Political instability throughout many of Mozambican rural areas in the latter years of Portuguese rule deterred the growth of land transportation routes in the country's northern half. Today, northern and central areas have few road and rail connections, instead relying largely on air travel. Linhas Aéreas de Moçombique (Mozambique Airlines) provides much of the nation's international and domestic air service, with major airports servicing Maputo, Beira, and Vilanculos. Maputo and Beira are also home to important seaports, with smaller ports serving other coastal cities such as Nacala, Pemba, and Inhambane.

Media & Communications

Mass media and communications have been slow to come to Mozambique. Television broadcasts in the nation did not begin until 1981, and as of 2003, only about 20 out of every 1,000 Mozambicans owned televisions. The only station available nationwide is the state-run Televisão de Moçambique (TVM), although many smaller stations have local and regional coverage. Portuguese-language broadcasts from Portugal and Brazil are also popular. The most significant radio broadcaster, also operated by the government, is Antena Nacional. Although many newspapers such as the *Noticias* and *Diario de Moçambique* are published on a daily or weekly basis, readership is relatively low due to widespread illiteracy.

The advent of cellular technology has somewhat improved telecommunications, which have historically been characterized by high cost and low distribution. Internet usage is growing steadily. The estimated 1.4 million Internet users at the beginning of 2014 represented a major increase over figures from only six years previously.

SOCIAL DEVELOPMENT

Standard of Living

In 2014, Mozambique ranked 178th on the United Nations Human Development Index, which measures quality of life and standard of living indicators.

Water Consumption

According to 2009 statistics from the World Health Organization, only slightly more than 50 percent of the population has access to an improved drinking water source, while just over 20 percent of the population has access to improved sanitation. For water consumption, Mozambique is highly reliant on shared and foreign water sources; over half of the country's water originates outside of the country's borders, including major rivers.

Education

The educational picture in Mozambique is bleak. Though the government has been attempting to institute reforms in the early 21st century, the educational system remains substandard at best.

Problems include a lack of trained or qualified teachers, teacher attrition, insufficient school facilities, and poor enforcement of school attendance. Mozambique's average literacy rate was reported as 58 percent in 2015 by the government, one of the lowest in the world (though international reports have listed the rate as low as 48 percent). The literacy rate is estimated as lower among females, with the illiteracy rate of rural woman between 70 and 80 percent. Education is free and compulsory until the age of twelve; however, in 2007, an estimated 1 million children did not attend school regularly, mostly in rural regions.

The situation has been exacerbated by Mozambique's dire AIDS\HIV situation (the country has one of the world's highest percentages of people living with HIV or AIDS). According to a 2010 report, an estimated 336 employees of the Ministry of Education are known to have died due to AIDS complications that year, 90 percent of which were teachers. Teachers continue to be at high risk for infection.

Eduardo Mondlane University in Maputo is one of the country's primary universities. Another primary university, Pedagogical University, is also located in the capital. Other universities include the Polytechnic University (ISPU), the Higher Institute of Science and Technology (ISCTEM), the Higher Institute of Public Administration (ISAP), the Higher Institute of International Relations (ISRI), the São Tomás University of Mozambique (USTM), and the Technical University (UDM). However, net enrollment in tertiary education is a mere one percent.

Women's Rights

Despite official prohibition of discrimination against women through both laws and ratification of the Convention on Elimination of all Forms of Discrimination against Women (CEDAW), Mozambican women continue to face many challenges. Crimes against women and sexual harassment are both common, and some traditional practices in rural areas severely limit the rights of women.

Domestic and spousal abuse is not specifically barred under Mozambican law, and many Mozambican women believe that their husbands hold the authority to assault them physically. A 2006 report showed that more than half of Mozambican women had been physically or sexually abused at some point, with slightly over one-fifth acknowledging such an incident within the preceding year. Spousal and familial abandonment of women with HIV/AIDS has been reported, as have accusations of witchcraft and subsequent punishment following the death of a husband from complications of HIV/AIDS. By 2008, the Mozambican government had begun efforts to encourage women to report domestic and sexual abuse by installing dedicated women's and children's police units and opening assistance centers at Maputo police stations.

In Mozambique, prostitution is legal and highly regulated. Mozambican women victimized by human traffickers are typically forced to work as domestic servants or prostitutes in South Africa, while forced labor by women and girls from other countries such as neighboring Zimbabwe have been reported within Mozambique. Women ensnared by traffickers who do not face strictly sexual servitude are nevertheless likely to be sexually abused by their captors. Although rape is a crime punishable by two to 12 years' imprisonment, the crime is rarely reported and prosecutions are practically nonexistent. Spousal rape in not a crime and is a widespread concern.

Rural Mozambican women particularly face challenges stemming from traditional cultural practices. The lack of ready access to the official governmental and judicial structures in the north prevents women from taking advantage of their full legal rights. Instead, decisions are made according to customary law, which bars women from certain types of inheritance. In some regions, a ritual sexual "purification" ceremony takes place after the death of a husband, and refusal to participate in this rite may bar women from receiving their inheritances. Urban women and others who hold non-farm jobs typically suffer pay discrimination and face extensive workplace sexual harassment.

The lack of adequate health care services negatively affects many women, particularly in rural regions. Insufficient medical care contributes to the high infant mortality rate, as well as to the number of women who die in childbirth. In 2007, the Mozambican government relaxed restrictions on abortion, due to the high number of fatalities caused by unsafe procedures—as many as 30 percent of women who faced complications following an illegal abortion died as a result of those complications.

Despite other social and cultural challenges, women have gained an increasingly significant role in Mozambican politics. In 2004, Luisa Dias Diogo (1958–) became the first female prime minister of the nation. As of 2008, women also held ninety-three of the 250 seats in the national assembly. Women also act as leaders in various ministerial departments, as well as within the governing bodies of the Mozambique government.

Health Care

The health care system in Mozambique is not equipped to meet the needs of the population. There are hospitals in Maputo, but most citizens do not receive adequate medical attention. The county also faces a severe shortage of health care workers; there are less than 900 doctors in the country, and only 1.26 workers per 1,000 people. Life expectancy is low, estimated at 53 years for women and 52 years for men (2015 estimate); however, this is almost a 10-year increase over the same statistics in 2009. In 2015, the infant mortality rate stood at 70 deaths per every 1000 births.

Mozambique has one of the world's highest percentages of people living with HIV or AIDS. About 10.5 percent of the adult population is infected with HIV/AIDS (2014 estimate), which causes roughly 44,900 deaths annually.

Mozambicans are at high risk for contracting numerous diseases, including bacterial and protozoal diarrhea, hepatitis A, typhoid fever, malaria, plague, and schistosomiasis. In addi-

tion, over one million active landmines left over from the civil war pose serious health and safety threats.

GOVERNMENT

Structure

Mozambique is an independent democratic republic. The president, elected to a five-year term, is the head of state. A prime minister, appointed by the president, is the head of government. The prime minister oversees the Council of Ministers, the appointed executive cabinet.

The legislative branch consists of a 250-member unicameral Assembly of the Republic, and the judicial branch consists of a Supreme Court. Officials are elected by secret ballot. The voting age is 18 in Mozambique. The constitution has been in effect since November 30, 1990.

Mozambique gained independence in 1975, after nearly five centuries of Portuguese rule and a 13-year resistance. In 1962, the Mozambique Liberation Front (Frelimo) rebelled against the Portuguese with violence, and eventually won. During the 1980s, the new government received aid from European communist nations. Anticommunist military groups joined with fundamental Christian groups to form the anticommunist Mozambican National Resistance (Renamo), a group dedicated to crippling Mozambique's communist government.

Using guerilla tactics, Renamo eventually instigated a full-blown civil war with Frelimo. When the Soviet Union disbanded, Mozambique's government followed South Africa's liberal reforms and drafted a peace accord between Frelimo and Renamo. The accord has been in effect since 1992, and both Frelimo and Renamo have become legitimate, nonviolent political parties.

Frelimo has won all successive elections, and Mozambique has undergone major social, political, and economic reforms during a decade of peace. These include shifting to a free-market economy, improving foreign relations, and promoting gender equity in the government. Nearly one-third of Mozambique's elected officials are women.

Political Parties

Mozambican politics is dominated by a two-party system. The Liberation Front of Mozambique party, or Frelimo, has ruled as the dominant party since 1975. Mozambican National Resistance, or Renamo, as part of an alliance of seven other parties, is the opposition party. Following the 2004 parliamentary election, the party captured ninety of the 250 seats in parliament. After the 2009 parliamentary elections, the number of seats held by Renamo fell to fifty-one, while the newly founded Democratic Movement of Mozambique immediately gained eight seats. In 2014, Frelimon retained a strong majority with 114 seats to Renamo's 89.

Local Government

Mozambique is divided into 10 provinces with Maputo, the capital, also holding provincial status. The provinces are then subdivided into 129 districts. The districts are further into administrative posts (Postos Administrativos), of which there are 405, and localities, both of which are governed by secretaries. Despite the established administrative divisions, many areas of the country have no established local governance. The 33 urban municipalities (in 23 cities and 10 towns) are governed by a municipal assembly and a municipal council. There are plans to extend this municipal form of governance to an additional 106 towns.

Judicial System

The Supreme Court is Mozambique's highest court. Lower courts operate on the provincial, district, and municipal levels. Criticism has been consistently leveled at the judicial system for its ineffectiveness in governing over commercial or industry matters. Reforms continue to address and transform the justice system in Mozambique.

Taxation

Mozambique's tax rates are high. The corporate tax rate is 32 percent (except for income derived from agriculture), while the highest income rate is also 32 percent. Other taxes levied include an inheritance tax and a value-added tax (or VAT, similar to a consumption tax).

Armed Forces

Officially called the Armed Forces for the Defence of Mozambique (FADM), the Mozambican military was formed from the warring remnants of the country's civil war, and consists of a land force, air force, and navy. Active personnel were reported as 11,200 strong in 2007.

Foreign Policy

Mozambique joined the United Nations (UN) in 1975, shortly after gaining independence from Portugal. The nation's earliest significant developmental partner was the Soviet Union, but by the mid-1980s, Mozambique had turned away from the Soviets in favor of Western aid. Since that time, the nation has become a member of many international bodies, including the African Union (AU), the World Bank, the International Monetary Fund (IMF), the Commonwealth, the Southern African Development Community (SADC), the Indian Ocean Rim-Association for Regional Cooperation (IOR-ARC), and the Organization of the Islamic Conference (OIC). In 1996, Mozambique also helped form the Community of Portuguese-Speaking Countries and served as the organization's first president.

Mozambique relies heavily on foreign developmental aid; according to the UN, about one-half of total government spending draws on international funding, making Mozambique the largest African recipient of foreign aid. Because much of the nation's food comes from local farmers, Mozambique is particularly dependent on foreign food aid in times of drought or other natural disasters. Much of the international funding for the nation comes from the United States. Relations between Mozambique and former colonizer Portugal, however, have been tenuous, but the two nations remain commercially and culturally linked. In 2007, Mozambique took formal control of the Cabora Bassa Dam, the last Portuguese-controlled public structure in the nation. However, this symbolic final victory for independence has brought significant economic and environmental costs to an already-struggling nation.

Mozambique has generally strong regional relations, despite regional instability, particularly in modern-day Zimbabwe and South Africa, contributing to political unrest in Mozambique during the 1980s. Since the end of the Mozambican civil war in 1992, the nation has increasingly worked to develop favorable diplomatic relationships with its geographical neighbors. Nonetheless, in 2008, thousands of Mozambicans fled South Africa because of attacks on foreigners in that nation, leading the Mozambican government to declare a state of emergency. Regional issues have also occasionally clouded diplomatic relations between Mozambique and some of its neighbors, including Malawi and Zimbabwe.

Although the country has no formal international grievances, it maintains a significant standing military—the Mozambique Armed Defense Forces, or FADM—comprising an army, navy, and air force. In the late 1990s, Mozambique instituted a two-year compulsory term of military service for Mozambican men. The nation's problems, however, remain largely internal rather than external; military efforts to safely remove and contain weapons dating from the Mozambican struggle for independence and ensuing war continue and are a topic of much concern in the country. Unintentional weapons explosions have occurred sporadically in the first years of the 21st century, injuring or killing many Mozambicans. Despite offers of assistance from the UN, Mozambique's government remains committed to handling the problem alone.

Human Rights Profile

International human rights law insists that states respect civil and political rights, and promote an individual's economic, social, and cultural rights. The United Nations Universal Declaration on Human Rights (UDHR) is recognized as the standard for international human rights. Its authors sought the counsel of the world's great thinkers, philosophers, and religious leaders, and were careful to create a document that reflects the core values shared by every world culture. (To read this document or view the articles relating to cultural human rights, visit http://www.udhr.org/UDHR/default.htm.)

Mozambique faces significant human rights challenges that stem largely from its years of civil war and high levels of poverty. Although both the Mozambican constitution and law officially prevent discrimination based on factors described UDHR, discriminatory practices against the disabled, women, and those afflicted with HIV/AIDS remain common. Acts of violence and killings by police, primarily in Maputo, are also not uncommon. Additionally, arbitrary arrests, lengthy detentions, and an inefficient criminal justice system have also been cited by international monitoring agencies. In 2008, murders by groups of private individuals seeking revenge for real or perceived crimes were on the rise and violence continues to be a major problem into 2015.

Freedom of speech and religion are constitutionally and legally protected. In practice, religious diversity is common and well accepted, with intrusions on freedom of speech occasionally committed. Government influence on the Mozambican press is strong; the state-controlled media has been accused of pro-government bias, and incidents of harassment of Mozambican journalists by local police have been reported. Speaking out against the president is outlawed. However, international media operate freely throughout Mozambique. Academic freedom is generally widespread, although instructors have at times felt pressured to promote a pro-government agenda.

In 2008, Mozambique formally outlawed the practice of trafficking in persons, or forcing people to work against their will. An ongoing problem in Mozambique, this trafficking is typically carried out by either South Africans or Mozambicans, and most often affects women and children. Most trafficking victims are forced to work in South Africa, with smaller numbers of victims transported to Zambia. The formal ban on this practice represents a significant step toward eliminating human trafficking in Mozambique.

Perhaps the brightest spot in Mozambique's human rights outlook is the nation's stated intentions of human rights protection through the ratification of numerous human rights treaties and protections. The nation is party to such significant agreements as the Convention on the Prevention and Punishment of the Crime of Genocide; the International Covenant on Economic, Social, and Cultural Rights; the Convention on the Rights of the Child; and the Convention on the Rights of Persons with Disabilities. In 2007, the UN acknowledged Mozambique's ongoing efforts to improve human rights and to protect ethnic diversity throughout the country.

ECONOMY

Overview of the Economy
Since gaining independence, Mozambique has abandoned its Marxist economy for free enterprise. The nation, once among the world's poorest, remains dependent on foreign aid. The International Monetary Fund (IMF) and the World Trade Organization (WTO) have helped Mozambique regulate foreign debt, spurring major developments and increasing the value of the metical. In 2014, the per capita gross domestic product (GDP) was estimated at $1,200 (USD).

Industry
Food processing, oil refining, and coal mining make up most of Mozambique's industrial activity. The Cahora Bassa Dam provides hydroelectric power, most of which is exported to South Africa and other neighboring nations. Manufactured and processed products include beverages, chemicals, fertilizer, aluminum, textiles, cement, glass, and asbestos.

Mozambique's main imports are machinery and equipment, vehicles, fuel, chemicals, metal, food, and textiles. Exports include cashews, aluminum, prawns, cotton, sugar, citrus, timber, and electricity. The country's main trading partners are Belgium, Italy, Spain, Germany, Zimbabwe, South Africa, Australia, and the United States.

Labor
Mozambique's labor force was estimated at 12.25 million in 2014. Most of the workforce is employed in agriculture. In general, the Mozambican labor force is poorly trained. Unemployment is estimated at 17 percent (sourced from data dating back to 2007).

Energy/Power/Natural Resources
In addition to the numerous natural harbors that are considered some of the best in Africa, Mozambique has a number of important natural resources. These include coal, natural gas, titanium, graphite, and tantalum. The Cahora Bassa Dam provides hydroelectric power, much of which is exported to neighboring nations.

Fishing
Artisanal fishing, where the catch is primarily used for domestic consumption or subsistence, comprises a large percentage of Mozambique's fishing industry. Among the commercialized industry, where domestic companies are typically small, shrimp, crabs, and lobster are the primary commercial species. Illegal fishing remains a huge concern, and foreign-chartered vessels from Spain and Japan operate in Mozambican waters.

Forestry
Mozambique was once known for its abundant forest resources, however, illegal cutting has contributed greatly to desertification in the country, and the government has turned to foreign aid for help with reforestation and establishing sustainability. In 2009, it was estimated that approximately 55.3 million hectares (136,649,275 acres) of Mozambique's land area was forest cover. As with other areas, data concerning the forestry industry is lacking. However, it is estimated that approximately 99 percent of all forestry companies or outfits operating in the sector were small or medium-sized enterprises.

Agriculture
Agriculture is the nation's largest economic sector, and most rural Mozambicans earn their livelihood on self-sufficient tribal farms. Mozambique

is the world's biggest exporter of cashews. In addition to cashews, cassava, cotton, coconuts, prawns, sugar cane, fish, tea, corn, tropical fruits, sisal, citrus, potatoes, sunflowers, beef, and poultry are the chief agricultural products.

Because the economy is heavily reliant on agricultural activity, economic success is dependent on the weather. The droughts and floods characteristic of Mozambique's climate often cause recessions. For this reason, Mozambique's government is working to diversify the economy in other sectors, particularly tourism.

Animal Husbandry

Cattle are the primary livestock in Mozambique. Other commercial livestock include goats, sheep, pigs, and rabbit. Historically, cattle farming supported the country's southeastern economy.

Tourism

While it does not generate enough revenue to be a substantial part of the economy, tourism in Mozambique has increased significantly since the civil war ended in 1992. The Mozambican government is expanding the tourism sector by building resorts and improving the country's transportation infrastructure. Foreign investment in the tourism sector has also increased. In 2009, it was reported that the country's tourism revenue had more than doubled over a five-year period dating back to 2004. A major investment in tourism in 2011, it is hoped, will strengthen the industry further.

One popular tourist destination is the Lago de Cahora Bassa, the large lake on the Zambezi River. Beach towns such as Tofo are popular for surfing, diving and snorkeling. Many tourists are drawn to Mozambique by the opportunity to view African wildlife. In addition to its elephant population, the Maputo Elephant Reserve is known for its tropical birds.

Vanessa Vaughn, Richard Means,
Beverly Ballaro

DO YOU KNOW?

- Maputo was once named Lourenço Marques, in honor of a Portuguese trader who came to the city in the 16th century.

- Mozambique's post-independence leaders changed the name of the capital to Maputo, to honor the indigenous chief Maputa. According to legend, Chief Maputa had been the sole ruler of the greater Maputo territory at the time the first Portuguese explorers landed on Mozambique's coast in the 16th century.

- Maputo's Praça dos Trabalhadores contains a sculpture honoring the sacrifices of Mozambican soldiers who fought in World War I. The monument depicts a cobra curling up from the feet of a woman. According to tradition, a local woman had heroically killed a rampaging cobra by plunging it into a pot of boiling porridge that she was balancing on her head.

Bibliography

Ana Mafalda Leite, et al., eds. "Speaking the Postcolonial Nation: Interviews with Writers from Angola and Mozambique." Bern, Switzerland: *Peter Lang*, 2014.

David C. King, "Mozambique." New York: *Marshall Cavendish Benchmark*, 2006.

George O. Ndege. "Culture and Customs of Mozambique." Westport, CT: *Greenwood Press*, 2007.

Juan Obarrio. "The Spirit of the Laws in Mozambique." Chicago: *University of Chicago Press*, 2014.

Mary Fitzpatrick, et al. "Zambia, Mozambique, Malawi." Oakland, CA: *Lonely Planet*, 2013.

Paolo Israel. "In Step with the Times: Mapiko Masquerades of Mozambique." Athens, OH: *Ohio University Press*, 2014.

Phillip Briggs. "Mozambique." Guilford, CT: *Globe Pequot*, 2014.

Works Cited

"2008 Human Rights Report: Mozambique." U.S. Department of State: Diplomacy in Action. *United States Department of State.* http://www.state.gov/g/drl/rls/hrrpt/2008/af/119015.htm.

"About Mozambique." United Nations Mozambique. *United Nations.* http://www.unmozambique.org/eng/About-Mozambique.

"Country Profile: Mozambique." *British Broadcasting Corporation.* http://news.bbc.co.uk/2/hi/africa/country_profiles/1063120.stm#media.

"Gorongosa National Park." *Gorongosa National Park.* http://www.gorongosa.net/.

"Instituto Nacional de Estatistica Moçambique." *National Statistical Institute.* Government of Mozambique. http://www.ine.gov.mz/Ingles.

"Island of Mozambique." UNESCO World Heritage Center. *UNESCO.* http://whc.unesco.org/en/list/599.

"Language of the Month: Xitsonga." *Government of South Africa.* http://www.saps.gov.za/docs_publs/publications/journal/june2006/pg14_15_language.pdf.

"Massukos." *Massukos.* 6 April 2009. http://www.massukos.org/.

"Mozambique Fears 'Exodus' from Violence in South Africa,' *New York Times, the Associated Press.* 24 May 2008. http://www.nytimes.com/2008/05/24/world/africa/24safrica.html?_r=1&scp=2&sq=mozambique&st=cse/.

"Mozambique." *Encyclopedia Britannica Online.* http://search.eb.com.ezproxy.libraries.wright.edu:2048/eb/article-9109711.

"Mozambique." World Data Analyst. *Encyclopedia Britannica.* http://www.world.eb.com.ezproxy.libraries.wright.edu:2048/wdpdf/Mozambique.pdf.

"Mozambique." The World Factbook. *Central Intelligence Agency.* https://www.cia.gov/library/publications/the-world-factbook/geos/mz.html.

"Mozambique." U.S. Department of State: Diplomacy in Action. *United States Department of State.* http://www.state.gov/r/pa/ei/bgn/7035.htm.

"Mozambique: Family." Panos, London. http://www.panos.org.uk/?lid=24492.

"Mozambique Homepage." United Nations Human Rights. *Office of the High Commissioner for Human Rights.* http://www.ohchr.org/EN/countries/AfricaRegion/Pages/MZIndex.aspx.

"Mozambique: Menus and Recipes from Africa." African Studies Department. *University of Pennsylvania.* http://www.africa.upenn.edu/Cookbook/Mozambique.html.

"Mozambique Set to Liberalise Abortion Law." *Bio-Medicine.* 10 June 2007. http://www.bio-medicine.org/medicine-news/Mozambique-Set-to-Liberalise-Abortion-Law-20778-1/.

"Niassa Wildlife Reserve." *Imagine Africa.* http://www.imagineafrica.co.uk/Mozambique/Niassa_Wildlife_Reserve.

"Núcleo de Arte-Arts into Art." Núcleo de Arte. http://www.africaserver.nl/nucleo/eng/index.html.

"Premio Camoes." *El Poder de la Palabra.* http://www.epdlp.com/premios.php?premio=Camoes.

"Rebelo, Jorge." *Encyclopædia Britannica Online.* 2009. http://search.eb.com.ezproxy.libraries.wright.edu:2048/eb/article-9062884.

"United Nations Member States." *United Nations.* http://www.un.org/members/list.shtml#m.

"The World Encyclopedia of Contemporary Theatre: Africa." http://books.google.com/books?id=TIgS_Eij8SEC&pg=PA202&lpg=PA202&dq=mutumbela+gogo&source=bl&ots=8V_kP0i67G&sig=zfR1S_tP77LLM-6ci1qQW1wglEc&hl=en&ei=v3vaSaacGI-aMprc-ewO&sa=X&oi=book_result&ct=result&resnum=2#PPA203,M1.

Alec Dubro. "Mozambique's Soggy Inheritance." *Foreign Policy in Focus.* http://www.fpif.org/fpiftxt/4922.

Barry Bearak. "In Mozambique, Singing a Song of Sanitation and Hoping to Change Habits," *New York Times,* 24 Oct. 2008. http://www.nytimes.com/2008/10/25/world/africa/25santos.html?scp=4&sq=mozambique&st=cse.

Bettina Holzhausen. "Youth Culture in Rural Mozambique: Summary." http://nestcepas.ch/_pdf/Youth_culture_in_rural_Mozambique_summary.pdf

Dean Foster. "The Global Etiquette Guide to Africa and the Middle East." New York: *John Wiley & Sons,* 2002.

Nicolas D. Kristof. "Decision Making: Mozambique," *New York Times,* 25 Aug. 2008. http://kristof.blogs.nytimes.com/2008/08/25/decision-making-in-mozambique/?scp=3&sq=mozambique&st=cse.

Sharon LaFraniere. "Fears Linger in Mozambique over Unexploded Weapons," *New York Times,* 29 May 2007. http://www.nytimes.com/2007/05/29/world/africa/29mozambique.html?pagewanted=2&sq=mozambique&st=cse&scp=6

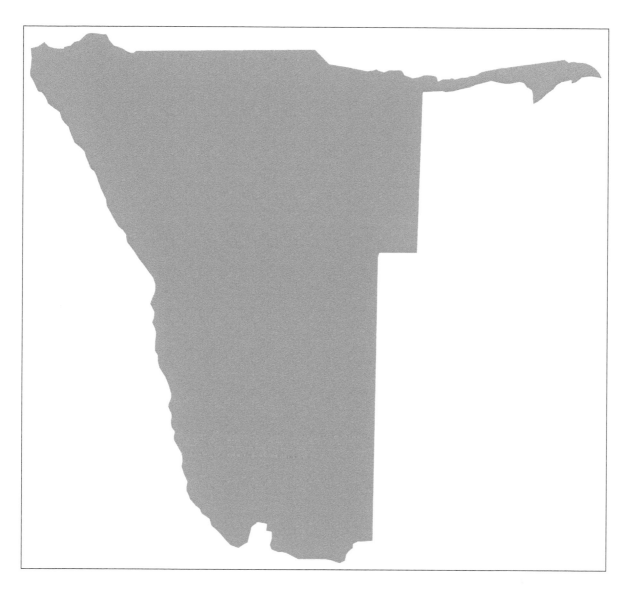

NAMIBIA

Introduction

The Republic of Namibia is a nation in south-western Africa. Namibia's western boundary is the Atlantic Ocean, while its land neighbors are South Africa to the south, Botswana to the east, and Angola and Zambia to the north.

Namibia gained its independence from South Africa in 1990. Since that time, Namibian tourism has grown extensively. The country's beautiful scenery and rich wildlife populations are major attractions. Ecotourists can view the country's wildlife in Etosha National Park or other reserves, while the country's game reserves attract hunters.

Namibia's population is largely black (87 percent), and a mix of native African groups. The Bushmen are an ethnic group who live in the Kalahari Desert, which spreads across Namibia as well as Botswana and South Africa. They are among the earliest inhabitants of southern Africa. The most populous group in Namibia is the Ovambo, who represent about half of the total Namibian population.

Namibia's cultural and artistic legacy dates back to early human history, as the country is home to some of the oldest hunting sites and petroglyphs in the world. In fact, the rock art at Twyfelfontein is recognized as a World Heritage Site.

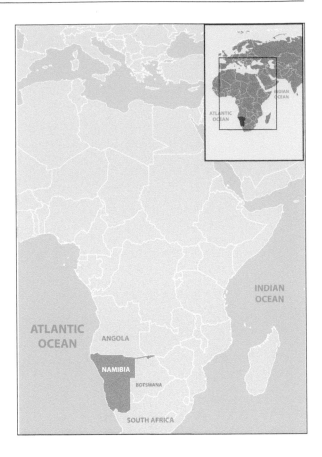

GENERAL INFORMATION

Official Language: English
Population: 2,212,307 (2015)
Currency: Namibian dollar (NAD)
Coins: The Namibian dollar is subdivided into 100 cents. Coins come in denominations of 5, 10, and 50 cents. There are also 1 and 5-dollar coins.
Land Area: 823,290 square kilometers (317,874 square miles)
Water Area: 1,002 square kilometers (386 square miles)
National Motto: "Unity, Liberty, Justice"
National Anthem: "Namibia, Land of the Brave"
Capital: Windhoek
Time Zone: GMT +1
Flag Description: The flag is divided by a red stripe edged in narrow bands of white that run from its lower left-hand (hoist) side to its upper right-hand (fly) side. The upper hoist triangle is blue with a yellow, twelve-rayed sun at its center. The lower fly triangle is green.

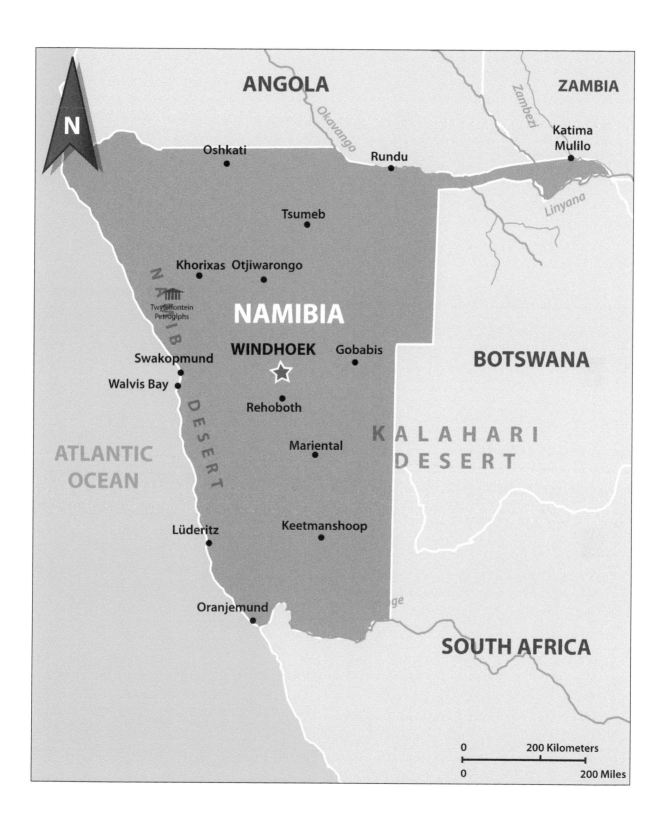

Principal Cities by Population (2012):

- Windhoek (334,580)
- Rundu (96,915)
- Walvis Bay (74,062)
- Swakopmund (35,675)
- Oshakati (35,144)
- Katima Mulilo (28,699)
- Okahandja (27,335)

Population

Namibia's population is largely black (87 percent), representing a mix of native African groups. The Bushmen, part of the Khoisan group, represent a grouping of peoples who live in the Kalahari Desert, which spreads across Namibia as well as Botswana and South Africa. They are among the earliest inhabitants of southern Africa.

The most populous group is the Ovambo, who represent about half of the total Namibian population, and the Kavango, who represent 9 percent. Other groups include Herero (7 percent of the population), Damara (7 percent), Nama (5 percent), Caprivian (4 percent), Bushmen (3 percent), and the Tswana (0.5 percent). The Baster, descendants of Cape Colony Dutch and black African women, along with other mixed-race people, make up 7 percent of the total population.

Whites of Afrikaner, German, Portuguese, and British background, make up around 6 percent of the population. Most whites speak Afrikaans, the language of South Africa's Dutch settlers.

In general, Namibia's population is very young, in part because of the high rates of death caused by disease. In 2015, the estimated average age was just 22 years. Less than five percent of the population was 65 years old or older.

Most of the population lives in the northern and central part of the country. The coastal and eastern parts of the country are largely deserts. Windhoek, the capital, is the largest city, with a population of 334,580 as of the 2015 census. Other major communities are the ports of Walvis

Bay and Luderitz, and the cities of Grootfontein and Oranjemund.

Languages

English is the official language. Afrikaans, the language of most white residents, was an official language until independence in 1990. German is also widely spoken among Namibian whites. The black population speaks several different native languages, with Oshivambo (the language of the Ovambo) being the most widely spoken.

Native People & Ethnic Groups

Today, the cultural make-up of Namibia is the result of nearly 30,000 years of migration, subjugation, and cultural reemergence. The San Bushmen are believed to be the first to settle in what is now Namibia; anthropological research suggests that they have lived there as long as 20,000 years. They themselves dislike the name "San," which means "outsider" in the language of the rival Khoikhoi people. The Nama and Damara peoples arrived later.

Constituting approximately 50 percent of the population, the Ovambo are the largest ethnicity and dominate national politics, though they have been Namibians for the shortest time, approximately 600 years ago. They are a traditionally mixed agrarian and cattle farming people, and are known for their dancing, singing, and ceramics.

The Kavango are the second largest group and mainly inhabit the eastern regions of the country. They are known for their traditional woodcarving. The Herero have diminished to the third largest ethnicity, and are known for their traditional dress, largely adopted during the German colonial period. This includes flat, horizontal hats believed to be inspired by the horns of cattle (the Herero are a traditional cattle-herding people).

Europeans first arrived in the region during the late 18th century, but full-scale colonization did not begin until the late 19th century. The Germans colonized the area in the 1880s and began arriving in the thousands during the last years before World War I, in order to farm and mine the land.

Friction between the whites and the local tribes was fueled by racial discrimination, and eventually led to open conflict. In 1904–1905, the Herero rose up against German rule and killed a number of German farmers. The German authorities suppressed the rebellion by massacring thousands of Herero, using tactics now seen as genocidal. In 2004, the German government apologized for the massacre, but has refused to pay compensation, despite the demands for it from the Herero.

Religions

Most Namibians (around 85 percent) are Christians. Lutheranism predominates, reflecting the country's history as a German colony. Between 10 and 20 percent of Namibians practice traditional religions, such as animism.

Climate

Namibia's climate is generally semi-arid, with desert conditions in many places. Around Windhoek, in the northeastern part of the country, conditions are subtropical; despite the heat, the high altitude makes conditions tolerable.

The average temperature ranges between 16° and 21° Celsius (60° and 70° Fahrenheit), with the cooler temperatures occurring mostly on the coast. In summer, temperatures can rise as high as 40° Celsius (1047° Fahrenheit). Winters, however, are often very cold, with temperatures below freezing.

Average annual rainfall is roughly 250 millimeters (10 inches), with higher amounts in the northern part of the country. The arid climate is due in part to ocean currents.

ENVIRONMENT & GEOGRAPHY

Topography

Namibia is mostly covered by high, dry plateaus and deserts. The extremely arid Namib Desert (from which the country takes its name) lies along the Atlantic coast. The immense, semi-arid Kalahari Desert, home of the Bushmen, lies to the east. Between the two lies the central plateau, which runs north to south. The highest point in Namibia is the Konigstein (also known as the Brandberg), at 2,606 meters (8,550 feet) above sea level.

Several large rivers run through Namibia, including the Zambezi and Okavango, as well as the Fish and Orange. The Caprivi Strip, part of Namibia since the German colonial period and named for the Imperial German chancellor, is a wildlife-rich strip of land that provides access to the Zambezi River. The inhabitants of the Caprivi Strip are mostly subsistence farmers.

Windhoek is located in a broad valley in Namibia's central Khomas region. It lies some 350 kilometers (217 miles) east of the Atlantic Ocean coastline and is bordered on the north by the Eros Mountains and on the south by the Auas Mountains.

The city's main thoroughfare, Independence Avenue, runs the length of the city, from the suburb of Ausspannplatz in the capital's southern end up to the former township of Katutura at the city's northern limits. The central business district is the commercial heart of the city. It features modern, upscale businesses as well as traditional open-air markets.

Plants & Animals

Wildlife is found in large numbers in Namibia, with many species living in national parks and game reserves in the savanna and woodland regions. One of the most important is Etosha National Park, which was established in the early 20th century, and is one of the world's largest game reserves. Private and communally owned game ranches, many of which cater to sport hunters, have helped conservation efforts by funding wildlife conservation programs.

Large game animals include the antelope, elephant, buffalo, giraffe, and rhinoceros, as well as large cats such as the cheetah, lion, and leopard. Despite the dryness of the desert regions, many plants and animals are still found in the less-arid regions, particularly small reptiles, and mammals.

Vegetation in the desert areas consists of shrubs, grasses, and other drought-resistant plants. The land becomes more heavily wooded toward the northeast.

CUSTOMS & COURTESIES

Greetings
Namibians are often characterized as elaborate greeters. Generally, when Namibians meet each other, they engage in a lengthy greeting that includes inquiries into another's well-being and family. As English is the national language, greeting are mostly done in English, though various ethnic languages are spoken in rural areas. Handshakes are the most common gesture of greeting.

Gestures & Etiquette
Namibia's culture of etiquette and gestures is very diverse. Handshaking and patting on the back are some of the universal friendly gestures of everyday life. In urban Namibia and among the Ovambo, it is common to see bowing and curtsying when greeting someone of authority. This may be an elder or someone with more education or status. Generally, children are required by cultural norms to bow or curtsy slightly when greeting adults, and this extends to accepting gifts. When a gift is exchanged, the receiver must accept it with both hands if it is sizable enough and bow or curtsy. If it is a small gift, it should be accepted with the right hand. When offering the right hand, either for greeting or to receive a gift, most Namibians might simultaneously touch their right elbow with their left hand, believed to imply gratitude and deference.

Eating/Meals
Namibian families generally eat three meals daily, depending on availability and socioeconomic status. Breakfast is traditionally light and eaten at home, and may be porridge, leftover dinner from the night before, or something from a small food stand. Lunch may also be eaten at home or purchased from a food stand. Though different ethnic groups dine differently, dinner generally involves the entire family. As dinner generally consists of a main starch and a single

or many sauces on the side, the family sits around a few communal dishes. Before dining, most families will wash their hands in a communal bowl of soapy water and pass around a towel to dry off. To eat, each diner first takes small pieces of starch, balls it up, and then dips it into one of the sauces.

Among the Ovambo peoples, children customarily prepare the food. Traditionally, they are also the last to eat, feeding their parents and the elders first, and are often excluded from the room. Once the adults finish eating in the oshoto, or outdoor socializing and dining area, children are allowed to reenter and eat their dinner together. Among the San Bushmen, equality is practiced at mealtimes. All the gathered food of a band is prepared and eaten together. This is especially important with a large kill, which is then divided evenly among all band members.

Visiting
Visiting in Namibia takes on a few forms, but there are some consistencies among all households. For example, nearly every Namibian home has a location where guests may be hosted. This may be a mat on the ground outside or it may be a sitting area inside one of the living units on a family's compound. When guests arrive, they are customarily offered something to drink. This may include water or soda, or local beers and wine. If visitors arrive during a meal, they must accept an offer to eat, as it might be perceived as disrespectful to decline.

Visiting among the hunter-gatherer groups of northern and central Namibia is a more formal affair. This is because visiting another's region is not common, except for the event of a marriage between two bands. The San Bushmen, for example, live in sectioned off regions. These sections are self-designated and determined based on their proximity to fresh water and sufficient food to sustain the entire band. Bands do not visit each other unless they request permission prior to arrival. Any deviation from this social requirement might be considered an act of hostility.

Among the Ovambo, visiting is now a major affair, especially among the rural and urban family members. When rural Ovambo visit their family members in the cities, urban Ovambo are expected to pay for the trip, while the rural family members are expected to bring some of their crops as a gift. When urban Ovambo visit their rural family they are expected to bring canned goods, clothes, and other items not readily available in smaller villages. These visits are long because it is both expensive and difficult to travel some of the vast distances in Namibia.

LIFESTYLE

Family

The traditional family structure in Namibia includes extended family and elders. Among some of Namibia's ethnic groups, this kin group also includes families hunting and gathering together. For the San Bushmen, these bands of adjoined families may number as many as 150 migrating people. The member families usually include a husband and his wife (or wives) and children, and bands are formed and modified through intermarriage. The San uphold strict guidelines as to the marrying between bands, the most important of which is the one outlawing marriage within a band. Despite this attempt to keep families distinct, many bands continuously intermarry because of diminished population. While there are typically no official leaders in these bands, the elder are customarily consulted for advice.

The Ovambo family structure is a product of their more stationary and agrarian lifestyle. An Ovambo family usually includes a husband and his wife or wives, and their children, plus cousins, the mother's brother and his family, and some elders. Ovambo are typically a matrilineal ethnic group; thus, the wife's eldest brother carries much weight. Because of economic hardship and increased unemployment, many Ovambo have fled their northern homes for urban areas. This has broken down many traditional households. In cities, Ovambo families generally live in a tighter nucleus of the father, mother(s) and children. Their rural family members then rely on

their financial support or generous gifts of food and clothing.

Housing

Housing in Namibia ranges from Bavarian style mansions to huts of straw. Most Namibians live in rural Namibia and construct their homes from the limited resources available. Materials range from mud, thatch, straw, and branches, to cement, corrugated tin, and bricks. In rural Namibia, the San Bushmen live in perhaps the most rudimentary homes because of their transitory lifestyle. They can construct homes in a matter of hours from straw or long grasses draped over and bound to posts planted in the ground. The posts are stripped tree branches that are typically gathered by the women. As many as five family members may live in one hut, depending on the number of people in the entire band and the space available.

The Ovambo, Herero, and Himba have begun a transition in housing style from mud and thatch housing to mud brick homes with corrugated tin roofs. However, many Himba and Herero have maintained their mud homes that they seal with a layer of cow dung. Fences constructed from stripped tree branches anchored deep in the ground encircle compounds.

In Windhoek and Swakopmund, remnants of German colonialism are extant. In fact, the centers of these large cities contain some of Africa's best-preserved colonial architecture, and some of Africa's only German architecture. Bavarian mansions were built in city centers and on the water as beachfront homes. Also on the outskirts of Windhoek, a growing number of middle class Namibians have led to the expansion of mid-size homes. These cement-walled homes are often ranch style, with many rooms. Some have indoor plumbing, and nearly all have electricity and brightly painted exteriors. Most families paint their homes bright hues of all shades.

Food

Namibian food, while diverse, shares some universal staples because of agricultural limitations. These include millet (or mahango), sorghum, and maize, vegetables such as squash, spinach (or ekaka), tomato, garlic, and onion, various ocean and freshwater fish, and meats such as lamb, goat, and beef. The Himba and Herero are famous cattle herders who have historically lived off the meat and milk of the animals.

Other than some diet discrepancies based on regional differences, most Namibians consume oshifima or mahangooshifima. These are types of dough-like paste made from pounded sorghum or millet, respectively. The grains are pounded with a giant pestle and mortar. Women are responsible for pounding the grain, and typically do so two or three at a time. When the women gather around the mortar, they take turns pounding the grain, one after the other, creating a musical rhythm. (They may often sing along with their own beats.) A stew or sauce is served alongside either of these starches. Oshiwambo is one of the more common stews and is made with spinach and beef and several other spices. Tomato sauces are all quite common. In the northwestern part of the country, okapenda or sardines are commonly eaten, as are many other fish.

Once a meal is over, many Namibians will partake in some social drinking. Oshikundu, a beer brewed from fermented millet; makatu, a watermelon wine; and tambo, a sweet drink made from fermented millet and cane sugar, are all commonly shared. Sweets are perhaps the greatest culinary legacy in Namibia leftover from German colonialism. Their konditoreien, or cake shops, are sprinkled throughout the major metropolises and produce delicious German pastries.

Life's Milestones

In Namibia, as in much of the rest of the world, birth, transition into adulthood, marriage, and death are often commemorated as life's major milestones. Following a new birth, the entire family gathers for the naming ceremony, during which the new baby is held up before the family and given a name by its father. Different ethnic groups add their own flavor to this tradition. For example, the Himba and Herero will place the baby's forehead against a cow for luck.

During transition to adulthood, young men often go through physical challenges and young women often are presented to society once they are ready to have children. Among the isolated Himba, hairstyle is indicative of a young woman's status. When she begins puberty, her hair is painted ochre (orange-yellow) and pulled to cover her face. When she then comes of childbearing age, her hair is swept to either side of her face.

The Herero have a marriage custom in which the father of the bridegroom will send beads to the potential bride asking for her hand to marry his son. If she accepts, the family makes arrangements. Weddings among all groups generally involve the bride gift, or the gift of money or goods to compensate the family of the bride.

CULTURAL HISTORY

Art

Namibia's cultural and artistic legacy dates back to early human history, as the country is home to some of the oldest hunting sites and rock art in the world. At roughly 28,000 years old, the first of these artistic contributions was made by the nomadic hunter-gatherers who decorated slabs of rock. These slabs were then moved from their original and unknown locations to the Huns Mountains in the southwestern region of the country. Referred to as the Apollo 11 cave site, scientists have uncovered images on the slabs depicting human forms and animals.

The Bushmen of Namibia are thought to have had a presence in the Kalahari Desert for nearly 30,000 years. For thousands of years they roamed central Namibia, forming only loose tribes of very small numbers that made them difficult to conquer, but easy to displace. However, they contributed much to the history of Africa, and their rock art of Twyfelfontein is perhaps the most astonishing example of their sophistication.

Architecture

Architecture in Namibia is at once modern and traditional, Western and African. One of the more striking features of Namibia's architecture is the pronounced and well-preserved German colonial architecture. In Windhoek, Swakopmund, and Walvis Bay, several buildings of Germanic design remain almost untouched by time. Among them are diverse representations of a few Germanic styles, namely the timbered and neo-Gothic designs. The Christuskirche and the Railway Station, both in Windhoek, were designed by the famous German architect Gottlieb Redecker (1871–1945). They reflect a unique blend of neo-Gothic, art nouveau, and classicist styles. Art nouveau design is inspired by elements of nature, including flowers and leaves, while neo-Gothic design is ornate and dramatic. The Windhoek Railway Station takes on a more classical style with its green roof and striking white exterior.

The indigenous architecture is strikingly distinct from German buildings. From the beehive houses of the Himba to the twig and leaf homes of the San Bushmen, Namibians have long relied on their environment for raw materials with which to construct their homes. As modern Namibia continues to rapidly develop, particularly in the capital of Windhoek, many modern high-rise modern buildings now dominate the urban skyline, and use modern materials such as steel, concrete, and glass.

Drama

Namibia has a thriving film industry. This is largely due to the Namibian Film Commission founded in 1997 by the national government. The commission has since made efforts to increase the number of nationally made films and international films shot in Namibia, as well as host international film festivals such as the Wild Cinema Festival. Every May, international filmmakers bring feature length, short, and documentary films for showing at the festival, and in 2006, there were over 6,000 attendees. The festival has proved to be a successful cinematic forum for Namibian directors such as Richard Pakleppa (1961–).

Music

Music is said to have begun among the San in Namibia. Guitars, drums, bows and lamellophones, or hollowed-out gourds fastened with reeds or tines that are then plucked, have been used for centuries. The seganpure is thought to be a more recent introduction to their instrumental repertoire, and strongly resembles the European violin. It is made from a flexible stick tied at each end with a strong string. The string can be tuned by twisting a fastened knob at the bottom of the instrument.

The Herero and Himba have also held fast to their long-held musical traditions. During their daily cattle herding, they could not use any instrument save their own voices. Thus, the Herero and Himba tradition is one of beautiful chanting in reverence of their most prized possession: the cattle.

Today in Namibia, the commercial music scene is starting to grow. It the past, popular music was exclusively imported from America, Europe, and South Africa. Hip-hop, reggae, rhythm and blues (R&B) and South African kwaito music are all common. Ngatukondje Nganjone (1975-), a Namibian musician known as Ngatu, is a skilled guitarist who blends Western styles such as reggae with traditional shumbo, or percussion music of the Ovambo.

Dance

The San Bushmen are famous for their traditional trance dancing. Any celebration among the San calls for ritualistic dancing in a circle around a fire. Men, the only dancers, circle the fire chanting and dancing for many hours. Toward the end of a celebration, from outright exhaustion they may begin to whirl uncontrollably and eventually pass out. Tribal ancestors attribute these "trances" and fits to being possessed.

Literature

Literature in Namibia can be divided into two distinct eras: the colonial era and the post-independence era. During Namibia's era of German occupation (1884–1915), literary works were exclusively dominated by the German colonists. Most works were written in Afrikaans or German and generally pertain to German observance and perception of indigenous Namibian life. German colonists largely withheld education from the vast majority of Namibians, and thus at the outset of independence, illiteracy was rampant.

In 1990, in an effort to avoid favoritism of one linguistic group over another, the newly independent nation decided on English as its official language, replacing Afrikaans and German. Most Namibian literature since independence has to do with the lives of individual Namibians and the transition from colonialism to independence. One of the most famous works to emerge during this post-colonial is *Born of the Sun* (1988) by Joseph Diescho (1955–). The novel is an autobiographical representation of the author's life, and details the protagonist's transition from village life to encountering Western religion and African politics.

CULTURE

Arts & Entertainment

The government has been active in the promotion of contemporary art and has endeavored to make the arts part of a unified Namibia. In 2001, the Namibian government declared a policy of "unity in diversity" among their many ethnic groups, and pledged to develop national arts and a unified national culture. This was supported through festivals, national forums, and arts patronage.

One particular festival, the annual Popular /Ae //Gams Arts and Cultural Festival, is held in the capital of Windhoek. (The name, read with clicking sounds native to the Khoisan languages indigenous to the region, translates to "Hot Springs" and was the original name given to Windhoek.) Each year has its own theme, which commonly involves a message pertaining to ethnic unity. Dance and music groups, renowned visual artists, Namibians, government officials, and tourists are all in attendance for the weeklong event. The government also supports the National Theatre of Namibia, headquartered in the heart of Windhoek. Performances range from ballet and African dance to opera, orchestra, choir, and traditional Namibian music groups. The Franco-Namibian Cultural Center is another critical venue for dance and music performance.

Namibia also has a rich tradition of landscape painting, dating back to German colonial rule, when only Europeans had access to artistic training. This early work was mostly characterized by pastels and soft, dreamlike portrayals of the country's natural beauty. However, certain artists began to make a dramatic shift from early European painting in Namibia. These include Nico Roos (1940–2008), a Namibian artist of European descent whose work emphasizes the natural and harsh landscape of Namibia, and Francois de Necker (1944–), an abstract painter who deconstructed nature into floating objects on hazy backdrops.

Outside of landscapes, native Namibian art is also thriving. The success of native Namibian artists can be largely attributed to the "father of Namibian art," John Ndevasia Muafangejo (1943–1987). Arguably Namibia's most famous artist, both domestically and internationally, Muafangejo used a medium called linocut in which the artist takes sheets of linoleum, often mounted on wood planks, and carves intricate designs into the surface. Linoleum is very soft, so it is easy to carve and does not leave any raised material on either side of the grooves. Once the slate is carved, the artist rolls ink over the surface and presses it, in Muafangejo's case to paper. His black and white prints are some of the most creative on the African continent and depict scenes from his daily life.

The government created the John Muafangejo Art Centre (JMAC) in Windhoek's parliament gardens. The center has since educated numerous contemporary Namibian artists. They include Fillipus Sheehama (1974–), a young artist intrigued by deadly car wrecks throughout Namibia. His works are also black and white and reminiscent of Muafangejo.

Namibia has a strong athletic tradition. Until 1990, Namibian athletes competed under the South African flag in international competitions. As in other African nations, soccer (football) is a popular sport. The Namibian Football Association belongs to several international soccer organizations, including the Fédération Internationale de Football Association (FIFA).

Namibia has distinguished itself in track-and-field events at the Olympics and other international events, thanks to Frankie Fredericks of Windhoek. He has received silver medals at the 1992 and 1996 Summer Olympics, as well as at the 1998 Commonwealth Games.

Mass media in Namibia are among the freest on the African continent, with a vibrant opposition press. The government operates its own daily newspaper, the *New Era*, but there are privately owned dailies not only in English, but also in Afrikaans (*Die Republikein*), German (*Allgemeine Zeitung*) and Oshivambo (*The Namibian*). Broadcast media include the state-owned Namibian Broadcasting Corp. (NBC) as well as several privately owned television and radio stations.

Cultural Sites & Landmarks

From some of the world's largest and most abundant nature reserves to some of humankind's oldest artifacts, Namibia's cultural significance is extensive.

In northwestern Namibia, mountains rise from the desert flatlands. In those mountains, a cavern known as Philips Cave contains one of Namibia's many cave drawings. The image, which depicts a hump-backed antelope (or possibly a camel) with an elephant superimposed inside, is thought to date back thousands of years. This painting is part of the larger "Bushman's Paradise" collection attributed to the San people who inhabited the region.

The United Nations Educational, Scientific, and Cultural Organization (UNESCO) recognized the universal importance of Namibia's ancient drawings and carvings. In 2007, it named Namibia's Twyfelfontein region as a World Heritage Site. Twyfelfontein contains over 2,000 rock petroglyphs, or engravings, including remarkably realistic images of animals and six painted rock shelters with human motifs. The San people were thought to have begun these drawings and carvings at the beginning of the Neolithic Age, around 9500 BCE.

The region of Kaokoveld, or Kaokoland, considered one of the last wilderness areas in the world, is home to the Himba. They have long preserved their culture and traditions through the isolation afforded them by the rugged terrain that surrounds their land. With increased tourism from Europe, however, more Himba are trying to profit from foreigners. Further inland are the cultural lands of the Ovambo. Despite their severe poverty, some efforts have been made to preserve their culture and land rights. Namibia is also home to Fish River Canyon, arguably the second-largest canyon in the world (behind the Grand Canyon). The canyon is one of numerous conservation parks in Namibia. Others include the Namib Naukluft Park, one of the largest national parks in Africa, and Waterberg Plateau, a nature reserve that was the site of significant battle between the Germans and the Herero. The graves of German soldiers remain, and a cultural center was established in the area to preserve the traditions of the Herero.

Libraries & Museums

The National Library of Namibia, which serves as the nation's legal depository, is located in Windhoek. Its collections include over 25,000 general reference materials, as well as 15,000 books and seventy-eight newspaper titles. The National Museum of Namibia is also located in Windhoek and houses collections on ethnography and natural history. The National Art Gallery of Namibia (NAGN) boasts one of the largest African art collections on the continent, though the works are nearly uniformly Namibian.

Holidays

Namibia's national holiday is Independence Day (March 21), which celebrates the country's gaining independence in 1990 from South Africa. As a predominantly Christian nation, Namibia also celebrates religious holidays such as Christmas and Easter.

Youth Culture

From very young ages, nearly all tribal groups, including the Ovambo, the Herero, Himba, and the San Bushmen, teach their youth their strict and respective roles in society. For young men, this often means learning the techniques of hunting or herding, while for women this traditionally means learning housewifery and other domestic responsibilities. In the case of the Himba people, for example, young boys are taken out very early on with the men of their clan to herd the cattle, and start by learning to wash the animals. Young Ovambo women are taught early on about childrearing, cooking, and basketry. (The Ovambo are known for weaving baskets.) However, these traditions are waning due to Western influences and increased education, as well as the spread of HIV/AIDS.

In most urban areas, more children are attending schools. However, among some of the more isolated ethnic groups such as the San and Himba, older women often remove girls from school as they see schooling as a disruption to a young girl's necessary education. The HIV/AIDS epidemic is also threatening to alter traditional roles of children. It is estimated that in the early 21st century, over 120,000 children have lost one or both parents, and nearly 60,000 of them lost both parents due to the epidemic. These orphaned children are often left by their families to be looked after by government-run youth programs or NGOs.

SOCIETY

Transportation

While walking is perhaps the preferred method of transportation—the main highways see very little traffic—scooters and mopeds are used for greater distances. Common modes of public transportation include taxis and minibuses. In recent years, the government has made efforts to phase out the widely used and overcrowded minibuses for state-run buses that are considered larger and safer. Often, bus routes may depend on the destination and the amount of passengers. In addition, the country's rail network, operated by the state-run TransNamib Railways, offers passenger service and links most major towns, but service is generally regarded as slow. Traffic in Namibia moves on the left-hand side of the road.

Transportation Infrastructure

Transportation infrastructure in Namibia is developing; in the early 21st century; there are approximately 40,000 kilometers (24,854 miles) of roadways in the country, including the Trans-Caprivi and Trans-Kalahari Highways, which connect Namibia to its neighboring countries. There are 2,300 kilometers (1,429 miles) of rail. The Hosea Kutako International Airport is located in Windhoek and is used for both passengers and freight transport.

Media & Communications

Namibia's constitution does not limit freedom of speech and the government generally allows for all manner of opinion in private press. In fact, Namibia has gained accolades from the international press community for a generally free and fair press. There are several dailies, including *The Namibia*, a privately owned and operated paper that runs stories in English and Oshiwambo; *The New Era*, which is government-owned and operated paper; and *Die Republikein*, which is privately owned and published in Afrikaans. There are numerous privately owned radio and television stations, and the state-run radio and television broadcaster is the Namibia Broadcasting Company (NBC).

The telecommunications infrastructure is generally considered to be above average, with mobile cellular telephones far outweighing mainline phones in use—an estimated 2.7 million mobile cellular phones in use in 2014, compared to an estimated 180,000 main telephone lines in use the same year. In addition there were an estimated 325,400 Internet users, representing less than 15 percent of the population.

SOCIAL DEVELOPMENT

Standard of Living

Namibia ranked 127th out of 187 countries on the 2014 United Nations Human Development Index, which measures quality of life and standard of living indicators.

Water Consumption

As the driest country is sub-Saharan Africa, Namibia relies heavily on groundwater to meet domestic demand. The vast majority of rivers in the country are seasonal, with the exception of some perennial rivers near the northern and southern borders of the country. Approximately 84 percent of the country's rural population and 98 percent of its urban population have access to improved water sources.

Rapid, unplanned migration into the Namibian capital has placed a severe strain on Windhoek's infrastructure and resources. Around a third of the capital's residents live in shantytowns that have pushed the city's boundaries steadily outward. Basic services to provide potable water and municipal trash collection and sewage disposal are lacking in most of the makeshift neighborhoods.

Education

The school system in Namibia comprises twelve years: four years of lower primary, three years of upper primary (during which time English instruction begins), three years of junior secondary, and two years of senior secondary. A very high proportion of all school-aged children, over 90 percent, enroll in primary school. Post-independence educational reform is credited with closing the gender gap in education; however, women still face difficulty in securing jobs traditionally held by men. The average literacy rate in Namibia is relatively high, at 84 percent for women and 79 percent for men.

Post-secondary education has been available since 1980, though no university existed until after independence. During the 1980s, professional education focused on business and teacher training. The University of Namibia (UNAM) was founded in 1993, along with the Polytechnic of Namibia and the Colleges of Education.

A comprehensive educational reform known as Vision 2030 was begun in the early 21st century to help strengthen Namibia education system. The reform seeks to increase the number of vocational training institutions in the country and restructure curricula so that more mathematics, science, and technology are taught.

Women's Rights

Women continue to play traditional roles in Namibia society. Most women are responsible for child rearing and domestic responsibilities, and many are involved in a polygamous marriage. Women make up only a minor fraction of the workforce and men mostly dominate high-level positions since they require more education or time away from family. The Ministry of Labor and Social Welfare and the Employment Equity Commissions have been established by the government to help improve equality.

Namibia is also famous for its recent rape legislation, which features groundbreaking practices and policies. This progressive legislation is broad in scope, and includes prosecution for marital rape, special protection measures for testifying victims, and the prosecution of boys as young as fourteen years of age. Despite these advances and efforts, Namibia still suffers from rampant domestic abuse and rape. Rape and spousal rape are against the law and carry a sentence ranging from five to forty-five years in length. Generally, the government prosecutes and convicts rapists on behalf of victims who see legal redress. However, societal perception of rape often deters women from coming forward.

The Married Person's Equality Act was established by the government in the late 1990s in an effort to rectify the desperate situation of wives widowed by the HIV/AIDS crisis. According to Namibian law, women and men have equal inheritance rights. However, in accordance with custom, women almost never received the rights to their land or to raise their children once their husbands had died. The act has made significant headway in allowing women to maintain their rights after the death of their husbands.

Statistics released in 2005 showed that women accounted or 55 percent of the nation's cases of HIV/AIDS. Many attribute this large number to the fact that the government struggled to dispel the superstition that a man can eradicate the disease by sleeping with a virgin. Under these assumptions, many infected men raped young girls and women, hoping to cure themselves.

There are countless ministries, commissions, non-governmental organizations (NGOs), and grassroots organizations working in Namibia to better the lives of women. The Ministry of Gender Equality and Child Welfare, the Ministry of Justice and Law, the Reform and Development Commission and the Married Person's Equality Act have all been established to handle various aspects of women's development in Namibia.

Health Care

Health care is poor in Namibia, and a large percentage of the population suffers from major infectious diseases, particularly HIV/AIDS. In 2014, it was estimated that over 15 percent of the adult population was infected with HIV/AIDS.

Other prevalent diseases include hepatitis A and typhoid fever, malaria, and schistosomiasis. The infant mortality rate is high, at 45 deaths per 1,000 live births. Average life expectancy at birth is 51 years; 52 years for men and 52 years for women (2015 estimate).

GOVERNMENT

Structure

Namibia's head of state is the president, chosen by popular election. The president serves a five-year term. The cabinet officers, headed by the prime minister, are appointed by the president from the ranks of the National Assembly.

Namibia has a two-house legislature: the National Council or upper house plays an advisory role, while the National Assembly or lower house handles most legislation. The National Council has 26 members, who serve six-year terms. Each of the thirteen regional councils sends two members. The National Assembly has 72 popularly elected members, who serve five-year terms and are elected on a proportional basis.

Under the policies of the ruling South West Africa People's Organization (SWAPO), all races are able to participate in government.

Prior to becoming an independent nation, the land now known as Namibia was governed by a variety of nations. It was a German colony from the 1880s until World War I, with the name German South West Africa. The British government occupied the territory in 1915. South Africa gained authority in 1920, and then annexed the region outright by the end of World War II. The annexation sparked international outrage, and fostered an independence movement. In 1966, Marxist guerrillas known as the South West Africa People's Organization (SWAPO) began a war for independence that lasted for the next several decades. During this period, South West Africa became known internationally as Namibia. In 1988, after decades of negotiation, South Africa finally agreed to withdraw from the territory, and Namibia became independent on March 21, 1990.

Political Parties

Political parties in Namibia include the South West Africa People's seventy-seven seats in the National Assembly; other parties, including the Rally for Democracy and Progress, and the Democratic Turnhalle Alliance, hold less than six seats each as of the 2014 elections. The ruling Swapo Party is led by Hage Geingob (1941–), who was elected president in 2014.

Local Government

The country is divided into 13 regions (Caprivi, Erongo, Hardap, Karas, Khomas, Kunene, Ohangwena, Okavango, Omaheke, Omusati, Oshana, Oshikoto, and Otjozondjupa), each of which is governed by an elected regional council. The head of a region is a governor, elected by regional councilors to a three-year term. Elected councils also govern at the municipal, town, and village levels, comprising forty-eight overall local bodies of governance.

Judicial System

The Namibian justice system, like that of South Africa, is based on Roman-Dutch law (though South Africa also uses English common law). The court system of Namibia comprises a

Supreme Court, High Court, and Lower Courts (such as Magistrate Courts, Community Courts, and Labor Courts).

Taxation

The top income tax rate and corporate tax rate are 35 percent; however, the oil and diamond industries are subject to a higher surtax. A value-added tax (VAT) is also levied.

Armed Forces

The armed forces of Namibia, known as the Namibian Defence Force, are relatively small but growing, and consist of a small air force, commissioned in 2005, and navy, recently commissioned in 2004, as well as an infantry-heavy army. The voluntary recruitment age is 18 for the armed forces. In 2010, the largest portion of the government budget was allocated to the Namibian Defence Force.

Foreign Policy

On April 1, 1989, Namibia became the last officially formed African nation after achieving independence from South Africa. Prior to independence, Namibia had been administered as South West Africa since World War I. Since 1990, Namibia has worked to establish an independent foreign policy and to strengthen relations and integration in the South African region. The country signed a mutual defense pact with neighboring Angola and, along with other African nations, intervened with military support in the Second Congo War in the Democratic Republic of Congo (DRC). Regionally, Namibia belongs to the South African Development Community (SADC), the African Union (AU), the African Development Bank (ADB), the Organization of African Unity (OAU), and the South African Customs Union (SACU).

Namibia is also emerging as an independent political actor on the international scene, largely due to the lucrative mining trade and the nation's oil reserves. Namibia joined the United Nations (UN) in 1990, and holds membership in the International Monetary Fund (IMF), the Non-Aligned Movement (NAM), and the World Trade Organization (WTO). Namibia is also a member of the British Commonwealth and maintains good relations with the United States. In July 2008, the Millennium Challenge Corporation (MCC), a U.S. governmental development fund, established a compact agreement with Namibia worth over $300 million.

Namibia is engaged in several international disputes, most notably the Caprivi conflict and the presence of Angolan refugees and rebel fighters in the country. The Caprivi situation is a conflict between the Namibian government and the Caprivi Liberation Army (CLA), a rebel group fighting for the secession of a narrow strip of land known as the Caprivi Strip. Namibia also continues to deal with the resettlement of Angolan refugees since the conclusion of that country's twenty-seven year civil war in 2002.

Human Rights Profile

International human rights law insists that states respect civil and political rights, and promote an individual's economic, social, and cultural rights. The United Nations Universal Declaration on Human Rights (UDHR) is recognized as the standard for international human rights. Its authors sought the counsel of the world's great thinkers, philosophers, and religious leaders, and were careful to create a document that reflects the core values shared by every world culture. (To read this document or view the articles relating to cultural human rights, visit http://www.udhr.org/UDHR/default.htm.)

In general, Namibia's human rights record is considered strong. For the most part, the freedom of religion, academic pursuit, culture, peaceful assembly, and free and fair elections were all protected in the constitution and upheld by the government. This unrepressed culture even extends to refugees—in 2007, Namibia was thought to be supporting upwards of 6,000—most of whom are found at the Osire Refugee Camp.

The Osire Refugee Camp was originally founded to help Angolans fleeing civil conflict throughout the 1980s and 1990s. Over time, and with increased conflict in the Democratic Republic of the Congo (DRC), refugees from

Burundi, Rwanda, and the DRC are also on the rise. The Namibian government has been credited with housing these refugees and maintaining their security in accordance with the Status of Refugee Rights outlined in a 1951 UN convention. Despite not actually signing the declaration on refugee rights, they provide shelter, education through the tenth grade and limited public health and HIV/AIDS initiatives. Human trafficking has recently also seen some attention with passage of anti-trafficking legislation in 2014.

However, other areas remained in need of further government oversight, particularly the justice and police forces, which suffer from human rights abuses and lack of resources. The national justice system, for example, must provide each accused criminal a free and fair trial. Prisoners must also be told what crime they are charged with within 48 hours of their detention. However, due to a limited number of judges and police inefficiency, detainees were often held for weeks without trial or knowledge of their accused crime. Police brutality and excessive force are also problems, and abuse is often employed as a method to elicit confessions.

Finally, prison conditions were often overcrowded and unsanitary. There were no health facilities to treat the sick or wounded and overcrowding led convicted criminals to share cells with suspects. Violence was also common and rarely stopped.

ECONOMY

Overview of the Economy
Although Namibia is considered a developing country, it has one of Africa's healthiest economies, with a strong free-market system. Namibia is trying to diversify its economy, increase foreign investment, and reduce dependence on South Africa, the country's major market. Major obstacles to growth include high unemployment (28.1 percent in 2014) and a lack of skilled workers. In 2014, the gross domestic product (GDP) was $13.35 billion (USD), and the per capita GDP was $10,800 (USD).

Namibia belongs to the South African Customs Union, a free-trade organization headquartered in Windhoek; the other members are South Africa, Botswana, Lesotho, and Swaziland. Although Namibia has its own currency (the Namibian dollar), it belongs to a monetary union with South Africa, and accepts the South African rand as legal tender.

Industry
Mining, commercial ranching and fishing, and tourism are Namibia's most important economic sectors. Overall, the mining industry accounts for more than 30 percent of GDP; service industries account for another 63 percent. There is little manufacturing activity. The country has few agricultural resources; the land is largely dry and non-arable, though many areas are suitable for grazing.

The main ports are at Luderitz and Walvis Bay; the latter has an excellent deepwater facility.

Labor
In 2014, the labor force of Namibia was estimated to be around 991,000. Approximately 61 percent work in the services industry, while 22 percent work in the industrial sector, and 16 percent work in the agricultural sector.

Energy/Power/Natural Resources
Namibia possesses considerable mineral wealth, particularly diamonds and precious metals such as gold. Key industrial minerals include lead, tin, nickel, uranium, and zinc. Namibia has made significant efforts to conserve the environment, including specifically mentioning environmental protection in the nation's constitution.

Fishing
Fishing is an important economic sector, because of the rich fishing grounds in the South Atlantic. Common species include anchovy, mackerel, and hake. Because of over-fishing in the pre-independence era, the Namibian government is working to conserve stocks. The industry employs approximately 14,000 workers.

Mining/Metals

Minerals account for roughly half of Namibia's exports. Diamond mining accounts for about five percent of GDP, with other mining valued at an additional two percent.

Agriculture

Namibia's agriculture is largely at the subsistence level, employing most of the population but contributing little to GDP. The main food crops are corn, millet, sorghum, and peanuts. Only about one percent of the land is arable; most of this is found in the country's better-watered northern section.

Animal Husbandry

In 2010, there were approximately 2.5 million head of cattle in the country, as well as 2.9 million sheep and 2.1 million goats. Most of the output from the livestock industry is exported. Many white farmers work as ranchers, either raising livestock commercially or operating game ranches to accommodate hunting safaris.

Tourism

Namibian tourism has grown extensively since independence. The country's beautiful scenery and rich wildlife populations are major attractions. Some visitors are ecotourists who want to view the country's wildlife in Etosha National Park or other reserves, while other visitors come as hunters to the country's many game ranches.

Kristen Pappas, Eric Badertscher,
Beverly Ballaro

DO YOU KNOW?

- The Namibian bush farmer N!xau (1944–2003) starred in the 1980 film *The Gods Must Be Crazy* and its sequels. He plays a Botswana bushman who encounters Western civilization, with unusual and sometimes humorous results.

- The name of Windhoek, Namibia's capital, means "windy corner" in Afrikaans.

- Windhoek was the first city in the world to produce potable water through the reclamation of domestic sewage.

Bibliography

Alan Murphy, et al. "Botswana and Namibia." Oakland, CA: *Lonely Planet*, 2013.

Chris McIntyre. "Namibia." Guilford, CT: *Globe Pequot Press*, 2015.

David P. Crandall. "The Place of Stunted Ironwood Trees: A Year in the Lives of the Cattle-Herding Himba of Namibia." New York: *Continuum International Publishing Group*, 2000.

Emmanuel Kreike. "Re-creating Eden: Land Use, Environment, and Society in Southern Angola and Northern Namibia." *Heinemann*, 2004.

Marion Wallace. "A History of Namibia: From the Beginning to 1990." New York: *Oxford University Press*, 2014.

Peter Joyce and Gerald Cubbit. "This Is Namibia." Johannesburg, S.A.: *Penguin South Africa*, 2014.

Robert Gordon and Stuart Sholto-douglas. "The Bushman Myth: The Making of a Namibian Underclass, Second Edition." *Westview Press*, 2000.

Works Cited

"Apollo 11 (ca. 25,500–23,500 B.C.) and Wonderwerk (ca. 8000 B.C.) Cave Stones." *The Metropolitan Museum of Art: Heilbrunn Timeline of Art History*.

"Background Note: Namibia." March 2009. *U.S. Department of State*. http://www.state.gov/r/pa/ei/bgn/5472.htm#history

"Country Profile: Namibia." *BBC World News*. http://news.bbc.co.uk/2/hi/africa/country_profiles/1063245.stm"Future of Namibian Film Industry Bleak." February 2009. *FilmContact.com*. http://www.filmcontact.com/namibia/future-namibian-film-industry-bleak

"Girls and Women in Namibia." *University of Minnesota: School of Kinesiology*. http://www.tc.umn.edu/~reim0037/girls.html

"History of the National Art Gallery of Namibia." *National Art Gallery of Namibia Website*. http://www.nagn.org.na/history.html

"John Muafangejo." *South African History Online: African Art and Craft in Kwazulu-Natal 1960-1990*. http://www. sahistory.org.za/pages/artsmediaculture/arts/visual/ never-too-early/muafangejo-john.htm

"Landscape and Wildlife Artists." *The Embassy/Mission of the Republic of Namibia in Vienna*. http://www. embnamibia.at/NAMIBIA/art/Landscape%20and%20 Wildlife%20Artis.pdf

"Malakani palms, oshanas and Owambo homesteads." *Flamingo*. http://www.flamingo.com.na/index. php?fArticleId=550

"Namibia." *National Geographic Music*. http://worldmusic. nationalgeographic.com/worldmusic/view/page.basic/ country/content.country/namibia_514

"Namibia." *City Population*. http://www.citypopulation.de/ Namibia.html

"Namibia: Country Reports on Human Rights Practices." March 2007. *U.S. Department of State*. http://www.state. gov/g/drl/rls/hrrpt/2006/78749.htm

"Popular /Ae Gams Arts and Cultural Festival Kicks Off." December 2008. *The Namibia Economist*. http://www. economist.com.na/index.php?option=com_content&v iew=article&id=8826%3Apopular-ae-gams-arts-and-cultural-festival-kicks-off&Itemid=65

"Rock Art of the Central Namib Desert." November 1998. *The Newsletter of The Prehistoric Society* – Past No. 30. http://www.ucl.ac.uk/prehistoric/past/past30.html

"Social Relations of Poverty: A Case-Study from Owambo, Namibia." *Michelsen Institute*, 1999. http://bora.cmi.no/ dspace/bitstream/10202/269/1/R1999.5%20Ingve%20 og%20Selma-07182007_1.pdf

"Twylfelfontein or /Ui-//aes." *UNESCO World Heritage Centre*. http://whc.unesco.org/en/list/1255

"Urbanization threatens Namibia's traditional Himba culture." February 2008. *The Christian Science Monitor*. http://www.csmonitor.com/2008/0205/p20s01-woaf. html?page=1

"Vision and Mission Statement." The National Theatre of Namibia. http://www.ntn.org.na/mission

Janette Deacon. "Human Beginnings in South Africa." *Rowman Altamira*, 1999. http://books.google.com/ books?id=zDurpMaICbYC&pg=PA95&lpg=PA95 &dq=namibia+stone+age&source=bl&ots=USOn_ lrtCl&sig=2yrb7634LQ__ZfOEgVLYMKOgMHc&hl= en&ei=eea3Sau5JKb0Mueh3OYK&sa=X&oi= book_result&resnum=7&ct=result#

McIntyre, Chris. Namibia. *Brandt Travel Guides*, 2007. http://books.google.com/books?id=Ky9G1y_johQ C&pg=PA24&lpg=PA24&dq=namibia+etiquette& source=bl&ots=MRElfEmjfR&sig=0uPRFJ-pyGg5 voigZ5KGTr26O70&hl=en&ei=gGG5SYO1DsK0-Abo94n7BA&sa=X&oi=book_result&resnum=10&ct= result#PPP1,M1

Phillipson, D.W. "African Archaeology." *Cambridge University Press*, 2005. http://books.google.com/ books?id=ZTcGszm-sN0C&dq=apollo+11+namibia& source=gbs_summary_s&cad=0

Tom Streissguth, "Namibia in Pictures." *Twenty-First Century Books*, 2009. http://books.google.com/books?id =QbZZFI51MIYC&pg=PA51&lpg=PA51&dq=shumbo +music+africa&source=bl&ots=vw-gYQ24PE&sig=O3 DWHKNzU0VdhGU5DiYGGPTYAnM&hl=en&ei=9ce 7SdbbAoHAMp3gragI&sa=X&oi=book_result&resnum =6&ct=result#PPP1,M1

Ada Obi Udechukwu. "Herero." s*The Rosen Publishing Group*, 1996. http://books.google.com/books?id=Uki-ri 3VJ70C&pg=PA29&lpg=PA29&dq=marriage++herer o&source=bl&ots=Y0TUNDleek&sig=cEgqllSbhcpSe lk-MBo5FcNbT4E&hl=en&ei=Ym3DScqQIcXfnQeAn L2ODg&sa=X&oi=book_result&resnum=1&ct=result# PPA27,M1

Sean Williams. "The Ethnomusicologist's Cookbook." *CRC Press*, 2006. http://books.google.com/books?id=1R 6xigawTekC&pg=PA25&lpg=PA25&dq=owambo+mea ls&source=bl&ots=eKYIYBOpA6&sig=D73n_tRqazK-R3ITPsBxuVGjC8k&hl=en&ei=O3a5SYXkLZX2MJ rf_J4I&sa=X&oi=book_result&resnum=2&ct=result# PPR5,M1

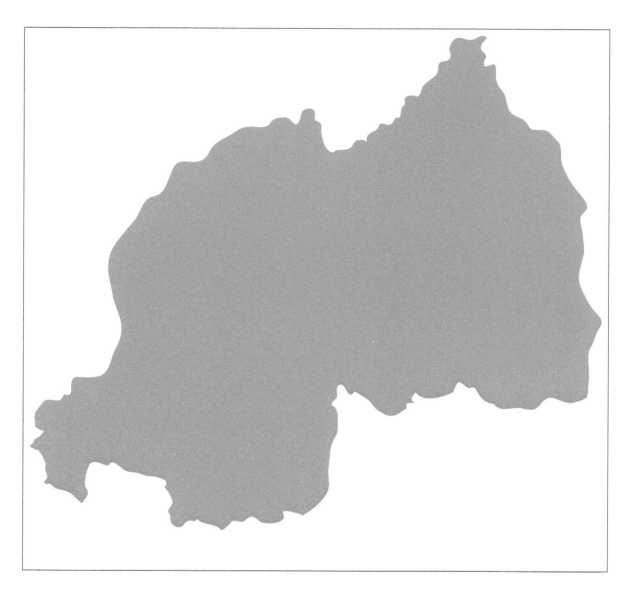

RWANDA

Introduction

Rwanda is an equatorial, landlocked country in east-central Africa. It borders the Democratic Republic of the Congo, Uganda, Tanzania, and Burundi. Kigali is the capital and largest city of Rwanda.

Rwanda is a country of renowned natural beauty and distinction, whose people suffered horrific genocidal ethnic violence in 1994. Rwanda represents the history of the African continent and of humanity in unique ways. It boasts one of Africa's oldest rainforests, as well as the one of the continent's largest mountainside natural parks, the Nyungwe Forest National Park and modern science reveals that the Twa people of Rwanda are one of the oldest races of people on the earth.

Music and dance has been an integral part of Rwandan society for centuries, ranging from royal songs and dances that transmit history, to traditional dances celebrating the harvest or marriage. Drums, in particular, are perhaps the most important instruments in Rwandan song and dance. These percussive instruments are revered not only for their musical value, but also for their cultural significance.

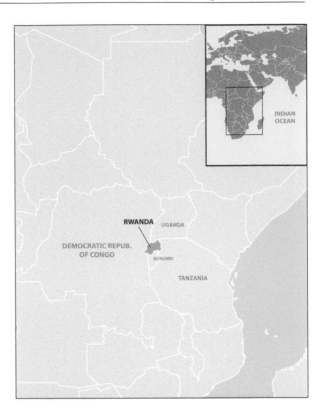

GENERAL INFORMATION

Official Language: Kinyarwanda, French, and English
Population: 12,661,773 (2015 estimate)

Currency: Rwandan franc
Coins: One hundred centimes equal one Rwandan franc. Coins are issued in denominations of 1, 2, 5, 10, 20, 50, and 100 francs.
Land Area: 24,668 square kilometers (9,524 square miles)
Water Area: 1,670 square kilometers (644 square miles)
National Motto: Ubumwe, Umurimo, Gukunda Igihugu ("Unity, Work, Patriotism")
National Anthem: "Rwanda nziza" (Kinyarwanda, "Rwanda, Our Beautiful Country")
Capital: Kigali
Time Zone: GMT +2

Flag Description: Rwanda's flag was adopted in 2001 and features a broad strip of blue, standing for peace and happiness, across most of the top half of the flag, with a sun shining in the right. Below the blue stripe is a stripe of yellow, signifying the country's current and potential economic development and another of green, representing the country's prosperity. The sun stands for the country's enlightenment.

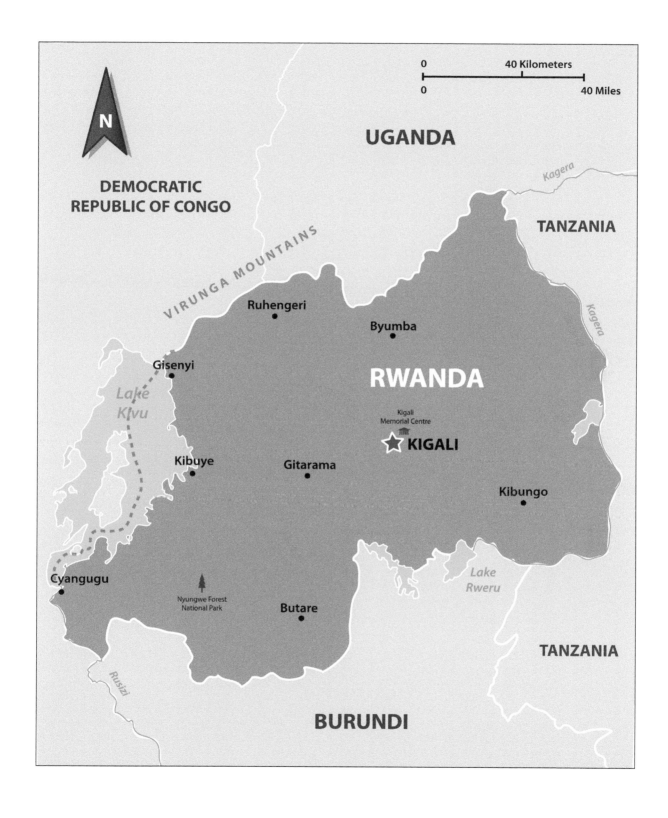

Principal Cities by Population (2012):

- Kigali (1,200,000)
- Ruhengeri (132,145)
- Gisenyi (127,587)
- Butare (115,704)
- Gitarama (86,741)
- Byumba (75,463)
- Cyangugu (69,992)

Population

Rwanda has one of the highest population densities in Africa. While many Rwandans live in urban areas, the country is still very rural in nature. Kigali, the capital, is the largest city, has more than 1.2 million inhabitants (2012 estimate). Other large cities include Gitarama, Butare, Ruhengeri, and Gisenyi. Rwanda has a large population of young people, with 43 percent of the population below the age of fourteen. Population estimates have taken into account the estimates the toll that HIV/AIDS infection has had on mortality, infant mortality, population growth rates and migration, as well as life expectancy.

Rwanda's demographics are unusual in that settlements center on homesteads found on the country's hillsides. These homesteads are family-centered. There are larger population concentrations around administrative centers.

Languages

There are three official languages in Rwanda: Kinyarwanda, French, and English. Kiswahili (Swahili) is also used in business and government.

Native People & Ethnic Groups

There are three ethnic groups in Rwanda: Hutu, Tutsi, and Twa. The Hutu are the majority group, accounting for 84 percent of the population. The Tutsi are the next largest, at 15 percent of the population. The Twa make up only one percent of the population.

The two chief ethnic groups are largely indistinguishable – they speak the same language, share similar cultures, and have a history of intermarriage. Belgian administrators, who used class conflict to control the population, emphasized the essentially arbitrary cultural distinction during the early 20th century.

Historically, the cultural division is economic: "Tutsi" referred to the upper class of cattle farmers, while "Hutu" was used for the peasant class. Under the Belgians, only the Tutsi could hold political office, which furthered hostility and resentment between the ethnic groups. By the time Rwanda gained its independence in 1962, the Hutu had become the dominant group.

The native people of Rwanda are the Twa, who now comprise only 1 percent of the total population. Sometimes referred to as "pygmies," the Twa are usually short in stature, and are seldom taller than 1.5 meters (five feet). The Twa were living in the mountains and forests of Rwanda before they were displaced by the arrival of the Hutu and Tutsi beginning in the 11th century.

Today, most Twa are farmers living in the Virunga Mountains, and some work as servants in Hutu and Tutsi homes. Both Hutus and Tutsis treat the Twa as social outcasts. In addition, the Twa are forced to navigate a dense bureaucracy just to receive basic services such as health care and education. During the 1994 genocide, more than 10,000 Twa were killed. Many surviving Twa are widows and orphans. Advocacy groups such as the Communauté des Autochtones du Rwanda (CAURWA), founded in 1995, have arisen to assist the Twa.

Despite their hardships, the Twa have made significant contributions to Rwandan culture. Their songs and dances are well known, and are integrated into modern music. They also have extensive knowledge of traditional medicine.

Religions

Nearly three-quarters of Rwandans are Christian, mostly Roman Catholic. There are small minorities of Muslims, as well as followers of traditional animist religions.

Climate

Despite its close proximity to the equator, Rwanda has a temperate climate due to its high elevation.

Though the temperature is usually mild, frost and snow are possible at high altitudes in the Virunga Mountains.

The average temperature in the central part of the country is around 20° Celsius (68° Fahrenheit), and varies little throughout the year. Temperatures are generally a few degrees cooler at higher elevations.

There are four seasons, though they only consist of mild temperature changes. The two rainy seasons occur between February and May, and between September and December. Rainfall amounts vary by region; the northeastern part of the country typically receives 102 centimeters (40 inches) annually, while the wetter southwest receives 152 centimeters (60 inches).

ENVIRONMENT & GEOGRAPHY

Topography

Rwanda is an equatorial country in central Africa. It borders the Democratic Republic of the Congo, Uganda, Tanzania, and Burundi. Rwanda lies on the East African plateau, and is characterized by grasslands, hills, valleys, and mountains. The grassy central plateau descends into swampland in the eastern part of the country, near the Kagera River.

Most of the country lies at an elevation of more than 1.5 kilometers (1 mile) above sea level. Its highest point is in the northwest Virunga volcanic mountain range, at the peak of Mount Karisimbi 4,507 meters (14,787 feet) above sea level. The country's lowest point is at the Ruzizi River, 914 meters (3,000 feet) above sea level.

The country's largest lake is Lake Kivu, along Rwanda's border with the Democratic Republic of the Congo. The Virunga Mountains lie between the Nile and Congo rivers. Other important rivers in Rwanda include the Akanyaru, the Kagera, and the Nyabarongo.

The capital of Kigali is located a few degrees south of the equator, on a range of four hills in the center of Rwanda between Mount Kigali and Mount Jali. The city lies on the bank of the Ruganwa River, just 80 kilometers (50 miles) east of Lake Kivu. The Nyabugogo river basin is also nearby. The city's high elevation gives Kigali a mild climate, with a year-round average temperature of 21° Celsius (70° Fahrenheit).

Plants & Animals

Lake Kivu, located in a warm valley surrounded by hills on the western border, is home to many species of plant and animal life. Most agriculture takes place in the fertile western region of the country. To the east, dry savannah takes over. Forests of acacia and bamboo, along with eucalyptus and banana trees, dominate the landscape.

More than half the world's remaining population of mountain gorillas lives in Rwanda's Volcano National Park. This endangered species is best known as the subject of study by American primatologist Dian Fossey. It is estimated that only about 600 of these gorillas are left in the world.

Rwanda is also home to such typical African animals as elephants, crocodiles, and hippopotamuses. Colobus monkeys and several species of orchids are found in the Nyungwe Forest. At one time, Rwanda had more protected national park land than any other country in Africa. This has changed since the 1994 war, however, with more areas being opened to settlement.

Mountain gorillas continue to be an endangered species due to expanding human settlements and poaching.

CUSTOMS & COURTESIES

Greetings

Rwandans are a friendly people. Like many African cultures, they are known for their warm greetings, and generally, shake hands or kiss on the cheek three times (alternating between the left and right cheek). Close friends and family may also embrace, and a pat on the back is also common. These physical greetings are customarily followed by general inquiries about family life and well-being, among other topics. Not adhering to this cultural protocol is impolite. Kinyarwanda (also known as Rwanda) is one of the official languages of Rwanda. (English and French are also official languages.) Common greetings include "Muraho" ("Hello") and "Amakuru?" ("How are you?").

Deference to elders is an important facet of Rwandan culture. Traditionally, youth are also expected to avert their eyes when greeting adults or elders, and are often expected to curtsy, for girls, or bow slightly, for boys.

Gestures & Etiquette

Rwanda was once a society of strict ethnic divisions and identity. During the Tutsi dynastic period, the Hutu were forbidden from acting in ways outside of their social status. During both the German and Belgian colonial periods, both ethnicities refrained from some traditional practices, including gestures, dancing, chanting, and tribal customs. Ethnic divisions and identity were further challenged during the 1994 genocide. Today, the matter of ethnicity still frames Rwandan culture and society. As part of national reconciliation, disparaging ethnic remarks or even mild ethnic comments are not allowed and are punishable by law.

Other elements of social etiquette in Rwanda include familial and gender roles. For example, women are expected to act reserved in public, and refrain from consuming alcohol and engaging in behavior perceived as masculine. Youth are also acclimated to gender roles within the family from birth. For young women, this includes learning modesty and conservatism in public and domestic responsibilities; for young men, it is learning their father's trade and the responsibilities of manhood. Children also learn that everyone in Rwandan society must contribute to the greater good. Not only are they responsible for contributing to their own nuclear family, but also to the clan and the greater community. While the genocide disrupted this long-held tradition, many families are rebuilding these social strata.

Eating/Meals

There are three meals corresponding to breakfast, lunch, and dinner in Rwandan culture, but Rwandans generally eat two meals per day. Simple meals are common, and include staples such as beans, corn, millet, fruit, potatoes, or cassava (manioc). Dinner is usually the largest or heaviest meal, while breakfast may consist of leftovers or common dishes such as toast and coffee or porridge. Meat is not commonly eaten in rural areas, and urban areas may follow Western patterns and eating customs. Small snacks, such as fried plantains and potatoes, roasted nuts, and fruit, are eaten throughout the day.

Women are traditionally expected to prepare family meals. Meals are communal in nature, including the sharing of a communal dish of water for diners to wash their hands, and communal dishes of food. Women are also tasked with the distribution of food, breaking up the food into pieces. While food is traditionally eaten with the hands, utensils are common in urban areas.

Visiting

Visiting in Rwanda is a frequent, if not daily, occurrence. Though food and other resources have been limited following the Rwandan genocide, Rwandans still maintain their strong sense of hospitality. Mealtimes are a particularly common time for receiving guests, and families were traditionally expected to prepare enough food for any unexpected visitors. This generosity is also expected to be reciprocal.

LIFESTYLE

Family

Large families have traditionally been the norm in Rwandan culture. Traditionally, Rwandans were linked by lineage and clan. The clan is a cluster of nuclear families that are generation-based. For example, several adult sons will most likely inhabit the same compound as their father, including their own wives and family. Historically, entire villages have been built around clans. Because of the strong familial link within some villages, families have outlawed marrying someone from their own village. The nuclear family, composed of a man, his wife, and their children, is now becoming increasingly common in Rwanda.

Housing

Historically, housing in Rwanda was clustered around the centralized home of a chief or head male. Traditional homes were circular structures built from mud and daub with a conical roof made from dense thatch. The floors inside of homes were made from tightly woven mats, often made by the female head of household. Several of these huts could comprise a single household and separate houses were built for functional rooms like the kitchen and the toilette. Homes were also generally separated by fencing or farmlands. Urban homes differ significantly from traditional styles, and are uniformly rectangular, with corrugated tin roofing and cement floors. In addition, as opposed to having many individual buildings on one property, urban Rwandans tend to have one building divided into several rooms.

Housing in Rwanda has also been affected by urbanization. To alleviate overcrowding, the government began involuntarily relocating Rwandans to established villages in 1997. The genocide also resulted in a severe housing shortage, particularly sparked after approximately 4 million refugees returned. In response, the government established a low-cost housing initiative, called "Imidugudu" locally, to resettle returning refugees.

Food

Rwandans eat a basic diet that depends on a few regional staples, such as cassava, plantains, bananas, corn, sorghum, beans, potatoes, and rice. Common meats include beef, chicken, and goat. Snacks include grilled corn on the cob, grilled beef and goat kebabs, and the very popular mizuzu, or fried plantains. Rwandan cuisine also has European influences from its colonial period; French fries, a notable Belgian culinary influence, are popular.

Dinner dishes often come with a starch, typically ubugali, or stewed cassava meal, makote, cooked plantain, or rice. Stews are served with the starches and often include peanuts, spices, cassava leaves or another deep green leaf. Igisafuriya is a dish of goat stewed in peanut sauce and served with makote. Isombe is another common dish and includes cassava leaves served with eggplant and cooked spinach.

Rural areas still suffer from serious nutritional deficiency and the government is working on alleviating the problem. One proposed solution is to inject food with nutritional supplements so that even if people are eating simple foods, those foods have added nutritional value.

Life's Milestones

Rwanda's religious demographics are mixed. Over half of the population identifies as Roman Catholic—56 percent, as estimated by the Rwandan government in 2006—and there are sizeable Protestant, Muslim, and Adventist populations. In general, commemorative milestones such as birth, transition into adulthood, marriage, and death are observed in accordance with the Christian faith. Different ethnic groups also have nuanced methods for commemorating each event, with some elements being universal.

For example, nearly every ethnicity observes the traditional practice of a bride gift prior to weddings. This gift, customarily consisting of money, livestock, foodstuff, and possibly even clothing, is presented to the bride's family on behalf of the groom and his family. The gesture, much needed in many cases, is meant to compensate the family for the loss of the young woman who will be leaving her home. Typically, weddings are long celebrations that may last up to a week. The entire family and even villagers may be invited to participate in the festivities.

CULTURAL HISTORY

Art

As in most early African cultures, traditional art in Rwanda was more functional than aesthetic. Crafts were beautifully adorned, but served a utilitarian purpose. Early art forms included wood and stone carving, textile weaving, metalworking, pottery, and basketry. Traditionally, men were the carvers, while women focused on woven crafts and ceramics. Men were also charged with creating drums and other instruments, usually carved from wood and gourds. While many art forms still maintain a functional role in contemporary Rwandan society, they have since become commercialized. For example, sculptures of royalty and religious figures serve a religious purpose in worship, but are purchased by tourists as decoration.

While the textile arts have fallen off in the 20th and early 21st centuries, replaced by Western-style dress and imported clothes, weaving remains a strong and important tradition. Perhaps that is due to the remarkable skill with which Rwandan baskets and mats are created. Baskets are traditionally made from the tightly coiled strands of bamboo strips, the fibers of the cypress and papyrus tree, or goosegrass, a native and wiry weed. Baskets and mats may be used for socializing, storing goods (including liquids), or as gifts for special occasions. The Tutsi, one of Rwanda's native ethnicities, are particularly known for their lidded baskets (agaseke).

Architecture

Rwanda's tendency to build compounds or households on the hills is a longstanding one. In Nyanza, the former royal capital of Rwanda, the king's palace is a traditional hut structure that has been recreated to reflect the early structure of the Rwandan household compound. The reconstructed hut is almost a pyramidal cone in shape, is covered in thatching, and is surrounded by outbuildings that house family members (wives and children), as well as foodstuffs. Some buildings serve a particular purpose, such as a kitchen or bathroom. Surrounding hillsides were populated by the king's extended family or associates.

In 21st-century rural Rwanda, houses still tend dot hillsides and are made from mud and daub. Most floors are dirt, the structures lack doors and windows, and there are no foundations. Roofs, thatched and metal, are largely inadequate. Because of this, the houses are often vulnerable to the elements and sometimes collapse.

Kigali itself was nearly destroyed by arson and gunfire, though international investors have rebuilt the city. With this modern and Western investment in the country, the architecture reflects those influences.

Drama

Rwanda has a fledgling film industry. The country's first feature film, *100 Days*, was released in 2001, four years after it was first filmed. The film deals with the genocide of 1994, providing a fictional account of the traumatic time. In fact, much of the films associated with the country, whether produced domestically or abroad, deal with the genocide. One of the more notable films is *Hotel Rwanda* (2004), a Western production that was filmed partly in Rwanda. The Academy Award-nominated historical drama portrays the efforts of a Rwandan hotelier who saves thousands of lives during the genocide. Other films about the genocide include the award-winning documentary *Shake Hands with the Devil* (2007) and the docudrama *Shooting Dogs* (2005), which employed survivors of the genocide. Rwanda also now hosts the Rwanda Film Festival (RFF), established with the focus of spreading social messages through film.

Music & Dance

Music and dance has been an integral part of Rwandan society for centuries, ranging from royal songs and dances that transmit history, to traditional dances celebrating the harvest or marriage. Drums, in particular, are perhaps the most important instruments in Rwandan song and dance. These percussive instruments are revered not only for their musical value, but also for their cultural significance. This is because the Tutsi directly linked the playing of drums with royalty, and the playing of the kalinga (royal sacred drum) honored Tutsi kings. It was believed that the number of drums playing could measure a king's power. These royal drums were housed in sacred places, and each king employed special drum makers. Other traditional instruments include the inanga (similar to a zither), ikembe (a type of lamellaphone or sound box, similar to a thumb piano), and umuduri (musical bow).

Certain traditional dances and styles of music have achieved international acclaim, including the intore style of dancing and the influential music of the Tutsi dynasties. The intore style achieved international fame through the traveling performances of Rwanda's Intore Dance Troupe. The dance style was first inspired by Tutsi warriors of the royal courts who would celebrate their victories with wild stomping movements. The dance developed structure and became integrated into Tutsi society. It was then performed by anyone wishing to honor warriors. Traditionally, the dance is accompanied by the beats of the ingoma drums.

Famous music styles have also been influenced by the Tutsi dynasties. Today, Rwandan music has three major classifications: indirimbo, imbyino, and ibitekerezo. Indirimbo combines musical instrumentation with voice to create a genre strictly aesthetic in its purpose. Imbyino is dominated by drums and is used as dance music. Ibitekerezo is a style in which lyrics are accompanied by music. These poetic lyrics are performed by skilled vocalists and are valued as important mechanisms for passing down history and cultural codes from one generation to the next. Originally used to honor Tutsi kings, Hutu and other regional and ethnic groups later adopted similar styles and adapted them to their own cultural needs.

Literature

Rwandan literature, like most other African cultures, is rooted in oral tradition. Storytelling and the memorization and recitation of folktales, legends, and histories are highly valued as a means of cultural preservation. Oral tradition, such as proverbs, riddles, and folklore, were also didactic in nature, and imparted morals and values while preserving a group's cultural heritage. Traditional Rwandan literature is said to be divided into three genres: pre-dynastic tales and mythology; royal documents (such as rituals and genealogy) and poetry used as a populist tool of the Tutsi royals; and informal folklore and legends used to preserve culture and history and impart lessons.

The Tutsi are particularly famous for their development of an oral literature, particularly their royal poetry. This rich tradition served to both commemorate the ascendency of royalty to the throne of Rwanda, as well as educate the masses on the natural right of the Tutsi royalty to hold power. With the influence of European culture and language on Rwandan society, written literature grew in popularity. The first Rwandan to introduce Rwandan poetry and history in the written form was Alexis Kagame (1912–1981). In 1951, he published *La Poésie dynastiqual au Rwanda*, which was a thorough collection of 176 of the Tutsi people's most valued poems.

Most contemporary Rwandan literature is published in English, Swahili, or most commonly French. An emerging body of work deals with the devastating Rwandan genocide of 1994 and the repercussive violence, much of it written by members of the Rwandan diaspora. Notable authors include Benjamin Sehene (1959–), who published a historical novel and ethnic study, among other works, about the Rwandan genocide, Immaculée Ilibagiza's (c. 1972–) autobiographical account of the genocide, titled *Left to Tell: Discovering God Amidst the Rwandan Holocaust* (2006), details her ninety-one days spent hiding during the ordeal in a small bathroom with seven other women.

CULTURE

Arts & Entertainment

Rwanda has a robust contemporary arts scene. Despite the loss of vast numbers of renowned artists during the 1994 genocide, artistic endeavors remain a priority. As a result, countless arts centers and initiatives are nurturing younger generations while allowing fully developed artists to display their work. In addition to venues for art exhibitions and performance art, Rwanda boasts East Africa's most modern and fully developed museum circuit. There are branches in numerous cities, and collections ranging from modern art to ancient artifacts.

Many modern Rwandan painters, photographers, sculptors and other artists find themselves touching in some way upon the genocide and its palpable after effects. Rwandan artists claim that the genocide eliminated an entire generation of Rwanda's best and brightest creative minds. Many dedicate works or entire exhibitions to remembering Rwanda's brutal history so that it may never happen again. Notable contemporary artists include Jean Bosco Bakunzi (1985–) and Richard Karekezi (1984–), whose works are characterized by bright oil paints contrasted against deep black outlines and traditional Rwandan scenes and designs. Painter Innocent Nkrunziza (1986–) is known for collages of close human forms.

Artist Colin Sekajugo (1980–) believes that Rwanda is overdue for a "Rwandan Renaissance" and has taken on the task of ushering in a new artistic era. In 2007, after traveling throughout East and West Africa representing Rwanda's young arts community and learning about the arts communities of other African nations, Sekajugo returned to Kigali. There, he founded Ivuka Arts Kigali, an arts institution dedicated to providing young aspiring artists a place where they can develop and display their skills. ("Ivuka" is the Kinyarwanda word for "birth.") Today, the center has many of Rwanda's top artists teaching younger generations about painting and traditional Rwandan arts. Not only do these artists work with the young, but they have also charged themselves with the task of bringing Rwandan art onto the international scene.

Traditional folk music is a significant part of Rwandan culture. The ikinimba is a native musical tradition that involves storytelling accompanied by stringed instruments, including the harp-like lulunga, and drums. The period of Belgian occupation added European influences to the country's traditional music, and modern Rwandan music is a combination of styles.

The centuries-old Intore Dance Troupe helps keep traditional Rwandan music and dance alive by performing throughout the country and abroad.

Football (soccer) is the most popular sport in Rwanda. The national football team, the Wasps, participated in the Africa Nations Cup tournament in 2004.

Cultural Sites & Landmarks

Rwanda is a country of renowned natural beauty and distinction. In fact, the country boasts one of Africa's oldest rainforests, as well as the one of the continent's largest mountainside natural parks, the Nyungwe Forest National Park. Located in the southwestern region of the nation, it is the youngest official park established by the Rwandan government. Volcanoes National Park, located in the northwestern region, is home to the Virunga Mountain Range, which boasts seven linked volcanoes. The range also contains a mountainside rainforest that contains one of the remaining populations of the endangered mountain gorillas. This forest was once home to a famous gorilla sanctuary and research station established by Dian Fossey (1932–1985), who studied the gorillas and was an outspoken advocate against poaching. Her grave remains at the research station she founded, alongside some of the gorillas killed by poaching.

Rwanda's genocide of the 1990s affects nearly every facet of life. Kigali itself was nearly destroyed by arson and gunfire, though international investors have rebuilt the city. Understandably, then, most recognizable landmarks in the capital and around the country are memorials to those killed in the genocide.

The Kigali Genocide Memorial Center at Gisozi is one of the most comprehensive of these sites. It traces the history of the ethnic conflict from pre-colonial times. Buried on the grounds of the site are some 250,000 victims of the 1994 genocide.

Other important sites are the Ntarama Church memorial, where more than 5,000 people were killed, and the Mille Collines hotel, which sheltered those fleeing the violence. The hotel was immortalized in the film *Hotel Rwanda* (2004), and is one of three major hotels in Kigali. The Bisesero, Nyamata, Ntarama, and Nyarubuye memorials are located all over the northwestern and southwestern regions of Rwanda, where the brutality was the most devastating.

Kigali also hosts a bustling nightlife, with numerous clubs and bars showcasing local bands. The BCDI tower and the Centenary House office block are among the more modern landmarks, and are both signs of the city's increasingly commercial outlook.

Libraries & Museums

Rwanda is home to many museums, including the National Museum of Rwanda, in Butare, considered to be the most comprehensive ethnographic museum in East Africa. Other museums include the Rukuri Ancient History Museum, which opened in 2008; the Rwesero Art Museum, housed in a converted palace; and the Living History Museum, which consists of a compound of sixteen traditional huts.

The Kigali Public library houses much of the history and information on the Rwandan Genocide, opened in 2007. The Bibliothèque nationale du Rwanda (National Library of Rwanda is in Kigali.

Holidays

National holidays observed in Rwanda include Kamarampaka Day (September 25), National Day (July 1), and Independence Day (July 4). Many traditional Christian holidays, such as Easter and Christmas, are also widely celebrated.

Youth Culture

According to early 21st century estimates, over 50 percent of Rwanda's population is under the age of 18, and an estimated 65,000 households are headed by youth. As such, the government has made it a crucial priority to focus on improving the lives of youngsters nationwide and have created numerous initiatives and ministries dedicated to determining avenues of youth development. Some of the more notable initiatives included a fee waiver for orphaned children to improve school attendance and programs aimed at reintegrating child soldiers into society and leveling the gender gap in education. The United Nations Children's Fund (UNICEF) funded many of these programs.

Still, Rwanda has been accused by the international community of using conflict with the DRC to abuse some orphaned children in northern and eastern regions. International human rights organizations have accused the Rwandan government of "adopting" children orphaned by conflicts in those regions and training them to be soldiers in Rwanda's national army. These children soon find themselves thrown back into the heart of conflicts they barely escaped.

Western influence has been widespread throughout Rwanda's youth culture since the late 20th century, and hip-hop culture has become particularly popular among Rwanda's youth. Many popular songs are reproductions of original material that are presented in a localized version. Other popular music genres include reggae, Afropop, and rhythm and blues (R&B). The local music industry in Rwanda has received increased focus in recent years, with 2008 concerts by international reggae acts Sean Paul (1973–) and Shaggy (1968–), the last of which was even attended by the president.

SOCIETY

Transportation

Buses, minibuses, and share taxis are the primary modes of public transportation in Rwanda. Minibuses are newer in Rwanda than in other nations, mainly because international aid has allowed more recent vehicle purchases. Shared taxis typically operate from bus stops, and will pick up additional passengers along the way. Roads between major towns are serviceable and larger buses end up being very comfortable means of traveling. For the vast majority of Rwandans, though, walking is the best means of travel. Other popular modes of transportation include motorcycle taxis known locally as boda-boda, scooters, and bikes.

Traffic in Rwanda travels on the right, and most cars have the steering wheel on the right, which is unusual for countries with right-hand travel.

Transportation Infrastructure
Rwanda has minimal water transportation services, and no passenger rail lines, though plans are in place to build rail networks. The country's main airport is Kanombe International Airport, located in Kigali. The national carrier is Rwandair Express. Kamembe Airport, in the city of Cyangugu, also offers passenger service. Only 10 percent of Rwanda's streets are paved.

Media & Communications
Radio is the most popular medium in Rwanda. The most popular station is the state-run Radio Rwanda. It airs programs in English, French, Swahili and various lesser-spoken indigenous languages, but generally portrays the government in a positive light. Numerous private stations that have sprung up since the 1994 genocide mainly run music and popular gossip programming. Television viewership remains limited, and is mainly concentrated in urban areas. The state-run network is Television Rwandaise (TVR).

The print media is also limited, and is subject to state harassment. As a result, self-censorship is common. International organizations such as Reporters Without Borders have also accused the highest government officials of obstructing freedom of speech and the press laws in their own interests. Nearly all print media is privately operated.

Since the turn of the 21st century, the Rwandan government has liberalized the telecommunications industry. As of October 2014, the country's mobile phone penetration was estimated at approximately 7.7 million subscribers, representing nearly 63 percent of the population. In addition, as of 2014, there were an estimated 1.1 million Internet users.

SOCIAL DEVELOPMENT

Standard of Living
In 2014, Rwanda ranked 151st out of 187 countries on the United Nations Human Development Index, which measures quality of life indicators.

Water Consumption
According to the African Development Bank, about 76 percent of Rwanda's population has access to clean water. About 23 percent have access to hygienic sanitation facilities. The goal for 2020 is to have 100 percent coverage for both water and sanitation.

Education
Education in Rwanda is free and compulsory for nine years. According to the Rwandan government, 15 percent of the national budget is spent on education. However, the average Rwandan receives less than three years of schooling, and only 40 percent of students reach the fifth grade level. Male children are more likely than female children to attend school are. Only 13,000 students can be admitted to the nation's more than 700 secondary schools, making admissions extremely competitive.

Christian missionaries run many schools in Rwanda. Most schools were closed during the ethnic violence that began in 1994, and many were destroyed in the fighting.

The University of Rwanda, founded in 1963, is the country's main institute of higher education. The average literacy rate among adult Rwandans is 70 percent (76 percent among men and 65 percent among women). More than 44,000 students attend university or pursue higher technical training.

Women's Rights

In many ways, Rwanda is on the forefront of women's development in the region, and women have seen their roles in society increase since the turn of the 20th century. Much of this is a result of Rwanda's recent violent past, as many women have been thrust into leadership roles they might not have assumed had their husbands and fathers not met a premature death. Regardless, no longer just tasked with domestic responsibilities, the women of Rwanda are playing a pivotal role in the rebuilding of their society.

Rwandan women have also benefitted from the application of microcredit (small loans designed to help the impoverished). As of 2006, over 200 microfinance institutions (MFI) had opened in Rwanda. With tens of thousands borrowing money in small amounts, typically between $50 and $400 (USD), women entrepreneurs have started a variety of businesses, ranging from craft making to farming. (Although men have also benefitted from loans, an estimated four out of every five males who borrow end up defaulting.) This economic pattern is leading to an overall cultural change; backed with economic success, Rwandan women are now looked upon as pillars of society and community leaders, and are no longer traditionally confined to subservient roles.

However, Rwandan women continue to face challenges and rights abuses, with domestic abuse and violence against women at the forefront. Like many African cultures, Rwandans generally believe that spousal abuse is the right of the husband. Further exacerbating the problem is the fact that constitutional law does not specifically prohibit domestic abuse (though a woman may charge her husband with general assault). In addition, despite having the capacity to file criminal charges, most women accept abuse, and refrain from reporting domestic violence due to social stigma. In addition, such minor crimes are often handled among extended family or

the local community, where an appointed male deliberates on such issues.

In an attempt to better the situation for women, Rwandan officials spearheaded a program in 2005 in which local police stations were newly equipped with a "gender station." These stations were staffed by at least one professionally trained official who would handle matters of abuse and rape. In the capital of Kigali, a more elaborate system was set up, including a hotline for women afraid to come directly to the police, counselors for victim treatment, and a special hospital that maintains the privacy of victims. Rape is criminalized, and the government has also stepped up efforts to combat the problem, but prostitution remains legal and widespread in Rwanda.

Outside of domestic abuse and violence, Rwandan women continue to face societal discrimination in the areas of education, property rights, and employment. Education remains unbalanced between men and women, and the government has worked to remedy this situation by establishing a scholarship program for families unable to send both their sons and daughters to school. (Traditionally, only sons were sent to school if the family could not afford to send both.) Since the 1994 genocide, the government has also addressed property rights, and has rewritten laws that prevent women from owning property. As a result, more women own their own land and businesses. The government also enacted the Family Code, which allowed women to inherit property and which established fair laws for child custody and divorce matters.

Health Care

According to recent estimates, less than half of Rwanda's population receives routine health care services. Rwanda has a national health care system that covers 92 percent of the population and costs only $2 per person. While all Rwandans are expected to pay into the system, a study conducted by Tropical Medicine & International Health indicates that 53 percent of health care funding comes from international sources. Because of the inconsistent nature of the funding, health care services can vary according to location and sponsoring organization.

Disease, often due to unsanitary conditions, is still the major cause of death. Common diseases include malaria, tuberculosis, dysentery, hepatitis, and schistosomiasis. Kwashiorkor, a disease caused by protein deficiency, is commonly found in many Rwandan children. The prevalence of preventable disease is due to the high rates of poverty and malnutrition throughout the country.

HIV/AIDS remains a problem in Rwanda, especially in urban areas, with an estimated 5 percent of the population infected. However, in recent years the government has developed an effective education and treatment program to combat the spread of the disease.

In recent years, the Catholic Church and other international groups have provided support for Rwandan hospitals and clinics. However, with limited access to modern medical care, many Rwandans resort to traditional remedies. Rwandan umufumu, or "witch doctors," provide herbal remedies and perform exorcisms.

GOVERNMENT

Structure

Rwanda is a republic with a multiparty government. Suffrage is universal for all Rwandans 18 and over. The executive branch consists of the president, prime minister, and cabinet.

Rwanda's legislature is the National Assembly, or Assemblee Nationale, which consists of 80, 53 of which are elected by popular vote and 24 that are elected by provincial councils and the remainder appointed. The Senate has 26 members made up of elected and appointed positions.

Prior to the 19th century, Rwanda was ruled for centuries by a monarchy, which expanded its territory by assimilating other peoples in the region. The country became part of German East Africa in the late 19th century, and was administered by Belgium after the First World War.

Belgium maintained the traditional structure of the monarchy, but the class distinctions fostered by the Belgians erupted into violence during the mid-20th century, as the Hutu population rose up against the Tutsi aristocracy. The monarchy was abolished, and Rwanda became independent in 1962.

A one-party military government was installed in 1978, and ethnic violence continued as exiled Tutsi began working to regain their footing in Rwanda. A new constitution was adopted in 1991, creating a multiparty, more representative system of government. The Hutu military regained control, however, with the genocide carried out against the Tutsi in 1994. Eventually, military action by the Tutsi Rwandan Patriotic Front (RPF) defeated the Hutu. Elections were held in 1999 and 2003 for a new, more inclusive government. In 2008, the parliamentary election resulted in the first female majority in a modern nation when forty-five of the seats went to women.

Political Parties

One party, the Rwandan Patriotic Front (RPF), dominates Rwandan politics. Other parties are allowed, but not believed to have the power to advance in the existing political climate. In the 2013 parliamentary elections, the RPF led a coalition that included the Islamic Democratic Party (PDI), the Christian Democratic Party (PDC), the Part for Progress and Concord (PPC), the Prosperity and Solidarity Party (PSP), the Democratic Union of the Rwandan People (UPDR), and the Rwandese Socialist Party (PSR). Other parties in that election include the Social Democratic Party and the Liberal Party.

Local Government

Rwanda adopted a decentralization policy in 2000. Rwanda is comprised of five provinces, which includes the city of Kigali. Provinces are divided into districts, of which there are 31 in the country. A provincial governor and a provincial executive secretary lead each province; each district is led by an executive secretary. The city of Kigali is administered by an executive secretary and a democratically elected mayor and an executive committee, with two vice-mayors.

Judicial System

The legal system of Rwanda is based on the civil law system, which differs from Western common law in that it relies on legislative decisions rather than legal precedent. The country is in the midst of a transition from the civil to a combined common and civil law system. The legal system is comprised of mediation committees, district courts, provincial courts, and high courts of the Republic. The Supreme Court is the country's highest court. Specialized courts, which included the gacaca courts, handle issues related to the genocide.

Taxation

Rwanda levies a graduated tax on personal income and a 35 percent tax on corporate income. Additionally, Rwandans pay a value-added, real or lump sum, loan, and property taxes.

Armed Forces

The Rwanda Defence Force (RDF) is made up of the High Command Council, the General Staff, the Rwanda Land Force, The Rwanda Air Force, and special forces, Many of those who served in the Rwandan Patriotic Army during the genocide now serve in the RDF, as those soldiers that previously served in the Rwandan Armed Forces (FAR) left Rwanda after the genocide.

Foreign Policy

Historically, Rwanda's internal politics have been defined by the relations between the Hutu and the Tutsi. Since the Tutsi tribes migrated into the region in the 16th century, they have maintained a minority rule over the majority Hutu. Because of the early efforts of the Tutsi to consolidate their power, Rwanda is one of the only African nations whose national boundaries had been defined long before the Europeans had a chance to determine them. Germany asserted its colonial governance over Rwanda from 1894 until 1918, annexing the nation into German East Africa. Following its defeat in World War

I, however, Germany turned all of its colonies over to other nations. As such, Belgium absorbed Rwanda and Burundi, then known as Ruanda-Urundi, and used ethnic tension between the Tutsi and Hutu groups to maintain control.

The desire for independence soon grew, and in 1961, Rwanda was declared a republic, with the dominant Party for Hutu Emancipation producing the first president. Out of fear of retribution from the newly appointed Hutu leadership, approximately 150,000 Tutsi fled north into Sudan and the Democratic Republic of the Congo (DRC). They would return in 1990 when the Tutsi-led Rwandan Patriotic Front invaded Rwanda from Uganda. In April 1994, following years of fighting and civil unrest between the Tutsi and Hutu, extremist Hutus executed their long-planned "ethnic cleansing" meant to rid the nation of the Tutsi minority. At the end of their brutal, three-month killing spree, over 800,000 Tutsi and Tutsi sympathizers were dead.

In the early 21st century, much of Rwanda's foreign relations have been framed by the effects of the 1994 genocide, including efforts to administer justice to those accused of committing the atrocities, receiving humanitarian and foreign aid to rebuild, and reintegrating the nation into the global political and economic scene. As such, Rwanda maintains a very active role in the United Nations, presiding over the United Nations Security Council (UNSC) in 1995. Rwanda has also established important bilateral relations with agencies such as the United States Agency for International Development (USAID) and the European Union (EU). Rwanda is also an active participant in the African Union (AU), and has sent peacekeeping forces to Darfur, Sudan. Rwanda also holds membership in the East African Community (EAC) and the African Development Bank (ADB), among other regional bodies.

One of the dominants aspects of Rwanda's foreign relations is its involvement with the Democratic Republic of the Congo (DRC). In 1998, Rwanda aided Congolese rebels attempting to overthrow the president, withdrawing troops only after a 2002 ceasefire was reached.

Six years later, in 2008, Rwanda and the DRC entered into a joint military operation against rebel forces in the region such as the Democratic Forces for the Liberation of Rwanda (FDLR), as well as General Laurent Nkunda (1967–), a former Congolese general and the leader of a rebel faction. (Rwandan forces captured Nkunda in 2009.) These efforts have improved Rwanda's international image and restored relations between the two nations. In 2009, Rwanda and the DRC resumed diplomatic relations when they appointed ambassadors in each other's capitals. Subsequently, Rwandan President Paul Kagame and DRC President Joseph Kabila met to discuss issues of common interest.

President Kagame has resumed limited relations with France, who backed the Hutu government during the genocide. French President Sarkozy visited Rwanda in 2010 and admitted to mistakes made by the French government in backing the Hutu government, but Sarkozy did not offer an apology for France's role in the genocide.

Human Rights Profile

International human rights law insists that states respect civil and political rights, and promote an individual's economic, social, and cultural rights. The United Nations Universal Declaration on Human Rights (UDHR) is recognized as the standard for international human rights. Its authors sought the counsel of the world's great thinkers, philosophers, and religious leaders, and were careful to create a document that reflects the core values shared by every world culture. To read this document or view the articles relating to cultural human rights, click here: http://www.udhr.org/UDHR/default.htm.

The human rights situation in Rwanda is perceived as poor, and the country continues to receive criticism for a range of human rights abuses. These include arbitrary arrest and prolonged detention; the use of torture and extrajudicial killings (state-sanctioned killings) by security forces; poor prison conditions; restrictions on the freedom of speech, press, assembly, and religion; human trafficking; the detention of political prisoners; child labor abuses; and discrimination and

violence against women. However, implications of human rights violations involving the Rwandan government have decreased in the early 21st century and the government has passed significant legislation to curb trafficking. In 2013, the government began opening centers aimed at aiding victims of gender-based exploitation.

The country is also still recovering from the brutal 1994 genocide. The genocide began as the "cleansing" of the Tutsi and moderate Hutu and Tutsi sympathizers at the hands of Hutu extremists, and ended with a backlash of violence directed against the Hutu. In a small, three-month window, over 800,000 men, women, and children were murdered throughout the nation, and the reverberations of the incident continue to be felt.

International human rights organizations have raised concerns over Rwanda's administration of justice to those accused of participating in the genocide. Many assert that the government is using trials as a means to maintain a repressive regime. Others accuse the government-started gacaca courts of invoking genocide by administering countless local and unofficial punishments. (Gacacas are local courts formed by the government to handle the overabundance of cases from the 1994 genocide.) In 1995, when the UN established the Rwanda Tribunal through the International Criminal Court (ICC), the vast number of cases flooded national and international courts, stalling judiciary proceedings. Rwandan and international officials then determined that local courts fashioned after traditional Rwandan tribal judiciary systems would decide the outcomes for smaller crimes affiliated with the genocide.

However, 15 years later, these gacaca courts are still holding trials without the presence of actual judges or official protocol for laying charges and administering punishment. Because of this lack of regulation, Rwandans and international observers alike have realized that the courts may try to punish individuals speaking out against the government, becoming tools for government suppression. International human rights organizations came out against such practices and encouraged Rwanda to end gacaca courts, which finally happened in 2012.

Another effect of the 1994 genocide is the ruling that "genocide ideology" was a criminal act punishable by law. As a result, Rwandans have experienced punishment for verbal expressions of dissatisfaction with the government. Expressing ethnic bias also carries a heavy sentence. While the government claims these policies eradicate ethnic tension, many human rights organizations maintain that these arbitrary policies have hindered Rwanda's progress.

Migration

Rwanda's net migration rate is 0.85 percent. Tutsi refugees, as well as others who had earlier fled Rwanda in any number of conflicts, continue to return to the country as the government remains stable and international investment continues to rebuild the country.

ECONOMY

Overview of the Economy

Rwanda remains one of the poorest countries in Africa, especially after the devastating ethnic violence in 1994. Roughly, 90 percent of the population is engaged in subsistence agriculture, and more than half the population lives below the poverty line. It is estimated that the overwhelming majority of the population lives on less than $0.43 (USD) a day.

The national economy relies on exports of coffee and tea. The country receives international economic aid, and is designated as a Heavily Indebted Poor Country (HPIC) by the World Bank and the International Monetary Fund (IMF). Foreign investment in Rwanda has picked up and the US Central Intelligence Agency estimates that the country is close to pre-1994 levels. A lack of transportation infrastructure has slowed economic growth.

In 2014, Rwanda's gross domestic product (GDP) was estimated at just over $8 billion (USD), with a per capita GDP of $1,700 (USD).

Industry

Rwandan industry is light, accounting for roughly 20 percent of GDP. Products manufactured in the country include beer and soft drinks, shoes and clothing, soap, cigarettes, and pharmaceuticals. Most goods and food are imported. In 2009, the industrial production rate was seven percent, showing growth.

Labor

Rwanda has a labor force of 4.4 million people. The unemployment rate, according to the OECD (Organization for Economic Co-operation and Development) in 2007, was "not a serious problem" except among the unskilled population.

Energy/Power/Natural Resources

In addition to arable land and hydropower, Rwanda has valuable deposits of gold, tin ore, and tungsten ore. The preservation of endangered animals, particularly the mountain gorilla population, is a major conservation issue in Rwanda. In addition, the large cattle population has put considerable strain on Rwanda's grasslands, and has contributed to soil erosion. The lingering effects of the war are still evident in Rwanda's natural areas. A great deal of arable land was lost in the fighting, and the return of Tutsi refugees has lead to a shortage of land. Recently, Rwanda's previously protected Kagera National Park was opened to settlement to help alleviate this crisis.

Forestry

Although more than 20 percent of the country's land is forested, deforestation is a major environmental concern, as more and more trees are cut down for fuel.

Mining/Metals

Rwanda's mining operations are generally small in scale, and mineral exports are not economically significant.

Agriculture

Agriculture is a lifestyle passed down through generations in Rwanda. Nearly all Rwandan farmers obtained their farmland through family inheritance. Droughts are a constant threat to the rural farming community. Overgrazing, deforestation, and soil erosion also threaten the nation's agriculture.

Roughly, one-third of Rwanda's land is arable, but this percentage is shrinking due to the strain placed upon the land by the growing cattle population and returning refugees. Overplanting in an attempt to ease food shortages has also eroded the country's available farmland.

Coffee and tea are the most important crops grown in Rwanda, though their prices fluctuate according to the world market. Animal products (mostly from cattle), especially meat and skins, are also important. These agricultural exports account for approximately half of the GDP.

Tourism

The combination of a lack of infrastructure and the specter of the 1994 genocide has prevented Rwanda from developing a profitable tourism sector. Despite its often violent and tumultuous history, Rwanda's capital Kigali is now considered one of the safest capital cities on the African continent, and is increasingly considered a major center of tourism and industry.

Rwanda's main attraction is its mountain gorilla population at the Parc National des Volcans, or Volcano National Park. The park is part of the Virunga Conservation Area located in the Virunga Mountains, in the northwestern part of the country. The bulk of Rwanda's tourism revenue comes from "gorilla tourism." Lake Kivu is another popular tourist destination.

Kristen Pappas, Rebekah Painter, Alex K. Rich

DO YOU KNOW?

- DNA analysis has proven that the Twa people of Rwanda are one of the oldest races of people on the earth.

- Rwanda is sometimes called by the French nickname "Pays des Mille Collines" ("Land of a Thousand Hills").

- The film *Hotel Rwanda* is based on events that took place in Kigali, but most of the filming took place in South Africa.

- Rwanda is the most densely populated country in Africa.

Bibliography

Adam Hochschild. "King Leopold's Ghost: A Story of Greed, Terror, and Heroism in Colonial Africa." Boston: *Mariner Books*, 1999.

Francois Soudan. "Kagame: Interviews with the President of Rwanda." New York: *Enigma Books*, 2015.

Jean Hatzfeld. "Machete Season: The Killers in Rwanda Speak." New York: *Farrar, Strauss and Giroux*, 2004.

Jean Hatzfeld and Linda Coverdale. *"Life Laid Bare: The Survivors in Rwanda Speak."* New York: *Other Press*, 2007.

Julius O. Adekunle. "Culture and Customs of Rwanda." *Greenwood Press*, 2007.

Philip Gourevitch. "We Wish to Inform You That Tomorrow We Will be Killed With Our Families: Stories from Rwanda." New York: *Picador USA*, 1998.

Rick Bass. "In My Home There Is No More Sorrow: Ten Days in Rwanda." San Francisco: *McSweeney's Books*, 2012.

Stephen Kinzer. "A Thousand Hills: Rwanda's Rebirth and the Man Who Dreamed It." Hoboken, NJ: *Wiley*, 2008.

Works Cited

"Country Profile: Rwanda." April 2009. *BBC* World. http://news.bbc.co.uk/2/hi/africa/country_profiles/1070265.stm#media

"Hotel Rwanda." *Imbd.com*. http://www.imdb.com/title/tt0395169/

"Life and etiquette in Rwanda." April 2009. http://www.monitor.co.ug/artman/publish/sunday_life/Life_and_etiquette_in_Rwanda_82291.shtml

"Partnering with Rwanda: United Nations in Rwanda." http://www.undg.org/docs/10003/*UN-Rwanda-Newsletter*, 3-2009.pdf

"Rwanda." *Encyclopedia Britannica Online*. http://www.britannica.com/EBchecked/topic/514402/Rwanda

"Rwanda." March 2006. *U.S. Department of State Human Rights Reports*. http://www.state.gov/g/drl/rls/hrrpt/2005/61587.htm

"Rwanda." *Citypopulations*, August 2002. http://www.citypopulation.de/Rwanda.html#Stadt_alpha

"Rwanda." *msn Encarta*. http://uk.encarta.msn.com/encyclopedia_761560996_4/Rwanda.html

"The power of horror in Rwanda." April 2009. *Human Rights Watch*. http://www.hrw.org/en/news/2009/04/11/power-horror-rwanda

"UN Rwanda addresses the rights and needs of youth." March 2009.

"Women Rise in Rwanda's Economic Revival." May 2008. *Washington Post*. http://www.washingtonpost.com/wp-dyn/content/story/2008/05/15/ST2008051504314.html

"The Rwandan National Museum." *Institute of National Museums of Rwanda*. http://www.museum.gov.rw/index.htm

"We Wish To Inform You That Tomorrow We Will Be Killed With Our Families." *Wikipedia Online Encyclopedia*. http://en.wikipedia.org/wiki/We_Wish_To_Inform_You_That_Tomorrow_We_Will_Be_Killed_With_Our_Families

David C. King, *Rwanda*. http://books.google.com/books?id=1yLx1zSuh_QC&pg=PA127&lpg=PA127&dq=rwanda+food+and+diet&source=bl&ots=DlqeNkyb83&sig=DL0uYPnTsYXZh55Yw26Qy2xncFs&hl=en&ei=Bh71Sc6kKZagMsrrkK0P&sa=X&oi=book_result&ct=result&resnum=3#PPA1,M1

Ivuka Arts Kigali. http://www.ivukaarts.com/index.php

Julius O. Adekunle, "Culture and Customs of Rwanda." http://books.google.com/books?id=g0FC40EQujwC&pg=PA81&lpg=PA81&dq=rwanda+cuisine&source=bl&ots=F2-0pxiUCA&sig=U06dxMmD5MqSjSBCBwrs_m0NFRU&hl=en&ei=67f0SZHHO5jMMqCVucAP&sa=X&oi=book_result&ct=result&resnum=9#PPR1,M1

The clock tower of Victoria, also known as "Little Big Ben," Seychelles.

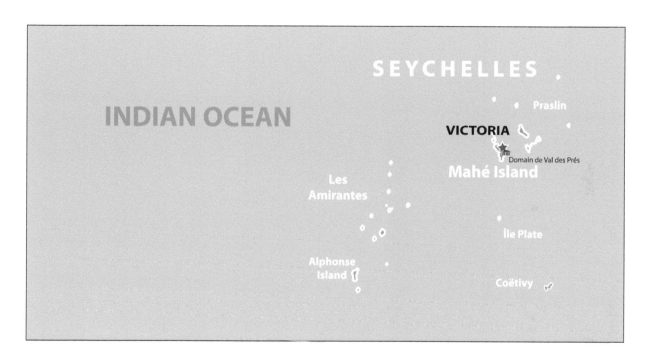

SEYCHELLES

Introduction

The Republic of Seychelles is a group of 115 small islands in the Indian Ocean, northeast of Madagascar, off the coast of Eastern Africa. It achieved independence from the United Kingdom on June 29, 1976. Once home to French privateers, escaped African slaves, and Asian traders, it has a racially mixed population and a rich cultural heritage, with its main languages being French, Seychellois Creole, and English. Its main industry is tourism, due to the islands' beautiful natural setting. However, it is transitioning to greater reliance on farming, fishing, and small-scale manufacturing in order not to become too fiscally dependent upon tourism. The Seychellois are active in environmental conservation efforts.

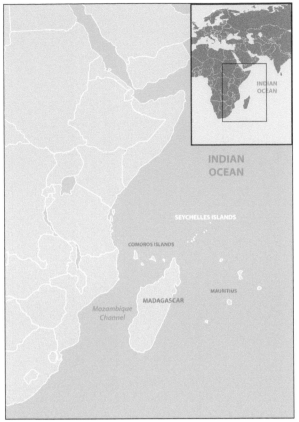

GENERAL INFORMATION

Official Language: French, English, Seychellois Creole (Seselwa Kreol)
Population: 92,430 (2015 estimate)
Currency: Seychelles rupee (also, Seselwa roupi)
Coins: There are 100 cents to one Seychelles rupee. Coins are available in denominations of 1, 5, 10 and 25 cents, and 1 and 5 rupees.
Land Area: 455 square kilometers (175 square miles)
National Anthem: "Koste Seselwa" ("Come Together Seychellois")
National Motto: "Finis Coronat Opus" ("The End Crowns the Work")
Capital: Victoria, on Mahé (also, Port Victoria)
Time Zone: GMT +4

Flag Description: The flag of Seychelles, adopted in January 1996, consists of five triangular bands of color that radiate outward like light rays from the lower hoist-side (left-hand) corner. These colored bands are, from left to right: royal blue (sky and sea), lemon yellow (sun), bright red (harmony), white (justice), and kelly green (lush terrain).

Population

Victoria is the capital and only city of the Seychelles. Almost all of the 92,430 Seychellois live in and around Victoria on the island of Mahé. The other two islands of note are Praslin and La Digue, with populations of 6,500 and 2,000, respectively (2015). About 85 percent of the population lives along the coasts. The remaining 115 islands are sparsely populated or uninhabited.

Citizens of Republic of Seychelles are called Seychellois. The average life expectancy in

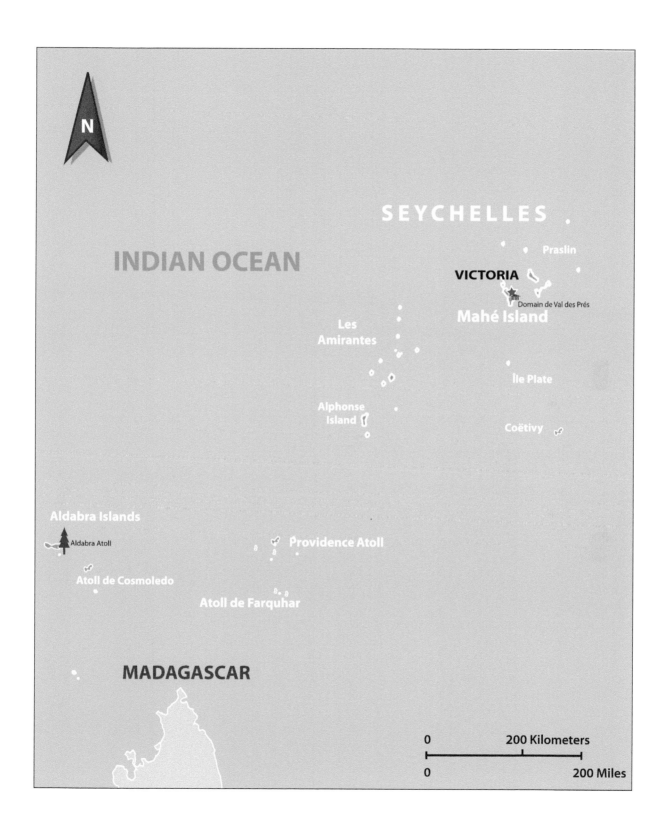

Principal Cities by Population (2012):

- Victoria (26,450)

Seychelles is 74 years, 70 for males, and 79 for females (2015 estimate). The island nation has no indigenous population.

Languages

The Seychellois Creole (or Seselwa Kreol) language is spoken by 89.1 percent of the population and developed from the French dialects spoken by the original settlers. It retains a mostly French vocabulary with a few Malagasy, Bantu, English, and Hindi words, and its grammar is a mixture of Bantu and French. The Kreol Institute has helped the government by developing a dictionary of the creole language, which was finished in 1981. The Seychellois Creole spoken in Seychelles is very similar to Mauritius Creole and Chagossian Creole. English (5.1 percent) and French (0.7 percent) are also official languages.

Native People & Ethnic Groups

The French settlers were the first inhabitants of the islands, arriving in the 18th century, but they were greatly outnumbered by the African slaves they brought with them. When slavery was abolished in 1834, many of the French slave owners left, taking their slaves with them.

New settlers arrived in very different circumstances. The British navy freed captured Africans from slave ships off the East African coast, and released them on Seychelles. In addition, small numbers of Asians also migrated to the islands. Intermarriage among the groups was common, and today few Seychellois families are of unmixed descent.

Ethnically, the Seychellois mostly are Creole, of mixed African, Asian, and European descent. Creole comprise more than 90 percent of the total population. British account for 3 percent, and French less than two percent. There are small Chinese (1.1 percent), Indian, Tamil, and Arab minorities, as well.

Religions

Most Seychellois (more than 76 percent) profess the Roman Catholic faith. More than six percent of the population is Anglican, while 1.5 percent is Pentecostal Assembly and 1.2 percent is Seventh-Day Adventist. Hinduism (2.4 percent) and Islam (1.6 percent) are practiced by a small percentage of the population.

Climate

Seychelles has a tropical marine climate. The weather is generally quite humid, often with 80 percent humidity, but with cool ocean breezes. The average temperature is between 24° and 32° Celsius (75° and 90° Fahrenheit).

The weather is cooler during the southeast monsoon season, from late May to September, and warmer during the northwest monsoon season, between March and May. Annual rainfall averages 2,213 millimeters (87 inches) at sea level in Mahé, and less on other islands.

Most of the islands lie outside the Indian Ocean cyclone belt, and until 2013, the islands' only recorded cyclone struck Mahé in 1862. However, in January 2013, a state of emergency was declared after Tropical Cyclone Felleng hit Mahé, Praslin, and La Digue, leading to the destruction of 150 homes. Pointe Au Sel received 184 mm of rain—a month's worth of precipitation—within a twenty-four-hour period.

ENVIRONMENT & GEOGRAPHY

Topography

The 115-island archipelago includes 43 Inner Islands—41 made of granitic rock and two of coral—and 72 coralline Outer Islands. The Mahé Group is comprised of granitic islands with narrow coastal strips, characterized by rocky hills and mountains that rise straight up from the sea. These islands are the peaks of the underwater Mascarene Plateau.

The highest point in Seychelles is Morne Seychellois, on Mahé, at 905 meters (2,969 feet). Other island groups include: the Amirantes Group; the Southern Coral Group (Île Platte and

Coëtivy Island); the Alphonse Group (Alphonse Atoll and St. François Atoll); the Farquhar Group (Farquhar Atoll, Providence Atoll, and St. Pierre Island); the Aldabra Group (Aldabra Atoll and Assumption Island); and the Cosmoledo Group (Cosmoledo Atoll and Astove Island).

Mahé, the largest island, is 25 kilometers (15.53 miles) long and 8 kilometers (4.97 miles) across at its widest point. Victoria, the island's only city and the capital of Seychelles, is an important port. Approximately 99 percent of the population lives on the granitic islands, with the majority (88 percent) living on Mahé.

The coralline islands are strung over a 1,200-kilometer (746-mile) radius from Île aux Vaches in the northeast to the Aldabra Atoll in the southwest. Unlike the granitic islands, the coralline islands are very flat, often only a few feet above sea level.

Plants & Animals

There are more than 1,170 varieties of flowering plants in Seychelles, along with many kinds of birds, mammals, reptiles, and insects. The islands are home to more than 100 species not found anywhere else in the world.

The waters surrounding the archipelago contain more than 900 types of fish, many of which live in the coral reefs. Unique birds found in Seychelles include the black paradise flycatcher, the black parrot, the brush warbler, and the flightless rail. Giant tortoises, as well as green turtles and hawksbill turtles, are found on many of the islands.

Common trees found on the islands include coconut palms, from which copra is harvested, and cinnamon trees. In keeping with the country's conservation efforts, the International Council for Bird Protection has established a bird sanctuary on Cousin Island, and there is a wildlife sanctuary in the Aldabra Atoll, which is home to 152,000 giant tortoises, the world's largest population. The Aldabra Atoll and its protected lagoon were inscribed as a UNESCO World Heritage Site in 1982. Off the east coast of Mahé, the Ste. Anne, Cerf, Île Cachée, Round, Long, and Moyenne islands form the Sainte Anne Marine National Park.

CUSTOMS & COURTESIES

Greetings

Seychellois culture is relaxed and easygoing, and greetings are generally informal and simple. When greeting, shaking hands is common, and close friends and family often kiss each other upon the cheek. Children are expected to present adults with a kiss on the cheek in greeting.

The three official languages of the Seychelles are English, French, and Seychellois Creole. Seychellois Creole is based primarily on 17th-century French, but also incorporates Malagasy, Bantu, English, and Hindi dialect. Local Creole, or Kreol Seselwa, is generally used for ordinary conversation, but English is the language of business and government. (Many Seychellois also speak German or Italian fluently.) Common greetings include "Bonzour" ("Hello") and "Ki dir?" or "Konman sava?" ("How are you?").

Gestures & Etiquette

The Seychellois are friendly and open, with few social restrictions; shyness should not be taken for aloofness. Personal space is not emphasized, and people commonly create less than an arm's length of distance between themselves. Touching is frequent during conversations to show engagement. People in the Seychelles speak directly, and eye contact is expected and appreciated. In addition, time is not as strict, and people are relaxed about punctuality. In general, the Seychellois are generous with their time.

The thumbs-up sign is a common way to express appreciation or satisfaction and is even employed when greeting others. When pointing at something, the Seychellois typically point with one finger.

Relations between men and women are conservative, and public displays of affection are not commonly seen in the Seychelles. While certain public affection is tolerated, anything beyond hand-holding will usually attract attention. The Seychellois usually have a relaxed dress code, in which a tie is rarely required. The one occasion for which all Seychellois don their finest is to attend church. While the dress code is relaxed in the Seychelles, it is not usually appropriate to wear bathing suits in public when not at the beach.

Eating/Meals

Seychellois eating habits vary widely. A few characteristics that many Seychellois share, however, are that breakfasts tend to be quick and casual, weekday lunches are also informal, while dinners tend to be quite formal. Breakfast is influenced by the French, and often consists of a croissant, bread and cheese, or eggs and meat (typically ham or bacon). For lunch and dinner, the most common meal is curry and rice. Coconut milk is often used in preparing the curries, and the wealthier Seychellois will include both fish and meat in their meals.

Dinner is a serious affair, for which people tend to dress nicely. Dressing in beachwear or sloppy attire implies to the host that one does not value their invitation and company. Aside from dressing well, proper table manners are expected. It is rude to pick at one's food, and one should never mix the foods together. Talking with one's mouth full is also considered disrespectful.

Snacks are common between lunch and dinner and are referred to as gajacks. Gajacks may also be served with pre-dinner drinks. On the weekends, lunches are more formal and are often occasion for families and friends to gather and catch up on the week. Restaurants will often even offer special weekend lunch menus.

Visiting

The Seychellois are very friendly and will often invite people over to their homes. Guests will often present a small gift for the host when they arrive. The Seychellois are also very fond of singing and may perform for each other casually when socializing. It is common to congregate on verandas, and leisurely games such as checkers, dominoes, and card games are popular.

While it is no longer necessary or important to be able to connect oneself to French roots as it was in the mid-1900s, skin color

and ethnicity remain indicators of status in the Seychelles. People tend to socialize primarily within their own set. The Seychellois terms for skin colors include ble (blue) and bla-rose (white-pink), which correlate with an obsolete class system that ranges from plantation worker to landowner. This is changing somewhat among younger Seychellois, but skin color remains a status symbol and continues to contribute to social stratification.

LIFESTYLE

Family

It is common in the Seychelles to live *en ménage*, or "in household," where a family may live together, but not be legally bound by traditional marriage. The mother is usually the center of the family unit, and is in charge of finances and child rearing. Children born out of wedlock will often recognize their fathers, and fathers will legally recognize and are bound by law to support their children financially. The Catholic Church, the dominant religious body, and the Seychellois government officially do not support unmarried couples living together, but these relationships and family units tend to be stable and have not resulted in negative social repercussions.

Housing

Many traditional homes are built on stilts, and coconut palm leaves are woven together to make cooling walls and roofs. Kitchens tend to be either outside or in separate buildings. Though living quarters are designed with sleeping quarters and communal space areas, most common areas are infrequently used, as the Seychellois prefer to spend their time outdoors. Because of the mild year-round weather, many buildings have large verandas; some even wrap entirely around the building.

Living rooms are often richly decorated and have many intricate carvings, and most of the furniture is made of wood featuring carved designs. Wood was once the most common building material, used both for exterior log façades and interior wood panels, but corrugated iron panels and concrete have become more popular as an inexpensive, durable, and easier building alternative.

Food

Seychellois cuisine is influenced by Chinese, Indian, and French culinary traditions, with distinct indigenous, or Seychellois Creole, roots. Typical Seychellois ingredients include fish, rice, coconut, breadfruit (a starchy, ovoid-shaped fruit with prickly outer skin), chilies, spices, and mangoes. Because Seychelles is an archipelagic nation, seafood is a dominant staple. Seafood is served in a variety of ways, and turtle meat was called "Seychelles beef" before authorities clamped down on turtle hunting. Although endangered by overfishing, bourzwa (red snapper) continues to be the most popular fish, and kordonnyen, a spiky trapfish, is common. Kari zourit is a creamy octopus curry dish prepared with coconut milk. A Seychellois favorite is "fisherman-style" rice and salted fish that is served in a banana leaf. Other specialties include a myriad of soups, satini rekin (dried shark chutney), and smoked fruit bat or sailfish.

Traditional dishes include soupe de tectec, a soup made with small white shellfish and pumpkin or, alternately, clams cooked with tomatoes, garlic, and ginger; poisson sale, salted dried fish; bouillon brèdes, which is spinach soup; and poisson grille, which is grilled fish marinated in onions, garlic, chilies, and ginger. A popular salad is the salade de palmiste, which uses thin, sliced rings of the heart of the cabbage palm tree. It is colloquially known as a "millionaire's salad" because the entire tree has to be cut down for a palm heart to be removed, and consequently, the trees are in decline due to over-harvesting. Popular Seychellois sauces include daube, a sweet sauce generally made from plantain, cinnamon, and coconut milk; rougaille, a tomato-based sauce; and cari coco, a mild coconut curry. A typical dessert would be a French pastry; an Indian sweet, like rasgulla (sweetened cottage cheese and semolina dumplings cooked in spiced sugar syrup); fresh fruit, or mousse.

Palm wine or calou, which is made from fermented sap taken from coconut palm leaves, is a popular Seychellois drink. Strong sugarcane liquor called bacca is often consumed during ceremonial events. While there is no specific meal or food eaten for ceremonies in the Seychelles, some kind of meat will usually be served.

Life's Milestones

There are three main religions in Seychelles: Hinduism, Christianity, and Islam. Roman Catholicism is the most influential sect, accounting for an estimated 76.2 percent in 2010. As such, many of the milestones observed in Seychellois culture are rooted in Catholicism, and include baptism, weddings, and funerary traditions.

Weddings in the Seychelles are traditionally large and joyous affairs, full of dancing, music, and singing. Weddings and funerals in the Seychelles are also often causes for lavish spending. Usually, the families of both the bride and the groom contribute financially to a wedding. Because of the many costly traditions, those who do choose to marry will often have a long engagement, ranging from six months to three years, to accumulate the necessary funding. This tradition of having a lavish wedding is also a large part of why living en ménage has become commonplace.

On the island of Mahé, three rounds of bell ringing, while simple funerals may have a single bell rung eleven times, mark expensive funerals. In either case, there will also be singing, organ music, and a sermon.

CULTURAL HISTORY

Art

Seychellois arts are a testimonial to the nation's pride. Regardless of ethnic origin, whether European, African, or Asian, almost all Seychellois will claim their Seychellois heritage first. Today, common themes in Seychellois art and literature include liberty, unity, and equality.

For example, once Seychellois Creole became one of the nation's official languages—the others being French and English—writing began to flourish. Antoine Abel (1934–2004) is considered the "father of Seychellois literature" and was the first Seychellois writer to bring its Creole culture to the rest of the world. He has written short stories and poetry, ranging from the lighthearted to the political and heavily emotional. He is best known for his stories of Soungoula, a mischievous combination of hero and villain who always comes through in the end. The Festival Kreol de Seychelles awards the Prix Antoine Abel each year to pay tribute to his work. In 2008, a Seychelles writers association called Lardwaz launched, established to nurture the growth of Seychelles literature. The non-governmental organization Lardwaz continues to foster a literary culture in Seychelles by hosting public readings and lectures, sometimes in conjunction with other organizations, like the Association for Media Practitioners Seychelles.

Musically, the Seychellois habit of incorporating other cultures into their own and embracing the hybrid is easily seen in seggae, a combination of reggae and local sega music. Jean-Marc Volcy (1966–) is one of the most popular musicians in the Seychelles, and his seggae music adds his own social commentary to popular themes, such as love and relationships. Volcy has been a chart-topping musician in Seychelles for decades and won the African Music Prize in 2000.

The fine arts such as painting and sculpture continue to flourish in the Seychelles. Well-known artists include Michael Adams (1937–), whose vivid paintings depict the island's beauty, and expatriate sculptor Tom Bowers (1936–), who works in bronze. Many other crafts and folk arts continue to be practiced as well, including stained glass, crafts made from coconut shells and husks, art works feature coral and seashells, and jewelry featuring pearl, wood, silver, and gold.

Every October, the Seychelles host the Creole Festival (or Festival Kreol), where artists of all kinds come together to highlight their work in Seychellois music, dance, art, fashion, performance, cuisine, and crafts. Visual artists use the natural beauty of the Seychelles in their work, and handicrafts are often nature-inspired as well. Tourists are often the consumers of Seychellois art, and local artists have become adept at using everything from watercolors and oils to metals and wood to seashells and coconut shells to create a wide variety of artistic souvenir options.

Architecture

Much of the architecture in the Seychelles derives from the influence of the country's French colonial past, often seen in lavish plantation homes or townhouses. These stately and historic houses are defined by characteristics such as a central courtyard, or lakou, decorative interior details, and winding stairs. Victorian architecture is also frequently seen in the townhouses, but they usually have thick iron roofs. Most buildings have pointed roofs to better weather the rain. Verandas are another popular architectural element, and traditional houses feature outdoor kitchens. Both are elements that have been adapted for tropical living. Another feature of architecture in Seychelles is the use of bright colors in both private and commercial property.

Music

Music of the Seychelles is as multicultural as its people, with African, Chinese, Arabic and European influences. Popular musical instruments include the stringed zeze from Madagascar; the East African kaskavel, similar to a rattle; the European accordion; and the banjo, which was derived from African stringed instruments and popularized by slaves in America. More recently, the violin and guitar have been incorporated into popular and traditional music. Choirs are plentiful and musical styles range from gospel, jazz, and hip-hop to reggae, country, and rock and roll. Recently, reggae and sega dance music have mixed to form the popular seggae, while moutia dance music and reggae have mixed to form mouggae.

Dance

Dance and music are central to Seychellois life, and both are influenced by African, Malagasy, and European culture. The two most popular dances in the Seychelles are the moutia and the sega. The moutia, an old tradition dating back to the days of slavery, is a combination of storytelling, singing, and movement. Often, two men begin the performance by exchanging stories of hard work, followed by women who dance and sing. Modern moutia uses traditional African rhythms, and the performers are usually skilled and respected. The dancing of the moutia was considered by the authorities to be too erotic and was banned during the colonial period, but has since become commonplace.

The sega, usually accompanied by guitars and drums, is a lively and elegant dance characterized by swaying hips and shuffling feet. It is accompanied by sega music, a blend of sounds indigenous to the Indian Ocean island culture yet similar to European dance music. Other popular dances include the kanmtole, which resembles the Scottish reel and is usually accompanied by the accordion, banjo, triangle, and violin. The contredanse is similar to the quadrille (precursor to square dancing) and comes from the French royal court of the 18th and 19th centuries, and is usually accompanied by the banjo and triangle. The sokoué dance is similar to dances seen in many other African countries, and involves dancing with masks and representing elements of nature, such as trees or birds.

Drama

Seychellois theater began to take shape in the mid-1900s, and its earliest incarnations were full of social messages. Dolfin César's (1928–) *Carolin et Carola* told the story of a woman who was punished for being unfaithful and was abandoned in the forest. After the Seychelles gained its independence in 1976, themes of the struggle for independence became popular. Two of the most celebrated are Marie-Thérèse Choppy's *Lalit en Pep* (*Struggle of a People*) and Patrick Victor's musical play *Kastor*. Marie-Thérèse Choppy later became the director-general of culture for the Seychelles.

Freedom of expression was more closely monitored in the Seychelles post-independence.

Since the 1990s, however, dramatists have been free to explore any and all social issues, including formerly taboo subject matter, like sexuality. Over time, as boundaries were pushed and Seychellois Creole performances became more popular, theater in the Seychelles truly became accessible to all. There is now one state-funded theater, the National Theater in Victoria, as well as three privately funded theaters. Christian Servina (1963–) is a modern playwright and director who pushes the envelope in dealing with political, sexual, and social issues in works like *Solisyon fatal* (*Fatal Solution*) and *Lo stenn* (*The Bus Station*).

Literature

Seychellois storytelling was a mostly oral tradition until very recently, and more written work is being produced in the Seychelles now than ever before. Many Seychellois stories and fables are both entertaining and enlightening. They are often about buried treasure (pirates are said to have used the islands frequently), ghosts, and other legends, or are didactic in nature. For example, comedy is often used to teach young and old alike how to live properly. Many fables are told about a character named Soungoula, a mischievous and clever hare that uses cunning to escape stronger—though often less intelligent—adversaries. These trickster tales borrow from African oral traditions (the trickster archetype is also present in Caribbean and American folklore).

The first literary work in Seychellois Creole was a translation of forty-nine fables by Jean de La Fontaine (1621–1695) by Rodolphine Young (1860–1932) in 1900; these were finally published in 1983. The first creole novel, *Fler Flétri* by Leu Mancienne (1958–), was published in 1985. Poetry and shorter fiction has been the preferred literary form in the Seychelles, and the Creole Institute has published many novellas and collections of poetry and short stories. Seychellois Creole is the most common language of Seychellois literature, though French is the language employed for writers seeking an international audience.

CULTURE

Arts & Entertainment

There is a single theater in Victoria, called Deepam Cinema, where films are shown and local plays are performed in Creole, French, or English. Victoria also boasts several museums, along with the National Library and the National Archives.

Traditional dances performed in Seychelles include the sega, a hip-swaying dance accompanied by guitars and drums; and the moutia, a traditional African dance accompanied by large drums made from goatskin. Contre is an imported dance from France, and kanmtole is similar to a Scottish reel. Seychellois groups such as the Waves and the Nouvelles Seychelles have recorded popular albums of Seychellois Creole music.

The Festival Kreol is held in Seychelles each year on October 28 (International Creole Day). The festival, filled with music, dance, and food, began as a way to increase awareness of Creole languages and culture.

The annual Seychelles International Underwater Festival is also held in October. Though this festival is meant to attract tourists, especially diving enthusiasts, it also aims to make the locals more aware of the importance of the marine life in Seychelles.

The most popular sport in Seychelles is football (soccer). The national stadium, Stade Linité, on the outskirts of Victoria, seats 10,000.

Cultural Sites & Landmarks

The Seychelles is home to two United Nations Educational, Scientific, and Cultural Organization (UNESCO) World Heritage Sites. The Aldabra Atoll was inscribed in 1982, and the Vallée de Mai Nature Reserve was inscribed in 1983. The Aldabra Atoll is the largest raised coral atoll on earth, comprised of four islands forming a rectangular oval around a shallow lagoon. Because of its remote location in the Indian Ocean—1,150 kilometers (714 miles) southwest of the island of Mahé, the largest island of the Seychelles, and 420 kilometers (260 miles) north of Madagascar—the

Aldabra Atoll has been left largely untouched. The atoll is home to many endangered species, including the world's largest population of giant tortoises, the largest number of nesting green turtles in the Indian Ocean, and the white-throated flightless rail (the last flightless bird species in the Indian Ocean).

Spanning 18 hectares (44 acres), the Vallée de Mai Nature Reserve is the smallest forest designated as a World Heritage Site. It is located on the second-largest island of Praslin. The Vallée de Mai resembles a natural primeval palm forest and is one of two places in the world—the other being the island of Curieuse, also in the Seychelles—where the endemic and rare coco de mer palm tree grows naturally. The coco de mer was once believed to grow deep in the ocean, and legend says it was the Tree of Knowledge in the Garden of Eden and has magical properties. It is considered a cultural icon of the Seychelles. Like the Aldabra Atoll, the Vallée de Mai Nature Reserve is also home to several self-sustaining endemic species of plants and animals, such as the Seychelles black parrot and the Pachypanchax playfairii, a freshwater fish.

The Seychelles also claims three national heritage sites: Patrimwann, of which Domaine de Val des Près is a part, and L'Union Estate. "Patrimwann" is a creole word that means "heritage trail." It encompasses several organizations that embrace the Seychellois Creole culture: the Creole Institute (sometimes the Kreol Institute), the Domaine de Val des Près, La Bastille, and the Ecomusée La Planie St. Andre (or simply the Ecomuseum).

Domaine de Val des Près is a craft village highlighting the Seychellois Creole culture, located on Mahé. Highlights include the Grann Kaz plantation house, dating back to approximately 1870, and the 20th-century working-class home La Kaz Rosa, which highlights traditional architecture. The Maison de Coco is a house built from and filled with coconut products, and the Vye Marmit is a restaurant serving traditional creole cuisine. There are also several craft ateliers, or workshops, displaying local arts and crafts.

L'Union Estate is a former coconut plantation located on the island of La Digue, where visitors can watch locals extract oil from copra (dried coconut flesh). The island is also home to one of the most photographed beaches in the world, the Anse Source d'Argent, famous for its pink and grey granite rocks, white sand, and calm turquoise water.

Libraries & Museums

The Seychelles' National Museum of History is a small museum in Victoria that consists of a single gallery. Among its collection are the Stone of Possession, which signified French control of the islands in 1756, as well as Creole furniture and traditional garb and instruments, among other historical artifacts. The National History Museum, also located in Victoria, is said to contain the world's heaviest nut.

The National Library of the Seychelles is located on the island of Mahé. A preceding library, the Carnegie Library, opened in 1910, and was changed to the National Library of the Seychelles in 1978, moving to a new facility the following year. (The library moved again in 1994.) An official logo and website for the national library was unveiled in 2004. There are several branch libraries.

Holidays

Government holidays observed in Seychelles include Liberation Day (June 5), Constitution Day (June 18), and National Day (June 29).

Youth Culture

Seychellois youth are often said to embody the easygoing attitude that pervades the archipelagic nation. Common recreational pursuits include dancing, and when dating, both girls and boys are equally forward. Youth are permitted to consume alcohol at 18 years of age.

From 1981 to 1998, Seychellois youth were required to participate in National Youth Service (NYS), a training program in which post-secondary students learned how to grow and prepare their own food, how to clean and keep a house properly, and how to care for animals, including

livestock. One of the goals was to keep young people from being unemployed. However, the program became controversial due to its socialist ideals and the fact that the Seychelles People's Progressive Front (SPPF) political party was at the program's core.

SOCIETY

Transportation

Roads in the Seychelles are generally well maintained, but narrow and winding, with few shoulders for pulling over. Taxis are available on the main islands but are generally expensive. Buses are the most popular means of transportation, especially on the island of Mahé. There are an estimated 176 motor vehicles per 1000 people in the Seychelles, making it the seventy-eighth country in the world for the number of vehicles per person. There are no private cars on the small island of La Digue, so locals and visitors alike often walk for short distances or use bicycles for slightly longer distances.

Traffic travels on the left side of the road.

Transportation Infrastructure

There are no railroads in Seychelles, and less than 300 miles of roads. There are fifteen airports, and Air Seychelles is the national airline. There is direct service between islands through small aircraft or ferries. Victoria serves as both the main port and main terminal. A transportation infrastructure project, funded through the World Bank was begun in 2007 and completed on June 30, 2011 at a cost of $2.11 million (USD). The project improved ports, waterways, and shipping infrastructure.

Media & Communications

The Seychellois government controls most media outlets, but freedom of speech has improved dramatically since the one-party system was overthrown in 1993. Despite tough libel laws, reporters for both private and opposition newspapers have been relatively open in their coverage, although harassment of journalists does in fact occur (see "Human Rights," below). *Seychelles Nation* is the state-run and only daily newspaper, *The People* is the weekly paper from the ruling political party, and *Le Nouveau Seychelles Weekly* and *Regar* are weekly newspapers supplied by the opposition parties.

Seychelles Broadcasting Corporation (SBC), also run by the government, owns both AM and FM radio stations. SBC-TV is the main television station provided by the government, but additional cable and satellite television stations are also available. There are four radio stations and 11 television channels, but satellite is offering a multitude of international entertainment options.

In 2007, there were 22,700 land-based telephone lines, and, as of 2014, there were an estimated 1,049 cell phones for every 1,000 people. Wireless broadband and 4G coverage became available in November 2014. While in 2008 there were 284 internet hosts, in 2012, Internet users comprised approximately 47 percent of the population. In addition, in 2014, Seychelles was ranked 72nd out of 197 countries for internet speed, the highest of all African countries. In May of 2014, available speed jumped from 2.92 Mbps to 11.32 Mbps, just below the global average of 18.52 Mbps.

SOCIAL DEVELOPMENT

Standard of Living

Seychelles is classified as a country with "high human development" by the United Nations (UN). In 2014, Seychelles ranked 71 out of 187 countries on the UN Human Development Index, which measures quality of life indicators.

Water Consumption

An estimated 95.7 percent of the Seychelles population has access to potable water. As of 2014, water demand was increasing at an annual rate of 8 to 10 percent. Groundwater sources throughout the island nation are limited, and rainwater is needed to ensure an adequate water supply. As of the early 21st century, there were four desalination plants: two on Mahé Island

(Providence, producing 5,000kl/day; Anse Boileau producing 2,500 kl/day) and one each on Praslin Island (600 kl/day) and La Digue Island (300 kl/day). The Indian Ocean Tuna Factory has its own desalination plant. As part of a water supply development plan, the Seychelles Public Utilities Corporation (PUC) plans to make water universally available and affordable throughout the island nation by 2030.

Education

The first schools opened in 1851. These were Catholic and Anglican mission schools, but in 1944, the government took over the administration of education, which has been free and compulsory for children between the ages of five and 16 since 1981. Students are taught to read and write in Creole first. In third grade, English is introduced, followed by French in sixth grade. As of 2012, the literacy rate for males aged 15 or older was reported as 91.4 percent. For females over 15, the literacy rate was slightly higher at 92.3 percent.

Participation in the government work program known as National Youth Service (NYS) was once mandatory for students wishing to attend The Seychelles Polytechnic. Since 1993, however, this unpopular prerequisite has not been necessary. Most students in Seychelles attend college for teacher training. Other courses offered include business studies, humanities and science, and hotels and tourism. Post-secondary institutions include the National College of the Arts, the Seychelles Tourism Academy, the National Institute for Health and Social Studies, the Farmers Training Centre, and the Maritime Training Centre.

The undergraduate University of Seychelles–American Institute of Medicine is based in Victoria. It is listed among the medical institutions approved by the World Health Organization (WHO).

Women's Rights

The Seychellois are a matriarchal society, and women hold power both in the nuclear family unit as well as in government and business. Women run many businesses and are generally empowered and free to do as they please. While there are no laws or cultural rules prohibiting women from any specific industries, women tend to avoid certain fields, such as fishing. In most other areas, men and women are represented fairly equally. In addition, women account for slightly more than half of the students at Seychelles Polytechnic, which represents the highest level of education available on the islands.

While the Seychelles is a strongly Catholic country with conservative views, sexuality is open and accepted. While consensual unions are common, marriage is not expected or desirable for many Seychellois. For those that do choose to marry, divorces are common. Over half of the pregnancies in the Seychelles are among women who are unmarried; many are girls under 20 years old. Girls are not allowed to attend school while pregnant, and many choose not to return to school once they have children.

Plantation living evolved into a sophisticated childcare system seen in all classes in which firstborn children were given to a maternal grandmother or aunt. Young women who gave their children to others to raise were later given other children to care for, from younger sisters or daughters. With women having fewer children, this fostering system is less common, and women usually care for their own children. Rape and domestic abuse are criminal offenses punishable by twenty years of imprisonment, but officials tend not to be as severe as they could be. Marital rape is also a recognized criminal act. However, since 2008, police officers generally have not pushed to arrest perpetrators unless a weapon was used and, once convicted, they were often given light sentences.

In 2005, along with fourteen other nations of the African Union, Seychelles ratified the Protocol to the African Charter on Human and Peoples' Rights on the Rights of Women in Africa, or more casually known as the Maputo Protocol. The protocol to the African Charter on Human and People's Rights (ACHPR) was designed to empower African women politically, give them equal rights as men, stop female genital mutilation (FGM), and allow them control over their reproductive rights and health.

Health Care

Malnutrition, poverty, and polluted water are the primary causes of poor health in many Seychellois children. Intestinal parasites and recurrent dengue fever outbreaks are also widely reported. Alcoholism and drug abuse have become major health issues.

Efforts to stop the spread of HIV/AIDS have so far been unsuccessful. In November 1992, the first case of acquired immune deficiency syndrome (AIDS) was confirmed; 20 people had tested positive for HIV in 1991. Reported cases of AIDS have been increasing in recent years, with more than 130 cases in 2001.

Medical treatment is free for all Seychellois. The largest medical institution is Victoria Hospital, on the main island of Mahé. There are other smaller hospitals and clinics on Mahé, and outpatient clinics on the main islands of Mahé, Praslin, and La Digue. Doctors and dentists usually come from other countries. In 2013, the country spent 4 percent of its GDP on health care. It also has 3.6 hospital beds and just over 1 physician for every 1,000 people.

GOVERNMENT

Structure

Today, the Republic of Seychelles is governed by a president who is both the chief of state and head of government. The president is elected by popular vote to a five-year term. The president appoints a Council of Ministers as the executive cabinet.

The legislative branch of government consists of the unicameral National Assembly, whose members serve five-year terms. Of the assembly's 34 seats, 25 are elected by popular vote, and nine are assigned on a proportional basis. The islands are divided into 25 administrative districts.

At first, Seychelles was governed under a single-party socialist system. Following several coup attempts during the 1980s, and because of pressure from foreign nations on whom the country was dependent for aid, a multi-party system was re-established in the early 1990s. Multiparty elections were first held in July 1993, after the approval of a new constitution a year earlier. Nevertheless, candidates from the People's Party (PL), formerly known as the Seychelles' People's Progressive Front (SPPF), have won both the presidency and the majority of the seats in the National Assembly in every election since 1993.

Political Parties

Politically, Seychelles has largely functioned as a two-party system, with the two dominant parties being the one-time Seychelles National Party (SNP)—which has been restructured to become the Popular Democratic Movement—and the socialist People's Party (PL), known as the Seychelles People's Progressive Front (SPPF) until 2009. In the 2011 parliamentary elections, PL secured 25 out of the 34 National Assembly seats and nearly 89 percent of the popular vote. The remaining seats are determined by proportional representation, and PL took six of these seats, bringing their total to 31 seats. Other political parties have achieved little to no success.

Local Government

The islands are divided into 25 administrative districts, and local government is state-appointed as opposed to being elected. The minister responsible for local governance oversees each municipal administration's activities. Local administrators serve under a two-year renewable contract.

Judicial System

The judicial branch includes the Court of Appeal and the Supreme Court. The president appoints judges to both courts. The legal system is based on English common law; French civil law, derived from Napoleonic codes; and customary law, all a result of the nation's colonial roots. France controlled Seychelles from the late 18th century until it ceded the islands to Britain in the 1814 Treaty of Paris. Seychelles finally obtained independence from Britain on June 29, 1976.

Taxation

The Seychelles has no personal income tax, but levies a corporate tax rate starting at 25 percent on the corporation's first million Seychelles rupees, and 30 percent on the remainder. Financial institutions, telecom companies, and alcohol manufacturers pay 33 percent on income in excess of one million Seychelles rupees. Other taxes include a 15 percent value added tax (VAT), which replaced the goods and services tax in January 2013.

Armed Forces

The armed forces of Seychelles consist of the Seychelles People's Defense Forces (SPDF), with paramilitary forces consisting of the Seychelles National Guard and the Coast Guard, which includes Naval Wing and Air Wing divisions. There is also the Seychelles Police Force and a presidential protection unit. In 2009, the Seychelles Armed Forces sought help from the Indian navy to help battle piracy in the region. In 2011 and 2013, India continued to provide troop support and equipment, including the furnishing of a Dornier 228 aircraft, outfitted with a thermal imaging sensor, surveillance radar, and satellite communications.

Foreign Policy

The Seychelles enjoys positive relations with its neighbors and the global community at large. As a member of the Non-Aligned Movement (NAM), it generally follows a principle of positive non-alignment, declining to align itself with any of the powerful nations or global regions. The Seychelles has supported reducing the superpower presence in the Indian Ocean in its push to have the Indian Ocean become a zone of peace. For example, the Seychellois have long advocated the removal of the American naval presence on Diego Garcia, an atoll in the British Chagos Archipelago, located about 3,057 kilometers (1,900 miles) northeast of Mahé. The United States Air Force had leased a parcel of land on Mahé for $4.5 million per year (USD) from the British.

The Seychelles has a record of supporting the more radical members of the Non-Aligned Movement, including Libya, Cuba, North Korea,

Iraq, and the former East Germany. However, tourism is such an important part of the country's economy that it never goes so far as to sever ties with any other nations. The Seychelles is a member of the United Nations (UN), the African Union (AU), International Monetary Fund (IMF), Indian Ocean Commission (IOC), Southern African Development Community (SADC), the Commonwealth of Nations, which is made up of former British colonies, and La Francophonie. In addition, on April 26, 2015, Seychelles became the 161st member of the World Trade Organization (WTO).

The Seychelles has an ambassador in New York who represents the island nation both in the UN and in foreign relations with the US and Canada. The US, in turn, has an ambassador who serves both Mauritius and Seychelles, but is located in Port Louis, Mauritius; the US has only a consular service in Seychelles at present. There is a Seychellois ambassador to France and Belgium and a corresponding embassy in Paris. In early 2007, the government announced plans for new diplomatic missions in South Africa, China, Italy, and India. Moreover, as of 2015, a high commissioner, representing the Seychellois people, is now stationed in Pretoria, South Africa, while India has established a high commission in Victoria and Seychelles now maintains a high commission in New Dehli. China, which now hosts a Seychelles embassy in Beijing, has been offered the opportunity by the Seychelles government to open a naval base intended to assist the archipelago in combatting piracy. Finally, Seychelles also participates in several international environmental pacts, especially in relation to biodiversity, climate change, desertification, endangered species, marine dumping, and ship pollution.

Human Rights Profile

International human rights law insists that states respect civil and political rights and promote an individual's economic, social, and cultural rights. The United Nations Universal Declaration on Human Rights (UDHR) is recognized as the standard for international human rights. Its authors sought the counsel of the world's great thinkers, philosophers, and religious leaders and were careful to create a document that reflects the core values shared by every world culture. (To read this document or view the articles relating to cultural human rights, visit http://www.ohchr.org/EN/UDHR/Pages/Introduction.aspx.)

The Seychelles generally has a positive human rights record and have ratified the African Charter on Human and Peoples' Rights (ACHPR). There were, however, a few cases of unlawful imprisonment and police brutality in 2008 and 2011. Moreover, as of 2013, prisons had not yet met international criteria due to sanitation and overcrowding issues. The Seychelles has also had problems upholding Article 19, which guarantees the right to freedom of opinion and expression without interference. In 2013, several opposition party members complained of having their emails, chatroom conversations, and blog posts monitored by the government. Others claimed they were harassed for posting comments critical of the government on social media. The U.S. State Department's Bureau of Democracy, Human Rights, and Labor cites the 2010 and 2012 arrests and detention of Michael Sabadin, site administrator for Gossip Corner Seychelles, after he posted similarly unfavorable website content.

The government owns nearly all of the main media outlets, including the local television and radio stations. While there are weekly newspapers that cautiously provide the perspective of the opposition parties, political parties and religious groups have traditionally been prohibited from obtaining radio licenses. Before 2013, steep licensing fees—approximately $185,000 (USD) annually—prevented many from voicing their opinions on broadcast radio. However, 2013 saw the reduction of these licensing fees, the launch of a private radio station, and the founding of a new print media outlet. Still, the watchdog group Freedom House ranks Seychelles as only "partially free" and has set the country's press freedom score at 52, with 100 reserved for the worst offenders. Often, journalists continue to practice self-censorship to avoid censure in the face of Seychelles' strict libel laws.

Political transitions have been smooth, even if a substantial portion of the population is unhappy with the results and claim Parti Lepep, formerly the Seychelles People's Progressive Front, exert undue control over political processes, government contracts, and municipal jobs. International election officials who observed the process in May 2011, when incumbent president James Michel was re-elected, have reported that it was conducted properly. When measuring life expectancy, education and literacy, and standard of living, the quality of life in the Seychelles was ranked in the UN Human Development Report (HDR) 71st out of 187 countries.

ECONOMY

Overview of the Economy

The economy of Seychelles has grown dramatically since independence in 1976. Most Seychellois depend on tourism and tuna fishing to make their living. However, since the country's 2008 default on interest payments related to a $230 million (USD) Eurobond, the government has made a number of significant reforms and is shifting their tourism-dependent economy to one with greater reliance on farming and small-scale manufacturing. In 2014, the gross domestic product (GDP) was estimated at $2.406 billion (USD), with a per capita GDP of $25,600 (USD).

Industry

Tourism is still the most important industry in Seychelles. Service industries accounted for 83.1 percent of the GDP in 2014, with industrial fishing, manufacturing, and construction making up the remainder. Manufacturing activity includes food processing (especially beverages), coir (coconut fiber) rope, boat building, printing, and furniture. Exports include canned tuna, frozen fish, petroleum products (as re-exports), copper bars, scrap iron, and fish oil.

Labor

The labor force was estimated at 39,560 in 2006, with 3 percent unemployment recorded in 2014.

Tourism is the primary source of employment in the Seychelles, occupying 30 percent of the labor force. As a whole, the services industry makes up 74 percent of the employed labor force, with industry and agriculture at about 23 percent and three percent, respectively.

Energy/Power/Natural Resources

As of 2011, electricity is generated entirely through fossil fuel consumption, and the country utilizes nearly 283 million kilowatts, while producing 304 million kilowatts. It neither imports nor exports electricity, but also has no hydroelectric, petroleum, or other renewable energy resources.

Many islands, such as Île aux Vaches, Île Denis, the Amirante Isles, Platte Island, and Coëtivy Island, are sand cays with large coconut plantations. Several islands are important breeding grounds for turtles and birds and were the sites of extensive guano deposits, now depleted. Tuna and other deep-sea fish are found in the surrounding waters.

Conservation problems include water pollution, caused by extensive import shipping and commercial tuna fishing. On Aldabra Island, goats are destroying much of the island's plant life, which the giant turtle population depends upon for food. A third problem is water shortages. Since rainwater collection, or catchment, is the source of most of the fresh water used in Seychelles, variations in rainfall or even short periods of little rain may result in serious water shortages. Small dams have been built on Mahé in an effort to guarantee a reliable water supply.

Conservation is important to the Seychellois. The Seychelles National Environment Commission oversees a system of national parks and animal preserves covering nearly half of the country's land area, as well as portions of the surrounding water. The country has also passed legislation to protect wildlife and outlaw environmentally dangerous practices.

Fishing

The fishing industry is overseen by the Seychelles Fishing Authority, part of the Seychelles Ministry of Environment, Natural Resources, and Transport. Fisheries employ 17 percent of the Seychelles population, and the sector is dominated by tuna fishing. Seychelles' only canning plant, Indian Ocean Tuna, Ltd, which is also one of the largest canning plant in the world, processes around 386 tons and 1.5 million cans of tuna daily and employs 2,300 people. Inland fisheries include The Prawn Farm on Coëtivy Island, The Pearl Oyster Farm on Praslin, and the nearby Giant Clam Farm, close to Praslin Airport. These, along with tuna, contribute $370 million USD annually to the Seychelles economy. As of 2014, foreign companies have begun paying licensing fees to trawl Seychelles' waters, providing the government with an additional revenue source.

Agriculture

Only 2.2 percent (about 988 acres) of land is arable on Seychelles' various islands, and just three percent of the total labor force works in agriculture. Seychellois farmers grow coconuts, cinnamon, vanilla, sweet potatoes, cassava (or tapioca), and bananas. Rice and grains do not grow well on the islands. Commercial agricultural companies produce mainly coconuts, cinnamon, and tea for export. Despite widespread home gardening and other subsistence farming, Seychelles' National Bureau of Statistics indicated that, in 2011, the country still imported 72 percent of its food, totaling $87.79 million. In in order to increase Seychelles' self-sufficiency, the government is currently developing the Seychelles National Agriculture Investment Plan (SNAIP), part of the Comprehensive Africa Agriculture Development Programme (CAADP).

Animal Husbandry

Pork and poultry production are the predominant livestock sectors, while some farms raise small numbers of goat and cattle. Many also keep chickens for both meat and eggs. Most livestock farms are specialized and commercial in nature. Increasing livestock production has been a growing issue, particularly in relation to food security in the island nation.

Tourism

Tourism has been the leading economic sector in Seychelles since 1975. However, world events, such as the 1991–92 Gulf War and the September 2001 terrorist attacks against the United States, have contributed to the volatility of the tourism sector.

Tourism-related businesses employ 30 percent of Seychelles' work force. In 2000, it was estimated that tourists spent $631 million (USD) in Seychelles. In addition, in 2013, 230,272 tourists visited the archipelago. Most of the country's visitors hail from Western Europe, particularly France, the UK, Germany, and Italy. The number of tourists from the United Arab Emirates is also steadily increasing.

In addition to the country's natural beauty, tourists are drawn to Seychelles' warm climate, unspoiled beaches, and stunning coral reefs. Popular attractions in Victoria include the La Digue Plantation Houses and the Botanical Gardens.

Jennifer Kan Martinez, Lois Bailey, M. Lee,
Savannah Schroll Guz

DO YOU KNOW?

- Seychelles is named after Viscount Jean Moreau de Séchelles, controller-general of finances and minister of state under France's King Louis XV.

- Seychellois are able to vote at the age of seventeen.

- During the Napoleonic Wars, the French surrendered Seychelles to the British numerous times. However, every time the British troops left the islands, the French pulled down the British flag and reinstated the French flag.

Bibliography

Carillet, Jean-Bernard. *Mauritius, Réunion & Seychelles*. London: Lonely Planet, 2014.

Carpin, Sarah & Paul Turcotte. *Seychelles*. Geneva, Switzerland: Editions Olizane, 2007.

Freedman, Maurice. *Social Organization: Essays Presented to Raymond Firth*. London, England: Routledge, 1967.

Gikandi, Simon. *Encyclopedia of African Literature*. London: Routledge, 2009.

Hawkins, Peter. *The Other Hybrid Archipelago: Introduction to the Literatures and Cultures of the Francophone Indian Ocean*. Rpt. Lanham, MD: Lexington Books, 2010. After the Empire: The Francophone World and Postcolonial France Ser.

Hughes, Alex & Keith Reader. *Encyclopedia of Contemporary French Culture*. London, England: Taylor & Francis, 2001.

Diakhaté, Ousmane; Hansel Ndumbe Eyoh; & Don Rubin, eds. *The World Encyclopedia of Contemporary Theatre: Africa*. Vol. 3. London, England: Routledge, 2015.

Metz, Helen Chapin. *Seychelles: A Country Study*. Washington: GPO for the Library of Congress, 1994.

Mancham, James. *Seychelles: The Saga of a Small Nation Navigating the Cross-Currents of a Big World*. St. Paul, MN: Paragon House, 2015.

Speake, Jennifer, ed. *Literature of Travel and Exploration: An Encyclopedia*. 2nd ed. London: Routledge, 2003.

Tingay, Paul. *Seychelles*. 6th ed. London: New Holland Publishers, 2015. Globetrotter Travel Packs Ser.

Works Cited

"2008 Country Reports on Human Rights Practices – Seychelles." U.S. Department of State. Refworld. *UN Refugee Agency*, 25 Jun. 2015. http://www.refworld.org/country,COI,,,SYC,,559bd53f12,0.html.

"2014 Human Development Report." United Nations Development Programme. *United Nations*, 2014. http://www.undp.org/content/undp/en/home/presscenter/events/2014/july/HDR2014.html.

"2014 Human Rights Report: Seychelles." 2014 Country Reports on Human Rights Practices. Bureau of Democracy, Human Rights, and Labor. *U.S. Department of State*, 25 Jun. 2015. http://www.state.gov/j/drl/rls/hrrpt/2014/af/236400.htm.

"2015 Investment Climate Statement – Seychelles." Bureau of Economic and Business Affairs. *U.S. Department of State*, May 2015. http://www.state.gov/g/drl/rls/hrrpt/2007/100502.htm.

"About Seychelles." *Information: Climate, People and Currency Converter for Seychelles*. Cerf Island Resort, 2014. http://www.cerf-resort.com/Seychelles.htm.

"Aldabra Atoll and Other Sites." *Aldabra Marine Programme*, 2015. http://www.aldabra.org/.

"Amazing Holidays to Seychelles." Just Seychelles. *Tropical Sky Ltd*, 2015. http://www.justseychelles.com/

"Human Rights Promotion Mission Undertaken by the African Commission on Human and Peoples' Rights to the Republic of Seychelles, from 6 to 10 April 2015." *ACHPR.org*. African Commission on Human and Peoples' Rights, 2009. http://www.achpr.org/.

"Home News." Seychelles Nation. *National Information Services Agency*, 2015. http://www.nation.sc/.

"IMF Executive Board Concludes 2013 Article IV Consultation with Seychelles." *International Monetary Fund*. IMF, 15 May 2013.

_____. "Statement at the Conclusion of an IMF Mission to Seychelles." *International Monetary Fund*, 13 Feb. 2009. http://www.imf.org/external/np/sec/pr/2009/pr0935.htm. http://www.imf.org/external/np/sec/pn/2013/pn1352.htm.

"Introducing La Digue." *La Digue Island Lodge*, 2014. http://www.ladigue.sc/.

"Introducing Seychelles." *Lonely Planet*, 2015. http://www.lonelyplanet.com/seychelles.

"Latest Tourism News." The Seychelles Islands: Official Tourism Destination Site. *Seychelles Tourism Board*, 2014. http://www.seychelles.travel.

National Bureau of Statistics. *National Bureau Statistics*. 2014. http://www.nsb.gov.sc/.

"Seychelles Bureau of Standards." Seychelles National Council for Children. *NCC*, 2015. http://www.ncc.sc/.

"Seychelles." Freedom of the Press 2014. *Freedom House*, 2015. https://freedomhouse.org/report/freedompress/2014/seychelles#.VfDVR2BRHVI.

"Seychelles Island Foundation." *Seychelles Island Foundation*, 2015.

"Seychelles." The World Factbook. *Central Intelligence Agency*, 2015. https://www.cia.gov/library/publications/the-world-factbook/geos/se.html.

"Seychelles: Transport Stats." NationMaster.com, 2015. http://www.nationmaster.com/country-info/profiles/Seychelles/Transport#2014. http://www.sif.sc.

"Seychelles National Library." IFLA Survey of National Libraries of Education. *Aarhus University Library/Jakob Andersen*, n.d. http://inet.dpb.dpu.dk/survey/seychelles_desc.html.

"Seychelles Profile." *BBC News*, 21 Jan. 2015. http://www.bbc.com/news/world-africa-14093816

"Seychelles." *UNESCO World Heritage Centre*, 2015. http://whc.unesco.org/en/statesparties/sc/.

"The African Union." Claiming Human Rights. http://www.claiminghumanrights.org/au.html. Office of the High Commissioner for Human Rights. *UNESCO*, 4 Jan. 2010.

"The Republic of Seychelles Ministry of Foreign Affairs." *Ministry of Foreign Affairs of the Republic of Seychelles*, 2015. http://www.mfa.gov.sc/.

"Universal Declaration of Human Rights." United Nations Human Rights. *OHCHR*, 2015. http://www.ohchr.org/EN/UDHR/Pages/Introduction.aspx.

"U.S. Relations with Seychelles." Bureau of African Affairs Fact Sheet. *U.S. Department of State*, 22 Jul. 2015. http://www.state.gov/r/pa/ei/bgn/6268.htm.

Virtual Seychelles." The Official website of the Government of Seychelles. *Virtual Seychelles*, 2013. http://www.virtualseychelles.sc/.

"WTO welcomes Seychelles as its 161st member" *World Trade Organization*, 27 Apr. 2015. https://www.wto.org/english/news_e/news15_e/acc_syc_27apr15_e.htm.

_____ and Sharon Uranie. "Seychelles is top in Africa for fastest internet speed." *Seychelles News Agency*, 6 Jun. 2014. http://www.seychellesnewsagency.com/articles/674/Seychelles+is+top+in+Africa+for+fastest+internet+speed.

Danny Faure. "Message from the Minister for Education and Youth Mr. Danny Faure." Education Page. *Ministry of Education Seychelles*, 2005. http://www.education.gov.sc/edupage/edupage/index.htm.

Els Slots. "Aldabra Atoll." *World Heritage Site*. Els Slots/WHS, 2015. http://www.worldheritagesite.org/sites/aldabra.html.

Hajira Amla. "Super-fast internet speeds ahead - 4G LTE technology now available in Seychelles." *Seychelles News Agency*, 28 Nov. 2014. http://www.seychellesnewsagency.com/articles/1850/Super-fast+internet+speeds+ahead+-+G+LTE+technology+now+available+in+Seychelles.

Jon Pedersen. "Seychelles." Countries and Their Cultures. *Advameg, Inc.*, 2015.http://www.everyculture.com/Sa-Th/Seychelles.html.

Kerstin Lisy. "The Maputo Protocol of the African Union." *Federal Ministry for Economic Cooperation and Development*, Germany, 2006. PDF. http://www.gtz.de/de/dokumente/en-fgm-maputoprotocol.pdf.

Sharon Meriton-Jean. "Boosting the agricultural sector to ensure food security." *Seychelles News Agency*, 13 Aug. 2014. http://www.seychellesnewsagency.com/articles/1159/Boosting+the+agricultural+sector+to+ensure+food+security++Seychelles+is+finalizing+national+agricultural+investment+plan.

Steff Gaulter. "State of Emergency Declared in Seychelles." Al Jazeera. *Al Jazeera Media Network*, 29 Jan. 2013. http://www.aljazeera.com/weather/2013/01/201312993838165255.html.

Somali refugee camp where thousands wait for food and water.

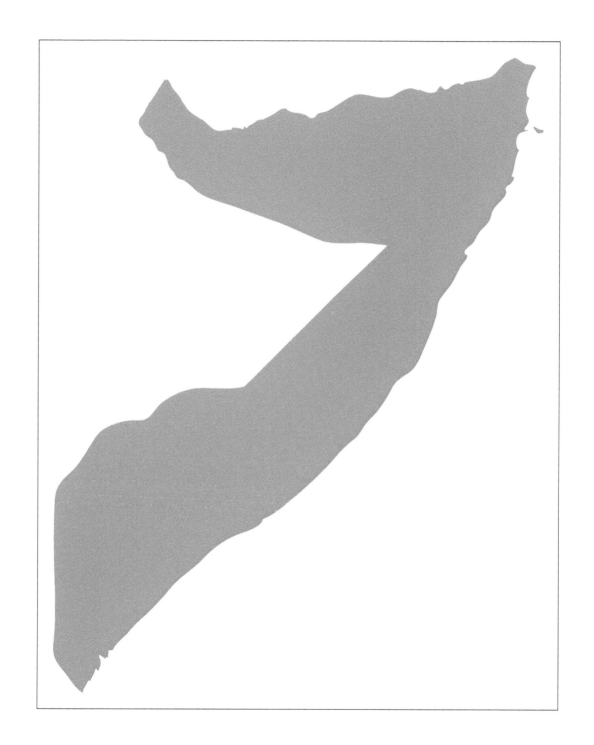

SOMALIA

Introduction

Somalia occupies the easternmost portion of the Horn of Africa. The region was known to the ancient Egyptians as the "Land of Punt," a place famed for its frankincense and myrrh. Somalis enjoy conversation and poetry and place a high value on a person's verbal skills. In fact, because the Somali language has yet to be documented or codified in a dictionary, poetry is the most important means of perpetuating the Somali language and culture.

During the 19th and 20th centuries, several colonial powers dominated the region to exploit Somalia's resources and protect trade routes through the Suez Canal. The region was united as a country in 1960; in 1991, it descended into civil war, following the overthrow of military dictator Siad Barre by clan-based, armed opposition groups. The Transitional Federal Charter of the Somali Republic, passed in February 2004 and distinct from the country's 1979 constitution, vested a Transitional Federal Government with supremacy of law over the country; defined its borders, religion, official languages, and rights to citizenship; and established Somalia as a sovereign state. Following lengthy negotiations between regional leaders and Mogadishu-based politicians, a provisional constitution was written in June 2012, which further defined the country's overarching executive, legislative, and judicial system. In August 2012, the country approved the new constitution by a 96 percent margin, and the country's various administrative regions subsequently became a federation, known as the Federal Republic of Somalia. However, some regions, like Somaliland, still declare their autonomy. Currently, Somalia is battling Al-Shebaab and Al-Qaeda-linked groups, which have gained significant footholds in the south-central portions of the country. Their violent activities, along with continued civil unrest, have made realizing a stable political environment and economic development extremely difficult.

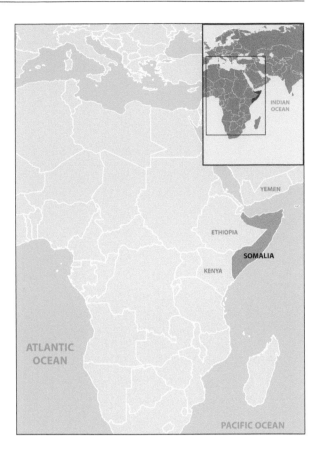

GENERAL INFORMATION

Official Language: Somali, Arabic
Population: 10,616,380 (July 2015 estimate)
Currency: Somali shilling
Coins: The Somali shilling can be subdivided into 100 senti. Coins are issued in denominations of 5, 10, and 50 cents and 1 Somali shilling. The

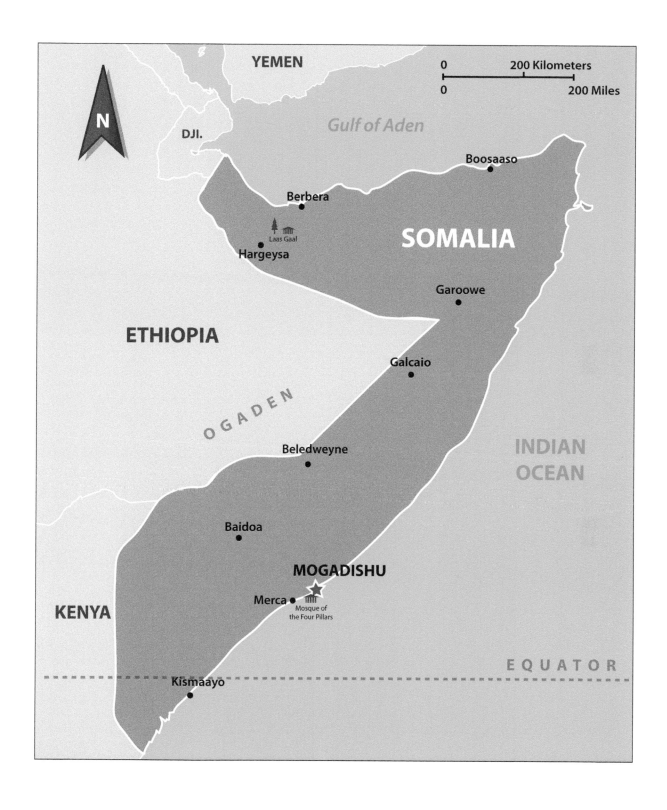

Principal Cities by Population (2015):

- Mogadishu (1,280,000)
- Hargeisa (1,200,000)
- Bosaso (formerly Bender Cassim) (400,321)
- Berbera (232,500)
- Jamaame (224,700)
- Kismayo (183,300)
- Baidoa (also Iscia Baidoa) (157,500)
- Galcaio (also Galkayo) (137,667)
- Burao (also Bur'o) (120,400)
- Afgooye (79,400)

northwestern Republic of Somaliland, a self-declared but mostly unrecognized independent state since 1991, has issued six coins. (The area ceased accepting the Somali shilling as currency and instead uses the Somaliland shilling, which is still internationally unacknowledged and, consequently, has no exchange rate.) Somalia has also issued various unusual commemorative coins, such as guitar-shaped coins issued in 2004, but the circulation and legal tender of such coins is questionable.

Land Area: 627,337 square kilometers (242,216 square miles)

Water Area: 10,320 square kilometers (3,984 square miles)

National Anthem: "Qolobaa Calankeed" ("Praise the Homeland")

Capital: Mogadishu

Time Zone: GMT +3

Flag Description: The flag of Somalia simply features a five-pointed white star centered in a light blue background. The five points of the white star are said to represent the five Somali regions within the Horn of Africa.

Population

Somalia's population is estimated at approximately 10,616,380 in 2015, with an estimated 3.5 million residing in the autonomous region of Somaliland. Approximately 39.6 percent of the population is urban, and a large percentage is nomadic. Mogadishu, with a population of almost 1.3 million, is the largest city. Other

urban centers include Hargeisa, the largest city (and capital) of Somaliland, and the port cities of Bosaso and Berbera.

Somalia's population is young and growing, with an average of nearly six children born per woman. The infant mortality rate is over 98 deaths for every 1,000 live births. Average life expectancy is 52 years; 50 years for males and 54 years for females (2015 estimate). Population density is seventeen persons per square kilometer (44 persons per square mile), but most non-nomadic peoples occupy the fertile south, near the country's two major rivers. Somalia is one of the least developed countries in the world.

Languages

Somali, the dominant language of the country, is an Eastern Cushitic language within the Afro-Asiatic language super-family. It has several dialects; Common Somali is the most widely spoken. Since 1973, it has been written in a modified Latin script. According to the 2004 Transitional Federal Charter of the Somali Republic, Arabic has also been designated as an official language. It is studied for religious purposes as well to facilitate study of the Koran. Other spoken languages include Italian and English.

Native People & Ethnic Groups

Ethnic Somalis have ancient roots in the Horn of Africa and arrived in the region before 100 CE. Despite the ethnic homogeneity of the population and a shared culture and religious background, loyalty is given foremost to one's clan rather than to a national identity. Intense rivalries between clans have long fostered political in-fighting and, in the most extreme case, sparked a long-running civil war.

Ethnic Somalis comprise the overwhelming majority of the population, around 85 percent. A Cushitic people, they organize their society according to ancient clan designations. Though there are many clans and sub-clans, most Somalis belong to one of five major clans (Hawiya, Ishaak, Darod, Dir, and Rahanwein). About 15 percent of the population is comprised of non-Somali minorities, including Arabs, of which there are approximately 30,000; Indians; and the Swahili-speaking Bantu peoples: the Shidle, Shabelle, Makanne, Eyle, Elay Baydabo.

Religions

Somalis accepted Islam around the eighth century, and today nearly 100 percent of Somalis are Sunni Muslims. According to the Transnational Federal Charter, passed in 2004, Islam is the country's official religion, and Sharia is its law. Before the rise of Islam, Somalis held animist beliefs, which they subsequently incorporated into the newer religious system. Radical Islam gained some adherents during the 1990s, though it is thought to be limited to a small percentage of the population.

Climate

Outside of the rainy seasons, one long and one short, most of Somalia has a hot and dry climate. Monsoon winds from the northeast dictate a very dry season between September and December, and rainy seasons between April and June and in October and November; rain patterns are variable, however. Average annual precipitation measures about 280 millimeters (11 inches), with some mountain areas receiving enough rainfall to sustain forests. In the northeast, annual rainfall is less than 100 mm (4 inches); in the central plateaus, it can run 200 to 300 mm (8 to 12 inches); and the southwest can have between 510 to 610 mm (20 and 24 inches).

Between the dry and rainy seasons, humidity is generally high. The average annual temperature is 28° Celsius (82° Fahrenheit), though the coastal plains can be much hotter and the northern mountains can experience night-time temperatures below freezing.

During the dry months, droughts are a serious problem threatening people, livestock and the already sparse vegetation; even deep wells can dry up. Sand storms are also common in this period. During the rainy season, floods can occur. The tsunami of 2004 killed several hundred Somalis and destroyed property along the coast of the Indian Ocean. In November 2013, Puntland, the region at the Horn of Africa's

tip, suffered devastation from a cyclone, which ruined crops and killed both people and mass numbers of livestock, creating a humanitarian crisis. At the same time, in Jowhar, the River Shabelle flooded to such a degree that 10,000 people were displaced.

ENVIRONMENT & GEOGRAPHY

Topography

Somalia occupies the easternmost portion of the Horn of Africa. Somalia is bordered by Djibouti, Ethiopia, and Kenya, with the Gulf of Aden to the north, and the Indian Ocean to the south.

Dry savannah-like plains and plateaus make up most of Somalia's terrain. Their elevation ranges from about 180 meters (600 feet) in the south to about 500 meters (1,640 feet) in the north. The Karkaar Mountains rise in the far north. They range in elevation between 915 and 2,135 meters (3,000 and 7,000 feet), or an average of 1,663 meters (5,456 feet). The range's high point is Shimbir Berris at 2,416 meters (7,927 feet). The mountains extend from the northwest to the tip of the Horn of Africa.

Somalia's coastline measures 3,025 kilometers (1,880 miles). It is predominantly straight, yielding few natural harbors. Wide sandy plains are common along both the coastline of the Gulf of Aden and the coastline of the Indian Ocean.

Somalia has approximately 10,320 square kilometers (3,985 square miles) of water and 200 nautical miles (230 miles) of territorial seas. Numerous small water courses flow along shallow valleys during the rainy season, but Somalia has few major rivers. Only the Jubba River in southern Somalia flows permanently, while the Shabelle River usually flows for about seven months of the year. Both rivers originate in the Ethiopian highlands and flow into southern Somalia, creating fertile river valleys on the plateau. The Jubba empties into the Indian Ocean, and the Shabelle disappears into the desert.

Mogadishu is part of the coastal region of Benadir. It is situated near the point where the Shabelle River changes its course and curves to become parallel to the coast and continues southward. "Shabelle" means "leopard" in the Somali language.

Plants & Animals

Few types of vegetation can withstand Somalia's arid climate. Acacia trees and coarse shrubs and grass predominate on the plains and plateaus, though a brief cover of grass and wildflowers is common after rains. In the higher elevations of the north, aloe plants, succulents, and various trees are found, including cedar, juniper, boswellia, and commiphora; from the latter two are derived frankincense and myrrh, respectively.

The country's two major rivers make the south the most verdant area. Mahogany, euphoria (also known as the longan tree), and eucalyptus trees grow there, in addition to shrubs and high grasses. Mangrove trees are found near the estuary of the Jubba River.

Elephants, cheetahs, lions, zebras, giraffes, rhinoceroses, antelopes, warthogs, wild asses, and crocodiles are found in Somalia. Somali hedgehogs, Somali elephant shrews and Somali golden moles, all endangered, are indigenous to the area. There are also populations of eagles, bustards, and storks, and several types of poisonous snakes, including the nocturnal red spitting cobra, which can project its venom up to seven feet. The African wild ass and the hartebeest are listed as critically endangered, while among those considered vulnerable are the African elephant, the lion, and the cheetah. The civil war has caused problems for the country's wildlife, and there is also a growing illicit trade in the rarer animals.

CUSTOMS & COURTESIES

Greetings

Greetings in Somalia are somewhat formal, especially between strangers. Handshakes between men are common, but women rarely extend their hands to men. Women may shake each other's hands—and in the southern part of the country, they often kiss the hand they have shaken—but generally refrain from shaking hands with the opposite sex. However, family members, especially those of the same sex, may typically embrace and kiss one another on the cheek. As Somalia is a Muslim country, women rarely make any physical contact with men who do not belong to the same family.

Customary greetings include "Salaam" ("Hello"), "Assalam Alaikum" ("Peace be upon you"), "Subah wanaagsan" ("Good morning"), and "Salab wanaagsan" ("Good afternoon"). Another common greeting may be "Ma nahad baa" ("Is there peace?"). Educated Somalis speak Arabic, English, and Italian, but more rural Somalis usually speak one of three dialects of the Cushitic language family, depending on their clan affiliation.

Gestures & Etiquette

In Somali culture, it is not uncommon for people to speak emphatically, using sweeping gestures with hands and arms. Arab customs and gestures have had a lasting influence on nonverbal communication in Somalia, especially to signal specific needs or requests. For example, to gesture for a person to "come here," a Somali will hold out the right hand while opening and closing it, as if to beckon. To do the opposite, Somalis will turn the right hand to face the ground and sweep it away from the body. To signal the most sincerity when greeting a person, Somalis will often place their right hand over their heart.

Certain gestures are considered taboo. For example, the "thumbs up" gesture commonplace in American culture is considered obscene in Somali culture. Also, Somalis refrain from curling the index finger inward as a gesture to beckon somebody else. Because of their Muslim heritage, many Somali gestures are dictated by Islamic culture. For instance, it is considered disrespectful to point the sole of one's foot at another. Somalis also typically refrain from using the left hand, whether to shake hands or simply pass an item, since that hand is associated with the cleansing of the body, and is thus considered impure.

Somalis often utilize their fondness for poetics in their daily interactions. They prefer subtle exchanges and place a high value on mastering communication skills. Before negotiating on a specific subject or asking for cooperation, Somalis might approach an issue indirectly, particularly to gauge the other person's perspective. If they suspect uncooperativeness, they might avoid the issue to avoid embarrassment. Generally, they are not blunt or direct about their needs and, in the same vein, do not appreciate a direct refusal to a request. Lastly, Somalis prize humor, as it reduces tension, especially in awkward situations.

Eating/Meals

The largest meal of the day is traditionally the midday meal. This may consist of a meat and sauce dish mixed with noodles or rice, or traditional soups served with bread. Breakfast is typically a light meal of porridge, cereals, and breads, or leftovers from other meals. Dinner also includes lighter fare such as salads, beans, and other simple dishes. Somali breads are a staple food item, and include muufo, a flat bread made with ground corn and commonly baked in patties; the crepe-like canjeero (also canjeelo); or the laxoox (also lahoh) a spongy, pancake-style bread.

Somali cuisine has distinct African, Arabic, Indian, and Italian influences and varies depending on the region, especially among nomadic Somalis and those living in coastal cities. For example, the eating customs of nomadic peoples are based on their agrarian way of life. Activities such as herding affect their mealtimes, and dishes commonly consist of simple or local foods such as yogurt, grains such as millet, and goat and camel meat. They also eat sesame, corn, and sorghum, which is a drought-resistant plant that is also used for animal feed.

Somalis in coastal areas and cities eat primarily seafood, as well as imported rice and local meat. In other cities and in rural areas, lamb, mutton, and goat are used in many dishes. Foreign influences are also more dominant in urban areas, such as pasta from Italian cuisine and Indian foods such as breads and curries. Indian ghee, which is clarified butter, is commonly used for cooking. Somalis do not eat vegetables frequently, as they are difficult to grow in the dry soil and expensive to import. Somalis do, however, eat tropical fruits, such as mangoes and bananas, which are used in fruit salads.

Beyond the immediate family, men and women typically eat in separate rooms, with women traditionally served after the men. A bowl of water may be provided so that everyone, including children, can wash their hands before and after eating. Rural Somalis eat with their right hand instead of with forks or spoons. Utensils in such areas may be considered indicators of wealth, and it is not uncommon for finely carved utensils to be displayed. Urban Somalis, however, most often eat with utensils, but many eat with their fingers. In rural areas, diners traditionally sit around a large communal dish. During the Muslim month of fasting, known as Ramadan, Somalis fast from dawn until dusk. During this period, the traditional three meals per day are replaced by an early morning meal (suhoor) that is eaten before sunrise, and an evening meal (iftar), which breaks the fast.

Visiting

Somalis are family-oriented and maintain close ties within families and clans. Hospitality is considered a hallmark of traditional Somali culture. While Somalis may be initially cautious with non-Muslims, they are known for their generosity and spend ample time visiting with one another. Visits to the home frequently occur in late afternoon or evening when the air begins to cool. Men are more likely to visit one another in coffee houses, while women often visit privately in the mornings. As with meals, women and men socialize separately in Somalia.

Hosts often serve guests a sweet spicy tea that has some milk. If the visit includes an offering of food, it is considered polite to accept. Likewise, it is not considered impolite to leave food on one's plate. Traditionally, Somalis leave a small amount of food on their plate to signify that they have been provided with enough food. Otherwise, an empty plate might indicate that the guest is still hungry.

LIFESTYLE

Family

Family life in Somalia centers on the clan structure. In fact, women do not traditionally change their name after marriage, but instead keep the name of their father and grandfather to maintain clan affiliation. However, as Somalis moved to urban areas during the second half of the 20th century, clans became fragmented and Somalis lost part of their rural social cohesion as they adapted to a new way of life. In recent years, civil war has ignited clan hostilities, causing many Somalis to return to their rural clans. In political situations, Somalis are obligated to their families and clans before choosing a side. Their loyalty and devotion to their families, whose members rely upon one another when necessary, is considered crucial to their larger clan and society.

Somalia is a patriarchal society in which a father's extended family takes precedence over the mother's. Though women own property in Somalia, unlike in other Muslim countries, the modern tradition of dating before marriage is not practiced. Parents still commonly arrange the marriages of their children, usually to form bonds between clans and strengthen their social and political network. However, divorce is common in Somalia, with women possibly marrying many men throughout their lifetime and bearing children with each of them. Polygamy, or the practice of multiple wives, is also common. In these situations, children are loyal to their mothers. If divorce occurs, the children stay with their mother.

Housing

Rural and nomadic Somali housing typically consists of temporary, one-story huts with thatched roofs and dirt floors called akals. They can be assembled and disassembled quickly for the nomadic life. The akal roof is formed by tying together sticks to form a dome that is then covered with either animal hide or tightly woven matting to keep out the rain. The hut's wall is a tubular structure of sticks that are sometimes plastered with mud for stability. Nomads can build and disassemble their huts in about two hours, allowing them to move quickly to find pasture for grazing animals.

Urban Somali housing ranges from permanent, two-room homes to refugee and settlement camps in which huts are assembled with cardboard, flattened tin, plastic, and cloth. Urban homes average about two rooms and in the interior are typically made of wood with metal roofs or with sun-dried bricks. Homes along the coasts are built with concrete, limestone, and even coral. Displaced Somalis and refugees have found housing shortages in urban areas, where two or more families often live in two-room houses.

Food

Meat (hilib), milk (caano), rice, pasta, and bananas are the basis of Somali food, which is influenced by East African, Arabic, Indian, and Italian cuisine. Goat and lamb meat is common in dishes such as Italian spaghetti with meat sauce, and goat is also used in traditional meat stews. Goat liver is often fried in ghee (clarified butter) with onions for breakfast. Camel meat, especially the hump, is a traditional meat that Somalis tend to serve only on special occasions. However, nomads keep otka, or dried camel meat much like jerky, handy for long journeys. For special feasts, they enjoy sambusas, which are spicy meat dumplings. Somali crabmeat stew, eaten along the coast, is made with white rice, crabmeat, spices such as curry and ginger, and onions. The most common seasonings for meat are cumin, coriander, and turmeric. Flatbread, a Somali staple, is served with most meals.

Somalis drink plenty of camel milk. In fact, nomadic herdsmen are known to drink about nine liters (2.37 gallons) a day. Somalis cook with ghee (clarified butter) made from cream and make a fermented yogurt dish called jinow. They even mix it with cooked grains, such as millet or rice for lunch. A southern Somali clan, called the Rahanweyn, cooks coffee beans in ghee. Sweet foods are easily found throughout the country, especially fruit such as bananas and dates. A semolina cake called basbousa includes buttermilk vanilla, lemon, and sugar. Somalis also love sweet Somali tea in the morning, during breaks, and after dinner. It is made with black tea, ground cinnamon, cardamom, cloves, peppercorns, ginger, and nutmeg, and sugar, and milk.

Life's Milestones

Somalia is a largely homogeneous country. Somalis are the only ethnicity and nearly 100 percent of the population is Sunni Muslim. As such, milestones are observed in accordance with Muslim customs and laws. In Somalia, marriage is considered an important link between two families. Such bonds are crucial for maintaining the strength of a clan. Men traditionally arrange marriages with the father of the bride-to-be. Traditionally, older Somalis often paid large sums of money (called bride wealth) to fathers to marry their young daughters. However, marriage arrangements are increasingly based on honor, respect, and love.

Traditional marriage celebrations in Somali can last three days, depending on whether the bride's family can afford the festivities. Friends and family visit the bride's home to dance and feast for the three days prior to the ceremony. The younger generations visit during the first couple of days, with everyone visiting the on last day. The families provide a large feast with special dishes, such as muqmad, which is dried meat in ghee. Somali women traditionally write a buraanbur to wish the couple a long life together with a strong family. The buraanbur also includes advice for preserving their culture throughout their life together. A sheikh, or religious leader, conducts the ceremony, during which the couple signs legal documents that describe settlement money or property.

Children are very important to young Somali families, as they are the next generation to carry on cultural traditions. As spoons are considered a sign of wealth in Somali culture, they are often given to a woman who has just given birth. These spoons are typically made of finely carved wood, ivory, or silver.

CULTURAL HISTORY

Art

Most Somali art is part of a nomadic lifestyle and is therefore functional, serving daily needs. Rural Somali women weave rugs and fabrics and make leather goods, such as sandals and water pitchers. They grow, pick, and seed the cotton, from which they make either fine thread or yarn that they then dye with natural pigments and weave on a loom. They make colorful macawis (ma'awiis), the sarongs that men wear around the waist, and guntiinos, which are long cloths that women tie over one shoulder.

Women also make ornamental jewelry, pottery, and woodcarving in traditional Somali culture. Traditionally, necklaces made of gold or silver were regarded as status symbols and are worn most often as bangle bracelets, but sometimes also as necklaces and anklets. As most Somalis cannot afford gold or silver, they wear jewelry made of stone, glass, or colored beads of wood. Henna, is also an important part of the Somali culture, and the art of henna tattooing on women's hands, arms, and necks are popular during weddings and other festivities, like Eid, which follows Ramadan. Women traditionally hand-build pottery, without using a potter's wheel, and they decorate it with plant dyes. They also carve wood into boxes, utensils, and decorative cups for drinking or holding face powders. In areas where Islam is followed less strictly, women decorate cups with animal forms and other images, such as boats (in coastal areas). In places where Islam is followed more strictly, decoration is largely aniconic, meaning representations of animals, people, and other elements of the natural world are absent. Islamic art is prevalent throughout Somalia and mosaics, carpets, tapestries, and pottery generally feature beautiful and intricately wrought patterns. Many of these pieces are designed and purchased by artists and collectors.

Architecture

Ancient architecture in Somalia ranges from tomb and monumental architecture (with dry stone construction common), to Islamic-influenced architecture of the country's medieval period, which saw the construction of fortresses, castles, and mosques. Throughout Somalia's history, the use of stone in architecture is predominant, including limestone, coral stone, and sundried bricks. Aside from Arabic influences, Somali architecture shows British and Italian influences, dating from the nation's colonial era. However, much of the country's architectural heritage and infrastructure has been damaged during civil war.

Drama

The Somali art of storytelling found a new medium in the 1970s and 1980s in film. Musical films became a way to convey the traditional art form into a new medium. However, in 2006, the Islamic government began closing down cinemas and arresting—and in some instances shooting—men, women, and children in cinemas. Television and music were also banned in certain areas, as well. By 2009, harsh tactics including violence and shootings had become more widespread throughout the country. This has continued in 2015 with violence perpetrated by groups adhering to the tenants of Islamic fundamentalism and allying themselves with larger militant groups, like Al-Shabaab. Some filmmakers managed to escape the war-torn country. Abdisalam Aato (1975–) left Somalia to come to the United States, where he makes films about the enormous political challenges and living conditions in Somalia. His film company, Olol Films, is based in Columbus, Ohio, which has become known in the film industry as "Somaliwood," in part because of Aato's efforts. His first feature-length Somali film, *Rajo* (*Hope*) was released in 2003.

Music

Music plays an important role in Somali culture and has been a part of daily routines for centuries. The many cultural influences in the country include a complex mix of African, African, and Indian rhythms. These range from traditional compositions for work and daily life, to modern styles such as jazz. Originally used with dance, Somali music was mostly sung while clapping and drumming. A simple reed flute was often used to accompany the singing and rhythms, with a greater range of instruments incorporated during the 20th century. Somali music also uses the Arabic oud, similar to the lute, along with the kaban, which is like a four-stringed guitar. Somali jazz, called kaban, includes melodic rhythms and lyrics and became popular during the last half of the 20th century.

Modern Somali music mixes poetry and music in many forms, some of which are distinctly urban, others rural. Beginning about the 1930s, these modern styles blended singing and various types of folk dance that is rhythmic. One form of popular Somali music, called balwo, combines poetry with African rhythms and originated in the northern areas of the country. Another, called hees (also heeso), is folk music played at weddings. Though Muslim fundamentalists have tried to suppress certain forms of musical expression in Somalia, music has been important throughout the 20th century. However, Islamic fundamentalism successfully suppressed cultural music until the beginning of the civil war in the 1990s.

Dance

Intricately connected with some of the country's community poetry is traditional dance. At public events during which poets compete, dancers also often perform. Many of the dances follow a similar structure in which a lead singer begins with an impromptu poetic composition and then sets a beat by clapping the hands or stomping the feet, often aided by a drum. In northern pastoral areas, the singer's voice and poetry are the focus. In southern areas of Somalia, the dancers' movements are more important. Some of the most common dances throughout Somalia are the batar and the dhaanto.

In the southern region along the Juba River, Bantu Somalis celebrate membership in a dance group. In fact, the importance of belonging to a dance group in this region is on par with the importance of kinship. Dance is used during important social rites of passage and is closely connected to the power that different individuals hold within the group. Muslim sheikhs in the area have, in the past, opposed such dancing and drumming because they considered them inappropriate for Islam. However, since the civil war began in 1991, Bantu dancers have been able to practice their tradition mostly uninterrupted.

Literature

The oral tradition of poetry and folk stories has been a crucial part of Somali culture for centuries. In fact, poetry became the main expression of Somali culture, earning the country the nickname the "nation of poets." In early times, a respected community member would compose a poem that communicated tribal decisions to the rest of the clan. This type of poem was called a gabaye and included alliteration to help make persuasive elements memorable. The poem had to be memorable since it was often repeated, but the poet would recite it to the community only once. Poetry was also used for daily routine tasks as well as for political and cultural uses. Poetry remains important in rural, nomadic cultures, where it is used in work songs and other daily activities.

Traditional Somali folk literature conveyed moral teachings about respect and good behavior, like *Dhegdheer the cannibal woman*, told to little children to instill self-restraint. Another common topic is immigrant life, represented by the popular story, *A Lion's Tale*. The importance of water in this parched desert region has been, and continues to be, the focus of many Somali stories and poems, as water is such a valuable resource. At the end of the 20th century, when a national literature began to emerge, Somali writers began transcribing traditional folk tales. Because Somalia did not officially adopt a modified Latin script until 1972, after it was developed by Somali linguist Shire Jama Ahmed (1935–1999), Somali writers only began writing novels and nonfiction in the late 20th century. Prominent writers include novelist Nuruddin Farah (1945–), who combines mythical elements with local histories in English, and Abdourahman A. Waberi (1965–), who studied in France and writes in French.

CULTURE

Arts & Entertainment

Somalis enjoy conversing with family and friends and place a high value on a person's verbal skills. In fact, because the Somali language has yet to be documented or codified in a dictionary, oral and written poetry remain the fundamental means of perpetuating the language and culture. Poetry has communicated Somali beliefs and sentiments about the political and cultural upheaval that has kept the country unstable for decades. It is also devotional toward Islam. Overall, Somali poetry is essentially about the people and culture and hundreds, even thousands of Somalis attend poetry readings. However, the main means of listening to poetry has been through cassette tapes, and now, more frequently, through internet resources.

The gabaye, which is a subset of the larger, classical poem genre about serious issues called maanso, has retained its place of importance in the culture and has continued to flourish in rural Somalia. Gabayes are recited on short-wave transistors, where listeners can discuss the poems and their effects. Poet Maxamed Xaashi Dhamac "Gaariye" (1949–) confronts both national and global issues, from Somalia's political turmoil to the South African anti-apartheid movement and nuclear weapons. Somali women write poetry called buraambur, which may be equally political. Early 21st-century Somali poetry, however, has turned the focus toward peace and the need to move forward from civil strife.

The music climate in Somalia has suffered not only because of the civil war, but also because of the fundamentalist crackdown on music and musicians, especially in the southern areas of the country. Because of this, much of Somalia's music is now created and played in other locales where exile Somali communities have grown. In London, England, Numbi—named for a traditional healing dance—is a large, annual Somali music and cultural festival that features hip-hop and traditional Somali music and poetry. Elsewhere, in communities in Toronto, Canada, and in the U.S., contemporary

Somali musicians create hip-hop, rap, and jazz music, and concentrate their lyrics on the turmoil in their homeland.

The traditional Arabic oud remains the primary instrument, accompanied by Indian tablas (small drums) for rhythm, African bongos, and American guitars and saxophones. The eclectic and adaptable music has maintained its traditional, gentle melodies. Even within Somalia, where almost 100 percent of the population is Muslim, music remains important to the people, though violent tactics against musicians and musical venues by Al-Shabaab and Al-Qaeda-linked groups have become increasingly widespread since 2009.

Cultural Sites & Landmarks

Somalia's mix of Arab, African, and European cultures is evident in coastal areas that have been important trading centers. The politically charged coastal city of Mogadishu has a history originating in 900 CE as an Arab trading port. The capital later came under Italian rule during the early 20th century. As a result, Mogadishu's architecture is a blend of both European and Arabic styles. However, much of the Italian colonial architecture had been destroyed, and many of the capital's historic buildings have been damaged by the extensive fighting that has occurred in the city since the 1990s. One particular landmark, the Arba-Rucun Mosque (Arba'a Rukun Mosque), or Mosque of the Four Pillars, still stands next to a large Roman arch and a Catholic cathedral.

Somaliland, an autonomous region, which remains unrecognized, is considered one of the safest regions of Somalia. Remnants from prehistoric times are painted on cave walls in Laas Geel (also Laas Gaal), and hundreds of Neolithic cave paintings in interconnected caves show well preserved and vividly painted horned cattle. The cow's importance to the Neolithic people is evident in these paintings. Ochre and red cows are depicted pregnant, grazing, and being milked. Near Laas Geel, the capital of the Somaliland region, the city of Hargeisa, has clean, white beaches. In early 20th-century Somalia, Hargeisa is considered one of the country's safest cities.

Somalia is also home to two national parks: Kismayo National Park, in the southwest, and Hargeisa National Park, in the north. Both parks are home to rare East African species of animals. The country also has roughly ten game reserves. It is not known to what extent these conservation areas have been damaged by poaching, lack of funding, and civil war.

Libraries & Museums

Since the government's collapse in 1991, cultural institutions in Somalia have seen little development or protection. Cultural institutions such as the National Museum and the National Library are located in the capital of Mogadishu; however, most of these museums have been looted. The Somali National Museum, for example, is reported to have lost its entire collection.

Holidays

Most holidays in Somalia are religious, relating to Islam. Ramadan, the annual month-long fast between dusk and dawn, is ended with the three-day celebration called Eid al Fitr. Another important holiday, Eid al Adha, commemorates the ancient patriarch.

Abraham's willingness to sacrifice his son Isaac to God. Both of these holidays are marked by gatherings of family and friends, large feasts, the donning of new clothes, prayers, dancing, and street festivals. Those who can afford it often kill an animal and distribute the meat to the poor.

The birth of the Prophet Mohammed, Maulid (Mawlid Nabi), is celebrated on the 12th day of Rabi'al-awwal, which is the third month in the Islamic calendar. When drought prevails, the ceremony of robdoon is performed. Koranic prayers are read in order to bring rain. Independence Day is marked on June 26, and the Foundation of the Republic is observed on July 1. Dab Shid, the beginning of the solar year, is celebrated at the end of July and is a remnant of pagan Somalia, often coinciding with harvest time.

Youth Culture

Growing up in a war-torn country, Somali youth generally suffer from a lack of social life and underachievement. Access to education is often sporadic at best; it is estimated that only 42 percent of primary-age children are enrolled in school and most of them are now girls. Many youth have become caught up in the aggression that has plagued the nation. In fact, the violence and gang culture they experience in their homeland has even carried over to refugee or exile communities, most notably in Minnesota (where a large number of Somalis settled in the 1990s) and in Great Britain, particularly in London. In recent years, programs oriented toward youth employment and skills training have become prioritized, and Islamic schools have also increased their sponsoring of youth education. However, many Somalis are wary of increasing Islamic extremism, especially among youth.

Sports continue to be an important pastime for youth in the war-torn nation of Somalia. During 16 years of Islamist rule, the government's sports ministry ceased to operate and females were banned from sports participation, a ban that was lifted in January 2007. However, the rise of Al-Shabaab has made participation in sports a life or death choice for many players, particularly females, since the extremist group has labeled sports a "satanic activity." Football (soccer) is the most popular sport, followed by volleyball, basketball, running, handball, and boxing. In 2009, sports initiatives were used to promote peace efforts; and upon becoming president in January 2009, Sharif Ahmed (1964–), whose tenure in office came to an end on August 20, 2012, met with the Somali football federation, the first civil society organization the president met with following elections.

Outside of sports, Somali youth enjoy spending time listening to and learning stories and poetry, particularly in rural areas. Before the crackdown on films and music, young Somalis in cities spent ample time at the cinema and listening to music. Urban Somali youth are also more exposed to modern and Western culture than their rural counterparts. Young men wear modern clothing, such as tailored shirts and sports jerseys with pants or shorts. Young women, though, most often wear traditional clothing, including the guntiino, a long, colorful dress that ties across one shoulder, leaving the other shoulder exposed.

SOCIETY

Transportation

In rural areas, walking is the main method of transportation for Somalis. Pick-up trucks also serve as a main method of transportation, and many rural Somalis still employ animals such as donkeys and camels to carry goods. Buses and taxis are also common modes of public transportation. In May 2015, 70,000 vehicles were registered in Puntaland alone. Traffic moves on the right side of the road in Somalia.

Transportation Infrastructure

At the turn of the 21st century, there was an estimated 21,830 kilometers (13, 565 miles) of roads, of which 2,757 kilometers (1,713 miles) were paved. Unpaved roads become mud-filled and difficult to travel during the rainy season. The country lacks a rail network and has experienced damage to other infrastructure since civil strife broke out in the late 20th century. As of 2012, there were 62 airports, of which seven had paved runways. In 2013, Somali Airlines relaunched after suspending operations in 1991. While Somali Airlines was grounded, six private airlines filled the void, offering domestic and international flights. These private airlines include: Daallo Airlines, Jubba Airways, African Express Airways, East Africa 540, Central Air, and Hajara. There are 15 ports in Somalia, including the major cargo hubs of Mogadishu, Bosaso, Berbera, and Kismaayo. However, piracy and armed robbery have made marine travel dangerous for commercial and private vessels.

Media & Communications

The media in Somalia is largely divided and subject to hostile treatment and censorship. In fact, Reporters Without Borders, a freedom of the press advocacy group, ranked Somalia as one of the worst countries in the world for journalists, rating them 172nd out of 180 countries in 2015. In fact, in September 2015, Abdullahi Ali Hussein, the English-language editor for the online news source *Waagasucub* was gunned down by unidentified gunmen in Mogadishu after leaving a mosque. Hussein often wrote articles critical of Somalia's violence and political unrest.

Radio is the popular medium, and there are numerous privatized radio services, including two official government-run radio stations. One of these is Radio Mogadishu, which was reestablished by the Transitional National Government in the early 2000s after being shut down in 1991. There are four main television broadcasters, one of which is the government-run, Mogadishu-based Somali National Television, known as SNTV, which broadcasts 24 hours per day. However, few people have televisions. Somalis in urban centers have more access to television, but usually in restaurants. The press remains limited, but includes private newspapers with a variety of viewpoints, a fact which has proved dangerous for many journalists. Beginning in 2003, online news sources began to multiply and, because they have proven more cost-effective, have begun to eclipse printed broadsheets. As of 2012, *Xog Doon*, *Xog Ogaal*, *Horyaal Sports* were the only remaining printed papers in Mogadishu.

Somalia's 29-year civil war has nearly destroyed the nation's public telecommunications system. Nonetheless, private telecom companies have begun operating fixed-line telephones in certain areas as well as wireless service for international calls. It is a growing industry with great promise, and Somalia's telecommunications system is considered one of the best in Africa. Somalis in large cities, such as Mogadishu, have access to cellular phone service. As of 2013, more than 52% of Somalis used cellular phones, but they also still rely on mail to communicate. Computers and Internet use is still relatively sparse, but continuing to grow. As of 2014, there were an estimated 163,185 Internet users, representing 1.51 percent of the population.

SOCIAL DEVELOPMENT

Standard of Living

Somalia is unranked on the United Nations Human Development Index for 2014, which measures quality of life indicators for 187 UN member states; this is due to unavailable data, though the country last had a classification of low human development. Somalia was, in fact, the lowest ranking country in 2001.

Water Consumption

Overall, Somalia is considered a water-scarce country. Environmental degradation remains a serious problem in Somalia, and contaminated water continues to be a primary source of a range of human health problems and epidemics. According to UNICEF, only an estimated 29 percent of the Somali population has access to an improved or safe water source and estimates just 39 percent of households have access to proper sanitation. According to 2011 UN statistics, the estimates are somewhat higher, with 69.6 percent of the urban population having access to an improved drinking water resource, but only 8.8 percent in rural areas. Similarly, in 2011, only approximately 23.6 percent of the population has access to improved or proper sanitation, with just 52 percent in urban areas and 6.3 percent in rural areas.

Education

Educational opportunities have been limited at all levels in Somalia since the country descended into civil war in 1991. As a result, most schools are closed, and the schools that do manage to function have low enrollment and only the most basic materials, especially in rural areas. (In the more stable Somaliland and Puntaland regions, enrollment rates are higher.) Previously, more boys than girls received an education, a fact once reflected in the literacy rate, which was higher for men than women. (Like most educational statistics, data varies, and the literary rate is estimated at between 20 and 40 percent of adults.) However, UNICEF reports indicate that this is changing: as of 2015, of the 42 percent of children enrolled in primary school (an estimated

710,860 children out of an estimated 1.7 million children), 36 percent of were girls. Still, only 15 percent of teachers are women. There is approximately one teacher to every 33 students.

In principle, free and compulsory education is provided for eight years. Secondary school lasts for another four years, and may entail a standard general education or vocational training. One of the country's main universities, the Somali National University in Mogadishu, which had been closed since the early 1990s, reopened in August 2014. For the most part, higher education is private.

Women's Rights

In Somalia's male-dominated and paternalistic society, women lack basic human rights, including the ability to make their own life choices. Cultural expectations for a woman often do not extend beyond domestic responsibilities, and men are primarily expected to earn in the workforce. It is also not uncommon for women to be removed from school when married—most marriages are arranged, and include older male suitors—and parents often sell their daughters to the highest bidder. In addition to lacking a voice in family matters, women lack political representation and generally have no decision-making abilities in business. Moreover, women risk immediate divorce should their husbands find fault with them; economic circumstances and social conventions force women to find another husband quickly in order to survive.

A majority of internally displaced persons (IDPs) in war-torn Somalia are minorities and women. Minorities typically do not belong to clans and, as a result, are unprotected either by militias or warlords. As such, minorities, particularly female minorities, are more vulnerable to rape, attack, and robbery. Women traveling alone are also highly susceptible to rape and assault. If raped, the woman must have four male witnesses who will speak on her behalf. Otherwise, she is considered guilty of causing adultery. Women and young girls have been stoned to death after being raped and unable to produce enough male witnesses to vouch for their innocence.

Somali women regularly face violence and discrimination. Spousal rape is not prohibited and there are no laws that address domestic abuse, which is widespread. Sexual violence is also prevalent in the home, as well as in refugee and urban areas. Women are also marginalized due to a lack of health care; it is estimated that forty-five women die every day during childbirth. Polygamy is allowed, and women are discriminated against in matters of inheritance and property ownership. The traditional practice of female genital mutilation (FGM) is also prevalent in Somalia. The process, often performed with non-sterile implements, has resulted in serious complications with both intercourse and childbirth. Some have even died from post-procedure infections, and many women live with life-long pain resulting from nerve damage. According to the United Nations Children's Fund (UNICEF), that prevalence is estimated at 95 percent, affecting girls between four and 11 years of age. In July 2013, UNICEF also reported that 63 percent of those who had undergone the procedure have been infibulated.

A pan-Somali women's movement called the Sixth Clan—in reference to the five traditional Somali clans—has worked to politically empower women in recent years. Officially recognized during the 2002 Somali Peace and Reconciliation conference in Eldoret, Kenya, the group is made up of women who have married across clans. Since its inception, this network of women has made progress toward the development of female participation in Somali politics. Because of this organization, Somali's transitional government included a provision in the Transitional Federal Charter (TFC) that required women fill 12 percent of the seats in parliament, totaling thirty-three seats. By 2004, however, only 8 percent of the seats were filled. Women have essentially been uninvolved in the peace-seeking coalitions in the country. The new provisional constitution, passed in 2012, calls for women to make up 30 percent of parliament, offering the prospect of more political engagement and participation.

Health Care

The war has destroyed Somalia's health care system. Hospitals, clinics, trained personnel, and medical supplies are all in short supply. As a result, the health of Somalis is generally compromised.

Unclean drinking water, poor sanitation, malnutrition, refugees, and a high infant mortality rate are all widespread problems. Many diseases are prevalent or have occasional outbreaks, including intestinal illnesses, malaria, cholera, measles, Rift Valley fever, tuberculosis, leprosy, and bilharzia. Because the humanitarian crisis has made doctors and hospital care scarce, if almost non-existent, many Somalis rely on folk medicine, which often employs practices based on superstition.

GOVERNMENT

Structure

Since a popular uprising ousted the Siad Barre regime in 1991, Somalia lacked a central government until August 20, 2012, when the Federal Republic of Somalia (Dowladda Federaalka Soomaaliya) was established. A national constitution, passed June 23, 2012—following much negotiation between national and regional leaders—made Somalia a federation. Parliament serves as the legislative branch, while the president, as chief of state; prime minister, as head of government; and the advisory cabinet together form the executive branch.

Before 2012, warlords and their clans battled each other for control. The south, including the capital Mogadishu, was largely lawless and still faces outbreaks of extreme violence now frequently perpetrated by Al-Shabaab and other Al-Qaeda-linked groups. The clans of the north and center have been able to form self-governing administrative units: Somaliland, which has declared independence, and Puntland, which has not. Somaliland has been largely stable since seceding from the troubled south. The federal government, however, does not recognize either region's autonomy and considers them part of the federation and subject to the new constitutional laws.

The Federal Parliament of Somalia (Golaha Shacabka Soomaaliya) elects the president and prime minister and can pass or veto laws. The bicameral legislature has a 275-seat lower house and a 54-seat upper house. A Technical Selection Committee elected the first parliamentary members in August 2012. By law, 30 percent must be women. A future electoral system is currently being determined.

Political Parties

Due to a lack of a centralized government, political systems have been largely ineffective in Somalia. Prior to civil war, there were numerous parties, but many have since transitioned into autonomous regions or states, or into militias. The federal government, established by the constitution in August 2012 has become a unifying force in the country, creating a federation, although some regions still seek sovereignty. The first democratic elections within the new Federal Republic of Somalia are yet to occur and the electoral process itself is still being sorted out by the current government. There are currently 22 recognized political parties, many of which are clan-, ethnic-, or religion-based.

The unrecognized Somaliland region of Somalia, which declared independence in 1991, has a multi-party system. As of the 2010 elections, there were four political parties represented in government: the United Peoples' Democratic Party (UDUB), the Peace, Unity and Development Party (KULMIYE), the For Justice and Development (UCID) party, and the Waddani (WDM) party. On May 11, 2015, a few weeks before a new general election was slated to take place, the Somali "elderates," known as the guurti, extended the current government by two years and postponed general elections until 2017, a decision that sparked significant controversy.

Local Government

Somalia is divided into eighteen administrative regions (gobolka), known since 2012 as Federal Member States. These states have some home-rule capabilities and maintain their own police and security forces. However, all are subject to the laws of the Federal Republic of Somalia, the country's president, and its national parliament.

Judicial System

Before 2012, judicial matters are handled at the local level. Some clans employed a secular system of arbitration, whereas others employ the Islamic system of Sharia law. In March 2009, however, the coalition government announced they would accept Sharia as the official judicial system of Somalia. And since the passing of the Provisional Constitution in August 2012, the Somali judiciary has been divided into three tiers: a Constitutional Court, federal level courts, and Federal Member State courts. A nine-member Judicial Service Commission appoints Constitution Court judges, which are ultimately approved by parliament, as well as judges serving in the federal courts. The new Constitutional Review and Implementation Commission, established in 2014, operates in conjunction with the Ministry of Justice to oversee all judicial activities.

Taxation

With no highly centralized form of government, tax collection was not enforced for some twenty-three years, following the collapse of Sid Barre's government in 1991. In 2009, Kenya agreed to collect tax revenue for the embattled Somali government by taxing goods on imports into Somalia through Kenya. And in March 2014, the Somali government agreed on a new, comprehensive taxation system, which they are in the process of implementing. Data on the system is not yet available.

Armed Forces

Since the outbreak of civil war, Somalia has had to reestablish and rebuild its military forces. By 2009, a national army and police force had been reestablished and reinstated as the Somali Armed Forces (Ciidamada Qalabka Sida). As of 2015, the SAF is comprised of an army, navy, air force, police force, and a National Intelligence

and Security Agency. Overall, the SAF, of which the president is commander in chief, numbers approximately 20,000 active personnel. The regions of Somaliland and Puntland still maintain their own police and security forces.

Foreign Policy

Somalia's foreign policy during the 1970s was aligned with communist powers such as the Soviet Union and China. During the 1980s, Somalia began to align with the West. This realignment also followed a dispute with Ethiopia over territory in the late 1970s. During that time and up to 1991, which marked the onset of the Somali Civil War, numerous Arab nations developed relationships with Somalia, which included military and financial support. Since the beginning of the war in 2006, in which Ethiopian and transitional government forces have been engaged with Islamic insurgents, the rival Islamic Courts Union (ICU) administration, and various other militia groups, the county's foreign relations have focused on the need for international recognition and support.

In 2007, American-backed Ethiopian forces invaded the southern region of Somalia to overturn Islamic factions that had alleged terrorist associations, particularly with al-Qaeda. Fighting expanded as Islamic insurgents attacked military forces and government officials, leading to intense fighting in Mogadishu. Since the spring of 2007, insurgents had taken control of more areas in southern areas, even with the additional help from soldiers of the greater African Union (AU) Mission to Somalia. Ethiopian forces withdrew in early 2009, leaving areas open to insurgent control. The continued fighting resulted in thousands of casualties, deaths, and displaced civilians, adding to the already tenuous situation in Somalia. An estimated 1,192,060 civilians have fled Mogadishu between 2007 and January 2015, with 1,012,960 of them internally displaced, according to the UN High Commissioner on Refugees.

The ongoing war and Somalia's previous lack of a cohesive, central governing authority has made the development of consistent foreign relations extremely difficult. During the early stages of the twenty-nine-year civil war, surrounding countries held conferences to attempt to reconcile the divisions. Nations such as Ethiopia, Kenya, Egypt, Yemen, and Italy all assisted in the effort. Djibouti, which was integral to the peace process since 2000 and was involved in the African Union Mission in Somalia in 2011, attended the inauguration of Somalia's new president in 2012, as did representatives from Ethiopia. Egypt, too, has expressed its support of the new Somali government and territory, as does Yemen, which maintains an embassy in Mogadishu.

Since independence from European powers, foreign relations between Somalia and the neighboring countries of Ethiopia and Kenya have been tense. Relations between Somalia and Ethiopia have been strained since the 1960s because of conflict over the Ogaden region in Ethiopia that borders Somalia. Large numbers of Somali nomads have lived in the region, causing a dispute over Somali self-determination on the land. A similar dispute occurred between Somalia and then-British-controlled Kenya over Kenya's Northern Frontier District. In January 2013, the United States reestablished diplomatic ties with Somalia that had been at least partially severed for almost twenty years. Prior to the 2013 bilateral talks, the US maintained contact with Somalia's Transitional Federal Government through the US embassy in Nairobi, Kenya.

Piracy off the coast of Somalia has escalated in the early 21st century, to the point that foreign states have had to intervene. For instance, in 2010, the US Central Intelligence Agency (CIA) has suggested the strategized use of covert operations. (One of the most notable examples of piracy, in fact, was the capture of MV *Maersk Alabama* in 2009, an incident which resulted in US intervention in the form of Navy SEALS, who killed three pirates.) Most of these attacks come in the Gulf of Aden, a strategic waterway; an estimated 90 percent of shipments by the World Food Programme, for example, arrive by ship. It was estimated that, in a twelve-month period dating from November 2007, pirate ransoms totaled $150 million—and an estimated $200 million

since 2008, a year in which 111 ships were attacked, resulting in forty-two hijackings. (In 2006, there were only a reported ten incidents.) In 2008, the UN Security Council passed a resolution in which military force could be used to suppress piracy in the region. Multi-national policing and military escorts have had some affect in lessening piracy off of Somalia.

Human Rights Profile

International human rights law insists that states respect civil and political rights and also promote an individual's economic, social, and cultural rights. The United Nations Universal Declaration on Human Rights (UDHR) is recognized as the standard for international human rights. Its authors sought the counsel of the world's great thinkers, philosophers, and religious leaders and were careful to create a document that reflects the core values shared by every world culture. (To read this document or view the articles relating to cultural human rights, visit http://www.ohchr.org/EN/UDHR/Pages/Introduction.aspx.)

The human rights situation in Somalia remains dire. General living conditions, including the health, safety, and welfare of Somalis, have greatly deteriorated since 2007, especially in the south. Though the government ratified a new constitution in 2012 and is attempting to reestablish the economy and general order, difficulties unifying the country continue because regional governments do not yet recognize the federal government's overarching authority. Moreover, the government and the transitional body that preceded it has been implicated in numerous human rights abuses. The Islamic extremist group Al-Shabaab, which controls a large area in southern Somalia, has added to the culture of violence, as they oversee public beatings and executions.

Since the beginning of 2007, when the U.S.-backed Ethiopian government and the African Union sent troops into southern Somalia to dislodge Islamist control in certain areas, more than 6,000 civilians had been killed and nearly 900,000 had become displaced as they fled the fighting in Mogadishu. As of January 2015, an estimated 1,192,060 Somalis were in need of humanitarian assistance, according to the UN Refugee Agency. Piracy off Somalia's northern shores and attacks on humanitarian aid workers have seriously inhibited getting necessary aid to civilians. Attacks against aid workers, activists, and journalists were frequent in 2008, and in early 2009, four UN workers were kidnapped in the southern town of Wajid, while 35 UN aid workers were killed and twenty-six others abducted from various conflict zones. Additionally, militias often brutally attack or murder civilians caught fleeing war-torn areas. The Somali National Intelligence and Security Agency (NISA) also frequently harasses, detains, and tortures journalists. And in 2014 alone, three media professionals, including two journalists were murdered. One, a reporter working for Mustaqbal Radio, was killed with a car bomb.

Police and military brutality as well as sexual violence is a widespread occurrence in Somalia. Police and government and military officials have been implicated in raping, murdering, and looting in Mogadishu, including schools. Police forces have also been known to kill civilians while fighting insurgents and arbitrarily arrest civilians for ransom, torturing them in a Mogadishu detention center that has deplorable conditions. The Ethiopian National Defense Force's (ENDF) indiscriminate use of weapons in Mogadishu and Beletweyne between early 2007 and early 2009 regularly destroyed homes and public buildings, killing innocent civilians. In January 2014, the ENDF merged with militias from Burundi, Uganda, Sierra Leone, Djibouti, and Kenya—which together form the African Union Mission to Somalia (AMISOM)—bringing troop numbers up to 22,126. Despite being a peacekeeping force, many of the AMISOM soldiers have been implicated in the rape and murder of civilians. Insurgent forces also accused of atrocities include militant Islamist groups linked to the group Al-Shabaab (which means "youth" in Arabic), which, on June 2, 2014, publically executed three men they accused of spying for the government. Such groups have also attacked Somali government officials and collaborators, as well as civilians thought to exhibit behavior considered un-Islamic. Attacks generally increase around Ramadan. Human trafficking and child labor—including child soldiers—are also prevalent human rights abuses, and the government has made little effort to curb rampant human trafficking and piracy.

The organization Human Rights Watch (HRW) has noted the lack of condemnation of NISA's and ENDF's actions by key international groups, such as the European Commission, the US, and the United Kingdom (UK). Though the UN became involved to oversee peace talks, insurgent factions persist in refusing to recognize any reconciliation or unification, despite the adoption of the 2012 provisional constitution. Mogadishu continues to be the epicenter of Somali violence and conflict. Since February 2009, African Union peacekeeping troops have been engaged in fighting with Islamic rebels in the city. This has hindered the work of the UN and other peacekeepers.

ECONOMY

Overview of the Economy

War, famine, drought, and some degree of international isolation have wreaked havoc with Somalia's already fragile economy. The number of people estimated to be living in extreme poverty is 43 percent in urban centers and 53 percent in rural areas. According to UN data, in 2012, Somalia's per capita gross domestic product (GDP) was estimated at $128 (USD) and its GDP to be $1,306 (USD). The labor force, which numbered 3.011 million in 2012, has few skilled laborers. Economic hardship, in fact, is one of the root causes of piracy in Somalia.

Industry

Industry accounts for 7.4 percent of the GDP and employs only a small percentage of the labor force. Many of Somalia's factories have been damaged in the war or dismantled and sold for scrap. The few that still operate depend on local agricultural products and include sugar refineries and textile production. Wireless communication technologies are a new and burgeoning industry in Somalia and show great promise. The presence of oil and natural gas reserves, as well as valuable minerals, also has the potential to attract foreign investors.

Labor
According to the U.S. Department of State, Somalia's workforce numbers 3.011 million, of which a miniscule number is considered skilled.

Energy/Power/Natural Resources
Though Somalia has proven reserves of many natural resources, the lack of infrastructure and the lengthy civil war have prevented exploration and exploitation. Tin, iron ore, gypsum, feldspar, kaolin, tantalum, gemstones, manganese, copper, quartz, silica, and bauxite, as well as salt, marble, uranium, oil and natural gas are present.

Somalia's environmental problems derive from the country's scarce resources. Overgrazing has led to soil erosion and, in the more arid regions, to desertification. Deforestation is also occurring since many Somalis rely on wood for fuel and cooking. These problems contribute to the country's frequent droughts and famines, which are increasing in intensity and length.

Fishing
Somalia's "economic zone" in terms of the national fishing industry has been a contentious issue. Without a strong, central government, European, Asian, and African fishing vessels have been able to exploit fishing waters off the coast of Somalia. Some analysts point to illegal fishing practices in Somali waters by foreign fleets and trawlers as one of the primary causes of piracy in Somalia. However, the increase in piracy has largely disrupted the local fishing industry, as well as the multi-billion-dollar tuna fishing industry of the Indian Ocean. The fishing industry also suffered greatly after the 2004 tsunami.

Forestry
Natural forest accounts for a small portion of Somalia's land area. The production of charcoal, a primary source of domestic fuel, is one of the main reasons for timber harvesting.

Mining/Metals
Somalia's mining sector is yet undeveloped. The country has unexploited deposits of iron ore, kaolin, limestone, quartz, tantalum, tin, and uranium, as well as natural gas. In 2006, Range Resources, Ltd. Of Australia negotiated with the Puntland region for the right to explore mineral and fuel deposits. However, the federal government invalidated the agreement, citing that Puntland did not have the sovereign authority to assign such rights. To date, gemstone and salt mining is still artisanal.

Agriculture
Agriculture accounts for 60.2 percent of the GDP and employs 71 percent of the labor force. The fertile south, along and between Somalia's two major rivers, is the center of cultivation, though significant rainfall in the northern highlands allows modest farming. According to the World Bank, approximately 70.3 percent of the country's total area was actually arable in 2012. The major crops are bananas, mangoes, coconuts, corn, sorghum, rice, sugarcane, sesame seeds, and beans.

Animal Husbandry
The raising of livestock has historically been, and remains, one of Somalia's most important economic activities, accounting for about 40 percent of the GDP and 50 percent of export revenue. Approximately 50 percent of the land is suitable for grazing, and traditional herding routes are well established between deep wells.

Cattle, sheep, goats and camels are the predominant livestock, with the camel being of particular importance given its ability to survive harsh climatic conditions and transport nomads and their gear. A ban in 2000 by the Persian Gulf States on livestock from the Horn of Africa, following an outbreak of Rift Valley Fever, dealt a serious blow to the sector; the ban was partially lifted in 2005. In 2014, thanks to disease prevention investments provided by the European Union and the United Kingdom, Somalia exported $5 million in livestock, particularly goats and sheep.

Tourism

Since the beginning of the civil war, Somalia has seen few tourists. A wrecked infrastructure, lawlessness, and violence (which has sometimes targeted Westerners) have put the hopes for significant tourist revenue far into the future. Hotels continue to operate, but employ private security militias. In September 2012, the non-profit organization, Somali Tourism Association (SOMTA), was founded in Mogadishu to help kick-start the industry and facilitate acceptance of tourism's value to Somali residents, who have, thus far, been largely resistant.

The country has the potential to offer many tourist attractions. These include camel treks, ancient rock paintings, a long, rugged coastline, and a range of big game animals.

Kathryn Bundy, Michael Aliprandi,
M. Lee, Savannah Schroll Guz

DO YOU KNOW?

- Although Mogadishu's location means that seafood is widely available, fish is not a favored part of the Somali diet because it is considered a food of the poor.

- There are several possible explanations for the origin of the name "Mogadishu." Some scholars believe it comes from the Persian phrase "Ma'qad Shah," which means "imperial seat of the shah." It is also possible that "Mogadishu" is an incorrectly pronounced version of a Swahili term "mwyu wa," which means "last northern city."

Bibliography

Abdullahi Mohamed Diriye. "Culture and Customs of Somalia." Westport, CT: *Greenwood Publishing Group*, 2001.

Ahmed Artan Hanghe. "Folktales From Somalia." Uppsala, Sweden: *Nordic Africa Institute*, 1998.

Ali Jimale Ahmed. "Daybreak Is Near: Literature, Clans, and the Nation-State in Somalia." Trenton, New Jersey: *Red Sea Press*, 1997.

Fran Osseo-Asare. "Food and Culture in Sub-Saharan Africa." Westport, CT: *Greenwood Press*, 2005.

Ioan Lewis. "Understanding Somalia and Somaliland: Culture, History, Society." 2nd ed. New York: *Columbia University Press*, 2011.

Mary Harper. "Getting Somalia Wrong?: Faith, War and Hope in a Shattered State." London: *Zed Books*, 2012. African Arguments Ser.

Mary-Jane Fox. "Political Culture in Somalia: Tracing Paths to Peace and Conflict." Uppsala, Sweden: *Uppsala Universitet*, 2000.

Stig Jarle Hansen. "Al-Shabaab in Somalia: The History and Ideology of a Militant Islamist Group." Oxford, UK: *Oxford UP*, 2013.

Susan M. Hassig and Zawiah Abdul Latif. "Somalia." New York: *Marshall Cavendish Benchmark*, 2007. Cultures of the World Ser.

Works Cited

_____. "News website editor gunned down in Mogadishu." *Reporters Without Borders*. Reporters Without Borders, 10 Sept. 2015. Web. http://en.rsf.org/somalia-news-website-editor-gunned-down-in-10-09-2015,48330.html.

_____. "Water, Sanitation, and Hygiene." UNICEF: Somalia. *UNICEF*, 2015. Web. http://www.unicef.org/somalia/wes.html.

2015 UNHCR country operations profile—Somalia." *UN High Commissioner for Refugees, 2015*. Web. http://www.unhcr.org/pages/49e483ad6.html.

"2015 World Freedom of the Press Index." *Reporters Without Borders*, 2015. http://index.rsf.org/#!/.

"About Us." Somali Tourism Association. *SOMTA*, 2015. http://somta.so/about-us/.

"Agricultural land (% of land area)." Data by Country. *The World Bank Group*, 2015. Web. http://data.worldbank.org/indicator/AG.LND.AGRI.ZS.

"Education in Somalia." *UNICEF: Somalia*. UNICEF, 2015. http://www.unicef.org/somalia/education.html.

"Operational Update No 03/13." *International Committee of the Red Cross*, 27 Nov. 2013. https://www.icrc.org/eng/resources/documents/update/2013/11-27-somalia-cyclone-puntland-middle-shabelle.htm.

"Maxamed Xaashi Dhamac 'Gaarriye.'" Poetry Translation Centre. *Somaliland Cyberspace*, n.d. http://www.mbali.info/doc273.htm.

"Somalia registers record exports of 5 million livestock in 2014." *Food and Agriculture Organization of the United Nations*. FAO,, 29 Apr. 2015. http://www.fao.org/news/story/en/item/283777/icode/.

"Somalia: Struggling in the face of twin natural disasters." International Committee of the Red Cross.

"Somalia: The new Constitution 2012." International Idea Institute for Democracy and Electoral Assistance. *ConstitutionNet*, 12 Jun. 2012. http://www.constitutionnet.org/vl/item/somalia-new-constitution-2012.

"Somalia" The World Factbook. *Central Intelligence Agency*, 2015. https://www.cia.gov/library/publications/the-world-factbook/geos/so.html.

"Somalia" UNData. *United Nations Statistics Division*, 2015. http://data.un.org/CountryProfile.aspx?crName=somalia.

"Somalia" *World Report 2015. Human Rights Watch*, 2015. https://www.hrw.org/world-report/2015/country-chapters/somalia .

"U.S. Relations with Somalia." Bureau of African Affairs. *U.S. Department of State*. US Department of State, 15 Jul. 2015. http://www.state.gov/r/pa/ei/bgn/2863.htm.

Abderazzaq Noor. "Muqmad (Preserved Meat)" *The Somali Kitchen*. The Somali Kitchen, 2015. http://www.somalikitchen.com/muqmad-preserved-meat.html/.

Abdulkadir Khalif, "Somalia reintroduces taxes after 23 years." *Africa Review*. Nation Media Group, 9 Mar. 2014. Web. http://www.africareview.com/News/Somalia-reintroduces-taxes-after-23-years/-/979180/2237214/-/14favcb/-/index.html.

Abdulkadir M. Wa'ays. "Bloodshed continues and music disappears." *Freemuse. Freemuse/Freedom of Musical Expression*, 4 Jul. 2008. http://freemuse.org/archives/1273.

Cedric Barnes. "Somaliland's Guurti Sparks a Crisis." Crisis Group: In Pursuit of Peace. *International Crisis Group*, 21 May 2015. http://blog.crisisgroup.org/africa/2015/05/21/somalilands-guurti-sparks-a-crisis/.

Mohamoud Ahmed Shunuuf. "History of Music in Somaliland." *The Somaliland Times,* 46 (7 Dec. 2002). http://www.somalilandtimes.net/Archive/46/4610.htm.

Susan M. Hassig and Zawiah Abdul Latif. "Somalia." New York: *Marshall Cavendish Benchmark*, 2007. Cultures of the World Ser.

Teo Kermeliotis. "Somali women defy danger to write basketball history." Cable New Network/Turner Broadcasting, 22 Dec. 2011. http://www.cnn.com/2011/12/22/sport/basketball-somalia-women-al-shabaab/.

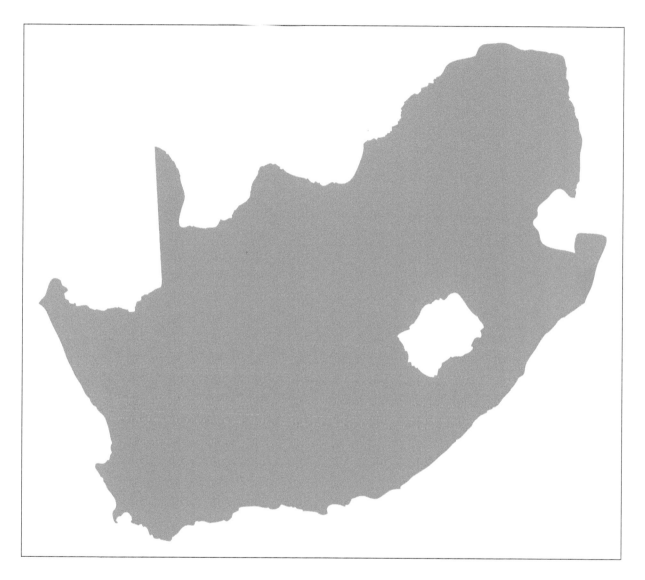

SOUTH AFRICA

Introduction

Situated at the southern tip of the African continent, the Republic of South Africa has been inhabited for well over 100,000 years. It spans the rise of prehistoric and indigenous culture, the emergence of the region's mineral wealth, European settlement, and an era of racial segregation known as apartheid, the end of which came with the 1994 general elections—the first with universal suffrage.

Unofficially founded in 1652 by Dutch traders who sought a layover point on the spice route, the country of South Africa has long been known for its cultural diversity, even earning the nickname "the rainbow nation." As such, the country maintains eleven official languages. Its modern culture embodies the influences of the country's traditional cultures, namely, the Nguni (Zulu and Xhosa peoples), Sotho, Shangaan-Tsonga, and Venda ethnic groups; its Afrikaner population, historically descended from northwestern European settlers; and its leading position, both politically and economically, in 21st-century Africa.

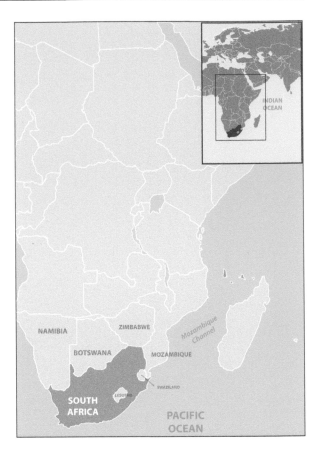

GENERAL INFORMATION

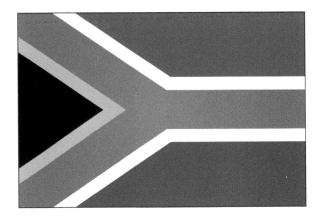

Official Languages: Afrikaans, English, Sepedi, isiNdebele, Sesotho, siSwati, Xitsonga, Setswana, Tshivenda, IsiXhosa, and IsiZulu
Population: 53,675,563 (July 2015 estimate)
Currency: Rand (ZAR)

Coins: 100 cents make one rand. Coins are available in denominations of 10, 20, and 50 cents, as well as in the value of 1 full rand, 2 full rands, and 5 full rands. Most transactions are rounded to the closest 5c. The minting of the one and two cent coins ceased in 2002. The 5 full-rand coin, with its two-metal design, was released in 2004.
Land Area: 1,214,470 square kilometers (468,909 square miles)
Water Area: 4,620 square kilometers (1,783 square miles)
National Motto: "Unity in Diversity"
National Anthem: "Nkosi Sikelel' iAfrika" ("God Bless Africa") combined with "Die Stem van Suid-Afrika" ("The Call of South Africa")
Capital: Pretoria (executive), Bloemfontein (judicial), Cape Town (legislative)
Time Zone: GMT +2
Flag Description: The flag of the Republic of South Africa features a centered horizontal green stripe, outlined in white, which breaks into a "Y"

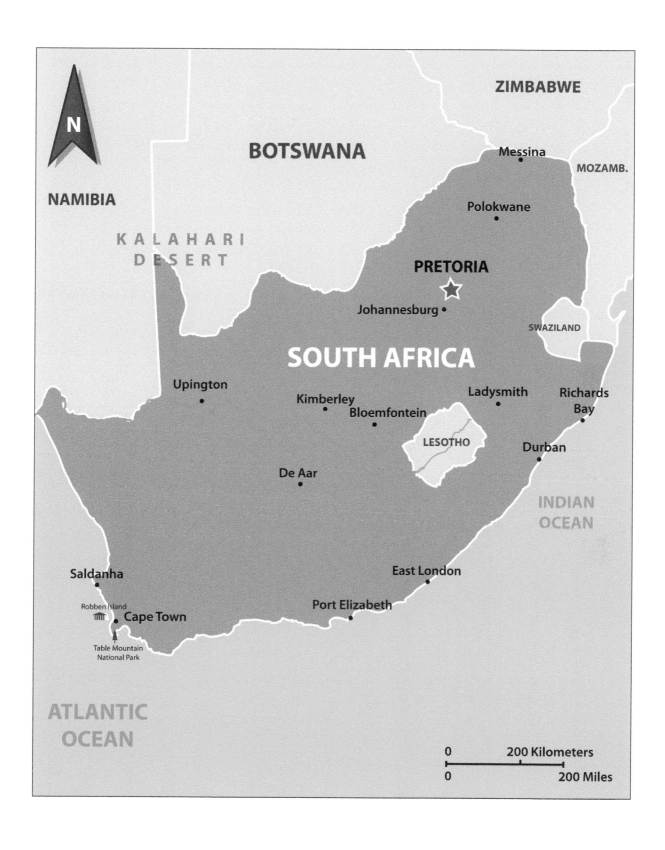

Principal Cities by Population (2011):

- Johannesburg (4,434,827)
- Cape Town (3,740,026)
- Durban (3,442,361)
- East Rand (3,178,471)
- Pretoria (2,921,488)
- Port Elizabeth (1,152,115)
- East London (755,200)
- Bloemfontein (747,431)
- Vanderbijlpark (721,662)
- Thohoyandou (618,462)

on the hoist (left) side. This "Y" creates a black equilateral triangle, outlined in yellow, against the hoist side. The green stripe is traced on both sides by equal horizontal bands of red, on the top, and blue, on the bottom. The flag symbolizes unity in its design: black, green, and yellow are the colors of the African National Congress, while the red, white, and blue reference both the Netherlands' tricolor flag and the British Union Jack.

Population

The country's most densely-populated areas are cities and the areas formerly known as Bantustans (homelands), which were reserved for ethnic Africans. In 2015, approximately 64.8 percent of the population lived in rural areas. Cape Town (population 3,740,026), Pretoria (population 2,921,488), and the township of Soweto (with a population now estimated between 3.5 and 6 million) are the largest urban centers. Whites, Asians, and those of mixed ancestry live predominantly in the cities.

Once in decline, South Africa's population has seen a sharp upturn and, in 2015, is growing by 1.33 percent. Currently, the average life expectancy is estimated at 61 for males and 64 for females. Conditions have indeed improved for South Africans, since the average life span in 2007 was 49 for men and 50 for women. Moreover, a 2008 United Nations Population Fund report, life expectancy for South Africans was lower than the average life expectancy in

continental Africa, and even lower than that of war-torn Iraq. This is no longer the case.

Languages

South Africa's eleven official languages are Zulu (IsiZulu, 22.7 percent); Xhosa (IsiXhosa, 16 percent); Afrikaans (13.5 percent); English (9.6 percent); Pedi (Sepedi, 9.1 percent); Tswana (Setswana, 8 percent); Sotho (Sesotho, 7.6 percent); Tsonga (Xitsonga, 4.5 percent); Swazi (siSwati, 2.5 percent); Venda (Tshivenda, 2.4 percent); Bdebele (isiNdebele, 2.1 percent). Sign language is also represented at 0.5 percent, although it is not one of the country's official languages. All of the native African languages are Bantu, a group of languages belonging to the Niger-Congo family. Several Indian languages (1.6 percent) are also spoken. The rate of multilingualism is high, with English serving as a second language for many South Africans. White South Africans who speak Afrikaans are known as Afrikaners and are usually descendants of 17th- and 18th-century Dutch settlers.

Native People & Ethnic Groups

Black Africans comprise 80.2 percent of the total population. They can be divided into several groups, including Zulu and Xhosa, which are the two largest. The Zulu people number an estimated nine to 10 million, while the Xhosa, concentrated primarily in the southeast, number just over 8 million; both ethnicities are unique to South Africa. Whites comprised an estimated 8.4 percent of the total population in 2014 and are mainly of Dutch and English descent. Those of mixed ancestry comprise 8.9 percent of the total, and Asians, including Indians and Malaysians, comprise roughly 2.5 percent.

One of the lasting legacies of South Africa's apartheid government is a strict division of all South African citizens into one of four racial groups: White, Black, Coloured, and Indian (all of which were capitalized under apartheid law). Before 1991, South Africa had strict laws relating to ethnicity, specifically in regards to which people could legally be called "Black." Although these laws have been abolished, people still adhere to these categories, both in terms of personal identity and social circumstance. Many mixed-race people with sub-Saharan ancestry are lumped together in a group referred to variously as "Coloured," "Bruinmense," "Kleurlinge," or "Bruin Afrikaners." Those who fall into the classification of "Coloured" have always unofficially accounted for the majority of South Africa's population because they represent a heterogeneous group.

Religions

Christians make up the single largest religious group, claiming 79.7 percent of the population. Denominations include Anglican (3.8 percent), Catholic (7.1 percent), Dutch Reform (6.7 percent), Zionist Christian (11.1 percent), Pentecostal/Charismatic (8.2 percent), Methodist (6.8 percent), and numerous independent African churches. Animists continue to account for 29 percent of the population, though this figure can also include syncretic religions, which combine Christian and animist elements. Islam (1.5 percent) and Hinduism (roughly 2.3 percent) remain minority religions.

Climate

South Africa is known for its pleasant, mild climate; long, sunny days and cool nights are the norm throughout much of the country. Overall, four different weather patterns prevail. The western coast, where it is generally warm and dry, is affected by the Benguela Current from the Atlantic Ocean between June and September. It brings light rainfall averaging 200 millimeters (eight inches) annually.

Temperatures in Cape Town average between 16° and 26° Celsius (61° and 79° Fahrenheit) in January and between 7° and 18° Celsius (44° and 64° Fahrenheit) in June. The subtropical eastern coast is hotter and more humid, affected by the warm Agulhas Current. Durban, typical of the region, experiences average temperatures between 21° and 28° Celsius (69° and 82° Fahrenheit) in January and 11° and 23° Celsius (52° and 73° Fahrenheit) in July.

In the Karroo Desert, conditions are hot and dry with low rainfall. Only the central

northwest region receives regular, heavy rainfall, an average of 600 millimeters (25 inches) falling between October and April. On the highest plateaus, mists, winter frosts, and occasional snowfall can occur.

In the regions where rainfall varies from year to year, long droughts can be followed by floods.

ENVIRONMENT & GEOGRAPHY

Topography

The Republic of South Africa occupies the southernmost tip of the African continent. The country borders Botswana, Lesotho, Mozambique, Namibia, Swaziland, and Zimbabwe. In fact, it surrounds Lesotho and nearly surrounds Swaziland. South African territory also includes several small islands in the Atlantic Ocean, namely Marion Island and Prince Edward Island. These two islands were created by a volcano that was last active in 2004.

Several natural regions make up the territory of South Africa. A high central plateau is the largest region. It can be divided into high, middle, and bushveld (Afrikaans, "rolling grasslands"). The highveld ranges in elevation between 1,200 and 1,800 meters (about 4,000 and 6,000 feet) and is bounded in the north by the Witwatersrand (Afrikaans, "ridge of white waters"), a massive, gold-bearing escarpment.

North of the Witwatersrand is the bushveld, an intensively cultivated area that has an average elevation of 1,200 meters (4,000 feet). Low mountains, including the Waterberg and Strypoortberg ranges, form the northern border of the bushveld. The middleveld, to the west and ranging in elevation between 600 and 1,200 meters (2,000 and 4,000 feet), is an arid, marginally populated area.

South of the veld is the Great Escarpment, which separates the central plateau from the coast in a semi-circle. The Drakensberg Mountains run along the southeastern coastline. The country's highest point, Mount Njesuthi (also Injesuthi Dome), rises in this range to 3,408 meters (11,181 feet). Along the southwestern coastline are the

Cedarberg Mountains, the Witsenberg Mountains, and the Great Winterhoek Mountains. Along the southern coastline are the Swartberg Mountains and the Langeberg Mountains. Some peaks in these ranges surpass 2,000 meters (over 6,500 feet).

South Africa's long, narrow coastal plain extends 2,798 kilometers (1,739 miles) along the South Atlantic and Indian Oceans.

South Africa has several rivers, but they are often dry because of low rainfall or drought. The Orange, Vaal, and Limpopo Rivers are the most significant. Natural lakes are few, but several artificial lakes have been made by damming rivers.

Cape Town gets its name from its position on the northern end of South Africa's Cape Peninsula. The city is home to more than seventy mountains, including the famous Table Mountain, which is believed to have once been an island. Table Mountain is a flat-topped mountain, more than a kilometer (3,300 feet) high. Cape Town is the largest city in South Africa by area, covering 2,499 square kilometers (965 square miles).

Plants & Animals

More than 22,000 plant species have been identified in South Africa. Savanna comprises the largest biome, covering roughly one-third of the country's total area. Various grasses and shrubs as well as acacia, baobab, and mopani trees characterize it. Vegetation varies greatly according to rainfall patterns.

Forests cover only 7.6 percent of the total area and tend to be scattered. Yellowwood, lemonwood, and ironwood are rare indigenous trees; pine and eucalyptus are non-indigenous trees grown for timber.

The Cape Floristic Kingdom, also known as the Cape Floral Region—a small fynbos (Afrikaans, "fine bush") biome, which resembles an English heath—is one of six floral kingdoms in the world and is located on South Africa's western coast. The area contains 8,700 plant species, 68 percent of them endemic to South Africa. The area was inscribed as a UNESCO World Heritage Site in 2004.

Wildlife is also extensive. The country boasts elephants, zebras, lions, monkeys, baboons, antelope, black and white rhinoceroses, cheetahs, and a sizable population of birds and reptiles. Approximately 15 percent of the total animal species are threatened, the black rhinoceros critically so. In fact, the World Wildlife Fund estimates that between 2007 and 2013, rhino poaching in South Africa alone increased from 13 to 1,004, driven by the Vietnamese demand for rhino horn, which is believed to be a cancer treatment and medicinal cure-all.

CUSTOMS & COURTESIES

Greetings

South Africa recognizes eleven official languages, including English, Afrikaans, Sesotho, Setswana, Xhosa, and Zulu. Afrikaans—a derivative of the Dutch language that took root during colonization in the 17th century—is the most widely used and encountered language. In addition to English, this is the language of informal conversation. Zulu, represented by an estimated 22.7 percent of the population, is most commonly spoken at home, followed by Xhosa. English is the dominant language of government and media. Other existing languages and dialects, though not official, are nonetheless considered relevant, as their existence helps to preserve the cultural identities of the communities and ethnicities they represent.

Greetings are an important aspect of South African culture, as they help to forge friendly connections that cultivate a profound sense of community. Exchanges are leisurely and not to be rushed, as South Africans like to include extensive exchange of pleasantries and social discussion. A typical greeting is "Hallo" ("Hello") followed by "Hoe gaan dit?" ("How are you?"). This exchange is commonly accompanied by a handshake. A more informal or colloquial greeting is "Howzit," a catch-all equivalent to "Hi," "How are you" and "What are you up to?" Generally, an informal response would be "Goed dankie" ("Fine, thank you"). Additionally, both "Asseblief" ("Please") and "Totsiens" ("Bye") commonly serve as a farewell.

Gestures & Etiquette

A handshake is the universal greeting in South Africa. However, interaction between men and women is typically modest, and it is not expected that a foreign male will extend his hand to a South African woman. A woman will instead likely nod her head in greeting. Family is an exception, as female relatives are often kissed on the cheek. Hand gestures while speaking are very common. However, pointing a finger at someone, standing to close to someone, or speaking to someone with hands in pockets is considered impolite. In addition, while racial and ethnic tensions are widespread, race and ethnicity are generally not considered taboo topics of conversation, as they are in other cultures.

Eating/Meals

A South African meal is certain to be a festive affair and can feature multiple courses over a leisurely few hours. Generally, South Africans eat three meals per day. Utensils are usually not offered; instead, the meal is served in a communal dish. In this fashion, each diner serves themselves from large dishes of food usually centered in the table. It is also important to use the right hand when passing or reaching for food, as the left hand is considered impure, and traditionally associated with the cleansing of the body.

Breakfast usually consists of "putu pap" (also, "krummelpap" a hot, crumbly cornmeal porridge), served with milk, coffee or tea. Corn, known as mealie, is a common crop, and mealie pap (corn porridge) is a staple food in South Africa. While considered bland on its own, it is often the foundation for an entrée of hearty sauce or stew. In urban areas, roasted mealie is a popular street snack, as is bunny chow (also, "bunny" or "kota"), which is half a bread loaf hollowed out and filled with curry, a fast food established by Durban Indians. In addition, lunch tends to be the biggest meal of the day in rural areas, whereas in urban areas dinner is a larger, more leisurely event. Rural meals also tend to be more modest—such as a base of mealie pap with stewed vegetables—due to widespread poverty and the availability of locally grown or raised produce and meat.

Additionally, wineries have been present in South Africa since the mid-17th century. While the wine is largely considered superb in quality and reasonably priced, beer is considered South Africa's national beverage. Eighteen is the legal drinking age.

Fruit juices and tea are other common beverages served at meals.

Visiting

In general, visiting is a casual or informal affair in South African culture. However, modesty is still emphasized, especially in terms of dress. If a guest has children, they are likely to be invited as well, and food and drink will be furnished for them. It is not inappropriate to offer to contribute a dish, though this should not serve as a hostess gift. Flowers, chocolates or wine are commonly given as gifts. However, the gift is customarily presented with the right hand.

Guests should expect to sample all food offered to them, as a sign of appreciation for a host's hospitality. However, if a guest does not drink alcohol, it is considered appropriate to politely decline. With respect to food preparation, the men of the house traditionally oversee the grilling, while the women prepare a variety of side dishes, including stuffed breads, bean salads, pickled vegetables, and spiced potatoes.

LIFESTYLE

Family

The idea of family is revered in South African culture. Traditionally, allegiance extends beyond the nuclear family—most commonly, a father, mother, and their children—to include extended relatives. This is particularly evident in tribal communities, where fellow tribal and family members often lend emotional and financial support during difficult times.

One challenge in the rural regions is the absence of male family members who leave to work in the cities. Their absences often place more pressure and responsibility on women to provide for their families. It is not uncommon for rural women to work long and laborious hours harvesting fruit to earn income. The routine domestic duties of cooking, cleaning, and parenting then, are often left to their daughters. Consequently, girls over the age of ten sometimes forfeit their education in order to stay home and contribute to their households. Education is typically made a priority for young boys, particularly in the hopes that this will equip them to provide for their family and community in the future.

In recent years, domestic violence, the spread of HIV/AIDS and a climbing divorce rate have raised concerns about a disintegrating family unit, particularly among urban families. National anxiety about the socio-economic repercussions of this breakdown has prompted the formation of organizations such as the South African National Council for Marriage Guidance and Counseling. This group, along with similar organizations, aims to encourage sound relationships and stable communities.

Housing

Upper class homes in the larger cities typically have linear European construction with white-washed walls. In recent years, a modified style of modern and classic architecture is prominent. Rural homes are more unique, as they feature the traditional beehive hut, characteristic of Zulu tribal homes and featuring layers of grass over a wooden framework. In recent years, these homes began incorporating mud and cement, which are easily constructed and slightly less vulnerable to unpredictable rains and floods. The huts are placed differently depending on the tribe. Zulu communities, for example, are typically arranged in a circle around a central cattle pen and then surrounded with a fence. Traditionally, these fortified villages are situated on a slope with the chief's hut at the highest point.

In recent years South Africa has experienced a significant housing shortage, prompting government action. In fact, since the early 1990s, the state has overseen the construction of nearly 1.5 million housing units. As of 2015, nearly 65 percent of the population resides in urban areas.

Food

Traditional cuisine in South African is largely a blend of indigenous and European influences, along with a blend of Asian and Middle Eastern traditions and techniques. South African cuisine was also shaped by the early presence of the Dutch East India Company, which used the Cape as an important stop on its trading routes. The company also brought in slaves from Malay and Java, who in turn introduced their distinct culinary styles. Native agricultural products such as corn (maize), squash, sweet potatoes, and wild fruits, as well as wild game and fish, feature prominently in South African food.

Typically, South African cuisine is characterized by the simple use of meat—beef, lamb and steak, as well as more distinctive local selections such as ostrich or crocodile—and corn. This is evident in staples such as mieliepap (cornmeal porridge), boerwors (spicy sausages)—introduced by the Dutch and the English—and biltong (dried, salted meats). Grilling is the most popular preparation method. Pickled fish stews are also enjoyed along the coast.

Potjiekos (literally "small pot food") is the most common entrée, named for the three-legged cast iron "potjie" in which it is prepared. Potjiekos is a general term for meat and vegetable stew, of which there are many variations. Usually, the meal consists of sautéed chopped onions, lamb, and diced bacon, combined with quartered potatoes, cabbage, water, lemon juice and mixed herbs. The stew is left simmering in a pot, with the result being a very tender meat in a savory sauce, usually served with side dishes of yellow rice or bean salad. Bobotie is a popular baked meal and typically consists of browned ground lamb complemented by onion and chopped tart apple, curry powder, raisins, slivered almonds, lemon juice, eggs, and turmeric, while an egg-based, custard-like topping covers this filling.

Life's Milestones

As family is considered the cornerstone of South African culture, milestones such as births, weddings, and funerals are customarily observed and practiced. Generally, births are observed with a small gift of food or money, while weddings are typically celebrated with dancing and feasting. In rural areas, dowries are commonplace, and usually consist of cattle and livestock. In addition, newly married women may wear colored beads in their hair and on their skirts to indicate their status.

Male circumcision remains an important tradition in tribal culture. It is most often performed at the age of sixteen and is considered a rite of passage, signifying the transition from boyhood to manhood. Once a boy is circumcised, he is eligible to marry, buy land, and participate in community hearings. However, traditional male circumcision has recently become a public health issue and has come under criticism for being a form of body mutilation.

Due to the AIDS epidemic, funerals are all too frequent—so much so that the country has to consider revising its burial rites. Traditionally, custom dictates that the deceased are buried in a coffin and the family of the dead slaughter an ox. The rising death rate, however, has frequently resulted in overcrowded burial sites and even bankruptcies due to onerous burial expenses. As a result, officials have adapted local custom to incorporate cremation, and communities have started burial societies that help residents cover the cost of funeral arrangements.

CULTURAL HISTORY

Art

South Africa has witnessed a dynamic cultural history rich with artistic expression. It began with the rock art of its nomadic cave dwellers and continued with the European influences of both the country's colonial period and the voices and expressions of the black revolutionaries who fought against it. In particular, South Africa's cultural history is rooted in the Khoekhoen nomads and Bantu-speaking people who are the ancestors of existing Zulu, Xhosa, Swazi, and Tswana tribes, among others. The cave dwellings of the first nomads—referred to as the "Bushman"

people—date back ten thousand years and contain numerous detailed paintings. Drawn in white, red, brown, and yellow pigments derived from indigenous plants, the scenes depict a range of domestic life and include representations of dark-skinned humans and animals. Most remarkable is the introduction of white figures on horseback in some of the more recent paintings, recognized as the earliest references to colonization.

As these tribal settlements evolved, they developed certain art traditions, such as ceramic sculptures, beaded jewelry, colorful textiles, and other woven or carved objects. These tribal settlements were sustained until the late 15th century, when Portuguese explorers set up ports of trade. The presence of the Portuguese attracted competition from the Dutch in the late 17th century, who brought their folk art traditions. By the end of the 18th century, Dutch trade had weakened and the British took hold of the coastline, strengthening the influence of European culture in the country. The Dutch who remained, called the Boers, moved inland, further displacing the Khoekhoen people and occupying Zululand (a historical region in southeastern South Africa).

During this colonial era, South African art focused largely on detailed portrayals of the people and landscape. Artists such as Thomas Baines (1820–1875) traveled the countryside to research everyday life in this "new world." They used paintings to record the people, landscapes, and wildlife. By the end of the 19th century, with colonialism deeply entrenched, artists began to explore the local community. Consistent with the European movements of the time, painters such as Jacobus Hendrik Pierneef (1886–1957), Jan Volschenk (1853–1936), and Hugo Naudé (1869–1941) desired to engage their environment and create pieces that expressed the "moment." The result was an unprecedented subjectivity: highly emotional color palettes and experimentation with light and shadow. South African-born female painters Irma Stern (1894–1966) and Maggie Laubser (1886–1973) are credited with bringing the German Expressionist style to South Africa.

During the apartheid era, visual arts were divided into two categories: traditional art, free of social or political influence, and abstract art that dealt with the issues at hand. Alternative media, such as cartoons and graffiti, were used to express discontent, and political art became a valued vehicle for opposition. Post-apartheid, black and white artists alike are exercising their freedom of expression, while also taking an opportunity to recall tradition. Folk art is becoming increasingly popular as artists reinterpret the tribal crafts of their heritage. While maintaining their domestic function, basketry, embroidery, beadwork, and ceramics are being abstracted to communicate the ambivalence and hope of the new era.

Architecture

During South Africa's apartheid years (1948–1994), art become more political. In addition, modern movements, such as abstract art, became increasingly popular, as did themes of nationalism and cultural identity and art dealing with the apartheid experience. Prominent artists from this period included Gerard Sekoto (1913–1993), considered the father of South African art, and abstract painter Walter Whall Battiss (1906–1982).

South African architecture is a direct reflection of its environment and colonial history. As such, it has distinct European influences, most notably Dutch and English. One particular architectural style is Cape Dutch architecture, which emerged during the late 17th century during Dutch colonization (1652–1795). The style is unique to the Western Cape Province—with Cape Town the capital—and is reminiscent of the architecture of the Netherlands. Characteristics of this particular style include the lime wash effect (whitewashed walls), ornamental gables, and thatched roofs, with the latter implemented to keep homes warm in winter and cool during the summers. This style is evident in the gabled homesteads, such as the Tulbagh Country House, which is now a hotel, in the Western Cape. With the arrival of the British in the late 18th and early 19th centuries, colonial British architecture began to blend with the Cape Dutch style, resulting in a hybrid, or blended, style.

With the discovery of gold and diamonds in the late 19th century, buildings became more grand and ornate, and featured a blend of various styles, from Victorian to Gothic to Neoclassical. This period was followed by the whimsical designs of the art deco movement (1925–1939), a decorative style exemplified by Cape Town's Greenmarket Square. However, the apartheid era was characterized by bland public structures. As the crime rate increased in urban areas, local architecture sacrificed aesthetics for security provisions, such as high walls and electric fences. Two exceptions are the modern and minimal Constitutional Court in Johannesburg and the somber Freedom Park in Pretoria.

Rural and traditional architecture was often earthen in origin and featured local resources such as thatched and woven grass, reeds, sandstone, and clay (wood was typically scarce). Often, rural architecture consisted of multifamily dwellings and communal style homesteads. One dominant style of this type of architecture is the beehive-shaped huts popularized by the Zulu peoples. These typically consist of a frame of wooden sticks or saplings bent and tied together to create a dome and then covered with grass and thatching. Other southern tribes built huts made largely of stone or mud, often with conical, thatched roofs. South Africa is also known for the wall paintings of the Ndebele. Beginning in the 18th century—when the Ndebele transitioned to mud or stone dwellings—they began painting vivid colors and geometric designs on their houses. The colorful patterns were largely considered both a cultural, as well as individual, form of expression.

Drama

South African theatre consisted mainly of European plays well into the 20th century, until black writers began expressing themselves at the local level. One of the most celebrated pieces from this time is *The Girl Who Killed to Save* by Herbert Dhlomo (1903–1956), considered one of the leading figures of South African literature. This drama garnered popularity despite the fact that the apartheid regime denied funds and resources to black playwrights.

The black theatrical scene flourished in the 1950s under the leadership of Athol Fugard

(1932–), who established several troupes in Johannesburg and Port Elizabeth. This movement set off a ripple of political theater that continued for the next two decades, the most acclaimed product being *Woza Albert!*, which depicted Jesus Christ visiting apartheid-era South Africa.

Music

The victory over apartheid has spawned an artistic rebirth, and there is no stronger evidence of this than the evolution of South African music. Crossing all genres, it has prompted some to return to traditional tribal a-cappella. Others have turned to gospel music, recalling the anthems of Dutch missionaries. One movement blends both indigenous harmonies and the church choir mbube (meaning "lion") style into isicathamiya (a type of music that originated with the Zulus, but identified with *a cappella* singing), which has been popularized internationally by the group Ladysmith Black Mambazo.

Contemporary pop music has also become an eclectic blend of styles, and none more so than the pop phenomenon kwaito. Kwaito, slang for "hot" or "dangerous" (but originating with the Afrikaans word kwaai, meaning "angry"), is largely considered South Africa's version of hip-hop and house music and is the country's most popular genre. It has become increasingly popular among youth since the music largely reflects a country in political transition and features themes of political and social struggle and restlessness. However, the music has become controversial due to its alleged objectification of women and sensationalized view of violence and urban life.

This style of music was largely pioneered by the band Boom Shaka, active from 1993 to 2000 and known to question in their lyrics the country's social hardships, such as poverty and domestic abuse. The band Bongo Maffin, founded in Cape Town in 1996, incorporates international sounds and spirituality into their music. They have furthered the kwaito tradition, helping it become a household name on the contemporary music scene. Today, kwaito has moved beyond the music industry to become indicative of South African pop culture, representing all eleven official languages and influencing fashion, television shows, and national ad campaigns

Legendary South African jazz musician Hugh Masekela (1939–) has spent the most recent incarnation of his sixty-year career rallying against the residual effects of apartheid. Exiled during the apartheid era, today he is credited with reinvigorating South Africa's recording scene and nurturing young talent. On the humanitarian front, he pioneered the Musicians and Artists Programme of South Africa, which develops drug rehabilitation initiatives for artists afflicted by addiction. Masekela also formed the first African-owned independent record label, Chissa, which has broadened to also include theatre, opera, and film.

Literature

Literature has been the pulse of South African society since the oral traditions of the first tribal settlers. The country's written literary history begins with the European immigrants who used fiction to cope with the discomfort and unfamiliarity of their new surroundings. This is illustrated by the 19th-century adventure stories of Sir Henry Rider Haggard (1856–1925), including the bestselling *King Solomon's Mines* (1885). Haggard's work, though sometimes criticized for romanticizing the colonists and casting native South Africans in antagonizing roles, continues to be influential. Olive Schreiner's (1855–1920) *The Story of an African Farm* (1883), with characters designed to represent each aspect of South African society, is considered the first truly South African work for its bold vision of a freethinking people.

The 20th century witnessed the emerging voices of black authors. The novel *Mhudi* (1930) by Solomon Tshekisho Plaatje (1876–1932) was one of the first books published in English by a black South African. Later, in 1948, Alan Paton (1903–1988) helped put South African literature on the map with the international bestseller *Cry, the Beloved Country* (1948). During the 1950s, *Drum* magazine emerged as a voice of black culture and the liberation movement. The magazine helped open the door for anti-apartheid literature through the next three decades. Prominent authors during this period include poet Mongane Wally Serote (1944–) and novelists Nadine Gordimer (1923–2014) and J. M. Coetzee (1940–), both Nobel laureates. In addition, writers such as Zakes Mda (1948–) began critically reflecting on the state of the new South Africa.

CULTURE

Arts & Entertainment

South Africans are devoted sportsmen and spectators. Cricket, football (soccer), and rugby are the most popular sports. With the end of apartheid, South African teams became racially mixed and were once again allowed to participate in international events.

Cultural Sites & Landmarks

South Africa is home to eight World Heritage Sites, as designated by United Nations Educational, Scientific and Cultural Organization (UNESCO). Included are geological sites, such as the Vredefort Dome, the oldest and largest impact crater on Earth; archaeological sites that feature the fossils of hominids (early humans); and cultural areas, such as the city of Mapungubwe, situated in northern South Africa.

South Africa features an extraordinary landscape. The Greater St. Lucia Wetland Park extends from Kosi Bay to the southern end of Lake St. Lucia. It is Africa's largest estuary, encompassing five different ecosystems. The Cape Floral Region Protected Areas are located in Cape Province and are made up of eight protected areas that house 20 percent of the country's flora. Besides its exquisite beauty, the area is also considered a precious resource for studying ecological and biological processes. It has been identified as one of the world's 18 biodiversity hotspots. In addition, the Sterkfontein Caves house one of the richest paleontological sites in the world and boast the discovery of the first adult skull, believed to be roughly 2.6 million years old.

Cape Town is home to numerous cultural sites and landmarks, including Table Mountain National Park, the Victoria & Alfred Waterfront, and Robben Island, which offers a historical overview of the apartheid movement. During its history, the island housed many political prisoners, including Nelson Mandela, who was incarcerated there for eighteen years. It was designated as a UNESCO World Heritage Site in 1999. (In addition, there is a Mandela Museum in Mthatha, which details Mandela's struggles.)

Cape Town is also home to the Victoria & Alfred Waterfront, an historic working harbor that is South Africa's most visited destination; and the town's Malay Quarter, which features a picturesque urban landscape of cobbled streets and colorful houses. Cape Town is also known for its modern architecture, as well as the unique Cape Dutch style that flourished during the nation's early colonial period.

Tourism authorities recognize the draw of South Africa's great topography and wildlife, and have made efforts to establish the nation as a premier ecotourism destination. However, increased water consumption coupled with sustained drought is rapidly depleting the water supply. Water levels at some South African parks and preserves have been at historic lows in recent years. These issues, combined with the environmental impact of tourism in general, have inspired some notable innovations. The Lynedoch Eco-Village, found just south of the Cape Winelands, is South Africa's first attempt at an ecologically designed, self-sufficient community. All the houses and community buildings are energy efficient and emphasize recycling. The intention is that such self-contained communities will control urbanization, preserve the environment, and protect the local economy.

Cape Town, often referred to as "Mother City" by locals, is the legislative capital of South Africa and the capital of the Western Cape Province of the country. Cape Town's natural landmarks and long coastline have helped make the city the most popular tourist destination in South Africa; many have called Cape Town one of the most beautiful cities in the world. Cape

Town's culture is a mixture of European and African influence, with a mixed population to match.

Libraries & Museums

Cape Town's South African Museum is considered the oldest museum in sub-Saharan Africa. A diverse cultural institution, its exhibits range from fossils and Stone Age tools to traditional 20th-century clothing. Other museums in Cape Town include the Slave Lodge, which focuses on Cape Town's unique history, and the South African National Gallery. In all, the country is home to over 300 museums.

The National Library of South Africa (Staats-Bibliotheek der Zuid-Afrikaansche Republiek), established in 1818, bills itself as the leading national library in Africa. A dual site—it is located in Cape Town and Pretoria—the library has over three million items in its collection.

Holidays

South Africans celebrate traditional religious holidays relating to different faiths and a number of political holidays commemorating the country's struggle for equality. They are marked by parades and rallies and include Human Rights Day (March 21), Freedom Day (April 27), Workers' Day (May 1), Youth Day (June 16), and Day of Reconciliation (December 16). National Women's Day is celebrated on August 9, while the Day of Goodwill is celebrated on December 26, the day after Christmas is observed.

South Africa also has an extensive calendar of art, music, and wine festivals. Among the most popular annual events are the National Festival of the Arts in Grahamstown, the One City Festival in Cape Town, and the Arts Alive in Johannesburg.

Youth Culture

Young people in South Africa are experiencing a newfound freedom of expression, as they represent the first generation to come of age in the post-apartheid era. As such, youth culture is becoming a major influence in the country's political and social rebirth. This is evident in the abundance of media that caters to young South Africans. One of the first stations to secure licensing post-apartheid was Johannesburg's 99.2 YFM radio. Targeting the "Y Generation," it is considered the most popular station for pop music's kwaito craze, which emerged in the 1990s. (The word kwaito is derived from the Afrikaans word kwaai, which means "angry.")

South African youth are also becoming more engaged socially and politically, again, largely through media influence. For example, *Y Magazine*, a counterpart to YFM radio, pushes the envelope by featuring articles that address the struggles of South Africa's urban youth culture. Ranging from fashion to education advocacy to government policy, *Y Magazine* has been applauded for moving beyond mainstream entertainment magazines to create a well-rounded political platform for black and white youth alike.

Sports also figure prominently into South African youth culture, most notably football (soccer). Bafana Bafana, the South African national soccer team, has a large youth following. South Africa hosted the 2010 FIFA World Cup, the first time the tournament was held in Africa. In addition, South Africa is known for its surf culture, which has grown in recent years. As such, it is not uncommon to see youth throughout the country dressed in clothing related to the sport.

SOCIETY

Transportation

Generally, cars are widely available in South Africa, but they are expensive and owned by only a few. In deep, rural areas, where motorized transport is either not available or not affordable, the government is promoting bicycle use. Targeting mainly women and children who need better access to work and school, the program plans a rollout of one million cycles over ten years. The government is also planning on providing cycling education and opening cycle shops.

However, public transport safety and reliability remain a challenge, and nearly 10,000 deaths result from traffic accidents each year. Many of these accidents are attributed to lax regulation, overworked drivers and the lack of traffic law enforcement. Consequently, drivers of mopeds, cars, and other private or commercial vehicles face similar problems. In response to this reality, the government has recently created the "Arrive Alive" campaign, which is aimed at promoting diver safety. And in 2011, the government committed to the UN's Decade of Action for Road Safety 2011–2020 to reduce traffic fatalities.

Driving is on the left-hand side of the road, with all vehicles being right-hand drive. Seat belt use is compulsory and using a hand-held cellular phone is prohibited. Toll roads represent nearly a quarter of all surfaced national roads.

Transportation Infrastructure

In general, South Africa has a well developed and extensive transportation infrastructure, with more than 20,384 km (12,666 miles). Rail transport is available nationwide, while buses and light rail systems are the popular modes of transportation in urban areas. The country's extensive rail network is considered the 10th longest in the world and offers links to Botswana, Lesotho, Namibia, Swaziland, and Zimbabwe. As of 2015, the railway connecting South Africa to Mozambique is under repair.

While popular in urban areas, buses arc also commonly used for rural travel. Overall, minibus taxis are the predominant mode of transport, serving 70 percent of the population. While there are more than 90 airports in South Africa, Johannesburg International Airport, known as O. R. Tambo International Airport, is the central hub for domestic and international flights and handles approximately 19,135,093 passengers annually.

In advance of the 2010 FIFA World Cup, South Africa announced a ZAR 9 billion investment in transportation infrastructure. This included a transformation of the bus industry and a taxi recapitalization program, as well as upgrades to the national airports. Between 2008 and 2012, the government spent in excess of ZAR 19.5 billion annually to improve rail infrastructure and ports.

Media & Communications

After decades of repression, South Africa is now considered a driving force in African media. Whereas the media once was a vehicle for white propaganda, it now provides a variety of programming for black South Africans and many tribal groups. State-run and commercial television networks broadcast nationally, and paid services such as satellite and cable TV are becoming increasingly popular, even in rural areas. In addition, a deregulated radio sector has led to an abundance of broadcasts, ranging from national programs by the South African Broadcasting Corporation (SABC) to small community stations aimed at specific ethnic groups.

With 11 recognized languages in South Africa, diversity is key in the country's media industry. This is particularly reflected in the print media, where newspapers are published in a variety of languages—most notably English and Afrikaans, as well as tribal languages such as Zulu—with many alternative publications available. South Africa's most popular dailies include the tabloid-style *Daily Sun, The Star,* and *The Sowetan*, all of which are published in English. The leading Afrikaans published newspapers include *Die Burger* and *Beeld*, which is published in both a daily and a Saturday format.

Freedom of the press is provided for in the constitution and is largely respected. State control of media content is moderate and journalists practice their investigations and reporting with little threat of repression. In fact, Reporters Without Borders has consistently ranked South Africa as one of top fifty countries in the world in the early 21st century in regards to freedom of expression. In their 2015 Freedom of the Press Index, they rated South Africa 39 out of 180 countries for journalistic liberty.

Additionally, Internet access continues to grow in South Africa and in 2015, an estimated 49 percent of the population—26,841,126 people—were Internet users. More important, the Internet is playing a greater role in the media, and South Africa is considered a continental leader in this regard.

SOCIAL DEVELOPMENT

Standard of Living

The country ranked 118th out of 187 UN member countries on the 2014 United Nations Human Development Index (HDI). The country is classified as having "medium human development."

Water Consumption

Rising demand and ageing or outdated infrastructure have affected water consumption and quality in South Africa in recent years. In fact, water demand is expected to increase by as much as 50 percent within the next 25 years. While improved water sources were available to 99.6 percent of urban populations and 81.4 percent of rural populations, overall water quality and pollution, ineffective or even non-existant sewage treatment, and a crumbling infrastructure, continue to be growing concerns in the second decade of the 21st century. Widespread cases of diarrhea in young children and an outbreak of cholera in 2001 have underlined these concerns. As of 2015, 30.4 percent of the urban population and 39.5 percent of the rural population still did not have proper sanitation systems.

Education

Since the end of apartheid, the South African government has made significant strides towards eradicating the legal discrimination that occurred under white minority rule. Inequalities still exist, but today ethnic Africans have better access to educational opportunities and training, a legal framework to guarantee their rights, and greater funding. Nonetheless, in poorer areas, shortages of teachers and materials, large classes and inadequate facilities are still problems.

Schooling is compulsory for 10 years, beginning at the age of seven. Instruction can be in any of the country's eleven official languages. Schools set tuition fees to complement government subsidies, but it is illegal to exclude students who are unable to pay. Education at private schools is widely available for those who can afford it. According to a report published by the South African government in 2012, there were approximately 25,826 educational institutions. Enrollment in all sectors of the educational system was numbered at 12,428,069 that same year.

South Africa has over 20 universities and numerous technical schools. In fact, the country has more institutions of higher learning than most African nations combined. Institutes of higher education are officially desegregated, and the language of instruction varies between institutions. Among the universities are the University of South Africa in Pretoria, the University of Cape Town, and the University of the Witwatersrand in Johannesburg.

As of 2015, literacy rates among South Africans over 15 are high—95.5 percent for men and 93.1 percent for women. The average literacy rate is 94.3 percent.

Women's Rights

Since the late 1990s, several key pieces of legislation have been enacted to ensure equal rights for women. These include the Domestic Violence Act of 1998 and the Promotion of Equality and Prevention of Unfair Discrimination Act of 2000. There is also increasing gender equality in government and the public sector. Nonetheless, barriers remain in the private sector, and women remain more economically disadvantaged than men, often working for lower wages or inferior positions. However, three significant issues affecting women's rights in South Africa are HIV/AIDS and sexual and domestic violence.

UNICEF estimates that, in 2012, South African women accounted for 3,400,000 of the nation's HIV-infected population. This represents the world's second highest concentration of infected women, surpassed only by India. Compromised rights make it seemingly impossible for women to surmount this epidemic. For example, the patriarchal family dynamic—as well as the threat of domestic violence—often prohibits women from making health decisions. In addition, men are permitted to take multiple wives, which increases transmission risks. In addition, South African men are normally reluctant to undergo HIV testing.

When women do become infected, they typically face abandonment, violence, and discrimination. Trying to access health care often brings abuse as spouses are in denial about their own status, and thus resent the treatment. If women are supported in pursuing care, treatment requires regular hospital visits and adequate food must be available to take medication. However, this level of treatment is frequently inaccessible to poor, rural women who lack access to proper nutrition and transportation. Furthermore, existing hospitals are severely understaffed.

The international community continues to press the South African government to implement legislation that combats the stigma and violence that infected women face. One priority is making care more accessible, though this effort is hampered significantly by cultural attitudes. Creative grassroots solutions are also emerging. Individual provinces reach out to women with programs such as "Gogo Grannies," which gives grandmothers who adopt orphaned grandchildren a plot of land to cultivate and farm. In addition, the Positive Women's Network is a forum for South African women living with HIV to discuss their anxieties about coping with the stigma. As many of these women have been abandoned, they are also taught basic business skills and income-generating crafts to help them provide for themselves.

In South Africa, it is estimated that a woman is raped every seventeen seconds. In addition, sexual violence is especially rampant in schools, and young girls are frequently assaulted by teachers and classmates alike, either as punishment or in exchange for food or better grades. Although it is mandatory to report abuse, victims who come forward are typically met with indifference and hostility. It is also widely believed that school authorities do not challenge the perpetrators, to avoid negative publicity. The criminal justice system is generally unwilling to assist those who report abuse. In addition, biases of surgeons and judges often inhibit proper medical and legal services, resulting in poor documentation of crucial medical evidence and rendering investigations incomplete.

Consequently, South African girls interrupt their education or refrain from joining the workforce because they feel vulnerable. The South African government acknowledges the severity of the issue, but only small actions have been taken. International rights groups remain concerned that these young women are accepting sexual violence as inescapable. The government now faces growing pressure to be more aggressive in implementing education policy that supports a safe environment free from gender discrimination.

Health Care
Though the health care situation in South Africa has improved, the system still reflects the socioeconomic divisions that typified the country during apartheid. Today, state hospitals provide comprehensive care to the majority of South Africans on a sliding scale. Pre-natal and postnatal care is free for mothers, and health care is free for children until the age of six.

Hospitals and clinics are primarily located in urban centers, and many people rely on traditional medicine. The wealthier class can afford treatment in private hospitals, where standards and costs are high. Still, hospitals are largely understaffed, and as of 2013, there was less than one physician (0.78) for every 1,000 people.

Hosts of illnesses afflict the poorer majority of ethnic Africans, for whom life expectancy is lower and infant mortality higher. Tuberculosis, malaria, and measles are all problems, and 6,836,500 people are living with HIV/AIDS as of 2014. Tuberculosis, which often accompanies HIV infection, accounted for 9.9 percent of deaths in 2012. However, government officials remain uncertain whether all TB deaths are actually reported as such, and, consequently, the percentage may be much higher.

GOVERNMENT

Structure
South Africa became a republic in 1961 and until the early 1990s, the white minority maintained apartheid in the face of increasing political pres-

sure within the country as well as the international community. The country's first fully democratic elections were held in 1994, and ethnic Africans finally won majority control. A new constitution guaranteeing equal rights was drafted on May 8, 1996; approved December 4, 1996; in force on February 4, 1997; and implemented over the next four years. It has been amended several times, most recently, in 2013.

The executive branch is presided over by a president, who is both head of state and head of government. He or she is elected to a five-year term from the majority party by the National Assembly. There is a two-term limit. The president is responsible for appointing a deputy president and a cabinet of ministers from within the National Assembly.

South Africa's bicameral legislature consists of the 400-member National Assembly and the ninety-member National Council of Provinces (ten members from each province), all of whom serve five-year terms. Members of the National Assembly are elected by proportional representation, whereas the National Council of Provinces are appointed at the provincial level. Pretoria is the executive capital, Cape Town is the legislative capital, and Bloemfontein is the judicial capital.

Political Parties

South Africa has a multiparty system, with 11 parties represented in parliament as of 2015. Parliamentary democracies often have a large number of political parties, which have a tendency to shift in terms of political platform and their alliance with other parties sharing common interests. Often, parliamentary systems are ruled by coalitions of two or more parties that unite to form a majority coalition. These coalitions differ in nature, with some coalitions having a lasting strength and others failing to govern at all. Additionally, it is not unusual for parties to dissolve because of personality conflicts within the organization.

The African National Congress (ANC) is the country's most popular and dominant political party; since the end of apartheid in 1994, it

has governed as the major portion of a coalition. As of 2015, it controls eight of the country's nine provinces; Western Cape was the only province not won by the ANC, but was carried instead by the Democratic Alliance (DA). Other parties include the Inkatha Freedom Party (IFP), United Democratic Movement (UDM), Economic Freedom Fighters (EFF), and the African Christian Democratic Party (ACDP). In 2015, the Democratic Alliance and the Economic Freedom Fighters were the two largest parties represented in parliament outside of the ANC, with 89 and 25 respective National Assembly seats. In the 2014 general elections, the ANC received 62.2 percent of votes.

Local Government

South Africa consists of nine provinces, which include Eastern Cape, Free State, Gauteng, KwaZulu-Natal, Limpopo, Mpumalanga, Northern Cape, North West, and Western Cape. Each of these provinces is administered by a provincial assembly. The provincial assemblies choose a premier to preside over the province's core executive council. Under the current constitution, the provinces are vested with wide-ranging powers.

Judicial System

On the uppermost tier of the judicial branch is the Supreme Court of Appeals, which consists of a court president and deputy president, along with 21 judges. This body is the highest authority on all non-constitutional matters. Also on the highest tier is the Constitutional Court, which consists of a chief justice, deputy chief justice, and nine judges. This branch of the judiciary has the highest authority on constitutional matters. Beneath these two courts are High Courts, Magistrates' Courts, labor courts, and land claims courts.

Taxation

Income tax is the main source of tax revenue in South Africa. Rates are progressive, with the maximum taxation rate being 42 percent. A flat tax rate of 28 percent is levied on domestic companies, while foreign companies 33 percent.

There is a secondary tax of 10 percent on all dividends. Other taxes include the value-added tax (VAT), of which the standard rate is 14 percent, capital gains tax, and customs and excise taxes. Taxation is overseen by the South African Revenue Service (SARS).

Armed Forces

The South African National Defence Force (SANDF) consists of the South African Army, the South African Air Force (SAAF), the South African Navy (SAN), and the South African Military Health Service. The armed forces are overseen by a commander, who in turn is accountable to the minister of defence. A regional superpower, South Africa voluntarily discontinued its nuclear weapons program. The SANDF is considered one of the largest contributors to UN peacekeeping missions, including operations in Eritrea, Ethiopia/Somalia, and Liberia. Service is voluntary, but lasts a minimum of two years. Women are eligible for service in non-combat positions. As of 2014, there were 78,707 active personnel and 15,107 reserves.

Foreign Policy

South Africa's foreign policy is largely rooted in the promotion of democracy and the betterment of the African continent through regional and international economic cooperation. Though it is still young in its nation-building efforts, South Africa has also increased its stature in the international community since apartheid was ended in 1994. It has acted as an important regional mediator, has regained membership into the Commonwealth of Nations (a group of over 50 independent states, mostly former British colonies), and holds a non-permanent position on the UN Security Council, having served between 2007 and 2008 and 2011 and 2012. Most notably, South African piloted a revolutionary foreign policy movement that has been a cornerstone of peaceful development in Africa and abroad: the Kimberley Process, which supports the regulation of the international diamond trade.

Conflict diamonds are rough diamonds sold by rebel movements and their allies to finance the destabilization of legitimate governments. The diamonds have long been used to generate funds for arms procurement and their trade has fueled wars in Angola, Sierra Leone, Cote d'Ivoire and the Democratic Republic of the Congo, with devastating socio-economic repercussions. In May 2000, Southern African diamond-purchasing states met in Kimberley, South Africa, to discuss ways to ensure that trade was not funding violence. Sanctioned by the UN and chaired by South Africa, The Kimberley Process Certification Scheme launched in 2003.

Involvement is open to any country willing to subscribe to its extensive requirements. Participating governments agree to trade controls and uphold full transparency of their operations. The scheme encompasses all facets of production, including the licensing of diamond mines that maintain strict security standards, but most notable is its standardization of the diamond trade itself. Diamonds that pass through stringent controls are ultimately issued a Kimberley Process Certification, which guarantees compliance with the scheme. Participating countries may only trade certified diamonds. Whereas before the Kimberley Process conflict diamonds accounted for over 15 percent of global diamond production, they now account for less than 1 percent.

As a member of the African Union (AU) and the Southern African Development Community (SADC), the country has been a leader in matters concerning the continent's infrastructure, finance, and defense. On the international front, South Africa has exercised its influence by pressuring the UN Security Council to select a permanent African member. As a member of the Non-Aligned Movement (NAM), the country collaborates with twenty-five nations worldwide on everything from agricultural development to disarmament programs. Acknowledging its impact on global economic health, the South African government is focusing intently on the eradication of poverty and the AIDS epidemic.

The global community has identified AIDS as a threat to international well-being and security, noting that the death toll of an epidemic as critical as that in South Africa erodes communities and military with grave destabilizing results. The Group of Eight (G-8) countries have stepped in to contribute funds and workers, concentrating on provisioning emergency clinics and training medical personnel. At the helm of this intervention has been the U.S., which has established itself as the single largest donor to South Africa's AIDS relief by committing over $750 million (USD). Since 2012, however, South Africa has begun to fund its own response, allocating $1 billion (USD) annually for AIDS-related programs. Still the U.S.'s commitment was further invigorated by the Emergency Plan for AIDS Relief (PEPFAR), a $15 billion (USD) initiative focusing on preventative education, medical care, and therapeutic support. Coupled with the international community's commitment to drive down pharmaceutical costs and accelerate vaccination research, relief for the infected is slow going but promising.

Human Rights Profile

International human rights law insists that states respect civil and political rights and promote an individual's economic, social, and cultural rights. The United Nations Universal Declaration on Human Rights (UDHR) is recognized as the standard for international human rights. Its authors sought the counsel of the world's great thinkers, philosophers, and religious leaders and were careful to create a document that reflects the core values shared by every world culture. (To read this document or view the articles relating to cultural human rights, visit http://www.ohchr.org/EN/UDHR/Pages/Introduction.aspx.)

One of the key components of South Africa's post-apartheid era has been an emphasis on human rights. South Africa's Truth & Reconciliation Commission became an international human rights model and proactively confronted the traumatic effects of apartheid's inequality and exploitation. It was a commission by South Africans, for South Africans. In fact, the commission's work of was an integral

element in the peaceful transition to black majority rule.

Despite this historical step toward combating inequity, the South Africa's human rights record is riddled with incidences of discrimination. An escalation in xenophobic violence (violence against foreigners) is receiving recent international attention. In defiance of Articles 2, 3, 9 and 14, asylum seekers (particularly Zimbabweans), migrant workers, and ethnic minorities are increasingly at risk of violent attacks and unlawful deportation.

Concentrated mostly in the cities, foreigners are the target of lootings, destruction of businesses, beatings, and even killings. In one high profile raid of a Johannesburg church, refugees sheltering there were subjected to arbitrary arrest and police brutality. Any who sustained injuries from the excessive force received delayed medical treatment or no treatment at all. Similarly, migrant workers, who are afforded rights under South Africa's employment law, are consistently abused and deprived of minimum or overtime wages.

In addition, these groups are being denied safe access to essential food, potable water, basic shelter, essential medical services, and sanitation. Thousands have been displaced because of relentless attacks, and a National Day of the Disappeared is observed each year to acknowledge the alarming number of enforced disappearances. Although the South African government has been collaborating with the UN to eliminate xenophobia-related violence, it has done little to instill confidence in international human rights watch groups. According to these groups, the government routinely ignores these attacks and acts of discrimination.

Disease poses another human rights challenge in South Africa. As of 2014, 18.2 percent of the population is HIV positive. This is the fourth highest rate of infection in the world, but represents one of the most severe HIV epidemics, as the rate of infection is increasing with no indication of slowing. This can be seen as a violation of Article 25, particularly as government inaction and cultural biases delay or derail the implementation of legislation and reform. For example, the constitutional court recently ordered the government to provide antiretroviral drugs, particularly to prevent mother-to child transmission during childbirth. The majority of the infected are still without treatment, however, as most provinces maintain a ban on distributing the drugs in state hospitals.

A great contributor to this epidemic, and other human rights issues, is the poverty rate. Unemployment is at 25 percent and nearly 36 percent of the population lives in extreme poverty. AIDS-related deaths have also ravaged the family unit, and in deep rural areas, food is scarce and there is limited opportunity to harvest. In addition, children who have access to schooling must endure compromised conditions, as nearly half of South Africa's educational institutions have no electricity or clean water.

International human rights organizations have implored the government to be more insistent in helping the general population to achieve a basic standard of living. Until this is realized, they allege that there is little hope of combating the continuing AIDS crisis.

Migration

Immigration policy has been, at times, a contentious topic in post-apartheid South Africa. In particular, critics contend that the government has not formulated an appropriate policy in an ever-increasing migratory region, while human rights groups criticize the country's deportation methods; between 1994 and 2006, an estimated 1.7 million undocumented workers were deported, with roughly 250,000 migrants arrested and deported in 2006 alone. While authorities claim that immigration policing has put a strain on budgets and work force in recent years, critics contend that rampant xenophobia is hampering immigration policy reform and public opinion on the matter. As of 2015, the UN Refugee Agency reports that an estimated 112,192 refugees and 463,940 asylum seekers currently reside within South Africa's borders, while just 962 South African nationals have fled the country as refugees.

ECONOMY

Overview of the Economy

South Africa is the most industrialized country on the African continent and thus its economic leader. Since the end of apartheid and the lifting of international sanctions, economic growth has been strong and major reforms have been implemented. Serious problems remain, however. Unemployment affects 25.1 percent of the labor force (2014 estimate), which numbers 20.23 million, and 35.9 percent of the population lives below the poverty line. In 2014, the gross domestic product (GDP) was estimated at $704.5 billion (USD), up from $693.9 billion (USD) in 2013.

Industry

Industry accounts for over 28.5 percent of the GDP and employs 18 percent of the labor force. Its major sectors are mining, manufacturing, and energy production. Mining remains a major source of revenue, though the sector has gone into decline. The services sector represents nearly 69.1 percent of the GDP, while agriculture accounts for under 2.4 percent.

Chemical and fertilizer production, automobile assembly, food processing, equipment and armament building, and textiles dominate the manufacturing sector. Through various energy resources, South Africa provides electricity to over half of the continent.

Labor

Unemployment affects 25 percent of the labor force (2014 estimate), which numbers an estimated 20.23 million people in 2014. By occupation, the services sector accounts for 66 percent of the labor force.

Energy/Power/Natural Resources

South Africa possesses reserves of natural gas. Environmental problems include water, air, and soil pollution from mining and other industries, inadequate sewage disposal and treatment and the widespread use of open fires.

Fishing

The commercial fishing industry provides fish for both the domestic and export markets. According to South African government statistics, the commercial fishing industry is valued at $6 billion ZAR annually. Hake, anchovies, sardines, mackerel, sole, tuna, rock lobster, and abalone make up the largest part of the domestic catch. As of 2015, approximately 27,000 people were employed in the fishing industry. The country has 22 commercial fisheries, focusing exclusively on wild catches. Aquaculture, or fish farming, has been neglected in the past. However, because of decline wild fish populations, the government has begun to make establishing this industry a priority.

Forestry

The timber industry is well developed, contributing one percent to the GDP, employing 165,900 people, and providing a total of 92,700 jobs. The paper and pulp industry provides another 24,200 jobs. While deforestation is a problem in some areas, the government has instituted municipal reforestation programs and aims to contribute 10,000 hectares (24,710 acres) of new forest annually.

Mining/Metals

In addition to being the world's largest producer of platinum, gold, chromium, manganese, vermiculite, and vanadium. The country also has vast quantities of uranium, tin, copper, fluorspar, andalusite, nickel, phosphates, iron ore, coal, and diamonds.

Agriculture

Agriculture accounts for 2.4 percent of the GDP and employs 4 percent of the labor force. Commercial farming is important to the export economy, and subsistence farming is important to a wide section of the population. Scarce water sources, combined with droughts, make production variable from year to year, and only 9.9 percent of the land is arable. Corn, sugarcane, fruits, grapes and wine, vegetables, and wheat are major crops.

Animal Husbandry

Poultry, cattle, goats, and sheep are South Africa's principal livestock, and these are raised for both subsistence purposes and for product exports, such as beef, mutton, wool, dairy products, and broiler chickens.

Tourism

Since the end of apartheid, South Africa's tourism industry has grown exponentially. The existing infrastructure in the tourism sector was already extensive, and in recent years, it has developed further. According to South Africa's Strategic Research Unit, in 2013, foreign visitors numbered 2,683,141.

Cultural attractions include Stone Age rock art, vineyards, early Dutch domestic architecture, and the nightlife and settings of Cape Town and Durban. Important collections about local pre-history and history are found in the National Museum in Bloemfontein, the Iziko South African Museum, and the National Cultural History Museum, both in Cape Town.

Natural attractions include beaches and nature reserves, particularly the Royal Natal National Park, the Kruger National Park, and the Kgalagadi Transfrontier Park, which highlight South Africa's diverse flora and fauna.

Heidi Liese Edsall, Michael Aliprandi,
Alex K. Rich, Savannah Schroll Guz

DO YOU KNOW?

- Nelson Mandela, the first president of a democratic South Africa, shared the 1993 Nobel Peace Prize with F.W. de Klerk, the country's last state president. Both men were instrumental in ending apartheid.

- South Africa ranks first in the world in gold, chromium, manganese, platinum, vanadium, and vermiculite extraction.

Bibliography

Donna Lee Bowen and Evelyn A. Early. "Everyday Life in the Muslim Middle East." Bloomington, IN: *Indiana University Press*, 2002.

Nancy L. Clark and William H. Worger. "South Africa: The Rise and Fall of Apartheid." 2nd ed. New York: *Routledge*, 2011. Seminar Studies Ser.

Kari A. Cornell. "Cooking the Southern African Way." Minneapolis, MN: *Lerner Publications Company*, 2005.

Bruce Donaldson. "Colloquial Afrikaans: A Complete Course for Beginners." Rev. ed. New York, NY: *Routledge*, 2015.

Lehla Eldridge. "The South African Illustrated Cookbook." Cape Town, South Africa: London: *Allison and Busby*, 2010.

Bruce Fish. "South Africa: 1880 to the Present." Philadelphia, PA: *Chelsea House Publishers*, 2001.

Mary Fitzpatrick. "South Africa, Lesotho & Swaziland." Victoria, Australia: *Lonely Planet*, 2006.

Nelson Mandela. "Long Walk to Freedom." New York: *Little, Brown*, 2013.

Magdaleen Van Wyk. "The Complete South African Cookbook." 3rd ed. Cape Town, South Africa: *Penguin Random House South Africa*, 2007.

Magdaleen Van Wyk and Pat Barton. "Traditional South African Cooking." 5th ed. Cape Town, South Africa: *Struik Lifestyle*, 2014.

Patti Waldmeir. "Anatomy of a Miracle: The End of Apartheid and the Birth of the New South Africa." New York, NY: *W.W. Norton & Company, Inc.*, 1997.

Frank Welsh. *South Africa: A Narrative History*. New York: *Kondansha America*, 1998.

Works Cited

_____. "Forestry." Official Website of the South African Government. *Government of South Africa*, 2015. Web. http://www.gov.za/about-sa/forestry.

_____. "Robben Island." *UNESCO World Heritage*, 2015. http://whc.unesco.org/en/list/916.

"2013 Arrivals." South African Tourism Strategic Research Unit. South African Tourism, 2015. http://www.southafrica.net/research/en/landing/research-home.

"2015 UNHCR country operations profile—South Africa." *The UN Refugee Agency*. UNHCR, 2015. Web. http://www.unhcr.org/pages/49e485aa6.html.

"Action Plan to 2014: Towards the Realisation of Schooling 2025." Basic Education, Republic of South Africa. *Department of Basic Education*, 2015. Web. http://www.education.gov.za/Curriculum/ActionPlanto2014/tabid/418/Default.aspx.

"Africa." *Internet World Stats. Miniwatts Marketing Group*, 19 Sept. 2015. Web. http://www.internetworldstats.com/africa.htm.

"Cape Floral Region Protected Areas." *UNESCO World Heritage Centre*. UNESCO World Heritage Centre, 2015. Web. http://whc.unesco.org/en/list/1007.

"Funding for HIV and AIDS." *AVERT: AVERTing HIV and AIDS. AVERT*, 2014. Web. http://www.avert.org/funding-hiv-and-aids.htm.

Karl Mathiesen, "Can anything stop the rhino poaching crisis?" *The Guardian. Guardian News and Media Limited*, 23 Jan. 2015. http://www.theguardian.com/environment/2015/jan/23/can-anything-stop-the-rhino-poaching-crisis.

"KP Basics." *Kimberly Process*. Kimberly Process, 2015. Web. http://www.kimberleyprocess.com/en/about.

"Launch of the Decade of Action for Road Safety 2011–2020." The United Nations and Road Safety. *UN Web Services Section*, 2009. http://www.un.org/en/roadsafety/.

Reporters Without Borders. "South Africa." *2015 World Press Index*. Reporters Without Borders, 2015. Web. https://index.rsf.org/#!/.

"South Africa." The World Factbook. *CIA*, 2015. Web. https://www.cia.gov/library/publications/the-world-factbook/geos/sf.html.

South African Government. "Fisheries." Official Website of the South African Government. *Government of South Africa, 2015*. Web. http://www.gov.za/about-SA/fisheries.

"Threats – Illegal Wildlife Trade." *World Wildlife Fund*, 2015. http://www.worldwildlife.org/threats/illegal-wildlife-trade.

UNICEF. "South Africa: Statistics." *UNICEF*. UNICEF, 31 Dec. 2013. Web. http://www.unicef.org/infobycountry/southafrica_statistics.html.

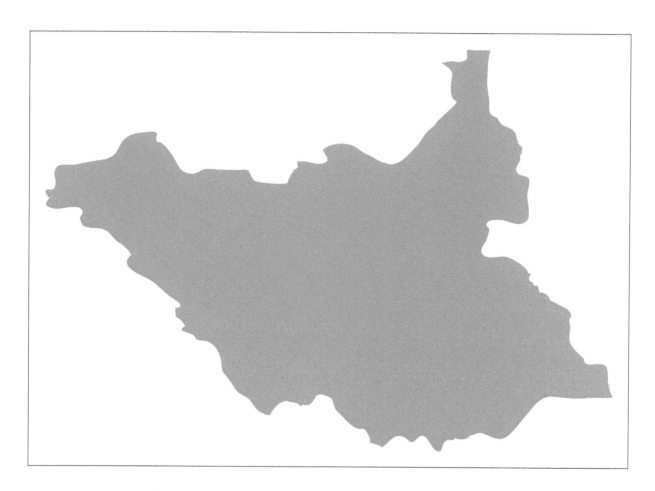

SOUTH SUDAN

Introduction

The world's newest country emerged from decades of civil war with Sudan on July 9, 2011 as part of the 2005 Comprehensive Peace Agreement, also known as the Naivasha Agreement. Signed by the government of Sudan and the Sudan People's Liberation Army/Movement (SPLA/M), the agreement paved the way for both an end to the Second Sudanese Civil War (1983–2005) and a referendum on autonomy for Sudan's ten southernmost states, which identify by tribal affiliation and are predominantly Animist and Christian.

Since December 2013, however, South Sudan has been mired in an internal conflict between Salva Kiir Mayardit, the country's democratically elected president and head of the SPLA/M, and opposition forces loyal to Salva Kiir's former vice president, Riek Machar. The individual power struggle has devolved into an ethnic conflict, with Kiir mobilizing the Dinka people and Machar mobilizing the Nuer. More than 10,000 people have been killed since the conflict erupted, and 2.25 million people have become refugees, 180,000 of them internally displaced. Others have fled to Uganda and Kenya. UNICEF reports that because civil unrest has prevented farmers from planting subsistence crops, famine looms. As of mid-September 2015, a peace agreement, signed by both sides, is slated for ratification.

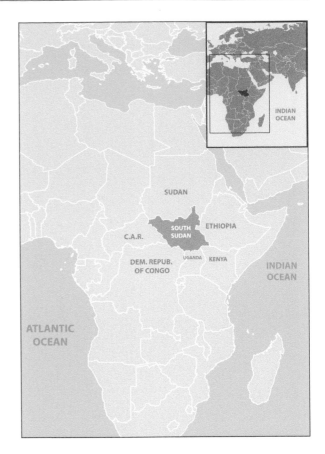

GENERAL INFORMATION

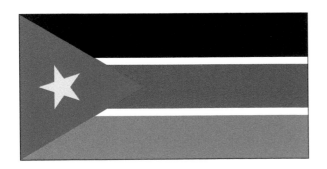

Official Language: English
Population: 12,042,910 (July 2015)
Currency: South Sudanese pound

Coins: One hundred piasters equal one South Sudanese pound. Coins are issued in denominations of 1, 5, 10, 25, and 50 piasters.
Land Area: 644,329 square kilometers (248,776 square miles)
National Motto: "Justice, Liberty, Prosperity"
National Anthem: "South Sudan Oyee!" ("South Sudan Hooray!")
Capital: Juba
Time Zone: GMT +3
Flag Description: The flag of Sudan consists of three horizontal bands of red, white, and black, separated by thinner white stripes. A blue equilateral triangle with a yellow star at its center rests against the hoist (left) side of the flag, and its tip reaches one quarter of the way across the flag's width, its apex in the red band. The flag's colors symbolize the blood shed for freedom (red), peace after many years of struggle (white), the people of Sudan (black;

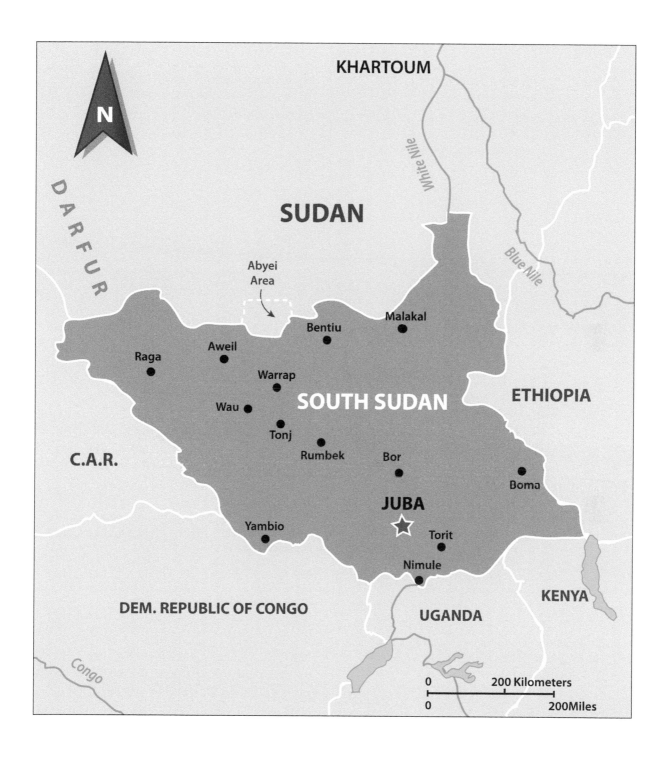

Principal Cities by Population (2015):

- Juba (321,000)
- Yei (185,000)
- Malakal (160,765)
- Wau (151,320)
- Pajok (Parjok) (49,000)

Sudan means 'black' in Arabic), and the country's natural resources, or verdant land (green). The blue in the triangle represents the waters of the Nile, and yellow the unity of the states that comprise the country.

Population

As of July 2015, South Sudan's population was approximately 12,042,910 and very young. In fact, the median age is seventeen years old, with 45 percent below the age of 14 and 20 percent between the ages of 15 and 24. Only 5 percent are over 54 years old. While each woman has an average of five children, the country's infant mortality rate is extremely high, with more than 66 deaths per 1,000 live births. Still, the country's population growth was just over four percent in 2015.

Languages

English is the official language. However, Arabic, including both Juba (a localized pidgin Arabic) and Sudanese dialects, are also spoken, particularly in more developed areas, like the capital. There are an estimated 60 other regional languages, including Dinka, Nuer, Bari, Zande, Shilluk, Murle, and Luo. Most of these indigenous languages are part of the Nilo-Saharan linguistic family, while those spoken in the west and southwest are part of the Ubangi and Niger-Congo families.

Native People & Ethnic Groups

South Sudan has more than 60 ethnic groups, the largest of which are the Dinka (36 percent), of which there are five geographically oriented tribal subdivisions; the Nuer (15.6 percent);

and the Shilluk. However, the country is also populated by other Nilotic (Nile Valley) peoples, including the Azande, Bari, Kakwa, Kuku, Murle, Mandari, Didinga, Ndogo, Bviri, Lndi, Anuak, Bongo, Lango, Dungotona, and Acholi. These groups often live in tribes, which, in times of food shortages, become nomadic. Such peripatetic searches for food and other resources often lead to tribal hostilities, particularly between the smaller ethnic groups and the larger Dinka and Nuer populations. The Dinka call themselves "Moinjaang" (People of the people), and the term "Moinjaang" is the equivalent of the word 'male' in English.

Religions

The population of South Sudan primarily follows Animist or Christian beliefs, and some have even merged the Animist worldview with the traditional Christian faith. Although each tribe may have individualized rituals and beliefs, the term Animism generally refers to an indigenous population's belief that spirits exist in the material world, especially within inanimate objects and animals. The Dinka ethnic group, which comprises 36 percent of the country's population, is monotheistic and believes in Nhialic, or Creator, who is responsible for life and death. Ritual sacrifices of cattle are made to honor Nhialic's works.

Climate

South Sudan is a largely equatorial climate. Between late April and early November, the country experiences a rainy season, during which flooding is common. Yambio, in the country's extreme south, can have as much as 114.2 cm (450 inches) of rain between April and December. From November to April, the country is dry and hot, influenced by arid, northeastern weather patterns. The heat is particularly oppressive in January and February, and the sky is cloudless. In Juba, the country's capital, temperatures can reach as high as 37 degrees Celsius (100 degrees Fahrenheit) in February and as low as 18 degrees Celsius (65 degrees Fahrenheit) in July.

ENVIRONMENT & GEOGRAPHY

Topography

South Sudan borders Ethiopia to its east, Kenya to its southeast, Uganda to its south, the Democratic Republic of the Congo to its southwest, and the Central African Republic to its west. It also shares a 2,100 km (1,305 mile) border with Sudan, to its north.

The Abyei Area, a contested territory that South Sudan claims, is 10,546 square kilometers (4,072 square miles). It is located along the border South Sudan shares with Sudan, to the north.

In the north-central region is South Sudan's largest swamp, the Sudd, formed by the confluence of the Mountain Nile (Baḥr al-Jabal) and the White Nile, South Sudan's longest river. Although variable—depending on precipitation and inflow from Lake Victoria—the swamp covers around 30,000 square kilometers and is one of the world's largest freshwater wetlands.

The Imatong Mountains are located in the southeast and stretch into neighboring Uganda. Mount Kinyeti, part of the Imatong range, is the country's highest point, at 3,187 meters (10,456 feet).

The country's lowest point is Ironstone Plateau (Jabal Hadid), named for its rusty-red soil, rich in iron and aluminum. It is 800 to 1,000 meters (2,600 to 3,300 feet) above sea level and runs parallel to the country's border with Central African Republic. It begins in South Sudan's west and extends into the south.

The country boasts nearly 30 rivers, mostly tributaries of the White Nile and its related marshlands, into which some rivers flow.

Plants & Animals

Because of the country's precipitation and temperature fluctuations, many of South Sudan's mammals take part in the Serengeti migrations, during which they search for vegetation and water. This generally occurs during the November-to-April dry season, when animals move south, where grasses remain lush. The animals taking part in these vast migrations include white-eared kob antelope, tiang antelope, mongalla gazelle, elephant, and buffalo.

Boma National Park, in the west; the swampy Sudd wetland, in the north-central Nile basin; and the Southern National Park, in the southwest, provide habitats for giraffes, elephants, buffalo, lions, and various types of antelope, including hartebeests, kob, topis, and bongo. The Imatong Mountain rage is densely forested, although this is partially endangered by the advance of logging and subsistence farming, which has led to soil erosion. Still, giant forest hogs, chimpanzees, and various monkeys populate these wooded areas.

CUSTOMS & COURTESIES

Greetings

Handshakes are the standard South Sudanese greeting, and even men and women shake hands with one another. It is disrespectful not to offer or accept a handshake. If hands are wet or dirty, touching wrists is practiced. It is not uncommon for a pat on the shoulder to precede a handshake. Women may exchange three kisses on alternating cheeks with both males and females whom they know well. In addition, embracing close friends and relatives is common.

Bari greeting phrases are generally used, even in urban areas. These include: "Do pure" ("Good morning") or "Do parana" ("Good afternoon"). "Gwon ada?" ("How are you?") or the Arabic "Kief?" ("How is it?") generally follow greetings, to which one might respond "Kweis" ("Okay"), "Tamam" ("Good"), or "Miya miya" ("Excellent"). Superiors are addressed by surname, and the expression "comrade" is often used by members of the Sudan People's Liberation Army. Husbands and wives refer to each other not by first name or by endearments, but as "mother of" or "father of" their eldest child's name.

In Dinka, the word for "Hello" is "Kudual," and the more formal expression "I greet you" is "Yïn ca muɔɔth." When asking after someone's well-being, Dinka would inquire, "Looi adï kennë yïn?" The appropriate response and a reciprocal inquiry is "Acïn kë rac, alɛɛc, ku looi adï." ("Fine, thanks, and how are you?") A person of high esteem in the Dinka community is addressed as "beny" (leader).

Gestures & Etiquette

In South Sudan, nodding the head downward means 'yes,' while nodding upward means 'no.' Maintaining unbroken eye contact with someone, particularly between opposite genders, is considered rude, as is remaining seated while greeting an elder. Additionally, insulting an elder is believed to result in a curse on the person delivering the offense. In some tribal communities, the tongue is used to point to someone nearby, particularly when the person pointing has ill feelings towards the person indicated. However, pointing directly at someone with a finger is considered impolite and generally reserved for heated discussion. Finally, South Sudanese never gesture or pass things to others with the left hand, always the right.

Eating/Meals

Generally, the South Sudanese eat only twice each day. Breakfast is usually a millet (awuou) porridge (asida), which is sweetened with honey and served with milk. Tea is drunk throughout the day, and to curb hunger, fruit is eaten or sugar cane stems chewed. Between 2 pm and 3 pm, the day's principal meal is served, which consists of meat and vegetables, prepared in a stew form. These are eaten either with a fermented sorghum flatbread (kisra) or with asida.

Meals are often eaten family style, from the same bowl, often a hollowed-out kalabash gourd in rural areas. Fathers are served first. Torn into pieces, kisra is used as a utensil—always in the right hand, never the left—to dip stew from the communal bowl. Following dinner, tea is generally served.

Visiting

Family and community ties are maintained by visiting, and long stretches without visitation is considered an insult. Particularly in Dinka culture, visits frequently occur between families who may be united by the marriage of children, and this is part of the pre-marital 'screening' process. Hosts never ask visitors what they would like to drink, as this is considered impolite. Instead, tea or beer is immediately offered. If visitors arrive at dinnertime, they are provided with a portion of the food, and if there is not enough, hosts will forfeit their own helping for the guests' benefit. It is considered disrespectful to refuse it. Visiting in-laws always bring gifts of goat, fish, flour, or drinks. There are no proscriptions on mingling of the sexes; men and women freely socialize together.

LIFESTYLE

Family

In South Sudan, families are patrilineal, meaning wealth and bloodlines descend from the father through his male children. Marriages, particularly tribal marriages, are often polygamous, and very wealthy men have been known to have as many as thirty wives, although urban families are much smaller, sometimes even nuclear. Children of one father are raised communally. Moreover, while each mother is responsible for her own biological children, childcare is often shared among the wives, who divide responsibilities. Women also fetch water and firewood, maintain the home, prepare all meals, and herd cattle. Because respect for elders is a vital part of South Sudan's culture, a man's parents will often live with him and be cared for by wives. Meanwhile, men provide for the family financially and, in rural areas, care for livestock. Younger widows take over the male's role, and because of the civil war, there is an ever-increasing number of them.

Housing

As of 2013, a reported 93 percent of houses in South Sudan were grass-thatched mud huts, called tukuls, which last roughly three years before succumbing to the elements. Seeking to facilitate the construction of more durable concrete homes that can withstand the country's long rainy season, the government has initiated a mortgage system with South Sudan's central bank, which will work in conjunction with the newly-established Housing Development Corporation (HDC).

The government owns 20 percent of HDC, while foreign investors own 49 percent and South Sudan's private sector owns 31 percent. In early 2014, the company China Jiangsu, one of the 100 registered Chinese companies currently investing in South Sudan's development, began providing capital and manpower for the construction of low-cost concrete houses in Juba. Other companies, like South Africa-based Moladi, employ patented plastic forms for cost-effective residential construction.

Food

Because of the ongoing civil unrest within South Sudan, food scarcity is rampant. As of June 2015, the multinational aid organization World Food Program (WFP) reported that South Sudan is seeing the worst levels of food insecurity in history, with an estimated 4.1 million affected, 180,000 of whom are internally displaced and entirely reliant on airdrops and other food deliveries.

However, traditional foods are still available in some areas. Ground millet porridge (asida) is a staple in the South Sudanese diet, as is a crepe-like, fermented-sorghum flatbread (kisra). In Juba, a beer-like beverage (merisa) is made by further fermenting kisra in water. Other popular starches include cassava fritters and a heavy cornbread (gurassa).

Goat, beef, camel, sheep (mutton), and chicken are the most common meats, and, although South Sudan is not a Muslim country and wild hogs populate the country's wooded areas, pork is not consumed. Meats are either grilled or cooked to tenderness in stews. Perhaps the most common dish is goat stew, which consists of chopped goat meat served in a gray or red sauce spiced with chili powder. Popular especially in the Nile River basin is perch, which is either smoked whole on a stick or chopped and deep-fried. Peanuts, known in South Sudan as groundnuts, also figure prominently in many stews.

Popular in Juba is kudura (also koodra)—a leafy green that resembles lettuce, but has the tough texture of collard greens. It, too, appears in stews, sometimes mixed with kombo (ash from the oven, diluted in water), which both tenderizes it and thickens broths. Other common vegetables are cassavas; molokhia (jute leaves); sweet potatoes; the starchy root, taro; onions; tomatoes; and okra (bamia). Sugarcane and sorghum stalks are often chewed as a sweet snack. Available fruits include mango, watermelon, and guava. Desserts are few, but peanut macaroons (ful Sudani) are a rare treat. Besides merisa, a popular beverage is a red tea made by steeping hibiscus flowers (karkadeh, also kakaday). A homemade gin, called Siko, is also occasionally brewed, but poor distillation practices make it unsafe.

Life's Milestones

Births are a celebrated event among South Sudanese tribes. Boys are prized for their ability to carry on the family lineage and girls are prized for their ability to secure wealth for the family via the "bride price" each groom must pay. Girls who have undergone female circumcision (see "Women's Rights") command a higher bride price.

Among Dinka males, the "initiation" ritual is performed between 10 and 16 years of age. During the ritual, six deep gashes are made in the boy's forehead, often down to the skull bone and in patterns that signify tribal affiliation. These result in lifelong scars. To cry or flinch brings dishonor. The marks mean that the boy is now a warrior and must no longer milk cows or cart manure. Boys' names also change upon initiation. At birth, a child is usually named for a significant individual characteristic or circumstances specific to their delivery. Upon reaching young adulthood, particularly with the agripastoral Dinka, birth names are changed to "bull names," which honors a quality associated with the cattle the men herd.

Another rite of passage is marriage. While most Dinka and Murle men—particularly those who have converted to Christianity—take only one wife, tribal tradition calls for numerous brides, particularly so that the husband may produce as many children as possible and thereby continue his bloodline. To secure a bride, a man must offer "bride wealth" in the form of cattle, which is considered currency in South Sudan's various tribal cultures. The usual bride price is thirty to forty cattle, and this hefty sum has led to tribal wars, since cattle are often stolen so that bride wealth can be secured. It is estimated that 2,000 people are killed each year as a result of cattle raids and ensuing violence. Dinka must marry outside their own clan, in order to create alliances with communities beyond their own tribal borders.

CULTURAL HISTORY

Art

Many minor tribes in South Sudan—like the Bongo and Belanda, who migrated from Chad and Congo to South Sudan's Bahr el Ghazal state—are known for their funerary sculpture. Works appearing on tombs are carved out of tree trunks and feature highly stylized representations of the deceased. These are anchored 24 to 30 inches in the ground and appear, surrounded by stones, either on top or in front of the burial mound. Depending on the figure's community prominence, similar statues were placed at the village entrance or near important public buildings, while a smaller sculpture is made to be displayed in the home.

Another form of traditional South Sudanese art is also ornamental in nature: the Dinka corset (Manlual). In certain Dinka clans, Manlual, comprised of hundreds of strings of colored glass seed beads, are sewn around males while they are still young. As they age and accrue wealth, additional beads are sewn into the design while it is still being worn. The higher the corset back, the richer the male wearing it. Generally, these are removed upon marriage. Dinka women also enjoy similar personal ornamentation in the form of intricate necklaces (Alual), which drape over the shoulders like a poncho. Its size is a public display of her family's wealth. Alual sometimes contain cowerie shells, believed to enhance fertility. These, too, are worn without being removed until the woman is married.

Art has also become an important record of the Sudanese diaspora as well as a method of coping with the difficulties of exile. Contemporary South Sudanese painters who have passed through Kenya's Kakuma refugee camp include James Aguer Garang, Samuel Ajok, Atem Aleu, Ajang Atem Awuol, Atem Benjamin, Peter Makuol Maketh, and Ajok Mayol, all of whom identify as Dinka. Other one-time Kakuma resident painters, like Mario Lual Deng and Stephenal Takiy, are Nuer. The works of all these artists depict traditional cultural symbols and, in some cases, reveal how these rituals have been devastated by decades of civil war.

Music & Dance

Music, coupled with dance, has been central to each tribal community, as it promotes social cohesion and is a valued form of personal expression. In Dinka culture, songs prepare boys for the pain of initiation, prime warriors for battle, or celebrate tribal ancestors. The Dinka's traditional Aweil dance is characterized by rhythmic chanting, drums, and foot stamping. Sticks and spears are carried during such dances, and Dinka men throw their hands upward to mimic the movements of their oxen's horns.

Since the 1960s, Western musical styles, like jazz, have had a significant influence on South Sudanese popular music, which is often played in Juba-based clubs. Groups like the Skylarks and Rejaf Jazz experienced a swell of popularity during the mid-twentieth century. Today, artists continue to be inspired by Western sounds, and some even use YouTube to disseminate their work and develop their identity. Pop singer Yaba Angelosi blends electronica with tribal rhythms, while the pop duo the Freedom Boys and the vocalist Ciara Mazakwe employ auto-tuned vocals and address subject matter that demonstrates the influence of American hip-hop. Similarly, Emmanuel Kembe's album *Shen* (*Cry for South Sudan*) is strongly influenced by reggae.

Literature

The Dinka have a strong oral literary tradition that includes poetry and legends, many of which feature Aweil Longar, a river spirit that takes human form and has the ability to create or destroy life. To date, however, very few of these narratives have been recorded. Despite relentless war and its attendant dislocations, South Sudan does have a nascent literary culture. Among the country's prominent writers are Jacob J. Akol (1947–), author of the 2005 semi-autobiographical novel *I Will Go the Distance*, and Francis Mading Deng (1938–), the country's first UN ambassador and author of nine books, including the 1989 novel *Cry of the Owl*. Another contemporary South Sudanese writer is Abel Alier (1933–), a human-rights activist and Christian lawyer, who served as Sudan's vice president between 1971 and 1982. His book *Southern Sudan: Britain's Ithaca Press published Too Many Agreements Dishonoured* in 1999.

Sports

The country's Dinka population often engages in mock sparring using spears, sticks, and shields. These war-games are intended to hone fighting abilities in preparation for actual tribal combat. Another highly popular sport is Dinka wrestling, which even has sponsors, like South Sudan Wrestling Entertainment (SSWE). In addition to professionalizing South Sudanese wrestling, SSWE's mission is to help quell the deadly violence between herding tribes through such inter-tribal matches. Many Dinka wrestlers, who are often identified by their tribal affiliations—specifically the Dinka Bor of South Sudan's Jonglei State, the Mundari of Central Equatoria, and the Aliap and Atuot of the Lakes (al-Buhayrat) State—have a stature similar to American athletes.

As of 2015, Bright Star, the nickname for the South Sudan Football Association (SSFA), is ranked 195th among FIFA members. In July 2012, the team played its first international match against Uganda and thus became part of FIFA's international ranking system. In addition, in 2014, SSFA entered its first international tournament, the 2015 Africa Cup of Nations, although the team failed to qualify. In late 2015, SSFA will attempt to qualify for the 2018 FIFA World Cup.

CULTURE

Cultural Sites & Landmarks

Because of the ongoing civil war, the government has devoted little time to identifying cultural sites, even though South Sudan has been inhabited since the Paleolithic era and likely has numerous important archeological sites. Still, a few locations have been recognized for their potential cultural draw. On the Boma Plateau in the states of Jonglei and Eastern Equatoria, *coffea arabica* grows wild, and the area itself is largely unexplored. Boma plateau is also known to be the site of spectacular annual animal migrations. The Nimule Rapids, also known as the Fulla Rapids, is a patch of whitewater along the White Nile that extends 0.7 km (0.43 miles). In Juba, important religious sites include All Saints Cathedral, St. Joseph's Catholic Church, St. Theresa Cathedral, and Juba's Main Mosque.

National Parks in South Sudan include Bandingilo, running between Central and Eastern Equitoria; Boma, near the Ethiopian border; Lantoto, near the border with Democratic Republic of Congo; Nimule, near Uganda; Shambe, in the country's center; and Southern, not far from the Central African Republic. Among the country's protected game reserves are: Ashana, Bengangai, Bire Kpatuos, Boro, Chelkou, Ez Zeraf, Fanikang, Juba, Kidepo, Mushra, Mbarizunga, and Numatina. All are sites that boast populations of giant eland; buffalo; giraffe; many varieties of antelope, both large and small; the critically endangered white rhino; lion; and the black-and-white colobus monkey.

Libraries & Museums

In 2014, UNESCO launched an initiative to assist the South Sudanese government in establishing their own cultural sector by founding a museum that would celebrate the country's rich cultural and ethnic diversity. As of 2015, the museum is in its "pilot phase" and a traveling exhibition of cultural artifacts is moving among three of South Sudan's ten states, Eastern Equatoria, Western Equatoria, and Western Bahr el Ghazal. The National Museum project is co-sponsored by the country's Ministry of Culture, its Youth and Sports (MoCYS) organization, Open Society East Africa (OSIEA), and the French government.

Holidays

South Sudan's national holidays include Peace Agreement Day on January 9, which commemorates the Comprehensive Peace Agreement signed in 2005. May 16 is SPLA day, which celebrates the founding of the Sudan People's Liberation Army. July 9 is the country's Independence Day, when South Sudan officially gained autonomy. July 30 is Martyr's Day, which memorializes the political leader who initiated the rebellion leading to South Sudan's independence: John Garang de Mabior.

Youth Culture

Because of the civil war, South Sudanese youth are consistently subjected to violence and sexual abuse at the hands of the various militia groups. Child kidnapping, trafficking, and prostitution are all prevalent in conflict zones. Orphaned boys often join rebel forces for food and shelter, while orphaned girls opt for prostitution as a means of survival.

In some tribes not disrupted by civil unrest, families continue to teach traditional ideals of bravery and honor, while milking and cleaning dung are daily responsibilities assigned to the clan's young males prior to their initiation ceremony. Girls, meanwhile, are taught to cook and perform the many domestic responsibilities related to caring for extended families.

Some South Sudanese children become members of the Sudan People's Liberation Movement Youth League (SPLM–YL), although no statistics are available concerning membership numbers. In January 2014, the group rallied in Yambio, where adult administrators accused the UN Mission in South Sudan (UNMISS) of interfering with rather than aiding refugees and smuggling arms to rebel forces. Some civil

rights activists accuse the ruling SPLM party of exploiting Youth League members for political ends.

SOCIETY

Transportation

Because of the poor condition of country's roadways, of which only a total of 155 miles are paved, motor bikes (boda boda) are a popular mode of transport. Even in Juba, there are very few asphalted roads, and during the country's rainy season, from late April to early November, these roads become impassable. For this reason, transportation disruptions are common. Around urban areas like Juba, privately owned minibuses (matatus), are common and more popular than taxis, which are unmetered and expensive. Traffic moves on the right-hand side of the road.

Transportation Infrastructure

South Sudan has 248 km (154 mi) of railroad track running from Sudanese border to the northwestern city of Wau. As of 2015, there are plans to extend the tracks from Wau to Juba, the country's capital, and ultimately to link up with the Ugandan and Kenyan railway system.

There are 25 airports in South Sudan, the busiest of which is Juba International, a civilian, military, and cargo hub that also services incoming and outgoing United Nations aid flights. As of July 2014, a 30-month expansion project to repave and extend the runway by 700 feet, as well as create additional terminals, was underway. The country's second largest airport, and the country's only other international airport is Malakal Airport, situated near the Sudanese and Ethiopian borders. Like Juba International, Malakal serves as an operation hub for UN aid transports.

Media & Communications

The civil war, poverty, widespread illiteracy, and poor infrastructure have contributed to the South Sudan's underdeveloped media, which is concentrated primarily around Juba. Freedom of the press is guaranteed by the South Sudanese constitution. However, journalists have been subjected to harassment and abuse from SPLA/SPLM representatives, who have also confiscated newspapers or threatened to close radio stations unsympathetic to their cause. Arabic language newspapers have similarly been restricted. Journalists are required to register with the government and the government is drafting a restrictive new media law. In 2015, the watchdog group Reporters Without Borders ranked South Sudan 125th out of 180 countries in press freedom.

Radio listening is considered a community activity, and local stations are often funded by churches and international aid organizations. The UN, for example, has set up Radio Miraya in Juba through their UN Mission in South Sudan (UNMISS). South Sudan Radio Network, run by the government, operates stations broadcasting between four to six hours each day. These stations include Radio Juba, Radio Wau, Radio Malakal, and Radio Rumbek. Most broadcasts are conducted in English, with some programming in Nilotic languages, like Zande and Ma'di. Other radio stations include Catholic Radio Network, Nairobi-based Sudan Radio Service, USAID-financed Internews, and BBC World Service.

Juba-based South Sudan Television Station (SSTV), run by the government, broadcasts six hours each day, and has smaller stations in Aweil, Wau, Malakal, and Rumbek. The recently launched Citizen Television (CTV), owned and operated by *The Citizen* newspaper, broadcasts five hours each day in Juba only.

With high poverty and illiteracy rates, newspapers to do not enjoy broad circulation. Because the country only has two presses, one of which is owned by the government, some newspaper outlets print in Nairobi and fly them to Juba for distribution. South Sudan's dailies include *The Citizen* and the *Juba Monitor*. The country's only Arabic daily, *Al-Maugif*, was launched in June 2014. Weeklies include *The New Nation*, *The Pioneer*, *The Southern Eye*, *The Star*, and *The New Times*. Other news agencies, like Winnepeg-based *New Sudan Vision* and Paris-based *Sudan Tribune*, offer online-only coverage.

As of June 2014, there were only an estimated 100 internet users in South Sudan.

SOCIAL DEVELOPMENT

Standard of Living

As of 2015, South Sudan was not yet ranked on the Human Development Index, and the new country stood with Somalia, North Korea, San Marino, the Marshall Islands, and Monaco in its absence of social indicators. Moreover, because of the civil war, South Sudan is not expected to achieve any of the UN's Millennium Development Goals.

Water Consumption

Only nine percent of the country has access to improved sanitation facilities, with just 15.7 percent in urban areas and 7.3 percent in rural areas. People generally purchase water extracted from the Nile and brought into communities via tanker trucks. Those who are very wealthy have wells or external tanks from which water is drawn. The 501(c)3 organization Water for South Sudan actually works to drill wells for underprivileged communities. Since 2003, the organization has drilled 177 wells. Each costs $15,000 (USD) and involves the sweat-equity of villagers, who determine the well's location.

Education

Because of war and internal displacement, illiteracy continues to be widespread, and the educational system is virtually nonexistent. Just 27 percent of the population is literate, with 40 percent of males and only 16 percent of females capable of reading and writing. To foster a more literate culture, UNESCO, working in conjunction with South Sudan's Ministry of Education, Science, and Technology, began training literacy teachers in the Eastern Equatorial Province.

Women's Rights

The civil war has cast a dark shadow over women's rights. Since the war's eruption in late 2013, humanitarian organizations have reported numerous accounts of rape perpetrated by soldiers from both rebel militias and government forces. The continued conflict and high refugee numbers have prevented both an accurate statistical record and treatment for victims. Female refugees, many of whom are widowed and traveling alone, are easy prey, and aid organizations have noted the probability that a majority of rapes go unreported.

Even within more insulated tribal culture, however, women face significant challenges. Early and forced marriages have long been custom in rural clans. Traditionally, brides are, on average, twelve or thirteen years old, a tradition imposed to maximize a couple's reproductive period. Similarly, the customary bride price placed on tribal women is also a cause of disagreement for women's rights activists, who argue that because husbands feel they have bought and paid for their wives, they can freely abuse them. Moreover, many activists feel bride prices make women little more than commodities passed between families in exchange for tribal currency.

Female circumcision, the process by which genitalia are excised and the vaginal opening is sewn very small, continues to be a pervasive practice in South Sudan. Also termed 'female genital mutilation' (FGM) by human rights activists, the ritual usually takes place when female infants are seven weeks old and is often performed without sterile instruments. Deaths from post-procedure infections are not uncommon. The procedure generally causes heavy scarring, nerve damage, frequent renal and gynecological infections, and complications with both sexual intercourse and childbirth. The practice persists because women who have undergone the procedure are considered more hygienic and, therefore, command higher bride prices.

Health Care

In 2013, government health care expenditures amounted to 2.2 percent of the GDP, although many are entirely reliant on humanitarian aid, as there are neither hospitals nor resident doctors. Because transportation problems make

humanitarian outreach challenging, folk medicine is often the only option for rural populations.

War, unclean drinking water, poor sanitation, famine, chronic malnutrition, lack of vaccinations, and the ever-present refugee crisis have allowed largely preventable diseases, such as tuberculosis, malaria, dysentery, typhoid, meningitis, hepatitis, cholera, and even polio to surge. The number of AIDS cases is also growing, with 2.24 percent of the adult population infected as of 2013.

GOVERNMENT

According to its 2011 constitution, South Sudan's legislature is bicameral, with a 50-seat Council of States—30 of which are appointed by the president and 20 of which are carry-over members from the Comprehensive Peace Agreement era—and a 332-seat National Legislative Assembly, 170 of which were elected in April 2010 and took office in July 2011, following independence. The president, upon democratic election, serves as both chief of state and head of government, serving a constitutionally defined, four-year term. Because of the continued unrest and attendant humanitarian crisis, elections scheduled for 2015 have been delayed until 2018.

Political Parties

South Sudan's ruling part is the Sudan People's Liberation Movement (SPLM), which originally fought for independence from the north under the name Sudan People's Liberation Army (SPLA). In the country's first 2011 democratic elections, SPLM leader Salva Kiir Mayardit won by 93 percent. The Sudan People's Liberation Movement–Democratic Change (SPLM–DC), represented by former Sudanese Lam Akol, ran against Salva Kiir and took only seven percent. In the parliamentary elections, SPLM took 251 of the 332 seats, while SPLM–DC took six, the Sudan African National Union (SANU) took four, the nationalist-oriented United Democratic Front achieved four seats, and the National Congress Party (NCP) took three. The civil war has stimulated the development of an opposition party: the Sudan People's Liberation Movement-in-Opposition (SPLM-IO), mainly comprised of Nuer and those opposing Salva Kiir's government. Members of this party are referred to as AGFs, or anti-government forces. Other active political parties with South Sudan include the Labour Party South Sudan (LPSS), the South Sudan Democratic Forum, the South Sudan Liberal Party, the Communist Party of South Sudan, the United South Sudan Party, and the South Sudan People's Liberal Party (PLP). Suffrage is universal; anyone 18 and older can vote.

Local Government

The country's 2011 constitution provides for a decentralized government, and consequently, South Sudan is divided into three administrative regions: Bahr el Ghazal, Equatoria, and Greater Upper Nile. Within these regions are a total of 10 states and 86 counties. In rural areas, local government is conducted at the county, district (payam), and village (boma) levels. In urban areas, like Juba, a city council oversees local affairs. At present, local authorities rely entirely on the country's government to share oil revenues, as there is no local taxation system and consequently no local revenue. This fact, along with the ongoing conflict, has resulted in the virtual destruction of the decentralized, local government structure.

Judicial System

The Judiciary of South Sudan (JOSS) is a constitutionally established branch that administers the country's court system. The country's highest court is the Supreme Court of South Sudan, and its chief justice answers directly to South Sudan's president. Beneath the Supreme Court are courts of appeals; high courts; county courts; and, finally, town and rural courts. Courts of appeal for the Great Upper Nile province are based in Malakal, for the Equatoria province in Juba, and for Bahr el Ghazal province in Rumbek. Each of the 10 states has their own high court and county court.

Taxation

On November 4, 2014, the Taxation Act of 2009 was signed into law and amends previous tax legislation, including that passed under the Taxation Amendment Act of 2012. South Sudan imposes sales, excise, withholding, and income taxes. Corporations pay a flat rate of 15 percent, while sales tax is also 15 percent. Employees pay 8 percent in social security withholding, while employers pay 17 percent in social security withholding on all gross wages. There is also a 15 percent state-imposed and 0.5 percent national fuel tax.

Armed Forces

Founded as a guerilla movement in Sudan in 1983, the Sudan People's Liberation Army (SPLA) is now the official army of South Sudan and has an air division, known as the South Sudan Air Force, which is equipped primarily with Russian Mil Mi-17 helicopters. In 2013, the SPLA was estimated to have 210,000 active soldiers. However, because of many casualties, in 2015, there are only an estimated 180,000 active personnel.

Foreign Policy

On July 13, 2011, South Sudan became an official member of the United Nations and joined the African Union later that month. The country currently seeks membership in the East African Community (EAC), the International Monetary Fund (IMF), and the World Bank. In addition, while it has been assured membership in the Arab League, it has not pursued this opportunity.

South Sudan's independence from Sudan was amicable, and Sudan was the very first country to recognize its independence following the successful passing of the 2011 referendum. Following secession, South Sudan retained 75 percent of Sudan's oil reserves. However, refineries and the pipeline to the Red Sea are in Sudan, and Sudan began charging enormous fees for the processing and transport of South Sudan's crude oil. Tensions increased in 2012, culminating in the Heglig Crisis, named for the border town that South Sudan invaded and briefly held before the Sudanese Army pushed back. South Sudan also ceased oil production, cutting off a major revenue source for Sudan. A resolution was finally signed between the two countries on September 26, 2012, which ended the conflict.

The Abyei Area, an oil-rich region shared with Sudan, is a continuing point of contention. Heglig is part of this area. Disputes over boundary demarcation and residency rights stymied the region's independence referendum. In May 2011, the North Sudanese military seized the region, further preventing an election that would determine to which country the area legally belongs. Since the Abyei Area was granted "special administration status" by the 2004 Abyei Protocol, part of the 2005 Comprehensive Peace Agreement, it operates largely by its own laws, and its status is yet undetermined.

Because South Sudan is mired in civil conflict, it has had little chance to form alliances or engage in disputes with other countries, and thus far, its principal attentions have been internal. The United States and European Union have imposed sanctions against both President Salva Kiir and opposition leader Riek Machar, but to date, it has had little impact on the conflict.

Human Rights Profile
International human rights law insists that states respect civil and political rights and promote an individual's economic, social, and cultural rights. The United Nations Universal Declaration on Human Rights (UDHR) is recognized as the standard for international human rights. Its authors sought the counsel of the world's great thinkers, philosophers, and religious leaders and were careful to create a document that reflects the core values shared by every world culture. (To read this document or view the articles relating to cultural human rights, visit http://www.ohchr.org/EN/UDHR/Pages/Introduction.aspx.)

The civil war has fostered a culture of extreme violence throughout the country, and both government soldiers and rebel forces, known as the White Army, have both been accused of war crimes and crimes against humanity, including gang rapes, the murder of civilians, the looting and destruction of private property, and the burning of homes with occupants still alive inside. Additionally, there have been reports of arbitrary mass arrests in the states of Eastern, Central, and Western Equatoria. Most of those arrested are young men, who are accused—often without evidence—of sympathizing with rebel forces. Once detained, the men are tortured for several days and ultimately executed. Human rights groups are now condemning the South Sudanese government—particularly President Salva Kiir—for killing 600 such political prisoners in Juba on August 25, 2015. One detainee, who survived a similar experience after having been left for dead in the Central Equatoria town of Rajaf, reported having been held in the "White House," a now notorious military detention center. There, he described confinement with 900 other prisoners, who were physically tortured and sexually abused by government agents. Human Rights Watch also reports the targeted killing or castration of members of the Nuer ethnic population, with the arrest and mass execution of between 200 and 400 Nuer males on the night of December 15, 2013.

The government's National Security Services (NSS), which has the power to arrest, detain, surveil, search, and seize property, has also severely limited freedom of expression by harassing and detaining journalists who report on controversial stories or interview government opposition figures. The government has also shut down a radio station and confiscated several print runs in order to control information distribution.

In October 2014, 10,500 UN troops were deployed to South Sudan to assist in the peacekeeping mission and help to minimize violence around the UN bases, which accept civilians seeking asylum.

Migration
Despite the civil war and refugees moving into neighboring countries, such as the 730,000 reported entering Ethiopia and 46,000 flooding into Kenya's Kakuma refugee camp in 2015, South Sudan is still experiencing a positive migration rate, with nearly 12 incoming

migrants—mostly from conflict sites in Sudan's Blue Nile and South Kordofan states—for every 1,000 people.

ECONOMY

Overview of the Economy

Because oil represents 98 percent of South Sudan's revenue, the country's economy is on the brink of collapse, attributable in large part to the drop in oil prices, a decrease in oil production due to fee-disputes with Sudan, and the toll of ongoing civil war. As of July 2015, the country is producing just 160,000 barrels per day, down from 350,000 barrels per day in 2011. Moreover, because Sudan controls processing and export channels, South Sudan is unable to regulate production and sale of its own natural resources.

The South Sudanese pound has also become increasingly unstable. In fact, there are two currency values: the official value and a parallel value, set by South Sudan's Central Bank, far exceeding the official value. An unsanctioned black market has developed, through which a select few with connections and special bank credit letters gain access to the official value, while all others must pay the inflated parallel value. This has led to many companies becoming incapable of securing the capital necessary to conduct business. Further complicating the issue is the fact that South Sudan's Central Bank also began printing additional currency, which led to soaring inflation that peaked at 79 percent in May 2012. While in 2014, that rate fell to –0.7 percent, the country was still operating with a budget deficit of –15.3 percent. As of 2014, the country's GDP was $25.96 billion and the per capita GDP was $2,300. Important to note is that South Sudan's government is increasingly reliant on foreign aid. The World Bank's International Development Association (IDA) alone sent $29.39 million (USD) in grants as of July 31, 2015.

Industry

South Sudan seeks to construct a pipeline within its Unity state and connect to the Uganda-Kenya Crude Oil Pipeline. Such a move would allow South Sudan to regain control of its crude oil production and bypass disputes over transit fees imposed by the Sudanese government, a disagreement that resulted in a 2012 production shutdown. As of 2014, no headway has been made on the project because of interruptions caused by the civil war. Although South Sudan seeks to explore gold and other mineral resources, very little related industry has developed to date.

Labor

Currently, labor statistics are not maintained. However, reports indicate that there are very few paying jobs outside the government. Moreover, among the agripastoral tribes, conventional employment is not sought. Rather, livestock functions as both livelihood and currency. Nonetheless, the CIA estimates that over 50 percent of the country's population lives below the poverty line because there is so little gainful employment.

Energy/Power/Natural Resources

While South Sudan holds an estimated 75 percent of Sudan's oil reserves following secession, it is largely dependent on Sudan for its processing, refining, and export channels. While oil revenues made up 98 percent, or $7.4 billion USD, of South Sudan's budget in 2011, this income source was curbed in 2012, when Sudan initiated disputes over export fees for the use of its pipelines.

Only about one percent of the population has access to electricity, although it is not constant. Moreover, just seven percent of urban areas are electrified. The diesel-run Kapoeta Power Station, completed in 2011 and in the Eastern Equatoria State, is on the Narus River and produces .9 MW of power. The diesel-run Maridi Power Station, also completed in 2011, is on the River Maridi in the Western Equatoria State and produces .9 MW. Only the Juba power station, completed in 2006, creates 5.0 MW. Ultimately, hydropower must be increased to 230 MW in order to meet current energy demands.

Fishing

Artisanal river fishing is common and generally involves rowboats and gill nets. As of 2013, the UN's Food and Agriculture Organization (FAO) estimated that South Sudan had approximately 208,000 subsistence anglers and about 12,000 commercial anglers. Species most often caught include Claris catfish, Nile perch, Tigerfish, Nile carp, Moonfish, and Elephant Snoutfish. The Nile tilapia, according to FAO, represents 20 percent of all catches. Problematic for artisanal fishers are losses due to the absence of preservation capabilities. Fish caught along the Nile are often taken to fish traders who, in turn, deliver the fish in burlap sacks lined with ice to restaurants in urban areas. Often, 40 percent of the catch is spoiled on arrival. As of 2012, the FAO began teaching South Sudanese fishers to smoke, salt, and sun-dry their catches to lengthen its marketability.

Fish farming is also growing in South Sudan. Popular farmed species include tilapia and Nile perch. Some farms, like Akorogbodi in Western Equatoria, have not only begun to produce fish for hotels and restaurants, but also raise the fingerlings needed to stock other developing farms. In February 2015, there were eighteen fish farms in Western Equatoria alone, thirteen of them newly established. Currently, the government has no management or data collection practices in place, so statistics on the burgeoning sector are few.

Forestry

Forests cover an estimated 29 percent of South Sudan. However, deforestation, due in part to subsistence farming, civil war, and resettlement of refugees has become a serious problem. This is particularly true of residents who cut trees to use as firewood and clear areas to grow crops. Tree farming itself has been impacted. The first teak plantation began in Central Equatoria in 1919. By the 1940s, plantations spread across the Equatorias and Bahr el Ghazal states. As of 2007, 18 teak plantations were identified; each having trees between 35 and 50 years old. However, since 2011, the SPLA has pillaged plantations to fund its activities, selling trees to Uganda in a move referred to by humanitarian organizations as "blood teak." The UN Food and Agriculture Organization (FAO) has estimated that each year, the country loses 2,776 square kilometers (1,072 square miles) of forested land.

Mining/Metals

South Sudan's Ministry of Energy and Mining oversees mining. The country is rich in minerals, metals, and gemstones, which have been untouched for 50 years. These resources include iron ore, talc, marble, copper, chromium ore, zinc, tin-tungsten, mica, uranium, silver, gold, and diamonds. In light of petroleum-export disputes, which have hampered the South Sudanese economy, the government has begun to investigate other income sources, like its metals and precious gems. A mining bill was ratified in late 2012, which facilitates exploration of these unexploited resources, allows for issuance of new corporate mining licenses, and prohibits untaxed artisanal mining.

Agriculture

The South Sudanese are primarily reliant on subsistence farming. Rather than exporting agricultural goods, they are mainly produced for individual use. Chief crops include sorghum, maize, rice, millet, wheat, sugarcane, mangoes, papayas, bananas, sweet potatoes, sunflower seeds, cotton, sesame seeds, cassava, beans, and peanuts (groundnuts). Some vegetables, like tomatoes and onions, are imported from Uganda, Kenya, and Sudan.

Animal Husbandry

Cattle herding is central to many of South Sudan's indigenous cultures. Moreover, the CIA estimates that the country currently boasts between 10 and 20 million head of cattle, nearly all of them raised by agripastoral tribes, like the Dinka. Yet, cattle-raiding feuds between tribal groups in the state of Jonglei alone have led to hundreds of deaths since independence.

Tourism

As of September 2015, the U.S. State Department has issued a security warning admonishing travelers to avoid South Sudan due to clashes between Sudan Armed Forces (SAF) and the Sudan People's Liberation Army (SPLA). The bulletin also identifies seven rebel militia group involved in violent clashes with the SPLA, further broadening already wide conflict areas. Because of the civil war, there is very little data on foreign and domestic tourism, or even how many people travel through the Juba airport. However, if tourists choose to brave the conflict, the Ministry of Wildlife and Tourism oversees seven national parks and 12 game reserves within the country. These parks and reserves are home to bongos (a type of gazelle), elephants, buffaloes, giraffes, red river pigs, chimpanzees, forest monkeys, hippos, hyenas, gazelles, zebra, and lions. Within Juba, there are several hotels, like the Tulip Inn and Acacia Village, which receive high marks for service and Westernized food options. Outside Juba, however, there are few, if any, hotel accommodations.

Savannah Schroll Guz

DO YOU KNOW?

- Rendered cow brains, which have a naturally high fat content, are often used to grease cooking pans, and are considered vital to the ritual of making kisra, South Sudan's fermented-sorghum flatbread.

Bibliography

"South Sudan's New War: Abuses by Government and Opposition Forces." New York: *Human Rights Watch*, 2014.

Andrew S. Natsios. "Sudan, South Sudan, and Darfur: What Everyone Needs to Know." Oxford, UK: *Oxford UP*, 2012.

Angela Fisher and Carol Beckwith. "Dinka: Legendary Cattle Keepers of Sudan." New York: *Rizzoli*, 2010.

Benjamin Ajak, Benson Deng, Alephonsion Deng, and Judy A. Berstein. "They Poured Fire on Us from the Sky: The True Story of Three Lost Boys from Sudan." New York: *PublicAffairs*, 2006.

Edward Thomas. "South Sudan: A Slow Liberation." London, UK: *Zed Books*, 2015.

James Copnall. "A Poisonous Thorn in Our Hearts: Sudan and South Sudan's Bitter and Incomplete Divorce." London, UK: *Hurst*, 2014.

John Young. "The Fate of Sudan: The Origins and Consequences of a Flawed Peace Process." London, UK: *Zed Books*, 2012.

Kuirë Garang. "South Sudan Ideologically: Tribal Socio-Democracy, SPLM Ideologues, Juba Corruptocrats, Khartoum Theocrats and their Time-Frozen Leadership." Calgary, Alberta: *Nile Press*, 2013.

Matthew Arnold and Matthew LeRiche. "South Sudan: From Revolution to Independence." London, UK: *Oxford University Press*, 2013.

Peter Adwok Nyaba. "The Politics of Liberation in South Sudan." Kampala, Uganda: *Fountain Publishing*, 1996.

Works Cited

_____. "South Sudan: Economic Overview." The World Bank. *World Bank Group*, 2015. http://www.worldbank.org/en/country/southsudan/overview.

_____. "The potential of fishing in South Sudan." *FAO in emergencies*. FAO, 14 Aug. 2012.

_____. "UNESCO Investing in Literacy Teachers in South Sudan." *UNESCO Media Services*, 25 Jun. 2014. http://www.unesco.org/new/en/media-services/single-view/news/unesco_investing_in_literacy_teachers_in_south_sudan/#.VeXjLGBRHmS.

"About South Sudan." United Nations in South Sudan. *United Nations*, 2011. http://ss.one.un.org/country-info.html.

"About Women in South Sudan." *Women for Women International*, 2015. http://www.womenforwomen.org/what-we-do/countries/south-sudan.

"Africa: South Sudan." The World Factbook. *Central Intelligence Agency*, 6 Aug. 2015. https://www.cia.gov/library/publications/the-world-factbook/geos/od.html.

"China Jiangsu is Constructing Low Cost Houses in Juba." *Sudan Tribune*, 27 Jan. 2014. http://southsudantribune.org/states-news/19-china-jiangsu-is-constructing-low-cost-houses-in-juba.

"Communities of South Sudan Build their National Museum." *UNESCO Media Services*. UNESCO, 19 Jun. 2014. http://www.unesco.org/new/en/media-services/single-view/news/communities_of_south_sudan_build_their_national_museum/#.VdymNmBRHIU.

"Fishery and Aquaculture Country Profiles: The Republic of South Sudan." *Fisheries and Aquaculture Department*, 2015. http://www.fao.org/fishery/facp/SSD/en.

"Gurtong: Bringing South Sudanese Together." The Judiciary of South Sudan. *Gurtong*, 2014. http://www.gurtong.net/Governance/JudiciaryofSouthSudan/tabid/344/Default.aspx.

"Making Kisra." Green Shakes in Sudan: Food Experiences & Understandings, Southern Sudan 2009–2010. *Blogger.com*, 23 Jul. 2009. http://greenshakesinsudan.blogspot.com/2009/07/making-kisra.html.

"More than 2.25 million now displaced in South Sudan and across its borders." The UN Refugee Agency. *United Nations High Commissioner for Refugees*, 7 Jul. 2015. http://www.unhcr.org/559bdb0e6.html.

"Paying Taxes in South Sudan." Doing Business: Measuring Business Regulations. *World Bank Group*, 2015. http://www.doingbusiness.org/data/exploreeconomies/south-sudan/paying-taxes.

"Republic of South Sudan: IMF Country Report 14/345." Washington, DC: *International Monetary Fund*, 2014. PDF file.

"S. Sudan president denies killing of over 600 political prisoners." *Sudan Tribune*, 2 Sept. 2015. http://www.sudantribune.com/spip.php?article56267.

"Small Hydro World." World Small Hydropower Development Report 2013. *United Nations Industrial Development Organization & International Center on Small Hydro Power*, 2013. http://www.smallhydroworld.org/index.php?id=420.

"South Sudan Profile: Overview." *BBC News*, 18 Aug. 2015. http://www.bbc.com/news/world-africa-14069082.

"South Sudan." Participatory Local Democracy. *The Hunger Project*, n.d. http://localdemocracy.net/countries/africa-east/south-sudan/.

"South Sudan." Wildlife Conservation Society, 2015. *WCS.org*. http://www.wcs.org/where-we-work/africa/southern-sudan.aspx.

"South Sudan: Events of 2014." World Report 2015. *Human Rights Watch*, 2015. https://www.hrw.org/world-report/2015/country-chapters/south-sudan.

"South Sudan's National Museum." *Lost Boys Center for Leadership and Development*, 30 Jun. 2014. http://www.lbcld.org/south-sudans-national-museum/.

"SPLM youth call for stability and reconciliation." *Sudan Tribune*. Sudan Tribune, 31 Jan. 2014. http://www.sudantribune.com/spip.php?article49781.

"Tourismus." *Die Botschaft der Republik Südsudan in Deutschland. Embassy of South Sudan*, 2014. http://embassy-southsudan.de/geschaft-wirtschaft/tourismus/.

"Transport in South Sudan." South Sudan Travel: Your Guide to South Sudan. *African Sudanese, 2014.* http://www.africansudanese.org/travel-tips/sudan-transport.html.

Abraham Nhial. "Fish Farming in South Sudan's Western Equatoria." World Vision South Sudan. *World Vision International*, 1 Feb. 2015. http://www.wvi.org/south-sudan/article/fish-farming-south-sudan%E2%80%99s-western-equatoria.

Alexander Dziadosz and Hereward Holland. "South Sudan Mining Law to Kick-Start Exploration." *Thompson Reuters*, 18 Sept. 2012. http://www.reuters.com/article/2012/09/18/ozabs-southsudan-mining-law-idAFJOE88H02C20120918.

Catherine Soi. "Little to celebrate on South Sudan's fourth anniversary." *Al Jazeera Media Network*, 9 Jul. 2015. http://www.aljazeera.com/blogs/africa/2015/07/south-sudan-independence-anniversary-150709043259183.html.

Charlton Doki. "Forests Dying in South Sudan Violence." *IPS: Inter Press Service News Agency.* IPS-Inter Press Service, 26 May 2012. http://www.ipsnews.net/2012/05/forests-dying-in-south-sudan-violence/.

Flavia Krause-Jackson. "Cows-for-Bride Inflation Spurs Cattle Theft in South Sudan." *BloombergBusiness.* Bloomberg, 26 Jul. 2011. http://www.bloomberg.com/news/articles/2011-07-26/cows-for-bride-inflation-spurs-cattle-theft-among-mundari-in-south-sudan.

Laura Bridle. "Female Genital Mutilation in South Sudan." Doctors Without Borders. *MSF USA*, 27 Feb. 2015. http://blogs.msf.org/en/staff/blogs/msf-in-south-sudan/female-genital-mutilation-in-south-sudan.

Sasha Martin. "About the Food of South Sudan." *Global Travel Adventure. Global Travel Adventure*, 9 Apr. 2013. http://globaltableadventure.com/2013/04/09/about-the-food-of-south-sudan/.

Simona Foltyn. "Independent South Sudan's economic woes." Al Jazeera. *Al Jazeera Media Network*, 9 Jul. 2015. http://www.aljazeera.com/indepth/features/2015/07/independent-south-sudans-economic-woes-150705112843046.html.

SWAZILAND

Introduction

Swaziland, a small country in southeastern Africa known for its rolling veldts and longstanding monarchy, achieved independence from Britain in 1968 and adopted a constitution in 2006. The country is landlocked and nearly completely surrounded by the country of South Africa. The only portion of the country that is not bordered by South Africa is the northeastern region, which borders Mozambique.

Swaziland has been affected more than any other African nation by the HIV/AIDS epidemic. AIDS, drought, poverty, and starvation have brought much suffering to the country. The United Nations has worked with the Swazi government to try to alleviate some of these problems.

Swaziland has two capitals. Mbabane is the administrative capital, while the city of Lobamba, only 16 kilometers (10 miles) to the south, remains the country's traditional capital. Lobamba serves as the legislative seat of Swaziland, as well as the residence of the Ndlovukazi, or queen mother, the king's partner as joint head of state. Although advances have been made toward a more democratic governmental system, political parties and political representation have not yet successfully gained a foothold in the country.

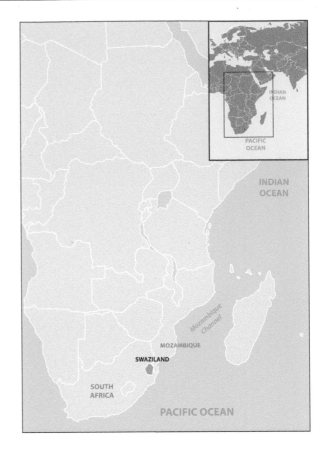

GENERAL INFORMATION

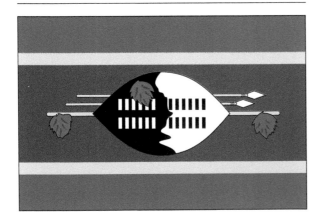

Official Language: English (used for official, government business) and SiSwati

Population: 1,435,613 (July 2015 estimate)

Currency: Swazi Lilangeni (plural Emalangeni) and South African Rand

Coins: One hundred cents equal one lilangeni. Coins are issued in denominations of 1, 2, 5, 10, 20, and 50 cents, as well as 1 lilangeni, and 2 and 5 emalangeni.

Land Area: 17,204 square kilometers (6,642 square miles)

Water Area: 160 square kilometers (61 square miles)

National Motto: "Siyinqaba" ("We are the fortress")

National Anthem: "Nkulunkulu Mnikati wetibusiso temaSwati" ("Oh God, Bestower of the Blessings of the Swazi")

Capital: Mbabane (administrative) and Lobamba (royal/legislative)

Time Zone: GMT +2

Flag Description: The flag of the Kingdom of Swaziland features five horizontal bands of

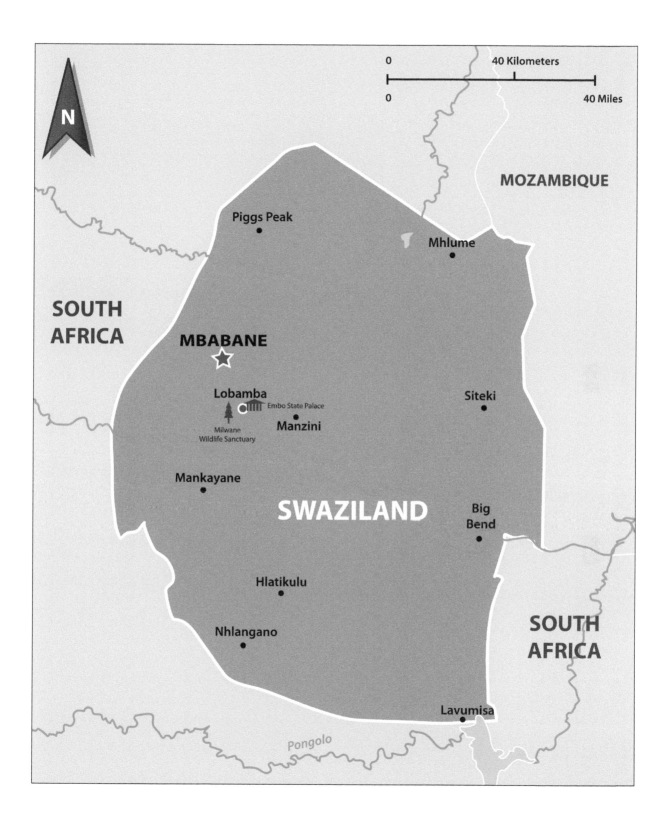

Principal Cities by Population (2015):

- Manzini (110,537)
- Mbabane (76,218)
- Big Bend (10,342)
- Malkerns (9,724)
- Nhlangano (9,016)

color: a wide central red band flanked by two thinner yellow bands and then two sky blue bands, one on the top and one on the bottom. The red stands for past battles; the blue represents peace and stability; and the yellow signifies the country's natural resources. Centered in the red band are a traditional ox-hide shield of Swazi Emasotsha Regiment in black and white, to signifying racial harmony, and staff, as well as two spears. Two feathers, from the lisakabuli (widow bird) and ligwalagwala (lourie) birds, adorn the staff.

Population

Almost every estimate on Swaziland's population includes a note that discusses the high rate of HIV/AIDS infection and its impact on the country's death rate and population. According to UNICEF (United Nations Children's Fund), the Joint United Nations Programme on HIV/AIDS and the Government of Swaziland, between 200,000 and 230,000 people were living with HIV infection in 2012; 22,000 children were living with HIV; 78,000 children have been orphaned by HIV/AIDS. Among the fifteen to twenty-four year age group for women, there is a 20 percent infection rate; for men between the ages of fifteen and twenty-four , the infection rate is 10.3 percent. HIV/AIDS has an impact not only on population, but on the economy.

Approximately 97 percent of people living in Swaziland are Swazis, an ethnic group that belongs to the Bantu language group. Traditionally, the Swazi people have been subsistence farmers, as most of the population (78.7 percent) lives in rural areas. Many people, though, now have to supplement that income in other occupations. While Swaziland produces

many well-educated professionals, many leave to find better job opportunities abroad.

A small proportion of the population, roughly 3 percent, is non-Swazi, and includes refugees from Mozambique and Zulu, as well as some Europeans who work in the business sector.

Languages

SiSwati is a Bantu language, part of the Niger-Congo language family. It is most closely related to Ndebele, but also shares many similarities with the Zulu and Xhosa languages, which are also spoken in South Africa. SiSwati is the official language of Swaziland, along with English. However, English is used for communication purposes in most government and business affairs. About 76,000 Swazis speak Zulu.

Native People & Ethnic Groups

Some of the earliest people to settle in the region were related to the Ngwane, who were the ancestors of the modern Swazi people. In the 15th century, they migrated south from central Africa and reestablished themselves in the area that is occupied today by Mozambique.

By the 19th century, the powerful Zulu nation and the Ndwandwe clan in the south were a growing threat to the Swazis, so they established their kingdom in lands further to the north, in the region that is known today as Swaziland. The first king of the modern Swazi state was King Mswati II (also known as Mavuso III, ca. 1820–1868; r. 1840–1865). The name "Swaziland" was derived from the name "Mswati."

The Swazi population predominates, representing over seventy clans.

Religions

The major religions in the country are African Zionist (a mix of Christianity and indigenous practices and accounting for 40 percent of the population) and Roman Catholicism (20 percent), and Muslim (10 percent). Thirty percent of the population identifies with a series of other faiths, ranging from Judaism, Baha'ism, and other Protestant religions, including the Methodist and Mormon faiths.

Climate

Swaziland has a subtropical climate, which ranges from sub-humid and temperate in the higher regions to semi-arid and warm in the lower-lying areas. Subject to various wind conditions and air masses, which in part affect rainfall and temperature in the country, Swaziland occasionally experiences weather patterns like cyclones and drought. In the semi-arid areas of the country, drought is part of a cyclical climate pattern.

Temperatures in Swaziland average around 16.9° Celsius (62.4° Fahrenheit). The hottest month is January, with temperatures ranging from 22° Celsius (71° Fahrenheit) in the highveldt to 34° Celsius (93° Fahrenheit) in the eastern lowveldt. June is the coldest winter month, with temperatures ranging between 8° and 12° Celsius (46.4° and 53.6° Fahrenheit).

The highveldt region typically experiences frost conditions in the winter. Higher elevations tend to receive more rainfall, averaging from around 800 to 1,400 millimeters (25 to 55 inches). The middleveldt receives from 650 to 1,000 millimeters (25 to 39 inches), while the lowest-lying regions receive around 550 to 800 millimeters (21 to 31 inches) of rainfall per year.

ENVIRONMENT & GEOGRAPHY

Topography

Swaziland is a landlocked country, bordered by South Africa and Mozambique. The western region tends to have higher elevations, with lower plains in the east. The country consists of four separate regions
the highveldt, the middleveldt, the lowveldt, and the Lebombo plateau. Each region extends between the country's northern and southern borders.

In the west, the highveldt covers one-third of the country's land area. It consists of plateaus, hills, valleys, and basins. The highveldt is part of an escarpment that is connected to the Transvaal plateau.

The middleveldt, which is around 14 percent of the country's area, contains eroded plateaus and hills, while the rolling lowveldt plains make up around 11 percent of the land. On the eastern border of the country, the Lebombo Ridge is a plateau that makes up 8 percent of Swaziland's total area.

The country's highest point is Emlembe at 1,862 meters (6,108 feet). Emlembe is part of the east uKhahlamba (also known as Drakensberg) mountain range, right on the border with South Africa. The country's lowest point is in the Great Usutu River (also called the Maputo River), where there is a depth of just 21 meters (69 feet) above sea level.

Plants & Animals

Plant life in Swaziland varies according to elevation. The highveldt consists of grassland and some forested areas, while the middleveldt and the lower-lying areas have savanna with taller grasses, trees, and shrubs. Some species of flower that are native to Swaziland include Aloe kniphofioides, Dierama galpinii (also known as Angels' Fishing Rods), Strelitzia caudate (called Wild Banana), and Pimpinella caffra (or Ibheka).

Swaziland is home to a number of large animal species, including lions, elephants, rhinoceroses, leopards, and giraffes. Crocodiles and hippopotamuses can be found in the country's rivers, and different species of monkey, baboons, jackals, honey badgers, and mongooses may be found throughout the land. The rolling grasslands are home to herds of antelope, African buffalo, black wildebeests, zebras, and impalas. While many large mammals live in the parks and reserves, much of the habitat outside of these areas has been degraded or destroyed. Habitat destruction also affects the country's bird life. Swaziland has over 400 species of birds, many of which can be found in its reserves. Among these species are eagles, vultures, the lanner falcon, the pied kingfisher, the white-faced duck, and the purple-crested lourie, which is Swaziland's national bird.

CUSTOMS & COURTESIES

Greetings

The official languages of Swaziland are SiSwati, which originated with the Bantu people who migrated throughout southern Africa thousands of years ago, and English, spoken widely in Mbabane and Manzini. (English is considered the language of business.) SiSwati shares some of the same vocal characteristics and phrasing as many other African tribal dialects. A typical greeting begins with "Sawubona" ("I see you" or "Hello"), followed by "Unjani?" ("How are you?"). Common parting phrases include "Sala kahle" ("Be well") or "Hamba kahla" ("Good journey"). In general, the Swazi people value an opportunity to connect with each other. The notion of "people first" is a core value in Swazi culture. At its heart, the simple act of greeting is a ritualistic way of acknowledging the dignity of the individual.

Handshakes typically accompany a greeting. When extending one's hand, it is most respectful to shake with one's right hand while placing your left hand, palm upward, under your right forearm, an old custom indicating that you hold no weapons and come in peace. (Additionally, as with Muslim culture, the left hand is associated with the cleansing of the body, and thus considered impure; the right hand is exclusively used for interacting.). Important to note is that these handshakes last considerably longer than in Western culture, sometimes even as long as several minutes. It is important to greet each person that one meets and also to acknowledge when someone is extending a greeting, as it is considered rude to avoid or ignore a neighbor. Although greetings are friendly and frequent, the Swazi are mindful of eye contact, particularly in the more traditional rural regions. As a sign of respect, children customarily do not make eye contact with adults. Likewise, when greeting an elder or someone or a higher status, it is customary to bow slightly.

Gestures & Etiquette

Swazi culture is very social and demonstrative. However, social interactions between men and women are modest. Although urban areas are more progressive, proper codes of conduct are still observed in the more traditional rural areas. (Traditionally, a young woman's reputation and chastity were tied to her standing in the community.) For example, women and men seldom make eye contact and tend to segregate for socializing and eating. In the urban areas, friendly handshakes are tolerated, but interactions between men and women are generally public, preferably with the young woman's family present. Between members of the same sex, interactions are very warm and affectionate; men may hold hands or link arms, and women frequently embrace each other.

It is important to not show the soles of one's feet to another, as this is considered disrespectful. Also when socializing, it is not unusual for everyone to sit or stand with virtually no space in between each other, as the Western concept of "personal space" is not observed.

Eating/Meals

The Swazi people traditionally eat three meals a day. Meals generally consist of simple and rustic fare, prepared using mainly local produce and livestock. Breakfast is light, usually a bowl of sitfubi (porridge made of hot milk and cornmeal) or sishwala (porridge of cornmeal and beans, sometimes even served with meat or vegetables), or bread with peanut spread, as well as tea or coffee. Lunch is the largest meal of the day and taken when children return home from school. It might consist of a stew of vegetables served over cornmeal porridge or with cornbread. Dinner is a lighter meal and might consist of leftovers. In the cities, some families share a large Sunday meal of rice, roasted meat, salad, fruit, and custard.

Snacks are typically fermented milk, fresh fruit, or roasted peanuts. Umncweba (also biltong) is a popular treat of cured dried meat—most often beef, game, goat, or ostrich—sold by street vendors. Traditional tea and coffee are staple drinks, as is tjwala, a home-brewed beer made from ground sorghum and maize (corn).

Visiting

Time is fluid in Swazi culture and schedules are rarely adhered to. However, visits to another's home generally occur at the agreed upon time. Guests are generally expected to remove their shoes upon entering and to traditionally ask "Sikhulekile ekhaya," which requests permission to enter the house and shows deference to the host family. Though it is not expected, giving a small token to the host is appreciated, particularly specialty items, like chocolates or candy.

Guests will likely be seated on the floor, as the majority of Swazi households are rural and offer sparse furnishings. When eating, it is expected that everyone will separate according to gender and age. The head of the household eats first, followed by the women and children. Hands are washed before the meal, as utensils are rarely used. It is likely that a guest would be served a meat stew with porridge, which is served in individual wooden bowls, and eaten by using the right hand to shape the porridge into balls.

LIFESTYLE

Family

The traditional Swazi family is large, with extended family joining the homestead as members marry. Swaziland is traditionally a polygamous society and men may take several wives on payment of a dowry, known as lobola, which normally entails giving cattle to the bride's parents. An acceptable number of cattle is fifteen, and payment can be made in what Westerners might call "installments." Wives typically move into the homestead of their husband's family. However, which children join the family depends entirely on the original dowry. For example, if the father did not offer any cattle, then he forfeits rights to fatherhood and any children stay with the mother's family.

Domestic duties are generally segregated; males tend to agrarian and outside affairs, while females are responsible for child rearing, cooking, and maintaining the household. The father is considered the head of the household and, therefore, earns great respect. The elderly are perceived as being very wise and are also held in high esteem. They are often consulted in family

affairs and their guidance is revered. Discipline is highly valued and children are taught that obedience to one's superiors is a virtue. Children are also highly valued in traditional Swazi culture, and women who cannot reproduce are subject to social stigmas.

Housing

In the urban areas of Mbabane and Manzini, Swazi homes are generally simple concrete structures with basic access to water and electricity. In the rural outskirts, where the vast majority of Swazi families reside, traditional homesteads (shared by extended family) are still common. These traditional homesteads feature three beehive-shaped huts: one used for cooking, one for sleeping, and one for socializing. The huts are typically made of dry grass and straw. More affluent homesteads may also include a separate hut for guests or a room for men to gather. In polygamous families, each wife has her own hut and a fenced-in yard.

Homesteads also have a cattle corral or a separate area for livestock. The hut belonging to the head of the household is always situated opposite the corral, as livestock are considered an indicator of wealth and prosperity. Running water and electricity are rare; generally, a community shares a common tap and collects from it the water they need each day.

Food

Swazi cuisine is largely characterized by the use of cultivated cereal foods (sorghum, millet, maize, and rice) and traditional fruits and vegetables, as well as milk (particularly from cattle), and groundnuts (the region's word for peanuts). Meals are traditionally very simple, such as stews and starch-based dishes, and rely on locally harvested staples such as sugar cane, peanut oil, citrus fruits, pumpkins, and vegetables such as carrots, cabbages, onions, tomatoes, okra, and potatoes. Meat is a commodity, as livestock are used primarily for production of milk, eggs, and wool, though beef, chicken, goat, and lamb are eaten on special occasions, particularly in stews. (Cattle, traditionally seen as a symbol of wealth and used as currency among tribal members, were not kept for consumption, and fish were historically disdained.) Meals are generally flavored with chilies (especially piri-piri, known as the African bird's eye chili), peanuts, and onions. Since most staple food is locally cultivated, the months of November and December are particularly lacking, as food stockpiles may be exhausted and summer crops are not ready.

Traditional dishes include sishwala, a thick porridge customarily served with meats or vegetables; incwancwa, which is sour porridge made with fermented mealie (cornmeal); umncweba, which is dried and uncooked meat (also called biltong); sishibo, which is stew made with onions, potatoes, green beans, green peppers, tomatoes, salt and either chicken or beef; and emasi emabele, which is ground sorghum mixed with sour milk. Traditional porridges are also made of mashed groundnuts, pumpkin, and beans.

Life's Milestones

Marriages are customarily arranged by the parents of the bride and groom. One of the goals of a marriage is to advance in the class system. (Swazi society operates based on a clan system; the clan of the highest rank is the Dlamini, to which the king always belongs.) A dowry of cattle is given to the bride by her groom and the public marriage ceremony unfolds over several days, culminating in the anointing of the bride, which seals the union.

Another important family ritual is the choosing of the sangoma, a divine healer and guide. The sangoma is believed to be elected by family ancestors and becomes a resource for the family at times of emotional turmoil, sickness, and death. After being selected, the sangoma is trained in meditation (for the purpose of diagnosis) and the graduation ceremony is commemorated with music and a celebratory meal. Sangoma are distinct from inyanga, who are doctors using traditional folk medicines and homemade compounds to heal.

Traditionally, common citizens are buried at their homestead, while kings are interred in mountain caves. Extended family generally gathers for the funeral. One month after the funeral, the extended family traditionally meets again to ritualistically purge themselves of the contamination of death.

CULTURAL HISTORY

Art

Human habitation in Swaziland dates back to the early Stone Age, and the country is home to numerous sites displaying evidence of prehistoric or primitive art. Lion Cavern, considered the world's oldest mine, is one of the country's richest archeological resources. A wealth of prehistoric artifacts such as Stone Age tools (choppers, picks, and hammer stones) and beaded jewelry has been collected there. In addition, archeologists have found quantities of specularite, a form of iron ore with hematite flakes and angularly shaped crystals that create a glittering effect. It is believed that ancient spiritual leaders would grind the ore and smear the glittering paste on their body and hair when dressing for special ceremonies.

One of the more mysterious and dramatic early art forms in Swaziland are the Nsangwini rock paintings, housed at the Nsangwini Rock Art Shelter. The rock paintings, which depict mainly human and animal forms, have been traced back 4,000 years to the Bushmen (or San, the indigenous hunter-gathers of southern Africa). Some of the paintings incorporate natural formations, such as cracks in the rock, in the illustrations. For example, one painting depicts a wildebeest emerging from behind the crack. Similarly, another painting shows a headless human form emerging from a crack, which is seemingly the source of the figure's decapitation. Researchers believe this indicates a mystical figure, and is likely the depiction of a shaman in an altered spiritual state. The most intriguing paintings, mainly because their significance is unclear, are those illustrating two winged figures that are half-bird or insect and half-human. One on the right appears to be flying and the other is merely hovering as four human figures file toward a crack in the rock. Rock paintings also exist in other locations, and depict hunting and battle scenes, as well as dance rituals.

Swaziland is renowned for its traditional craftworks and handicraft industry, and the government has called its contemporary arts and crafts and traditional markets one of the nation's greatest attractions. These various traditional crafts include wooden sculpture, soapstone carvings, glassblowing, ceramics, and the textile arts (tapestries, grass and mohair weaving, and the art of batik). However, these arts and crafts are mainly done by women as a means to generate income, and many are perceived as souvenirs rather than art. Nonetheless, a movement to develop and fund the fine arts, such as painting, sculpture, and theater, has gained traction in the early 21st century, including the development of a national arts center and the country's first performance art festival. Since it opened in February 2011, Yebo! Contemporary Art Gallery, located in Ezulwini, has featured and represents the work of over seventy contemporary painters, sculptors, and craftspeople. In 2012, Yebo! published Swaziland's first visual arts book and began hosting classes and workshops as part of a program called "ArtReach" intended to enrich the community.

Architecture

The traditional "beehive" huts that feature predominantly in Swazi homesteads are made from bent branches, with dried grasses forming the shell, and raised thatched roofs. These collections of homes are typically surrounded by reed fences.

Dance

Dance has been an integral part of Swazi spiritual rituals for centuries. These ceremonies often last for several hours and are accompanied by traditional instruments such as the kudu horn (from the kudu antelope), calabash (a round and dried hollowed fruit filled with seeds), rattle, and reed flute. One notable dance is the Umhlanga dance (also referred to as the Reed Dance), a tradition that was designed as a showcase of marriageable young women for the king to choose from, should he seek another wife (the king is entitled to take as many wives as he desires). Because of weather and the maturation of the reed, the traditional dance usually takes place in August. Thousands of eligible young women—mostly teenagers who are childless—from across the country set off to the outskirts of Lobamba to gather fresh reeds and to pay homage to the Queen Mother (iNdlovukazi, literally "She-Elephant"). The dance ritual, which is now more about celebrating the virtues of young women, lasts eight days. It culminates in the actual dance, attended by the king, in which the dancers are attired in ceremonial jewelry and feathers and short beaded skirts.

The Incwala ceremony (also called the "First Fruits" ceremony) is a sacred ritual that takes place in December or January and culminates with the king's blessing of the New Year harvest. Several weeks in advance, young men from across the country harvest lusekwane branches and hike to the Engabezweni royal residence. Arriving at dawn, they work together to build a kraal (an enclosure usually used for livestock). Ceremonial songs permitted only for this occasion are sung as the men work and the bemanti (national priests, literally "men of water") bring water from the rivers. On the third day, a bull is sacrificed, and on the fourth day the king emerges to dance for the people. He eats a pumpkin to signal the beginning of the New Year's crops. Days later, anything used in the ceremony is burned in a ritual designed to bring rain.

In contrast to the ancient ritual dances that remain a part of Swazi tradition, sibhaca dancing is generally performed for fun at special occasions and is often incorporated as an extracurricular school activity. Young boys, dressed in colorful fabric and furs, form teams and trade turns performing choreography that involves stomping and chanting to traditional music. These dances generally go on at length, sometimes lasting for several hours.

Music

Drums often accompany vocals in Swazi folk and dance music. A Makhweyane, a single metal-stringed instrument with a gourd sound box, is played by tapping the string with a reed, and herders often carve flutes out of a piece of wood. Other regional instruments include the kudu horn and the calabash.

Contemporary Swazi music is really part of a greater regional southern African music movement, which has experienced a reciprocal sharing of both style and instruments with contemporary Western music. This is evident in the music of artists like Paul Simon, who has collaborated with Ladysmith Black Mambazo, a male choral group that has gained an international following of its own. In 2013, the group's album *Live: Singing For Peace Around The World* won a Grammy for Best World Music CD

Within Swaziland, jazz, hip hop, reggae, rock and rap music are all thriving.

Literature

Swaziland has a strong oral tradition, characterized by the inganekwane (folk tale). Knowledge of these spoken stories is considered essential to the moral and traditional upbringing of any child. The use of praise poems or tibongo has been used to support the royal family's version of history, particularly throughout the reign of King Sobhuza II (1921–1982).

In the 20th century, writers such as J. S. M. (James Shadrack Mkhulunyelwa) Matsebula (1918–1993) began a wave of postcolonial literature, presenting historical perspectives of the Swazi experience, as well as poetry. Later, authors like Stanley Muza N. Matsebula (1958–), an economist and novelist, wrote about issues of gender and equality. Salayedvwa Modison Magagula (1958–) is a short story writer and playwright who founded the first traveling theater group in the country. Elias Adam Bateng Mkhonta (1954–2001), also a novelist, wrote of the social problems plaguing the nation.

CULTURE

Arts & Entertainment

Swaziland's handicraft industry has grown significantly in recent years, thanks to a government movement supporting handicraft production.

Rural women in particular are benefiting from government-sponsored training, as many of the trades (including candle making, woodworking, glassblowing, weaving, dyeing, and sculpting) are traditionally feminine and passed down through generations. These women are capitalizing by organizing at the local level to share the cost of materials and help each other sell the wares outside the village confines.

Woven goods are becoming one of the most important crafts, and include basic baskets and mats woven from simple sisal, and more durable baskets woven from bark. Functional items are woven from grass, such as the sitja bowl and mats and baskets. The sitja bowl consists of grass fibers spun by hand into thread, and then tightly woven in intricate patterns so that the absorbent fibers render the bowl watertight.

Artists are also sought after on a global scale. Johan Mhlanga (1930–) is a master wood sculptor of Swaziland whose work is collected around the world. Swaziland has also produced many talented painters and artists. An accomplished painter, Lucas Mlambo's (1959–) work is internationally known. Lucas Macie (1960–), a refugee from Mozambique, also creates paintings that are sought after by international collectors.

Encouraged by the efforts of the Department of Commerce and Trade, local art establishments are reinventing themselves to improve business practices, while giving back to the community. One example is Ngwenya Glass, near Mbabane. Known for its production of glass-blown tableware, vases, and ornaments, the shop (comprised solely of Swazi artisans) has teamed with local school children to clean up the streets and benefit their environment by collecting discarded glass (mostly soda bottles) to be recycled as glass for the studio. The store's inventory is produced entirely from recycled glass. This program has proved so effective that it has now grown to include a system that exchanges student volunteerism (primarily roadside cleanup) for sponsorship of their local interests, like the community soccer team.

Swaziland does not generate much original contemporary music, as Swazis tend to listen to the artists of neighboring South Africa (many Swazi artists record and perform in South Africa). Furthermore, only gospel singers traditionally earned a living as musical artists, since they could use the church to market their music. However, Western-style music such as hip-hop is becoming increasingly popular.

Traditional Swazi sports include kugwaza inzema (javelin throwing), butjoki (archery), and wrestling (kubambana ngemandla). The National Sports Council was created in 1999 and is responsible for sports development in the country. Other popular sports include football (soccer), golf, rugby, swimming, and volleyball.

Cultural Sites & Landmarks

Despite Swaziland's small size—at only 17,364 square kilometers (6,704 square miles) it is the smallest country in the southern hemisphere—the country offers a range of cultural sites and landmarks. Swaziland is also home to a range of beautiful natural habitats, such as mountains, savannahs, and rainforests, and contains several important game and nature reserves. Swaziland also has one site being considered for the list of World Heritage Sites maintained by the United Nations Educational, Scientific, and Cultural Organization (UNESCO): the ancient Ngwenya Mines, located in the province of Hhohho, was submitted for consideration on December 31, 2008. The site is home to the earliest mining activity in the world.

The heart of Swazi tourist activity is in the Ezulwini Valley, which contains the Mlilwane Wildlife Sanctuary, Swaziland's oldest protected area. The sanctuary houses a small museum and a diversity of wildlife, including nearly thirty species of large game. The valley is also home to Mantenga Cultural Village, dubbed "Ligugu Lemaswati" ("Pride of the Swazi People") by King Mswati III. Located in the Mantenga Nature Reserve, it consists of sixteen huts that depict Swaziland's mid-19th century life. In Lobamba, the Swazi royal residence includes the Embo State Palace, built by the British for King Sobhuza II (1899–1982); the Lozitha State House, the king's contemporary dwelling; the Royal Kraal, one of the royal residences and host

to the Incawala and Umhlanga ceremonies; and the National Museum.

Swaziland is also home to several declared national monuments, including a sacred pool in Mbabane and a tree under which Ngwane V (1876–1899), referred to as King Bhunu and also as Mahlokohla, was put on trial for murder by the neighboring South Africa Republic (1881–1902). The historic chief of Swaziland remains a colorful part of Swaziland's history, including his sudden death at the age of twenty-three during the famed Incwala ceremony. Other landmarks include the Houses of Parliament, King Sobhuza II Memorial Park, and the country's various rock art sites.

Libraries & Museums

The Kingdom of Swaziland's National Museum was built in 1972 and houses important cultural artifacts, photographs, a natural history exhibit, and a Swazi village exhibit. The museum library contains a collection of significant Swazi books and printed material. The library also boasts a mobile museum that travels to schools throughout the country.

Holidays

In addition to the many Christian holidays observed in the country, Swaziland also celebrates the traditional holidays of Incwala ("Festival of First Fruits") and Umhlanga ("Reed Dance"). Incwala is traditionally held in December and lasts for four days; the exact dates are determined by astrologers. It celebrates the country's fertility with a number of rituals, including one in which the king blesses the country's produce.

Umhlanga is held in late August or early September in the Ludzidzini Royal Village and lasts approximately eight days. It includes some rituals that reinforce the expectation of young women's chastity and others that honor the queen mother. In one event, young women perform traditional dances before the royal family. Independence or "Somhlolo" Day is celebrated annually on September 6. On April 19, the birthday of current king Mswati III is celebrated, and the birthday of the late king Sobhuza is celebrated on July 22.

Youth Culture

There remains a noticeable gap between rural and urban youth in Swaziland. The youth in Swaziland's rural regions live simply and have limited exposure to modern conveniences. Domestic duties and socialization are segregated; girls generally gather together at home to work on handicrafts, while young boys might simulate football (soccer) matches. In fact, the national football team is popular among young males, and teens may congregate at home or in local coffee shops to watch games on television or listen on the radio. Youth culture is more progressive in urban areas, and young people may socialize together at nightclubs and other venues. However, relationships between boys and girls are usually rather modest. Like most young people the world around, Swaziland's urban youth enjoy Western pop culture such as films and music.

As of 2015, an estimated 36 percent of the population was under the age of fifteen. However, the staggering HIV/AIDS rate and unemployment rate—at an estimated 28 percent and 40 percent respectively—is having a devastating effect on Swazi youth in the 21st century. (As of 2008, the country also had the highest rate of notified tuberculosis [TB] cases, and in 2014, Doctors Without Borders estimated that over 80 percent of those infected with IIIV also suffer from TB, often drug-resistant strains.) Families are unable to provide for their children, and thousands of children and young people have been orphaned due to the national crisis of HIV/AIDS. In addition, because the Swazi government is more focused on a traditional lifestyle, urban children who are orphaned or poverty-stricken are increasingly not benefitting from social welfare. International aid also is primarily directed at rural areas.

SOCIETY

Transportation

Kombies (mini-bus taxis) running between Manzini and Mbabane are very inexpensive and are the most widely used mode of transport in those urban areas. Taxis can be hired, but they are very costly and considered relatively unnecessary (as are personal cars), as the cities and towns are small enough that one can travel by foot. Buses between towns are rarely used as they are considered infrequent and unreliable. There is a railroad, Swazi Railway, but it is for cargo, not passengers. Cars in Swaziland are driven on the left hand side of the road.

King Mswati-III International Airport, located outside Manzini, was inaugurated in March 2014. Built at a cost of $150 million (USD), to which Taiwan contributed $22 million (USD), it has a runway 11,810-foot paved runway and the capacity to handle 300,000 passengers annually. However, no airline has yet utilized the airport, and it does not yet have an operation license from the International Air Transport Association. Matsapha Airport is the only other paved airport in Swaziland (there are as many as twelve other unpaved air fields, however). Its paved runway is 8, 530 feet, and it mainly handles chartered flights to O. R. Tambo International Airport in Johannesburg.

Until the King Mswati-III International Airport is functioning, Swaziland has no international flights and connects to South Africa via plane and Mozambique bus. South Africa-based Airlink connects flights from South Africa and Swaziland's flag carrier, Swaziland Airlink, flies within the kingdom.

Transportation Infrastructure

According to the Swazi Ministry of Public Works and Transport, the Swazi transportation system is comprised of 3,770 kilometers (6067 miles) of roads and 301 kilometers (187 miles) of railway. Through its participation with the South African Development Community, the Swazi government has agreed to support regional transport development (including road, rail, port, telecommunications and port side infrastructures) corridors between Swaziland, South Africa, and Mozambique.

Commerce is aided by an extensive roadway system throughout the country that facilitates transport among Swaziland's neighbors South

Africa and Mozambique. Rural, or district, roads are not considered to be well maintained and have a direct impact on economics, as well as access to foodstuffs for those populations.

Media & Communications

Swaziland's absolute monarchy has significant influence over the country's media. Swazi TV is run by the Swaziland Television Authority. The Swaziland Broadcasting and Information Service is also state-run, offering three channels (the SiSwati channel, the English channel, and the Information Service channel). The two most prominent daily newspapers are the *Swazi Observer* and the privately owned *Times of Swaziland*, although both—like the radio and television programming—do not exercise freedom of the press, as expressing opposition to the throne is strictly prohibited. Therefore, journalists consistently self-censor and cover stories that reflect well on the monarchy.

Household computers are becoming more common, but Internet cafés continue to offer access in more urbanized areas, like Mbabane and Manzini. According to the World Bank, as of 2014, internet penetration in Swaziland was 27.1 percent. Cell phones are relatively inexpensive, but seen almost exclusively in urban areas.

SOCIAL DEVELOPMENT

Standard of Living

Swaziland ranked 148th out of 187 countries on the 2014 United Nations Human Development Index, which measures quality of life indicators. The UN classifies the country as having "low human development."

Water Consumption

The World Health Organization (WHO) reports that as of 2015, 74.1 percent of the country had improved access to clean drinking water. Rural areas suffered from less access, at only 70 percent of the population, while urban households had an 93.6 percent access rate. Additionally, the country's average for access to improved

sanitation stands at 57.5 percent as of 2015. That breaks down into 63.1 percent in urban areas and 56 percent in rural areas.

The Ministry of Natural Resources and Energy has allocated €30 million for the Disaster Relief Fund, which brings potable water to residents in rural areas. Additionally, the Ministry of Economic Planning and Development is implementing a micro-projects programme to develop local water management plans.

Education

Education in Swaziland consists of primary, secondary, and university levels. Primary education lasts from age six to thirteen, and addresses basic literacy and mathematics skills. In 2010, the government began to provide free education for grades one and two, with plans to progressively institute free education to higher grades in the future. As of 2011, education expenditures represented 7.8 percent of the GDP.

In the past, and in grades beyond one and two, families paid the cost of their children's education, although the government provided free textbooks. The lack of free education has, in some families, forced them to choose to educate only one child or to rotate the education of their children one year at a time. When the government instituted the government-funded first and second year educations, they had to turn some students away because of a shortage of classrooms, teachers, and materials.

After primary school, students take examinations that assess whether they will move on to secondary education, which lasts for four or five years. According to the CIA's *World Factbook*, school life expectancy in Swaziland is an average of eleven years, twelve for males and eleven for females. Prior to 2010, the only post-secondary institution in Swaziland was the University of Swaziland, based in the capital of Mbabane, with campuses in Luyengo and Kwaluseni. However, in 2010 the Limkokwing University of Creative Technology was founded. Also in 2010, the government announced that university students would be responsible for paying for 50 percent of their tuition costs.

Before the HIV/AIDS crisis struck sub-Saharan Africa in the 1980s, Swaziland had been building a successful educational system and had achieved a high rate of school attendance among young people in the country. However, HIV/AIDS has had a devastating effect on education in Swaziland. A large percentage of teachers have died from AIDS, while many others have retired out of fear of contracting the disease. Often, students who are AIDS orphans must stay home from school to care for their younger siblings and themselves. The Ministry of Education is attempting to integrate HIV/AIDS education into school curricula.

Women's Rights

Family dynamics in Swazi culture traditionally marginalize women and empower men. Arranged marriages are still prevalent and women marry young—often under the age of eighteen—limiting their educational and employment opportunities. Women are traditionally responsible for domestic duties and child rearing, while men represent the primary earners and assume control over the finances and the household in general. Adultery is culturally acceptable among men, and traditional marriages also allow for polygamy, or the practice of multiple wives (civil marriages do not).

Further marginalizing women is the imposing of umchwasho, a Swazi chastity rite that bans unmarried women from sexual relations with men. The women are required to wear woolen tasseled scarves: girls under the age of eighteen wear blue and yellow, and are not permitted any physical contact with men; women ages nineteen and older wear scarves with red and black tassels and are permitted only limited contact. Disobedience carries with it a fine—usually one cow, the nation's unstated currency—in addition to the stigma women face for being publically reprimanded. The women of Swaziland are especially affected by the country's HIV/AIDS epidemic—studies show that over 54 percent of the population that is infected are women. This rite was most recently active from 2001 to 2005 due to the king's assertion that it would help to curb the spread of HIV.

Although the 2006 constitution awarded equal rights to both men and women, civil law does not yet support these amendments. For example, Swazi women do not have the right to seek a divorce. Furthermore, children are granted their father's citizenship at birth, preventing a mother from custody rights should the marriage dissolve. Inheritance rights are also bestowed upon male children, but not female. In addition, women customarily require a husband's permission to obtain a passport, establish a bank account, or even leave the country.

Increasingly problematic is the frequency of domestic violence, which has become alarmingly commonplace despite traditional restrictions against its practice. Beatings and marital rape are perceived as acceptable assertions of a husband's authority and subject to family rather than legal intervention, and many women generally have no recourse as victims. However, women do reserve the right to press charges against abusive husbands, and this is becoming a more frequent occurrence in urban areas. While rape is considered criminal, it is often underreported due to social stigma. An estimated one in three women experiences sexual violence before the age of 18.

Swazi women are uniting to make the best of their circumstances and exercise empowerment. This is particularly evident in the business sector. Women were recently awarded the right to take out bank loans without a man's approval. This has prompted a growing number of women's groups to organize small business ventures. Capitalizing on the crafting traditions that have been passed down for generations, Swazi women are pooling their resources to produce and sell handmade items at local markets. Some are even using the money they earn to partner with aid organizations on literacy programs, community farms, and other enrichment programs that bolster the status of women.

Health Care

The Ministry of Health and Welfare provides a number of public health programs, clinics, and support and outreach services throughout the country. There are seven hospitals in Swaziland, as well as a number of smaller clinics and public outreach sites. The largest hospital is the Mbabane Government Hospital, which is located in the capital. Some of the non-governmental medical clinics are run by private for-profit agencies, Christian missionaries, and non-governmental organizations (NGOs).

Because of a shortage of health resources, widespread poverty, and a population that is largely affected by HIV/AIDS, Swaziland's health infrastructure has been weakened considerably. Problems such as a lack of access to clean water and proper sanitation also affect public health in the country.

In 2013, the government spent 8.4 percent of its gross domestic product (GDP) on health services. The urban population tends to benefit more from government health spending and health programs than the rural population does, although the government is attempting to improve access to health services in rural areas.

In order to address the growing HIV/AIDS problem, the government has instituted a number of educational programs. These include the Swaziland National AIDS Program and the Schools HIV/AIDS Partnership Education. There is also a movement to educate the tinyanga, or traditional Swazi healers, about the dangers of the disease.

Because of its widespread health problems, life expectancy in Swaziland is fifty-one years (2015 estimate).

GOVERNMENT

Structure

Today, Swaziland is an absolute monarchy. The government tends to be repressive, and civil liberties, such as freedom of the press, are not guaranteed. Political parties are not permitted. The monarch has power over what bills will become law, must approve appointees to the office of prime minister, and is at the head of the judicial branch of government, although the 2006 constitution gave the judicial branch greater autonomy from the king. However, this has created a power

struggle between the king and Swaziland's chief justice, which has resulted in the chief justice's suspension. As of May 2015, this issue remains unresolved.

Appointed by the monarch, the prime minister is the head of the government, which consists of a cabinet and a parliament. Parliament (Libandla), located in the city of Lobamba, consists of two houses; there are sixty-five seats in the House of Assembly and thirty in the Senate. The country also has a traditional court system, and a system of chiefs administering sub-regional districts.

Swaziland emerged as a kingdom in the early 19th century under King Mswati Dlamini II. When he died, the country became a protectorate of South Africa from 1894 to 1902. It then became a protectorate of Great Britain until 1968. From the beginning of British rule through the early 1960s, the country's king did not have sovereign power.

The European Advisory Council helped the British government to rule in the region. Britain had initially planned for Swaziland to become part of South Africa after it granted the neighboring country independence; however, the growth of racial tensions and racist policies in South Africa caused Britain to prepare Swaziland for independence instead.

The British government put a temporary constitution in place in 1963 to ensure fair elections in 1964. One influential Swazi political party at this time was the Imbokodvo National Movement (INM). When Swaziland was finally granted independence from Britain on September 6, 1968, the INM party gained power. Supporters of the INM wanted an absolute monarchy. The Ngwane National Liberatory Congress, an opposition party, pushed for a constitutional monarchy.

Throughout the 1980s, the political opposition clamored for democratic reform; the People's United Democratic Movement was an active underground opposition movement. In 1996, a Constitutional Review Commission was established to draft a new constitution. The draft of the constitution was brought before parliament in 2004 and adopted in 2006.

Political Parties

Political parties were outlawed in Swaziland in 1973, by King Sobhuza II. The 2006 constitution purportedly changed this, but Article 25 only guarantees freedom of association. As a result of Article 25, Swaziland's High Court required that the following three associations register with authorities: African United Democratic Party (AUDP), Ngwane National Liberatory Congress (NNLC), and People's United Democratic Movement (PUDEMO). At the time, an attorney before the court argued that while these organizations could exist, candidates for election had to enter the race without party or organization affiliation, standing as individuals. However, in 2007, King Mswati III reiterated the ban on political parties and the chair of the Elections and Boundaries Commission confirmed this prior to the 2008 House of Assembly election.

After political activists tried to blow up a bridge near the king's home, the king enacted the Suppression of Terrorism Act, 2008. The act banned political activism and several groups were identified by the government as terrorist organizations and some of their members detained. As of 2015, no political parties are registered in Swaziland; AUDP, NNLC, and PUDEMO are still considered associations.

Local Government

Swaziland is divided into four provinces: Hhohho, Lubombo, Manzini, and Shiselweni. Each of these is led by a regional administrator. These provinces are further divided into 55 districts (tinkhundlas) and 360 administrative subdivisions (imiphakatsi). Tinkundlas are similar to townships in the Western world and are comprised of representative boards comprised of local chiefs, who are elected for five year terms. Imiphakatsi are overseen by a tribal chief or elder. Municipal governments, responsible for larger cities, have a mayor and council. Generally, local government is responsible for housing, planning and development, water and sanitation infrastructure, and environmental issues.

The World Bank continues to work with the Swazi government to implement the Swaziland Local Government Project (SLGP). The three point grant project aims at providing financial and technical assistance to growing population centers, existing town governments, and municipalities as they develop infrastructure and development planning.

Judicial System

The highest court in Swaziland is called the Supreme Court of the Judicature, which is comprised of the Supreme Court, its five justices and chief justice, and the High Court, composed of four justices and an ex officio chief justice. Lower courts include the magistrates' and National Swazi Courts, for cases relating to traditional laws and customs. In 2006, the new national constitution vested the judiciary with autonomy from the monarch, although the monarch, King Mswati III, has strenuously fought against this loss of control.

Taxation

The Swazi government levies a graduated personal income tax, ranging from 20 to 33 percent and based on rate of income. Non-residents are subject to withholding tax on royalties, rental revenue, dividends, trusts, and interest earned in the country. Sales, value-added, and fringe-benefits taxes are in place, as are duties. Corporate taxes stand at 27.5 percent of taxable income since July 1, 2013.

Armed Forces

The Swazi armed forces, known as Umbutfo Swaziland Defense Force (USDF), is currently comprised of Ground Force, of which Air Wing Force is a part. While this branch of the Dwazi military previously had Israeli-provided planes, as of 2013, it no longer has operational aircrafts. They do not participate in actions outside of the country. There is also no conscription, and both women and men are eligible for service upon turning eighteen. HIV testing is mandatory, and only those with HIV-negative tests are accepted for service.

Foreign Policy

Swaziland possesses the world's only absolute monarchy, in which the king has the power to rule by royal decree. King Sobhuza II (1899–1982) reigned for sixty-one years, and his son, King Mswati III (1968–), took the throne in 1986. During his reign, King Sobhuza had thrown out the original 1968 national constitution because it was drawn up by the British and didn't reflect Swazi culture. Sobhuza instituted a new version in 1978. In 2005, successor King Mswati III signed a new constitution to replace his father's. Effective as of February 2006, the new version states that the absolute monarchy is a cornerstone of Swazi culture. In light of the government's position on this matter, there is no expectation that the monarchy will be replaced in the near future, despite the peaceful influences of neighboring democracies in South Africa and Mozambique.

Swaziland's main foreign policy objectives are to maintain diplomatic relations with the international community and to promote trade relations. Swaziland is member of the United Nations (UN), the African Union (AU), the Common Market for Eastern and Southern Africa (COMESA), Commonwealth of Nations, the Southern African Development Community (SADC), and the Southern African Customs Union (SACU), which partners with Botswana, Namibia, Lesotho, and South Africa in a free trade agreement with the United States. Swaziland's foreign relations and integration with South Africa are particularly significant, as the country receives 90 percent of its imports from South Africa and also sends 60 percent of its exports to South Africa.

Swaziland's foreign policy is particularly impacted by the country's HIV/AIDS crisis—the virus claims just over one-quarter of the population, the highest infection rate in the world. These epidemic proportions are putting intense strain on the government's ability to provide adequate health care and financial assistance. In addition, the population is losing an average of 10,000 adults each year, which is severely depleting the workforce. The US has responded by contributing funding and manpower for initiatives through the US Agency for International Development (USAID), the Centers for Disease Control (CDC), the Peace Corps, and the African Development Foundation (ADF). The US is also the most significant contributor to the Global Fund, which is Swaziland's foremost funding source for HIV/AIDS programming. Beginning in 2008 and continuing into 2015, the European Union (EU), through the European Development Fund (EDF), is also providing targeted support to curb HIV/AIDS and tuberculosis infections, as well as improve irrigation and sanitation services.

Human Rights Profile

International human rights law insists that states respect civil and political rights and also promote an individual's economic, social, and cultural rights. The United Nations Universal Declaration on Human Rights (UDHR) is recognized as the standard for international human rights. Its authors sought the counsel of the world's great thinkers, philosophers, and religious leaders and were careful to create a document that reflects the core values shared by every world culture. (To read this document or view the articles relating to cultural human rights, go to: http://www.ohchr.org/EN/UDHR/Pages/Introduction.aspx.)

Swaziland's most pressing human rights concern is the right to an adequate standard of living, as the seemingly insurmountable rate of HIV infection, over a quarter of the population, is the highest in the world and growing, as is a concomitant, drug-resistant TB outbreak. The US, joined by the other G8 countries (Canada, France, Germany, Italy, Japan, Russia, and the United Kingdom), has committed funding to control (and ultimately reverse) the spread of HIV/AIDS. However, the majority of the money from international organizations is channeled into education, prevention, medical services, and antiretroviral drugs, which do not address the political and socio-economic contributors such as unemployment and malnutrition. In addition, nearly 120,000 Swazi children are orphaned because of AIDS in 2012.

The most serious contributing factor in Swaziland's AIDS crisis is the country's dire poverty rate. According to the UN's World Food Programme (WFP), one-half of the population is considered "food-insecure," which is to say that they do not have the means to meet basic dietary needs. An estimated 70 percent of the population relies on subsistence agriculture in 2014, and the rampant AIDS mortality rate leaves a depleted agrarian workforce (drought has also been a factor in agrarian production). Poverty in Swaziland therefore simultaneously decreases income and food production, creating a vicious cycle in which Swazi families are incapable of providing for themselves. This increase in poverty affects the public's ability to seek medical care, as those who are infected are further weakened by malnutrition and rendered physically unprepared to fight the virus.

In addition, as poverty and malnutrition ravage the villages, pursuit of basic medical care is simply neglected. Families face critical responsibilities at home that make it nearly impossible to pursue health care services, so many of the infected go untreated. Particularly in the rural areas, which account for the majority of the population, health clinics are inaccessible—sometimes a day's walk or more away—and ill prepared. Many lack running water and a consistent staff, providing little incentive for infected citizens to travel to seek care.

Many human rights organizations criticize the king for not taking a more active role in remedying this situation. Although he has declared the epidemic "a national disaster," only a small percentage the national budget is committed to fighting HIV/AIDS. In addition to this poor political support, human rights organizations also disapprove of the king's polygamous lifestyle, which they say glorifies reckless behavior and contradicts messages about prevention.

Other problem human rights areas in Swaziland include arbitrary arrests and killings by authoritative bodies, as well as lengthy pretrial detainment; limits of the freedom of speech, particularly in regard to the media; restrictions on political activism and freedom of assembly; and lack of government transparency and the inability for citizens to change the government. In 2008, the king enacted a Suppression of Terrorism Act, which has allowed him to widely apply the term terrorism to various anti-government acts and, therefore, confiscate property or otherwise impose punitive measures on those who speak out against the government. In 2013, Human Rights Watch drafted an open letter to the country's Minister of Justice and Constitutional Affairs, urging him to work to amend the act so that it will conform to the Swazi Constitution.

Human trafficking has also been a concern, and Swaziland has been suspected as a country of origin, transit, and destination for trafficking for the purposes of sexual exploitation and forced labor.

ECONOMY

Overview of the Economy

At one time, Swaziland enjoyed the status of being one of the wealthier countries in Africa, and this was due in part to the success of foreign investments there. However, during the 1990s, the country began to experience an economic slowdown. The most important industry is the United States-backed soft drink concentrate industry, and sugar is a major export. The sugar growing and processing industry has created a large number of jobs in the country, but as was evident in the 1990s, the industry is subject to the vagaries of sugar prices on the world market. In 2010, the outlook for the industry looked good, as the European Union sugar market eliminated duties and quotas for Least Developed Countries. As of 2015, according to the the Swaziland Sugar Association, the country's principal sugar markets have been the EU; the Southern African Customs Union; and, to a lesser degree, the United States.

In order for real growth in the country, the government must address the HIV/AIDS issue that is depleting the workforce and creating a society dominated by older generations and HIV orphans. Additionally, the government spends more than 55 percent of its budget on wages.

Swaziland's transportation system allows it to transport goods through South Africa and Mozambique. The Port of Maputo in Mozambique is an important shipping center for Swazi goods. The country's major markets are the European Union, South Africa, and the United States. In 2014, the gross domestic product (GDP) of Swaziland was $8.621 billion USD, and the per capita GDP was $7,800 USD.

Industry

Manufacturing is important to Swaziland's economy, accounting for around 47.4 percent of GDP in 2014. The sugar refining industry has become the largest sector with the closure of wood pulping facilities and the country's iron ore mine. Some of the products manufactured in the country include cotton products and related apparel, textiles, processed foods, soft drink concentrates, and sugar processing. Backed by foreign investment, the textile and garment industry is growing in Swaziland.

Swaziland is rich in mineral resources, such as coal and diamonds. There is also a quarry stone industry, which serves the domestic market. Swaziland's rich wildlife resources are important to its tourist industry.

Labor

In 2012, the labor force in Swaziland numbered 435,500. The HIV/AIDS epidemic, which was estimated to affect one-qaurter of the population in 2013, has compromised the number of able-bodied people. And in the second decade of the 21st century, as in the first, unemployment continued to hover around 40 percent.

Energy/Power/Natural Resources

Electrical capacity has been an issue for Swaziland in the early 21st century, and the country depends on electricity imports to satisfy its domestic needs. These capacity issues have a direct impact on manufacturing and mining efforts in the nation. In response to domestic capacity needs, the Swaziland Electricity Company (SEC) is engaged in the development and construction of two coal-powered and one hydro-powered electrical plants.

Forestry

Timber is grown for export, and until the end of 2009, wood pulp, sawn wood, and wood products represented the second largest export earners into the country following sugar processing. However, when the London-based owner of Usutu Pulp closed operations in January 2010, the production of 200,000 tons of pulp and 550 Swazi-based jobs were lost. The closure Swazi Paper Mills and the significant scaling back of Peak Timbers caused a domino effect into other sectors, like the railway, as timber-cargo transports slowed. Black wattle, a type of acacia tree, is still grown, primarily for its bark, which is a cash crop and is exported to South Africa.

Mining/Metals

Because the country's only iron ore mine closed in 2014, its principal mining activity now involve gold, diamonds, coal, and quarry stone. Tin and iron ore had once been important natural resources for Swaziland, with Mbabane serving as a primary distribution center into neighboring South Africa and Mozambique. However, most of this sector is in currently in decline and has become largely artisanal, particularly those activities related to gold and diamonds.

Agriculture

Agriculture accounts for around 7.2 percent of Swaziland's GDP and employs 70 percent of the population. Some of the primary agricultural exports are sugarcane, corn, tobacco, citrus fruits, cotton, rice, sorghum, and groundnuts (peanuts). The Swazi government owns and controls 60 percent of the country's land, while the rest is privately owned.

Subsistence farming is common, although agricultural export industries, such as the sugarcane industry, employ many people. Natural disasters like droughts and floods can make farming in Swaziland difficult. Other problems facing agriculture include overgrazing and soil depletion.

Animal Husbandry

The farmers of Swaziland primarily engage in livestock herding. And while they are highly valued by the Swazi people, they are often malnourished and left to roam, sometimes being struck and killed by vehicles. As of 2012, Swaziland had a hormone-free beef quota export program with the EU. However, the EU reported that they consistently failed to provide the requisite numbers. In September 2012, approximately 10,000 cattle died from chronic malnutrition and cold temperatures. It was the highest mass death of cattle, since the outbreak of rinderpest (also known as cattle plague), which killed 90 percent of the country's cattle in the 1890s.

Tourism

Before the end of apartheid, unrestricted travel between South Africa and Swaziland enabled many South Africans to visit the country each year. The tourism sector has suffered in part because the end of apartheid in South Africa has meant that fewer South Africans are traveling to Swaziland.

However, because of its natural wildlife resources and its location in sub-Saharan Africa, Swaziland has become a popular destination for international tour groups; in 2014, 435,599 tourists visited the country, most of them coming from other parts of Africa and Western Europe.

In an effort to increase tourism, Swaziland built a number of casinos during the 1990s, including the more remote The Orion Piggs Peak Hotel and Casino and The Royal Swazi Spa Valley Casino & Resort in Mbabane. The Ministry of Tourism, Environment, and Communications was created in 1996. In 2000, the government drafted a National Tourism Policy to help develop tourism in the country.

Tourist attractions in Swaziland include Hlane Royal National Park, which features safaris that offer viewing of big game animals like elephants, lions, rhinos, and leopards. Other wildlife preserves include the Mlilwane Wildlife Sanctuary and the Mkhaya Game Reserve. Because of its diverse bird population of more than 500 species, Swaziland is also a popular destination for bird enthusiasts. Some of the country's famous bird sanctuaries are part of the Hlane, Mlawula, and Phophonyane nature reserves.

Heidi Edsall, Christina Healey,
Lynn-nore Chittom, Savannah Schroll Guz

DO YOU KNOW?

- The primitive cycad plant, a living fossil that has existed virtually unchanged for 240 million years—that is, since the Jurassic period—grows in Swaziland.

- Swaziland is the smallest country in Africa and one of the smallest in the Southern Hemisphere.

- Mbabane is home to the Waterford-Kamhlaba United World College (UWC) of Southern Africa, one of the thirteen locations of the international United World Colleges. The school, like other UWC schools, brings together exceptional students from around the world to foster peace and international understanding.

- Mbabane was named after Chief Mbabane Kunene, a local clan chief from the 1880s. The name Mbabane means "something sharp and bitter," but the exact meaning and translation that this holds for the city of Mbabane is unknown.

Bibliography

Bainbridge, James & Kate Armstrong. *South Africa, Lesotho & Swaziland*. Victoria, Australia: Lonely Planet, 2009.

Cheney, Glenn Alan. *Love and Death in the Kingdom of Swaziland*. Hanover, CT: New London Librarium, 2012.

Cornell, Kari A. *Cooking the Southern African Way*. Minneapolis, MN: Lerner Publications Company, 2005.

Duignan, Peter & Lewis Henry Gann. *Colonialism in Africa, 1870–1960*. New York, NY: Cambridge University Press, 1973.

Fitzpatrick, Mary. *South Africa, Lesotho & Swaziland*. Victoria, Australia: Lonely Planet, 2006.

Jacob, Jeanne & Michael Ashkenazi. *The World Cookbook for Students*. Westport, CT: Greenwood Press, 2007.

Kalipeni, Ezekiel, Susan Craddock, Joseph R. Oppong, & Jayati Gosh, eds. *HIV and AIDS in Africa: Beyond Epidemiology*. 2nd ed. Malden, MA: Blackwell Publishing, 2008.

Works Cited

"About Yebo! Gallery" *Yebo! Contemporary Art Gallery*. Yebo Contemporary Art Gallery, 2015. Web. http://yeboswaziland.com/yebo_gallery/.

Amnesty International. "Swaziland and Human Rights." *Amnesty International*. Amnesty International USA, 2015. Web. http://www.amnestyusa.org/our-work/countries/africa/swaziland.

"Birdwatching." *The Kingdom of Swaziland: A Royal Experience*. GeoGroup, 18 Jun. 2013. Web. http://www.thekingdomofswaziland.com/pages/activities/activity.asp?Activity=Bird+Watching.

Bowen, Jenny. "Swazi Etiquette." *The Kingdom of Swaziland: A Royal Experience*. GeoGroup, 18 Jun. 2013.Web. http://www.thekingdomofswaziland.com/pages/blog_01/blog_item.asp?Blog_01ID=7.

Doctors Without Borders. "Treating HIV and TB in Swaziland: "We didn't know what to expect." *Médecins Sans Frontières*. Médecins Sans Frontières, 30 Jun. 2014. Web. http://www.msf.org/article/treating-hiv-and-tb-swaziland-%E2%80%9Cwe-didn%E2%80%99t-know-what-expect%E2%80%9D

Government of the Kingdom of Swaziland. Government of the Kingdom of Swaziland, 2015. Web. http://www.gov.sz/.

"HIV & AIDS in Swaziland." *AVERT: AVERTing HIV and AIDS*. AVERT, 2014. Web. http://www.avert.org/hiv-aids-swaziland.htm.

Human Rights Watch. "Swaziland: Letter to the Swazi Government relating to amendments to the Suppression of Terrorism Act." *Human Rights Watch*. Human Rights Watch, 21 Nov. 2013. Web. https://www.hrw.org/news/2013/11/21/swaziland-letter-swazi-government-relating-amendments-suppression-terrorism-act.

"Mantenga Swazi Cultural Village—Ligugu Lemaswati." *Swaziland National Trust Commission*. SNTC, 2015. http://www.sntc.org.sz/cultural/cultvillage.asp.

Mavhinga, Dewa. "Dispatches: The Opportunity Behind Swaziland's Judicial Crisis." *Human Rights Watch*. Human Rights Watch, 28 May 2015. https://www.hrw.org/news/2015/05/28/dispatches-opportunity-behind-swazilands-judicial-crisis.

Ngwenya Glass. Ngwenya Glass, 2015. Web. http://www.ngwenyaglass.co.sz.

"Nsangwini Rock Shelter." The Kingdom of Swaziland: A Royal Experience. Geo Group, 2013. Web. http://www.thekingdomofswaziland.com/pages/attractions/the_attraction.asp?AttractionsID=16.

Official Page for Ladysmith Black Mambazo. Ladysmith Black Mambazo, 2015. Web. http://www.mambazo.com/index.

"Swaziland." *USAID*. USAID, 2015. Web. https://www.usaid.gov/swaziland.

"Swaziland: Cattle die in the thousands." *IRIN: Humanitarian News & Analysis*. IRIN, 20 Sept. 2012. Web. http://www.irinnews.org/report/96353/swaziland-cattle-die-in-the-thousands.

"Swaziland Economic Overview." *How We Made it in Africa*. Maritz Africa, 30 Jul. 2010. Web. http://www.howwemadeitinafrica.com/swaziland-economic-overview/2982/.

Swaziland National Trust Commission. SNTC, 2015. Web. http://www.sntc.org.sz http://www.gov.sz

Swaziland Sugar Association. "Sales by Market." *Swaziland Sugar Association*. Swaziland Sugar Association, 2015. Web. http://www.ssa.co.sz/industry-statistics/2013-12-11-06-16-55/sugar.

Swaziland Revenue Authority. "Swaziland Income Tax." *Swaziland Revenue Authority*. SRA, 2015. Web. http://www.sra.org.sz/index.php?option=com_content&view=article&id=88&Itemid=216.

UNICEF. "Swaziland Statistics." *UNICEF*. UN, 2015. Web. http://www.unicef.org/infobycountry/swaziland_statistics.html.

UN Women. UN Women, 2015. Web. http://www.unwomen.org/en.

UNESCO. "Ngwenya Mines." *UNESCO World Heritage Convention*. UNESCO, 2015. http://whc.unesco.org/en/tentativelists/5421/.

"Visit Swaziland." *The Kingdom of Swaziland: A Royal Experience*. Geo Group, 2013. www.welcometoswaziland.com

World Bank, The. "Internet users (per 100 people)." *The World Bank World Development Indicators*. The World Bank Group, 2015. Web. http://data.worldbank.org/indicator/IT.NET.USER.P2.

Elephants and baobab trees are common among the grasslands of Tanzania.

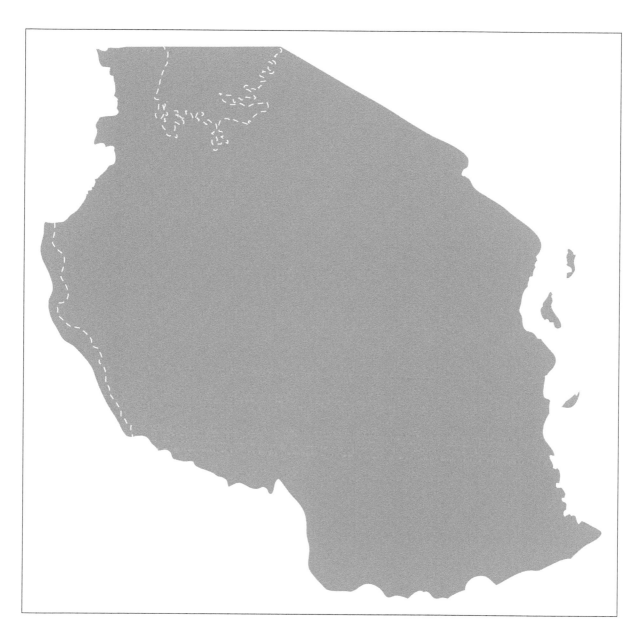

TANZANIA

Introduction

Tanzania is the largest East African nation. Located on the southeastern coast of Africa, it contains some of the most beautiful and famous natural sites in the world, including Mount Kilimanjaro, Lake Victoria, the Zanzibar Archipelago, and wild game preserves such as the Serengeti National Park.

Originally called Tanganyika, present-day Tanzania gained independence from Britain on December 9, 1961. Zanzibar and its offshore island of Pemba gained their independence on December 10, 1963, and on April 26, 1964, Tanganyika and Zanzibar united to form a single nation. Its current constitution was adopted on April 25, 1977. The country has faced severe domestic challenges, but it is effecting positive change in education, public health, literature and the arts.

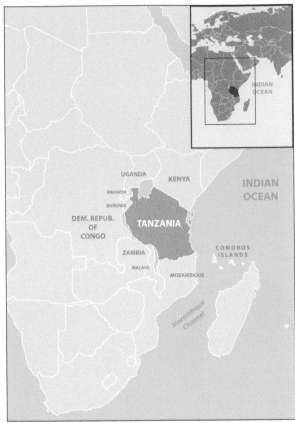

GENERAL INFORMATION

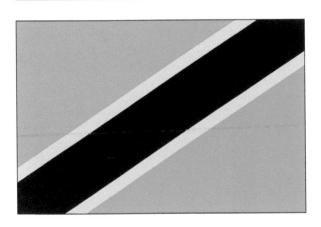

Official Language: English (used for all official government business and commerce) and Kiswahili (also called Kiunguja in Zanzibar)

Population: 51,045,882 million (July 2015 estimate)

Currency: Tanzanian shilling

Coins: The Tanzanian shilling is divided into 100 senti, and coins are available in denominations of 50, 100, 200, and 500 shilingi, the last of which was newly issued in late 2014.

Land Area: 885,800 square kilometers (342,009 square miles)

Water Area: 61,500 square kilometers (23,745 square miles)

National Motto: "Uhuru na Umoja" ("Freedom and Unity")

National Anthem: "Mungu ibariki Afrika" ("God Bless Africa")

Capital: Dodoma

Time Zone: GMT +3

Flag Description: The flag of Tanzania is divided diagonally by an ascending black stripe outlined on both sides in yellow (the stripe originates in the lower hoist [left] side). The flag's upper-left triangle is green, representing vegetation or agriculture, and the lower-right triangle is light blue, symbolizing the country's water resources, namely its position next to the Indian Ocean.

Population

Tanzania's population is quite diverse. Among the ethnic groups represented are 130 African groups, or tribes, most of which are Bantu. About

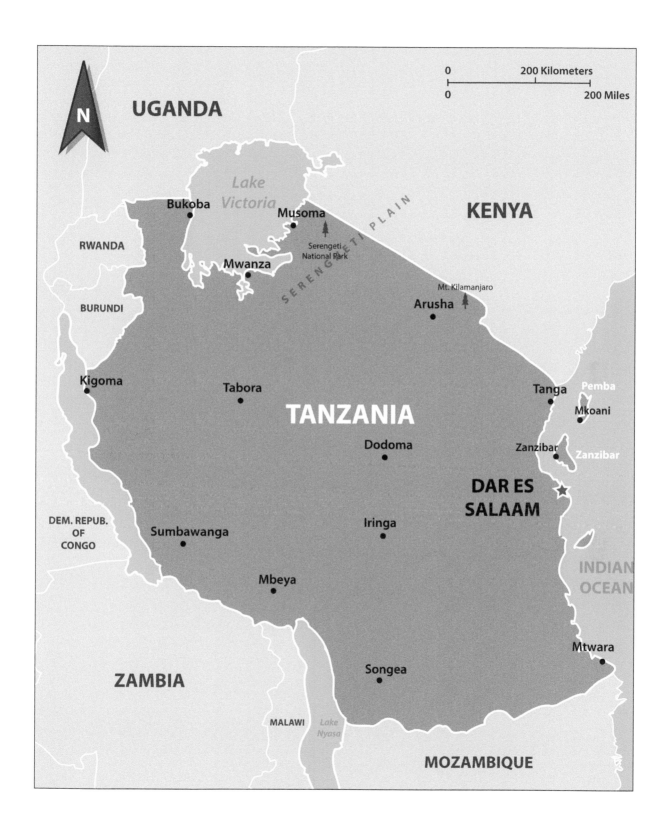

Principal Cities by Population (2012):*

- Dar es Salaam (4,364,541)
- Mwansa (706,453)
- Arusha (416,442)
- Dodoma (410,956)
- Mbeya (385,279)
- Morogoro (315,866)
- Tanga (273,332)
- Zanzibar (223,033)
- Kigoma-Ujiji (215,458)
- Moshi (184,292)

*These population numbers reflect urban localities and do not include larger municipal districts with the same name.

1 percent of the population is comprised of a mix of Asian, Indonesian, Indian, European, and Arab ethnicities. A majority of the country's Arab population resides on the island of Zanzibar, where there is also a mixed Arab-African population. Dar es Salaam is the country's largest city, and home to over one-third of Tanzania's total urban population; an estimated 31.6 percent of the total population lives in urban areas. As of 2015, the population growth rate was approximately 2.79 percent.

Languages
Kiswahili (Swahili) is one of the many ethnic Bantu dialects. Swahili's vocabulary has been developed from contact with a variety of languages and dialects, including English and Arabic (spoken widely on the island of Zanzibar). English remains the official language of administration, commerce, and higher education. Kiunguja is the local name for Swahili in Zanzibar. There are also many local languages spoken throughout Tanzania.

Native People & Ethnic Groups
In 1960, paleoanthropologist Louis Leakey discovered remains that he named *homo habilis* ("handy man," referencing the hominid's toolmaking aptitude) in Olduvai Gorge. Dated around two million years old, this prehistoric man may be considered the first native of Tanzania.

Tanzania's population is 99 percent native African, 95 percent of which are Bantus that identify with more than 130 individual tribes. The first Bantu ancestral groups migrated to the area between 2000 and 1000 BCE. The word "Bantu" means "the people," and of the many different Bantu-speaking groups, the Sukuma, who live south of Lake Victoria, are the largest. Once warriors, they are now peaceful farmers who raise cattle and cultivate crops in Mwanza. The Nyamwezi, living in the grasslands (savannahs), were one of the most powerful tribes in the early nineteenth century. The Bena and Chagga, who dwell on Kilimanjaro's rise, often work as tour guides and run flourishing farms and coffee plantations. The Gogo, near Dodoma, raise herds and crops, but their land has little water, and it is a hard living. The Hehe were once feared and warlike. Their name comes from the war cry of a chief who led the resistance against German colonizers. Now they work as rangers and guides. The Makonde, famous woodcarvers, live near the Mozambique border.

Non-Bantu tribes include the Masai, a proud, nomadic people who move freely between Kenya and Tanzania. They prize their cattle, subsisting mostly on the blood and milk. Asian, Indonesian, Indian, Arab, and European populations make up the remaining one percent of the population.

Religions
Christians account for 30 percent of Tanzania's population and Muslims, 35 percent. About 35 percent of the population adheres to traditional indigenous beliefs. On Zanzibar, more than 99 percent of the population is Muslim.

Climate
Tanzania has a tropical climate with high temperatures and humidity on the coast and islands. Daytime temperatures average around 15°–20° Celsius (59°–68° Fahrenheit) from June to September and 25°–31° Celsius (77°–88° Fahrenheit) from December to March. Summer is the dry season in Tanzania, and lasts from

December until March. Winter, from March to May, corresponds with the rainy season. There are short rains, called Vuli, from October to December and long rains, called Masika, from March to May.

Annual rainfall is more than 1,000 millimeters (40 inches), although the central plateau is much drier than the rest of the country, and usually receives only 250 millimeters (10 inches) or rain each year.

On peaks above 1,500 meters (5,000 feet) there is a semi-temperate climate, with permanent snow on the highest peaks. Temperatures on Mount Kilimanjaro and Meru regularly drop below freezing.

ENVIRONMENT & GEOGRAPHY

Topography

The largest country in East Africa, Tanzania consists of the mainland plus the Indian Ocean islands of Zanzibar, Pemba, and Mafia off its east coast. Mainland Tanzania has borders with Kenya, Uganda, Rwanda, Burundi, the Democratic Republic of the Congo, Malawi, Mozambique, and Zambia.

The mainland can be divided into three types of terrain. The northeastern and southwestern mountain regions include the dormant volcanic mountain, known as Mount Kilimanjaro, which is the highest point in Africa at 5,895 meters (19,341 feet). The name Kilima Njaro means "Shining Mountain." The lowest point in Tanzania is, of course, the Indian Ocean.

The large central high plateau has an average altitude of about 1,200 meters (4,000 feet) and is split by the Great Rift Valley, a 9,656-kilometer (6,000-mile) fissure that reaches from Lebanon to Mozambique. The low coast region includes the islands of Zanzibar, Pemba, and Mafia.

Dodoma is located on the plateau of central Tanzania, roughly 480 kilometers (300 miles) inland from Africa's Indian Ocean coastline. Dodoma's selection as Tanzania's capital was based principally on conveniences of location and climate. The city sits at an elevation of 1,135

meters (3,720 feet) above sea level, an altitude that creates a cooling effect.

Lake Tanganyika lies on the western border of Tanzania and extends from Burundi, along the border with the Democratic Republic of Congo, and into Zambia. Lake Nyasa is on the southwest border and is shared with Malawi and Mozambique. Lake Victoria, in the northwestern corner of the country, also lies partly in Uganda and Kenya. Major rivers in Tanzania include the Pangani, Rufiji, Ruvuma, and Malagarasi.

Plants & Animals

Plant life in Tanzania varies with the country's geography. The mainland plateau is mostly grassland, and evergreen forests cover the mountains. Mangrove trees grow alongside coastal rivers, and rainforests thrive near Lake Victoria. The islands are mainly brush and grassland, though some rainforests have developed in extremely wet sections.

Examples of Tanzania's more interesting trees include the ubiquitous umbrella acacia tree and the unusual baobab tree, one of the world's largest tree species. The branches of the baobab are said to resemble roots, leading to the folk belief that the tree grows upside down.

Tanzania's 16 national parks, thirteen game reserves, and the Ngorongoro Conservation Area, a UNESCO World Heritage Site since 1979, are home to a wide variety of wildlife. The country boasts over 1,000 bird species, including flamingos, African spoonbills, African paradise flycatchers, cattle egrets, saddle-billed storks, hoopoes, ostriches, and parrots.

Common mammals found in Tanzania include warthogs, leopards, elephants, wildebeests, lions, zebras, chimpanzees, baboons, monkeys, crocodiles, buffalos, dik-diks (very small, 10-pound antelopes), and kudus (a considerably larger antelope species).

There are several species of poisonous snakes found throughout Tanzania, including black mambas, puff adders, and red and black spitting cobras. Boa constrictors and pythons also abound. Most of these dangerous snakes avoid humans, when possible.

CUSTOMS & COURTESIES

Greetings

A notable feature of Tanzanian culture is the greeting that precedes any conversation in daily life. When greeting older individuals, Tanzanians always begin with the Kiswahili word "Shikamoo," which translates as "I hold your feet" or "I show my respect." This is then followed by the title-appropriate word. For example, an elderly man is referred to as "Babu," or grandfather, and an elderly woman is called "Bibi," which means grandmother. For a man, "Baba," or father, is commonly used, and for a woman it is "Mama," or mother, though "Mwalimu" can be used for someone of academic standing. If ever addressed as such, the appropriate response is "Marahaba," meaning, "I am delighted."

Otherwise, the most common greeting in Tanzania is "Hujambo?" or "Hello, how are you?" To which someone might reply "Nzuri," which translates to "I am fine." When speaking to a younger person, it is then appropriate to use less formal terms. Terms such as "Vipi" and "Mambo," both roughly translated to "What's up?" can be answered with the common expressions of "Poa," "Bomba" or "Gado," all slang for "Cool."

When meeting anyone for the first time, whether it is a lifelong friend or simply someone for directions, it is appropriate to use one of these commonly accepted greetings. Longer greetings are favorable because they express a genuine interest in the life of the person approached for conversation. Generally, conversation on all levels is conducted along these guidelines and is a great source of pride for Tanzanians. Should the greeting be forgotten, the other person will commonly be reminded, and the greeting will commence so that a conversation can then take place.

On Zanzibar, and in some coastal regions, the influence of Muslim culture is evident. In these regions, the Arabic greeting of "Salaam alaikum," translated as "Peace be unto you," is commonly used, followed by the appropriate response of "Mualaikum salaam," meaning "Peace also be unto you." In addition, Tanzanian women commonly curtsy, or respectfully bow, slightly when greeting, while the men shake hands. This is done while always using the right hand and grasping right forearms or wrists with the left hand for a more formal gesture.

These aforementioned greetings and formalities reflect the Tanzanians' general devotion to the respectful treatment of all people in public venues. There is deep value placed on human interaction as a means to a functioning society. It is no wonder that when introduced, most Tanzanians call themselves Tanzanians first and foremost, favoring to identify with their countrymen as opposed to one of the over 130 tribes represented in Tanzania.

Gestures & Etiquette

Conduct in Tanzania is generally characterized by a combination of stoicism, or impassiveness, and discipline in public conduct. As a result, it is considered inappropriate for couples to show affection in public places. Holding hands is occasionally acceptable, but is generally reserved for two males who do so as a sign of friendship. Frivolous or temperamental behavior is generally frowned upon in the public arena, though it is becoming more common in urban areas.

When greeting one another, men are generally expected to shake hands, being very careful to extend only the right hand. Often this handshake is held much longer than in Western cultures. The preference for the right hand comes from a long held belief, particularly exemplified in Muslim culture, that the right hand is pure while the left hand is impure. When accepting a gift, the same customs apply. It must be accepted either with both hands or with the right hand extended and the left hand holding the wrist of the right arm.

Eating/Meals

Before beginning a meal, it is customary for each diner at the table to rinse his or her hands in a washbasin located in the dining room. This is an important point of etiquette, as food is commonly eaten with the hands. Generally, a communal dish is served from which all diners will partake using only their rights hands to scoop small portions. Typically, the main course served is ugali, Tanzania's most widely consumed dish. Ugali is generally made with maize flour, sorghum flour, or millet flour cooked in water to a thick, porridge-like consistency.

In various regions, the eating styles differ slightly. For example, people living near the ocean or Tanzania's lakes often sit on mats to eat. In addition, Muslim families are often known to have women and men eat meals separately, only allowing interaction between the sexes to take place before and after the food is consumed. Women generally eat with their children, while the men may dine alone or with other men in the family or community.

Visiting

When visiting a private home in Tanzania, the proper course of action upon arriving, whether announced or unannounced, is to call out "Hodi," or "Hello and May I come in?" Upon hearing "Karibu," or "Welcome," the visitor may enter. Entering without adhering to this custom is considered impolite and out of line with a Tanzanian's code of conduct.

When visiting a Tanzanian home, it is also a general custom to bring a gift for the host and the host's family. The main reason for this custom is practicality. A guest is most likely to be eating with the hosts, so naturally, he or she should bring something to contribute to the meal. Men tend to prefer tobacco, while women commonly appreciate household gifts. For example, any item that will help with daily chores, such as soap, rice, milk, sponges, or paper and pen, is commonly accepted. If there are children at the home, sweets are acceptable. However, as is the case with many cultures, these types of gifts are customarily given to the mother first for her to distribute.

LIFESTYLE

Family

Marriage (ndoa) in Tanzania was once strictly arranged along tribal lines. However, in recent years, arrangements are decreasing and intermarriage among cultures and tribes is quite common. When a couple gets married, tradition dictates that a dowry be given by the bridegroom's family to the bride.

The structure of the family in Tanzania is considered synonymous with the word jamaa or ujamaa, which means community, as it involves a collective spirit. This may involve several generations in the same home caring for each other. It also generally involves active participation of all community members in each other's lives, especially in child rearing. Due to economic hardship in recent decades, however, this tradition is waning, leaving many women as the sole caretakers of their children.

Within the family, the male is generally still responsible for earning income, while the woman manages the home, cooks, and cares for the children. It is such an essential role for the woman that she might often be traditionally referred to by the name of her eldest child. "Mama Kibo" would be an example for a mother giving birth to a son named "Kibo." As the children grow older and if finances permit, they may enroll in school. However, if there is not enough money, the male children will be favored for school, while the females stay at home to learn domestic skills.

Another factor having a profound impact on the structure of the family is the HIV/AIDS infection in Tanzania. In 2012, an estimated 1.2 million children in Tanzania had lost one or both parents to AIDS. This surge in orphaned children has led to an increase in child labor, prostitution, and crime. Services are slowly being introduced and many organizations are starting orphanages to help get these children off the streets.

Housing

The majority of Tanzanians live in rural areas. The prevalent housing style is the tembe, or the mbavu za mbwa. It is constructed from a wooden foundation and covered with mud, which dries in place like cement. The roof is often constructed of corrugated tin or, more commonly, thatch. The floor is simply the earth upon which the home was built. Generally, these homes consist of a single room in which all facilities, aside from the bathroom, are located. That means families sleep, eat, and cook in the same multipurpose room, often in close quarters. Bathroom facilities are most often located outside and are generally shared among several family homes. It is common for families to decorate the outsides of their homes with bright colors or patterns.

Because of such basic living arrangements, many of the materials used in construction do not adequately protect against the elements and natural threats to the area. Specifically, mosquitoes often breed in the pools of water that accumulate on floors during heavy rains. This, in addition to sharing the use of a common bathroom, is a major contributor to the spread of malaria, dysentery, typhoid, and other parasitic infections.

Food

The morning meal in Tanzania typically includes soups, porridges, and sweet breads. Supu is a light, brothy soup usually stewed from the parts of an animal not used in the previous night's stew. Hooves, bones, and intestines are all common ingredients. Supu is sometimes served with rice.

Eating in the evening in Tanzania almost always includes ugali, a thick, pasty porridge made from cassava, corn, sorghum, or millet flour cooked in water. This is often served with a fish, lamb, goat, beef, or vegetable stew. On the coast, it is more common to see rice served as the starch; this sometimes takes the form of a delicious cinnamon, clove, and cardamom-flavored rice dish called pilau.

The average Tanzanian eats two relatively large meals daily, but may snack on various foods sold by vendors during the day. These include sugar cane, samosas, chapattis (or "Tanzanian pizzas" without the tomatoes), peanuts (called groundnuts in Africa), grilled meat skewers, or grilled corn on the cob.

Otherwise, the crops native to various regions dictate the local cuisine. In the north and in the southern highlands, plantains are widely eaten and are prepared by frying. In Zanzibar, spices native to the island, including cloves, turmeric, cumin, and curry, lend more heat to dishes.

Coconut milk is often used in cooking to complement these intense spices.

Life's Milestones

In Tanzania's urban population, the milestones are consistent with those of other developing nations. For example, birth, childhood, marriage, and childbearing often take on the characteristics of religious belief, with Islam and Christianity being the most popular religions. With the spread of Christianity, it is now common for Tanzanian families to come together for a traditional Christian wedding ceremony.

In rural areas, tribal rites of passage are still widely practiced. Perhaps one of the most famed and pronounced example is among the Masai people, who practice the circumcision of teenage and young adult boys. According to this rite of passage, the boy must suffer the procedure without anything to numb the pain. He must also do so with his father standing by and without making a single sound. Once the procedure is over, he then moves into a neighboring village with other young men. The village has none of the protections of his family's village, and during his years there, he must learn to how to fulfill his role as village protector.

CULTURAL HISTORY

Art

Tanzania's history of artistic expression dates back to prehistoric times, when some of the first examples of art in human history were discovered. Inscribed as a UNESCO World Heritage Site in 2006, the Kondoa Rock-Art Sites, in particular, include upwards of 1,600 different drawings. These images have been naturally preserved for thousands of years on the rock shelters, or vertical slabs of rock, in caves in the Kondoa region. The skillfully crafted drawings are thought to date back as far as 30,000 years, with the most recent drawings added only 100 to 200 years ago.

The drawings are believed to have captured the unfolding of human history in the region. The images mainly display "round headed" humans in pursuit of prey, holding ceremonies, or dancing. The figures are famous for the distortion of the human forms—many only having three fingers—while animals are drawn anatomically correct. Many of the drawings are said to still have a spiritual value for some of the tribes in surrounding areas, including the Masai and Hadzabe peoples.

Woodcarving has also long been a tradition among some Tanzanian peoples. The Makonde people, in particular, are renowned for their intricate and expressive designs. In fact, a Makonde legend claims that a man suffering from great loneliness did the first woodcarving. According to the legend, he carved a female figure and left it to rest overnight, only to find that in the morning the figure had come to life. Over time, the sculptures have transitioned from mainly functional tools to expressions of creativity. The sculptures are unique for being artfully carved from single pieces of ebony, a very hard dark wood. Most sculptures today are of the ujamaa, the community, or family. This subject is known as the "tree of life" motif. These works typically show some arrangement of humans and animals around their common ancestor. Masks are also common and still used in tribal celebration.

Architecture

In most major cities along Tanzania's coast, architecture is a mixture of indigenous and foreign influences. For example, in the city of Dar es Salaam, the country's largest city, mosques represent the influence of Arabic architecture, Lutheran churches represent the influence of German architecture, and the various homes and commercial buildings represent the influence of British architecture. In addition, Zanzibar's history as a British protectorate is evident in the island's Victorian architecture.

Dar es Salaam is further representative of the rise of modern architecture in Tanzania in the 1950s and 1960s. This movement, largely attributed to Tanzanian architect Anthony Almeida (1921–), helped define local architecture in Tanzania's post-colonial period. In fact,

the architectural heritage of Dar es Salaam is explored in the documentary *Many Words for Modern* (2007) by Dutch filmmaker and architect Jord Den Hollander.

Outside of urban areas, where a large percentage of Tanzanians live, the vast majority of structures are residential. These structures can range from one-room edifices built from stone or mud and wood, with a ribbed tin or more complex thatched roof, to another form of suburban dwelling is called the Swahili house. This term, used in Tanzania and Kenya, can refer to this type of typical Tanzanian home, or to something more upscale and on a hillside, as in Kenya.

In addition, each ethnic group has its own traditional architecture or style of housing. They exist in various forms depending upon the geographic region in which they were built. The Nyakyusa of central Tanzania, for example, have used a style of home characterized by its cylindrical design and conical thatched roofs. These roofs were important because they allowed for rain run-off. In recent years, more European-style houses—in which a wider variety of materials such as brick and wood is used with the native building materials of earth and thatch—are becoming the norm.

Film

Tanzanian cinema has had a strong representation, despite the lack of a large film industry. Tanzania's documentary filmmaking is renowned for the internationally acclaimed documentary *These Hands* (1992), directed by Flora M'mbugu-Schelling. The film portrays the life of refugee women from Mozambique working in a quarry outside Dar es Salamm. Other Tanzanian films include *Maangamizi* (2001) and *Mama Tumani* (1986), or "Women of Hope," both directed by Tanzanian Martin M'hando.

While Tanzania's locally-produced films are limited in number, a few famous American films have been shot in Tanzania, including *The African Queen* (1951), starring Humphrey Bogart and Katherine Hepburn; *Mogambo* (1953), starring Clark Gable, Ava Gardner and Grace Kelly; *Hatari!* (1962), filmed in Arusha National Park and starring John Wayne; *Mountains of the Moon* (1990), a bulk of which was also filmed in Kenya; and *Congo* (1995). In addition, Zanzibar's Stone Town hosted its first annual international film festival in 1998. The festival acts primarily as a forum for filmmakers in the Indian Ocean region, but also highlights films from all over the world.

Music

The two oldest forms of music in Tanzania are taraab, mainly played on Zanzibar (the largest of a group of islands off the Tanzanian coast) since the mid-19th century, and ngoma, played throughout the Tanzanian mainland. Ngoma ya kiasili, or "music of the ancestors," was in earlier days a primary form of recording and passing on history from one generation to the next. In this style of music, each performer is involved in delivering the message, be it the history of a tribe, intricate personal anecdotes, or educational messages for younger generations. In addition, the music is always delivered against the backdrop of drums. The Masai people, whose ngoma music is known for its chanting and hypnotic effects, are said to transcend the physical world, bridging the space between life and death. This is done in the hopes of evading mortality by always communicating with the departed.

Taraab music, in contrast, is mainly performed on Zanzibar and includes the use of drums, but also of instrumental accompaniment. This style of music also represents a blend of cultures, as African and Arab musical styles blend with Indian strings to form a truly unique style. Dramatic theatrical acting involving the audience also accompanies most taraab performances.

Literature

Tanzania's history is characterized by hundreds of years of foreign rule. As such, language and expression in Kiswahili or Swahili, the national language, was often limited not only in daily life, but also in the literary world of Tanzania. The use of Kiswahili in published literature finally emerged following Tanganyikan independence in 1961, with Zanzibar following closely behind in 1963. With the later introduction of the culture policy "Sera Ya Utamaduni" in 1997, writing in Kiswahili vastly expanded. The policy emphasized the importance of national publications being written and published in the national language. This bolstered a sense of national pride in writing in Kiswahili.

Shabaan Bin Robert (1909–1962) is the nation's most famous writer, both nationally and abroad. His famous poem "Utenzi wa vya Uhuru" recounts Tanzania's struggle for freedom from ages of foreign rule. Other famed authors include Edwin Semzaba, a national playwright working at the University of Dar es Salaam, and Abdulrazak Gurnah (1948–), who was born in Zanzibar and whose writings reflect his multicultural background as a Muslim in Africa.

CULTURE

Arts & Entertainment

Historically, the arts in Tanzania have evolved from tribal expressions to primarily functioning as a source of quick income for artists, with little development in between. Stylistically, much of the visual works done, especially in the Tingatinga painting style, are valued by tourists as reminders of their journeys to such foreign lands. The Tingatinga style was developed in the 1960s and is exemplified by high gloss paints and animal themes. These designs have been produced in Tanzania for decades and are highly recognizable. Thus, many of Tanzania's artists limit their designs to what will appeal to travelers. Without the support to create unique designs, there is little innovation and much reproduction.

Contemporary arts culture in Tanzania is still dominated by a strong link to that past. However, with the introduction of a new arts initiative, this is changing slowly. Traditional forms of expression, including dance, music, and visual arts, are being redefined. The creation of the non-profit organization Mfuko wa Utamaduni Tanzania (Tanzania Culture Trust Fund) in 1998 was the first major step in this direction. The organization's goal is to categorize art forms in Tanzania, while expanding on them. This includes gathering artists into forums to discuss work, categorizing artists by medium and general audience, educating artists and the general population, and making the arts more accessible to the public through performances and exhibitions. As of 2015, Mfuko wa Utamaduni Tanzania is partnered with the government of Sweden in funding arts and cultural efforts by artists from Zanzibar and mainland Tanzania.

In addition, grants are now provided for individuals and smaller organizations throughout the country. These grants support anything from a 2006 Painters Exhibition in the Neyerere Cultural Center to training seminars in countless media, including pottery, painting, drawing, beadwork, clothes design, and performing arts. Again, these programs are rooted in the fundamentals and traditions, but also aim to expand education beyond customary styles.

Tanzanians enjoy football (soccer), cricket, and the half marathon. There are several major football clubs for continental competition. Cricket has been played in Tanzania since colonial times, but the first official game dates back to 1890, in Zanzibar. Internationally successful long-distance runners from Tanzania include Martin Sulle (1982–) and Fabiano Joseph Naasi (1985–). Runner John Yuda Msuri (1979–) holds several international championships.

Annual events and festivals held in Tanzania include the Festival of the Dhow in Zanzibar, which features an international film festival.

Cultural Sites & Landmarks

Because of its large size, the country encompasses some of East Africa's most famous and majestic natural landmarks, including the Zanzibar Archipelago, a group of islands off the coast in the Indian Ocean. These islands feature a rich blend of cultures, which evolved from Zanzibar's historic reputation as the "Spice Island" and its role as a major trade hub for East Africa.

A particular reminder of the cultural value of Zanzibar lies in Stone Town (also Mji Mkongwe), the historic center of Zanzibar City, the island's capital. This white-walled monument of African, Arab, and European influence is considered the only historical town in East Africa still in operation. The site exhibits traces of early Arab traders (c. 700 CE), whose distinct homes and famous carved wooden doors line the streets. Stone Town was designated as a United Nations Educational, Scientific, and Cultural Organization (UNESCO) World Heritage Site in 2000. Landmarks in Stone Town include the Livingstone House, the base camp of the famous Christian missionary explorer and anti-slavery advocate David Livingstone (1813–1873). It was from this camp that Livingstone embarked on his final exploration of East Africa in search of the source of the Nile.

On the mainland, Dar es Salaam, Swahili for "abode of peace," embodies the same cultural fusion as Zanzibar. Once the capital, it still has the largest concentration of government buildings and remains the nation's center of commerce. Of particular note is the National Museum, which houses the fossils of Zinjanthropus, a male humanoid believed to be one of the oldest human relatives. These fossils were excavated from eastern Africa's Olduvai Gorge, known as the "cradle of civilization," in 1959.

North of Dar es Salaam, majestic Mount Kilimanjaro rises to the sky. It is an extinct volcano and Africa's highest mountain. Kilimanjaro's highest summit, Kibo, reaches a height of 5,895 meters (19,340 feet). Hans Meyer first reached Kibo's snowy reaches on October 6, 1889, offering evidence to refute the many scholars of the day who considered it impossible for snow to form and last in a region so close to the equator.

Another volcanic site is the Ngorongoro Crater. Formed from a collapsed volcano roughly 2.5 million years ago, the crater is 18 kilometers (11 miles) across. Located in the Ngorongoro Conservation Area (NCA), it is the world's largest perfect crater, and considered a natural wonder due to its beauty and extensive ecosystem. Also inside NCA are several other craters, the Olduvai Gorge, settlements of the Masai people, and an array of wildlife including gazelle, buffalo, zebra, giraffe, eland, wart hog, elephant, hyena, lion, cheetah, and leopards.

Tanzania's Serengeti region is home to one of the last remaining examples of extensive migration of Africa's plant-eating animals and their predators. The region encompasses nearly 30,000 kilometers (11,583 square miles), mapped out according to the path of its migrating herbivores. In addition to containing a protected territory known as the Serengeti National Park, the Serengeti also contains two UNESCO World Heritage Sites: the Serengeti National Park and the NCA, as well as two biosphere reserves. In this ecosystem, every inhabitant serves a purpose, from the termites to the grass to the grazers and their predators, all of which depend on the rains.

Libraries & Museums

Tanzania's national museum, the National Museum and House of Culture, is located in Dar es Salaam. It is the country's largest museum, housing exhibits that range from archeology and ethnography to fine art and biology. The museum is home to some of the fossil discoveries of renowned archaeologist Louis Leakey. Other museums in Tanzania include the Arusha Museum of Natural History (also known as the Old Boma Museum); the Sukuma Museum, which celebrates the traditional arts and culture of the Sukuma people, Tanzania's largest ethnicity; and the Mwalimu Nyerere Museum Centre in Butiama, dedicated to Julius Nyerere, Tanzania's first president.

The National Central Library, located in Dar es Salaam, is the acting headquarters of the Tanzania Library Services Board (TLSB), which oversees seventeen regional libraries and numerous divisional and district libraries. The country is also home to over fifteen academic libraries and several corporate libraries.

Holidays

Secular, government-sponsored holidays in Tanzania include Union Day (April 26), celebrating the union of Tanganyika and Zanzibar; Karume Day (April 7), which memorializes the 1972 assassination of Zanzibar's president Abeid Karume; Independence Day (December 9); Zanzibar Revolution Day (January 12); Nane Day (Farmers' Day, August 8); Human Rights Day (March 21); Family Day (date varies); Youth Day (June 16); Women's Day (August 9); and Day of Reconciliation (December 16).

Nyerere Day (October 14) is celebrated in honor of Tanzania's first president, Julius Kambarage Nyerere (1922–1999), and marks the climax of the Uhuru Torch Race.

Major Christian and Muslim holidays are celebrated in Tanzania. Mwaka Kogwa, which marks the beginning of the Persian New Year, is observed in southern Zanzibar.

Youth Culture

Today's youth culture in Tanzania is largely an expression of the crossroads between tradition and the future. For example, Tanzania has seen its own successful hip-hop culture grow after a significant influx of Western hip-hop in the 1980s. However, Tanzania has its own unique form of hip-hop, known as Bongo (Kiswahili for "brains"), which includes Kiswahili lyrics. In addition, the subject matter, which artists and youngsters claim make the music better than its Western counterpart does, often addresses issues relevant to Tanzanian youth. These include sex and its consequences, inequality, HIV/AIDS, joblessness, orphans, and politics. Tanzanian rappers have used their popularity to spread the word on safe sex and abstinence practices.

SOCIETY

Transportation

Driving is done on the left-hand side of the road in Tanzania, and international traffic signs are used. Overall, speeding, and reckless driving, are common and, coupled with unpaved roads, can create very unsafe conditions. In addition, flooding in the rainy season from March through May often completely washes away rural roads, rendering them impassable and stranding people.

Despite these hazards, most Tanzanians travel by bus between cities and towns. Minibuses or dala dalas (also referred to as *thumni*; mini-vans) are used to travel within cities and run along specified routes. To know the specific route, a passenger must look at the markings and coloring of the dala, which indicates where it stops. Names of locations are not widely used. Many times these vehicles will not leave on their routes until the van is considered "full," or carrying upwards of 25 passengers.

There are two major railways that serve Tanzania. The Tan-Zam, or TAZARA Line, travels from Dar to Zambia off the southwest border, while the Central Line travels to western Tanzania. Train service is not known for its timeliness and is often a haven for petty criminals. However, with few options for secure road travel, it is a preferred option for those who can afford it.

Transportation Infrastructure

As of 2014, Tanzania's road network was estimated at nearly 91,049 kilometers (about 56,575 miles), of which only 6,578 kilometers (4,087 miles) was paved. Much of the existing infrastructure has been upgraded in recent years, including the tarring of roads in remote regions to help promote tourism and easy accessibility. (Local government authorities maintain District, city, and feeder roads.) It is estimated that the country's road network is, even as of 2015, still responsible for the transportation of approximately 75 percent of internal freight and over 80 percent of passenger traffic.

Tanzania has three primary sea ports—Dar es Salamm, Tanga, and Mtware—and several inland ports. The country has twenty-five airports, four of which are international, including Julius Nyerere, Kilimanjaro, Zanzibar, and Mwanza. Air Tanzania Corporation (ATC) is the major provider of domestic flights.

Media & Communications

In Tanzania most of the large media institutions—radio, print and television—are state-run and located in Kiswahili. Despite this trend, there are still a number of privately run communications firms. Television has seen a growth in popularity since 2001, when the state launched its own programming. Until then, Tanzania had regarded television a luxury, per the opinion of former President Julius Nyerere (1922–1999),

who served as Tanzania's first president from 1964 until 1985. It was the former president's opinion, carried out in policy, that access to television only furthered the income gap in Tanzania.

The early 21st century has witnessed the introduction of a mix of private and public television stations such as Tanzania Broadcasting Corporation (TBC), which is state-run; Independent Television (ITV), a widely-watched private network; Star TV, a private and widely popular for its sports and dramatic broadcasts; and TV Zanzibar, state-run and giving limited service to the island. Radio Tanzania (RTD) still serves roughly 60 percent of the population, and includes broadcasts in Kiswahili and English. It broadcasts local, regional, and international news, with the latter coming from international sources such as the British Broadcast Corporation (BBC) and American sources. Radio is seeing a decline as more and more people are able to access television. In addition, Tanzania has several Internet providers, though the government has been criticized for not encouraging private growth in this sector. Internet cafés are also becoming increasingly popular in urban areas and cities.

Like many African nations, Tanzania has at times struggled with the concept of freedom of the press. However, Tanzania has made some headway in this area with the election of President Jakaya Kikwete (1950–) in 2005. During the campaign, many opposing parties were able to use radio and television to campaign and even discredit corrupt politicians, free of punishment from the government. In spite of this progress, there is still rampant bribery, intended to prevent the reporting of crime and corruption. There are even sanctions against and arrests of reporters and informants who report on corrupt police practices.

SOCIAL DEVELOPMENT

Standard of Living

Tanzania has deliberately remained a country of small villages and farms; its urban communities cannot support the large number of people who come from the rural areas. According to a 2011 estimates, nearly 68 percent of the population lives below the poverty line. Tanzania ranked 159th out of 187 countries on the 2014 UN Human Development Index (HDI). The UN classifies the country as having "low human development."

Water Consumption

For the most part, access to safe water and basic sanitation remains a challenge in Tanzania, despite recent reforms to improve infrastructure. It is estimated that, as of 2015, 77.2 percent of the urban population has access to a clean or improved water resource, but only 45.5 percent have the same level of access in rural areas. Access to water is also a primary concern in Dar es Salaam, where only an estimated 25 percent of the population has access to piped city water, which was privatized in 2003 as part of the government's National Water Sector Development Strategy. However, the government terminated this 10-year lease contract in 2005, following allegations of corruption, deteriorating service, and retributory practices against citizens by the private, multinational consortium known as City Water. Moreover, a majority of residents in Dar es Salaam live in unserved settlements or unplanned areas, such as slums and shantytowns. The country also suffers from a number of environmental problems, and water quality varies across regions.

Education

The Ministry of Education and Vocational Training is responsible for the quality of education in Tanzania. Primary educations spans seven years, while secondary education spans six years (four years of junior secondary and two years of senior secondary). Tertiary education can last up to three years and includes institutions of higher learning. Education is compulsory for seven years, until students reach the age of fifteen.

There are nearly 30 public and private postsecondary institutions throughout the country. The largest of these is the University of Dar es Salaam. Specialty schools in Tanzania include the Sokoine University of Agriculture in Morogoro and the International Medical and Technological University in Dar es Salaam. St. Augustine University of Tanzania in Mwanza is one of the country's prominent private institutions. The island of Zanzibar also has its own university.

Primary school enrollment, teacher-to-student ratios, and school funding remain challenges in the Tanzanian education system. Still, UNICEF places primary school enrollment at just over 98.2 percent in 2012. According to the World Bank, the teacher-to-student ratio in 2014 was estimated to be, on average, one teacher for every forty-three students, just above the standard of one teacher per forty students. As of 2015, the adult literacy rate in Tanzania was an average of nearly 71 percent.

Women's Rights

Tanzania's constitution prohibits discrimination based on nationality, ethnicity, political affiliation, race, or religion, but makes no mention of discrimination based on gender, age, or disability. As a result, gender inequalities exist in both rural and urban areas.

In general, the vast majority of women in Tanzania manage the household or farm. Certain laws are in place to limit the amount of time a woman may work. For example, women in Tanzania may not work from the hours of 10 pm to 6 am. Even after receiving wage-earning jobs in more urban areas, women are often subject to sexual harassment and lower wages.

Despite the requirement of seven years of compulsory education, it is growing ever more expensive to send children to school. As a result, families often choose to send only some of their children to school. In this, male children are usually preferred. Not surprisingly perhaps, the literacy rate among women is only 65.4 percent, while the male literacy rate is over 75.9 percent.

In addition to professional and economic inequalities, many Tanzanian women suffer physical abuse that goes unpunished. There are no established laws addressing domestic abuse. The Marriage Act of 1971 only condemns the act. While Tanzania's constitution does prohibit the general act of assault, the law does not specifically prohibit domestic abuse. As a result, many cases are never reported. A woman who does report abuse may be granted a divorce on those grounds. However, this is difficult to enforce in rural areas, or in Zanzibar, where Islamic tradition influences civil law.

Rape is also prevalent throughout Tanzania; however, only roughly 5 percent of reported cases ever go to trial. Female genital mutilation (FGM), also known as female circumcision, is still practiced in Tanzania. Often performed by a layperson using non-sterile instruments, the procedure is considered a human rights violation that has serious, sometimes even fatal physical and mental repercussions, including chronic pain from nerve damage, recurring renal and gynecological infections, and painful complications during both intercourse and childbirth. While Tanzanian law prohibits this practice for females under the age of eighteen, UNICEF estimates that, as of 2013, roughly 15 to 18 percent of young women in Tanzania still endure the procedure.

Health Care

The greatest health concerns facing Tanzania are malaria, human sleeping sickness caused by tsetse flies, and large bloodsuckers, which can transmit trypanosomes, some of which are responsible for a few major diseases in humans. Female genital mutilation (FGM), extremely painful and sometimes even fatal due to post-procedural infections, is still practiced among the Masai (See also "Women's Rights"). Bilharzia, caused by parasitic worms, is common in tropical areas, but is easily diagnosed and treated.

HIV/AIDS is spreading in Tanzania, and affects everyone, old and young. However, in 2007, because of an ambitious public health initiative, the Dodoma region recorded one of the country's lowest rates of new infections. Hoping to replicate this success in hard-hit parts of Tanzania, more than 100 high-ranking elected officials, including the Tanzanian president and his wife, publicly underwent HIV testing in Dodoma's Mwalimy Nyerere Square to kick off a five-year nationwide HIV/AIDS prevention and care program. As of 2014, 5.34 percent of the adult population lives with HIV/AIDS.

GOVERNMENT

Structure

In 1967, the new government wrote the Arusha Declaration, which emphasized the need to educate the people in socialism. Tanzania's constitution was adopted in 1977, modified in 1984, and amended again in 2012. A national referendum on a new constitution, drafted in 2014 and passed by the National Assembly, will occur in October 2015. Tanzania has been moving toward multiparty democracy since 1990.

The new republic has faced several serious challenges, such as the failure of socialism in the villages, increasing taxation and corruption, infrastructure problems, bankruptcy, and the 1978 war with Uganda.

The United Republic of Tanzania is lead by the president, who is both chief of state and the head of government. A vice president serves as the chief executive of Zanzibar. The president and vice president are elected by popular vote to five-year terms, with a two-term limit. The cabinet is appointed by the president from among the members of parliament.

The prime minister, appointed by the president, serves as the leader of the National Assembly. The unicameral National Assembly are elected to five-year terms by popular vote. Of the 357 seats, 239 members are elected by popular majority vote, 102 women are elected by proportional representation, five are elected by a House of Representatives majority vote, 10 are appointed by the president, and one is held for the attorney general.

Zanzibar has its own 81-member House of Representatives (Baraza La Wawakilishi), which has jurisdiction over all non-union matters for the island.

Political Parties

Chama Cha Mapinduzi (Revolutionary Party), known as CCM, is the ruling party of Tanzania and, until 1992, was the only legal party in the country. Because of the party's political dominance, Tanzania is considered a one-party dominant state. Other political parties represented in Parliament, though by small margins, include Chama Cha Demokrasia na Maendeleo (Party of Democracy and Development), or CHADEMA; the Civic United Front, or CUF; National Convention for Construction and Reform—Mageuzi, or NCCR–M; the Tanzania Labour Party, or TLP, and the United Democratic Party, or UDP. In March 2014, the parties CUF, CHADEMA, and NCCR-Mageuzi merged to form Umoja wa Katiba ya Wananchi (Coalition for the People's Constitution), or UKAWA. As of 2015, Tanzania had twenty-two registered political parties, although the majority are perceived as structurally weak.

Local Government

For administrative purposes, Tanzania is divided into 30 administrative regions (*mkoa*), with 25 on the mainland and five on Zanzibar. These regions are subdivided into districts (*wilaya*), and further divided into divisions (*mgawanyiko*), and local wards (*wodi*), which are categorized as either urban wards (*mitaa*) or rural villages (*kijiji*). Local governance includes thirty urban councils and 169 district councils. Local government had been abolished in the 1970s, but local governance has seen reform since then, such as the establishment of city, municipal, and town councils in urban areas, and district, township, and village councils in rural areas. Education, health care, road maintenance, water management, and agriculture all fall under the purview of local government.

Judicial System

The country's highest judicial authority is the Court of Appeal of the United Republic of Tanzania, which consists of fourteen justices and a chief justice. Under the Court of Appeal is the High Court of the United Republic for Mainland Tanzania with a principal judge and thirty judges that adjudicate cases involving land, labor, and commercial interests. There is also a High Court of Zanzibar, which is similarly organized. Under these bodies are magistrate courts; Kadhi courts, for Islamic matters, and finally, district and primary courts.

Taxation

Personal, investment, and corporate income are all taxed in Tanzania. Personal income is taxed at a progressive rate, from 11 percent up to 30 percent depending on income level. For non-residents with some earnings in Tanzania, the rate is 20 percent on their total personal income. The corporate tax rate is 30 percent. Other taxes include excise tax, sales tax (on services and goods), stamp duty, and the value-added tax (VAT), levied at 18 percent.

Armed Forces

The Tanzania Peoples' Defence Force (Jeshi la Wananchi la Tanzania, JWTZ) represents the armed forces of Tanzania. It consists of an Army; the Naval Wing (which includes the Coast Guard); an Air Force Command, which includes an Air Wing division, although, as of 2014, most of the Air Wing's planes are no longer flight-capable. Military service is not compulsory, and active duty soldiers are estimated at approximately 27,000, with 80,000 reserve personnel (2013).

Foreign Policy

Formerly two separate entities, Tanganyika and Zanzibar were formally unified as the Republic of Tanzania in 1964. The United Republic of Tanzania has been a participating member of the United Nations (UN) since its re-inception in April 1964 and is a member of the Commonwealth of Nations, an intergovernmental organization of 53 states that were once British territories. Tanzania had to be reinstated because it had originally been a participating member under the separate names of Tanganyika with Zanzibar. Between January 2005 and December 2006, Tanzania served on the UN Security Council. Tanzania's primary issues of focus in the UN have been moderating conflict within the East African region and elevating the rights of refugees and HIV/AIDS victims.

A founding member of the Non-Aligned Movement, Tanzania often plays the role of a mediator in regional conflicts due to its political stability. Furthermore, it has maintained a consistent faithfulness to participating in regional agreements and talks. For example, Tanzania was involved in the 1999 formation of the East African Cooperation Treaty with neighbors Kenya and Uganda. This in turn led to the formation of the Customs Union in 2005, which now includes Burundi and Rwanda. The goal of the treaty and resulting union is eventually to operate on a similar regional economic scale as seen in Europe with the European Union (EU) or the Southern Cone of South America. Tanzania also regularly partners with the United Nations High Commissioner for Refugees to host asylum seekers and those fleeing violence in neighboring countries, like Mozambique, Democratic Republic of Congo, Burundi, and Rwanda.

A considerable portion of Tanzania's foreign policy depends on foreign aid for development. The US, through the organization the U.S. Agency for International Development (USAID) is responsible for donating roughly $20 million (USD) annually for international development. Additional funds have also gone to fighting AIDS and malaria. Former U.S. President George W. Bush highlighted this policy during his spring 2008 visit to Tanzania. The country still holds President Bush in high regard for the assistance his administration provided for the sick. Moreover, the Peace Corps regularly sends workers to the country to help with humanitarian efforts, and as of 2015, 147 Peace Corps members are stationed in Tanzania.

Human Rights Profile

International human rights law insists that states respect civil and political rights and promote an individual's economic, social, and cultural rights. The United Nations Universal Declaration on Human Rights (UDHR) is recognized as the standard for international human rights. Its authors sought the counsel of the world's great thinkers, philosophers, and religious leaders and were careful to create a document that reflects the core values shared by every world culture. To read this document or view the articles relating to cultural human rights, visit http://www.ohchr.org/EN/UDHR/Pages/Introduction.aspx.

Regarding human rights, Tanzania measures up to some international standards, but falls short of others. In accordance with Article 2 of the UDHR, Tanzania has declared that any form of discrimination based on race, nationality, ethnicity, political affiliation, or religion is prohibited. However, these prohibitions neglect the disabled, elderly, and female populations. As a result, most of the prevalent human rights violations in Tanzania affect these groups. There is also a common custom among indigenous populations to trade in the amputated body parts of albinos, who are believed to have magical properties. According to *National Geographic*, since 2000, there have been 72 documented murders of Tanzanian albinos. Little has been done by the national or local governments to combat the practice or prosecute those who commit the acts. Additionally, Albinos regularly claim that they are treated as less than human in their communities.

Articles 5 and 6 of the UDHR declare that a person is entitled to recognition as an equal human before national law and should not be punished in an inhuman fashion or tortured. The enforcement of police regulations in Tanzania is, however, weak, or nearly non-existent in some cases. In addition, brutality and murders by police are relatively common. Torturing prisoners with caning and harsh beatings is the most frequent method. Furthermore, jails or detention facilities are known to be disease-ridden and corrupt. Reasonable cause and due process are rarely enforced, as police initiate an arrest policy based solely on suspicion. This is a direct violation of Article 9 in the UDHR. Since journalists are discouraged from exposing police corruption, it usually goes unpunished.

In rural areas, the elderly are sometime accused of witchcraft and brutally beaten. Public stoning and beatings are difficult to prosecute because the actual perpetrators are rarely turned in. The penal system's inability to seek out and prosecute such individuals is in violation of Article 3 of the UDHR. Tanzania's general inability to deal with this issue and that of violence against women is a significant human rights issue.

Despite these problems and infractions, Tanzania has a strong human rights record compared to neighboring countries. Tanzania's election in 2010 was generally considered free and fair by the global community. The next election is slated for mid-October 2015.

Tanzania is struggling to abolish discrimination against those suffering from HIV/AIDS. This discrimination often takes the form of unwillingness to employ or house those even suspected of having the disease. In accordance with Article 9 of the UDHR, the Tanzanian government is seeking to punish companies found guilty of such discriminatory practices. The president and his wife, in an effort to show the people the importance of confronting the disease, underwent HIV tests in public.

Migration

Up until the turn of the 21st century, Tanzania had one of the largest refugee populations—an estimated 680,000—on the African continent, namely from the Democratic Republic of Congo, Rwanda, and Burundi. In 2010, the Tanzanian government granted citizenship to some 162,000 long-term Burundi refugees. As of December 2014, the UN Refugee Agency estimates there are 252,357 refugees currently in Tanzania's borders, and 883 of them are seeking asylum there. Tanzania, which borders eight countries, has been home to thousands of refugees for nearly five decades, but became more restrictive in terms of refugees' freedom of movement in the 1990s.

ECONOMY

Overview of the Economy

Tanzania, once considered one of the world's poorest countries, has seen significant economic developments thanks to its natural resources

and burgeoning tourism industry. Once largely agriculture-reliant, with over half of its GDP derived from agrarian products, the country has begun to shift its economic structure, and as of 2014, agriculture comprises just 27 percent of its GDP, while 48 percent is devoted to the service industry. However, agriculture still employs 80 percent of the work force. (Yet, only 16.6 percent of the land is devoted to cultivated crops, while 27.1 percent is permanent pasture.) The country's GDP is $127.1 billion, and its per capita GDP is $2,700 (USD) (2014).

Industry

The industrial sector accounts for only 25.2 percent of Tanzania's GDP. Manufacturing activity includes processed agricultural goods, like sugar, beer, tobacco cigarettes, paper, refined petroleum, fertilizer, aluminum goods, and construction materials (especially cement). Clove oil and woven goods are also produced.

Labor

The labor force was estimated at approximately 25 million in 2014. The agriculture sector remains the main provider of employment. As of 2015, there are currently no statistics available on Tanzania's unemployment rate. However, it was estimated to be 11.7 percent in 2006, when the last official labor survey was conducted. As of 2009, that number had increased to around 13 percent.

Energy/Power/Natural Resources

Tanzania's chief natural resources include large mineral deposits (including gold), natural gas, and vast parklands and nature preserves. None of these resources have been exploited to their full economic potential, however.

Fishing

According to official statistics, the commercial fishing industry employs some 80,000, but only accounts for 10 percent of Tanzania's total catch. Primary exports include prawns, sardines, and perch. Dynamite fishing, or blast fishing, which is popular because it can net up to 400 fish at a time, has ruined offshore coral reefs, and threatened the fishing industry in the early 21st century. Fishers who are found guilty of fishing with dynamite may serve up to five years in prison. Some have turned to harvesting seaweed at low tide to supplement their incomes, particularly along Zanzibar's coasts, although warming ocean waters are making both seaweed and fish less plentiful.

Forestry

Approximately 37 percent of Tanzania is covered in forest. The abundance of trees found in Tanzania, including mahogany, teak, ebony, camphor wood, and mangrove, fuel the country's timber and wood products industry. However, land deforestation to provide fuel and to create farms has created conservation issues, particularly soil loss, which has caused the formation of desert areas. As a result, the blackwood tree, among others, is nearly extinct. NGOs, like the British-based aid organization Farm Africa, are working with district governments and communities within the Nou Forest to provide other means of making a living, like beekeeping, mushroom-farming and running tree nurseries. These activities are part of a more sustainable forestry management model. As of 2015, Farm America conducted programs with 23,000 community members from the Babati and Mbulu districts.

Mining/Metals

Diamonds, tanzanite, rubies, and garnets are mined in Tanzania, along with gold, salt, gypsum, phosphates, kaolin, tin, coal, uranium, nickel, copper, cobalt, silver, limestone, soda ash, and iron ore. Tanzania is a significant producer of diamonds and the fourth largest producer of gold in Africa, after South Africa, Ghana, and Mali. Current gold yields are 44 tons annually, while copper comes in at 3284 tons, and silver is 11 tons. Tanzania also boasts an average annual diamond yield of 112,670 carats. The Tanzanian Chamber of Minerals and Energy projects mining to account for 10 percent of the country's GDP by 2025.

Agriculture

Tanzanian agriculture consists of both plantations for commercial profit and subsistence farming. The country's principal exported crops are cloves and copra (from which coconut oil is extracted), as well as coffee, tea, pyrethrum (insecticide made from chrysanthemums), sisal (agave), rice, peanuts, tobacco, sugarcane, cotton, cashews, cassava, and bananas.

Subsistence farming, practiced by most of the population to feed families, produces corn, wheat, millet, sorghum, vegetables, bananas, and cassava.

Animal Husbandry

The livestock industry is a primary sector of agriculture in Tanzania, accounting for approximately eight percent of the country's agricultural GDP. Tanzanian farmers raise livestock such as cattle, sheep, poultry, goats, and pigs. Tanzania ranks fourth in East Africa's in livestock production—after Rwanda, Kenya, and Burundi—with cattle accounting for approximately 75 percent of all animals raised. Commercial ranches and dairy farms account for an estimated one percent of the livestock subsector.

The tsetse fly, fatal to cattle as well as humans, prevents farmers and herdsmen from settling vast sections of land across Tanzania. Many parts of Tanzania would be open to cultivation if eradication of the tsetse fly becomes a reality, but most eradication programs have not been practical because the pesticides used damage the environment.

Tourism

Like many of its natural resources, Tanzania's tourism industry has gone largely unexploited, but has begun to show signs of development. According to World Bank statistics, the number of inbound visitors has increased every year, climbing from 754,000 in 2010 to 1,063,000 in 2013. Those tourists who do visit mainland Tanzania and Zanzibar are drawn to wildlife safaris in the Serengeti, as well as the beautiful scenery of Kilimanjaro and the island beaches. There are several large resorts along the coast, near Dar es Salaam. Divers enjoy exploring the waters of the Indian Ocean off Tanzania, home to interesting marine life and coral reefs such as Wambe Shando.

Following the 2008 global recession, an estimated 30 percent of tour guides in Tanzania—approximately 900—lost their jobs. These layoffs have extended to the hotels and lodging sector as well. Tourism, nonetheless, remains a primary contributor to Tanzania's GDP—an estimated 17.2 percent as of 2009. In 2013, the industry employed 11 percent of the country's labor force, providing 1,189,300 jobs and generating $4.48 billion (USD) in revenue.

Kristen Pappas, Lois Bailey, Beverly Ballaro,
Savannah Schroll Guz

DO YOU KNOW?

- There are many myths surrounding the unusually shaped baobab tree, which can be found in Tanzania. A traditional Tanzanian belief holds that God planted the tree upside down, while Arab legend suggests that the uprooting is the work of the Devil. Some botanists believe that certain specimens are thousands of years old.

- The Uhuru (Swahili, "Freedom") Torch, placed atop Mount Kilimanjaro in 1961, is considered a symbol of freedom and light in Tanzania.

- Dar es Salaam is the largest city in Tanzania. Its name translates into English as "abode of peace."

- Dodoma is the center of Tanzania's wine industry, which took root during the early 1980s. It is also the only location in the world that enjoys two grape-growing seasons every year. Dodoma wines are popular among British wine enthusiasts and, as of 2014, have begun to provide a serious to challenge the long-standing dominance of South African wines.

- There are several legends surrounding the origins of the capital's name. The most popular account relates that an elephant that came to drink at a stream became stuck in the mud, prompting some locals to dub the place "Idodomya" ("the place where it sank"), a name eventually transformed into Dodoma.

Bibliography

Dorothy L. Hodgson. "Once Intrepid Warriors: Gender, Ethnicity, and the Cultural Politics of Maasai Development." Bloomington, IN: *Indiana U P*, 2004.

Gregory H. Maddox and James L. Giblin, Eds. "In Search of a Nation: Histories of Authority & Dissidence in Tanzania." Eastern African Studies Ser. Athens, OH: *Ohio U P*, 2006.

James R. Brennan. "Taifa: Making Nation and Race in Urban Tanzania." New African Histories Ser. Athens, OH: *Ohio U P*, 2012.

John Ndembwike. "Tanzania: The Land and Its People." Dar es Salaam: *New Africa Press*, 2006.

Kelly Askew. "Performing the Nation: Swahili Music and Cultural Politics in Tanzania." Chicago Studies in Ethnomusicology Ser. Chicago: *U Chicago P*, 2002.

Liisa H. Malkki. "Purity and Exile: Violence, Memory, and National Cosmology among Hutu Refugees in Tanzania." 1995.

Mary Fitzpatrick, Tom Parkinson, and Nick Ray. "*East Africa.*" Victoria, Australia: *Lonely Planet Publications Ltd*, 2006.

W. H. Ingrams. "Zanzibar: Its History and Its People." London: *Stacey International*, 2007.

"Spectrum Guide to Tanzania." New York: *Interlink Publishing Group Inc.*, 2002.

"Tanzania Country Studies: A brief, comprehensive study of Tanzania." CIA & U.S. State Department. Covington, WA: *Zay Publishing*, 2012.

"Tanzania: Foreign Policy and Government Guide." 2nd ed. Washington, DC: *International Business Publications*, 2009.

Works Cited

_____. "Seaweed and Blast Fishing Ban Help Protect Tanzania's Fisheries and Mariculture." The World Bank. *The World Bank Group*, 15 Sept. 2015. http://www.worldbank.org/en/news/feature/2015/09/15/seaweed-and-blast-fishing-ban-help-protect-tanzanias-fisheries-and-mariculture.

_____. "Tanzania country profile—Overview." *BBC News*, 20 Apr. 2015. http://news.bbc.co.uk/2/hi/africa/country_profiles/1072330.stm.

_____. "Tanzania, United Republic of: Statistics." *UNICEF*, 31 December 2013. http://www.unicef.org/infobycountry/tanzania_statistics.html.

"2015 UNHCR country operations profile–United Republic of Tanzania" *The UN Refugee Agency*, 2015. http://www.unhcr.org/pages/49e45c736.html.

"Children Orphaned by HIV and AIDS." http://www.avert.org/children-orphaned-hiv-and-aids.htm.

"Cultural Norms and Respect: Tanzanian Style." *Global Basecamps*, 2011. http://blog.globalbasecamps.com/cultural-norms-and-respect-tanzanian-style.

"Female Genital Mutilation and Cutting: A Statistical Overview and Exploration of the Dynamics of Change." New York: *UNICEF*, 2013. PDF.

"Figures: David Livingstone 1813–1873." *BBC History*, 2014. http://www.bbc.co.uk/history/historic_figures/livingstone_david.shtml

"Forest management in Tanzania." *Farm Africa Limited*, 2015. http://www.farmafrica.org/tanzania/forest-management-in-tanzania.

"Hatari!" (1962) Perf. John Wayne. *IMDB*. http://www.imdb.com/title/tt0056059/.

"Makonde Sculpture." For African Art Gallery. *ForAfricanArt.com*, 2015. http://www.forafricanart.com/Makonde-Sculpture_ep_65-1.html.

"Overview of the Mining Sector." *Tanzanian Chamber of Minerals and Energy*, n.d. http://www.tcme.or.tz/mining-in-tanzania/industry-overview/.

"Security Council." Permanent Mission of the United Republic of Tanzania to the United Nations. *United Republic of Tanzania & UN*, 2015. http://tanzania-un.org/?page_id=62.

"Tanzania." The World Factbook. *Central Intelligence Agency*, 2015. https://www.cia.gov/library/publications/the-world-factbook/geos/tz.html

"Tanzania National Parks: The Official Website." *Tanzania National Parks*, 2012. http://www.tanzaniaparks.com/.

"The EAC Livestock & Fisheries Sector: Overview." East African Community Agriculture and Livestock. *EAC Agriculture*, 11 Feb. 2015. http://www.eac.int/agriculture/index.php?option=com_content&view=article&id=77&Itemid=108.

Aamera Jiwaji. "Tanzania: Developing a good nose for wine." *African Business Magazine. IC Publications*, 25 Jul. 2014. http://africanbusinessmagazine.com/uncategorised/developing-good-nose-wine/.

Dan Gilgoff. "As Tanzania's Albino Killings Continue, Unanswered Questions Raise Fears." National Geographic. *National Geographic Society*, 10 Oct. 2013. http://news.nationalgeographic.com/news/2013/10/131011-albino-killings-witch-doctors-tanzania-superstition/.

Gladys Njoroge. "Blast fishing destroying Tanzania's marine habitats." *BBC News*, 4 Sept. 2014. http://www.bbc.com/news/world-africa-29049264.

John Ndembwike. Tanzania: The Land and Its People. Dar es Salaam, Tanzania: *New Africa Press*, 2006.

"Kondo Rock-Art Sites." *UNESCO World Heritage Centre*, 2015. http://whc.unesco.org/en/list/1183.

Daily life unfolds in the main taxi park in Kampala, Uganda.

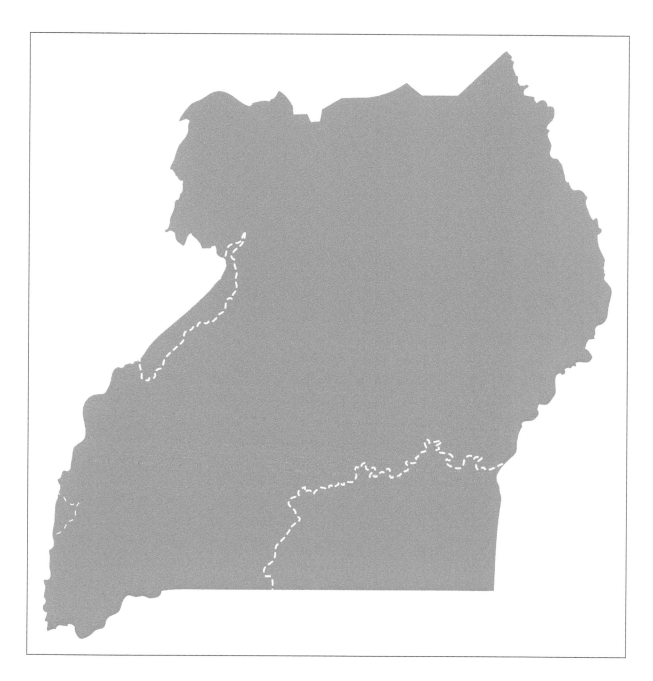

Uganda

Introduction

The Republic of Uganda is located in Eastern Africa. Famous for its vast savannah plains and diverse wildlife, Uganda obtained its independence from British rule in 1962. The country's social and economic structure has been severely compromised by brutal governments, like that of the country's third president Idi Amin, who reportedly killed some 300,000 members of his opposition, and long-time Ugandan politician Milton Obote, under whose later five-year regime an estimated 100,000 people died. Ongoing civil conflicts, guerrilla uprisings, and large refugee populations have further inhibited the country's development and prevented foreign investment. Yoweri Museveni—in office since 1986 and a pivotal part of movements that lead to the overthrow of both Amin and Obote—has brought relative balance to the country, with some significant exceptions, and has been effective in dealing with the country's long-running AIDS crisis.

Uganda's cultural legacy includes a unique and ancient textile craft practiced by the Baganda people of southern Uganda, the making of bark cloth. In 2005, the United Nations Educational, Scientific, and Cultural Organization (UNESCO) proclaimed the creation of bark cloth one of the Masterpieces of the Oral and Intangible Heritage of Humanity. Uganda also maintains several important cultural sites and wildlife preserves, including the last remaining natural habitats for mountain gorillas.

GENERAL INFORMATION

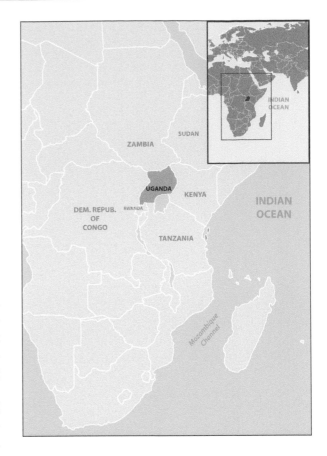

Official Language: English
Population: 37,101,745 (July 2015 estimate)
Currency: Ugandan shilling
Coins: Before 2013, 100 cents equaled one shilling. However, as of 2013, the shilling is no longer subdivided. Shilling coins come in the following denominations: 10, 50, 100, 200 and 500, the last three of which are most often used. The American dollar is widely accepted, as is the pound sterling and the euro.
Land Area: 197,100 square kilometers (76,100 square miles)
Water Area: 43,938 square kilometers (16,964 square miles)
National Motto: "For God and My Country"
National Anthem: "Oh Uganda, Land of Beauty"
Capital: Kampala
Time Zone: GMT +3
Flag Description: The Ugandan flag features six horizontal stripes, a repeating pattern of black (on the top), yellow, and red. Emblazoned in the center

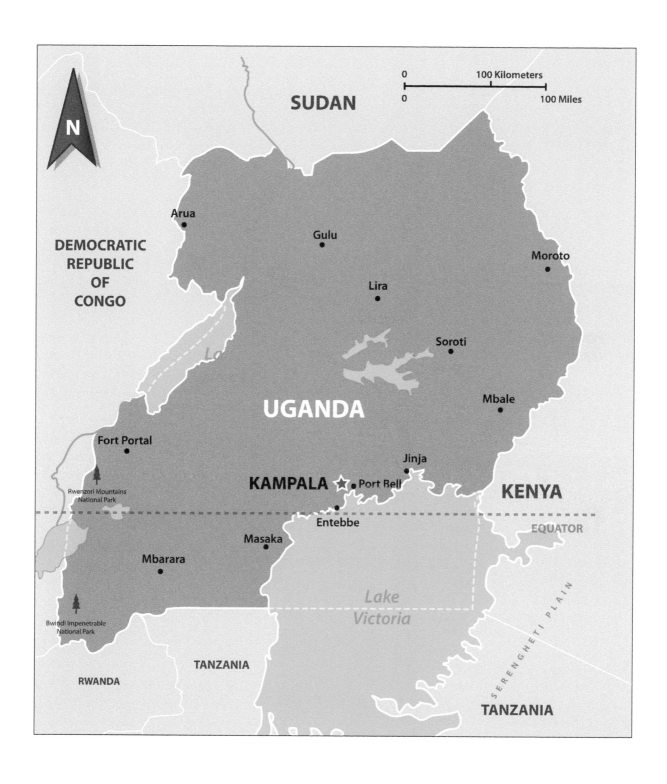

Principal Cities by Population (2014):

- Kampala (1,516,210)
- Jinja (468,256)
- Kira (313,761)
- Masaka (296,649)
- Mbarara (195,013)
- Gulu (152,276)
- Nansana (144,441)
- Kasese (101,679)
- Lira (99,059)
- Mbale (96,189)
- Entebbe (69,989)

of the flag is a white circle with a grey crowned crane. The crane is noted for its gentle nature and was the symbol of Ugandan military forces during British rule. The color of the flag's stripes are symbolic of the people (black), the sun (yellow), and the blood that connects all Africans (red).

Population

As of 2015, around 84 percent of Uganda's population lives in rural areas. Population density is greatest around Lake Victoria, in the southeastern corner of the country.

The country's capital, Kampala, in the southeast of the country, is also its largest city, with a population of approximately 1.5 million. The overcrowded lower portions of Kampala feature bustling streets that reflect the city's vibrancy and its problems. The thriving shops, street markets, street vendor stalls, low-end motels, and eateries attest to the city's economic growth during the past two decades. However, the slum neighborhoods and the presence of large numbers of street children are evidence of Kampala's ongoing struggles against poverty.

Kampala's population growth has led to the development of shantytowns, where the lack of indoor plumbing, potable water supplies, and trash collection has created a public health crisis. In particular, the unsanitary conditions have triggered a number of cholera outbreaks since the late 20th century, the most recent of which was in

April 2013 in the districts of Hoima, Nebbi, and Buliisa, where there was a reported 3.2 percent fatality rate among the population.

In 2007, the Ugandan and Belgian governments embarked on a joint five-year campaign aimed at building roads, drainage ditches, sanitary facilities, and water lines, as well as planting thousands of trees in some of Kampala's worst slums. The goal is to make these areas more habitable for residents and attractive to outside investors. Similarly, in 2013, Denmark became involved in working to ensure rural Ugandans can more easily obtain potable water. Allocating DKK 450 million for the period of 2013 to 2018, the government of Denmark is currently leading a program called the Joint Water and Environment Sector Support Programme (JWESSP) to build pipelines and improve sanitation.

Languages

While English is the official language, Bantu languages such as Ganda and Luganda are also taught and are used in native language publications distributed in Kampala. Arabic is also spoken, although not by a large part of the population. Swahili is also widely spoken and was made an official language in 2005. The move was controversial, as Swahili is spoken largely among the military and was the country's official language during the reign of President Idi Amin (1971–1979), a brutal dictator who was responsible for the deaths of about 300,000 people.

Many of the indigenous languages are closely related enough to be mutually understood.. For instance, a speaker of Luganda can easily communicate with a speaker of Lusoga, Lunyoro, and Kinyaruanda. Generally, Uganda's indigenous languages are either part of the Niger-Congo or Nilo-Saharan language families.

Native People & Ethnic Groups

Uganda has a rich and diverse ethnic heritage. The area has been inhabited since the first millennium BCE, originally by Bantu and Luo speakers. Europeans did not arrive until the 19th century.

Resident tribes include the Baganda (16.9 percent of the population), the Ankole (9.5 percent), the Basoga (8.4 percent), the Bakiga (6.9 percent), the Iteso (6.4 percent), the Langi (6.1 percent), the Bagisu (4.6 percent), the Acholi (4.7 percent), the Lugbara (4.2 percent), and the Bunyoro (2.7 percent). The Alur, Bagwere, Bakonjo, Batoro, Jopodhola, Karamojong, Rwanda, and Rundi, as well as Europeans, Asians, and Arabs, round out the remainder of the total population (a total of 29.6 percent).

Religions

Eighty-four percent of Uganda's population adheres to Christianity, split evenly between Roman Catholicism and Protestantism at 42 percent each. Of those who practice Protestantism, nearly 36 percent are Anglican, 4.6 percent are Pentecostal, and 1.5 percent are Seventh-Day Adventist. Muslims account for 12.1 percent of the population, and there are some people (3.1 percent) who have retained animistic indigenous beliefs. Nearly one percent do not identify with any faith.

Climate

Uganda's climate is tropical, with temperatures ranging between 16° and 28° Celsius (60° to 83° Fahrenheit). Conditions are generally wet and rainy, but there are two dry seasons, from December to January and June to August. Otherwise, there is little seasonal variation in the weather.

Most of Uganda's rainfall occurs near Lake Victoria and Lake Albert, and ranges between 114 centimeters (45 inches) per year in those areas and 89 centimeters (35 inches) in the short-grass savannahs. The heaviest rains fall between March and May, and lighter rainfall occurs between August and December. The northwestern part of the country is semi-arid.

ENVIRONMENT & GEOGRAPHY

Topography

The Republic of Uganda is located in Eastern Africa, east of the Democratic Republic of the Congo, south of South Sudan, west of Kenya, and north of Rwanda and Tanzania. Most of Uganda's land is plateau, consisting of low

savannah with a tall reed-like grass known as elephant grass (*Pennisetum pupureum*). The plateau is surrounded by mountains, and there are some small areas of equatorial forest. Much of this land is ideal for growing coffee (which is native to the area), as well as tea, bananas, plantains, cotton, tobacco, and other crops.

Buganda, in the southeast area of the country, is an eroded plateau dotted with small hills and valleys that are filled with papyrus swamp and an occasional forest. Fertile bands of red clay, ideal for farming, surround the hills. Other areas are not farmed, but may provide grasses for thatch and grazing livestock. Uganda's highest point is Margherita Peak on Mount Stanley, at 5,110 meters (16,675 feet). The lowest point is Lake Albert, at 621 meters (2,037 feet).

Chief among Uganda's inland bodies of water are Lake Victoria (the source of the Nile River's longest branch, the White Nile), Lake Albert, Lake Edward, and Lake Kyoga. There are harbors on Lake Victoria at Entebbe, Jinja, and Port Bell.

The capital, Kampala, lies in the southern-central portion of Uganda, on Lake Victoria's northern shore.

Plants & Animals

There are 343 species of mammals to be found in Uganda. Of these, nearly half are large animals, such as apes and monkeys, lions, leopards, cheetahs, golden jackals, hippos, buffaloes, and twenty-nine different species of antelope. Smaller mammals include bats, rodents, and shrews.

Uganda's Bwindi Impenetrable Forest is home to about 300 mountain gorillas—nearly half the world's current mountain gorilla population. They are critically endangered and threatened with extinction. Uganda is also home to the Eastern chimpanzee.

Like other African countries, Uganda is home to a wide variety of bird life. More than 1,000 different species of birds nest in the country. Common reptiles include the Nile crocodile.

Of the 18 plant kingdoms found in Africa, seven thrive in Uganda, more than in any other nation on the continent.

For decades, the area around Lake Victoria was infested with water hyacinth, a weed from South America that, within seven years of its first sighting, clogged 80 percent of Uganda's waterways, prevented fishing boats from navigating the lake or making catches and serving as rich breeding ground for the snails that carry the fatal schistosomiasis parasite. The introduction of Neochetina weevils in 1997 succeeded in killing off the water hyacinth, but not before more than half of the lake's 500 fish species were driven to extinction.

CUSTOMS & COURTESIES

Greetings
When Ugandans greet each other, the most common gesture is the handshake, which is customarily softer than in Western culture. Women may embrace each other, as do close male friends, and children may bow or curtsy in a sign of deference to their elders. English and Swahili are the official languages, but the primary language in Uganda is Luganda. Common phrases of greeting in Luganda include the informal "Ki kati" ("Hi"); "Wasuze otya nno?" ("Good Morning" or literally, "How was your night?"); and "Oli Otya" ("How are you?"), to which one might respond "Gyendi" ("I'm okay"). Customarily, inquiries into one's family and well-being will follow greetings.

Gestures & Etiquette
An important facet of social etiquette in Uganda is deference to the elderly. Older people are traditionally considered wise and strong. Customarily, they are served first at meals, counted on for family advice, and generally cared for by their children and other younger family members. Other important aspects of etiquette include male/female interaction. For example, dating is generally nuanced; public affection is generally frowned upon and introducing someone to one's parents is traditionally considered a sign of marital intentions.

Ugandans have adopted many aspects of Western culture, with the most significant being dress. Urban Ugandans have a heightened fashion sense, with many dressing almost exclusively in Western-style clothing. Nonetheless, it is still a cultural requisite that one dresses formally when leaving the house on any business. Ugandans also appreciate a neat appearance and conservative dress for women.

Eating/Meals
The majority of Ugandan families eat two meals per day, one at lunch and one at dinner. Meals generally involve the entire family. Customarily, hands are communally washed prior to eating, and the family sits upon mats surrounding a communal center dish. Food is eaten with the right hand only, as the left is associated with personal cleansing and considered inherently unclean. Moreover, items are always passed with either the right hand or both hands, but never with the left alone.

Generally, meals consist of a main starch with sauce. Other commonly consumed foods include grilled meats, roasted nuts, fried dough, and fruit. The women are expected to prepare meals and are further charged with the tasking of breaking up and rationing out the food.

Dinner etiquette is also very important to Ugandans, who value a sense of community at meal times. When eating, it is only appropriate to reach to food in the nearest section. In addition, everyone is expected to stay seated on the mat until all diners are finished with their meal. Many Ugandans refrain from consuming water or other beverages until after the meal is finished.

Visiting
Visiting is a common and daily occurrence in Uganda. They also frequently occur during mealtimes, where women are expected to prepare enough food for the family and any unexpected guests. When a guest arrives for a meal, they are traditionally treated and served as if family, and are expected to reciprocate such respect at a later date.

When visiting, guests are customarily escorted to an area reserved for socializing. These areas, whether they are inside of a building or under the shade of a tree, are generally furnished with mats for seating. Popular activities include watching football (soccer), the national sport.

LIFESTYLE

Family

Traditionally, families in Uganda consisted of a nuclear family (husband, wife, and their children) and extended members related to the male head of the household. This might include the husband's parents, siblings, and nieces and nephews, all who may live in the same compound and share in the domestic responsibilities. Families are traditionally patriarchal as well. Among the Baganda people, largest ethnic group in the country, the man makes all decisions for the home and is never challenged by any other member. Baganda also tend to send their children off to family friends to begin working from very young ages. This male-based and very work-oriented structure is said to derive from the days of kingdoms, in which the king was revered and unchallenged. Polygamy (practice of multiple wives) is common among all ethnicities.

Most ethnic groups in Uganda are patrilineal, or traced through the male members. A lineage is based from a nuclear family and traced from one generation to the next through any sons that are born. Essentially, sons keep the family name while daughters are absorbed into their husband's families. Among the Acholi and Langi, two smaller ethnic groups in the north, families are also patrilineal and fixated on their relation to decedents of past kings. Among all ethnic groups, lineages derive from single nuclear families, while clans are made up of several related lines.

Housing

Housing in Uganda is relatively uniform, except for those living in displaced persons camps in the northern regions of the country. In those camps, homes may range from rectangular structures built from mud bricks and cement to homes made from scrap metal. These homes are generally lined up in rows so that one room shares a wall with the next. In these rows, any sort of previously used material may be recycled and used as additional insulation to fortify the home.

In greater Uganda, homes are generally rectangular or cylindrical in shape (like huts) and made from available materials such as sunbaked mud bricks, with roofs made from corrugated tin or thatch. Buildings are nearly always one-room structures that may be shared among as many as six children or two or more wives. The head of the household traditionally maintains his own room. Generally, the kitchen and the bathroom are also individual structures, and mainly all grouped into a compound. In the past, when many ethnic groups were organized into kingdoms separated into smaller chiefdoms, villages were tightly settled around a chief's home. Today villages are scattered, affording families more room within which to create their compounds. Many families also have expanded space to include their subsistence farms or livestock.

Urban housing is more modern, and generally built from brick and cement. European architecture is also common, and the urban landscape also features high-rise style buildings constructed from steel and cement. As the urban population increases, shantytowns (informal settlements) are becoming more common, and feature dwellings made of poor materials. Such temporary structures, often made of found objects and other recycled elements, also lack of proper sanitation and electricity.

Food

The staple foods of the Ugandan diet include cassava (manioc), potatoes and yams, millet, matoke (similar to plantain), and groundnuts (peanuts). Common vegetables include cabbage, onions, pumpkins, and tomatoes, while commonly grown fruits include lemons, oranges, and pawpaws (in Africa, a yellow, melon-like fruit similar to papayas). Most dishes are starch-based and accompanied by sauces which are often meat-heavy and spicy. These sauces are similar to stews, and commonly feature vegetables, butter, and spices (such as curry or salt).

Generally, Ugandans eat less fish and have small variations on regional dishes. The first and most significant variation is on the regional dish ugali, which Ugandans call posho or sima. Ugali is served throughout East Africa and is made from cooked maize, sorghum, or millet that has been pounded to a fine powder. It is sometimes stewed with cassava, which serves as a starchy thickener. Matoke (also known as Ugandan plantains) many popular Ugandan dishes. These fruits, which are sweet and have a starchy quality, are harvested while still green, pounded in a large mortar and pestle, and then fried or stewed and served with a spicy sauce.

The northern diet is slightly different and people generally eat far more grains, such as millet, sorghum, and cornmeal with vegetable sauces. Due to ongoing conflict-related destabilization, most food there has come from international aid organizations over the past twenty years. In addition, some of the oldest ethnic groups who have been herding cattle for centuries still gain most of their nutrition from the animals they raise; cow products, such as beef, milk, butter, and even blood, are essential staples in their diets.

Life's Milestones

Christianity is the dominant religion in Uganda. According to government estimates in 2014, approximately 84 percent of the population identified with a Christian denomination. As such, milestones commemorating birth, transition into adulthood, marriage, and death are generally observed in accordance with the Christian faith. Different ethnic groups have nuanced methods for commemorating each event, though some elements remain universal.

The tradition of a bride price or gift is nearly universal among all Ugandan ethnicities prior to a wedding. This gift, typically consisting of money, livestock, foodstuff, and possibly even clothing, is traditionally presented to the bride's family on behalf of the groom and his family. The gesture is meant to substitute for the young woman who will be leaving her home, and is thus no longer able to contribute in her parents' household. Under Ugandan law, the groom's family may no longer seek to reclaim the bride gift should he and his bride split up or should she pass away. Customarily, weddings are long celebrations that may last up to a week in length. The entire family and even villagers are all invited to participate in the festivities.

CULTURAL HISTORY

Art

Traditional arts in Uganda originally served a utilitarian purpose before they were valued and created for their aesthetics. These traditional handicrafts range from ceramics and textile arts to metalworking and have mainly been imported with the various peoples who migrated to the region over time. For example, the Bantu peoples brought their superior ironworking skills several hundred years ago, while Southeast Asian immigrants, particularly those from Indonesia and Java, are thought to be responsible for importing batik (a type of textile art) to the region. Batik is a process by which people use wax to create patterns on cloth before they dye it. Hot wax is drizzled over a fresh cloth to create a pattern, and the fabric is then dipped in dye several times to create deep shades and blends. Finally, the fabric is dipped into a solution that dissolves the wax leaving the un-dyed fabric as a bright pattern amid the deeply dyed portions. Other traditional arts include basketry, beadwork, wood carving, and body painting and scarification.

One unique and ancient craft, practiced by the Baganda people of southern Uganda, is the making of bark cloth. The technique used to make the bark cloth is prehistoric, and believed to predate the first weaving techniques. The cloth is made using the inner bark of the mutuba tree (*Ficus natalensis*), which is then beaten to achieve a certain color and texture. Bark cloth made for royalty was traditionally dyed black or white. In 2005, the United Nations Educational, Scientific, and Cultural Organization (UNESCO) proclaimed this practice of making bark cloth as one of the Masterpieces of the Oral and Intangible Heritage of Humanity.

Architecture

Traditional architecture throughout Uganda is mostly characterized by the use of rudimentary and available materials. These materials are usually limited to mud, thatch, mud bricks (such as adobe), and scrap metal. Most structures in rural

Uganda are simple, one-room and one-story buildings made from mud walls or mud bricks cemented together. Roofs are either thatch or corrugated tin. Some buildings are cylindrical in shape, which proves effective for protecting against wind and other natural elements. In urban Uganda, primarily Kampala, modern architecture and high rises featuring glass and steel construction are now common, including state-of-the-art buildings owned by Chinese and European interests.

Drama

Uganda maintains a fledgling and costly film industry in the early 21st century. The country lacked a heralded professional film school, resulting in a lack of quality productions and international acclaim. The Uganda Federation of Movie Industry (UFMI) recently developed a training program to meet the needs of young students interested in film. The country has also opened itself up to Western productions in recent years. The award-winning *The Last King of Scotland* (2006), a fictional account of the brutal regime of Ugandan leader Idi Amin (c.1923–2003), was the first Western film shot in Uganda since 1990. (Incidentally, the last Western film shot in Uganda was *Mississippi Masala,* which references Amin's expulsion of Uganda's Asian population in the 1970s.)

Many acclaimed documentaries have also been made about Uganda since the turn of the 20th century, including *Uganda Rising* (2006), which details the conflict in northern Uganda, and *War Dance* (2007), which traces the lives of three Acholi children as they struggle to cope with war and devastation. *War Dance* relates the real-life accounts of Rose, Nancy, and Dominic—all three who have lost parents due to the conflict in Uganda and are being raised by abusive relatives. However, all three children are also members of a local vocal performance group that qualifies for the national musical competition held in the capital of Kampala. The moving story has helped to further the human rights causes among international donors and organizations for its heartwarming and personal tale.

Music

Traditional Ugandan music generally involves of the use of the marimba (xylophone), lamellaphone (hand-held piano played by plucking metal tines), and the lyre (stringed instrument). The blend of these traditional instruments with rhythmic dancing and chorus singing are characteristic of most, if not all, national music. Various subgroups, however, have their own instruments and musical styles.

The Acholi in northern and northwestern Uganda have channeled their suffering from 20 years of guerilla warfare into their traditional musical style. Employing the adungu (also ekidongo), or the indigenous Acholi harp, this group has developed musical styles at once celebratory and solemn. Their traditional chanting and stomping has also won them national and international acclaim from an American documentary tracing the story of three Acholi children participating in a national performance arts competition (*War Dance*). In addition to traditional music, Congolese music has been popular in nightclubs and dance halls since the 1970s, when groups began performing their distinctive combination blues, jazz, big band, and traditional African hybrid style in neighboring countries.

Literature

The literature of Uganda is rooted in the strong oral traditions that have sustained and preserved the many cultures of Africa for centuries. The ability to memorize and perform poignant stories and history during gatherings is considered a sign of wisdom and respect among Africa's shared cultural heritage. Oral literature, which includes tales, songs, poems, riddles, and proverbs, were also didactic in nature, and imparted important societal values and moral lessons. With increased Middle Eastern and European influence, written literature became more integral to Ugandan society. The majority of contemporary authors write in English, Swahili, and Ganda (or Luganda), the most widely spoken languages throughout the country.

One of Uganda's more notable authors is Moses Isegawa, which is the pseudonym for Sey Wava (1963–). Isegawa joined the seminary, but was expelled and went on to teach in the Netherlands. There, he suffered from bouts of depression and even attempted suicide before completing his most celebrated work, *The Absyssian Chronicles*, first published in Amsterdam in 1998 and then in the UK and US in 2001. The book tells the story of a young man who comes of age during the repressive regime of Idi Amin. The work is thought to be largely autobiographical and has been translated into nine languages. Other notable Ugandan writers include poet Okot p'Bitek (1931–1982), who achieved acclaim for the epic poem *Song of Lawino* (1966), which deals with the effects of colonization, and Taban Lo Liyong (1938–), a well-known literary critic, poet, and fiction writer.

CULTURE

Arts & Entertainment

Traditional art, much of which is now created for the tourist market, still forms the basis of contemporary Ugandan art. Traditional crafts include wood carving, textile arts, and ceramics. While many of artistic products produced from these traditional arts are still utilitarian in nature, they are frequently being created and sold for aesthetic purposes and decoration. Many Ugandans, however, believe these goods, once exclusively used for practical, daily life, become something other than what they are meant to be when they are bought for decorative purposes.

The contemporary visual art scene in Uganda is dominated primarily by European-trained artists. One of the more famous Ugandan painters was Henry Michael Lutalo Lumu (known as HMLL, 1939–1989). He was noted for his passion for studying the realist styles of Old Masters, like Jan Vermeer, but was also an enthusiast of VanGogh and Gauguin. His younger brother, David Kibuuka, now a Canadian citizen, borrowed from traditional African art while incorporating Western styles such as impressionism and expressionism. Kibbuka is considered to be one of the founders of "modern batik art painting." One of the artist's most important themes is the

Maasai people of Kenya, among whom Kibuuka lived for six years. These paintings generally show a single individual with detailed musculature and bodily features; the backdrops are almost always thick with beautiful and sweeping skies. Other modern artists include sculptor Francis Nnaggenda (1936–). His most famous work, *War Victim*, was created in honor of those who died during Idi Amin's reign of terror.

In the world of dance, Uganda has seen much progress in the recent past. The foundation of the Kampala Dance Studio (formerly the Kampala Ballet and Modern Dance School) in August 2004 helped solidify the dedication to using the arts as a means of national reconciliation. The studio is the first of its kind nationwide and determined to teach formal ballet and modern dance to Ugandan children regardless of race, ethnic background, socioeconomics, and gender. It is currently the only professional dance studio of its kind in Uganda and teaches ballet, tap, jazz, salsa, modern, and hip-hop. Traditional dance, unique to each ethnic group in Uganda, is preserved through the Ndere Troupe, a national and international performing group headquartered at the Ndere Cultural Centre, located in Kampala. The dance troupe has developed performance pieces representing traditional dance styles of several of the diverse ethnic groups inhabiting Uganda.

Uganda also has a rich tradition of folk music. Large, sacred drums are commonly-used instruments, along with the entongoli, similar to a lyre, and adunga, a harp-like instrument; the endingidi, a single-stringed instrument played with a bow; the amadinda, a xylophone; and the lukeme, a thumb piano.

Choruses and other group vocals are typical of most styles of Ugandan music. The popular modern music style known as takeu combines elements from Ugandan, Tanzanian, and Kenyan music.

Acholi poet Okot p'Bitek (1931–1982) is one of the best known authors in Ugandan literature. Originally written in the Luo language, then translated into English in 1966, his epic *Song of Lawino* draws on local folklore and traditional songs.

Cultural Sites & Landmarks

Uganda is home to numerous sites both naturally beautiful and culturally rich. This includes three World Heritage Sites as designated and administered by UNESCO: Bwindi Impenetrable National Park, Ruwenzori Mountains National Park, and Kasubi Tombs. Bwindi Impenetrable National Park was recognized as a World Heritage Site for its diverse ecosystems and species. The park is home to one of the remaining populations of the endangered mountain gorilla, as well as over 350 species of birds, and numerous other fauna, others of which are also endangered. There is also over an estimated 130 species of trees.

The Rwenzori Mountains National Park is in the northwestern region of the country, on the border with the Democratic Republic of the Congo (DRC). It is the largest state park in the nation and encompasses the majority of the Rwenzori Mountain range; in fact, the park is home to Mount Stanley which, at 5,109 meters (16,763 feet) is Africa's third tallest peak. The park boasts staggering views of the blue mountain range, glaciers, and the dramatic pine forests that sweep up the foothills and mountainsides. Inhabiting these forests are a diverse array of endemic and endangered flora and fauna, including four primate species and nearly 100 species of birds. Other national parks include the Mgahinga Gorilla National Park, the only other park in which the mountain gorilla is found.

The Kasubi Tombs are the burial grounds for the kabakas (kings) of the Kingdom of Buganda, or the kingdom of the Buganda people, Uganda's largest ethnicity. The kingdom, which rose to power in the 19th century, was abolished after Buganda achieved independence in the 1960s, and was not restored until 1993. The four tombs are situated on a hill, and the site's main building is a domed, circular structure. UNESCO recognized the site for its organic architecture, particularly the thick thatching technique, and cultural and spiritual importance. The site remains an active religious site among the Buganda people.

Other manmade sites of cultural significance in Uganda include the Nyero rock paintings; Bigo bya Mugyenyi, the site of an ancient aqueduct system; and Kibiro village, the site of historic salt mining. The Nyero rock paintings date back to the Iron Age, and their origins are unknown. Some of the paintings seem to resemble planetary bodies. The excavated earthworks at Bigo bya Mugyenyi, which include an inner and outer trench for agricultural purposes, were built by the people of the Bacwezi Empire during the 14th and 16th centuries. The salt-producing village of Kibiro is located on the shores of Lake Victoria. The Kibiro are famous for their unique salt extracting methods, which they developed because of a lack of arable farmland. They mix the salty earth with regular soil and use the properties of the soil as a natural draw on the salt. All three sites are currently on the UNESCO World Heritage Sites' "Tentative List."

Libraries & Museums

The Uganda Museum in Kampala features exhibits of traditional culture, archeology, history, science, and natural history, as well as a collection of traditional musical instruments that visitors are allowed to play. Founded in 1964 following a 1959 act of Parliament, the National Art Gallery of Uganda, also known as the Nommo Art Gallery, is located in Kampala and showcases the work of both Ugandan and foreign artists. Both Nommo and the National Theatre, which features a live-performance stage as well as a cinema, are part of the Uganda National Cultural Centre (UNCC).

Holidays

Ugandans celebrate their Independence Day each year on October 9, as they gained their freedom from Britain on that date in 1962. Other holidays include Heroes' Day (June 9) and Martyrs' Day (June 3). Women's Day is celebrated in early March.

Youth Culture

According to recent estimates, Uganda's youth population dominates the national demographics, with just over 48 percent of the population aged fourteen years old or younger. An additional 21.16

percent of the population is between the ages of fifteen and twenty-four. This staggering demographic carries with it numerous social concerns for Uganda's youth. One of the most distinctive and striking aspects of this is the prevalence of child soldiers in the nation's northern provinces. Throughout twenty years of domination over the northern regions of Uganda, the militant LRA was responsible for kidnapping and intentionally orphaning tens of thousands of children. Many were forced to become child soldiers or prostitutes. Now free, many of these Ugandan children have been shunned by their families and communities, and are working with numerous NGOs to reintegrate themselves into society.

Different aspects of Ugandan culture pose a number of challenges for girls and young women, especially those who live in rural areas. Education has always been highly valued in Uganda, and, according to UNICEF, an estimated 81.3 percent of primary-aged children are enrolled in school. However, as age increases, the number of females enrolled in school decreases. This is largely due to inherent cultural traditions and the early marriages of young women. While the constitution sets the legal minimum age for marriage at eighteen, young girls are married between the ages of twelve and fifteen in many rural areas. In addition, among the Sabiny and Pokot ethnicities, female genital circumcision initiation ceremonies are common among young women between the ages of fourteen and sixteen (see also "Women's Rights").

SOCIETY

Transportation

Buses and minibuses (matatus) are the common modes of public transportation throughout Uganda. Buses generally connect major towns and cities, while minibuses connect greater distances. For local travel, bicycle and motorcycle taxis (boda-bodas) are common, and special-hire taxis are also available.

In Uganda, vehicles are driven on the left-hand side of the road.

Transportation Infrastructure

There is no passenger rail service in Uganda, and despite having 1,244 km of track and a stalled rehabilitation program dating to 1995, Uganda Railways Corporation remains mostly inoperative. Roads being the overall primary mode of transportation. The roads themselves are not well-maintained and are riddled with pot holes. Many are composed of hard earth which can be impassable in a rain storm. The primary international airport of Uganda is Entebbe International Airport.

Media & Communications

Uganda was one of the first African nations to liberalize its media, doing so in the early 1990s. While the state has often been critical of private broadcasters, often using defamation and the incitement of civil unrest as motives to suppress the media, they are generally free to control their own opinions and programming.

Radio is the primary medium in Uganda. The most wide-reaching station is UBC Radio, a public broadcaster run by the Uganda Broadcasting Corporation (UBC). The UBC operates five stations, and runs news in English and local languages across the country. There are numerous private stations, including over 50 private radio stations in and around the capital of Kampala. The public television broadcaster is UBC TV, and there are also numerous private TV stations, some of which broadcast programming from the British Broadcasting Corporation (BBC) and from France. The print media consists of the leading state-run *New Vision*, as well as private dailies such as *Red Pepper*, *The Daily Monitor*, and *The Weekly Observer*. *Bukedde* is also a state-run newspaper that is published in the Luganda language.

Despite being mostly a rural nation, Uganda has a well-developed and competitive telecommunications infrastructure and industry. Uganda's largest telecommunications provider is Uganda Telecom. According to the company, it operates a mobile network that, as of 2015, covers forty-one of the country's districts. Along with MTN Uganda, it is one three telecom companies that operate in the country and offers 4G service. Overall, as of 2012, around 45.9 percent of the population were mobile phone subscribers. Also as of 2012, an estimated 14.7 percent of the population were Internet users.

SOCIAL DEVELOPMENT

Standard of Living

Uganda ranked 164th in the 2014 United Nations Human Development Index listing of 187 countries. The UN classifies the country as having "low human development."

Water Consumption

In 2015, Uganda's water and environment minister reported that in rural areas, 76 percent of the population had access to clean water, while 95.5 percent of the population in urban areas had the same. Further, coverage is spotty, with some areas of the country where only 10 percent of the population has access (particularly in the north), and others (such as in the southwest) where access reaches 95 percent. Climate change, environmental degradation, and a growing population due to development were threats to expanded coverage; additionally, corruption in the water sector is thought to have absorbed 10 percent of water expenditures. In 2015, just 17.3 percent of the population had access to improved sanitation, while the urban area was not significantly higher, at 28.5 percent.

Education

Since 1997, primary education in Uganda has been free, but not compulsory. As a result of the Universal Primary Education (UPE) policy instituted that year, primary school enrollment increased by 70 percent. By 2012, UNICEF estimated that nearly 94 percent of Ugandan children were enrolled in primary schools. The government continues to work to improve access to the country's 1,200 secondary schools (half of which are private institutions), which was similarly made free in 2007. Again, according to UNICEF, in 2012, only about 17.4 percent of those who attend primary school go on to secondary school, 16.2 percent for boys and 18.7 for girls.

In 2010, a parliamentary committee called for a review of the educational system, claiming that the government was overwhelmed by the enrollment numbers seen at both the primary and secondary levels. The result, it claimed, was a shortage of teachers and student resources, such as desks and books. The teacher to student ratio is still a staggering 1:200. Uganda's National Curriculum Development Centre is also currently in the process of revising and updating lower secondary (that is, grades six through ten) programs of study.

In the first decade of 21st century, Uganda's literacy rates revealed a significant disparity between men and women. Before 2010, only a little more than half the female population—that is, 58 percent—were literate, while men had a 77 percent literacy rate. However, women have begun to close the gap. As of 2015, women's literacy rates have climbed to 71.5 percent, while men's are 85.3 percent. And since 2010, when enrolled, males and females both complete around ten years of education.

Of Uganda's seven universities, Makerere University in Kampala is the oldest in Uganda and established in 1922. The largest university in the region, it attracts students from all over East Africa. Today, there are more than 40,000 students enrolled there as of 2015.

Women's Rights

Since the late 1980s, the Ugandan government has mandated improving and enforcing women's rights nationwide. Working in conjunction with numerous international and national non-governmental organizations (NGOs), the Ugandan government has adopted new legislation and developed national workshops aimed at educating women on their rights under law. By 1994, women were making progress and Uganda elected the first female vice president in sub-Saharan Africa. In the second decade of the 21st century, women now hold 131 of the 375 parliamentary seats, which amounts to 35 percent. Additionally, female MPs in Uganda joined forces in 1989 to create the Women's Parliamentary Association, which supports women's political participation and mobilize resources for women's welfare throughout the country. Also promising is that school attendance amongst girls had increased, indicating an even brighter future for Ugandan women. However, despite drastic improvements, Uganda continues to experience serious challenges and deficiencies in regards to women's rights.

The traditional role of women in Ugandan society has been slow to adapt and change. Typically, women are expected to be subordinate to men. As a result, women lag behind men in terms of education and employment opportunities. They typically face discriminatory practices during hiring, and are afforded fewer privileges, such as promotions, then men. Due to their limited role in the professional sector, many women even turn to prostitution. In addition, sexual harassment continues to be a problem, though it is prohibited by law.

Beyond the employment sector, women still suffer from discriminatory practices in marriage, property ownership, and child custody. For example, women must build a substantial case in order to be granted a divorce and polygamy (practice of multiple wives) is allowed. Furthermore, under traditional law and custom, a woman is neither permitted child custody nor allowed any property following a divorce or the death of her husband. Traditionally, the next male descendent, whether it is an eldest son or a relative of the deceased, would retain any property. This forces some women to marry the individual who inherits her husband's property. In fact, this is upheld as customary law in some cultures and rural areas.

According to UNICEF, female circumcision—called Female Genital Mutilation (FGM), by human rights activists—is still performed on 1 percent of the Uganda's female population. Usually performed without sterile instruments in a home environment by non-professionals, the process can lead to post-procedure infections and even death. Women also suffer from life-long nerve damage, difficulty with intercourse and childbirth, and chronic gynecological and renal problems. And while the procedure persists, driven largely by traditional values and its association with hygiene, it is falling out of favor thanks to educational programs launched

by Doctors Without Borders and UNICEF. As of 2015, Uganda has the lowest rate of those countries known to advocate and practice FGM.

Domestic abuse continues to be a significant issue in Ugandan society. Much of the problem stems from the fact that domestic abuse is an ingrained part of the culture. For example, a 2006 national survey estimated that 60 percent of men and 70 percent of women acknowledged that it was a husband's right and responsibility to use violence to maintain order in the household. In 2012, the Uganda Bureau of Statistics released a report indicating that almost half of all females in Kampala have experienced some form of domestic violence, either physical or sexual. There is also no specific law that protects women from spousal abuse, and women who prosecute may charge their husbands with general assault. However, social stigma and police bias have limited the number of reported and prosecuted domestic abuse cases. Furthermore, police often treat domestic abuse as a private affair, and refrain from intervening.

Health Care

According to the World Health Organization, Uganda's health care system ranked 161st out of 186 countries in 2012, an improvement from previous rankings. The system is still plagued by poor drug distribution, lack of medical equipment and trained medical personnel—there are only 0.117 doctors and 1.3 nurses for every 1,000 people—and economic constraints. According to the *Guardian*, 51 percent of the population does not have access to health care, with rural areas suffering the most.

The infant mortality rate in Uganda is high, at about 59 deaths per 1,000 live births. Average life expectancy for men is 54 years, and approximately 56 years for women (2015 estimate).

In 2014, it was estimated that 7.25 percent of Uganda's population was living with HIV and/or AIDS, and 32,900 people died from the disease that year.

The risk for contracting food or waterborne diseases such as bacterial diarrhea, hepatitis A, and typhoid fever is quite high. The chances of contracting malaria, schistosomiasis, and sleeping sickness (African trypanosomiasis) are also high in certain parts of the country.

GOVERNMENT

Structure

Uganda was a British colony from 1894 to 1962, when it was granted independence. Several decades of coups and military rule followed, most notoriously during the 1970s. Under the regime of President Idi Amin, the country's economic structure was shattered. Between 1971 and 1979, an estimated 300,000 Ugandans were killed by the regime. A period of guerilla war followed under the rule of Milton Obote, the country's first president who returned to power in 1980.

Uganda's president is both chief of state and head of government and is elected by popular vote to a five-year term. The president selects his cabinet from among the elected senators. A prime minister supervises the cabinet and assists the president as needed.

The legislature is a unicameral National Assembly composed of 338 members, 238 of which are elected by popular vote, and 100 who are nominated by government-recognized special interest groups. All legislators serve five-year terms. There are 111 districts and one capital city-district (Kampala) within the four regions in Uganda.

Political Parties

The dominant political party in Uganda is the National Resistance Movement (NRM), led by President Yoweri Museveni (1944–), also known simply as the "Movement." While other smaller parties exist, they were disenfranchised between 1986 and 2005. The 2006 presidential election saw the rise of several new parties, the most powerful being the Forum for Democratic Change (FDC), a splinter party that was formed by disenchanted NRM members centered on president Museveni's primary rival, Kizza Besigye (1956–). In the 2011 presidential elections, their candidate Besigye garnered 26 percent of the vote to Museveni's 68.4 percent.

Other political parties that have risen once again are the Democratic Party—a moderate-conservative party that gained twelve seats in the National Assembly—and the Independent Party, which gained 43 seats. The Uganda People's Congress (the party of former Prime Minister and President Milton Obote, from the north of the country) and Uganda People's Defense Force each took 10 seats.

Local Government

Local government in Uganda is overseen by the Ministry of Local Government, under which there are administrative unit councils that oversee each of the 111 districts and one capital city, which together comprise Uganda. In rural areas, under these districts are sub-counties run by councils. In urban areas, there are city councils headed by mayors that similarly manage local affairs. Local administrators are working towards government decentralization and face the challenge of increasing demand for services with limited funds. Managing HIV infection rates is a particular challenge for Ugandan local officials.

Judicial System

The highest court in Uganda is the Supreme Court, which is comprised of seven justices and one chief justice. Justices are appointed by the president (and approved by the National Assembly) based on recommendations made by the Judicial Service Commission, an independent advisory board consisting of nine members. Under this are the Court of Appeal; the High Court, which consists of ten circuit courts and seven high-court divisions; the Chief Magistrate; and court levels, known as Grade One and Grade Two.

Taxation

Residents of Uganda pay income tax of 40 percent, a value-added tax (VAT), tax on rental income, and other fees and duties. Income for corporations is also taxed.

Armed Forces

As of 2013, The Uganda People's Defense Force (UPDF) is comprised of Land Forces, which includes a Marine Unit, and the Uganda Air Force. There is currently no military conscription. Once enlisted voluntarily, there is a nine-year service obligation. The UPDF faces continued threat in the north of the country against the Lord's Resistance Army (LRA), although a truce was negotiated between the two organizations in 2008.

Foreign Policy

Uganda achieved official independence in the mid-20th century, but was plagued by political unrest for the next 40 years, including the ushering in of some of Africa's most notorious dictatorships, including the brutal reign of Idi Amin. During this period, Uganda suffered from isolation, as the politics of Amin and his successors drew the ire of the international community. (When Amin waged war on neighboring Tanzania as a distraction from his failed policies, he was overthrown by the superior military force of his opponent, further hampering foreign relations.)

In 1986, Yoweri Museveni (c. 1944–) assumed the presidency, and has maintained a mixed following since. Internationally, his reputation has becoming increasingly tarnished as he enacts legislation concerning term limits that have framed what appears to be a president-for-life scenario, as well as his involvement in the Democratic Republic of the Congo's (DRC) civil war and his treatment of Rwandan refugees in the late 1980s. However, he has gained international praise for his privatization efforts and his work with the Organization of African Unity (OAU). Nonetheless, he has proved powerless in disrupting the guerilla tactics of the rebel faction fighting in northern Uganda since the late 20th century.

Despite political unrest and a devastating human rights record, Uganda has maintained their economic growth in the long run. Their adherence to World Bank and International Monetary Fund (IMF) regulations that privatized national companies and placed the Ugandan currency on the international market has improved economic conditions. In 1991, the nation also began an Investment Code that offered tax incentives to international firms for investing in Ugandan

industry and commerce, the result of which has set Uganda apart. While most other nations have seen international investment dry up because of strict and arbitrary regulations that funnel earnings to the ruling class, Uganda has seen international investment increase, although this has been hampered somewhat by conflicts with the Lord's Resistance Army (LRA).

Uganda maintains membership in the UN and the Commonwealth. Regionally, the country maintains membership in the East African Intergovernmental Authority on Development (IGAD), a seven-member organization; the East African Community (EAC); the Common Market for Eastern and Southern Africa (COMESA); and the African Union (AU). Uganda maintains tenuous relations with some of its neighbors, including the DRC, Burundi, and Rwanda. This mostly stems from Uganda's involvement in conflicts in each country and border relations. Uganda also supports the AU through troop involvement and sent troops to Somalia to support that nation's peace process. Uganda has also been involved in mediatory efforts in Burundi, Sudan, and Kenya. Uganda receives significant humanitarian aid from both the United States and the European Union (EU).

Human Rights Profile

International human rights law insists that states respect civil and political rights and also promote an individual's economic, social, and cultural rights. The United Nations Universal Declaration on Human Rights is recognized as the standard for international human rights. Its authors sought the counsel of the world's great thinkers, philosophers, and religious leaders and were careful to create a document that reflects the core values shared by every world culture. (To read this document or view the articles relating to cultural human rights, visit http://www.ohchr.org/EN/UDHR/Pages/Introduction.aspx.)

Internationally, Uganda's human rights record is regarded as poor. This reputation stems from the notorious reign of terror imposed upon Uganda in the 1970s by ruthless leader Idi Amin. Amin unleashed a brutal and systematic form of mass killing, particularly targeting the Langi and Acholi groups whom he suspected of harboring allegiance to the former disposed president, Milton Obote (1925–2005). It is estimated that between 300,000 and 500,000 people were murdered during Amin's brutal reign. Amin was also known for his anti-Semitism and for exiling the entire Asian population from Uganda. Since Amin's reign ended, numerous other leaders have also been suspected of mass killings.

One particular dire human rights situation in Uganda involves the conflict in the northern part of the country. The conflict involves fighting between the rebel group Lord's Resistance Army (LRA) and the government of Uganda (the LRA wants to establish a theocratic state). The LRA has been accused of many human rights abuses during this longstanding conflict, including torture; the forced enslavement of children, for both soldiering and prostitution; abduction; murder; physical mutilation, such as cutting off womens' lips; and rape. The region is also home to roughly 29,776 million internally displaced persons (IDP) as of May 2015 and some are still unable to return to their villages or find secure locations to rebuild their lives, as pockets of the LRA persist in their persecution of civilians. Many remain in displaced-person camps, where they lack appropriate food, water, healthcare, and security.

There have also been reports of government security authorities acting independently of the government. The Uganda People's Defense Force (UPDF) is the body responsible for external security and resolving the crisis in the north; the police force and the Local Defense Units (LDUs) are responsible for local security. Both groups have been accused by the public or arbitrary arrest, brutality, torture, and extrajudicial killing. Generally, these tactics were used to break up mass demonstrations. Despite such brutality, these security forces were mostly immune to prosecution under the law.

Other human rights abuses concern the limited of constitutional rights, such as freedom of speech and the press, poor prison conditions, and discrimination against homosexuals and the disabled. Uganda is also considered an origin and destination country for human trafficking, particularly for the purposes of sexual exploitation and forced labor. The availability of healthcare also continues to be a concern. However, the Ugandan government has made significant progress in fighting the spread of HIV/AIDS and in 1998, Uganda became the first African nation to report that cases of the disease had actually dropped. As of 2014, 7.25 percent of the population is reported to be infected.

Migration

The UN Refugee Agency (UNRA) estimates that, in 2015, Uganda has accepted 385,513 refugees, of which 35,475 are asylum-seekers. Nearly 125,000 of these are South Sudanese refugees. Conversely, Ugandan refugees have fled into South Sudan to the north and the Democratic Republic of the Congo to the west. In 2010, the Ugandan government banned Rwandan refugees from cultivating crops in an effort to encourage those refugees to return to Rwanda. As of 2015, only a few Rwandans remain and have not been formally accounted for in the (UNRA report).

ECONOMY

Overview of the Economy

Despite its many natural resources, Uganda remains one of the world's poorest, least-developed countries due to continuing political instability. However, thanks to economic reform policies, inflation has been steadily declining since the late 1980s. Uganda is also eligible for significant international debt relief and in 2012, it received $1.7 billion USD assistance, $80 million of which was humanitarian aid. In that year, it was the twenty-seventh largest aid recipient in the world.

In 2014, Uganda's gross domestic product was an estimated $76.94 billion USD. The per capita GDP was $2,000 USD. The service sector provides approximately 51.3 percent of the GDP, agriculture accounts for 21.9 percent, and industry accounts for 26.7 percent.

Industry

Most of Uganda's industrial activity is related to the agricultural sector. Important manufacturing categories include food processing, textiles, animal feed, fertilizers, other horticultural products, gold, and leather goods. Most consumer goods are manufactured for export, and this alone counts for 26.7 percent of the country's GDP. As part of ongoing economic reforms, Uganda is attempting to diversify its industrial activity. There has been some progress in resuming the manufacture of construction materials and household goods. Uganda's primary import partner is the United Arab Emirates, followed by Rwanda, Kenya, Germany, Netherlands, Italy, and Belgium.

Labor

The labor force in Uganda numbers 18 million people. The Uganda Bureau of Statistics reports that in urban areas, unemployment is at 9.5 percent; in rural areas, unemployment is at three percent. Most of the population finds work in the agricultural sector, but reports indicate that low compensation in that sector is driving rural agricultural workers to urban areas, straining resources, adding to temporary housing populations, and creating unrest.

Energy/Power/Natural Resources

Uganda's population does not have adequate access to electricity—only about 20 percent of the urban population was connected to the electricity grid and only three percent of the rural population. This results in extremely low energy consumption: an estimated 215 kWh per capita per year. By comparison, Sub-Saharan Africa requires, on average, 552 kWh per capita. However, to fill the gap left by inadequate infrastructure, many use alternative methods, such as diesel generators and car batteries—expensive ways of generating electricity. Moreover, Uganda pays for emergency power at a very high cost, which takes away from dollars that could be spent in developing a more efficient power infrastructure.

Biomass and hydropower are the largest sources of energy generation in Uganda. Nalubale Power Station has ten generators that produce a maximum 150 MW, while the newer Kiira station produces 200 MW. Other stations include Kanungu Power Station (6.4 MW), Mpanga Power Station (16.4 MW), and the 2012-constructed Bujagali (250 MW), all of which belong to Ugandan Electricity Generation Company Limited (UEGCL). To date, only about 15 percent of the potential hydropower is harnessed and exploitation of biomass (trees and shrubs) is having a detrimental impact on the environment. The government has developed a Hydropower Development Master Plan, which will explore large and small hydropower development possibilities, and the Uganda Photovoltaic Pilot Project for Rural Electrification is exploring solar alternatives.

In 2010, a study was commissioned to explore energy challenges and develop a master plan for East Africa. Among the ideas was a shared energy grid for nations such as Uganda, Ghana, Namibia, and Kenya, as well as the development of renewable energy sources. In 2015, Japan International Cooperation Agency (JICA) has continued work with the government on the Hydropower Development Master Plan, and estimates that it will have harnessed 2,000 MW, developed new power stations, and constructed isolated grids to assist with distribution by 2023.

Large deposits of copper and cobalt are Uganda's most important natural resources, along with arable land and regular rainfall. Just over 25 percent of the land is arable, and 13 percent of the land is comprised of wetlands.

Fishing

As a landlocked country, Uganda total area is about 18 percent water, including the benefits of several lakes regions. These resources have suffered in the past from overfishing, invasive plant species, and pollution. As a result, the Ugandan fish industry, which previously boasted 300 varieties of fish, now only cultivates twenty-three species. Efforts at developing the nation's aquaculture are aimed at addressing threats to this industry.

Forestry

According to the African Development Bank, Uganda experienced a decline in woodland cover, going from 16.5 percent to 11.5 percent between 1990 and 2005—a 27 percent decline. Other estimates indicate that between 1990 and 2010, some 19,360 square kilometers (7,474 square miles)—equaling 39 percent of extant forested area—was lost. Woodlands have suffered as the ever-expanding population utilizes the available biomass for fuel and construction and stymies reforestation efforts, resulting in environmental degradation, landslides, and famine.

Mining/Metals

Minerals mined in Uganda include copper, cobalt, gold, limestone, and salt.

Agriculture

Agriculture drives the national economy, employing 82 percent of all Ugandans, mostly on small farms, and comprising 22 percent of the GDP. Uganda leads all African nations in coffee production, and the crop accounts for more than one-quarter of all the country's exports. Other important crops include tea, cassava, corn, cotton, potatoes, cut flowers, pulses (beans and peanuts), millet, and tobacco. Sorghum and gourds are also grown locally.

Animal Husbandry

Livestock farming, which includes poultry, goats, and cattle (beef and dairy), is also important to the agricultural sector.

Tourism

The Uganda Tourist Board bills Uganda as "The Pearl of Africa," and the industry is overseen by the Ministry of Tourism, Wildlife and Antiquities, which estimates that in 2013, 1,206,334 foreign visitors spent time in Uganda. Before Idi Amin came to power in 1971, Uganda enjoyed an even more robust tourist trade. However, due to continuing violence and political instability, the tourist industry has declined and has yet to fully recover.

Tourists visit Uganda to enjoy the natural beauty of its lakes and mountains and to go on safari in the country's national parks and game reserves. Popular attractions include the volcanic Rwenzori Mountains (known as the "Mountains of the Moon"), Mount Elgon, and the Virunga Volcanoes. Adventurous tourists enjoy whitewater rafting near the Murchison Falls on the Nile.

Most visitors enter the country through the international airport in Entebbe. The best time to visit Uganda is during the dry season between December and February.

Kristen Pappas, C. Todd White,
Beverly Ballaro, Savannah Schroll Guz

DO YOU KNOW?

- The name Kampala comes from the Kiganda phrase kasozi k'impala, or "the hills of the impalas (antelopes)." The area's grassy hills and swamps provided an excellent habitat for the impala herds, which once made the site of present-day Kampala rich hunting grounds for the local Bugandan kings.

- Mountain Gorillas were first discovered by Friedrich Robert von Beringe (1865–1940), in the Virunga Mountains of southwest Uganda, in 1902. It is estimated that, as of 2015, half of the world's 700 remaining mountain gorillas are located there.

- Uganda's national bird is the Crested Crane (*Balearica regulorum gibbericeps*).

- Lake Victoria, which Uganda shares with Kenya and Tanzania, is the largest lake in Africa and the second largest freshwater lake in the world (after Lake Superior and Lake Baikal).

Bibliography

Aili Mari Tripp. *Museveni's Uganda: Paradoxes of Power in a Hybrid Regime.* Boulder, CO: *Lynne Rienner Publishers*, 2010.

Bernard Atuhaire. "The Uganda Cult Tragedy: A Private Investigation." Cambridge, UK: *Janus Publishing Company*, 2006.

Goretti Kyomuhendo. "Waiting: A Novel of Uganda's Hidden War." Women Writing in Africa Ser. New York: *Feminist Press*, 2007.

Gregory Barz. "Singing for Life: HIV/AIDS and Music in Uganda." New York: Routledge: *Taylor & Francis Group*, 2006.

Joshua B. Rubongoya. "Regime Hegemony in Museveni's Uganda:Pax Musevenica." New York: *Palgrave Macmillan*, 2007.

Michael Sweikar. Mzungu: "A Notre Dame Student in Uganda." Nashville, TN: *Cold Tree Press*, 2007.

Opiyo Oloya. "Child to Soldier: Stories from Joseph Konys Lord's Resistance Army." 3rd ed. Toronto: *University of Toronto P*, 2013.

Peter Eichstaedt. "First Kill Your Family: Child Soldiers of Uganda and the Lord's Resistance Army." Reprint ed. Chicago, IL: *Chicago Review P*, 2009.

Richard Sobol. "Abayudaya: The Jews of Uganda." New York: *Abbeville Press*, 2002.

Susanne Buckley-Zistel. "Conflict Transformation and Social Change in Uganda: Remembering after Violence." Rethinking Peace and Conflict Studies Ser. Hampshire and New York: *Palgrave Macmillan*, 2008.

Works Cited

_____. "Uganda Demographic and Health Survey 2011." Kampala: *Uganda Bureau of Statistics*, 2012. PDF.

_____. "Uganda." *UNICEF Statistics*, 31 Dec. 2013. http://www.unicef.org/infobycountry/uganda_statistics.html.

"2015 UNHCR country operations profile–Uganda." United Nations High Commissioner on Refugees. *The UN Refugee Agency*, 2015. http://www.unhcr.org/pages/49e483c06.html.

"Africa: Uganda." The World Factbook. *Central Intelligence Agency*, 9 Sept. 2015. https://www.cia.gov/library/publications/the-world-factbook/geos/ug.html.

"Biography." *Kibuuka*. David Kibuuka, n.d. http://www.kibuuka.com/pages.asp?muidx=3003&menu=About+The+Artist.

"Country Profile: Uganda." *BBC News*, 21 May 2015. http://news.bbc.co.uk/1/hi/world/africa/country_profiles/1069166.stm#media.

"Danish support for water and sanitation in Uganda (2013–2018)." Denmark in Uganda. *Ministry of Foreign Affairs of Denmark*, 2015. http://uganda.um.dk/en/danida-en/water-and-sanitation/.

"Female Genital Mutilation/Cutting: A Statistical Overview." New York: *UNICEF*, 2013. PDF.

"Labour Force and Time Use." *Uganda National Household Survey Report. Uganda Bureau of Statistics*, 2010. http://www.ubos.org/UNHS0910/chapter4_%20time%20use.html.

"Properties Inscribed on World Heritage List: Uganda." UNESCO World Heritage Convention. *UNESCO World Heritage Centre*, 2015. http://whc.unesco.org/en/statesparties/ug.

"Sector Statistical Abstract, 2014." Ministry of Tourism, Wildlife and Antiquities. *Republic of Uganda*, 2015. http://tourism.go.ug/index.php?option=com_phocadownload&view=category&id=4&Itemid=282.

"The Last King of Scotland: About the Film." *FOX Searchlight Online*. Twentieth Century Fox Film, 2015. http://www.foxsearchlight.com/thelastkingofscotland/.

"Uganda IDP Figures Analysis." Internal Displacement Monitoring Centre. *Norwegian Refugee Council*, 2013. http://www.internal-displacement.org/sub-saharan-africa/uganda/figures-analysis.

"Uganda: Cholera Outbreak—May 2013." *ReliefWeb*, 2015. http://reliefweb.int/disaster/ep-2013-000058-uga.

"Uganda Energy Situation." *Energypedia*, 28 Feb. 2015. https://energypedia.info/wiki/Uganda_Energy_Situation.

"U.S. Relations with Uganda." Bureau of African Affairs. *US Department of State*, 8 Oct. 2013. http://www.state.gov/r/pa/ei/bgn/2963.htm.

"Virunga Gorillas." National Geographic. *National Geographic Society*, 2015. http://animals.nationalgeographic.com/animals/great-apes/.

Mukasa E. Ssemakula. "Luganda Phrasebook: Small Talk." Dr. Mukasa E. Ssemakula *Buganda.com*. n.d. http://www.buganda.com/phrssmlt.htm.

Paul Mukasa-Ssali. "Henry Michael Lutalo Lumu (HMLL)." *The Ugandan Masters*, 27 Jul. 2009. http://www.theugandanmasters.com/Henry_Lumu.html.

Steven Charles. "The Music of their Harps." World Music: Wabash College. *Wabash College*, n.d. http://www.wabash.edu/magazine/index.cfm?news_id=3603.

Tanya Abramsky. "'Beating Your Wife is a Sign of Love'—Changing Norms to End Domestic Abuse." The Guardian. *Guardian News and Media Limited*, 2015. http://www.theguardian.com/global-development-professionals-network/2014/aug/29/domestic-violence-uganda.

ZAMBIA

Introduction

The Republic of Zambia is a landlocked country in South Central Africa, located just south of the equator. Since the mid-1990s, the Zambian government has been working with international charitable organizations, the World Bank, and foreign governments to improve education, health care, and the national economy, all of which have been challenged by a postcolonial legacy of poverty, debt, corruption, and disease.

Zambia is home to approximately thirty-five ethnic groups and seventy-two different tribal groups. Perhaps, as a result, Zambian culture encourages communities to strengthen social bonds through frequent conversation. The concept of family in Zambia is so community-oriented that many of the local languages do not even have separate terms for fathers and uncles, mothers and aunts, brothers and sisters, or even cousins.

Nature also defines the country's culture. Victoria Falls—named for the late 19th-century British monarch by the explorer David Livingstone—is one of the largest and most striking waterfalls in the world. The falls straddle the border between southwestern Zambia and Zimbabwe, and were once called "shungu mumi" ("the life falls") by early hunter-gatherers. Locals in Zambia now refer to the falls as Mosi-oa-Tunya, meaning "the smoke that thunders."

GENERAL INFORMATION

Official Language: English
Population: 15,066,266 (July 2015 estimate)

Currency: Zambian kwacha (ZMW)
Coins: One kwacha can be subdivided into 100 ngwee. On January 1, 2013, new coins were minted in denominations of 5, 10, and 50 ngwee and 1 kwacha.
Land Area: 743,398 square kilometers (287,027 square miles)
Water Area: 9,220 square kilometers (3,550 square miles)
National Motto: "One Zambia, One Nation"
National Anthem: "Lumbanyeni Zambia" ("Stand and Sing of Zambia, Proud and Free")
Capital: Lusaka
Time Zone: GMT +2
Flag Description: The Zambian flag design consists of a pea-green field on which a block of three vertical bands of red, black, and orange (arranged left to right) is situated on the outer (right-hand) edge. The green represents the nation's vegetation. Red symbolizes the struggle for freedom. Black represents the country's people,

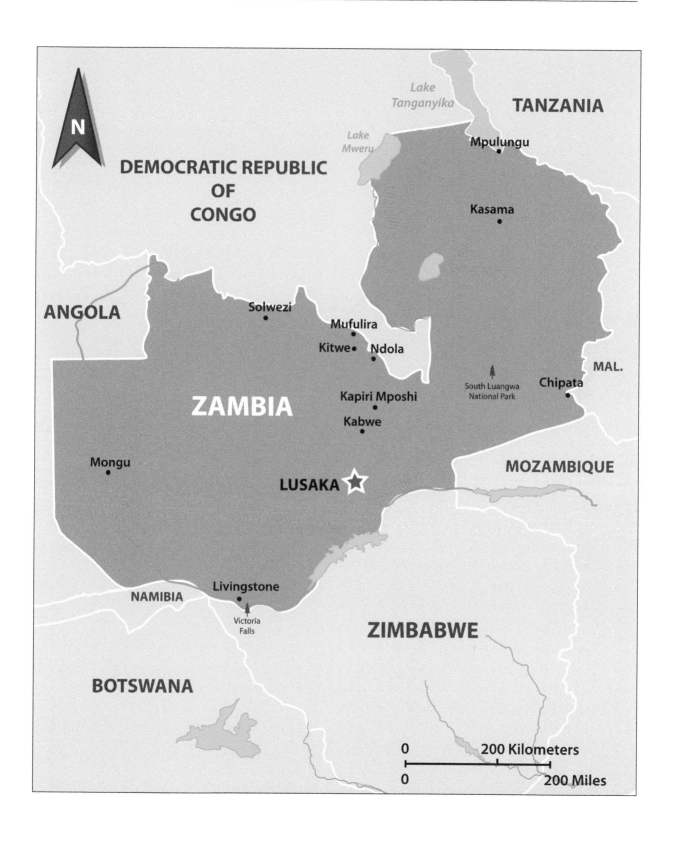

Principal Cities by Population (2010):

- Lusaka (1,742,979)
- Kitwe (522,092)
- Ndola (455,194)
- Chipata (452,428)
- Kasama (238,035)
- Chingola (210,073)
- Kabwe (202,914)
- Mufulira (161,601)
- Luanshya (153,117)
- Livingstone (142,034)

and orange signifies the country's natural and mineral resources. Above these vertical bands is an orange eagle in flight, symbolizing liberty and the peoples' ability to transcend problems.

Population

According to United Nations' estimates, Zambia has a population exceeding 15 million in 2015, nearly 41 percent of which lives in urban areas. In 2013, the World Bank reported that population density was 19.56 persons per square kilometer. Overall, Zambia is home to about thirty-five African-descended ethnic groups, comprising about 82 percent of the population. The remaining 13.8 percent are generally of European or Asian (primarily Indian and Chinese) extraction and are mostly concentrated in urban areas, while the remaining 0.4 percent is of unspecified ethnic descent.

Living conditions in most of Zambia reflect the prevalence of HIV/AIDS and other diseases. As of 2014 estimates, approximately 12.37 percent of Zambia's population (more than 1,150,400 people) lives with HIV/AIDS. Zambia's birthrate of more than 42.13 births per 1,000 and death rate of slightly more than 12.67 deaths per 1,000 has created population growth of just over 2.88 percent as of 2015 estimates.

Languages

Zambia is home to over 70 regional dialects, but the official language is English. In the north and

central areas of the country, the Bemba people, speakers of the Bemba language, dominate at 33.4 percent. In the south and east, Tonga and Nyanja speakers are most prevalent, at 11.4 percent and 14.7 percent respectively. The Lozi can be found predominantly in the west and account for 5.5 percent. Other regional and tribal languages include Chewa (4.5 percent), Nsenga (2.9 percent), Tumbuka (2.5 percent), Lunda (1.9 percent), Kaonda (1.8 percent), Lamba and Lala (both 1.8 percent), Luvale (1.5 percent), Mambwe (1.3 percent), Namwanga (1.2 percent), Lenje (1.1 percent), and Bisa (one percent), along with an estimated 54 other dialects.

Native People & Ethnic Groups

Anthropologists believe that there have been humans living in the Lusaka area of Zambia since the early emergence of *Homo sapiens* about 100,000 years ago. Since that time, the area has witnessed the settlement and migration of early Swahili-Arab slave traders from the coast, Bantu-speaking tribes from neighboring countries, and European traders beginning in the 18th century.

Most of the 35 native ethnic groups and seventy-two tribes currently living within Zambia's borders are believed to derive from Bantu-speakers who arrived in the 14th through 16th centuries. In the 19th century, these groups were joined by—and in some cases forcibly relocated by—refugees from the Zulu wars to the south.

According to the 2000 Zambian census, 99.5 percent of the Zambian population was of African origin, with high concentrations of people from Angola (nearly 38,000), the Democratic Republic of the Congo (18,000), and Zimbabwe (about 9,000). However, these figures changed significantly by the 2010 census with the ongoing implementation of neighboring Zimbabwe's controversial land redistribution policies. Many white farmers, ejected from their Zimbabwean properties, moved to Zambia. Also within the last decade, some 10,000 Asians and Southeast Asians, primarily Chinese and Indians, have created dynamic communities within Zambia's urban areas, significantly changing the country's demographics.

Religions

The largest religious faith in Zambia is Christianity, of which 75.3 percent are Protestant and 20.2 percent are Roman Catholic. Islam, Buddhism, Hinduism, and Baha'i are also significant faiths in the country, accounting for 2.7 percent of the population according to government estimates. All of these faiths tend to become intermixed with local indigenous faith practices, which still shape the lives of most Zambians. An estimated 1.8 percent identify with no religious faith.

Climate

Zambia lies only 10 to 18 degrees latitude south of the equator and is categorized as humid subtropical. However, the country's altitude keeps the climate generally temperate and dry and there are portions of the country that qualify as semi-arid steppe. Throughout most of the country, temperatures average 21° to 35° Celsius (70° to 95° Fahrenheit) in the summer and 6° to 22° Celsius (43° to 72° Fahrenheit) in the winter. Winter falls between May and August and tends to be dry, during which bushfires become widespread. Summertime temperatures reach their peak between September and November.

Average rainfall is about 950 millimeters (37 inches) during the rainy season, from November to April in most of the country. The Eastern highlands receive heavy rainfall year round.

In the Zambezi and Luangwa River valleys, the weather tends to be extreme, and temperatures have risen to 40° Celsius (104° Fahrenheit) with high humidity in October, the peak of summer. Zambia is prone to occasional droughts.

ENVIRONMENT & GEOGRAPHY

Topography

Located in South Central Africa, Zambia is landlocked and borders the countries of the Democratic Republic of Congo, Tanzania,

Malawi, Mozambique, Zimbabwe, Botswana, Namibia, and Angola. Most of the country sits on a plateau between 1,060 and 1,363 meters (3,478 and 4,472 feet) above sea level. Small, granite hills dot the plateau.

Northeastern Zambia rises to over 4,000 meters (13,123 feet) above sea level on the Nyika Plateau. The Zambezi River cuts across the high plateau, fed by the Kafue and Luangwa rivers. Along the riverbeds, large valleys and waterfalls mold the surface of the plateau.

In the south, Victoria Falls dominates the border with Zimbabwe at the town of Livingstone. In the north near Congo and Tanzania, Kalambo Falls spills into Lake Tanganyika, the second largest and second deepest freshwater lake in the world. The Luangwe River Valley actually forms part of the Great African Rift Valley, a massive fault system extending from southwest Asia across east Africa.

At 2,150 meters (7,050 feet), Mwanda Peak is said to be the highest point of elevation in Zambia, although some claim the terrain reaches 2,301 meters (7,549 feet) somewhere in the Mafinga Hills. The country's lowest point is approximately 329 meters (1,079 feet) in the Zambezi Riverbed.

Plants & Animals

Zambia's wildlife parks are internationally renowned for their rare and impressive animal and plant species. Baobab trees, sometimes thousands of years old, grow in the river valleys.

Lions, elephants, hippopotamuses, water buffalo, giraffes, baboons, warthogs, wild dogs, zebra, hyenas, and mongooses thrive in Zambia's moist savannah woodlands and the bushveld covers of the dry southwest. Zambia has twenty national parks and thirty-four game reserves—representing 30 percent of the country's total land area—to help preserve its incredible array of wildlife.

Zambia is also famous among birdwatchers. Hundreds of bird species can be spotted in the wetlands, woodlands, and dry lowlands of the country.

CUSTOMS & COURTESIES

Greetings

Zambian greetings are steeped in formalities and cultural habits. The type of greeting one person gives another reflects the respective social standings of both individuals. During important events, especially those involving people of high social rankings, people will always address each other using family names accompanied by honorific titles. When greeting an elder or person of status, women and children will frequently kneel, while a man will sometimes curtsy in front of a senior person. Zambian salutations can also become complex after a standard greeting, and include inquires into another's family, health, employment, community, or idle small talk.

Greetings in Zambia differ depending on geographic area and local languages. Regional greetings include "Mwabonwa" ("Good to see you"), common in the south; "Mulibwanji" ("How are you?"), heard around the capital of Lusaka; and "Mwapoleni" ("Welcome"), which is commonly heard around the central Copperbelt region. The shaking of hands is a common gesture of greeting, and Zambians might use the left hand to support the right hand. This is considered a sign of respect. In western and northwestern areas, in addition to Luapula province, some Zambians greet each other with a light squeeze of the thumb. Traditionally, men and women refrain from public contact and will regularly greet each other by standing apart and clutching their own hands in front of their chests.

Gestures & Etiquette

Zambian culture encourages communities to strengthen social bonds through frequent conversation. As such, verbal interactions in Zambia are often lengthier and more involved than in Western cultures. Zambians also tend to be indirect and will often avoid touchy subjects or merely allude to them metaphorically. Oftentimes, Zambians will avoid answering in the negative and may only offer a prolonged pause instead. Rituals are important, and it is considered proper to call someone by their title and last name, especially when conducting business. It is polite to address someone by his or her first name only after being invited to do so.

Respect for elders is a central element in Zambian society. It is necessary to identify the eldest or highest ranked people in a room, and to ensure that they are greeted first and treated with the deference traditionally ascribed to them. For example, a traditional, respectful greeting given to an elder involves kneeling on one leg, bowing the head, and clapping the hands three times in succession. A person speaking to an elder should be wary of looking him directly in the eyes, since this is considered rude. Avoiding eye contact is a sign of deference.

Gender also affects the way in which Zambians interact with one another. Women generally do not touch men while conversing, and people of different genders take care to give each other enough personal space when talking. If two people of the same gender are speaking to each other, however, they often stand close, and there is usually some interactive, conversational touching. However, public displays of affection are frowned upon. On the other hand, holding hands is seen as a sign of friendship between two men or two women. It is also considered offensive to touch someone's head, or to summon someone by whistling or motioning with the finger raised and beckoning; both of these techniques are reserved solely for animals. Instead, Zambians call each other over by motioning with their palm down and their fingers moving back and forth.

Eating/Meals

Habits and formalities shown during mealtimes are an extension of general Zambian etiquette. Just as use of the left hand is avoided during regular social interactions—it is associated with personal cleansing and considered impure—Zambians take care not to use their left hand when eating. Utensils are not traditionally employed at mealtimes, and the right hand, carefully washed prior to eating, is used. This usually involves a bowl of water that is circulated around the table by one of the youngest children. If there are guests present, the guests will be offered the water to wash their hands before anyone else. Otherwise, the bowl is passed around based on the status of each family member. When the meal is finished, the ritual of washing hands is repeated and the wife and youngest children clean. Traditionally, Zambians talk little while eating.

Women are customarily responsible for cooking. In the past, men and women would eat separately, with any son over the age of seven eating with the father, while the daughters and son younger than seven would eat with their mother. Although some traditional families and communities still refrain from sharing a meal, families in more urban settings often eat together.

Visiting

When entertaining a visitor, a host will commonly offer food or refreshments, such as tea, soda, and beer. It is considered polite to accept such an offering, as declining food or drink might be interpreted as discourteous, especially if the guest does not know the host well. In addition, a guest should never ask or demand anything from their hosts, and guests are expected to refuse any offers by their host to prepare food on their behalf.

Gift giving is a traditional practice, and customarily occurs once greetings and small talk are finished; it is considered impolite for guests to immediately present a gift upon arrival. Guests should bring a gift that is generally useful to the household, such as a decoration, or one that can be consumed. When handing a gift over to hosts, it is important for guests to also employ modesty, perhaps mentioning the small size of the gift. Gifts are often given and received with both hands.

LIFESTYLE

Family

In Zambian society, the extended family plays an important role in shaping and maintaining the local community. Relatives create a support structure that helps kin in times of crisis, such as when a family member has fallen ill or when there is a poor agricultural season. In the case of parents passing away, relatives traditionally assume the responsibility of raising the orphaned children. The concept of family in Zambia is so community-oriented that many of the local languages do not even have separate terms for fathers and uncles, mothers and aunts, or brothers, sisters, and cousins.

In rural, more traditional environments, the entire community or village will provide an extensive support network for families. The community is responsible for nurturing and educating all of the children. The HIV/AIDS epidemic has placed a heavy burden on these social structures, since many children have been left without a mother, father, or both. In 2015, it was estimated that the spread of HIV/AIDS has created between 290,000 and 680,000 orphans between the ages of several months to 17 years of age.

The development of urban centers has also threatened the traditional Zambian home environment. Cities separate families from their extended kin system, which results in children learning less about their specific community's culture and language. The nuclear family (mother, father and their children) is also becoming more common in urban areas.

Housing

Housing in Zambia reflects the country's widening economic disparity. Large, lavish houses with expansive yards, which were once reserved for European colonialists, are built in residential areas known as mayadi. Such dwellings are common in Zambia's cities and are occupied by the country's rich elite. In contrast, many of those same cities are home to dilapidated and overcrowded shantytowns. These informal settlements often consist of shelters made from cement or cinder blocks and covered by a corrugated tin roof. Rural homes generally consist of mud huts with thatched grass roofs. These huts will normally house an entire family in one room, and the sleeping area will serve as a cooking area.

Housing for urban poor is a widespread problem for the government, which has been attempting to improve conditions with the help of the World Bank and governmental loan schemes. Poverty and the HIV/AIDS pandemic are the main reasons for deteriorating living conditions and overcrowding. The migration of people to urban areas in search of better jobs and a higher standard of living has also resulted in congested shantytowns, since cities are not prepared to support the rising number of inhabitants.

Food

Zambia's cuisine is mild rather than spicy and relies heavily on maize (corn), which is at the heart of the country's most popular dish, nsima (also nshima). Nsima is made out of cornmeal, or dried kernels of corn that are ground very fine. Zambians refer to the cornmeal as "mielie-meal." The cornmeal has to be boiled in water and pressed down with a paddle until it has attained a thick texture. This dish is commonly eaten for lunch and dinner. Zambians generally eat nsima by forming it into a ball and then dipping it into a sauce, referred to as a "relish."

Nsima, like other popular dishes, is often served with meat sauces made from cows, goats, sheep, or fish. Vegetables are also added to these sauces or served separately in their own sauce. The vegetables that are commonly used include pumpkin, cassava, cabbage, tomatoes, and onions. Rural communities do not always have access to meat, and so their nsima is generally served with more vegetables and beans. Zambians also have other methods of cooking and utilizing maize in their dishes. For example, the maize can be pounded into a medium texture and cooked with rice. Zambians also enjoy grinding up the corn enough that the kernels shed their outer layer. The corn that remains is boiled separately or it is sometimes combined with peanuts or beans.

Life's Milestones

For Zambians, a funeral represents the time when a person's soul is believed to be most active. Generally, many funerals will last days, allowing people to travel long distances to attend. It is common for men to sit outside, separate from the women, socializing with each other and drinking. The women are generally expected to display overt expressions of grief. Local traditions differ according to the specific beliefs held by Zambia's

ethic groups, which number over seventy. For the Lenje people, the malila anene (big funeral ceremony) indicates the end of the funeral period and signifies a transition point where the spouse of the deceased is no longer expected to mourn and is once again an independent person in society. The ceremony typically incorporates traditional song and dance, including men and women dancing with mansangwa and buyombo—rattles worn on the legs and waist, respectively. In other clans, such as the Lamba community, ukupianika (cleansing) marks the death of a husband. Traditionally, this involves the village chief assigning the closest male relative of the husband the task of looking after and supporting the wife of the deceased and her children.

Another unique milestone is the mukanda, an initiation ritual practiced by the Luvale, Chokwe, Luchazi, and Mbunda peoples of western Zambia. The ritual customarily occurs in the dry season and involves young boys between the ages of eight and twelve living in isolation for up to three months at a bush camp. The completion of the ritual is acknowledged with a ceremony that includes the "Makishi Masquerade." In 2005, UNESCO proclaimed this unique dance and pantomime-like performance as one of the Masterpieces of the Oral and Intangible Heritage of Humanity.

CULTURAL HISTORY

Art

Zambia's tradition of basket weaving is an intricate and delicate art. Many baskets are a representation of the natural environment from which the basket originated, and feature a large range of designs and materials interwoven together. Most baskets are constructed out of grass reeds, although baskets can also be woven out of bamboo, roots, grasses, vines, papyrus palm leaves, bark, and sisal (a plant known for its large, tough leaves). Baskets may also be decorated and dyed with brightly colored soil, bark, leaves, and roots. Traditionally, both men and women could practice basket weaving.

Traditional weaving techniques not only produce decorative items, but utilitarian items used in the traditional Zambian household. For example, woven items, such as baskets, can be used as containers, fishing traps, and sieves for cooking, while woven mats are used for cooking, eating, and sleeping. Although the art of basketry has waned in modern times, there are organizations that strive to both preserve and inspire Zambia's woven crafts and artistic traditions. These organizations include the Nayuma Museum in Mongo, the Choma Museum, and Craft Centre in Choma, the Moto Museum in Mbala, and the Zintu Handicrafts Center in Lusaka.

Music

Music has traditionally formed the backbone of Zambian culture. Songs and melodies serve as fundamental elements in rituals and ceremonies and are used as teaching tools and for entertainment purposes. In rural villages, instruments are often unnecessary, as many songs are sung and clapped by the community while they sit or stand in a circle.

Although the popularity of traditional Zambian music has declined with the emergence of pop and contemporary forms of music, characteristics of traditional music have become infused in the contemporary music scene. The "call and response" technique used in traditional music is heard in most modern Zambian songs. Call and response involves an unprompted interaction between the singer and the audience, with the singer calling out a statement or question to be answered or accentuated by the audience. The call and response technique is commonly utilized during religious worship and song. Dance and drums have also been integrated into some Christian ceremonies in Zambia.

Zambia has a variety of distinct instruments, including the silimba, which contains a series of wooden blocks in various sizes that produce varying notes when struck, much like a xylophone. Other instruments include the thumb piano, which is a small hollowed-out box with a row of metal strips, and the kalumbu, a type of single-stringed instrument. The kalumbu is played against a stick that is attached to a calabash gourd for both stability and resonance; young men to announce publicly their readiness for marriage traditionally used it. Lastly, drums play a fundamental role in creating the rhythm intrinsic to dances. Different drums have different purposes in Zambian society, and their shapes and sounds can be dramatically dissimilar to each other.

Dance

Zambian music and dance are closely entwined. Dance uses music to further its own expressive purposes, usually by synchronizing movements to percussive beats. Similar to Zambian traditional music, dance is steeped in tradition and folklore that articulate the identity of Zambia's ethnicities and communities. For example, the Luvale people from northwestern Zambia perform Makishi at the end of Mukanda, which is an annual rite of passage for boys, during which they leave the village for a short period to become men. Makishi is elemental to the ceremonial process and celebrates manhood and ancestry. The dance at the conclusion of the ceremony entails a pantomime involving a number of masks. Each mask is symbolic of a section of tribal history and mythology.

The majority of Zambian traditional dances follow a particular routine. Most are performed outside with musicians and singers surrounding the dancers in a sizeable circle. Often an entire community may be involved, and those without a specific role will join in the singing. Dances usually begin with singing, which is often accompanied by clapping. The dance will generally begin at a slower pace and increase to a climax that is characterized by faster rhythms and intense movements of the body. At the conclusion, the dancers will often begin singing again to mark the beginning of a new sequence of dancing or the end of the dance.

Literature

Zambia's literature has been used to express the desire for Africa's political and cultural freedom from colonialism. For example, *The Tongue of the Dumb* (1971), by Dominic Mulaisho (1933–2013), focuses on the country's struggle against colonialism, and was Zambia's first popular English-language novel. It follows how colonists attempted to impose their power on Africa through control over religious and political affairs and how African communities resisted. Other Zambian works that explore issues of colonialism include Andreya Masiye's (1922–) *Before Dawn* (1970), and Binwell Sinyangwe's (1956–) *A Cowrie of Hope* (2000).

CULTURE

Arts & Entertainment

Zambia experienced a new period of musical development after independence in 1964. Congolese rumba increasing in popularity and zam-rock, characterized by guitar-based rhythms and songs that used English lyrics, emerged. The Zambia Broadcasting Service was particularly instrumental in providing access to these new styles of music. In an attempt to promote a unique, national identity in the late 1970s, President Kenneth Kaunda (1924–) instructed that 95 percent of all of the music played on the radio had to be songs by Zambian artists. This provided an opportunity for more Zambian artists to be heard by their fellow citizens. Kaunda's order resulted in a new wave of artists, who suddenly had the radio exposure necessary to popularize their music.

One of the emerging forms from this era was kalindula music, which became a fashionable form of modern Zambian pop music in the mid-1980s and is now a general term referring to Zambian pop music. Kalindula music is known for its catchy up-tempo rhythms created by the kalindula bass guitar, a four-stringed bass guitar also known as the mbabadoni. Kalindula has a homespun quality that originates from its instruments. The music often incorporates both hand-made drums and a unique guitar referred to as a "banjo" (pronounced "bahn-jo"). Zambians do not follow set specifications when creating their banjos, so banjos usually come in a wide

range of sizes and shapes. The body is most often constructed from wood, but variations of the typical banjo are created out of tin cans, with the strings usually collected from used radial tires. Oftentimes musicians will play their banjos and kalindula guitars using a two-finger and three-finger picking style reminiscent of techniques adopted from traditional Zambian music. Modern kalindula bands will frequently include modern drums and electric guitars, in addition to the more customary kalindula and banjo. Serenje Kalindula Band is credited with being the first Zambian band to establish the sounds that would exemplify kalindula.

Dance is fundamental to life in Zambia. Historical events, spiritual beliefs, and social mores are encoded into group dances. Each year, members of the Nyau brotherhood—a secret society of Chewa men—still participate in Gule Wamkulu, a ritual dance that has been held following harvests, initiation ceremonies, and weddings since the 17th century. Missionaries once attempted to ban the dance, but it persists into the present day. The rumba, imported from the Congo, has become one of the most popular dances for entertainment.

Although traditional Zambian visual art generally refrains from political and social commentary, the Zambian modern art scene is making progress toward forming an extensive and reflective arts community. The Art Academy Without Walls project, established in 1996, provides aspiring artists from Zambia with the education and environment to further their art through workshops in Zambia and an exchange program with Norway. Artists participating in the program have used the opportunity to create projects aimed at tackling pertinent issues through installations and other artistic works. Some of the most pressing issues that Zambian artists are addressing include HIV/AIDS awareness, the status of refugees, poverty, and the large orphan population.

Soccer has become Zambia's most popular sport, and most of the country's towns and villages sponsor a soccer team for local and national competition. However, soccer is usually limited to boys, with girls playing a game called netball that is closely related to basketball. Boxing is also popular in Zambia, along with rugby, badminton, tennis, and golf. In the country's many lake areas, fishing is a family pastime and the basis for national competitions. Isolo, a traditional African board game, is common in small villages and large towns throughout Zambia.

Cultural Sites & Landmarks

Victoria Falls is one of the largest and most striking waterfalls in the world. The falls straddle the border between southwestern Zambia and Zimbabwe, and were once called "shungu mumi" ("the life falls") by early hunter-gatherers. Locals in Zambia now refer to the falls as Mosi-oa-Tunya, meaning "the smoke that thunders." The powerful presence of the falls is due to the effect of water crashing down upon basalt gorges. These gorges are composed of volcanic rock, and as the water collides with the rocks, it produces a distinct, thunderous sound. Another result of the impact of water on rock is the formation of a rising, shimmering mist, which can be detected from over 20 kilometers (12 miles) away. The United Nations Educational, Scientific, and Cultural Organization (UNESCO) inscribed the falls as a World Heritage Site in 1989 for their geographical and ecological importance.

Along with its natural landscapes, Zambia is known for the diversity and abundance of its wildlife. South Luangwa National Park is an example of the country's intact natural environment and is a popular destination for walking safaris. The park, located in eastern Zambia, was originally founded in 1938 as a game reserve and became a national park in 1972. The park stretches over 9,050 square kilometers (3,494 square miles) and primarily contains areas of woodland savanna, a type of grassland characterized for its flat ground. Common inhabitants include zebra, giraffe, hippopotami, leopards, wildebeest, impalas, and elephants. However, the elephant population continues to be under occasional threat from poaching.

Lower Zambezi National Park is situated on the northwestern side of the Zambezi River in southeastern Zambia. It is best known for its flood plain, the smooth grassland floors that are adjacent to river bodies and often flooded. The park is generally toured via boat along the river or through the floodplains themselves. Highlights of the park include the varieties of large trees endemic to the area, which include the miombo and the mopane, known for its butterfly-shaped leaves. The floodplain is also the focal point of the park for its inhabitants, which include elephants, hippos, antelope, buffalo, lions, leopards, crocodiles, and a wide variety of birds. The once pervasive black rhino were extirpated around the time of the park's foundation in 1983.

Libraries & Museums

The national museum of Zambia is the Lusaka National Museum, which opened in 1996 and features a wide range of ethnographic exhibits. The museum is divided into four primary sections: ethnography, witchcraft, cultural history, and contemporary art. Other museums include the Railway Museum in the colonial city of Livingstone; Mbala's Moto Museum, which opened in 1974 and celebrates Zambian culture and folklore; the Livingstone Museum, which has four galleries—archaeology (prehistoric exhibits), ethnography and art, cultural history, and natural history—as well as exhibits dedicated to European explorer David Livingstone; and the Choma Museum and Crafts Project, in the market town of Choma, dedicated to the cultural heritage of the Tonga tribe.

Like many African nations, organized libraries were first established in Zambia during the nation's colonial period. While there is no national library, the government maintains the National Archives of Zambia. In the absence of a national library, the University of Zambia Library was designated as Zambia's national reference library.

Holidays

Zambia officially recognizes many of the holidays familiar in Western countries: Good Friday, Easter, Easter Monday, Christmas, and New Year's Day on January 1. The country also celebrates Youth Day (March 12), Labor Day (May 1), African Freedom Day (May 25), Heroes Day and Unity Day (first Monday and Tuesday in July), Farmer's Day (first week in August), and Independence Day (October 24) memorializes the country's independence from Britain in 1964.

Zambians also celebrate a number of regional festivals. Near the town of Mongu in western Zambia, Lozi people ferry their chief and his family across the Zambezi River in a state barge, called Nalikwanda and painted black and white, like the country's coat of arms. The chief and his family are transported in this way from a palace in Lealui to one in Limulungathe. Called Kuomboka (literally "to get out of water" in Lozi), the festival surrounding the event marks the end of the rainy season.

The Ngoni celebrate N'Cwala in the eastern town of Mutenguleni in late February. The festival is accompanied by music, dancing, and feasting all to commemorate the arrival of the Ngoni in Zambia in 1835.

Youth Culture

Many of Zambia's youth struggle to find a balance between adhering to the traditional values and customs of their culture and a desire to follow modern trends. Teenagers in urban areas are increasingly adopting Western popular culture, such as fashion and music, but this often creates conflict within the home environment.

Zambian society is conservative with regard to dress. According to Zambian customs, the thigh area is considered one of the most private areas on a woman's body and should not be revealed in public. Society dictates that women should publicly wear a chitenge (also kitenge), a strip of cloth traditionally worn as a skirt, or another conservative outfit, such as a long skirt or dress. Since most young women are trained from a young age to wear a chitenge at home and a school uniform at school, many are experimenting with miniskirts as a form of rebellion. Still, few choose to wear a miniskirt in public, and will only wear a miniskirt at home, due to the belief that it is a sign of disrespect to one's elders, in addition to its associations with immorality.

SOCIETY

Transportation

Both the highway system and the rail network function as important ways of connecting the Zambia's main cities and towns, and often run alongside each other throughout the country. The Lusaka-Copperbelt Road is the most frequently used interprovincial roadway. Zambia Railways Limited (ZRL) is the country's primary rail network, although there are others, like the binational TAZARA Railway, which connects Zambia to Tanzania. Buses and minibuses are common modes of public transportation, with express-style buses servicing main routes. Zambians drive on the left-hand side of the road.

Transportation Infrastructure

Lusaka serves as the junction for every mode of transportation within Zambia (each of the four primary highways for the nation radiate from the city center). The capital is home to the junction of the Great North Road, which leads to Tanzania, the Great East Road, which leads to Malawi, and rail connections which transport people and goods to the historic cities of Livingstone and Ndola (Zambia's second largest city), as well as the country of Tanzania.

Lusaka also serves Zambia with the nation's only international airport, Kenneth Kaunda International (before 2011, Lusaka International), which is located 27 kilometers (16 miles) to the east of the city. In 2012, the airport served an estimated 787,000 people. Besides Kaunda International, there are seven other paved airports and 80 unpaved airfields. After the national airline, Zambian Airways, ceased operations in January 2009, the government has allowed air charter companies to handle transports of people, cargo, mining equipment, and humanitarian aid.

Since Zambia is a landlocked country, it relies on its neighbors for seaports and shipping. This dependence on other countries for the transportation of goods is vital to Zambia's economy. The political conflict that has occurred in neighboring countries, such as Angola and the

Democratic Republic of the Congo, has caused Zambia to reconsider its transportation system.

Media & Communications

Zambia's media is largely state-run and limited, but private media outlets have been steadily establishing their own voice since the United National Independence Party (UNIP) was politically defeated in 1991. The government also operates several popular print sources as well, including the *Zambia Daily Mail* and *Times of Zambia*. These resources publish articles from a pro-government stance, rather than including opposing viewpoints. The state also runs a single TV channel and three primary radio stations through the Zambia National Broadcasting Corporation (ZNBC). However, there are approximately twenty-four privately owned radio stations operating within Zambia. Poverty and illiteracy are obstacles preventing the media from reaching the general Zambian population.

There are a few laws that have been utilized by the government to keep journalists in check. For instance, insulting or defaming the president publicly was formerly considered a criminal offense and has been used to censure the media. Reporters, who cover stories on fraud and corruption within the Zambian government, must still be wary of the information they release to the public. In March 2009, the draft for a new constitution contained provisions that would prohibit such regulation of the media, and would promote the freedom of the press. However, Freedom House, an independent, international watchdog group, has downgraded Zambia's press from "Partly Free" in 2013 to "Not Free" in 2014, citing the late president Michael Sata's repeated arrests and detention of independent journalists and media outlet representatives, his blocking of websites, and his denial of broadcasting licenses to some media outlets.

According to 2012 estimates, cellular phone usage far eclipsed landline telephone usage, with 82,500 landlines and 10.5 million mobile phones. As of June 2013, there were an estimated 1.9 million Internet users, representing 13.5 percent of the population. The Zambian government keeps a close eye on the Internet reaching citizens and has previously worked to close down sites, like *Zambian Watchdog*, that provide content unfavorable to the government. *Zambian Watchdog*, however, is hosted outside Zambia, and efforts to take the site down were unsuccessful.

SOCIAL DEVELOPMENT

Standard of Living

Zambia ranked 141st on the 2009 United Nations Human Development Index (HDI), which measures quality of life indicators. The UN classifies the country as having "medium human development."

Water Consumption

Access to safe water and poor sanitation are prevalent issues in Zambia and are cited as two fundamental reasons for continued poverty and illness. According to a 2015 report, 51.3 percent of rural households had access to safe drinking water, but only 35.7 percent had access to improved sanitation. In cities and towns, 2015 statistics indicate that 85.6 percent of these urban households had access to safe water, while just 55.6 percent of that same population had access to improved sanitation. In these urban areas, where potable water is more available, broken infrastructure remains a persistent problem, making water distribution and sanitation increasingly complicated as the infrastructure continues to age.

According to the government, Zambia has an adequate supply of either groundwater or surface water resources, but the extraction of these resources, particularly in a sustainable or efficient manner, remains an issue.

Education

Zambian children are required to complete seven years of education (four years of lower primary school and three years of upper primary) beginning at age six. Students may then attend two years of junior secondary school and three years of senior secondary school. Students must pass national competitive examinations created by the Examination Council of Zambia at the end of seventh, ninth, and twelfth grade in order to progress to the next level of education. The country's two major public universities, the University of Zambia and Copperbelt University, provide four-year college degree programs. The University of Zambia also provides graduate degrees. Ten other universities—including the University of Lusaka, founded in 2007; the Seventh-Day Adventist Rusangu University, established in 2002; and the public Mulungushi University—demonstrate the continued development of Zambia's education system.

Despite pervasive poverty and disease, attendance in the compulsory years of primary school has improved and, according to UNICEF, stands 81.3 percent for males and 81.8 percent for girls. However, only 38.2 percent of boys and 35.6 percent of girls proceed from primary school to secondary school, and, in 2015, the literacy rate was less than 71 percent among adult men and just 56 percent among adult women.

Zambia's education system remains strained by the country's demographics. A high mortality rate (associated with HIV/AIDS) and a high fertility rate have left Zambia with a very young population. The median age in the country is 16.7 years.

Women's Rights

Zambian society has created and maintained a restricted environment for women. In urban households, women are generally relegated to domestic responsibilities, such as cooking, cleaning, and child rearing. Likewise, women living in rural areas have similar tasks and are further expected to perform agrarian duties as well. Even though Zambian society reserves the utmost respect for its oldest generations, Zambia's patriarchal hierarchy still values men over elderly women. This means that elderly women are still placed in a subordinate role, and are generally expected to cater to men. Interesting to note, however, is that women, ages 16 to 49, are classified as "manpower" for the Zambian Defence Force, although there is no conscription now. Yet,

upon serving, female soldiers carry out the same duties as their male counterparts.

Zambian law indeed espouses equality for men and women, but women experience discrimination in work and academic environments. There are no formal laws regarding sexual harassment against women, and sexual harassment at work is a common occurrence. Few companies will allow women to borrow money, which has kept women reliant on their husbands for financial matters. The imbalance between the rights of men versus women is especially conspicuous when it comes to property, marriage, and inheritance. Traditionally, the estate of any man that has passed away will be divided according to the wishes of his family. This frequently allows relatives to assume parts of an estate without any legal repercussions. By law, the children of the man will divide half of his property, while the widow and the man's parents both are given 20 percent, respectively, and the remaining relatives receive 10 percent. If a man were married to more than one woman, the 20 percent allocated to the widow would be divided equally between all the wives.

In January 2015, newly elected president Edgar Chagwa Lungu (1956–) appointed Inonge Mutukwa Wina (1941–) vice president of the country. Wina is the first women ever to hold such a prominent position in the country, a fact that bodes well for the progress of women's rights, both political and social, within the country.

Domestic violence is a prevalent issue, especially since there are no laws explicitly protecting women from domestic abuse. Law does not prohibit marital rape. Although the police intervene in cases of abuse in the home, they often try to mediate the situation rather than filing a public report and taking legal action. The unwillingness by authorities to interfere in cases of domestic violence is indicative of larger cultural reservations and traditional gender roles. Women will rarely report any cases of domestic abuse themselves and will often not cooperate with authorities or humanitarian groups when questioned about abuse.

The narrow freedoms allowed Zambian women have also exacerbated the HIV/AIDS epidemic. Women interviewed for a 2007 Human Rights Watch (HRW) study claimed that they frequently chose not to participate in free HIV testing and counseling services because they feared the reactions of their husbands. Fear of violent reprisals was also cited as a reason for avoiding HIV treatment, a concern that persists in 2015. Since women have little control or say over issues of sexual relations, programs to curb the spread of the virus have had little success. Husbands are still encouraged to engage in as many relationships as they would like without consequence, and women are encouraged to obey their husbands.

Health Care

Zambia's health care system has undergone significant changes since 1963. After gaining its independence from Britain, Zambia experienced an economic boom that allowed the government to provide free basic health care to its citizens. Following a long period of recession in the late 1970s and 1980s and the increase of HIV/AIDS in the region, Zambia's health system became one of the most understaffed and overstretched systems in the world.

Since the early 1990s, Zambia's government has been working with international charitable organizations and the World Bank to redesign the health care system. At present, Zambia's health centers and district hospitals work under district supervision with grants provided by the state or by charitable organizations. These health centers and local hospitals provide basic health care needs at some charge based on the patient's ability to pay. Patients may opt for pre-paid health care accounts or for private health insurance to assist with future health care costs. In 2013, health care expenditures accounted for 5 percent of the GDP. In addition, while there were two hospital beds for every 1,000 people, there was less than one doctor for the same number of patients.

Malaria, plague, bacterial diarrhea, typhoid, hepatitis A, and schistosomiasis (a water-borne parasite carried by snails) are common in certain areas of the country. As a result, the infant mortality rate stands at nearly 65 deaths for every 1,000 live births (2015 estimate). Life expectancy for men is nearly 51 years, and for women, it is 54 years.

GOVERNMENT

Structure

Introduced to the European empires by 18th-century Portuguese explorers, Zambia developed into a colonial center of mining under the British South Africa Company in the last years of the 19th century. Under the British, the country became known as Northern Rhodesia, and most of its resources were used to support the colonial administration in Southern Rhodesia (now Zimbabwe). Northern Rhodesia did not gain its independence until 1964, when it took the name Zambia. Since 1964, the young African republic has battled government corruption and one failed coup in 1997.

The first multiparty election took place in 2001. Of the 158 total members of Zambia's National Assembly, 150 are elected by popular vote to five-year terms, and the president appoints an additional eight. Zambia's president serves as both chief of state and head of government. The president is elected by popular vote to a maximum of two five-year terms. The vice president is appointed by the president.

Political Parties

Between 1972 and 1991, Zambia was a one-party state, dominated by the United National Independence Party (UNIP) led by Kenneth Kaunda (1924–), who was the country's first president, from 1964 to 1991. All other political parties were banned during this period. However, 1991 marked the reintroduction of a multiparty system, a change spearheaded by Frederick Chiluba (1943–2011) and his Movement for Multiparty Democracy (MMD), founded in 1990 as opposition to UNIP. Many UNIP members ultimately defected to MMD, and Chiluba became

Zambia's second president. Currently, the left wing, democratic-socialist Patriotic Front (PF) is in power, with its leader Edgar Chagwa Lungu installed since January 2015 as the country's sixth president. Since the 2015 election, PF currently holds 72 parliamentary seats, the socialist-democratic MMD holds 34 seats, and the liberal United Party for National Development (UPND) has 32, while one seat each went to the Alliance for Democracy and Development (ADD) and the Forum for Democracy and Development (FDD).

Local Government

Since 2013, local government is divided among the country's ten provinces: Eastern, Central, Luapula, Muchinga, Northern, Northwestern, Copperbelt, Western, Southern and Lusaka provinces. These provinces, previously divided into 72 districts, are now subdivided into 103 districts, each with a local council or municipal authority that oversees them. District distribution is as follows: Central Province has 11; Copperbelt has 10; Eastern has nine; Luapula has 11; Lusaka has eight; the country's newest province, Muchinga, has seven; Northern has nine; North-Western has 11; Southern has 13; and Western has 16 districts.

Judicial System

Zambia's judicial system consists of a Supreme Court, a High Court, and an Industrial Relations Court. There are numerous subordinate (magistrates) and local courts. The Supreme Court is the final court of appeal, and Supreme Court judges are appointed by the president, based on recommendations made by the nine-member Judicial Service Commission headed by the chief justice. Ultimately, the National Assembly vets and ratifies each appointment. In March 2010, the government launched a computerization of its judicial system—the Zambia Justice Information System (ZAJIS)—the first of its kind in Africa. However, after failing to secure continued donor funding, neglecting to follow internationally recognized records management standards, and encountering difficulty with digital storage issues, the government abandoned the plan.

Taxation

The Zambia Revenue Authority oversees taxation. Personal income can be taxed at a graduated rate of 25, 30, and 35 percent, depending on income level, while a value-added tax (VAT) is levied at a flat rate of 16 percent. Corporate taxation is levied at a 35 percent rate, for both resident and non-resident businesses. Other administered taxes include import and excise duties, withholding tax (20 percent), and property transfer tax (three percent). The agriculture, mining, and banking industries pay slightly different rates than the standard percentage imposed on other business' corporate income: agriculture and chemical fertilizer companies pay fifteen percent, mining pays 30 percent, and banks pay 40 percent. There is no tax on capital gains. However, a new mineral royalty tax was implemented on January 1, 2015.

Armed Forces

The Zambian Defence Force (ZDF) is made up of the Zambia Army, the Zambia Air Force, and the Zambian National Service (ZNS), which was established in 1968 with food security and agriculture as two of its primary objectives. In 2008, the armed forces numbered approximately 15,100, a number that has remained largely unchanged since 2003. Military service is not compulsory in Zambia. There is no conscription. However, all must register nationally upon turning sixteen, at which age anyone may volunteer with parental consent. Both males and females may otherwise voluntarily serve between 18 and 25 years of age. Zambia citizenship and a certificate verifying graduation from grade twelve is required. HIV testing is mandatory upon enlistment.

Foreign Policy

Zambia joined the United Nations (UN) a month after it gained independence in 1964, and has participated as a member in a number of international organizations, including the Commonwealth of Nations, the African Union (AU), the International Monetary Fund (IMF), and the World Health Organization (WHO). During his inauguration speech in November

2008, President Rupiah Banda (1937–), who was president from 2008 to 2011, declared that Zambia would remain an active participant in the AU, the Southern African Development Community (SADC), and the Common Market for Eastern and Southern Africa (COMESA) under his administration. This has indeed continued into 2015 under the presidency of Edgar Lungu (1956–). Zambia has supplied troops in support of UN peacekeeping missions in Rwanda, Angola, Mozambique, and Sierra Leone.

Zambia relies on foreign investment for future development. According to the Zambian government, foreign investment rose from $255 million (USD) in 2003 to over $4.25 billion (USD) in 2008. By 2013, this figure rose to $1,630,364,000 (USD). China is one of the many countries contributing hundreds of millions of dollars toward Zambia's development, including the construction of the Tan-Zam (now TAZARA) Railway in the 1970s, maintenance, and development of Zambia's copper mines since the turn of the 21st century. In 2006, the Chinese government was alleged to have tried to sway the presidential election by implying that it would end all diplomatic relations and stop all investments indefinitely if Michael Sata (1937–2014), the favored non-incumbent, was voted into office. (Sata antagonized China by implying that he would recognize Taiwan as a sovereign state and publicizing the mistreatment of workers in mines run by Chinese nationals.)

Zambia is surrounded by eight countries, including Zimbabwe, Angola, Mozambique, Tanzania, and the Democratic Republic of the Congo (DRC). Since Zambia is a landlocked nation, it considers it a priority to maintain friendly relations with its neighbors, particularly since it must rely on these neighbors for transportation of exports. In the past, the country has experienced territorial disputes, especially in the areas around the Zambia-DRC border, and the land where Namibia, Botswana, Zimbabwe, and Zambia meet. Nevertheless, Zambia remains in good stead with its neighbors and has supported them in times of political unrest and war.

The government never adopted the refugee laws as established by the 1951 UN convention, but it created its own unique protocol for protecting refugees and offering them asylum. As of 2009, Zambia was housing an estimated 85,000 refugees from the DRC, Angola, Rwanda, and Burundi. Zambia was also responsible for the repatriation of around 10,000 refugees from the DRC in 2008. By 2014, the number of refugees from DRC had nearly doubled to 18,598. The Zambian government worked in association with the UN High Commissioner for Refugees (UNHCR) and other international humanitarian organizations when supplying shelter and governmental protection to refugees.

Human Rights Profile

International human rights law insists that states respect civil and political rights and promote an individual's economic, social, and cultural rights. The United Nations Universal Declaration on Human Rights (UDHR) is recognized as the standard for international human rights. Its authors sought the counsel of the world's great thinkers, philosophers, and religious leaders and were careful to create a document that reflects the core values shared by every world culture. (To read this document or view the articles relating to cultural human rights, visit http://www.ohchr.org/EN/UDHR/Pages/Introduction.aspx.)

The Zambian government generally tries to adhere to basic international law regarding human rights, and its constitution provides for many of the freedoms articulated in the UDHR. However, Zambia still exhibits a large number of human rights violations. As of 2012, these continued to include cases of arbitrary arrest and detention, torture, extrajudicial killings (unauthorized killings by authoritative and government officials), governmental immunity from the law, and a lack of freedom of speech, among other injustices.

Although Zambian laws call for a tolerance and equal treatment of all its citizens, there are no laws explicitly protecting the physically or mentally disabled. Disabled persons often face considerable hurdles due to societal prejudices, which they encounter when attending school, when applying for jobs, and when trying to acquire healthcare. Additionally, there are few buildings that are handicapped-accessible, and public services or support groups for the mentally and physically disabled are scarce. HIV/AIDS is a sensitive subject, and those with HIV/AIDS have a strong stigma attached to them, which manifests into marginalization in the workplace and society.

Article 5 of the UDHR prohibits the use of torture or inhumane methods of punishment. Although these rights are reflected in the Zambian constitution, the Zambian police force often fails to adhere to these laws. Police brutality is common, and the Human Rights Commission (HRC) reported in 2006 that police often use torture as a means of interrogation. Zambia's prisons have also been overwhelmed with issues of overcrowding and squalid living conditions. The prison system is known for poor sanitation, which is only worsened by the high number of inmates. For example, Lusaka Central Prison, built to house only 200 prisoners, contained more than 1,500 inmates in 2008 and 1,738 in 2010. In addition, prisoners are often deprived of medical treatment, and the medical facilities within the prison walls are consistently rated poorly. These prisons have also been criticized for combining a prisoner's food rations into one daily meal. This technique for distributing food has led to severe cases of malnutrition among prisoners.

According to Article 12, there should be no concern for random intrusions by the government into a person's private and home life. While Zambian law usually requires police and governmental authorities to have a warrant when arresting a person, there are exceptions to the rule. For instance, if a person is suspected of treason, slander against the president, illegal assembly, and inciting a riot or rebellion, then authorities are not obligated to obtain a warrant under law. In general, the police rarely arrest people with warrants, and the police force has been criticized for arbitrarily detaining, arresting, and sometimes abusing, family members or acquaintances of criminal suspects.

Article 20 of the UDHR involves the right to form a peaceful assembly. Citizens are allowed to assemble publicly, although there are limitations to this right, as established by the government. The government has the power to choose when and where public demonstrations will be held, and who may participate. Police have also been known to use armed force to break up rallies. During a University of Zambia protest in May 2008, two students were shot and killed by police. In 2014, the Inter-Parliamentary Union called for an amendment to a Public Order Act (POA) that prevents parliamentary officials from meeting outside the parliamentary context and permits their harassment by police. In 2014, Dora Siliya, Maxwell Mwale, and Hastings Sililo all opposition party MPs, were charged with illegal political practices and disqualified from serving in the National Assembly because they met outside the accepted legislative context. In May 2015, however, MMD member Dora Siliya defected to the Patriotic Front.

ECONOMY

Overview of the Economy

Zambia's gross domestic product (GDP) was estimated to be $61.05 billion (USD) in 2014, a significant increase from the country's $12.3 billion GDP of 2009. The country remains one of the most urbanized sub-Saharan nations, and, for this reason, its GDP growth rate is expected to be higher than the average for the sub-Saharan region—six percent as compared to two percent—moving forward. As of 2014, this growth rate stood at 5.4 percent, down slightly from 6.7 percent in 2013 and 6.8 in 2012.

Industry

Zambia's 20th-century economy was built on copper mining and processing, originally operated by the colonial government. The industry was privatized in 2002, to the benefit of the Zambian economy. Several smaller industries have appeared in recent decades, including emerald mining, construction, and the production of foodstuffs, beverages, chemicals, textiles, fertilizer, and horticulture. Together, these comprise nearly 33 percent of the GDP.

Labor

Zambia's workforce as estimated at 6.338 million in 2014, with approximately 85 percent working in the agricultural sector, six percent in the industrial sector, and nine percent in the services sector. Zambia's unemployment rate was roughly 50 percent at the turn of the 21st century. In 2008, it dropped to 15 percent, but it continues to be an area of significant concern, as it contributes to both Zambia's widespread poverty, which stands at 60.5 percent, and overall lack of development.

Energy/Power/Natural Resources

Zambia's natural resources include copper, cobalt, zinc, lead, coal, emeralds, gold, silver, uranium, and more recently, hydropower. After decades of decline due in part to falling prices on the international market, Zambia's copper industry has rebounded. The industry was privatized in 2002, and copper exports have since increased by roughly 25 percent. In fact, copper and corn saw the country through the worst parts of the 2008 global economic recession. Still, the metal's economic productivity faltered for Zambia slightly in 2014 in the face of competition from the Democratic Republic of Congo, which surpassed Zambia in copper production. As of January 1, 2015, a new mineral royalty tax is expected to significantly increased government revenue.

Forestry

As of 2011, an estimated 66.3 percent of Zambia was forested. However, unsustainable forestry practices have been a concern. In recent years, the forestry and timber industries have become privatized. Soft and hardwood timber make up the bulk of forestry products.

Mining/Metals

Zambia's 20th-century economy was built on copper mining and processing. After decades of decline due in part to falling prices on the international market, the country's copper industry has rebounded. The industry was privatized in 2002, and copper exports have since increased by roughly 25 percent. Other natural resources include cobalt, zinc, lead, coal, emeralds, gold, silver, and uranium.

Agriculture

According to early 21st-century statistics, approximately 85 percent of the population labors in the agricultural sector, but it accounts for 11 percent of the GDP. Zambia's temperate climate and fertile soils provide good conditions for agricultural production, although the increase in agricultural activities in recent decades has meant a decline in the country's valuable woodlands. Still, the UN estimates that only 4.8 percent of Zambia's land is arable, while nearly 27 percent is dedicated to pasture and grazing areas.

Small farmers and large-scale farms typically produce corn, sorghum, rice, peanuts, sunflower seed, vegetables, flowers, tobacco, cotton, sugarcane, coffee, and cassava.

Animal Husbandry

Farmers raise cattle, goats, pigs, sheep, and poultry for the production of meat, milk, eggs, and hides.

Tourism

Historically, tourism has had little impact in Zambia, due in part to the political policies and economic collapse of the 1970s and 1980s in the country. However, between 2000 and 2008, the country reported a 28 percent increase in hotel numbers. Large-scale investments continue to grow the country's hospitality and tourism industry, and in 2008, despite the ongoing global economic crisis, the country recorded a five percent increase in tourists, resulting in an almost eight percent increase in tourism revenue. Numbers continue to increase: in 2013, the World Bank estimates that the country saw 915,000 international inbound visitors, an increase of 56,000 people from the previous year. Guided tours in Zambia generally focus on Victoria Falls, the Zambezi River, and the wealth of wildlife that still inhabits Zambia's plains and forests.

Danielle Chu, Amy Witherbee, Lynn-nore Chittom, Savannah Schroll Guz

DO YOU KNOW?

- Zambia takes its name from the Zambezi River. Its name under British colonization, Southern Rhodesia, was taken from English executive and mining magnate, Cecil Rhodes.

- Victoria Falls, called Mosi-oa-Tunya ("the smoke that thunders") by locals, is said to be longest curtain of water in the world at 1,708 meters (5,604 feet) high. In 1855, Scottish missionary and explorer David Livingstone found the falls, which are located along the Zambezi River that borders both Zambia and Zimbabwe. He named the falls in honor of Queen Victoria, but its indigenous name is Mosi-oa-Tunya.

Bibliography

Andrew Sardanis. "Zambia: The First 50 Years." London, UK: I.B. International Library of African Studies Ser. *Tauris*, 2014.

Christina Lamb. "The Africa House: The True Story of an English Gentleman and His African Dream." Internat. Ed. New York: *HarperCollins Publishers*, Inc., 2004.

Dan O'Brien. "The Struggle for Control of Education in Zambia: From the Colonial Period to the Present." Lewiston: *Mellen Press*, 2006.

Douglas G. Anglin. "Zambian Crisis Behaviour: Confronting Rhodesia's Unilateral Declaration of Independence, 1965–1966." Montreal: *McGill-Queen's University Press*, 1994.

Kate Crehan. "The Fractured Community: Landscapes of Power and Gender in Rural Zambia." Perspectives on Southern Africa Ser. London: *University of California Press*, Ltd., 1997.

Marcia Burdette. "Zambia: Between Two Worlds." Boulder: *Westview Press*, 1988.

Mwelwa Musambachime. "Basic Facts on Zambia." Bloomington: *AuthorHouse*, 2005.

Patrick E. Idoye. "Theatre and Social Change in Zambia: The Chikwakwa Theatre." Lewiston: *Mellen Press*, 2006.

Robert I. Rotberg. "The Rise of Nationalism in Central Africa: The Making of Malawi and Zambia, 1873–1964." 2nd ed. Cambridge: *Harvard University Press*, 1972.

William D. Grant. "Zambia, Then and Now: Colonial Rulers and Their African Successors." 2nd ed. New York: *Routledge*, 2014.

Works Cited

_____. "Mosi-oa-Tunya/Victoria Falls." *UNESCO World Heritage Centre*, 2015. http://whc.unesco.org/en/list/509.

"Art Academy Without Walls Zambia." *Zambia National Visual Arts Council/Statens Kunstakademi*, 2015. http://www.aaww-zambia.com/.

"International tourism, number of arrivals." The World Bank Data. *The World Bank Group*, 2015. http://data.worldbank.org/indicator/ST.INT.ARVL.

"Dora Silva Officially Defects to the PF." *Lusaka Times*, 3 May 2015. https://www.lusakatimes.com/2015/05/03/dora-siliya-officially-defects-to-pf/.

"IPU urges Zambia to protect MPs right to assemble freely." Press Briefing Note. *Inter-Parliamentary Union*, 26 Sept. 2014. http://www.ipu.org/press-e/pressnote201409262.htm.

"Introducing Lower Zambezi National Park." *Lonely Planet*, 2015. http://www.lonelyplanet.com/zambia/southeastern-zambia/lower-zambezi-national-park.

"Southern Africa: Rupiah Banda off to Swaziland for SADC Summit." Times of Zambia. *AllAfrica*, 30 Mar. 2009. http://allafrica.com/stories/200903300157.html.

"The Makishi Masquerade." Third Proclamation of Masterpieces of the Oral and Intangible Heritage of Humanity. *UNESCO World Heritage Center*, 2005. http://www.unesco.org/culture/intangible-heritage/42afr_uk.htm.

"Zambia: Enact law to curb sexual violence." *Human Rights Watch*, 10 Dec. 2008. http://www.hrw.org/en/news/2008/12/10/zambia-enact-law-curb-sexual-violence.

"Zambia: HIV and AIDS estimates (2014)" *UNAIDS*, 2015. http://www.unaids.org/en/regionscountries/countries/zambia.

"Zambia: Statistics." *UNICEF*, 31 Dec. 2013. http://www.unicef.org/infobycountry/zambia_statistics.html.

"Zambian Watchdog." *Zambian Watchdog*, 2015. http://www.zambiawatchdog.com/.

"Zambia." Freedom of the Press. *Freedom House*, 2015. https://freedomhouse.org/report/freedom-press/2014/zambia.

Celia W. Dugger. "Report Calls Zambia's Prisons 'Death Traps'." *New York Times Company*, 27 Apr. 2010. http://www.nytimes.com/2010/04/28/world/africa/28zambia.html?_r=0.

Ernest Douglas Brown. "Drums of Life: Royal Music and Social Life in Western Zambia." *University of Washington*, 1984.

Hugh Tracy. "Ngoma: An Introduction to Music for Southern Africans." London: *Longmans*, 1948.

Jean Marie Allman,. "Fashioning Africa: Power and the Politics of Dress." Bloomington: *Indiana University Press*, 2004.

Jeffrey Jensen Arnett, Ed. "International Encyclopedia of Adolescence: A Historical and Cultural Survey of Young People Around the World." 2 vols. London: *Routledge*, 2006.

Karen Tranberg Hansen. "Getting Stuck in the Compound: Some Odds against Social Adulthood in Lusaka, Zambia." *Africa Today* 51.4 (2005): 2–16.

Kelvin Kachingwe. "Zambia: Media Resists Calls for State Regulation." *IPS News*. Inter Press Service News Agency, 30 Mar. 2009. http://ipsnews.net/news.asp?idnews=46322.

Michael Joseph Gross. "Travel: Chasing the Ultimate Waterfall." *New York Times Company*, 18 Mar. 2007. http://query.nytimes.com/gst/fullpage.html?res=9C07E1D71031F93BA25750C0A9619C8B63&sec=travel&spon=&pagewanted=all .

Pat Coate. "Refugees living in Zambia will receive continued assistance, UN official pledges." *Great News Network*. GNN, 22 Aug. 2007. http://www.greatnewsnetwork.org/index.php/news/article/refugees_living_in_zambia_will_receive_continued_assistance_un_official_ple/?source=rss.

Rupiah Banda. "Zambia/Inauguration speech by President Rupiah Banda." African Press Organization. *Wordpress*, 2 November 2008. http://appablog.wordpress.com/2008/11/02/zambia-inauguration-speech-by-president-rupiah-banda-november-2-2008/.

Simon Gikandi. "Encyclopedia of African Literature." London: *Taylor & Francis*, 2003.

Stephen D. Glazier. *"Encyclopedia of African and African-American Religions."* London: *Taylor & Francis*, 2001.

Scott D. Taylor. "Culture and Customs of Zambia." Santa Barbara: *Greenwood Press*, 2000.

Wilson Zimba. "Managing humanitarian programmes in least-developed countries: the case of Zambia." *Humanitarian Exchange Magazine* 34 (July 2006). ODI HPN, 2011. http://www.odihpn.org/report.asp?id=2819.

The mbira, also known as a thumb piano, is a traditional instrument of Zimbabwean music.

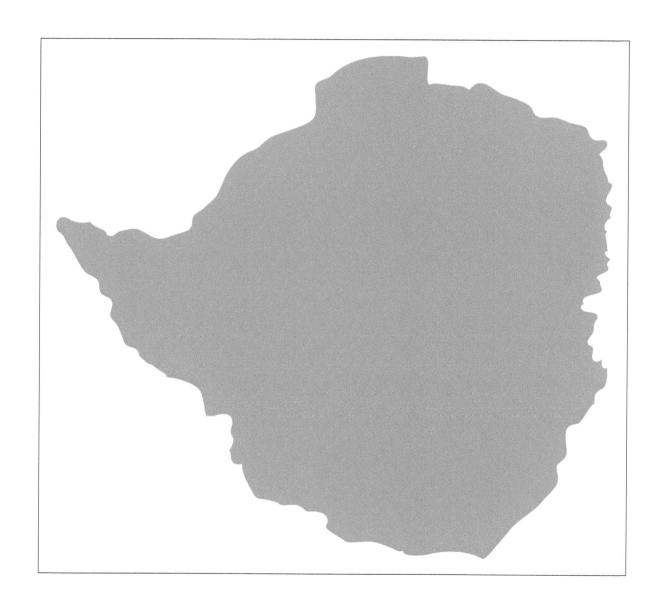

ZIMBABWE

Introduction

The Republic of Zimbabwe is a small landlocked country in southern Africa. It is bordered on the north and northwest by Zambia, on the southwest by Botswana, on the east by Mozambique, and on the south by South Africa.

Zimbabwe consists of eight provinces and two cities with provincial status. Provinces include Manicaland, Mashonaland Central, Mashonaland East, Mashonaland West, Masvingo, Matabeleland North, Matabeleland South, Midlands. The two city-provinces are Bulawayo and Harare.

Formerly known as Rhodesia, the country gained its independence from the United Kingdom in 1980. In the years since independence, international officials have accused President (and former Prime Minister) Robert Mugabe of election tampering, including intimidation and outright violence against opposition party members, as well as other human rights abuses. Mugabe has also been criticized for the country's economic collapse following his introduction of a controversial 1997 land redistribution plan, which caused an exodus of white farmers from the country. He also imposed price controls in 2007, which created a financial panic. In 2013, a new constitution was passed by 95 percent referendum vote. The new constitution will limit the president to two five-year terms. However, the constitutional mandate is not retroactive, making Mugabe again eligble for election. And indeed, Mugabe again ran and won in July 2013, although there were widespread accusations political intimidation and election fraud.

Still, despite the country's inhospitable government and difficult economic environment, one of the greatest challenges facing Zimbabwe in the 21st century is the HIV/AIDS epidemic, which affects nearly 17 percent of the adult population.

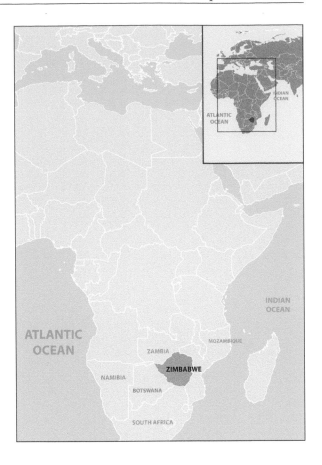

GENERAL INFORMATION

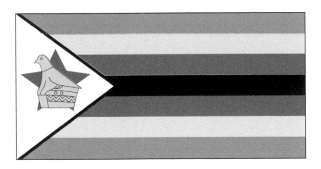

Official Languages: English, *Shona*, Ndebele, twelve tribal dialects, and sign language.
Population: 14,229,541 (July 2015 estimate)
Currency: US Dollar (as of June 12, 2015; the Zimbabwean dollar was abandoned on April 12,

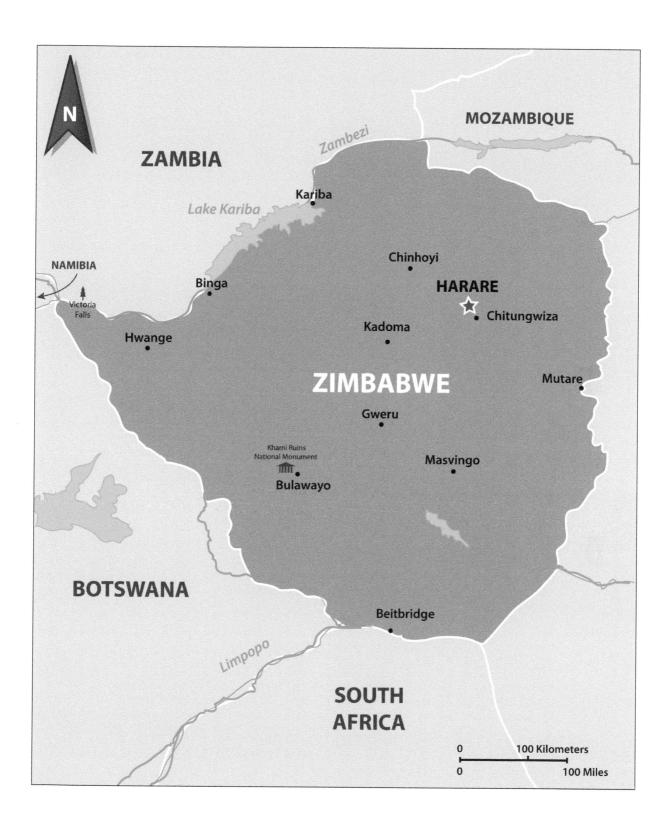

Principal Cities by Population (2012):

- Harare (1,485,231)
- Bulawayo (653,337)
- Chitungwiza (356,840)
- Mutare (187,621)
- Gweru (157,865)
- Kwekwe (100,900)
- Kadoma (92,469)
- Masvingo (87,886)
- Chinhoyi (77,929)
- Marondera (61,998)

2009, following a period of hyperinflation; a six-currency system of legal tender was adopted between 2009 and 2015).

Coins: Zimbabwean Bond Coins were issued on December 18, 2014. They exist in denominations of 1, 5, 10, and 25 cents and correspond to US coin values. In March 2015, a 50-cent coin was also issued.

Land Area: 386,847 square kilometers (149,362 square miles)

Water Area: 3,910 square kilometers (1,510 square miles)

National Anthem: "Blessed Be the Land of Zimbabwe" (Ndebele: "Kalibusiswe Ilizwe leZimbabwe"; Shona: "Simudzai Mureza wedu WeZimbabwe")

National Motto: "Unity, Freedom, Work"

Capital: Harare

Time Zone: Central Africa Time (CAT)/GMT +2

Flag: The flag of Zimbabwe features three horizontal bands of green, yellow and red, and one central black band. The green represents agriculture and the yellow represents mineral wealth. The red represents the blood lost in the struggle to achieve independence, and the black represents the country's native people. On the hoist side of the flag, inside a white equilateral triangle, a stylized yellow bird sits over a five-pointed red star. The red star represents Marxism, while the yellow bird represents a soapstone statuette found at the ruins of Great Zimbabwe, a historic city in the country's southeastern hills.

Population

More than 99 percent of the population of Zimbabwe is African. The Shona constitute the majority of the population, at more than 70 percent; the Ndebele account for approximately 16 percent. White Europeans account for 0.4 percent of the population and, until recently, held a disproportionate amount of power and wealth in the country.

As of 2015, more than 32.4 percent of the population lives in urban areas, and the rate of urbanization between 2010 and 2015 was 32.4 percent. The two major cities are Harare, the capital (population 1,485,231), and Bulawayo (population 653,337).

The HIV/AIDS epidemic has devastated Zimbabwe's population, but has improved slightly since 2009, when infection numbers were extremely high. As of 2013, approximately 15 percent of the population is infected, and 63,900 died from the disease in 2013. This is down from 160,000 in 2009.

The average age in the country is twenty, and 38 percent of the population is under the age of fifteen. Average life expectancy was fifty-seven years in 2015, down from sixty-one years in 1990. As of 2015, the infant mortality rate was 26 deaths per 1,000 live births.

Languages

As of 2015, Zimbabwe has sixteen official languages. The three major languages are English, Shona, and Ndebele. Twelve tribal dialects are also acknowledged with official status, including: Chewa, Chibarwe, Kalanga, Koisan, Nambya, Ndau, Shangani, Sotho, Tonga, Tswana, Venda, and Xhosa. Finally, sign language is also recognized as an official language. Shona is the most widely spoken, followed by Ndebele, and then English, which is used for official government business.

Native People & Ethnic Groups

Over 85 percent of the population of Zimbabwe belongs to two major ethnic tribal groups. The Shona are, Zimbabwe's largest, and comprise more than 70 percent of the population. The

Shona are the most closely related to the country's native people. Bantu-speaking Shona ancestors migrated to Zimbabwe more than 2,000 years ago, during the Iron Age. Languages that the Shona speak include the own Niger-Congo language, also called Shona (and one or more of its five dialects—Korekore, Zezuru, Manyika, Karanga, and Ndau); English; and, sometimes, Portuguese.

The Ndebele make up approximately 16 percent of the population. The group's origins in the region date to the late 1830s. They clashed with the Shona, and were subsequently dominated by British military forces in 1890. The Northern Ndebele people of Zimbabwe have their own language, known as Sindebele (or isiNdebele).

The British colonial interests grew, including the creation of the British South Africa Company, which established gold mining operations. Britain subsequently named its new territory Southern Rhodesia, after English businessman Cecil Rhodes. The company conscripted the native population as a labor force in the mines.

Religions
Nearly 76 percent of Zimbabweans are Protestant, with 38 percent Apostolic, 21 percent Pentecostal, and 16 percent identifying with another Protestant sect. Just over 8 percent practice Roman Catholicism, while 8.4 percent identify with another Christian denomination. Just over 1 percent are practicing Muslims. A small population of 6.1 percent identifies with no religion at all.

Climate
Zimbabwe's climate is tropical, though its high elevation tends to moderate temperatures. The central plateau experiences the most consistent and comfortable temperatures throughout the year.

Because of its location in the southern hemisphere, Zimbabwe's summer occurs from October to April. During the summer, the average temperature is between 28° and 31° Celsius (82° and 88° Fahrenheit), but can climb as high as 35° Celcius (95° Fahrenheit). Summer evening

temperatures in the capital often drop to around 15° Celsius (59° Fahrenheit) overnight.

Winter lasts from May to August, and the season's average temperature drops to between 15° and 20° Celsius (59° to 68° Fahrenheit), although nighttime temperatures can fall even further, to 5° Celcius (41° Fahrenheit). In Harare, the weather is typically dry and sunny.

Zimbabwe's rainy season lasts from November until March. Rainfall is greatest in the cooler Highveld, where precipitation averages about 1,780 millimeters (70 inches) each year. The southern region is hotter and drier, and typically receives less than 653 millimeters (26 inches) of rain a year. In general, rainfall is erratic, and droughts are frequent, making agriculture difficult.

ENVIRONMENT & GEOGRAPHY

Zimbabwe is bordered by Botswana to the southwest, Mozambique in the east, South Africa to the south, and Zambia to the north.

The country features a high plateau, known as the Highveld, which is a grassland covering roughly one-quarter of the country's area. The Highveld is flanked by the Zambezi River on the north and the Limpopo River on the south. Situated along the Highveld and surrounded by beautiful game parks, natural reserves, recreational lakes, and farmland is the nation's capital of Harare.

The less-populated lowveld contains the Limpopo River Valley, which surrounds the Limpopo River on both the Zimbabwean and South African sides. This valley is characterized by dry savanna and has been the subject of debate between those who want to use the land for agriculture and those who desire to conserve and protect its ecosystem.

Topography
The highest region in Zimbabwe is the Eastern Highlands. The country's highest point, at the peak of Mount Inyangani, is 2,592 meters (8,506 feet) above sea level.

The Highveld plateau region is approximately 80 kilometers (50 miles) wide and ranges in altitude from 1,220 to 524 meters (4,000 to 5,000 feet) above sea level. Harare sits at an elevation of over 1,483 meters (4,865 feet), and covers an area of 960.6 square kilometers (370.9 square miles).

The junction of the Runde and Save Rivers is the lowest point in Zimbabwe, at only 162 meters (531 feet) above sea level.

Plants & Animals

Zimbabwe's fertile Highveld region is covered by savanna grassland. Common trees found in the lowveld region include baobab, mahogany, mukwa, teak, mopani (or balsam), and fig trees.

Plant and animal life is preserved in Zimbabwe's many national parks and reserves. The country's largest, Hwange National Park (formerly known as the Wankie Game Reserve), covers an area of 14,651 square kilometers (5,567 square miles), and is primarily known for its opportunities to view wild game animals.

Zimbabwean wildlife is typical of that found in most African countries. It includes giraffes, lions, monkeys, baboons, and African elephants. Six hundred bird species call Zimbabwe home, including the giant kingfisher and the great egret. Poaching, particularly for the purpose of harvesting ivory, is a continuing threat to the animals of Zimbabwe, especially to elephants and rhinoceroses. It is responsible for the decline of the black rhinoceros population, among other species.

CUSTOMS & COURTESIES

Greetings

Generally, introductions are a bit more formal in Zimbabwe than in Western cultures. Common expressions of greeting include "Mhoro" ("Hello") in Shona and "Isawubona" ("Hello") in Ndebele. Additionally, a typical morning greeting in Shona is "Mangwanani, mamuka sei?" ("How did you wake?"), to which the appropriate response would be "Ndamuka, mamukawo" ("I slept well if you slept well"). In Ndebele, the equivalent expression is "Uvuke njani?" Traditionally, children wait for elders to greet them before speaking in both cultures.

Because Zimbabwe is a multilingual country, deciding what language to use is important. Although most people speak or at least understand English, using the language native to the area (whether it is Shona or Ndebele) shows respect. Thus, it is often considered disrespectful to switch to another language that the listener doesn't understand.

Gestures & Etiquette

Because of clearly defined traditional gender roles, men and women avoid touching each other in public, although handshakes are common. In business situations, men may shake hands with men and women with women, but men and women typically only nod to each other. Men in Zimbabwe also have more physical contact with each other than what is customary in Western cultures, and they often embrace or pat one another on the back. While direct eye contact is considered polite, children will often avoid direct eye contact with a person of authority as a sign of respect.

Formal attire is common throughout Zimbabwe. Children wear uniforms to school, while women typically wear skirts or dresses. Men in white-collar positions wear suits. The concept of "business casual attire" that exists in the United States is not used in Zimbabwe.

Eating/Meals

The culinary influence of Zimbabwe's British colonial past is prevalent. For example, it is common for those in urban areas to follow a schedule that includes a substantial breakfast, a late morning tea, a hot lunch followed by an afternoon tea, and dinner between five and seven o'clock. In certain hotels and restaurants, the custom of "high tea," an early evening meal in British culture, is observed. In rural areas, meals are less structured; people usually have an early, small breakfast and a large lunch, with later meals dependent upon economic circumstances. Traditionally, meals are served communally. It is considered impolite to eat or serve with the left hand.

Visiting

Hospitality is important in Zimbabwe, and guests are treated with respect in both Ndebele and Shona cultures. Guests are typically afforded the best a household has to offer. This may include certain seating in the house, or food that is being saved for special occasions. Visitors usually bring a gift for the host, and hosts may also present a gift to visitors. During a meal, the guest is expected to consume whatever is offered as a sign of courtesy. Visiting, however, is generally not formal, and it is acceptable for friends and family to visit unannounced. In rural areas, visits are very relaxed and can last for hours.

LIFESTYLE

Family

As in many African cultures, the Shona and Ndebele people have traditionally lived in a large family system, with immediate and extended families sharing space and responsibilities. Beyond the extended family, ties to communities—villages and ethnic groups (formerly known as tribes)—are very strong. The well-being of the group is considered more important than that of the individual, and the concept of individuality is not particularly engrained in the ethnic culture of Zimbabwe. For example, the Shona use totems (mitupo) to identify different clans, and there are currently as many as twenty-five different totems identified; historically, these symbols were associated with animal names and helped form certain laws and social customs.

Respect for elders is an important part of both Ndebele and Shona cultures. Grandparents and aunts traditionally took an active part in parenting the children of the extended family, and taking care of the elderly was a community responsibility. Ancestors were also not forgotten, and were considered to be very much still with a family in spirit after their death. Arranged marriages are still common in Zimbabwe, with the wife typically residing with the husband's immediate family. If death or divorce should arise, the wife is then expected to return to her own family. Mothers, however, remain respected members of the family.

In the late twentieth and early twenty-first centuries, traditional family structures have been weakened by economic circumstances. This is particularly true as more male family members have migrated away from rural areas for employment. This has created many single-parent households in which the women have also assumed responsibility for agricultural production, in addition to child rearing and domestic duties. The rate of HIV/AIDS infection has also had a profound impact on Zimbabwean family structure in recent years, leaving many children orphaned. While an estimated 90 percent of Zimbabwe's orphans are cared for by relatives and extended families, it is believed that the remaining 10 percent reside in orphanages or live as street children because of the economic hardship they represent to relatives.

Housing

The traditional Shona dwelling is a kumusha (the Shona word for home), which is a round mud or clay house. Distinctive characteristics include a cone-shaped thatched roof and separate houses for sleeping and for cooking. Traditional Ndebele homes are of very similar construction, but are often slightly wider and lower than Shona homes. This type of traditional housing is still common in rural areas, but more modern, rural dwellings tend to be small, one-story structures made of cinderblock, brick, or stucco with corrugated metal roofing.

In urban areas, colonial architecture is still prominent, and many large homes are of European design, often protected with high walls or gates. Urban high-rise apartment buildings range from luxury apartments to low-income housing. Shantytowns, or informal settlements, are common in poor areas, and feature structures made out of discarded materials, including scrap metal and cardboard.

In 2005, it was estimated that half of the population of metropolitan Harare lived in substandard housing. In an effort to reduce the appearance and influence of poverty in Harare, the Mugabe government began Operation Marambatsvina, or "drive out rubbish," and destroyed most of the city's illegal shanty housing and roadside markets. This and similar programs displaced close to 2 million people. Critics questioned the authenticity of the government's concern for the poor, while civil unrest within the city increased because of the widespread displacement.

As of 2015, under ZIMASSET (Zimbabwe Agenda for Sustainable Socio-Economic Transformation), the government, specifically in Harare, has begun to make housing more durable and affordable for a greater number of people. In early 2015, Harare's city council and the Zimbabwe mortgage company, CABS, cut deposit amounts for 240- to 300-square meter homes in the new Budiriro housing development from 25 percent to 10 percent. Two-room houses in Zimbabwe's urban areas cost $22,000, while four room houses cost $27,000.

Food

The hyperinflation that has occurred in the Zimbabwean economy over recent years has resulted in a severe shortage of available food-stuffs. Any items that are available in grocery stores are often exorbitantly priced.

Traditional Zimbabwean cuisine is a blend of African and British influences. The staple of the Zimbabwean diet is sadza (called isitshwala in the Ndebele language), a thick maize-based porridge often referred to as mealie-meal. It is eaten at breakfast, lunch or dinner, either as a meal with gravy or vegetables or as a side dish with meat (then called sadza ne nyama, or sadza with meat). Sadza is still cooked in a large pot over an open fire in rural areas.

Chicken, beef and goat are common meat dishes, but Zimbabweans also eat game such as kudu (a kind of gazelle), crocodile, ostrich, and impala (African antelope). Biltong—a South African term that describes dried, cured meat of many varieties—is a common and inexpensive snack. In general, fruits and vegetables are limited, and beans, roasted maize, and stews feature prominently. The British influence is evident in the availability of an English breakfast (including fried eggs, toast, baked beans, sausage, and tomatoes) in urban areas. Additionally, Zimbabwean still enjoy drinking hot tea at mid-morning and in the afternoon, often accompanied by biscuits (cookies) or other sweets.

Life's Milestones

Ancestry is an important aspect of both Shona and Ndebele culture. Traditionally, after a death occurs in a Ndebele family, the family is cleansed after the funeral in order to prevent any bad omen associated with the death. One year later, the family holds a ceremony for the spirit of the deceased, who is then welcomed as an ancestor. A similar ceremony is also traditionally practiced by the Shona.

Other unique traditional customs include the burial of the umbilical cord near the entrance of a traditional Shona kitchen hut (separate from the sleeping hut) in order to maintain ties to the land throughout life. A rite of passage experienced by Ndebele boys lasts four years and involves the adoption of a new name and learning a language not understood by women. While these traditions have declined to the point that they are no longer widely observed, ceremonial dances done at initiation rituals are still performed on special occasions.

CULTURAL HISTORY

Architecture & Art

Zimbabwe's archeological heritage dates back to the early dwellings of the early Shona, a cluster of people native to modern-day Zimbabwe and southern Mozambique. (They were not united under the umbrella name "Shona" until the late nineteenth century.) These early dwellings were constructed of grass, which allowed their inhabitants to move them quickly in case of an attack or other necessity. During the twelfth to sixteenth centuries, ancestors of the Shona residing in modern-day eastern Zimbabwe built what is often considered the first pre-colonial stone buildings in southern Africa. The ruins of these stone buildings, referred to as Great Zimbabwe, are now a national monument. Soapstone carvings of birds found at the site are some of the earliest forms of art found in Zimbabwe, and the image of the birds has become a symbol of the country and is included on Zimbabwe's flag.

Most art created by the early people of Zimbabwe was for utilitarian or ceremonial purposes. Masks, headdresses, and jewelry worn during rituals have been made with the same techniques for centuries, and replicas of these traditional items are still made today. The Shona are known for their carving in stone (particularly soapstone) and wood, as well as their metalwork. Zimbabwe's Ndebele, who broke off from the Zulu of South Africa during the nineteenth century, are known for their colorful beadwork and woven basketry. Both cultures also have an historic tradition of decorative ceramics and textile art.

Dance & Drama

Dance was important to the early cultures of Zimbabwe. It developed as a form of communication and storytelling, with different gestures and steps assigned meanings that were commonly known. Dance was part of all sacred rituals, whether celebratory or mournful in nature. It was also part of social gatherings, harvest celebrations, or as preparation for hunting or going into battle. Specific clothing or masks are associated with different dances, and certain dances are segregated by gender. Masked dancers held a very prestigious position, as it was believed that the act of putting on the mask allowed the spirit of the ancestors to enter the dancer.

In 2008, the United Nations Educational, Scientific and Cultural Organization (UNESCO), which endeavors to protect cultural heritages through its list of "Masterpieces of the Oral and Intangible Heritage of Humanity," named the Mbende Jerusarema Dance, a dance of the Shona people of eastern Zimbabwe, as an Intangible Cultural Heritage (ICH). It is an ancient fertility dance that involves one drummer, with no songs or lyrics, and is characterized as acrobatic and explicit. Other important traditional dances are the Muchongoyo, which is always accompanied

by drums, and Dinhe, believed to conjure spirits. Mbakumba was usually performed following harvests, but is now presented primarily for entertainment purposes.

In Shona and Ndebele cultures, there was no distinction between storytelling, dance and music; all the elements combined to create dramatic performances. Performers typically wore costumes in the form of ritual headdresses or animal skins and jewelry, and recited well-known words or stories. Often, these performers held many different roles within the community.

Music

Early Zimbabwean music was performed by a variety of traditional instruments and borrowed and blended the sounds of neighboring African cultures, as well as the cultures of the Caribbean and Europe. Some of the most important traditional instruments include the mbira, marimba and the drums. The mbira, perhaps the most important instrument in Shona culture, is a small wooden instrument with rows of metallic keys which make a melodic bell-like sound (it is sometimes called a thumb organ). Traditionally, the mbira was used in sacred ceremonies for contacting ancestors and guardian spirits. The instrument also figured prominently in rainmaking ceremonies, weddings and funerals, and has become incorporated into contemporary music as well. Mbira singing often accompanied the music.

The marimba is a typical Zimbabwean instrument which consists of a series of flat wooden keys (similar to a xylophone) mounted on top of a table-like platform with wooden or metal resonators underneath. The keys are struck with a mallet to produce a hollow-sounding rhythm. Drums (ngoma) have also always been an important part of Shona and Ndebele music. There are dozens of different kinds of drums in Zimbabwe and learning to play them is considered an art form that should be learned from a master.

Literature

Because both Shona and Ndebele cultures relied on oral tradition and storytelling for thousands of years, a written tradition in Zimbabwe did not develop until the arrival of European settlers. During the colonial period, when Zimbabwe was known as Southern Rhodesia, most native literature was written by those of European descent. British writers such as Doris Lessing (1919–2013), who lived in Zimbabwe for many years and won the Nobel Prize in Literature in 2007, wrote about colonial life in Africa. However, a tradition of literature among the Ndebele and Shona people did not start until the mid-nineteenth century, with the establishment of the Southern Rhodesia African Literature Bureau in 1954.

Many early works were historical narratives written as vernacular literature. Patrick Chakaipa (1932–2003), often regarded as the "father of Shona literature," published his first book, an adventure story entitled *Karikoga Gumiremiseve*, in 1958. Later works of Ndebele and Shona literature began to move more into social commentary and African nationalism. This includes the work of Charles Mungoshi (1947–), who writes in both Shona and English and whose most recent book was *Branching Streams Flow in the Dark*, published by the University of California Press in 2013. Dambudzo Marechera (1952–1987) is famous for his short story collection, *The House of Hunger* (1978), which gave the reader a portrait of the country's colonial ghettos. Marechera is also known for his experimentation with form, and is considered to be one of the most influential modern Zimbabwean writers.

CULTURE

Arts & Entertainment

In Harare, culture reflects both British colonialism and the tribal influences of the rest of Zimbabwe. Zimbabwe's most popular sports are soccer, basketball, and cricket, while the traditional crafts, such as soapstone and wood carving, ceramics, and basket weaving still reflect the native African culture.

Rooted in the strong oral storytelling traditions of the Shona and Ndebele cultures, performance poetry continues to be a strong force in Zimbabwe. Dub poetry, a 1970s West Indian

form of spoken word poetry accompanied by music, has been embraced by Zimbabwean poets, most notably Albert Nyathi (1962–). One of Zimbabwe's best-known poets, Nyathi wears traditional Ndebele clothing as he performs his poems accompanied by musicians, adding dance steps into the mix. While his words reflect modern life, his style imitates the ancient Ndebele "praise poets," who would perform for chiefs, singing their praises.

Music is an important part of Zimbabwean culture. The traditional music of the Shona people is played on a mbira, a type of thumb piano. The instrument is also used in a genre of protest music native to Zimbabwe, called Chimurenga, which roughly translates to "revolutionary struggle." Popular music in the country is a mixture of African and Western influences.

Modern music in Zimbabwe is a blend of various sounds, ranging from Afropop (a pan-African form of popular music influenced by the African diaspora) and American jazz, hip-hop, and rhythm and blues, to Caribbean reggae, salsa, and rumba. In the 1980s, bands such as the Bhundu Boys popularized jit, a type of guitar and mbira-based music particular to Zimbabwe. More widely popular is sungura or museve music, which incorporates Congolese rumba music, drums and guitars to create a fast, danceable rhythm. One of Zimbabwe's most internationally acclaimed musicians is Thomas Mapfumo (1945–), known as "The Lion of Zimbabwe," who developed the musical style known as Chimurenga noted above. Mapfumo's songs often incorporate traditional instruments and have political influences, dealing with issues such as national identity and human rights.

During the 1990s, the Zimbabwean government cracked down on what it considered excessive influence of foreign culture in Zimbabwe by requiring that two-thirds of music played on radio stations (which are state-run) be from local artists. While this regulation was later reversed, it helped create a new genre of music in Zimbabwe known as "urban groove," which is a style of hip-hop sung mostly in Shona or Ndebele, or mixed with English. However, many perceive this type of music as cultural imitation.

Zimbabwean music is also popular internationally; the Zimbabwean Music Festival is held each summer in the United States' Pacific Northwest, and Zimbabweans from around the world join in a celebration of traditional and modern Zimbabwean music.

Shona sculpture is internationally acclaimed, having emerged as a dominant art form beginning in the mid-nineteenth century. The city of Harare boasts a sculpture park called Chapungu Sculpture Park, with a US sister site in Loveland, Colorado. Renowned sculptor Nicholas Mukomberanwa (1940–2002) is known for incorporating elements of Shona spirituality in his work. Other famous Zimbabwean sculptors include Tapfuma Gutsa (1956–), and Joseph Muzondo (1953–).

Despite the repressive regime of Robert Mugabe, who assumed power in 1980 (first as prime minister and later as president in 1987), theater and literature in Zimbabwe continue to thrive. Though playwrights are required to register new material with the government, they have found ways to make theater socially and politically relevant. The Amakhosi Theater for Social Change in Bulawayo, for example, uses theater for AIDS education and to inspire community action. Cont Mdladla Mhlanga, a Zimbabwean writer and director, wrote *The Good President* as a satire of a fictional Mugabe-like president in 2007. The play was performed in Harare, but later all of Mhlanga's works were banned in Zimbabwe. In 2008, Mhlanga was a co-winner of the international ArtVenture Freedom to Create Prize for his work, calling attention to the issue of censorship in his home country.

Since achieving independence in 1980, writers in Zimbabwe have continued to experiment with different forms and content, helping to build a new literary tradition. Moving beyond the largely protest-oriented literature that dominated the period of the civil war (1971–1979), contemporary Zimbabwean literature embraces a range of themes. Many Zimbabwean writers write in both English and either Shona or Ndebele, sometimes using both languages to reflect the reality of life in a multilingual, multicultural nation. Additionally, while in the past literature was dominated by men, a new generation of women writers such as Yvonne Vera (1964–2005) and Tsitsi Dangarembga (1959–) have gained recognition in their own country and abroad.

Other Famous Zimbabwean authors include Chenjerai Hove (1956–2015), who writes in both English and Shona. Yvonne Vera, author of *Under the Tongue* (1997) and *The Stone Virgins* (2002), received the Commonwealth Writers Prize for Africa, the German LiBeraturpreis, the Swedish PEN Tucholsky Prize, and the first Macmillan Writers' Prize for Africa.

Cultural Sites & Landmarks

Victoria Falls, located at the Zimbabwe-Zambia border, is perhaps the premiere tourist attraction on the African continent. The largest falls in the world (based on overall width and height), they were listed as a UNESCO World Heritage Site in 1989. While the dramatic appearance of the falls is distinctive in itself, they are also known for frequent rainbows and the surrounding wildlife. Famed British explorer David Livingstone (1813–1873) was the first European to see the falls in 1855. After Cecil Rhodes (1853–1902) founded Rhodesia, the town of Victoria Falls was established and a railroad station was built to accommodate tourists. In recent years, environmental and political concerns have threatened the site's status on the World Heritage List.

The ruins of a stone city at Great Zimbabwe National Monument are all that remains of a thriving medieval trading society, once the most prosperous in sub-Saharan Africa. The buildings, thought to have been occupied between the 12th and 16th centuries, were part of a city with a population estimated between 10,000 and 20,000. Great Zimbabwe is remarkable in that it proves that ancient Africans had a sophisticated society much earlier than anyone had previously thought. The inhabitants of Great Zimbabwe are believed to have accumulated great wealth and remnants of Chinese pottery and beads of Indian origin have been found at the site. It was declared a World Heritage Site in 1986.

Zimbabwe is also home to three other World Heritage Sites, including the ruined city of Khami, also a national monument, inscribed by UNESCO in 1986. Like Great Zimbabwe, which was abandoned in the mid-16th century, the Khami ruins are of particular archaeological importance, and both European and Chinese objects have been unearthed there.

The Mana Pools wildlife conservation area makes up the Mana Pools National Park; and Matobo National Park, which contains Matobo Hills, a series of distinctive granite formations and wooded valleys that have geological and cultural significance. An important concentration of wildlife is found at the Mana Pools site and the surrounding safari areas. Matobo Hills has evidence of human settlement dating back to the Stone Age, including rock paintings and caves.

Hwange National Park, situated between Bulawayo and Victoria Falls, is the largest game reserve in Zimbabwe, and is home to one of the largest concentrations of elephants in Africa. Once a hunting ground for the Ndebele kings and European settlers, the area was never suitable for farming and never developed, thus allowing wildlife to flourish. While elephants are the main attraction, the park also has an abundance of giraffes, rhinos, baboons and other wildlife.

Just outside of the nation's capital, there are a variety of safari-style animal reserves, including the Lavron Bird Gardens, the Lion and Cheetah Park at Norton, and the Lake Chivero Mukuvisi Woodlands Recreational Park. Harare is also home to the National Botanical Garden, which includes more than 900 species of wild trees and shrubs from all over Zimbabwe.

Harare also has more modern landmarks, namely the Sam Levy's Village in Borrowdale and the Ster-Kinekor Westgate shopping malls. These metropolitan shopping centers are popular destinations for both city residents and visitors. For more traditional shopping, the popular Mbare open-air market features a variety of handmade goods by local craftsmen, including baskets, clothing, soapstone carvings, wooden sculptures, and wickerwork.

Libraries & Museums

Harare is home to the Zimbabwe parliament and government buildings, as well as many of the nation's libraries and museums, including the Queen Victoria National Library and the Queen Victoria Museum. The Zimbabwe National Archives includes a collection of Zimbabwean and African artifacts, including diaries, notebooks, and reports from missionaries and explorers. Additionally, the National Art Gallery features a collection of Shona soapstone carvings, as well as a variety of traveling international exhibits.

Holidays

The major Zimbabwean national holiday is Independence Day (April 18), which celebrates the country's independence from British rule. Africa Day (May 25) celebrates the anniversary of the formation of the Organization of African Unity in 1963. On National Heroes' Day, celebrated on the second Monday in August, many Zimbabweans visit National Heroes Acre, where officers killed in the line of duty are buried. The Second Tuesday in August is Defense Forces Day, while December 22 is Unity Day, which was instituted in 1997 and celebrates the two political parties representing Shona and Ndebele interests.

Youth Culture

The youth culture of Zimbabwe is very much influenced by Western culture, particularly American music, cinema, and fashion. Additionally, because of the historical connection, British music and sports are also popular with young Zimbabweans. This has even resulted in a cultural backlash in which Zimbabwe youth from suburban or urban areas have been criticized for being overly American or British, often speaking with an "African American" or English inflection.

In cities and suburban areas, cell phones and other electronic devices have become increasingly common, though personal computers remain somewhat of a luxury for most families or students. As such, young people typically access the Internet through Internet cafés, schools and other public institutions. Most young people in Zimbabwe can read and speak at least some English in addition to Shona or Ndebele. Although they are better educated than previous generations of Zimbabweans, economic and political crises in recent years have caused many to leave their country for South Africa or other neighboring nations in search of a better life.

SOCIETY

Transportation

Few Zimbabweans in rural areas can afford cars and rely on bus service or "bush taxis," which are privately owned cars or vans. Some bush taxis offer scheduled or "semi-scheduled" service, but many operate on an irregular basis. In the larger cites, bus service is the most common mode of popular transportation, and many people use motorbikes and scooters.

There are a total of 97,267 km (60,438 miles), 18,481 km (11,483 miles) of which are paved. Paved roads include a variety of national toll roads, like the A1, which extends from Harare to Kariba, and the A5, which travels from Harare to Bulawayo. Roads are maintained by the Zimbabwe National Road Authority (ZINARA).

Automobiles in Zimbabwe drive on the left-hand side of the road. It is illegal in Zimbabwe to drive while using a cellular phone. Travelers to Zimbabwe should use caution while driving at night because roads are poorly lit and many cars do not use headlights or taillights.

Transportation Infrastructure

British colonization left behind a fairly extensive system of major roads, also known as trunk roads. Most international travel to neighboring countries is done by bus, and there are domestic flights within Zimbabwe that connect the major cities. However, transportation in the country does have its shortcomings.

Zimbabwe remains one of the few countries in the world that still operates steam trains for commuter use. Often, these trains operate at night

due to their inefficiency, and they use sleeping cars dating back to the 1920s. Furthermore, while Harare includes all of the transportation options of a major metropolitan city, including buses, taxis, trains, and an international airport, widespread gas shortages, electrical power outages, and subsequent government regulation adjustments have affected their efficiency.

There are 196 airports in Zimbabwe as of 2013. However, only seventeen of them have paved runways.

Media & Communication

The majority of the media in Zimbabwe is state-run and subject to censorship. In 2003, the government forced the largest independent newspaper to shut down, leaving only two independent weekly newspapers in operation. As a result, some Zimbabweans have also begun printing newspapers outside of the country, and then having them flown in for distribution. Additionally, Zimbabweans have started broadcasting from foreign countries, such as the United Kingdom, Madagascar, and the US on short and medium-wave frequencies that can be picked up in Zimbabwe, which is why shortwave radios have been confiscated by Zimbabwe's police force. Even so, many of the journalists who report for these outlets are afraid to use their own names and thus adopt on-air monikers. The government has jammed transmissions of such radio broadcasts.

In 2005, the international organization Committee to Protect Journalists (CPJ) named Zimbabwe the third worst place in the world to be a journalist. And a decade later, in 2015, Reporters Without Borders directly accuses Mugabe of, among other things, barring independent radio broadcasting start-ups in a bid to ensure Zimbabwe Broadcasting Corporation (ZBC) is the principal media source and preventing the proper function of the power-sharing government, so that reforms cannot be achieved. Even following the ratification of the new constitution, those who publish stories without a license are subject to arrest, and such licenses can be revoked by the government for arbitrary reasons.

In recent years, journalists have been harassed, arrested, and abducted by the police. Foreign media are not allowed to be based in Zimbabwe, and in 2008, the government charged an accreditation fee of $10,000 (USD) to be allowed to work in the country. In 2008, Zimbabwe was ranked in the bottom percentile (151st out of 173) of the World Press Freedom Index compiled by Reporters Without Borders (RWB). However thanks to the power-sharing government and the efforts of MDC leader Morgan Tsvangirai in 2009, the country's draconian media restrictions relaxed somewhat, and previously banned newspaper, like *Daily News*, *Financial Gazette*, and *NewsDay* recommenced publication. However, in 2015, RWB still categorized Mugabe as a "predator" and devotes a special webpage to his abuses. Zimbabwe was 131 of 180 in the 2015 World Press Freedom Index.

In 2009, the Mugabe-Tsvangirai power-sharing government established the Ministry of Information and Communications Technology to develop internet potential. And, as of 2013, an estimated 40 percent of Zimbabwe's population has Internet access, compared to just 15 percent in 2011. The government has not yet intervened in the publication of online magazines or journals, but Zimbabwean communications law states that service providers must allow the government access to private emails upon request.

SOCIAL DEVELOPMENT

Standard of Living
Due in part to the prevalence of HIV/AIDS, Zimbabwe is ranked 156th out of 187 countries on the 2014 United Nations Human Development Index, which measures quality of life indicators.

Water Consumption
Zimbabwe suffers from serious problems related to the availability of clean water. Pollution, widespread poverty, and lack of infrastructure upkeep and development have all seriously damaged public utilities and fresh water sources. Proper sanitation is not common, and much of the waste

in Harare is relegated to makeshift landfills and open sewers. In fact, just 3 percent of urban areas have access to improved sanitation, while rural areas are somewhat better, with 32.7 percent enjoying improved sanitation facilities. Power shortages often hamper the work of the water treatment facility in Harare, which also suffers from a lack of resources such as water treatment chemicals. In 2015, government corruption continues to delay efforts to repair or rebuild the country's plumbing and sewage infrastructure.

Education
In 2015, Zimbabwe's average adult literacy rate was estimated at 86.5 percent (88.5 percent among men and 84.6 percent among women), the highest rate in Africa. This is due in part to the fact that primary school is free for every Zimbabwean and that most children, even in rural areas, attend at least primary school. In 2010, education expenditures represented 2 percent of the country's GDP.

Until 1979, around the time of Zimbabwe's independence, the school system was segregated between Africans and Europeans. Schools are now racially integrated, and the school system extends beyond the primary grades to teach students trades through technical programs and apprenticeships.

There are sixteen post-secondary schools in Zimbabwe, three of them major universities. The largest, the University of Zimbabwe, is located north of Harare. The university's College of Medicine is located in Parirenyatwa Hospital. The National University of Science and Technology in Bulawayo also hosts the Bulawayo College of Health Sciences. The country's third largest university is Africa University in Mutare.

Women's Rights
Zimbabwe signed the UN's Convention on the Elimination of All Forms of Discrimination against Women (CEDAW), which is often referred to as the international bill of human rights for women. However, the government has been slow to ensure the equal treatment of

women, and Zimbabwe's previous constitution referred to customary law (the traditions of the people) rather than the modern legal system in regard to family, or internal, matters. However, the new constitution passed in March 2013 ratified in May, included provisions that outlaw discrimination against women. Zimbabwe now must realign some 400 relevant laws to reflect these new constitutional guidelines.

If a woman is married in a civil ceremony, she has a right to own property and to inherit that property if her husband dies. A woman also has a right to a portion of the couple's assets in the case of divorce. However, according to customary law, women can't possess property independent of men, and they cannot inherit property. Thus, under customary law, a woman must forfeit her home and property to her husband's closest male relative upon her husband's death unless an agreement was signed in advance. The new constitution and greater representation by women in parliament may effect a change in these customary policies. In rural areas, land is communally owned, and although women work the land, their only claim on it is through their husbands.

Domestic violence is one of the major issues still facing women in Zimbabwe. Women's rights advocates report that one in four Zimbabwean women will suffer some sort of abuse in her lifetime and even in 2013, over half of married women have experienced spousal rape. Police have traditionally regarded abuse as a family matter, and women often do not report it. In 2007, the government introduced a public awareness campaign to address the problem and introduced laws to prevent domestic violence. The laws include a ban on forced marriage, a definition of abuse as including psychological or economic abuse, and a policy that allows police to make an arrest without a warrant if a woman's life is at risk. In December 2013, the country also observed "16 Days of Activism Against Gender-Based Violence" a movement to raise additional awareness the continuing problem, since men convicted of rape still receive light sentences, often community service only. Human trafficking also remains a significant concern.

While educational and employment opportunities have improved since colonial times, women still hold few positions of power in Zimbabwe. The majority of women work in agriculture or the informal sector. Women in Zimbabwe also have among the lowest life expectancy in the world. This is due in part to the HIV/AIDS epidemic and the worsening economic crisis which has decreased access to health care and proper nutrition and sanitation.

Health Care

Zimbabwe's health care system is under severe strain from the number of people infected with HIV/AIDS. Health care coverage was briefly made available to all Zimbabweans, though this privilege has been revoked in light of the growing rate of infection. The government has also raised income taxes to help fund care for HIV-infected Zimbabweans, though the impact on public health has been minimal due to the misallocation of funds and government corruption. Still, a 3 percent AIDs tax is levied on all corporate and personal income.

Most health services are concentrated in Zimbabwe's urban areas, yet it is estimated that more than 90 percent of the population live within a day's walk of a health facility. The quality of health care has suffered, along with disease education programs, due to the country's economic problems. Tuberculosis was on the rise in Zimbabwe, with the number of cases increasing four-fold between 1995 and 2000. However, diseases plaguing the country as of 2013 are bacterial diarrhea, hepatitis A, dengue and typhoid fevers, malaria, schistosomiasis (a water-borne parasite, carried by snails, causing chronic illness and death), and rabies.

GOVERNMENT

Structure

In the twentieth century, white-ruled Rhodesia voted for independence from Britain in 1965. The British refused to recognize independence without majority rule for the colony's black African population. The white population and some black nationalist groups resisted efforts at majority rule until 1980, when a constitution was drafted and elections were held. Robert Mugabe became the first prime minister of the new country, now known as Zimbabwe and later its president. He has maintained power ever since, despite a new constitution, passed in May 2013, that limits presidential terms.

Today, Zimbabwe is a multiparty parliamentary democracy, despite Mugabe's socialist tendencies. The executive branch of government currently includes the president, his two vice presidents, and a cabinet. The legislative branch is bicameral consisting of a Senate, comprised of eighty seats, and the House of Assembly, which has 270 seats. Sixty seats are reserved for women in the House of Assembly, to which they are elected by proportional representation vote. Members serve five year terms. The next election is slated for 2018.

Political Parties

Zimbabwe is a multi-party system, but has long been dominated by two political parties: Zimbabwe African National Union-Patriotic Front (ZANU-PF), headed by Mugabe since independence, and the Movement for Democratic Change (MDC). In 2009, the MDC fractured into two disparate entities that share the MDC name but are led respectively by Morgan Tsvangirai (leader of the MDC-T) and Arthur Mutambara (who heads the MDC-N). Nonetheless, the MDC promotes democratic socialism, while the ZANU-PF considers itself to be the country's nationalist party. Other political parties in Zimbabwe include the International Socialist Organization, the Zimbabwe People's Democratic Party, the Zimbabwe African People's Union, Patriotic Union of Mandebeleland, National Alliance for Good Governance, and the Zimbabwe Youth in Alliance.

Local Government

Zimbabwe is divided into eight administrative provinces and two cities, Harare and Bulawayo, with provincial status. These provinces, each headed by a provincial governor, are further subdivided into 59 districts and 1,200 municipal wards. At the federal level, local government is represented by the Ministry of Local Government, Rural and Urban Development.

Judicial System

The judicial branch of the Zimbabwean government is headed by the chief justice of the Supreme Court and four other judges, all selected by the president as recommended by the Judicial Service Commission (JSC). The JSC is comprised of chief justice, the Public Service Commission chairman, the attorney general, and between two and three presidentially-appointed members. The country's legal system is a mixture of Roman-Dutch law and English common law. Judges generally preside until they are age sixty-five, although can extend service until the age of seventy. High courts and regional magistrate courts serve under the Supreme Court. In recent years, the Zimbabwean judicial and legal system has come under widespread criticism due to allegations of corruption and political favoritism.

Taxation

The government of Zimbabwe imposes a corporate tax of 25 percent on a company or trust's income, with special rates for mining operations. This tax alone accounts for approximately half the country's revenue. Additional revenue is gained through a 25 percent tax on personal income tax, which offers a tax-free threshold of $300 for the Pay-As-You-Earn (PAYE) plan, Zimbabwe's by-paycheck taxation system. Anyone who earns over $20,000 per month, must pay 50 percent in taxes as of January 2014. Income from pension funds is taxed at a rate of 15 percent. Also imposed are customs and excise duties as well as sales and value-added taxes. Dividends earned by companies incorporated outside the country are taxed at a rate of 20 percent. In addition to all other taxes, there is a 3 percent AIDS levy to support the work of the National AIDS Council in Zimbabwe. The country also receives a significant amount of international aid and its government also borrows a large amount money. In June

2009, China agreed to a loan to Zimbabwe in the amount of $950 million (USD).

Armed Forces

The armed forces of Zimbabwe is known as the Zimbabwe Defense Forces (ZDF), which consist of the Zimbabwe National Army (ZNA) and the Air Force of Zimbabwe (AFZ). The country, which is landlocked and without a coastline, does not have a navy. The budget for the Zimbabwean military was 2.79 percent of the country's GDP in 2014. The Zimbabwe Republic Police (ZRP) is also considered a wing of the armed forces. This branch includes the paramilitary Police Support Unit, equipped for riots and civil unrest. There is no conscription, and females are able to serve beginning at age eighteen. There are approximately 29,000 active military members and 21,800 paramilitary members in the country's armed forces.

Foreign Policy

Zimbabwe was granted independence from the British government on April 18, 1980, after nearly a decade of civil war that resulted from the ruling white party's refusal to allow majority rule. The new nation was immediately recognized by the international community, with the US establishing an embassy in Harare that same day. (Zimbabwe also has an embassy in Washington, DC.) Zimbabwe then became a member of the UN in 1980, followed by membership in the African Union (AU), the Commonwealth of Nations (a group mostly made up former British colonies), the Organization of African Unity (OAU), the IMF (International Monetary Fund), the World Bank (which closed its Zimbabwe office in 2004), the World Trade Organization (WTO), and the Southern African Development Community (SADC).

However, since independence, Zimbabwe has been the subject of international criticism resulting from the oppressive regime of Robert Mugabe. In 2002, Zimbabwe was suspended from the Commonwealth of Nations due to its unfair elections and land reform policy (Zimbabwe would withdraw from the organi-

zation in 2003). That same year the European Union (EU) imposed an arms embargo on the country, while both the US and the EU imposed economic sanctions against members of the ruling party, the Zimbabwe African National Union-Patriotic Front (ZANU-PF). The official response to these decisions and other forms of international criticism has been one of defiance and accusation and has led to Zimbabwe establishing a "Look East" policy and closer ties with countries such as China and Russia. Mugabe has also consistently relied on South Africa for support since the end of apartheid in 1994.

During the 2008 presidential elections, in which Morgan Tsvangirai of the opposition Movement for Democratic Change (MDC) party gained the majority vote, there were reports of widespread violence, intimidation, and voter fraud. Furthermore, Mugabe refused to leave office, drawing strong international condemnation. Italy withdrew its ambassador from the country and called for other EU members to do the same, and the prime minister of Kenya urged the AU to suspend Zimbabwe's membership. Due to increasing pressure from the AU and the UN, Mugabe agreed to power-sharing deal with the opposition party in September 2008, with South African president Thabo Mbeki serving as a the mediator. Previously, when several rounds of negotiations resulted in failure of the power-sharing agreement to move forward, many prominent African and international leaders started to call for Mugabe's removal (including neighboring Zambia, Botswana, Angola, and Namibia), and South Africa moved to withhold aid from the Zimbabwe until talks resumed. In the final agreement, however, Mugabe retained control of the army, which Human Rights Watch has reported is being used to intimidate opposition figures and civil society activists.

Human Rights

International human rights law insists that states respect civil and political rights and also promote an individual's economic, social, and cultural rights. The United Nations Universal Declaration on Human Rights is recognized as the standard for international human rights. Its authors sought the counsel of the world's great thinkers, philosophers, and religious leaders and were careful to create a document that reflects the core values shared by every world culture. (To read this document or view the articles relating to cultural human rights, visit: http://www.ohchr.org/EN/UDHR/Pages/Introduction.aspx.)

Since achieving independence in 1980, the Zimbabwean government has, in a short time, developed a history of instituting repressive policies. Though Mugabe promised a democracy with free and fair elections, the country has developed into an authoritarian state that does not tolerate dissent. There is virtually no freedom of speech, assembly or of the press in Zimbabwe, and laws exist which restrict freedom to enter and exit the country. According to Human Rights Watch, Zimbabwean police even confiscate shortwave radios, which can reach stations beyond government-dominated broadcasting frequencies, as well as harass and imprison civil society activists. The freedoms of nongovernmental organizations (NGOs), labor organizations, and human rights groups have also been greatly curtailed in recent years. In 2008, the US State Department named Zimbabwe to its list of the world's ten worst human rights offenders.

Independent international human rights groups report that Mugabe continues to exert control over the judicial system, having fired any judges who made rulings against him. Arbitrary arrests and detentions are also widespread, and those arrested can be denied the opportunity for bail, trial or appeal. Zimbabwe's prison conditions are said to be dismal, with little to no food or water available for prisoners and horrible sanitation conditions which lead to the spread of disease. In April 2009, the government appealed for international aid—specifically clothing, food, and legal assistance—after a documentary exposed dire conditions with Zimbabwean prisons, along with the allegation that inmates die from starvation and disease on a daily basis. Additionally, Zimbabwe's National Youth Service has been cited as a program which ultimately trains child

soldiers. Little has changed in these respects with the passing of the new constitution.

While land ownership reform was one of the priorities for Mugabe's government, the process of reform amounted to little more than forced expulsion of white landowners from their properties. Many white farmers were attacked or killed by ZANU-PF militias and had to flee their land with little or no compensation. The Mugabe government has also been cited by international human rights observers for discrimination against minority groups. In addition, the government demolished the homes and businesses of over 2 million people living and working in Harare and other urban areas, arresting over 10,000 people and sending the rest to provisional "camps." The government claimed this action was to eradicate illegal activities, but international organizations condemned the move as an effort to break up strongholds of political opposition.

Human rights abuses were further highlighted in Zimbabwe during the presidential elections of 2008. It was alleged that supporters of the opposition party MDC were threatened, arrested, tortured, and prohibited from staging rallies or protests. International voting observers reported that those who do not support Mugabe were intimidated or attacked at polling stations, and newly elected leaders from the opposition party had to go into hiding because Mugabe militias attacked them in their homes.

As of 2015, even following passage of the new constitution, the Access to Information and Protection of Privacy Act (AIPPA) and the Public Order and Security Act (POSA)—both of which limit civil rights—have yet to be repealed. These two acts alone, along with continued partisan activity exercised by the police and security forces severely limit freedom of the press, freedom to assemble, and freedoms of association and expression.

Migration

Government corruption, political conflict and economic conditions have resulted in many Zimbabweans choosing to leave the country.

The International Organisation for Migration (IOM) has estimated that the largest number of emigrants have fled to the United Kingdom. A smaller number have fled to nearby Botswana and South Africa. According the UN Refugee Agency, approximately 500,000 people have emigrated from Zimbabwe. Approximately 136,000 of these migrants are refugees, 278,000 asylum-seekers, and nearly 1,700 returnees who are still internally displaced. However this number represents only official, legally sanctioned emigration. It is estimated that some two million Zimbabweans have fled to South Africa illegally and remain there as of 2015.

ECONOMY

In 2014, Zimbabwe's per capita gross domestic product (GDP) was estimated at $2,000 USD. In 2012, approximately 72.3 percent of the population was living below the poverty line.

Overview of the Economy

Between 1998 and 2008, Zimbabwe's economy ground to a virtual halt. Inflation, the highest in the world, has increased prices more than 900 percent. Although much of the country's money was lost in the 1998–2002 war in the Democratic Republic of the Congo, it is widely believed that corruption and illegal spending within the Mugabe regime is to blame for the country's economic situation. Between 2010 and 2013, the economy began growing at a remarkable rate of 10 percent, but leveled off to 3.2 percent in 2014. The contraction, due to poor harvests, decreased investments, and meagre returns in the diamond trade, seems to portend a continued slowdown. Zimbabwe continues to work with the International Monetary Fund to aid in the country's economic expansion, but is struggling to make any of its Millenium Development Goals. Moreover, foreign investors are consistently deterred by Mugabe's 2008 Indigenization and Economic Empowerment Act, which gives Zimbabweans the right to take over foreign-owned companies and property.

The country's economy depends upon mining agriculture, although the government's poorly executed land reform scheme has weakened agricultural production. Flooding and drought, in addition to food shortages and allegations of government corruption, have thus far crippled Zimbabwe's economy in the twenty-first century.

Industry

Manufacturing is the largest industry, accounting for just over one-quarter of the GDP. Most industrial activity is concentrated in Harare and Bulawayo.

Zimbabwe's industrial products include iron, steel, wood products, cement, chemicals, fertilizer, textiles and clothing, footwear, processed foods, and beverages.

The country's major exports include platinum, cotton, tobacco, gold, ferroalloys, textiles, and clothing. Zimbabwe imports more products than it exports, with $3.263 billion in exports and $5.135 billion in imports in 2014.

Labor

In 2014, an estimated 95 percent of Zimbabwe's work force of more than 5.634 million was unemployed.

Energy/Power/Natural Resources

Hydroelectricity is generated for Zimbabwe and its neighbors by the Kariba Dam. Most of Zimbabwe's mineral resources are found in a mountainous region known as the Great Dyke in the Highveld.

Forestry

There are 15,624,000 million hectares (38,607,745 million acres) of forest in Zimbabwe. Hardwood trees such as teak and mahogany are exploited by the timber industry.

Deforestation is an environmental concern, as many Zimbabweans depend upon wood for fuel and cooking. Between 1990 and 2010, Zimbabwe lost 29.5 percent of its forest cover, or 6,540,000 ha (16,160,691 acres).

Mining/Metals

Mining accounts for roughly 4 percent of Zimbabwe's GDP. The country's gold mining industry uses the capital of Harare as a major distribution center, and although the industry is in decline in the early twenty-first century, gold is still the nation's second largest export item after coal. Other valuable minerals and metals mined in Zimbabwe include iron ore, chromium, silver, copper, nickel, lithium, clay, platinum, diamonds, and tin.

The country's mining operations cause pollution and toxic waste, which jeopardize public health and welfare.

Agriculture

Agriculture accounts for just over 20 percent of Zimbabwe's GDP and employs 66 percent of the work force. Farmers are routinely forced to contend with drought, soil erosion, and pollution. Just 10.9 percent of Zimbabwe's land is arable, while 31.3 is best used for pasture and grazing.

Common crops grown in Zimbabwe include cotton, tobacco, wheat, coffee, tea, sugarcane, and peanuts. Corn is also widely grown, and is the staple crop for domestic use.

Historically, the majority of Zimbabwe's farmland has been owned by the white minority population. In 2000, President Robert Mugabe embarked upon a controversial plan to seize land from white farmers and give it to black settlers. As a result, most black workers lost their jobs on white-owned farms. The new black settlers did not receive the supplies and training promised by the government, and were unable to sustain agricultural production.

Animal Husbandry

Zimbabwean farmers raise cattle, sheep, pigs, goats, and chickens. Donkeys and horses are also kept and remain important to Zimbabwe's agrarian production.

Tourism

There are many tourist attractions in *Zimbabwe*, especially in the country's many national parks. Domboshawa National Park north of Harare contains many ancient rock paintings. Artifacts from Zimbabwe's late Iron Age may also be viewed at the Great Zimbabwe ruins and archaeological site.

Victoria Falls, also known as Mosi-oa-Tunya, or "the smoke that thunders," is an enormous waterfall, considered one of the greatest natural wonders in the world and was, along with the Mosi-oa-Tunya National Park, inscribed as a UNESCO World Heritage site in 1989. Lake Kariba is another favorite tourist attraction, offering opportunities for fishing and sightseeing.

In recent years, political unrest and safety concerns have kept tourists away from Zimbabwe, and many airlines and hotel chains have discontinued service in the country.

Joanne O'Sullivan, Lynn-nore Chittom,
Rebekah Painter, Savannah Schroll Guz

DO YOU KNOW?

- Harare was officially known as Salisbury until 1982. When a small British military force, called the Pioneer Column, first arrived in the country in September 1890, they established Fort Salisbury as their base of operations. It had been named in honor of British Prime Minister Lord Salisbury.

- Harare is also known as the "Sunshine City" for its year-round nice weather.

- During the 1950s the Kariba Dam was constructed along the Zambezi River to generate electricity for Harare. The dam created Lake Kariba, which is also a tourist attraction.

Bibliography

Barclay, Philip. *Zimbabwe: Years of Hope and Despair.* New York: Bloomsbury USA, 2011.

Bourne, Richard. *Catastrophe: What Went Wrong in Zimbabwe.* London: Zed Books, 2011.

Chataway, N. H., ed. *The Bulawayo Cookery Book.* London: Jeppestown Press, 2006.

Chinula, Tione & Vincent Talbot. *Lonely Planet Zimbabwe.* London, UK: 2002.

Hooker, John. *Working Across Cultures.* Cambridge: Stanford Business Books, 2003.

Meredith, Martin. *Mugabe: Power, Plunder, and the Struggle for Zimbabwe's Future.* New York: PublicAffairs, 2007.

Mlambo, Alois S. *A History of Zimbabwe.* Cambridge, UK: Cambridge University Press, 2014

Nyangoni, Wellington. *African Nationalism in Zimbabwe.* Washington DC: University Press of America, 1978.

Owowoyela, Oyekan. *Customs and Culture of Zimbabwe.* Westport, CT: Greenwood, 2002.

Smith, Ian. *Bitter Harvest: Zimbabwe and the Aftermath of its Independence.* London: John Blake Publishing, Ltd., 2008.

Works Cited

BBC. "Zimbabwe approves new constitution." *BBC News.* BBC, 19 Mar. 2013. Web. http://www.bbc.com/news/world-africa-21845444.

_____. "Zimbabwe country profile—Overview." *BBC News.* BBC, 12 Jun. 2015. Web. http://www.bbc.com/news/world-africa-14113249.

Brulliard, Karin. "Power-Sharing Deal Is Signed In Zimbabwe." *The Washington Post.* The Washington Post, 16 Sept. 2008. http://www.washingtonpost.com/wp-dyn/content/article/2008/09/15/AR2008091500504.html.

Bureau of African Affairs. "U.S. Relations with Zimbabwe" *US Department of State.* Office of Website Management, Bureau of Public Affairs, 30 Jan. 2014. Web. http://www.state.gov/r/pa/ei/bgn/5479.htm.

CABS. "CABS mortgages for Budiriro scheme—new conditions." *Personal Banking, Loans, Mortgages.* CABS, Old Mutual Group, 2015. Web. http://www.cabs.co.zw/personal-banking/loans/mortgages.

Chuma, Wallace. "On the Arts: Zimbabwe Youth Are Mimicking American Culture, Minus the Context." *Pittsburgh Post-Gazette.* PG Publishing Co., Inc., 4 Aug. 2002. Web. http://old.post-gazette.com/ae/20020804onarts0804fnp6.asp

Curnow, Robyn. "'Long Arm' of The Government Threatens Media in Zimbabwe." 2 May 2005. *International Herald Tribune.* Dr. Ted Schwalbe, SUNY Fredonia, Fall 2006. Web. http://www.fredonia.edu/department/communication/schwalbe/zimbab.htm.

_____. "Thousands of Zimbabwean Youth Flee To South Africa." *CNN News.* Cable News Network/Turner Broadcasting, 19 Dec. 2008. Web. http://www.cnn.com/2008/WORLD/africa/12/18/zimbabwe.children/index.html.

Dugger, Celia. "White Farmers Confront Mugabe in Legal Battle." *New York Times.* The New York Times Company, 27 Dec. 2008. Web. http://www.nytimes.com/2008/12/28/world/africa/28farmers.html?pagewanted=all&_r=0.

Economic and Social Development Department. "Fact Sheet: Zimbabwe—Women, Agriculture, and Rural Development." *FAO Corporate Document Repository.* FAO Food and Agriculture Organization of the UN, 1994. http://www.fao.org/docrep/v9101e/v9101e00.htm.

Gwertzman, Bernard. "Lyman: Zimbabwe a 'Terrible Tragedy' Under Mugabe Rule." *Council on Foreign Relations.* Council on Foreign Relations, 7 Apr. 2005. http://www.cfr.org/zimbabwe/lyman-zimbabwe-terrible-tragedy-under-mugabe-rule/p7992.

Hufstader, Chris. "Zimbabwe Looks To New Domestic Violence Law." *Oxfam America.* Oxfam America, Inc., 16 Jan. 2007. Web. http://www.oxfamamerica.org/explore/stories/zimbabwe-looks-to-new-domestic-violence-law/.

Human Rights Watch. "Our Hands Are Tied." *Human Rights Watch.* Human Rights Watch, 19 Nov. 2008. Web. https://www.hrw.org/report/2008/11/08/our-hands-are-tied/erosion-rule-law-zimbabwe.

Itano, Nicole. "Despite Promises, Zimbabwean Women Not Given Land." *Women's eNews.* Women's eNews Inc, 10 Jan. 2002. http://womensenews.org/story/the-world/021001/despite-promises-zimbabwean-women-not-given-land.

"Kenya urges AU to Suspend Mugabe." *BBC News.* BBC, 30 Jun. 2008. Web. http://news.bbc.co.uk/2/hi/africa/7481857.stm

Krog, W. "The Progress of Shona and Ndebele Literature." *Southern Rhodesia Native Affairs Department Annual* (1979). Internet Archive, n.d. Web. http://archive.org/stream/TheRhodesiaNativeAffairsDept.AnnualFor1979/NADA2_djvu.txt.

Langa, Veneranda. "Shocking statistics on gender-based violence." *NewsDay.* NewsDay Zimbabwe, 2 Dec. 2013.

Lesser, Howard. "Mugabe Government in Zimbabwe One of Worst Offenders of Housing Rights." *Voice of America News.* VOA, 1 Dec. 2005. http://m.voanews.com/a/a-13-2005-12-01-voa28/301570.html.

MacAskill, Ewan. "UN Report Damns Mugabe Slum Clearance As Catastrophic." *The Guardian.* Guardian News and Media Limited, 23 Jul. 2005. Web. http://www.theguardian.com/world/2005/jul/23/zimbabwe.ewenmacaskill.

McLaughlin, Abraham. "In Zimbabwe, People Power Fails to Ignite." *Christian Science Monitor.* The Christian

Science Monitor, 22 Mar. 2008. Web. http://www. csmonitor.com/2005/0322/p01s04-woaf.html.

Meekers, Dominique. "The Noble Custom of Roora: The Marriage Practices of the Shona of Zimbabwe." *Ethnology* 32.1 (Winter 1993): 35–54.

Muchemwa, Kizito Z. & Musaemura B. Zimunya. "An Overview of Post-Independence Zimbabwean Poetry." *Poetry International Rotterdam*. Poetry International Rotterdam, 16 Oct. 2008. Web. http://www.poetryinternationalweb.net/pi/site/cou_article/item/13089/An-Overview-of-Post-Independence-Zimbabwean-Poetry.

"Mugabe Criticizes 'Stupid' West." *BBC News*. BBC, 23 Dec. 2008. Web. http://news.bbc.co.uk/2/hi/7797424.stm.

Murungu, Solomon. "Shona Religion and Beliefs." *Zambuko*. Solomon Murungu & Zambuko Projects Unlimited, 2004. Web. http://www.zambuko.com/mbirapage/resource_guide/pages/culture/shona_religion.html.

Musengeyi, Itali. "Extended Family Breaking Up Fast in Zimbabwe." *PanAfrican News Agency*. PANGAEA, 11 Oct. 1996. Web. http://pangaea.org/street_children/africa/zimba2.htm.

Nordqvist, Christian. "Zimbabwe Life Expectancy Lowest in The World." *Medical News Today*. MediLexicon International Limited. Web. 10 Apr. 2006. Web. http://www.medicalnewstoday.com/articles/41339.php.

Peel, Tony & Boo Peel. "The Legend of the Zimbabwe Bird." *Victoria Falls Guide*. Tony & Boo Peel, 2015. Web. http://www.victoriafalls-guide.net/zimbabwe-bird.html.

Reporters Without Borders. "2015 World Press Freedom Index." *Reporters Without Borders*. Reporters sans Frontières, 2015. https://index.rsf.org/#!/index-details/ZWE.

_____. "Predators: Indictment Zimbabwe—Robert Mugabe, president." *Reporters Without Borders*. Reporters sans Frontières, 2015. http://en.rsf.org/predator-zimbabwe-robert-mugabe-president,44532.html.

"Shona Information." *Art & Life in Africa*. University of Iowa Museum of Art, 2015. https://africa.uima.uiowa.edu/peoples/show/Igbo.

"South Africa Witholds Aid To Zimbabwe; Health Crisis Grows." *PBS Newshour*. NewsHour Productions LLC, 20 Nov. 2008. Web. http://www.pbs.org/newshour/updates/africa-july-dec08-zimbabwe_11-20/.

Thornycroft, Peta. "Women's Rights Activists Face Danger in Zimbabwe." *National Public Radio*. NPR, 13 Jul. 2007. Web. http://www.npr.org/templates/story/story.php?storyId=15806122.

United Nations High Commissioner on Refugees. "Zimbabwe." *2015 UNHCR subregional operations profile–Southern Africa*. UNHCR, 2015. http://www.unhcr.org/pages/49e485c66.html.

Whitaker, Raymond. "The Brutal Reality of Family Life in Zimbabwe." *The Independent*. The Independent, 14 Dec. 2008. Web. http://www.independent.co.uk/news/world/africa/the-iiosi-christmas-appeal-the-brutal-reality-of-family-life-in-zimbabwe-1066101.html.

Winter, Joseph. "Zimbabwe's Shattered Dream." *BBC News*. BBC, 11 Apr. 2000. Web. http://news.bbc.co.uk/2/hi/africa/701275.stm.

World Bank. "Data: Zimbabwe." *The World Bank*. The World Bank Group, 2015. Web. http://data.worldbank.org/country/zimbabwe.

ZIMRA. "PAYE Explained" *Zimbabwe Revenue Authority*. ZIMRA, 2014. Web. http://www.zimra.co.zw/index.php?option=com_content&view=article&id=1649&Itemid=193.

"Zimbabwe Denies Muzzling Media." *BBC News*. BBC, 1 Feb. 2002. Web. http://news.bbc.co.uk/2/hi/africa/1795125.stm.

"Zimbabwe Forest and Information Data." *Mongabay.com*. Rhett Butler, 2011. http://rainforests.mongabay.com/deforestation/2000/Zimbabwe.htm

"Zimbabwe: Internet Usage and Marketing Report." *Internet World Stats: Usage and Population Statistics*. Miniwatts Marketing Group, 30 Sept. 2012. http://www.internetworldstats.com/af/zw.htm.

Appendix One:
World Governments

Commonwealth

Guiding Premise

A commonwealth is an organization or alliance of nations connected for the purposes of satisfying a common interest. The participating states may retain their own governments, some of which are often considerably different from one another. Although commonwealth members tend to retain their own sovereign government institutions, they collaborate with other members to create mutually agreeable policies that meet their collective interests. Some nations join commonwealths to enhance their visibility and political power on the international stage. Others join commonwealths for security or economic reasons. Commonwealth members frequently engage in trade agreements, security pacts, and other programs. Some commonwealths are regional, while others are global.

Typical Structure

A commonwealth's structure depends largely on the nature of the organization and the interests it serves. Some commonwealths are relatively informal in nature, with members meeting on a periodic basis and participating voluntarily. This informality does not undermine the effectiveness of the organization, however—members still enjoy a closer relationship than that which exists among unaffiliated states. Commonwealths typically have a president, secretary general, or, in the case of the Commonwealth of Nations (a commonwealth that developed out of the British Empire), a monarch acting as the leader of the organization. Members appoint delegates to serve at summits, committee meetings, and other commonwealth events and programs.

Other commonwealths are more formal in structure and procedures. They operate based on mission statements with very specific goals and member participation requirements. These organizations have legislative bodies that meet regularly. There are even joint security operations involving members. The African Union, for example, operates according to a constitution and collectively addresses issues facing the entire African continent, such as HIV/AIDS, regional security, environmental protection, and economic cooperation.

One of the best-known commonwealths in modern history was the Soviet Union. This collective of communist states was similar to other commonwealths, but the members of the Soviet Union, although they retained their own sovereign government institutions, largely deferred to the organization's central leadership in Moscow, which in turn deferred to the Communist Party leadership. After the collapse of the Soviet Union, a dozen former Soviet states, including Russia, reconnected as the Commonwealth of Independent States. This organization features a central council in Minsk, Belarus. This council consists of the heads of state and heads of government for each member nation, along with their cabinet ministers for defense and foreign affairs.

Commonwealth structures and agendas vary. Some focus on trade and economic development, as well as using their respective members' collective power to address human rights, global climate change, and other issues. Others are focused on regional stability and mutual defense, including prevention of nuclear weapons proliferation. The diversity of issues for which commonwealths are formed contributes to the frequency of member meetings as well as the actions carried out by the organization.

Role of the Citizen

Most commonwealths are voluntary in nature, which means that the member states must choose to join with the approval of their respective governments. A nation with a democratic government, therefore, would need the sanction of its popularly elected legislative and executive bodies in order to proceed. Thus, the role of the private citizen with regard to a commonwealth is indirect—the people may have the power to vote for or against a legislative or executive candidate based on his or her position concerning membership in a commonwealth.

Some members of commonwealths, however, do not feature a democratic government, or their respective governmental infrastructures are not yet in place. Rwanda, for instance, is a developing nation whose 2009 decision to join the Commonwealth of Nations likely came from the political leadership with very little input from its citizens, as Rwandans have very limited political freedom.

While citizens may not directly influence the actions of a commonwealth, they may work closely with its representatives. Many volunteer nonprofit organizations—having direct experience with, for example, HIV/AIDS, certain minority groups, or environmental issues—work in partnership with the various branches of a commonwealth's central council. In fact, such organizations are frequently called upon in this regard to implement the policies of a commonwealth, receiving financial and logistical support when working in impoverished and/or war-torn regions. Those working for such organizations may therefore prove invaluable to the effectiveness of a commonwealth's programs.

Michael Auerbach
Marblehead, Massachusetts

Examples
African Union
Commonwealth of Independent States
Commonwealth of Nations
Northern Mariana Islands (and the United States)
Puerto Rico (and the United States)

Bibliography
"About Commonwealth of Independent States." *Commonwealth of Independent States*. CIS, n.d. Web. 17 Jan. 2013.
"AU in a Nutshell." *African Union*. African Union Commission, n.d. Web. 17 Jan. 2013.
"The Commonwealth." *Commonwealth of Nations*. Nexus Strategic Partnerships Limited, 2013. Web. 17 Jan. 2013.

Communist

Guiding Premise

Communism is a political and economic system that seeks to eliminate private property and spread the benefits of labor equally throughout the populace. Communism is generally considered an outgrowth of socialism, a political and economic philosophy that advocates "socialized" or centralized ownership of the economy and the means of production.

Communism developed largely from the theories of Karl Marx (1818–83), who believed that a revolution led by the working class must occur before the state could achieve the even distribution of wealth and property and eliminate the class-based socioeconomic system of capitalist society. Marx believed that a truly equitable society required centralized control of credit, transportation, education, communication, agriculture, and industry, along with eliminating the rights of individuals to inherit or to own land.

Russia (formerly the Soviet Union) and China are the two largest countries to have been led by communist governments during the twentieth and twenty-first centuries. In both cases, the attempt to bring about a communist government came by way of violent revolutions in which members of the former government and ruling party were executed. Under Russian leader Vladimir Lenin (1870–1924) and Chinese leader Mao Zedong (1893–1976), strict dictatorships were instituted, curtailing individual rights in favor of state control. Lenin sought to expand communism into developing nations to counter the global spread of capitalism. Mao, in his form of communism, considered ongoing revolution within China a necessary aspect of communism. Both gave their names to their respective versions of communism, but neither Leninism nor Maoism managed to achieve the idealized utopia envisioned by Marx and other communist philosophers.

The primary difference between modern socialism and communism is that communist groups believe that a social revolution is necessary to create the idealized state without class structure, where socialists believe that the inequities of class structure can be addressed and eliminated through gradual change.

Typical Structure

Most modern communist governments define themselves as "socialist," though a national communist party exerts control over all branches of government. The designation of a "communist state" is primarily an external definition for a situation in which a communist party controls the government.

Among the examples of modern socialist states operating under the communist model are the People's Republic of China, the Republic of Cuba, and the Socialist Republic of Vietnam. However, each of these governments in fact operates through a mixed system of socialist and capitalist economic policies, allowing private ownership in some situations and sharply enforcing state control in others.

Typically, a communist state is led by the national communist party, a political group with voluntary membership and members in all sectors of the populace. While many individuals may join the communist party, the leadership of the party is generally selected by a smaller number of respected or venerated leaders from within the party. These leaders select a ruling committee that develops the political initiatives of the party, which are thereafter distributed throughout the government.

In China, the Communist Party elects both a chairperson, who serves as executive of the party, and a politburo, a standing committee that makes executive decisions on behalf of the party. In Cuba, the Communist Party selects individuals who sit for election to the National Assembly of People's Power, which then serves directly as the state's sole legislative body.

In the cases of China, Cuba, and Vietnam, the committees and leaders chosen by the communist party then participate directly in electing leaders to serve in the state judiciary. In addition, the central committees typically appoint individuals to serve as heads of the military and to lower-level, provincial, or municipal government positions. In China, the populace elects individuals to local, regional, and provincial councils that in turn elect representatives to sit on a legislative body known as the National People's Congress (NPC), though the NPC is generally considered a largely ceremonial institution without any substantial power to enact independent legislation.

In effect, most modern communist states are controlled by the leadership of the national communist party, though this leadership is achieved by direct and indirect control of lesser legislative, executive, and judicial bodies. In some cases, ceremonial and symbolic offices created under the communist party can evolve to take a larger role in state politics. In China, for instance, the NPC has come to play a more important role in developing legislation in the twenty-first century.

Role of the Citizen

In modern communist societies, citizens have little voice in selecting the leadership of the government. In many communist states, popular elections are held at local and national levels, but candidates are chosen by communist party leadership and citizens are not given the option to vote for representatives of opposing political parties.

In most cases, the state adopts policies that give the appearance of popular control over the government, while in actuality, governmental policies are influenced by a small number of leaders chosen from within the upper echelons of the party. Popularly elected leaders who oppose party policy are generally removed from office.

All existing communist states have been criticized for human rights violations in terms of curtailing the freedoms available to citizens and of enacting dictatorial and authoritarian policies. Cuba, Vietnam, and China, for instance, all have laws preventing citizens from opposing party policy or supporting a political movement that opposes the communist party. Communist governments have also been accused of using propaganda and misinformation to control the opinion of the populace regarding party leadership and therefore reducing the potential for popular resistance to communist policies.

Micah Issitt
Philadelphia, Pennsylvania

Examples
China
Cuba
Laos
North Korea
Vietnam

Bibliography
Caramani, Daniele. *Comparative Politics*. New York: Oxford UP, 2008. Print.
Priestland, David. *The Red Flag: A History of Communism*. New York: Grove, 2009. Print.
Service, Robert. *Comrades! A History of World Communism*. Cambridge: Harvard UP, 2007. Print.

Confederation/Confederacy

Guiding Premise

A confederation or confederacy is a loose alliance between political units, such as states or cantons, within a broader federal government. Confederations allow a central, federal government to create laws and regulations of broad national interest, but the sovereign units are granted the ultimate authority to carry out those laws and to create, implement, and enforce their own laws as well. Confederate governments are built on the notion that a single, central government should not have ultimate authority over sovereign states and populations. Some confederate governments were born due to the rise of European monarchies and empires that threatened to govern states from afar. Others were created out of respect for the diverse ideologies, cultures, and ideals of their respective regions. Confederations and confederacies may be hybrids, giving comparatively more power to a federal government while retaining respect for the sovereignty of their members. True confederate governments are rare in the twenty-first century.

Typical Structure

Confederate governments are typically characterized by the presence of both a central government and a set of regional, similarly organized, and sovereign (independent) governments. For example, a confederate government might have as its central government structure a system that features executive, legislative, and judicial branches. Each region that serves as members of the confederation would have in place a similar system, enabling the efficient flow of lawmaking and government services.

In some confederations, the executive branch of the central government is headed by a president or prime minister, who serves as the government's chief administrative officer, overseeing the military and other government operations. Meanwhile, at the regional level, another chief executive, such as a governor, is charged with the administration of that government's operations.

Legislative branches are also similarly designed. Confederations use parliaments or congresses that, in most cases, have two distinct chambers. One chamber consists of legislators who each represent an entire state, canton, or region. The other chamber consists of legislators representing certain populations of voters within that region. Legislatures at the regional level not only have the power to create and enforce their own laws, but also have the power to refuse to enact or enforce any laws handed down by the national government.

A confederation's judiciary is charged with ensuring that federal and regional laws are applied uniformly and within the limits of the confederation's constitutional framework. Central and regional governments both have such judicial institutions, with the latter addressing those legal matters administered in the state or canton and the former addressing legal issues of interest to the entire country.

Political parties also typically play a role in a confederate government. Political leadership is achieved by a party's majority status in either the executive or the legislative branches. Parties also play a role in forging a compromise on certain matters at both the regional and national levels. Some confederations take the diversity of political parties and their ideologies seriously enough to create coalition governments that can help avoid political stalemates.

Role of the Citizen

The political role of the citizen within a confederate political system depends largely on the constitution of the country. In some confederacies, for example, the people directly elect their legislative and executive leaders by popular vote. Some legislators are elected to open terms—they may technically be reelected, but this election is merely a formality, as they are allowed to stay in office until they decide to leave or they die—while others may be subject to term limits or other reelection rules. Popularly elected legislators and executives in turn draft, file, and pass new laws and regulations that ideally are favorable to the voters. Some confederate systems give popularly elected legislators the ability to elect a party leader to serve as prime minister or president.

Confederations are designed to empower the regional government and avoid the dominance of a distant national government. In this manner, citizens of a confederate government, in some cases, may enjoy the ability to put forth new legislative initiatives. Although the lawmaking process is expected to be administered by the legislators and executives, in such cases the people are allowed and even encouraged to connect and interact with their political representatives to ensure that the government remains open and accessible.

Michael Auerbach
Marblehead, Massachusetts

Examples

European Union
Switzerland
United States under the Articles of Confederation (1781–89)

Bibliography

"Government Type." *The World Factbook.* Central Intelligence Agency, n.d. Web. 17 Jan. 2013.

"Swiss Politics." *SwissWorld.org.* Federal Department of Foreign Affairs Presence Switzerland, n.d. Web. 17 Jan. 2013.

Constitutional Monarchy

Guiding Premise

A constitutional monarchy is a form of government in which the head of state is a monarch (a king or queen) with limited powers. The monarch has official duties, but those responsibilities are defined in the nation's constitution and not by the monarch. Meanwhile, the power to create and rescind laws is given to a legislative body. Constitutional monarchies retain the ceremony and traditions associated with nations that have long operated under a king or queen. However, the constitution prevents the monarch from becoming a tyrant. Additionally, the monarchy, which is typically a lifetime position, preserves a sense of stability and continuity in the government, as the legislative body undergoes periodic change associated with the election cycle.

Typical Structure

The structure of a constitutional monarchy varies from nation to nation. In some countries, the monarchy is predominantly ceremonial. In such cases, the monarch provides a largely symbolic role, reminding the people of their heritage and giving them comfort in times of difficulty. Such is the case in Japan, for example; the emperor of that country was stripped of any significant power after World War II but was allowed to continue his legacy in the interest of ensuring that the Japanese people would remain peaceful. Today, that nation still holds its monarchical family in the highest regard, but the government is controlled by the Diet (the legislature), with the prime minister serving in the executive role.

In other countries, the sovereign plays a more significant role. In the United Kingdom, the king or queen does have some power, including the powers to appoint the prime minister, to open or dissolve Parliament, to approve bills that have been passed by Parliament, and to declare war and make peace. However, the monarch largely defers to the government on these acts. In Bahrain, the king (or, until 2002, emir or hereditary ruler) was far more involved in government in the late twentieth and early twenty-first centuries than many other constitutional monarchs. In 1975, the emir of Bahrain dissolved the parliament, supposedly to run the government more effectively. His son would later implement a number of significant constitutional reforms that made the government more democratic in nature.

The key to the structure of this type of political system is the constitution. As is the case in the United States (a federal republic), a constitutional monarchy is carefully defined by the government's founding document. In Canada, for example, the king or queen of England is still recognized as the head of state, but that country's constitution gives the monarch no power other than ceremonial responsibilities. India, South Africa, and many other members of the Commonwealth of Nations (the English monarch's sphere of influence, spanning most of the former British colonies) have, since gaining their independence, created constitutions that grant no power to the English monarch; instead, they give all powers to their respective government institutions and, in some cases, recognize their own monarchs.

A defining feature of a constitutional monarchy is the fact that the monarch gives full respect to the limitations set forth by the constitution (and rarely seeks to alter such a document in his or her favor). Even in the United Kingdom itself—which does not have a written constitution, but rather a series of foundational documents—the king or queen does not step beyond the bounds set by customary rules. One interesting exception is in Bahrain, where Hamad bin Isa Al-Khalifa assumed the throne in 1999 and immediately implemented a series of reforms to the constitution in order to give greater definition to that country's democratic institutions, including resuming parliamentary elections in 2001. During the 2011 Arab Spring uprisings, Bahraini protesters called for further democratic reforms to be enacted, and tensions between the ruler and his opposition continue.

Role of the Citizen

In the past, monarchies ruled nations with absolute power; the only power the people had was the ability to unify and overthrow the ruling sovereign. Although the notion of an absolute monarchy has largely disappeared from the modern political landscape, many nations have retained their respective kings, queens, emperors, and other monarchs for the sake of ceremony and cultural heritage. In the modern constitutional monarchy, the people are empowered by their nation's foundational documents, which not only define the rights of the people but the limitations of their governments and sovereign as well. The people, through their legislators and through the democratic voting process, can modify their constitutions to expand or shrink the political involvement of the monarchy.

For example, the individual members of the Commonwealth of Nations, including Canada and Australia, have different constitutional parameters for the king or queen of England. In England, the monarch holds a number of powers, while in Canada, he or she is merely a ceremonial head of state (with all government power centered in the capital of Ottawa). In fact, in 1999, Australia held a referendum (a general vote) on whether to abolish its constitutional monarchy altogether and replace it with a presidential republic. In that case, the people voted to retain the monarchy, but the proposal was only narrowly defeated. These examples demonstrate the tremendous power the citizens of a constitutional monarchy may possess through the legislative process and the vote under the constitution.

Michael Auerbach
Marblehead, Massachusetts

Examples

Bahrain
Cambodia
Denmark
Japan
Lesotho
Malaysia
Morocco
Netherlands
Norway
Spain
Sweden
Thailand
United Kingdom

Bibliography

Bowman, John. "Constitutional Monarchies." *CBC News.* CBC, 4 Oct. 2002. Web. 17 Jan. 2013.

"The Role of the Monarchy." *Royal.gov.uk.* Royal Household, n.d. Web. 17 Jan. 2013.

Constitutional Republic

Guiding Premise

A constitutional republic is a governmental system in which citizens are involved in electing or appointing leaders who serve according to rules formulated in an official state constitution. In essence, the constitutional republic combines the political structure of a republic or republican governmental system with constitutional principles.

A republic is a government in which the head of state is empowered to hold office through law, not inheritance (as in a monarchy). A constitutional republic is a type of republic based on a constitution, a written body of fundamental precedents and principles from which the laws of the nation are developed.

Most constitutional republics in the modern world use a universal suffrage system, in which all citizens of the nation are empowered to vote for or against individuals who attempt to achieve public office. Universal suffrage is not required for a nation to qualify as a constitutional republic, and some nations may only allow certain categories of citizens to vote for elected leaders.

A constitutional republic differs from other forms of democratic systems in the roles assigned to both the leaders and the citizenry. In a pure democratic system, the government is formed by pure majority rule, and this system therefore ignores the opinions of any minority group. A republic, by contrast, is a form of government in which the government's role is limited by a written constitution aimed at promoting the welfare of all individuals, whether members of the majority or a minority.

Typical Structure

To qualify as a constitutional republic, a nation must choose a head of state (most often a president) through elections, according to constitutional law. In some nations, an elected president may serve alongside an appointed or elected individual who serves as leader of the legislature,

such as a prime minister, often called the "head of government." When the president also serves as head of government, the republic is said to operate under a presidential system.

Typically, the executive branch consists of the head of state and the executive offices, which are responsible for enforcing the laws and overseeing relations with other nations. The legislative branch makes laws and has overlapping duties with the executive office in terms of economic and military developments. The judicial branch, consisting of the courts, interprets the law and the constitution and enforces adherence to the law.

In a constitutional republic, the constitution describes the powers allotted to each branch of government and the means by which the governmental bodies are to be established. The constitution also describes the ways in which governmental branches interact in creating, interpreting, and enforcing laws. For instance, in the United States, the executive and legislative branches both have roles in determining the budget for the nation, and neither body is free to make budgetary legislation without the approval of the other branch.

Role of the Citizen

In a constitutional republic, the citizens have the power to control the evolution of the nation through the choice of representatives who serve on the government. These representatives can, generally through complicated means, create or abolish laws and even change the constitution itself through reinterpretations of constitutional principles or direct amendments.

Citizens in a republic are empowered, but generally not required, to play a role in electing leaders. In the United States, both state governments and the federal government function according to a republican system, and citizens are therefore allowed to take part in the election of leaders to both local and national offices. In addition, constitutional systems generally allow individuals to join political interest groups to further common political goals.

In a constitutional democratic republic such as Guatemala and Honduras, the president, who serves as chief of state and head of government, is elected directly by popular vote. In the United States, a constitutional federal republic, the president is elected by the Electoral College, whose members are selected according to the popular vote within each district. The Electoral College is intended to provide more weight to smaller states, thereby balancing the disproportionate voting power of states with larger populations. In all constitutional republics, the citizens elect leaders either directly or indirectly through other representatives chosen by popular vote. Therefore, the power to control the government is granted to the citizens of the constitutional republic.

Micah Issitt
Philadelphia, Pennsylvania

Examples

Guatemala

Honduras

Iceland

Paraguay

Peru

United States

Uruguay

Bibliography

Baylis, John, Steve Smith, and Patricia Owens. *The Globalization of World Politics: An Introduction to International Relations.* New York: Oxford UP, 2010. Print.

Caramani, Daniele. *Comparative Politics.* New York: Oxford UP, 2008. Print.

Garner, Robert, Peter Ferdinand, and Stephanie Lawson. *Introduction to Politics.* 2nd ed. Oxford: Oxford UP, 2009. Print.

Hague, Rod, and Martin Harrop. *Comparative Government and Politics: An Introduction.* New York: Palgrave, 2007. Print.

Democracy

Guiding Premise

Democracy is a political system based on majority rule, in which all citizens are guaranteed participatory rights to influence the evolution of government. There are many different types of democracy, based on the degree to which citizens participate in the formation and operation of the government. In a direct democratic system, citizens vote directly on proposed changes to law and public policy. In a representative democracy, individuals vote to elect representatives who then serve to create and negotiate public policy.

The democratic system of government first developed in Ancient Greece and has existed in many forms throughout history. While democratic systems always involve some type of majority rule component, most modern democracies have systems in place designed to equalize representation for minority groups or to promote the development of governmental policies that prevent oppression of minorities by members of the majority.

In modern democracies, one of the central principles is the idea that citizens must be allowed to participate in free elections to select leaders who serve in the government. In addition, voters in democratic systems elect political leaders for a limited period of time, thus ensuring that the leadership of the political system can change along with the changing views of the populace. Political theorists have defined democracy as a system in which the people are sovereign and the political power flows upward from the people to their elected leaders.

Typical Structure

In a typical democracy, the government is usually divided into executive, legislative, and judicial branches. Citizens participate in electing individuals to serve in one or more of these branches, and elected leaders appoint additional leaders to serve in other political offices. The democratic system, therefore, involves a combination of elected and appointed leadership.

Democratic systems may follow a presidential model, as in the United States, where citizens elect a president to serve as both head of state and head of government. In a presidential model, citizens may also participate in elections to fill other governmental bodies, including the legislature and judicial branch. In a parliamentary democracy, citizens elect individuals to a parliament, whose members in turn form a committee to appoint a leader, often called the prime minister, who serves as head of government.

In most democratic systems, the executive and legislative branches cooperate in the formation of laws, while the judicial branch enforces and interprets the laws produced by the government. Most democratic systems have developed a system of checks and balances designed to prevent any single branch of government from exerting a dominant influence over the development of governmental policy. These checks and balances may be instituted in a variety of ways, including the ability to block governmental initiatives and the ability to appoint members to various governmental agencies.

Democratic governments generally operate on the principle of political parties, which are organizations formed to influence political development. Candidates for office have the option of joining a political party, which can provide funding and other campaign assistance. In some democratic systems—called dominant party or one-party dominant systems—there is effectively a single political party. Dominant party systems allow for competition in democratic elections, but existing power structures often prevent opposing parties from competing successfully. In multiparty democratic systems, there are two or more political parties with the ability to compete for office, and citizens are able to choose among political parties during elections. Some countries only allow political parties to be active at the national level, while other countries allow political parties to play a role in local and regional elections.

Role of the Citizen

The citizens in a democratic society are seen as the ultimate source of political authority. Members of the government, by contrast, are seen as servants of the people, and are selected and elected to serve the people's interests. Democratic systems developed to protect and enhance the freedom of the people; however, for the system to function properly, citizens must engage in a number of civic duties.

In democratic nations, voting is a right that comes with citizenship. Though some democracies—Australia, for example—require citizens to vote by law, compulsory participation in elections is not common in democratic societies. Citizens are nonetheless encouraged to fulfill their voting rights and to stay informed regarding political issues. In addition, individuals are responsible for contributing to the well-being of society as a whole, usually through a system of taxation whereby part of an individual's earnings is used to pay for governmental services.

In many cases, complex governmental and legal issues must be simplified to ease understanding among the citizenry. This goal is partially met by having citizens elect leaders who must then explain to their constituents how they are shaping legislation and other government initiatives to reflect constituents' wants and needs. In the United States, citizens may participate in the election of local leaders within individual cities or counties, and also in the election of leaders who serve in the national legislature and executive offices.

Citizens in democratic societies are also empowered with the right to join political interest groups and political parties in an effort to further a broader political agenda. However, democratic societies oppose making group membership a requirement and have laws forbidding forcing an individual to join any group. Freedom of choice, especially with regard to political affiliation and preference, is one of the cornerstones of all democratic systems.

Micah Issitt
Philadelphia, Pennsylvania

Examples

Denmark
Sweden
Spain
Japan
Australia
Costa Rica
Uruguay
United States

Bibliography

Barington, Lowell. *Comparative Politics: Structures and Choices*. Boston: Wadsworth, 2012. Print.

Caramani, Daniele. *Comparative Politics*. New York. Oxford UP, 2008. Print.

Przeworski, Adam. *Democracy and the Limits of Self Government*, New York: Cambridge UP, 2010. Print.

Dictatorship/Military Dictatorship

Guiding Premise

Dictatorships and military dictatorships are political systems in which absolute power is held by an individual or military organization. Dictatorships are led by a single individual, under whom all political control is consolidated. Military dictatorships are similar in purpose, but place the system under the control of a military organization comprised of a single senior officer, or small group of officers. Often, dictatorships and military dictatorships are imposed as the result of a coup d'état in which the regime in question directly removes the incumbent regime, or after a power vacuum creates chaos in the nation. In both situations, the consolidation of absolute power is designed to establish a state of strict law and order.

Typical Structure

Dictatorships and military dictatorships vary in structure and nature. Some come about through the overthrow of other regimes, while others are installed through the democratic process, and then become a dictatorship as democratic rights are withdrawn. Still others are installed following a complete breakdown of government, often with the promise of establishing order.

Many examples of dictatorships can be found in the twentieth century, including Nazi Germany, Joseph Stalin's Soviet Union, and China under Mao Tse-tung. A number of dictatorships existed in Africa, such as the regimes of Idi Amin in Uganda, Charles Taylor in Liberia, and Mu'ammar Gadhafi in Libya. Dictatorships such as these consolidated power in the hands of an individual leader. A dictator serves as the sole decision-maker in the government, frequently using the military, secret police, or other security agencies to enforce the leader's will. Dictators also have control over state institutions like legislatures. A legislature may have the ability to develop and pass laws, but if its actions run counter to the dictator's will, the latter can—and

frequently does—dissolve the body, replacing its members with those more loyal to the dictator's agenda.

Military dictatorships consolidate power not in the hands of a civilian but in an individual or small group of military officers—the latter of which are often called "juntas." Because military dictatorships are frequently installed following a period of civil war and/or a coup d'état, the primary focus of the dictatorship is to achieve strict order through the application of military force. Military dictatorships are often installed with the promise of an eventual return to civilian and/or democratic control once the nation has regained stability. In the case of North Korea, one-party communist rule turned into a communist military dictatorship as its leader, Kim Il-Sung, assumed control of the military and brought its leadership into the government.

In the late twentieth and early twenty-first centuries, dictatorships and military dictatorships are most commonly found in developing nations, where poverty rates are high and regional stability is tenuous at best. Many are former European colonies, where charismatic leaders who boast of their national heritage have stepped in to replace colonial governments. National resources are typically directed toward military and security organizations in an attempt to ensure security and internal stability, keeping the regime in power and containing rivals. Human rights records in such political systems are typically heavily criticized by the international community.

Role of the Citizen

Dictatorships and military dictatorships are frequently installed because of the absence of viable democratic governments. There is often a disconnect, therefore, between the people and their leaders in a dictatorship. Of course, many dictatorships are identified as such by external entities and not by their own people. For example, the government of Zimbabwe is technically identified as a parliamentary democracy, with Robert Mugabe—who has been the elected leader of the country since 1980—as its president. However, the international community has long complained that Mugabe "won" his positions through political corruption, including alleged ballot stuffing. In 2008, Mugabe lost his first reelection campaign, but demanded a recount. While the recount continued, his supporters attacked opposition voters, utilizing violence and intimidation until his opponent, Morgan Tsvangirai, withdrew his candidacy, and Mugabe was restored as president.

By definition, citizens do not have a role in changing the course of a dictatorship's agenda. The people are usually called upon to join the military in support of the regime, or cast their vote consistently in favor of the ruling regime. Freedom of speech, the press, and assembly are virtually nonexistent, as those who speak out against the ruling regime are commonly jailed, tortured, or killed.

Michael Auerbach
Marblehead, Massachusetts

Examples

Belarus (dictatorship)
Fiji (military dictatorship)
North Korea (military dictatorship)
Zimbabwe (dictatorship)

Bibliography

Clayton, Jonathan. "China Aims to Bring Peace through Deals with Dictators and Warlords." *Times* [London]. Times Newspapers, 31 Jan. 2007. Web. 6 Feb. 2013.

"Robert Mugabe—Biography." *Biography.com.* A+E Television Networks, 2013. Web. 6 Feb. 2013.

Ecclesiastical

Guiding Premise

An ecclesiastical government is one in which the laws of the state are guided by and derived from religious law. Ecclesiastical governments can take a variety of forms and can be based on many different types of religious traditions. In some traditions, a deity or group of deities are considered to take a direct role in the formation of government, while other traditions utilize religious laws or principles indirectly to craft laws used to manage the state.

In many cultures, religious laws and tenets play a major role in determining the formation of national laws. Historically, the moral and ethical principles derived from Judeo-Christian tradition inspired many laws in Europe and North America. Few modern governments operate according to an ecclesiastical system, but Vatican City, which is commonly classified as a city-state, utilizes a modernized version of the ecclesiastical government model. All states utilizing an ecclesiastical or semi-ecclesiastical system have adopted a single state religion that is officially recognized by the government.

In some predominantly Islamic nations, including the Sudan, Oman, Iran, and Nigeria, Islamic law, known as sharia, is the basis for most national laws, and government leaders often must obtain approval by the leaders of the religious community before being allowed to serve in office. Most modern ecclesiastical or semi-ecclesiastical governments have adopted a mixed theocratic republic system in which individuals approved by religious authorities are elected by citizens to hold public office.

Typical Structure

In an ecclesiastical government, the church or recognized religious authority is the source of all state law. In a theocracy, which is one of the most common types of ecclesiastical governments, a deity or group of deities occupies a symbolic position as head of state, while representatives are chosen to lead the government based on their approval by the prevailing religious authority. In other types of ecclesiastical governments, the chief of state may be the leading figure in the church, such as in Vatican City, where the Catholic Pope is also considered the chief of state.

There are no modern nations that operate on a purely ecclesiastical system, though some Islamic countries, like Iran, have adopted a semi-ecclesiastical form of republican government. In Iran, the popularly elected Assembly of Experts—comprised of Islamic scholars called mujtahids—appoints an individual to serve as supreme leader of the nation for life, and this individual has veto power over all other governmental offices. Iranian religious leaders also approve other individuals to run as candidates for positions in the state legislature. In many cases, the citizens will elect an individual to serve as head of government, though this individual must conform to religious laws.

In an ecclesiastical government, those eligible to serve in the state legislature are generally members of the church hierarchy or have been approved for office by church leaders. In Tibet, which functioned as an ecclesiastical government until the Chinese takeover of 1951, executive and legislative duties were consolidated under a few religious leaders, called lamas, and influential citizens who maintained the country under a theocratic system. Most modern nations separate governmental functions between distinct but interrelated executive, legislative, and judicial branches.

Many modern semi-ecclesiastical nations have adopted a set of state principles in the form of a constitution to guide the operation of government and the establishment of laws. In mixed constitutional/theocratic systems, the constitution may be used to legitimize religious authority by codifying a set of laws and procedures that have been developed from religious scripture.

In addition, the existence of a constitution facilitates the process of altering laws and governmental procedures as religious authorities reinterpret religious scriptures and texts.

Role of the Citizen

Citizens in modern ecclesiastical and semi-ecclesiastical governments play a role in formulating the government though national and local elections. In some cases, religious authorities may approve more than one candidate for a certain position and citizens are then able to exercise legitimate choice in the electoral process. In other cases, popular support for one or more candidates may influence religious authorities when it comes time to nominate or appoint an individual to office.

In ecclesiastical governments, the freedoms and rights afforded to citizens may depend on their religious affiliation. Christians living in a Christian ecclesiastical government, for instance, may be allowed to run for and hold government office, while representatives of other religions may be denied this right. In addition, ecclesiastical governments may not recognize religious rights and rituals of other traditions and may not offer protection for those practicing religions other than the official state religion.

Though religious authority dominates politics and legislative development, popular influence is still an important part of the ecclesiastical system. Popular support for or against certain laws may convince the government to alter official policies. In addition, the populace may join local and regional religious bodies that can significantly affect national political developments. As local and regional religious groups grow in numbers and influence, they may promote candidates to political office, thereby helping to influence the evolution of government.

Micah Issitt
Philadelphia, Pennsylvania

Examples

Afghanistan
Iran
Nigeria
Oman
Vatican City

Bibliography

Barrington, Lowell. *Comparative Politics: Structures and Choices.* Boston: Wadsworth, 2012. Print.

Hallaq, Wael B. *An Introduction to Islamic Law.* New York: Cambridge UP, 2009. Print.

Hirschl, Ran. *Constitutional Theocracy.* Cambridge, MA: Harvard UP, 2010. Print.

Failed State

Guiding Premise

A failed state is a political unit that at one point had a stable government that provided basic services and security to its citizens, but then entered a period marked by devastating conflict, extreme poverty, overwhelming political corruption, and/or unlivable environmental conditions. Often, a group takes hold of a failed state's government through military means, staving off rivals to fill in a power vacuum. The nominal leadership of a failed state frequently uses its power to combat rival factions, implement extreme religious law, or protect and advance illicit activities (such as drug production or piracy). Failed states frequently retain their external borders, but within those borders are regions that may be dominated by a particular faction, effectively carving the state into disparate subunits, with some areas even attaining relative stability and security—a kind of de facto independence.

Typical Structure

Failed states vary in appearance based on a number of factors. One such factor is the type of government that existed prior to the state's collapse. For example, a failed state might have originally existed as a parliamentary democracy, with an active legislature and executive system that developed a functioning legal code and administered to the needs of the people. However, that state may not have adequately addressed the needs of certain groups, fostering a violent backlash and hastening the country's destabilization. An ineffectual legislature might have been dissolved by the executive (a prime minister or president), and in the absence of leadership, the government as a whole ceased to operate effectively.

Another major factor is demographics. Many states are comprised of two or more distinct ethnic, social, or religious groups. When the ruling party fails to effectively govern and/or serve the interests of a certain segment of the population, it may be ousted or simply ignored by the marginalized faction within the state. If the government falls, it creates a power vacuum that rival groups compete to fill. If one faction gains power, it must remain in a constant state of vigilance against its rivals, focusing more on keeping enemies in check than on rebuilding crippled government infrastructure. Some also seek to create theocracies based on extreme interpretations of a particular religious doctrine. Frequently, these regimes are themselves ousted by rivals within a few years, leaving no lasting government and keeping the state in chaos.

Failed states are also characterized by extreme poverty and a lack of modern technology. Potable water, electricity, food, and medicine are scarce among average citizens. In some cases, these conditions are worsened by natural events. Haiti, for example, was a failed state for many years before the devastating 2010 earthquake that razed the capitol city of Port au Prince, deepening the country's poverty and instability. Afghanistan and Ethiopia—with their harsh, arid climates—are also examples of failed states whose physical environments and lack of resources exacerbated an already extreme state of impoverishment.

Most failed states' conditions are also worsened by the presence of foreigners. Because their governments are either unable or unwilling to repel terrorists, for example, failed states frequently become havens for international terrorism. Somalia, Afghanistan, and Iraq are all examples of states that failed, enabling terrorist organizations to set up camp within their borders. As such groups pose a threat to other nations, those nations often send troops and weapons into the failed states to engage the terrorists. In recent years, NATO, the United Nations, and the African Union have all entered failed states to both combat terrorists and help rebuild government.

Role of the Citizen

Citizens of a failed state have very little say in the direction of their country. In most cases, when a faction assumes control over the government, it installs strict controls that limit the rights of citizens, particularly such rights as freedom of speech, freedom of assembly, and freedom of religion. Some regimes allow for "democratic" elections, but a continued lack of infrastructure and widespread corruption often negates the legitimacy of these elections.

Citizens of failed states are often called upon by the ruling regime (or a regional faction) to serve in its militia, helping it combat other factions within the state. In fact, many militias within failed states are comprised of people who were forced to join (under penalty of death) at a young age. Those who do not join militias are often drawn into criminal activity such as piracy and the drug trade.

Some citizens are able to make a difference by joining interest groups. Many citizens are able to achieve a limited amount of success sharing information about women's rights, HIV/AIDS and other issues. In some situations, these groups are able to gain international assistance from organizations that were unable to work with the failed government.

Michael Auerbach
Marblehead, Massachusetts

Examples

Chad
Democratic Republic of the Congo
Somalia
Sudan
Zimbabwe

Bibliography

"Failed States: Fixing a Broken World." *Economist*, 29 Jan. 2009. Web. 6 Feb. 2012.
"Failed States." Global Policy Forum, 2013. Web. 6 Feb. 2012.
"Somalia Tops Failed States Index for Fifth Year." *CNN.com*. Turner Broadcasting System, 18 June 2012. Web. 6 Feb. 2012.
Thürer, Daniel. (1999). "The 'Failed State' and International Law." *International Review of the Red Cross*. International Committee of the Red Cross, 31 Dec. 1999. Web. 6 Feb. 2012.

Federal Republic

Guiding Premise

A federal republic is a political system that features a central government as well as a set of regional subunits such as states or provinces. Federal republics are designed to limit the power of the central government, paring its focus to only matters of national interest. Typically, a greater degree of power is granted to the regional governments, which retain the ability to create their own laws of local relevance. The degree to which the federal and regional governments each enjoy authority varies from nation to nation, based on the country's interpretation of this republican form of government. By distributing authority to these separate but connected government institutions, federal republics give the greatest power to the people themselves, who typically vote directly for both their regional and national political representation.

Typical Structure

A federal republic's structure varies from nation to nation. However, most federal republics feature two distinct governing entities. The first is a central, federal government, usually based in the nation's capital city. The federal government's task is to address issues of national importance. These issues include defense and foreign relations, but also encompass matters of domestic interest that must be addressed in uniform fashion, such as social assistance programs, infrastructure, and certain taxes.

A federal republic is comprised of executive, legislative, and judicial branches. The executive is typically a president or prime minister—the former selected by popular vote, the latter selected by members of the legislature—and is charged with the administration of the federal government's programs and regulations. The legislature—such as the US Congress, the Austrian Parliament, or the German Bundestag—is charged with developing laws and managing government spending. The judiciary is charged with ensuring that federal and state laws are enforced and that they are consistent with the country's constitution.

The federal government is limited in terms of its ability to assert authority over the regions. Instead, federal republics grant a degree of sovereignty to the different states, provinces, or regions that comprise the entire nation. These regions have their own governments, similar in structure and procedure to those of the federal government. They too have executives, legislatures, and judiciaries whose foci are limited to the regional government's respective jurisdictions.

The federal and regional segments of a republic are not completely independent of one another, however. Although the systems are intended to distribute power evenly, federal and regional governments are closely linked. This connectivity ensures the efficient collection of taxes, the regional distribution of federal funds, and a rapid response to issues of national importance. A federal republic's greatest strength, therefore, is the series of connections it maintains between the federal, regional, and local governments it contains.

Role of the Citizen

A federal republic is distinguished by the limitations of power it places on the national government. The primary goal of such a design was to place the power of government in the hands of the people. One of the ways the citizens' power is demonstrated is by participating in the electoral process. In a federal republic, the people elect their legislators. In some republics, the legislators in turn elect a prime minister, while in others, the people directly elect a president. The electoral process is an important way for citizens to influence the course of their government, both at the regional and federal levels. They do so by placing people who truly represent their diverse interests in the federal government.

The citizen is also empowered by participating in government as opposed to being subjected to it. In addition to taking part in the electoral process, the people are free to join and become active in a political party. A political party serves as a proxy for its members, representing their viewpoint and interests on a local and national level. In federal republics like Germany, a wide range of political parties are active in the legislature, advancing the political agendas of those they represent.

Michael Auerbach
Marblehead, Massachusetts

Examples
Austria
Brazil
Germany
India
Mexico
Nigeria
United States

Bibliography
"The Federal Principle." *Republik Österreich Parlament.* Republik Österreich Parlament, 8 Oct. 2010. Web. 6 Feb. 2013.

"The Federal Republic of Germany." *Deutscher Bundestag.* German Bundestag, 2013. Web. 6 Feb. 2013.

Collin, Nicholas. "An Essay on the Means of Promoting Federal Sentiments in the United States." *Friends of the Constitution: Writings of the "Other" Federalists, 1787–1788.* Ed. Colleen A. Sheehan and Gary L. McDowell. Online Library of Liberty, 2013. Web. 6 Feb. 2013.

Federation

Guiding Premise

A federation is a nation formed from the unification of smaller political entities. Federations feature federal governments that oversee nationwide issues. However, they also grant a degree of autonomy to the regional, state, or other local governments within the system. Federations are often formed because a collective of diverse regions find a common interest in unification. While the federal government is installed to address those needs, regions with their own distinct ethnic, socioeconomic, or political characteristics remain intact. This "separate but united" structure allows federations to avoid conflict and instability among their regions.

Typical Structure

The primary goal of a federation is to unify a country's political subunits within a national framework. The federal government, therefore, features institutions comprised of representatives from the states or regions. The representatives are typically elected by the residents of these regions, and some federal systems give the power to elect certain national leaders to these representatives. The regions themselves can vary considerably in size. The Russian Federation, for example, includes forty-six geographically large provinces as well as two more-concentrated cities as part of its eighty-three constituent federation members.

There are two institutions in which individuals from the constituent parts of a federation serve. The first institution is the legislature. Legislatures vary in appearance from nation to nation. For example, the US Congress is comprised of two chambers—the House of Representatives and the Senate—whose directly elected members act on behalf of their respective states. The German Parliament, on the other hand, consists of the directly elected Bundestag—which is tasked with electing the German federal chancellor, among other things—and the state-appointed Bundesrat, which works on behalf of the country's sixteen states.

The second institution is the executive. Here, the affairs of the nation are administered by a president or similar leader. Again, the structure and powers of a federal government's executive institutions varies from nation to nation according to their constitutional framework. Federal executive institutions are charged with management of state affairs, including oversight of the military, foreign relations, health care, and education. Similarly diverse is the power of the executive in relation to the legislative branch. Some prime ministers, for example, enjoy considerably greater power than the president. In fact, some presidents share power with other leaders, or councils thereof within the executive branch, serving as the diplomatic face of the nation but not playing a major role in lawmaking. In India, for example, the president is the chief executive of the federal government, but shares power with the prime minister and the Council of Ministers, headed by the prime minister.

In order to promote continuity between the federal government and the states, regions, or other political subunits in the federation, those subunits typically feature governments that largely mirror that of the central government. Some of these regional governments are modified according to their respective constitutions. For example, whereas the bicameral US Congress consists of the Senate and House of Representatives, Nebraska's state legislature only has one chamber. Such distinctive characteristics of state/regional governments reflect the geographic and cultural interests of the region in question. It also underscores the degree of autonomy given to such states under a federation government system.

Role of the Citizen

Federations vary in terms of both structure and distribution of power within government institutions. However, federal systems are typically democratic in nature, relying heavily on the participation of the electorate for installing representatives in those institutions. At the regional level, the people vote for their respective legislators and executives either directly or through political parties. The executive in turn appoints cabinet officials, while the legislators select a chamber leader. In US state governments, for example, such a leader might be a Senate president or speaker of the House of Representatives.

The people also play an important role in federal government. As residents of a given state or region, registered voters—again, through either a direct vote or through political parties—choose their legislators and national executives. In federations that utilize a parliamentary system, however, prime ministers are typically selected by the legislators and/or their political parties and not through a direct, national vote. Many constitutions limit the length of political leaders' respective terms of service and/or the number of times they may seek reelection, fostering an environment in which the democratic voting process is a frequent occurrence.

Michael Auerbach
Marblehead, Massachusetts

Examples

Australia
Germany
India
Mexico
Russia
United States

Bibliography

"Federal System of India." *Maps of India*. MapsOfIndia. com, 22 Sep. 2011. Web. 7 Feb. 2013.

"Political System." *Facts about Germany*. Frankfurter Societäts-Medien, 2011. Web. 7 Feb. 2013.

"Russia." *CIA World Factbook*. Central Intelligence Agency, 5 Feb. 2013. Web. 7 Feb. 2013.

Monarchy

Guiding Premise

A monarchy is a political system based on the sovereignty of a single individual who holds actual or symbolic authority over all governmental functions. The monarchy is one of the oldest forms of government in human history and was the most common type of government until the nineteenth century. In a monarchy, authority is inherited, usually through primogeniture, or inheritance by the eldest son.

In an absolute monarchy, the monarch holds authority over the government and functions as both head of state and head of government. In a constitutional monarchy, the role of the monarch is codified in the state constitution, and the powers afforded to the monarch are limited by constitutional law. Constitutional monarchies generally blend the inherited authority of the monarchy with popular control in the form of democratic elections. The monarch may continue to hold significant power over some aspects of government or may be relegated to a largely ceremonial or symbolic role.

In most ancient monarchies, the monarch was generally believed to have been chosen for his or her role by divine authority, and many monarchs in history have claimed to represent the will of a god or gods in their ascendancy to the position. In constitutional monarchies, the monarch may be seen as representing spiritual authority or may represent a link to the country's national heritage.

Typical Structure

In an absolute monarchy, a single monarch is empowered to head the government, including the formulation of all laws and leadership of the nation's armed forces. Oman is one example of a type of absolute monarchy called a sultanate, in which a family of leaders, called "sultans," inherits authority and leads the nation under an authoritarian system. Power in the Omani sultanate remains within the royal family. In the event of the sultan's death or incapacitation, the Royal Family Council selects a successor by consensus from within the family line. Beneath the sultan is a council of ministers, appointed by the sultan, to create and disseminate official government policy. The sultan's council serves alongside an elected body of leaders who enforce and represent Islamic law and work with the sultan's ministers to create national laws.

In Japan, which is a constitutional monarchy, the Japanese emperor serves as the chief of state and symbolic representative of Japan's culture and history. The emperor officiates national ceremonies, meets with world leaders for diplomatic purposes, and symbolically appoints leaders to certain governmental posts. Governmental authority in Japan rests with the Diet, a legislative body of elected officials who serve limited terms of office and are elected through popular vote. A prime minister is also chosen to lead the Diet, and the prime minister is considered the official head of government.

The Kingdom of Norway is another example of a constitutional monarchy wherein the monarch serves a role that has been codified in the state constitution. The king of Norway is designated as the country's chief of state, serving as head of the nation's executive branch. Unlike Japan, where the monarch's role is largely symbolic, the monarch of Norway has considerable authority under the constitution, including the ability to veto and approve all laws and the power to declare war. Norway utilizes a parliamentary system, with a prime minister, chosen from individuals elected to the state parliament, serving as head of government. Though the monarch has authority over the executive functions of government, the legislature and prime minister are permitted the ability to override monarchical decisions with sufficient support, thereby providing a system of control to prevent the monarch from exerting a dominant influence over the government.

Role of the Citizen

The role of the citizen in a monarchy varies depending on whether the government is a constitutional or absolute monarchy. In an absolute monarchy, citizens have only those rights given to them by the monarch, and the monarch has the power to extend and retract freedoms and rights at will. In ancient monarchies, citizens accepted the authoritarian role of the monarch, because it was widely believed that the monarch's powers were derived from divine authority. In addition, in many absolute monarchies, the monarch has the power to arrest, detain, and imprison individuals without due process, thereby providing a strong disincentive for citizens to oppose the monarchy.

In a constitutional monarchy, citizens are generally given greater freedom to participate in the development of governmental policies. In Japan, Belgium, and Spain, for instance, citizens elect governmental leaders, and the elected legislature largely controls the creation and enforcement of laws. In some countries, like the Kingdom of Norway, the monarch may exert significant authority, but this authority is balanced by that of the legislature, which represents the sovereignty of the citizens and is chosen to promote and protect the interests of the public.

The absolute monarchies of medieval Europe, Asia, and Africa held power for centuries, but many eventually collapsed due to popular uprisings as citizens demanded representation within the government. The development of constitutional monarchies may be seen as a balanced system in which the citizens retain significant control over the development of their government while the history and traditions of the nation are represented by the continuation of the monarch's lineage. In the United Kingdom, the governments of Great Britain and Northern Ireland are entirely controlled by elected individuals, but the continuation of the monarchy is seen by many as an important link to the nation's historic identity.

Micah Issitt
Philadelphia, Pennsylvania

Examples

Belgium

Bhutan

Japan

Norway

Oman

United Kingdom

Bibliography

Barrington, Lowell. *Comparative Politics*: *Structures and Choices*. Boston: Wadsworth, 2012. Print.

Dresch, Paul, and James Piscatori, eds. *Monarchies and Nations: Globalisation and Identity in the Arab States of the Gulf*. London: Tauris, 2005. Print.

Kesselman, Mark, et al. *European Politics in Transition*. New York: Houghton, 2009. Print.

Parliamentary Monarchy

Guiding Premise

A parliamentary monarchy is a political system in which leadership of the government is shared between a monarchy, such as a king or queen, and the members of a democratically elected legislative body. In such governments, the monarch's role as head of state is limited by the country's constitution or other founding document, preventing the monarch from assuming too much control over the nation. As head of state, the monarch may provide input during the lawmaking process and other operations of government. Furthermore, the monarch, whose role is generally lifelong, acts as a stabilizing element for the government, while the legislative body is subject to the periodic changes that occur with each election cycle.

Typical Structure

Parliamentary monarchies vary in structure and distribution of power from nation to nation, based on the parameters established by each respective country's constitution or other founding document. In general, however, parliamentary monarchies feature a king, queen, or other sovereign who acts as head of state. In that capacity, the monarch's responsibilities may be little more than ceremonial in nature, allowing him or her to offer input during the lawmaking process, to approve the installation of government officials, and to act as the country's international representative. However, these responsibilities may be subject to the approval of the country's legislative body. For example, the king of Spain approves laws and regulations that have already been passed by the legislative branch; formally appoints the prime minister; and approves other ministers appointed by the prime minister. Yet, the king's responsibilities in those capacities are subject to the approval of the Cortes Generales, Spain's parliament.

In general, parliamentary monarchies help a country preserve its cultural heritage through their respective royal families, but grant the majority of government management and

lawmaking responsibilities to the country's legislative branch and its various administrative ministries, such as education and defense. In most parliamentary monarchies, the ministers of government are appointed by the legislative body and usually by the prime minister. Although government ministries have the authority to carry out the country's laws and programs, they are also subject to criticism and removal by the legislative body if they fail to perform to expectations.

The legislative body itself consists of members elected through a democratic, constitutionally defined process. Term length, term limit, and the manner by which legislators may be elected are usually outlined in the country's founding documents. For example, in the Dutch parliament, members of the House of Representatives are elected every four years through a direct vote, while the members of the Senate are elected by provincial government councils every four years. By contrast, three-quarters of the members of Thailand's House of Representatives are elected in single-seat constituencies (smaller districts), while the remaining members are elected in larger, proportional representation districts; all members of the House are elected for four-year terms. A bare majority of Thailand's senators are elected by direct vote, with the remainder appointed by other members of the government.

Role of the Citizen

While the kings and queens of parliamentary monarchies are the nominal heads of state, these political systems are designed to be democratic governments. As such, they rely heavily on the input and involvement of the citizens. Participating in legislative elections is one of the most direct ways in which the citizen is empowered. Because the governments of such systems are subject to legislative oversight, the people—through their respective votes for members of parliament—have influence over their government.

Political parties and organizations such as local and municipal councils also play an important role in parliamentary monarchies. Citizens' participation in those organizations can help shape parliamentary agendas and build links between government and the public. In Norway, for example, nearly 70 percent of citizens are involved in at least one such organization, and consequently Norway's Storting (parliament) has a number of committees that are tied to those organizations at the regional and local levels. Thus, through voting and active political involvement at the local level, the citizens of a parliamentary monarchy help direct the political course of their nation.

Michael Auerbach
Marblehead, Massachusetts

Examples
Netherlands
Norway
Spain
Sweden
Thailand
United Kingdom

Bibliography
"Form of Government." *Norway.org*. Norway–The Official Site in the United States, n.d. Web. 17 Jan. 2013.
"Issues: Parliament." *Governmentl.nl*. Government of the Netherlands, n.d. Web. 17 Jan. 2013.
"King, Prime Minister, and Council of Ministers." *Country Studies: Spain*. Lib. of Congress, 2012. Web. 17 Jan. 2013.
"Thailand." *International Foundation for Electoral Systems*. IFES, 2013. Web. 17 Jan. 2013.

Parliamentary Republic

Guiding Premise

A parliamentary republic is a system wherein both executive and legislative powers are centralized in the legislature. In such a system, voters elect their national representatives to the parliamentary body, which in turn appoints the executive. In such an environment, legislation is passed more quickly than in a presidential system, which requires a consensus between the executive and legislature. It also enables the legislature to remove the executive in the event the latter does not perform to the satisfaction of the people. Parliamentary republics can also prevent the consolidation of power in a single leader, as even a prime minister must defer some authority to fellow legislative leaders.

Typical Structure

Parliamentary republics vary in structure from nation to nation, according to the respective country's constitution or other governing document. In general, such a system entails the merger of the legislature and head of state such as a president or other executive. The state may retain the executive, however. However, the executive's role may be largely ceremonial, as is the case in Greece, where the president has very little political authority. This "outsider" status has in fact enabled the Greek president to act as a diplomatic intermediary among sparring parliamentary leaders.

While many countries with such a system operate with an executive—who may or may not be directly elected, and who typically has limited powers—the bulk of a parliamentary republic's political authority rests with the legislature. The national government is comprised of democratically elected legislators and their appointees. The length of these representatives' respective terms, as well as the manner by which the legislators are elected, depend on the frameworks established by each individual nation. Some parliamentary republics utilize a constitution for this purpose, while others use a set of common laws or other legal precepts. In South Africa, members of the parliament's two chambers, the National Assembly and the National Council of Provinces, are elected differently. The former's members are elected directly by the citizens in each province, while the latter's members are installed by the provincial legislatures.

Once elected to parliament, legislators are often charged with more than just lawmaking. In many cases, members of parliament oversee the administration of state affairs as well. Legislative bodies in parliamentary republics are responsible for nominating an executive—typically a prime minister—to manage the government's various administrative responsibilities. Should the executive not adequately perform its duties, parliament has the power to remove the executive from office. In Ireland, for example, the Dail Eireann (the House of Representatives) is charged with forming the country's executive branch by nominating the Taoiseach (prime minister) and approving the prime minister's cabinet selections.

Role of the Citizen

A parliamentary republic is a democratic political system that relies on the involvement of an active electorate. This civic engagement includes a direct or indirect vote for representatives to parliament. While the people do not vote for an executive as well, by way of their vote for parliament, the citizenry indirectly influences the selection of the chief executive and the policies he or she follows. In many countries, the people also indirectly influence the national government by their votes in provincial government. As noted earlier, some countries' parliaments include chambers whose members are appointed by provincial leaders.

Citizens may also influence the political system through involvement in political parties. Such organizations help shape the platforms of parliamentary majorities as well as selecting candidates for prime minister and other government positions. The significance of political parties varies from nation to nation, but such organizations require the input and involvement of citizens.

Michael Auerbach
Marblehead, Massachusetts

Examples

Austria
Greece
Iceland
Ireland
Poland
South Africa

Bibliography

"About the Oireachtas." *Oireachtas.ie*. Houses of the Oireachtas, n.d. Web. 7 Feb. 2013.

"Our Parliament." *Parliament.gov*. Parliament of the Republic of South Africa, n.d. Web. 7 Feb. 2013.

Tagaris, Karolina, and Ingrid Melander. "Greek President Makes Last Push to Avert Elections." *Reuters*. Thomson Reuters, 12 May 2012. Web. 7 Feb. 2013.

Presidential

Guiding Premise

A presidential system is a type of democratic government in which the populace elects a single leader—a president—to serve as both head of state and the head of government. The presidential system developed from the monarchic governments of medieval and early modern Europe, in which a royal monarch, holder of an inherited office, served as both head of state and government. In the presidential system, the president does not inherit the office, but is chosen by either direct or indirect popular vote.

Presidential systems differ from parliamentary systems in that the president is both the chief executive and head of state, whereas in a parliamentary system another individual, usually called the "prime minister," serves as head of government and leader of the legislature. The presidential system evolved out of an effort to create an executive office that balances the influence of the legislature and the judiciary. The United States is the most prominent example of a democratic presidential system.

Some governments have adopted a semi-presidential system, which blends elements of the presidential system with the parliamentary system, and generally features a president who serves only as head of state. In constitutional governments, like the United States, Mexico, and Honduras, the role of the president is described in the nation's constitution, which also provides for the president's powers in relation to the other branches of government.

Typical Structure

In most modern presidential governments, power to create and enforce laws and international agreements is divided among three branches: the executive, legislative, and judicial. The executive office consists of the president and a number of presidential advisers—often called the cabinet—who typically serve at the president's discretion and are not elected to office. The terms of office for the president are codified in the state constitution and, in most cases, the president may serve a limited number of terms before he or she becomes ineligible for reelection.

The president serves as head of state and is therefore charged with negotiating and administering international treaties and agreements. In addition, the president serves as head of government and is therefore charged with overseeing the function of the government as a whole. The president is also empowered, in most presidential governments, with the ability to deploy the nation's armed forces. In some governments, including the United States, the approval of the legislature is needed for the country to officially declare war.

The legislative branch of the government proposes new laws, in the form of bills, but must cooperate with the executive office to pass these bills into law. The legislature and the executive branch also cooperate in determining the government budget. Unlike prime ministers under the parliamentary system, the president is not considered a member of the legislature and therefore acts independently as the chief executive, though a variety of governmental functions require action from both branches of government. A unique feature of the presidential system is that the election of the president is separate from the election of the legislature.

In presidential systems, members of the legislature are often less likely to vote according to the goals of their political party and may support legislation that is not supported by their chosen political party. In parliamentary systems, like the government of Great Britain, legislators are more likely to vote according to party policy. Presidential systems are also often marked by a relatively small number of political parties, which often allows one party to achieve a majority in the legislature. If this majority coincides with the election of a president from the same party, that party's platform or agenda becomes dominant until the next election cycle.

The judicial branch in a presidential system serves to enforce the laws among the populace. In most modern presidential democracies, the president appoints judges to federal posts, though in some governments, the legislature appoints judges. In some cases, the president may need the approval of the legislature to make judicial appointments.

Role of the Citizen

In a democratic presidential system, citizens are empowered with the ability to vote for president and therefore have ultimate control over who serves as head of government and head of state. Some presidential governments elect individuals to the presidency based on the result of a popular vote, while other governments use an indirect system, in which citizens vote for a party or for individuals who then serve as their representatives in electing the president. The United States utilizes an indirect system called the Electoral College.

Citizens in presidential systems are also typically allowed, though not required, to join political parties in an effort to promote a political agenda. Some governmental systems that are modeled on the presidential system allow the president to exert a dominant influence over the legislature and other branches of the government. In some cases, this can lead to a presidential dictatorship, in which the president may curtail the political rights of citizens. In most presidential systems, however, the roles and powers of the legislative and executive branches are balanced to protect the rights of the people to influence their government.

In a presidential system, citizens are permitted to vote for a president representing one political party, while simultaneously voting for legislators from other political parties. In this way, the presidential system allows citizens to determine the degree to which any single political party is permitted to have influence on political development.

Micah Issitt
Philadelphia, Pennsylvania

Examples

Benin
Costa Rica
Dominican Republic
Guatemala
Honduras
Mexico
United States
Venezuela

Bibliography

Barington, Lowell. *Comparative Politics: Structures and Choices.* Boston: Wadsworth, 2012. Print.

Caramani, Daniele. *Comparative Politics.* New York: Oxford UP, 2008. Print.

Garner, Robert, Peter Ferdinand, and Stephanie Lawson. *Introduction to Politics.* 2nd ed. Oxford: Oxford UP, 2009. Print.

Republic

Guiding Premise

A republic is a type of government based on the idea of popular or public sovereignty. The word "republic" is derived from Latin terms meaning "matters" and "the public." In essence, a republic is a government in which leaders are chosen by the public rather than by inheritance or by force. The republic or republican governmental system emerged in response to absolute monarchy, in which hereditary leaders retained all the power. In contrast, the republican system is intended to create a government that is responsive to the people's will.

Most modern republics operate based on a democratic system in which citizens elect leaders by popular vote. The United States and Mexico are examples of countries that use a democratic republican system to appoint leaders to office. However, universal suffrage (voting for all) is not required for a government to qualify as a republic, and it is possible for a country to have a republican government in which only certain categories of citizens, such as the wealthy, are allowed to vote in elections.

In addition to popular vote, most modern republics are further classified as constitutional republics, because the laws and rules for appointing leaders have been codified in a set of principles and guidelines known as a "constitution." When combined with universal suffrage and constitutional law, the republican system is intended to form a government that is based on the will of the majority while protecting the rights of minority groups.

Typical Structure

Republican governments are typically led by an elected head of state, generally a president. In cases where the president also serves as the head of government, the government is called a "presidential republic." In some republics, the head of state serves alongside an appointed or elected head of government, usually a prime minister.

This mixed form of government blends elements of the republic system with the parliamentary system found in countries such as the United Kingdom or India.

The president is part of the executive branch of government, which represents the country internationally and heads efforts to make and amend international agreements and treaties. The laws of a nation are typically created by the legislative branch, which may also be composed of elected leaders. Typically, the legislative and executive branches must cooperate on key initiatives, such as determining the national budget.

In addition to legislative and executive functions, most republics have a judiciary charged with enforcing and interpreting laws. The judicial branch may be composed of elected leaders, but in many cases, judicial officers are appointed by the president and/or the legislature. In the United States (a federal republic), the president, who leads the executive branch, appoints members to the federal judiciary, but these choices must be approved by the legislature before they take effect.

The duties and powers allotted to each branch of the republican government are interconnected with those of the other branches in a system of checks and balances. For instance, in Mexico (a federal republic), the legislature is empowered to create new tax guidelines for the public, but before legislative tax bills become law, they must first achieve majority support within the two branches of the Mexican legislature and receive the approval of the president. By creating a system of separate but balanced powers, the republican system seeks to prevent any one branch from exerting a dominant influence over the government.

Role of the Citizen

The role of the citizen in a republic depends largely on the type of republican system that the country has adopted. In democratic republics, popular elections and constitutional law give the public significant influence over governmental development and establish the people as the primary source of political power. Citizens in democratic republics are empowered to join political groups and to influence the development of laws and policies through the election of public leaders.

In many republican nations, a powerful political party or other political group can dominate the government, preventing competition from opposing political groups and curtailing the public's role in selecting and approving leaders. For instance, in the late twentieth century, a dominant political party maintained control of the Gambian presidency and legislature for more than thirty years, thereby significantly limiting the role of the citizenry in influencing the development of government policy.

In general, the republican system was intended to reverse the power structure typical of the monarchy system, in which inherited leaders possess all of the political power. In the republican system, leaders are chosen to represent the people's interests with terms of office created in such a way that new leaders must be chosen at regular intervals, thereby preventing a single leader or political entity from dominating the populace. In practice, popular power in a republic depends on preventing a political monopoly from becoming powerful enough to alter the laws of the country to suit the needs of a certain group rather than the whole.

Micah Issitt
Philadelphia, Pennsylvania

Examples
Algeria
Argentina
Armenia
France
Gambia
Mexico
San Marino
South Sudan
Tanzania
United States

Bibliography
Caramani, Daniele. *Comparative Politics*. New York: Oxford UP, 2008. Print.
Przeworski, Adam. *Democracy and the Limits of Self-Government*. New York: Cambridge UP, 2010. Print.

Socialist

Guiding Premise

Socialism is a political and economic system that seeks to elevate the common good of the citizenry by allowing the government to own all property and means of production. In the most basic model, citizens cooperatively elect members to government, and the government then acts on behalf of the people to manage the state's property, industry, production, and services.

In a socialist system, communal or government ownership of property and industry is intended to eliminate the formation of economic classes and to ensure an even distribution of wealth. Most modern socialists also believe that basic services, including medical and legal care, should be provided at the same level to all citizens and not depend on the individual citizen's ability to pay for better services. The origins of socialism can be traced to theorists such as Thomas More (1478–1535), who believed that private wealth and ownership led to the formation of a wealthy elite class that protected its own wealth while oppressing members of lower classes.

There are many different forms of socialist philosophy, some of which focus on economic systems, while others extend socialist ideas to other aspects of society. Communism may be considered a form of socialism, based on the idea that a working-class revolution is needed to initiate the ideal socialist society.

Typical Structure

Socialism exists in many forms around the world, and many governments use a socialist model for the distribution of key services, most often medical and legal aid. A socialist state is a government whose constitution explicitly gives the government powers to facilitate the creation of a socialist society.

The idealized model of the socialist state is one in which the populace elects leaders to head the government, and the government then oversees the distribution of wealth and goods among the populace, enforces the laws, and provides for the well-being of citizens. Many modern socialist governments follow a communist model, in which a national communist political party has ultimate control over governmental legislation and appointments.

There are many different models of socialist states, integrating elements of democratic or parliamentary systems. In these cases, democratic elections may be held to elect the head of state and the body of legislators. The primary difference between a socialist democracy and a capitalist democracy can be found in the state's role in the ownership of key industries. Most modern noncommunist socialist states provide state regulation and control over key industries but allow some free-market competition as well.

In a socialist system, government officials appoint leaders to oversee various industries and to regulate prices based on public welfare. For instance, if the government retains sole ownership over agricultural production, the government must appoint individuals to manage and oversee that industry, organize agricultural labor, and oversee the distribution of food products among the populace. Some countries, such as Sweden, have adopted a mixed model in which socialist industry management is blended with free-market competition.

Role of the Citizen

All citizens in a socialist system are considered workers, and thus all exist in the same economic class. While some citizens may receive higher pay than others—those who work in supervisory roles, for instance—limited ownership of private property and standardized access to services places all individuals on a level field with regard to basic welfare and economic prosperity.

The degree to which personal liberties are curtailed within a socialist system depends upon the type of socialist philosophy adopted and the degree to which corruption and authoritarianism play a role in government. In most modern communist governments, for instance, individuals are often prohibited from engaging in any activity seen as contrary to the overall goals of the state or to the policies of the dominant political party. While regulations of this kind are common in communist societies, social control over citizens is not necessary for a government to follow a socialist model.

Under democratic socialism, individuals are also expected to play a role in the formation of their government by electing leaders to serve in key positions. In Sri Lanka, for instance, citizens elect members to serve in the parliament and a president to serve as head of the executive branch. In Portugal, citizens vote in multiparty elections to elect a president who serves as head of state, and the president appoints a prime minister to serve as head of government. In both Portugal and Sri Lanka, the government is constitutionally bound to promote a socialist society, though both governments allow private ownership and control of certain industries.

Citizens in a socialist society are also expected to provide for one another by contributing to labor and by forfeiting some ownership rights to provide for the greater good. In the Kingdom of Sweden, a mixed parliamentary system, all citizens pay a higher tax rate to contribute to funds that provide for national health care, child care, education, and worker support systems. Citizens who have no children and require only minimal health care benefits pay the same tax rate as those who have greater need for the nation's socialized benefits.

Micah Issitt
Philadelphia, Pennsylvania

Examples

China
Cuba
Portugal
Sri Lanka
Venezuela
Zambia

Bibliography

Caramani, Daniele. *Comparative Politics*. New York: Oxford UP, 2008. Print.

Heilbroner, Robert. "Socialism." *Library of Economics and Liberty*. Liberty Fund, 2008. Web. 17 Jan. 2013.

Howard, Michael Wayne. *Socialism*. Amherst, NY: Humanity, 2001. Print.

Sultanate/Emirate

Guiding Premise

A sultanate or emirate form of government is a political system in which a hereditary ruler—a monarch, chieftain, or military leader—acts as the head of state. Emirates and sultanates are most commonly found in Islamic nations in the Middle East, although others are found in Southeast Asia as well. Sultans and emirs frequently assume titles such as president or prime minister in addition to their royal designations, meshing the traditional ideal of a monarch with the administrative capacities of a constitutional political system.

Typical Structure

A sultanate or emirate combines the administrative duties of the executive with the powers of a monarch. The emir or sultan acts as the head of government, appointing all cabinet ministers and officials. In Brunei, a sultanate, the government was established according to the constitution (set up after the country declared autonomy from Britain in 1959). The sultan did assemble a legislative council in order to facilitate the lawmaking process, but this council has consistently remained subject to the authority of the sultan and not to a democratic process. In 2004, there was some movement toward the election of at least some of the members of this council. In the meantime, the sultan maintains a ministerial system by appointment and also serves as the nation's chief religious leader.

In some cases, an emirate or sultanate appears similar to a federal system. In the United Arab Emirates (UAE), for example, the nation consists of not one but seven emirates. This system came into being after the seven small regions achieved independence from Great Britain. Each emirate developed its own government system under the leadership of an emir. However, in 1971, the individual emirates agreed to join as a federation, drafting a constitution that identified the areas of common interest to the entire group of emirates. Like Brunei, the UAE's initial government structure focused on the authority of the emirs and the various councils and ministries formed at the UAE's capital of Abu Dhabi. However, beginning in the early twenty-first century, the UAE's legislative body, the Federal National Council, has been elected by electoral colleges from the seven emirates, thus further engaging various local areas and reflecting their interests.

Sultanates and emirates are at times part of a larger nation, with the sultans or emirs answering to the authority of another government. This is the case in Malaysia, where the country is governed by a constitutional monarchy. However, most of Malaysia's western political units are governed by sultans, who act as regional governors and, in many cases, religious leaders, but remain subject to the king's authority in Malaysia's capital of Kuala Lumpur.

Role of the Citizen

Sultanates and emirates are traditionally nondemocratic governments. Like those of other monarchs, the seats of emirs and sultans are hereditary. Any votes for these leaders to serve as prime minister or other head of government are cast by ministers selected by the emirs and sultans. Political parties may exist in these countries as well, but these parties are strictly managed by the sultan or emir; opposition parties are virtually nonexistent in such systems, and some emirates have no political parties at all.

As shown in the UAE and Malaysia, however, there are signs that the traditional sultanate or emirate is increasingly willing to engage their respective citizens. For example, the UAE, between 2006 and 2013, launched a series of reforms designed to strengthen the role of local governments and relations with the people they serve. Malaysia may allow sultans to continue their regional controls, but at the same time, the country continues to evolve its federal system, facilitating multiparty democratic elections for its national legislature.

Michael Auerbach
Marblehead, Massachusetts

Examples

Brunei
Kuwait
Malaysia
Qatar
United Arab Emirates

Bibliography

"Brunei." *The World Factbook*. Central Intelligence Agency, 2 Jan. 2013. Web. 17 Jan. 2013.

"Malaysia." *The World Factbook*. Central Intelligence Agency, 7 Jan. 2013. Web. 17 Jan. 2013.

"Political System." *UAE Interact*. UAE National Media Council, n.d. Web. 17 Jan. 2013.

Prime Minister's Office, Brunei Darussalam. Prime Minister's Office, Brunei Darussalam, 2013. Web. 17 Jan. 2013.

Theocratic Republic

Guiding Premise

A theocratic republic is a type of government blending popular and religious influence to determine the laws and governmental principles. A republic is a governmental system based on the concept of popular rule and takes its name from the Latin words for "public matter." The defining characteristic of a republic is that civic leaders hold elected, rather than inherited, offices. A theocracy is a governmental system in which a supreme deity is considered the ultimate authority guiding civil matters.

No modern nations can be classified as pure theocratic republics, but some nations, such as Iran, maintain a political system largely dominated by religious law. The Buddhist nation of Tibet operated under a theocratic system until it was taken over by Communist China in the early 1950s.

In general, a theocratic republic forms in a nation or other governmental system dominated by a single religious group. The laws of the government are formed in reference to a set of religious laws, either taken directly from sacred texts or formulated by religious scholars and authority figures. Most theocratic governments depend on a body of religious scholars who interpret religious scripture, advise all branches of government, and oversee the electoral process.

Typical Structure

In a typical republic, the government is divided into executive, legislative, and judicial branches, and citizens vote to elect leaders to one or more of the branches of government. In most modern republics, voters elect a head of state, usually a president, to lead the executive branch. In many republics, voters also elect individuals to serve as legislators. Members of the judiciary may be elected by voters or may be appointed to office by other elected leaders. In nontheocratic republics, the citizens are considered the ultimate source of authority in the government.

In a theocratic republic, however, one or more deities are considered to represent the ultimate governmental authority. In some cases, the government may designate a deity as the ultimate head of state. Typically, any individual serving as the functional head of state is believed to have been chosen by that deity, and candidates for the position must be approved by the prevailing religious authority.

In some cases, the religious authority supports popular elections to fill certain governmental posts. In Iran, for instance, citizens vote to elect members to the national parliament and a single individual to serve as president. The Iranian government is ultimately led by a supreme leader, who is appointed to office by the Assembly of Experts, the leaders of the country's Islamic community. Though the populace chooses the president and leaders to serve in the legislature, the supreme leader of Iran can overrule decisions made in any other branch of the government.

In a theocratic republic, the power to propose new laws may be given to the legislature, which works on legislation in conjunction with the executive branch. However, all laws must conform to religious law, and any legislation produced within the government is likely to be abolished if it is deemed by the religious authorities to violate religious principles. In addition, religious leaders typically decide which candidates are qualified to run for specific offices, thereby ensuring that the citizens will not elect individuals who are likely to oppose religious doctrine.

In addition, many modern nations that operate on a partially theocratic system may adopt a set of governmental principles in the form of a constitution, blended with religious law. This mixed constitutional theocratic system has been adopted by an increasing number of Islamic nations, including Iraq, Afghanistan, Mauritania, and some parts of Nigeria.

Role of the Citizen

Citizens in a theocratic republic are expected to play a role in forming the government through elections, but they are constrained in their choices by the prevailing religious authority. Citizens are also guaranteed certain freedoms, typically codified in a constitution, that have been formulated with reference to religious law. All citizens must adhere to religious laws, regardless of their personal religious beliefs or membership within any existing religious group.

In many Middle Eastern and African nations that operate on the basis of an Islamic theocracy, citizens elect leaders from groups of candidates chosen by the prevailing religious authority. While the choices presented to the citizens are more limited than in a democratic, multiparty republic, the citizens nevertheless play a role in determining the evolution of the government through their voting choices.

The freedoms and rights afforded to citizens in a theocratic republic may depend, in part, on the individual's religious affiliation. For instance, Muslims living in Islamic theocracies may be permitted to hold political office or to aspire to other influential political positions, while members of minority religious groups may find their rights and freedoms limited. Religious minorities living in Islamic republics may not be permitted to run for certain offices, such as president, and must follow laws that adhere to Islamic principles but may violate their own religious principles. Depending on the country and the adherents' religion, the practice of their faith may itself be considered criminal.

Micah Issitt
Philadelphia, Pennsylvania

Examples

Afghanistan

Iran

Iraq

Pakistan

Mauritania

Nigeria

Bibliography

Cooper, William W., and Piyu Yue. *Challenges of the Muslim World: Present, Future and Past.* Boston: Elsevier, 2008. Print.

Hirschl, Ran. *Constitutional Theocracy.* Cambridge: Harvard UP, 2010. Print.

Totalitarian

Guiding Premise

A totalitarian government is one in which a single political party maintains absolute control over the state and is responsible for creating all legislation without popular referendum. In general, totalitarianism is considered a type of authoritarian government where the laws and principles used to govern the country are based on the authority of the leading political group or dictator. Citizens under totalitarian regimes have limited freedoms and are subject to social controls dictated by the state.

The concept of totalitarianism evolved in fascist Italy in the 1920s, and was first used to describe the Italian government under dictator Benito Mussolini. The term became popular among critics of the authoritarian governments of Fascist Italy and Nazi Germany in the 1930s. Supporters of the totalitarian philosophy believed that a strong central government, with absolute control over all aspects of society, could achieve progress by avoiding political debate and power struggles between interest groups.

In theory, totalitarian regimes—like that of Nazi Germany and modern North Korea—can more effectively mobilize resources and direct a nation toward a set of overarching goals. Adolf Hitler was able to achieve vast increases in military power during a short period of time by controlling all procedural steps involved in promoting military development. In practice, however, pure totalitarianism has never been achieved, as citizens and political groups generally find ways to subvert complete government control.

Totalitarianism differs from authoritarianism in that a totalitarian government is based on the idea that the highest leader takes total control in order to create a flourishing society for the benefit of the people. By contrast, authoritarian regimes are based on the authority of a single, charismatic individual who develops policies designed to maintain personal power, rather than promote public interest.

Typical Structure

In a fully realized totalitarian system, a single leader or group of leaders controls all governmental functions, appointing individuals to serve in various posts to facilitate the development of legislation and oversee the enforcement of laws. In Nazi Germany, for instance, Adolf Hitler created a small group of executives to oversee the operation of the government. Governmental authority was then further disseminated through a complex network of departments, called ministries, with leaders appointed directly by Hitler.

Some totalitarian nations may adopt a state constitution in an effort to create the appearance of democratic popular control. In North Korea, the country officially operates under a multiparty democratic system, with citizens guaranteed the right to elect leaders to both the executive and legislative branches of government. In practice, the Workers' Party of North Korea is the only viable political party, as it actively controls competing parties and suppresses any attempt to mount political opposition. Under Supreme Leader Kim Il-sung, the Workers' Party amended the constitution to allow Kim to serve as the sole executive leader for life, without the possibility of being removed from office by any governmental action.

In some cases, totalitarian regimes may favor a presidential system, with the dictator serving officially as president, while other totalitarian governments may adopt a parliamentary system, with a prime minister as head of government. Though a single dictator generally heads the nation with widespread powers over a variety of governmental functions, a cabinet or group of high-ranking ministers may also play a prominent role in disseminating power throughout the various branches of government.

Role of the Citizen

Citizens in totalitarian regimes are often subject to strict social controls exerted by the leading political party. In many cases, totalitarian governments restrict the freedom of the press, expression, and speech in an effort to limit opposition to the government. In addition, totalitarian governments may use the threat of police or military action to prevent protest movements against the leading party. Totalitarian governments maintain absolute control over the courts and any security agency, and the legal/judicial system therefore exists only as an extension of the leading political party.

Totalitarian governments like North Korea also attempt to restrict citizens' access to information considered subversive. For instance, North Korean citizens are not allowed to freely utilize the Internet or any other informational source, but are instead only allowed access to government-approved websites and publications. In many cases, the attempt to control access to information creates a black market for publications and other forms of information banned by government policy.

In some cases, government propaganda and restricted access to information creates a situation in which citizens actively support the ruling regime. Citizens may honestly believe that the social and political restrictions imposed by the ruling party are necessary for the advancement of society. In other cases, citizens may accept governmental control to avoid reprisal from the military and police forces. Most totalitarian regimes have established severe penalties, including imprisonment, corporal punishment, and death, for criticizing the government or refusing to adhere to government policy.

Micah Issitt
Philadelphia, Pennsylvania

Examples

Fascist Italy (1922–1943)
Nazi Germany (1933–1945)
North Korea
Stalinist Russia (1924–1953)

Bibliography

Barrington, Lowell. *Comparative Politics: Structures and Choices*. Boston: Wadsworth, 2012. Print.

Gleason, Abbot. *Totalitarianism: The Inner History of the Cold War*. New York: Oxford UP, 1995. Print.

McEachern, Patrick. *Inside the Red Box: North Korea's Post-Totalitarian Regime*. New York: Columbia UP, 2010. Print.

Treaty System

Guiding Premise

A treaty system is a framework within which participating governments agree to collect and share scientific information gathered in a certain geographic region, or otherwise establish mutually agreeable standards for the use of that region. The participants establish rules and parameters by which researchers may establish research facilities and travel throughout the region, ensuring that there are no conflicts, that the environment is protected, and that the region is not used for illicit purposes. This system is particularly useful when the region in question is undeveloped and unpopulated, but could serve a number of strategic and scientific purposes.

Typical Structure

A treaty system of government is an agreement between certain governments that share a common interest in the use of a certain region to which no state or country has yet laid internationally recognized claim. Participating parties negotiate treaty systems that, upon agreement, form a framework by which the system will operate. Should the involved parties be United Nations member states, the treaty is then submitted to the UN Secretariat for registration and publication.

The agreement's founding ideals generally characterize the framework of a treaty. For example, the most prominent treaty system in operation today is the Antarctic Treaty System, which currently includes fifty nations whose scientists are studying Antarctica. This system, which entered into force in 1961, focuses on several topics, including environmental protection, tourism, scientific operations, and the peaceful use of that region. Within these topics, the treaty system enables participants to meet, cooperate, and share data on a wide range of subjects. Such cooperative activities include regional meetings, seminars, and large-scale conferences.

A treaty system is not a political institution in the same manner as state governments. Rather, it is an agreement administered by delegates from the involved entities. Scientists seeking to perform their research in Antarctica, for example, must apply through the scientific and/or government institutions of their respective nations. In the case of the United States, scientists may apply for grants from the National Science Foundation. These institutions then examine the study in question for its relevance to the treaty's ideals.

Central to the treaty system is the organization's governing body. In the case of the Antarctic Treaty, that body is the Antarctic Treaty Secretariat, which is based in Buenos Aires, Argentina. The Secretariat oversees all activities taking place under the treaty, welcomes new members, and addresses any conflicts or issues between participants. It also reviews any activities to ensure that they are in line with the parameters of the treaty. A treaty system is not a sovereign organization, however. Each participating government retains autonomy, facilitating its own scientific expeditions, sending delegates to the treaty system's main governing body, and reviewing the treaty to ensure that it coincides with its national interests.

Role of the Citizen

Although treaty systems are not sovereign government institutions, private citizens can and frequently do play an important role in their function and success. For example, the Antarctic Treaty System frequently conducts large-scale planning conferences, to which each participating government sends delegates. These teams are comprised of qualified scientists who are nominated and supported by their peers during the government's review process. In the United States, for example, the State Department oversees American participation in the Antarctic

Treaty System's events and programs, including delegate appointments.

Another area in which citizens are involved in a treaty system is in the ratification process. Every nation's government—usually through its legislative branch—must formally approve any treaty before the country can honor the agreement. This ratification is necessary for new treaties as well as treaties that must be reapproved every few years. Citizens, through their elected officials, may voice their support or disapproval of a new or updated treaty.

While participating governments administer treaty systems and their secretariats, those who conduct research or otherwise take part in activities in the region in question are not usually government employees. In Antarctica, for example, university professors, engineers, and other private professionals—supported by a combination of private and government funding—operate research stations.

Michael Auerbach
Marblehead, Massachusetts

Example
Antarctic Treaty System

Bibliography

"Antarctic." *Ocean and Polar Affairs.* US Department of State, 22 Mar. 2007. Web. 8 Feb. 2013.

"About Us." *Antarctic Treaty System.* Secretariat of the Antarctic Treaty, n.d. Web. 8 Feb. 2013.

"United Nations Treaty Series." *United Nations Treaty Collection.* United Nations, 2013. Web. 8 Feb. 2013.

"Educational Opportunities and Resources." *United States Antarctic Program.* National Science Foundation, 2013. Web. 8 Feb. 2013.

Appendix Two:
World Religions

African Religious Traditions

General Description

The religious traditions of Africa can be studied both religiously and ethnographically. Animism, or the belief that everything has a soul, is practiced in most tribal societies, including the Dogon (people of the cliffs), an ethnic group living primarily in Mali's central plateau region and in Burkina Faso. Many traditional faiths have extensive mythologies, rites, and histories, such as the Yoruba religion practiced by the Yoruba, an ethnic group of West Africa. In South Africa, the traditional religion of the Zulu people is based on a creator god, ancestor worship, and the existence of sorcerers and witches. Lastly, the Ethiopian or Abyssinian Church (formally the Ethiopian Orthodox Union Church) is a branch of Christianity unique to the east African nations of Ethiopia and Eritrea.

Number of Adherents Worldwide

Some 63 million Africans adhere to traditional religions such as animism. One of the largest groups practicing animism is the Dogon, who number about six hundred thousand. However, it is impossible to know how many practice traditional religion. In fact, many people practice animism alongside other religions, particularly Islam. Other religions have spread their adherence and influence through the African diaspora. In Africa, the Yoruba number between thirty-five and forty million and are located primarily in Benin, Togo and southwest Nigeria. The Zulu, the largest ethnic group in South Africa, total over eleven million. Like Islam, Christianity has affected the number of people who still hold traditional beliefs, making accurate predictions virtually impossible. The Ethiopian or Abyssinian Church has over thirty-nine million adherents in Ethiopia alone.

Basic Tenets

Animism holds that many spiritual beings have the power to help or hurt humans. The traditional faith is thus more concerned with appropriate rituals rather than worship of a deity, and focuses on day-to-day practicalities such as food, water supplies, and disease. Ancestors, particularly those most recently dead, are invoked for their aid. Those who practice animism believe in life after death; some adherents may attempt to contact the spirits of the dead. Animists acknowledge the existence of tribal gods. (However, African people traditionally do not make images of God, who is thought of as Spirit.)

The Dogon divide into two caste-like groups: the inneomo (pure) and innepuru (impure). The hogon leads the inneomo, who may not sacrifice animals and whose leaders are forbidden to hunt. The inneomo also cannot prepare or bury the dead. While the innepuru can do all of the above tasks, they cannot take part in the rituals for agricultural fertility. Selected young males called the olubaru lead the innepuru. The status of "pure" or "impure" is inherited. The Dogon have many gods. The chief god is called Amma, a creator god who is responsible for creating other gods and the earth.

The Dogon have a three-part concept of death. First the soul is sent to the realm of the dead to join the ancestors. Rites are then performed to remove any ritual polluting. Finally, when several members of the village have died, a rite known as dama occurs. In the ritual, a sacrifice is made to the Great Mask (which depicts a large wooden serpent and which is never actually worn) and dancers perform on the housetops where someone has died to scare off any lingering souls. Often, figures of Nommo (a worshipped ancestral spirit) are put near funeral pottery on the family shrine.

The Yoruba believe in predestination. Before birth, the ori (soul) kneels before Olorun, the wisest and most powerful deity, and selects a destiny. Rituals may assist the person in achieving his or her destiny, but it cannot be altered. The Yoruba, therefore, acknowledge a need for ritual and sacrifice, properly done according to the oracles.

Among the Yoruba, the shaman is known as the babalawo. He or she is able to communicate with ancestors, spirits and deities. Training for this work, which may include responsibility as a doctor, often requires three years. The shaman is consulted before major life decisions. During these consultations, the shaman dictates the right rituals and sacrifices, and to which gods they are to be offered for maximum benefit. In addition, the Yoruba poetry covers right conduct. Good character is at the heart of Yoruba ethics.

The Yoruba are polytheistic. The major god is Olorun, the sky god, considered all-powerful and holy, and a father to 401 children, also gods. He gave the task of creating human beings to the deity Obatala (though Olorun breathed life into them). Olorun also determines the destiny of each person. Onlie, the Great Mother Goddess, is in some ways the opposite of Olorun. Olorun is the one who judges a soul following death. For example, if the soul is accounted worthy, it will be reincarnated, while the unworthy go to the place of punishment. Ogun, the god of hunters, iron, and war, is another important god. He is also the patron of blacksmiths. The Yoruba have some 1,700 gods, collectively known as the Orisa.

The Yoruba believe in an afterlife. There are two heavens: one is a hot, dry place with potsherds, reserved for those who have done evil, while the other is a pleasant heaven for persons who have led a good life. There the ori (soul) may choose to "turn to be a child" on the earth once more.

In the Zulu tradition, the king was responsible for rainmaking and magic for the benefit of the nation. Rainmakers were also known as "shepherds of heaven." They performed rites during times of famine, drought or war, as well as during planting season, invoking royal ancestors for aid. Storms were considered a manifestation of God.

The Zulu are also polytheistic. They refer to a wise creator god who lives in heaven. This Supreme Being has complete control of everything in the universe, and is known as Unkulunkulu, the Great Oldest One. The Queen of heaven is a virgin who taught women useful arts; light surrounds her, and her glory is seen in rain, mist, and rainbows.

The Ethiopian Church incorporates not only Orthodox Christian beliefs, but also aspects of Judaism. The adherents distinguish between clean and unclean meats, practice circumcision, and observe the seventh-day Sabbath. The Ethiopian (or Abyssinian) Church is monotheistic and believes in the Christian God.

Sacred Text

Traditional religions such as animism generally have no written sacred texts. Instead, creation stories and other tales are passed down orally. The Yoruba do have some sacred poetry, in 256 chapters, known as odus. The text covers both right action in worship and ethical conduct. The Ethiopian Church has scriptures written in the ancient Ge'ez language, which is no longer used, except in church liturgy.

Major Figures

A spiritual leader, or hogon, oversees each district among the Dogon. There is a supreme hogon for the entire country. Among the Yoruba, the king, or oba, rules each town. He is also considered sacred and is responsible for performing rituals. Isaiah Shembe is a prophet or messiah among the Zulu. He founded the Nazareth Baptist Church (also called the amaNazaretha Church or Shembe Church), an independent Zulu Christian denomination. His son, Johannes Shembe, took the title Shembe II. In the Ethiopian Church, now fully independent, the head of the church is the Patriarch. Saint Frumentius, the first bishop of Axum in northern Ethiopia, is credited with beginning the Christian tradition during the fourth century. King Lalibela, noted for authorizing construction of monolithic churches carved underground, was a major figure in the twelfth century.

Major Holy Sites

Every spot in nature is sacred in animistic thinking. There is no division between sacred and profane—all of life is sacred, and Earth is Mother. Sky and mountains are often regarded as sacred space.

For the Yoruba of West Africa, Osogbo in Nigeria is a forest shrine. The main goddess is Oshun, goddess of the river. Until she arrived, the work done by male gods was not succeeding. People seeking to be protected from illness and women wishing to become pregnant seek Osun's help. Ilé-Ifè, an ancient Yoruba city in Nigeria, is another important site, and considered the spiritual hub of the Yoruba. According to the Yoruba creation myth, Olorun, god of the sky, set down Odudua, the founder of the Yoruba, in Ilé-Ifè. Shrines within the city include one to Ogun. The shrine is made of stones and wooden stumps.

Mount Nhlangakazi (Holy Mountain) is considered sacred to the Zulu Nazareth Baptist Church (amaNazaretha). There Isaiah Shembe built a High Place to serve as his headquarters. It is a twice-yearly site of pilgrimage for amaNazarites.

Sacred sites of the Ethiopian Church include the Church of St. Mary of Zion in Axum, considered the most sacred Ethiopian shrine. According to legend, the church stands adjacent to a guarded chapel which purportedly houses the Ark of the Covenant, a powerful biblical relic. The Ethiopian Church also considers sacred the eleven monolithic (rock-hewn) churches, still places of pilgrimage and devotion, that were recognized as a collective World Heritage Site by the United Nations Educational, Scientific and Cultural Organization.

Major Rites & Celebrations

Most African religions involve some sacrifice to appease or please the gods. Among the Yoruba, for example, dogs, which are helpful in both hunting and war, are sacrificed to Ogun. In many tribes, including the Yoruba, rites of passage for youth exist. The typical pattern is three-fold: removal from the tribe, instruction, and return to the tribe ready to assume adult responsibilities. In this initiation, the person may be marked bodily through scarification or circumcision. The Yoruba also have a yearly festival re-enacting

the story of Obatala and Oduduwa (generally perceived as the ancestor of the Yorubas). A second festival, which resembles a passion play, re-enacts the conflict between the grandsons of these two legendary figures. A third festival celebrates the heroine Moremi, who led the Yoruba to victory over the enemy Igbo, an ethnicity from southeastern Nigeria, and who ultimately reconciled the two tribes.

Yoruba death rites include a masked dancer who comes to the family following a death, assuring them of the ancestor's ongoing care for the family. If the person was important in the village, a mask will be carved and named for them. In yearly festivals, the deceased individual will then appear with other ancestors.

Masks are also used in a Dogon funeral ritual, the dama ceremony, which is led by the Awa, a secret society comprised of all adult Dogon males of the innepuru group. During ceremonial times, the hogon relinquishes control and the Awa control the community. At the end of the mourning period the dama ceremony begins when the Awa leave the village and return with both the front and back of their heads masked. Through rituals and dances, they lead the spirit of the deceased to the next world. Control of the village reverts to the hogon at that point. The Wagem rites govern contact with the ancestors. Following the dama ceremony, the eldest male descendant, called the ginna bana, adds a vessel to the family shrine in the name of the deceased. The spirit of the ancestor is persuaded to return to the descendents through magic and sacrificial offerings, creating a link from the living to the first ancestors.

Ethiopian Christians observe and mark most typical Christian rites, though some occur on different dates because of the difference in the Ethiopian and Western calendars. For example, Christmas in Ethiopia is celebrated on January 7.

ORIGINS

History & Geography

The Dogon live along the Bandiagara Cliffs, a rocky and mountainous region. (The Cliffs of Bandiagara, also called the Bandiagara Escarpment, were recognized as a UNESCO World Heritage Site due to the cultural landscape, including the ancient traditions of the Dogon and their architecture.) This area is south of the Sahara in a region called the Sahel, another region prone to drought (though not a desert). The population of the villages in the region is typically a thousand people or less. The cliffs of the Bandiagara have kept the Dogon separate from other people.

Myths of origin regarding the Dogon differ. One suggestion is that the Dogon came from Egypt, and then lived in Libya before entering the the region of what is now Burkina Faso, Mauritania, or Guinea. Near the close of the fifteenth century, they arrived in Mali.

Among the Yoruba, multiple myths regarding their origin exist. One traces their beginnings to Uruk in Mesopotamia or to Babylon, the site of present-day Iraq. Another story has the Yoruba in West Africa by 10,000 BCE.

After the death of the Zulu messiah Isaiah Shembe in 1935, his son Johannes became the leader of the Nazareth Baptist Church. He lacked the charisma of his father, but did hold the church together. His brother, Amos, became regent in 1976 when Johannes died. Johannes's son Londa split the church in 1979 when Amos refused to give up power. Tangled in South African politics, Londa was killed in 1989.

The Ethiopian Orthodox Church is the nation's official church. A legend states that Menelik, supposed to have been the son of the Queen of Sheba and King Solomon, founded the royal line. When Jesuits arrived in the seventeenth century, they failed to change the church, and the nation closed to missionary efforts for several hundred years. By retaining independence theologically and not being conquered politically, Ethiopia is sometimes considered a model for the new religious movements in Africa.

Founder or Major Prophet

The origins of most African traditional religions or faiths are accounted for through the actions of deities in creation stories rather than a particular founder. One exception, however, is Isaiah Shembe, who founded the Nazareth Baptist Church, also known as the Shembe Church or amaNazarite Church, in 1910 after receiving a number of revelations during a thunderstorm. Shembe was an itinerant Zulu preacher and healer. Through his influence and leadership, amaNazarites follow more Old Testament regulations than most Christians, including celebrating the Sabbath on Saturday rather than Sunday. They also refer to God as Jehovah, the Hebrew name for God. Shembe was regarded as the new Jesus Christ for his people, adapting Christianity to Zulu practice. He adopted the title Nkosi, which means king or chief.

The Ethiopian Orthodox church was founded, according to legend, by preaching from one of two New Testament figures—the disciple Matthew or the unnamed eunuch mentioned in Acts 8. According to historical evidence, the church began when Frumentius arrived at the royal court. Athanasius of Alexandria later consecrated Frumentius as patriarch of the church, linking it to the Christian church in Egypt.

Creation Stories

The Dogon believe that Amma, the sky god, was also the creator of the universe. Amma created two sets of twins, male and female. One of the males rebelled. To restore order, Amma sacrificed the other male, Nommo, strangling and scattering him to the four directions, then restoring him to life after five days. Nommo then became ruler of the universe and the children of his spirits became the Dogon. Thus the world continually moves between chaos and order, and the task of the Dogon is to keep the world in balance through rituals. In a five-year cycle, the aspects of this creation myth are re-enacted at altars throughout the Dogon land.

According to the Yoruba, after one botched attempt at creating the world, Olorun sent his son Obatala to create earth upon the waters. Obatala tossed some soil on the water and released a five-toed hen to spread it out. Next, Olorun told Obatala to make people from clay. Obatala grew bored with the work and drank too much wine. Thereafter, the people he made were misshapen or defective (handicapped). In anger, Olorun relieved him of the job and gave it to Odudua to complete. It was Odudua who made the Yoruba and founded a kingdom at Ilé-Ifè.

The word *Zulu* means "heaven or sky." The Zulu people believe they originated in heaven. They also believe in phansi, the place where spirits live and which is below the earth's surface.

Holy Places

Osun-Osogbo is a forest shrine in Nigeria dedicated to the Yoruba river goddess, Osun. It may be the last such sacred grove remaining among the Yoruba. Shrines, art, sculpture, and sanctuaries are part of the grove, which became a UNESCO World Heritage site in 2005.

Ilé-Ifè, regarded as the equivalent of Eden, is thought to be the site where the first Yoruba was placed. It was probably named for Ifa, the god associated with divination. The palace (Afin) of the spiritual head of the Yoruba, the oni, is located there. The oni has the responsibility to care for the staff of Oranmiyan, a Benin king. The staff, which is eighteen feet tall, is made of granite and shaped like an elephant's tusk.

Axum, the seat of the Ethiopian Christian Church, is a sacred site. The eleven rock-hewn churches of King Lalibela, especially that of Saint George, are a pilgrimage site. According to tradition, angels helped to carve the churches. More than 50,000 pilgrims come to the town of Lalibela at Christmas. After the Muslims captured Jerusalem in 1187, King Lalibela proclaimed his city the "New Jerusalem" because Christians could no longer go on pilgrimage to the Holy Land.

AFRICAN RELIGIONS IN DEPTH

Sacred Symbols

Because all of life is infused with religious meaning, any object or location may be considered or become sacred in traditional African religions. Masks, in particular, have special meaning and

may be worn during ceremonies. The mask often represents a god, whose power is passed to the one wearing the mask.

Sacred Practices & Gestures

The Yoruba practice divination in a form that is originally Arabic. There are sixteen basic figures—combined, they deliver a prophecy that the diviner is not to interpret. Instead, he or she recites verses from a classic source. Images may be made to prevent or cure illness. For example, the Yoruba have a smallpox spirit god that can be prayed to for healing. Daily prayer, both morning and evening, is part of life for most Yoruba.

In the amaNazarite Church, which Zulu Isaiah Shembe founded, singing is a key part of the faith. Shembe himself was a gifted composer of hymns. This sacred music was combined with dancing, during which the Zulu wear their traditional dress.

Rites, Celebrations & Services

The Dogon have three major cults. The Awa are associated with dances, featuring ornately carved masks, at funerals and on the anniversaries of deaths. The cult of the Earth god, Lebe, concerns itself with the agricultural cycles and fertility of the land; the hogon of the village guards the soil's purity and presides at ceremonies related to farming. The third cult, the Binu, is involved with communication with spirits, ancestor worship, and sacrifices. Binu shrines are in many locations. The Binu priest makes sacrifices of porridge made from millet and blood at planting time and also when the help of an ancestor is needed. Each clan within the Dogon community has a totem animal spirit—an ancestor spirit wishing to communicate with descendents may do so by taking the form of the animal.

The Dogon also have a celebration every fifty years at the appearing of the star Sirius B between two mountains. (Sirius is often the brightest star in the nighttime sky.) Young males leaving for three months prior to the sigui, as it is called, for a time of seclusion and speaking in private language. This celebration is rooted in the Dogon belief that amphibious creatures, the Nommo, visited their land about three thousand years ago.

The Yoruba offer Esu, the trickster god, palm wine and animal sacrifices. Because he is a trickster, he is considered a cheater, and being on his good side is important. The priests in Yoruba traditional religion are responsible for installing tribal chiefs and kings.

Among the Zulu, families determine the lobola, or bride price. They believe that a groom will respect his wife more if he must pay for her. Further gifts are then exchanged, and the bride's family traditionally gives the groom a goat or sheep to signify their acceptance of him. The groom's family provides meat for the wedding feast, slaughtering a cow on the morning of the wedding. The families assemble in a circle and the men, in costume, dance. The bride gives presents, usually mats or blankets, to members of her new family, who dance or sing their thanks. The final gift, to the groom, is a blanket, which is tossed over his head. Friends of the bride playfully beat him, demonstrating how they will respond if he mistreats his new wife. After the two families eat together, the couple is considered one.

In the traditional Zulu religion, ancestors three generations back are regarded as not yet settled in the afterlife. To help them settle, offerings of goats or other animals are made and rituals to help them settle into the community of ancestors are performed.

Christmas is a major celebration in Ethiopian Christianity. Priests rattle an instrument derived from biblical times, called the sistra, and chant to begin the mass. The festivities include drumming and a dance known as King David's dance.

Judy A. Johnson, MTS

Bibliography

A, Oladosu Olusegun. "Ethics and Judgement: A Panacea for Human Transformation in Yoruba Multireligious Society." *Asia Journal of Theology* 26.1 (2012): 88–104. Print.

Barnes, Trevor. *The Kingfisher Book of Religions*. New York: Kingfisher, 1999. Print.

Dawson, Allan Charles, ed. *Shrines in Africa: history, politics, and society*. Calgary: U of Calgary P, 2009. Print.

Doumbia, Adama, and Naomi Doumbia. *The Way of the Elders: West African Spirituality*. St. Paul: Llewellyn, 2004. Print.

Douny, Laurence. "The Role of Earth Shrines in the Socio-Symbolic Construction of the Dogon Territory: Towards a Philosophy of Containment." *Anthropology & Medicine* 18.2 (2011): 167–79. Print.

Friedenthal, Lora, and Dorothy Kavanaugh. *Religions of Africa*. Philadelphia: Mason Crest, 2007. Print.

Hayes, Stephen. "Orthodox Ecclesiology in Africa: A Study of the 'Ethiopian' Churches of South Africa." *International Journal for the Study of the Christian Church* 8.4 (2008): 337–54. Print.

Lugira, Aloysius M. *African Religion*. New York: Facts on File, 2004. Print.

Mbiti, John S. *African Religions and Philosophy*. 2nd ed. Oxford: Heinemann, 1991. Print.

Monteiro-Ferreira, Ana Maria. "Reevaluating Zulu Religion." *Journal of Black Studies* 35.3 (2005): 347–63. Print.

Peel, J. D. Y. "Yoruba Religion as a Global Phenomenon." *Journal of African History* 5.1 (2010): 107–8. Print.

Ray, Benjamin C. *African Religions*. 2nd ed. Upper Saddle River: Prentice, 2000. Print.

Thomas, Douglas E. *African Traditional Religion in the Modern World*. Jefferson: McFarland, 2005. Print.

Bahá'í Faith

General Description

The Bahá'í faith is the youngest of the world's religions. It began in the mid-nineteenth century, offering scholars the opportunity to observe a religion in the making. While some of the acts of religious founders such as Buddha or Jesus cannot be substantiated, the modern founders of Bahá'í were more contemporary figures.

Number of Adherents Worldwide

An estimated 5 to 7 million people follow the Bahá'í faith. Although strong in Middle Eastern nations such as Iran, where the faith originated, Bahá'í has reached people in many countries, particularly the United States and Canada.

Basic Tenets

The Bahá'í faith has three major doctrines. The first doctrine is that there is one transcendent God, and all religions worship that God, regardless of the name given to the deity. Adherents believe that religious figures such as Jesus Christ, the Buddha, and the Prophet Muhammad were different revelations of God unique to their time and place. The second doctrine is that there is only one religion, though each world faith is valid and was founded by a ""manifestation of God" who is part of a divine plan for educating humanity. The third doctrine is a belief in the unity of all humankind. In light of this underlying unity, those of the Bahá'í faith work for social justice. They believe that seeking consensus among various groups diffuses typical power struggles and to this end, they employ a method called consultation, which is a nonadversarial decision-making process.

The Bahá'í believe that the human soul is immortal, and that after death the soul moves nearer or farther away from God. The idea of an afterlife comprised of a literal "heaven" or "hell" is not part of the faith.

Sacred Text

The Most Holy Book, or the Tablets, written by Baha'u'llah, form the basis of Bahá'í teachings. Though not considered binding, scriptures from other faiths are regarded as "Divine Revelation."

Major Figures

The Bab (The Gate of God) Siyyad 'Ali Mohammad (1819–50), founder of the Bábí movement that broke from Islam, spoke of a coming new messenger of God. Mirza Hoseyn 'Ali Nuri (1817–92), who realized that he was that prophet, was given the title Baha'u'llah (Glory of God). From a member of Persia's landed gentry, he was part of the ruling class, and is considered the founder of the Bahá'í faith. His son, 'Abdu'l-Bahá (Servant of the Glory of God), who lived from 1844 until 1921, became the leader of the group after his father's death in 1892. The oldest son of his eldest daughter, Shogi Effendi Rabbani (1899–1957), oversaw a rapid expansion, visiting Egypt, America, and nations in Europe. Tahirih (the Pure One) was a woman poet who challenged stereotypes by appearing unveiled at meetings.

Major Holy Sites

The Bahá'í World Center is located near Haifa, Israel. The burial shrine of the Bab, a pilgrimage site, is there. The Shrine of Baha'u'llah near Acre, Israel, is another pilgrimage site. The American headquarters are in Wilmette, Illinois. Carmel in Israel is regarded as the world center of the faith.

Major Rites & Celebrations

Each year, the Bahá'í celebrate Ridvan Festival, a twelve-day feast from sunset on April 20 to sunset on May 2. The festival marks Baha'u'llah's declaration of prophethood, as prophesized by the Bab, at a Baghdad garden. (Ridvan means Paradise.) The holy days within that feast are the first (Baha'u'llah's garden arrival), ninth (the arrival of his family), and twelfth (his departure from Ridvan Garden)—on these days, the Bahá'í do not work. During this feast, people attend social events and meet for devotions. Baha'u'llah referred to it as the King of Festivals and Most Great Festival. The Bahá'í celebrate several other events, including World Religion Day and Race Unity Day, both founded by Bahá'í, as well as days connected with significant events in the life of the founder. Elections to the Spiritual Assemblies, and the national and local administrations; international elections are held every five years.

ORIGINS

History & Geography

Siyyad 'Ali Muhammad was born into a merchant family of Shiraz in 1819. Both his parents were descendents of the Prophet Muhammad, Islam's central figure. Like the Prophet, the man who became the Bab lost his father at an early age and was raised by an uncle. A devout child, he entered his uncle's business by age fifteen. After visiting Muslim holy cities, he returned to Shiraz, where he married a distant relative named Khadijih.

While on pilgrimage in 1844 to the black stone of Ka'bah, a sacred site in Islam, the Bab stood with his hand on that holy object and declared that he was the prophet for whom they had been waiting. The Sunni did not give credence to these claims. The Bab went to Persia, where the Shia sect was the majority. However, because Muhammad had been regarded as the "Seal of the Prophets," and the one who spoke the final revelation, Shia clergy viewed his claims as threatening, As such, nothing further would be revealed until the Day of Judgment. The authority of the clergy was in danger from this new movement.

The Bab was placed under house arrest, and then confined to a fortress on the Russian frontier. That move to a more remote area only increased the number of converts, as did a subsequent move to another Kurdish fortress. He

was eventually taken to Tabriz in Iran and tried before the Muslim clergy in 1848. Condemned, he was caned on the soles of his feet and treated by a British doctor who was impressed by him.

Despite his treatment and the persecution of his followers—many of the Bab's eighteen disciples, termed the "Letters of the Living," were persistently tortured and executed—the Bab refused to articulate a doctrine of jihad. The Babis could defend themselves, but were forbidden to use holy war as a means of religious conquest. In three major confrontations sparked by the Shia clergy, Babis were defeated. The Bab was sentenced as a heretic and shot by a firing squad in 1850. Lacking leadership and grief-stricken, in 1852 two young Babis fired on the shah in 1852, unleashing greater persecutions and cruelty against those of the Bahá'í faith.

A follower of the Bab, Mirza Hoseyn 'Ali Nuri, announced in 1863 that he was the one who was to come (the twelfth imam of Islam), the "Glory of God," or Baha'u'llah. Considered the founder of the Bahá'í Faith, he was a tireless writer who anointed his son, 'Abdu'l-Bahá, as the next leader. Despite deprivations and imprisonments, Baha'u'llah lived to be seventy-five years old, relinquishing control of the organization to 'Abdu'l-Bahá before the time of his death.

'Abdu'l-Bahá, whom his father had called "the Master," expanded the faith to the nations of Europe and North America. In 1893, at the Parliament of Religions at the Chicago World's Fair, the faith was first mentioned in the United States. Within a few years, communities of faith were established in Chicago and Wisconsin. In 1911, 'Abdu'l-Bahá began a twenty-eight month tour of Europe and North America to promote the Bahá'í faith. Administratively, he established the spiritual assemblies that were the forerunner of the Houses of Justice that his father had envisioned.

During World War I, 'Abdu'l-Bahá engaged in humanitarian work among the Palestinians in the Holy Land, where he lived. In recognition of his efforts, he was granted knighthood by the British government. Thousands of people, including many political and religious dignitaries, attended his funeral in 1921.

'Abdu'l-Bahá conferred the role of Guardian, or sole interpreter of Bahá'í teaching, to his eldest grandson, Shoghi Effendi Rabbani. To him, all questions regarding the faith were to be addressed. Shoghi Effendi Rabbani was a descendent of Baha'u'llah through both parents. He headed the Bahá'í faith from 1921 to 1963, achieving four major projects: he oversaw the physical development of the World Centre and expanded the administrative order; he carried out the plan his father had set in motion; and he provided for the translating and interpreting of Bahá'í teachings, as the writings of both the Bab and those of Baha'u'llah and 'Abdu'l-Bahá have been translated and published in more than eight hundred languages.

Beginning in 1937, Shoghi Effendi Rabbani began a series of specific plans with goals tied to deadlines. In 1953, during the second seven-year plan, the house of worship in Wilmette, Illinois, was completed and dedicated.

Although the beliefs originated in Shi'ite Islam, the Bahá'í Faith has been declared a new religion without connections to Islam. To followers of Islam, it is a heretical sect. During the reign of the Ayatollah Khomeini, a time when Iran was especially noted as intolerant of diverse views, the Bahá'í faced widespread persecution.

Founder or Major Prophet

Mirza Husayn Ali Nuri, known as Baha'u'llah, was born into privilege in 1817 in what was then Persia, now present-day Iran. At twenty-two, he declined a government post offered at his father's death. Although a member of a politically prestigious family, he did not follow the career path of several generations of his ancestors. Instead, he managed the family estates and devoted himself to charities, earning the title "Father of the Poor."

At twenty-seven, he followed the Babis's movement within Shia Islam, corresponding with the Bab and traveling to further the faith. He also provided financial support. In 1848, he organized and helped to direct a conference that explained the Bab's teaching. At the conference, he gave symbolic names to the eighty-one followers who had attended, based on the spiritual qualities he had observed.

Although he managed to escape death during the persecutions before and after the Bab's death, a fact largely attributed to his upbringing, Baha'u'llah was imprisoned several times. During a four-month stay in an underground dungeon in Tehran, he realized from a dream that he was the one of whom the Bab had prophesied. After being released, he was banished from Persia and had his property confiscated by the shah. He went to Baghdad, refusing the offer of refuge that had come from Russia. Over the following three years a small band of followers joined him, including members of his family. When his younger brother attempted to take over the leadership of the Babis, Baha'u'llah spent two years in a self-imposed exile in the Kurdistan wilderness. In 1856, with the community near anarchy as a result of his brother's failure of leadership, Baha'u'llah returned to the community and restored its position over the next seven years.

Concerned by the growing popularity of the new faith, the shah demanded that the Babis move further away from Persia. They went to Constantinople where, in 1863, Baha'u'llah revealed to the whole group that he was "He Whom God Will Make Manifest." From there the Bahá'í were sent to Adrianople in Turkey, and at last, in 1868, to the town of Acre in the Holy Land. Baha'u'llah was imprisoned in Acre and survived severe prison conditions. In 1877, he moved from prison to a country estate, then to a mansion. He died in 1892 after a fever.

Philosophical Basis

The thinking of Shia Muslims contributed to the development of Bahá'í. The writings incorporate language and concepts from the Qur'an (Islam's holy book). Like Muslims, the Bahá'í believe that God is one. God sends messengers, the Manifestations of God, to instruct people and benefit society. These have included Jesus Christ, the Buddha, the Prophet Muhammad, Krishna, and the Bab. Bahá'í also goes further than Islam in accepting all religions—not just Judaism, Christianity, and Islam—as being part of a divinely inspired plan.

Shia Muslims believe that Muhammad's descendents should lead the faithful community. The leaders, known as imams, were considered infallible. The Sunni Muslims believed that following the way (sunna) of Muhammad was sufficient qualification for leadership. Sunni dynasties regarded the imams as a threat and executed them, starting with two of Muhammad's grandsons, who became Shia martyrs.

In Persia, a state with a long tradition of divinely appointed rulers, the Shia sect was strong. When the Safavids, a Shia dynasty, came to power in the sixteenth century, the custom of the imamate was victorious. One tradition states that in 873, the last appointed imam, who was still a child, went into hiding to avoid being killed. For the following sixty-nine years, this twelfth imam communicated through his deputies to the faithful. Each of the deputies was called bab, or gate, because they led to the "Hidden Imam." Four babs existed through 941, and the last one died without naming the next bab. The Hidden Imam is thought to emerge at the end of time to bring in a worldwide reign of justice. From this tradition came the expectation of a Mahdi (Guided One) to lead the people.

During the early nineteenth century, many followers of both the Christian and Islamic faiths expected their respective messiahs to return. Shia teachers believed that the return of the Mahdi imam was near. In 1843, one teacher, Siyyid Kázim, noted that the Hidden Imam had disappeared one thousand lunar years earlier. He urged the faithful to look for the Mahdi imam.

The following year in Shiraz, Siyyad 'Ali Mohammad announced that he was the Mahdi. (*Siyyad* is a term meaning descended from Muhammad.) He referred to himself as the Bab, though he expanded the term's meaning. Eighteen men, impressed with his ability to expound the Qur'an, believed him. They became the Letters of the Living, and were sent throughout Persia (present-day Iran) to announce the dawning of the Day of God.

In 1853, Mirza Husayn Ali Nuri experienced a revelation that he was "He Whom God Shall Make Manifest," the one of whom the Bab prophesied. Accepted as such, he began writing the words that became the Bahá'í scriptures. Much of what is known of the early days of the faith comes from a Cambridge academic, Edward Granville Browne, who first visited Baha'u'llah in the 1890. Browne wrote of his meeting, introducing this faith to the West.

The emphasis of the Bahá'í faith is on personal development and the breaking down of barriers between people. Service to humanity is important and encouraged. Marriage, with a belief in the equality of both men and women, is also encouraged. Consent of both sets of parents is required prior to marrying.

Holy Places

The shrine of the Bab near Haifa and that of Baha'u'llah near Acre, in Israel, are the two most revered sites for those of the Bahá'í faith. In 2008, the United Nations Educational, Scientific, and Cultural Organization (UNESCO) recognized both as World Heritage Sites. They are the first such sites from a modern religious tradition to be added to the list of sites. Both sites are appreciated for the formal gardens surrounding them that blend design elements from different cultures. For the Bahá'í, Baha'u'llah's shrine is the focus of prayer, comparable to the significance given to the Ka'bah in Mecca for Muslims or to the Western Wall for Jews.

As of 2013, there are seven Bahá'í temples in the world; an eighth temple is under construction in Chile. All temples are built with a center dome and nine sides, symbolizing both diversity and world unity. The North American temple is located in Wilmette, Illinois. There, daily prayer services take place as well as a Sunday service.

THE BAHÁ'Í FAITH IN DEPTH

Governance

Elected members of lay councils at international, national, and local levels administer the work of the faith. The Universal House of Justice in Haifa, Israel, is the location of the international nine-member body. Elections for all of these lay councils are by secret ballot, and do not include nominating, candidates, or campaigns. Those twenty-one and older are permitted to vote. The councils make decisions according to a process of collective decision-making called consultation. They strive to serve as a model for governing a united global society.

Personal Conduct

In addition to private prayer and acts of social justice, those of the Bahá'í faith are encouraged to have a profession, craft, or trade. They are also asked to shun and refrain from slander and partisan politics. Homosexuality and sexual activity outside marriage are forbidden, as is gambling.

The Bahá'í faith does not have professional clergy, nor does it engage in missionary work. However, Bahá'í may share their faith with others and may move to another country as a "pioneer." Pioneers are unlike traditional missionaries, and are expected to support themselves through a career and as a member of the community.

Avenues of Service

Those of the Bahá'í Faith place a high value on service to humanity, considering it an act of worship. This can be done through caring for one's own family or through one's choice of vocation. Within the local community, people may teach classes for children, mentor youth groups, host devotional programs, or teach adult study circles. Many are engaged in economic or social development programs as well. Although not mandated, a year or two of service is often undertaken following high school or during college.

United Nations Involvement

Beginning in 1947, just one year after the United Nations (UN) first met, the Bahá'í Faith was represented at that body. In 1948, the Bahá'í International Community was accredited by the UN as an international nongovernmental organization (NGO). In 1970, the faith received special consultative status with the UN Economic and Social Council (ECOSOC). Following World War I, a Bahá'í office opened in Geneva, Switzerland, where the League of Nations was headquartered. Thus the Bahá'í Faith has a long tradition of supporting global institutions.

Money Matters

The International Bahá'í Fund exists to develop and support the growth of the faith, and the Universal House of Justice oversees the distribution of the money. Contributions are also used to maintain the Bahá'í World Center. No money is accepted from non-Bahá'í sources. National and local funds, administered by National or Local Spiritual Assemblies, are used in supporting service projects, publishing endeavors, schools, and Bahá'í centers. For the Bahá'í, the size of the donation is less important than regular contributions and the spirit of sacrifice behind them.

Food Restrictions

Bahá'í between fifteen and seventy years of age **fast** nineteen days a year, abstaining from food and drink from sunrise to sunset. Fasting occurs the first day of each month of the Bahá'í calendar, which divides the year into nineteen months of nineteen days each. The Bahá'í faithful do not drink alcohol or use narcotics, because these will deaden the mind with repeated use.

Rites, Celebrations & Services

Daily prayer and meditation is recommended in the Bahá'í faith. During services there are mediations and prayers, along with the reading of Bahá'í scriptures and other world faith traditions. There is no set ritual, no offerings, and no sermons. Unaccompanied by musical instruments, choirs also sing. Light refreshments may be served afterwards.

Bahá'í place great stress on marriage, the only state in which sex is permitted. Referred to as "a fortress for well-being and salvation," a monogamous, heterosexual marriage is the ideal. To express the oneness of humanity, interracial marriages are encouraged. After obtaining the consent of their parents, the couple takes the following vow: "We will all, verily, abide by the will of God." The remainder of the service may be individually crafted and may also include dance, music, feasting, and ceremony. Should a couple choose to end a marriage, they must first complete a year of living apart while trying to reconcile differences. Divorce is discouraged, but permitted after that initial year.

Judy A. Johnson, MTS

Bibliography

Albertson, Lorelei. *All about Bahá'í Faith.* University Pub., 2012. E-book.

Bowers, Kenneth E. *God Speaks Again: an Introduction to the Bahá'í Faith.* Wilmette: Bahá'í, 2004. Print.

Buck, Christopher. "The Interracial 'Bahá'í Movement' and the Black Intelligentsia: The Case of W. E. B. Du Bois." *Journal of Religious History* 36.4 (2012): 542–62. Print.

Cederquist, Druzelle. *The Story of Baha'u'llah.* Wilmette: Bahá'í, 2005. Print.

Echevarria, L. *Life Stories of Bahá'í Women in Canada: Constructing Religious Identity in the Twentieth Century.* Lang, 2011. E-book.

Garlington, William. *The Bahá'í Faith in America.* Lanham: Rowman, 2008. Print.

Hartz, Paula R. *Bahá'í Faith.* New York: Facts on File, 2006. Print.

Hatcher, William S. and J. Douglas Martin. *The Bahá'í Faith: The Emerging Global Religion.* Wilmette: Bahá'í, 2002. Print.

Karlberg, Michael. "Constructive Resilience: The Bahá'í Response to Oppression." *Peace & Change* 35.2 (2010): 222–57. Print.

Lee, Anthony A. *The Bahá'í Faith in Africa: Establishing a New Religious Movement, 1952–1962.* Brill NV, E-book.

Momen, Moojan. "Bahá'í Religious History." *Journal of Religious History* 36.4 (2012): 463–70. Print.

Momen, Moojan. *The Bahá'í Faith: A Beginner's Guide.* Oxford: Oneworld, 2007. Print.

Smith, Peter. *The Bahá'í Faith.* Cambridge: Cambridge UP, 2008. Print.

Wilkinson, Philip. *Religions.* New York: DK, 2008. Print.

Buddhism

General Description

Buddhism has three main branches: Theravada (Way of the Elders), also referred to as Hinayana (Lesser Vehicle); Mahayana (Greater Vehicle); and Vajrayana (Diamond Vehicle), also referred to as Tantric Buddhism. Vajrayana is sometimes thought of as an extension of Mahayana Buddhism. These can be further divided into many sects and schools, many of which are geographically based. In Buddhism, these different divisions or schools are regarded as alternative paths to enlightenment (Wilkinson 2008).

Number of Adherents Worldwide

An estimated 474 million people around the world are Buddhists. Of the major sects, Theravada Buddhism is the oldest, developed in the sixth century BCE. Its adherents include those of the Theravada Forest Tradition. From Mahayana Buddhism, which developed in the third to second centuries BCE, came several offshoots based on location. In what is now China, Pure Land Buddhism and Tibetan Buddhism developed in the seventh century. In Japan, Zen Buddhism developed in the twelfth century, Nichiren Buddhism developed a century later, and Soka Gakkai was founded in 1937. In California during the 1970s, the Serene Reflection Meditation began as a subset of Sōtō Zen. In Buddhism, these different divisions or schools are regarded as alternative paths to enlightenment.

Basic Tenets

Buddhists hold to the Three Universal Truths: impermanence, the lack of self, and suffering. These truths encompass the ideas that everything is impermanent and changing and that life is not satisfying because of its impermanence and the temporary nature of all things, including contentment. Buddhism also teaches the Four Noble Truths: All life is suffering (Dukkha). Desire and attachment cause suffering (Samudaya). Ceasing to desire or crave conceptual attachment

ends suffering and leads to release (Nirodha). This release comes through following the Noble Eightfold Path—right understanding (or view), right intention, right speech, right conduct, right occupation, right effort, right mindfulness, and right concentration (Magga).

Although Buddhists do not believe in an afterlife as such, the soul undergoes a cycle of death and rebirth. Following the Noble Eightfold Path leads to the accumulation of good karma, allowing one to be reborn at a higher level. Karma is the Buddhist belief in cause-effect relationships; actions taken in one life have consequences in the next. Ultimately, many refer to the cessation or elimination of suffering as the primary goal of Buddhism.

Buddhists do not believe in gods. Salvation is to be found in following the teachings of Buddha, which are called the Dharma (law or truth). Buddhism does have saint-like bodhisattvas (enlightened beings) who reject ultimate enlightenment (Nirvana) for themselves to aid others.

Sacred Text

Buddhism has nothing comparable to the Qur'an (Islam's holy book) or the Bible. For Theravada Buddhists, an important text is the Pāli Canon, the collection of Buddha's teachings. Mahayana Buddhists recorded their version of these as sutras, many of them in verse. The Lotus Sutra is among the most important. The Buddhist scriptures are written in two languages of ancient India, Pali and Sanskrit, depending on the tradition in which they were developed. Some of these words, such as karma, have been transliterated into English and gained common usage.

Major Figures

Siddhartha Gautama (ca. 563 to 483 BCE) is the founder of Buddhism and regarded as the Buddha or Supreme Buddha. He is the most highly regarded historical figure in Buddhism.

He had two principle disciples: Sariputta and Mahamoggallana (or Maudgalyayana). In contemporary Buddhism, the fourteenth Dalai Lama, Tenzin Gyatso, is a significant person. Both he and Aung San Suu Kyi, a Buddhist of Myanmar who was held as a political prisoner for her stand against the oppressive regime of that nation, have been awarded the Nobel Peace Prize.

Major Holy Sites

Buddhist holy sites are located in several places in Asia. All of those directly related to the life of Siddhartha Gautama are located in the northern part of India near Nepal. Lumbini Grove is noted as the birthplace of the Buddha. He received enlightenment at Bodh Gaya and first began to teach in Sarnath. Kusinara is the city where he died.

In other Asian nations, some holy sites were once dedicated to other religions. Angkor Wat in Cambodia, for example, was constructed for the Hindu god Vishnu in the twelfth century CE. It became a Buddhist temple three hundred years later. It was once the largest religious monument in the world and still attracts visitors. In Java's central highlands sits Borobudur, the world's largest Buddhist shrine. The name means "Temple of Countless Buddhas." Its five terraces represent what must be overcome to reach enlightenment: worldly desires, evil intent, malicious joy, laziness, and doubt. It was built in the eighth and ninth centuries CE, only to fall into neglect at about the turn of the millennium; it was rediscovered in 1815. The complex has three miles of carvings illustrating the life and teachings of the Buddha. In Sri Lanka, the Temple of the Tooth, which houses what is believed to be one of the Buddha's teeth, is a popular pilgrimage site.

Some of the holy sites incorporate gifts of nature. China has four sacred Buddhist mountains, symbolizing the four corners of the universe. These mountains—Wǔtái Shān, Éméi Shān, Jiǔhuá Shān, and Pǔtuó Shān—are believed to be the homes of bodhisattvas. In central India outside Fardapur, there are twenty-nine caves carved into the granite, most of them with frescoes based on the Buddha's life. Ajanta, as

the site is known, was created between 200 BCE and the fifth century CE. Five of the caves house temples.

The Buddha's birthday, his day of death, and the day of his enlightenment are all celebrated, either as one day or several. Different traditions and countries have their own additional celebrations, including Sri Lanka's Festival of the Tooth. Buddhists have a lunar calendar, and four days of each month are regarded as holy days.

ORIGINS

History & Geography

Buddhism began in what is now southern Nepal and northern India with the enlightenment of the Buddha. Following his death, members of the sangha, or community, spread the teachings across northern India. The First Buddhist Council took place in 486 BCE at Rajagaha. This council settled the Buddhist canon, the Tipitaka. In 386 BCE, a little more than a century after the Buddha died, a second Buddhist Council was held at Vesali. It was at this meeting that the two major schools of Buddhist thought—Theravada and Mahayana—began to differ.

Emperor Asoka, who ruled most of the Indian subcontinent from around 268 to 232 BCE, converted to Buddhism. He sent missionaries across India and into central parts of Asia. He also set up pillars with Buddhist messages in his own efforts to establish "true dharma" in the kingdom, although he did not create a state church. His desire for his subjects to live contently in this life led to promoting trade, maintaining canals and reservoirs, and the founding a system of medical care for both humans and animals. Asoka's son Mahinda went to southern Indian and to Sri Lanka with the message of Buddhism.

Asoka's empire fell shortly after his death. Under the following dynasties, evidence suggests Buddhists in India experienced persecution. The religion continued to grow, however, and during the first centuries CE, monasteries and monuments were constructed with support from local rulers. Some additional support came from women within the royal courts. Monastic centers also grew in number. By the fourth century CE, Buddhism had become one of the chief religious traditions in India.

During the Gupta dynasty, which lasted from about 320 to 600 CE, Buddhists and Hindus began enriching each other's traditions. Some Hindus felt that the Buddha was an incarnation of Vishnu, a Hindu god. Some Buddhists showed respect for Hindu deities.

Also during this era, Mahavihara, the concept of the "Great Monastery," came to be. These institutions served as universities for the study and development of Buddhist thinking. Some of them also included cultural and scientific study in the curriculum.

Traders and missionaries took the ideas of Buddhism to China. By the first century CE, Buddhism was established in that country. The religion died out or was absorbed into Hinduism in India. By the seventh century, a visiting Chinese monk found that Huns had invaded India from Central Asia and destroyed many Buddhist monasteries. The religion revived and flourished in the northeast part of India for several centuries.

Muslim invaders reached India in the twelfth and thirteenth centuries. They sacked the monasteries, some of which had grown very wealthy. Some even paid workers to care for both the land they owned and the monks, while some had indentured slaves. Because Buddhism had become monastic rather than a religion of the laity, there was no groundswell for renewal following the Muslim invasion.

Prominent in eastern and Southeast Asia, Buddhism is the national religion in some countries. For example, in Thailand, everyone learns about Buddhism in school. Buddhism did not begin to reach Western culture until the nineteenth century, when the Lotus Sutra was translated into German. The first Buddhist temple in the United States was built in 1853 in San Francisco's Chinatown.

Chinese Communists took control of Tibet in 1950. Nine years later, the fourteenth Dalai Lama left for India, fearing persecution. The Dalai Lama is considered a living teacher (lama) who is to instruct others. (The term *dalai* means "great as the ocean.") In 1989, he received the Nobel Peace Prize.

Buddhism experienced a revival in India during the twentieth century. Although some of this new beginning was due in part to Tibetan immigrants seeking safety, a mass conversion in 1956 was the major factor. The year was chosen to honor the 2,500th anniversary of the Buddha's death year. Buddhism was chosen as an alternative to the strict caste structure of Hinduism, and hundreds of thousands of people of the Dalit caste, once known as untouchables, converted in a ceremony held in Nagpur.

Founder or Major Prophet

Siddhartha Gautama, who became known as the "Enlightened One," or Buddha, was a prince in what is now southern Nepal, but was then northern India during the sixth century BCE. The name Siddhartha means "he who achieves his aim." He was a member of the Sakya tribe of Nepal, belonging to the warrior caste. Many legends have grown around his birth and early childhood. One states that he was born in a grove in the woods, emerging from his mother's side able to walk and completely clean.

During Siddhartha's childhood, a Brahmin, or wise man, prophesied that he would grow to be a prince or a religious teacher who would help others overcome suffering. Because the life of a sage involved itinerant begging, the king did not want this life for his child. He kept Siddhartha in the palace and provided him with all the luxuries of his position, including a wife, Yashodhara. They had a son, Rahula.

Escaping from the palace at about the age of thirty, Gautama first encountered suffering in the form of an old man with a walking stick. The following day, he saw a man who was ill. On the third day, he witnessed a funeral procession. Finally he met a monk, who had nothing, but who radiated happiness. He determined to leave his privileged life, an act called the Great Renunciation. Because hair was a sign of vanity in his time, he shaved his head. He looked for enlightenment via an ascetic life of little food or sleep. He followed this path for six years, nearly starving to death. Eventually, he determined on a Middle Way, a path neither luxurious as he had known in the palace, nor ascetic as he had attempted.

After three days and nights of meditating under a tree at Bodh Gaya, Siddhartha achieved his goal of enlightenment, or Nirvana. He escaped fear of suffering and death.

The Buddha began his preaching career, which spanned some forty years, following his enlightenment. He gave his first sermon in northeast India at Sarnath in a deer park. The first five followers became the first community, or sangha. Buddha died around age eighty, in 483 BCE after he had eaten poisoned food. After warning his followers not to eat the food, he meditated until he died.

Buddhists believe in many enlightened ones. Siddhartha is in one tradition regarded as the fourth buddha, while other traditions hold him to have been the seventh or twenty-fifth buddha.

His disciples, who took the ideas throughout India, repeated his teachings. When the later Buddhists determined to write down the teachings of the Buddha, they met to discuss the ideas and agreed that a second meeting should occur in a century. At the third council, which was held at Pataliputta, divisions occurred. The two major divisions—Theravada and Mahayana—differ over the texts to be used and the interpretation of the teachings. Theravada can be translated as "the Teachings of the Elders," while Mahayana means "Great Vehicle."

Theravada Buddhists believe that only monks can achieve enlightenment through the teachings of another buddha, or enlightened being. Thus they try to spend some part of their lives in a monastery. Buddhists in the Mahayana tradition, on the other hand, feel that all people can achieve enlightenment, without being in a monastery. Mahayanans also regard some as bodhisattvas, people who have achieved the enlightened state but renounce Nirvana to help others achieve it.

Philosophical Basis

During Siddhartha's lifetime, Hinduism was the predominant religion in India. Many people, especially in northern India, were dissatisfied with the rituals and sacrifices of that religion. In addition, as many small kingdoms expanded and the unity of the tribes began to break down, many people were in religious turmoil and doubt. A number of sects within Hinduism developed.

The Hindu belief in the cycle of death and rebirth led some people to despair because they could not escape from suffering in their lives. Siddhartha was trying to resolve the suffering he saw in the world, but many of his ideas came from the Brahmin sect of Hinduism, although he reinterpreted them. Reincarnation, dharma, and reverence for cows are three of the ideas that carried over into Buddhism.

In northeast India at Bodh Gaya, he rested under a bodhi tree, sometimes called a bo tree. He meditated there until he achieved Nirvana, or complete enlightenment, derived from the freedom of fear that attached to suffering and death. As a result of his being enlightened, he was known as Buddha, a Sanskrit word meaning "awakened one." Wanting to help others, he began teaching his Four Noble Truths, along with the Noble Eightfold Path that would lead people to freedom from desire and suffering. He encouraged his followers to take Triple Refuge in the Three Precious Jewels: the Buddha, the teachings, and the sangha, or monastic community. Although at first Buddha was uncertain about including women in a sangha, his mother-in-law begged for the privilege.

Greed, hatred, and ignorance were three traits that Buddha felt people needed to conquer. All three create craving, the root of suffering. Greed and ignorance lead to a desire for things that are not needed, while hatred leads to a craving to destroy the hated object or person.

To the Four Noble Truths and Eightfold Path, early devotees of Buddhism added the Five Moral Precepts. These are to avoid taking drugs and alcohol, engaging in sexual misconduct, harming others, stealing, and lying.

The precepts of the Buddha were not written down for centuries. The first text did not appear for more than 350 years after the precepts were first spoken. One collection from Sri Lanka written in Pāli during the first century BCE is known as Three Baskets, or Tipitaka. The three baskets include Buddha's teaching (the Basket of Discourse), commentary on the sayings (the Basket of Special Doctrine), and the rules for monks to follow (the Basket of Discipline). The name Three Baskets refers to the fact that the sayings were first written on leaves from a palm tree that were then collected in baskets.

Holy Places

Buddhists make pilgrimages to places that relate to important events in Siddhartha's life. While Lumbini Grove, the place of Siddhartha's birth, is a prominent pilgrimage site, the primary site for pilgrimage is Bodh Gaya, the location where Buddha received enlightenment. Other pilgrimage sites include Sarnath, the deer park located in what is now Varanasi (Benares) where the Buddha first began to teach, and Kusinara, the city where he died. All of these are in the northern part of India near Nepal.

Other sites in Asia that honor various bodhisattvas have also become pilgrimage destinations. Mountains are often chosen; there are four in China, each with monasteries and temples built on them. In Japan, the Shikoku pilgrimage covers more than 700 miles and involves visits to eighty-eight temples along the route.

BUDDHISM IN DEPTH

Sacred Symbols

Many stylized statue poses of the Buddha exist, each with a different significance. One, in which the Buddha has both hands raised, palms facing outward, commemorates the calming of an elephant about to attack the Buddha. If only the right hand is raised, the hand symbolizes friendship and being unafraid. The teaching gesture is that of a hand with the thumb and first finger touching.

In Tibetan Buddhism, the teachings of Buddha regarding the cycle of rebirth are symbolized in the six-spoke wheel of life. One may be reborn into any of the six realms of life: hell, hungry spirits, warlike demons called Asuras, animals, humans, or gods. Another version of the wheel has eight spokes rather than six, to represent the Noble Eightfold Path. Still another wheel has twelve spokes, signifying both the Four Noble Truths and the Noble Eightfold Path.

Tibetan Buddhists have prayer beads similar to a rosary, with 108 beads representing the number of desires to be overcome prior to reaching enlightenment. The worshipper repeats the Triple Refuge—Buddha, dharma, and sangha—or a mantra.

The prayer wheel is another device that Tibetan Buddhists use. Inside the wheel is a roll of paper on which the sacred mantra—Hail to the jewel in the lotus—is written many times. The lotus is a symbol of growing spiritually; it grows in muddied waters, but with the stems and flowers, it reaches toward the sun. By turning the wheel and spinning the mantra, the practitioner spreads blessings. Bells may be rung to wake the hearer out of ignorance.

In Tantric Buddhism, the mandala, or circle, serves as a map of the entire cosmos. Mandalas may be made of colored grains of sand, carved or painted. They are used to help in meditation and are thought to have a spiritual energy.

Buddhism recognizes Eight Auspicious Symbols, including the banner, conch shell, fish, knot, lotus, treasure vase, umbrella, and wheel. Each has a particular significance. A conch shell, for example, is often blown to call worshippers to meetings. Because its sound travels far, it signifies the voice of Buddha traveling throughout the world. Fish are fertility symbols because they have thousands of offspring. In Buddhist imagery, they are often in facing pairs and fashioned of gold. The lotus represents spiritual growth, rooted in muddy water but flowering toward the sun. The umbrella symbolizes protection, because servants once used them to protect royalty from both sun and rain.

Sacred Practices & Gestures

Two major practices characterize Buddhism: gift-giving and showing respect to images and relics of the Buddha. The first is the transaction between laity and monks in which laypersons present sacrificial offerings to the monks, who in return share their higher state of spiritual being with the laity. Although Buddhist monks are permitted to own very little, they each have a begging bowl, which is often filled with rice.

Buddhists venerate statues of the Buddha, bodhisattvas, and saints; they also show respect to his relics, housed in stupas. When in the presence of a statue of the Buddha, worshippers have a series of movements they repeat three times, thus dedicating their movements to the Triple Refuge. It begins with a dedicated body: placing hands together with the palms cupped slightly and fingers touching, the devotee raises the hands to the forehead. The second step symbolizes right speech by lowering the hands to just below the mouth. In the third movement, the hands are lowered to the front of the chest, indicating that heart—and by extension, mind—are also dedicated to the Triple Refuge. The final movement is prostration. The devotee first gets on all fours, then lowers either the entire body to the floor or lowers the head, so that there are five points of contact with the floor.

Statues of the Buddha give a clue to the gestures held important to his followers. The gesture of turning the hand towards the ground indicates that one is observing Earth. Devotees assume a lotus position, with legs crossed, when in meditation.

Allowing the left hand to rest in the lap and the right hand to point down to Earth is a gesture used in meditation. Another common gesture is to touch thumb and fingertips together while the palms of both hands face up, thus forming a flat triangular shape. The triangle signifies the Three Jewels of Buddhism.

Food Restrictions

Buddhism does not require one to be a vegetarian. Many followers do not eat meat, however, because to do so involves killing other creatures. Both monks and laypersons may choose not to eat after noontime during the holy days of each month.

Rites, Celebrations, & Services

Ancient Buddhism recognized four holy days each month, known as *uposatha*. These days included the full moon and new moon days of each lunar month, as well as the eighth day after each of these moons appeared. Both monks and members of the laity have special religious duties during these four days. A special service takes place in which flowers are offered to images of the Buddha, precepts are repeated, and a sermon is preached. On these four days, an additional three precepts may be undertaken along with the five regularly observed. The three extra duties are to refrain from sleeping on a luxurious bed, eating any food after noon, and adorning the body or going to entertainments.

In Theravada nations, three major life events of the Buddha—birth, enlightenment, and entering nirvana—are celebrated on Vesak, or Buddha Day. In temples, statues of Buddha as a child are ceremonially cleaned. Worshippers may offer incense and flowers. To symbolize the Buddha's enlightenment, lights may be illuminated in trees and temples. Because it is a day of special kindness, some people in Thailand refrain from farm work that could harm living creatures. They may also seek special merit by freeing captive animals.

Other Buddhist nations that follow Mahayana Buddhism commemorate these events on three different days. In Japan, Hana Matsuri is the celebration of Buddha's birth. On that day, people create paper flower gardens to recall the gardens of Lumbini, Siddhartha's birthplace. Worshippers also pour perfumed tea over statues of Buddha; this is because, according to tradition, the gods provided scented water for Siddhartha's first bath.

Poson is celebrated in Sri Lanka to honor the coming of Buddhism during the reign of Emperor Asoka. Other holy persons are also celebrated in the countries where they had the greatest influence. In Tibet, for instance, the arrival of

Padmasambhava, who brought Buddhism to that nation, is observed.

Buddhists also integrate their own special celebrations into regular harvest festivals and New Year activities. These festivities may include a performance of an event in the life of any buddha or bodhisattva. For example, troupes of actors in Tibet specialize in enacting Buddhist legends. The festival of the Sacred Tooth is held in Kandy, Sri Lanka. According to one legend, a tooth of Buddha has been recovered, and it is paraded through the streets on this day. The tooth has been placed in a miniature stupa, or sealed mound, which is carried on an elephant's back.

Protection rituals have been common in Buddhism from earliest days. They may be public rituals meant to avoid a collective danger, such as those held in Sri Lanka and other Southeast Asia nations. Or they may be designed for private use. The role of these rituals is greater in Mahayana tradition, especially in Tibet. Mantras are chanted for this reason.

Customs surrounding death and burial differ between traditions and nations. A common factor, however, is the belief that the thoughts of a person at death are significant. This period may be extended for three days following death, due to a belief in consciousness for that amount of time after death. To prepare the mind of the dying, another person may read sacred texts aloud.

Judy A. Johnson, MTS

Bibliography

Armstrong, Karen. *Buddha*. New York: Penguin, 2001. Print.

Barnes, Trevor. *The Kingfisher Book of Religions*. New York: Kingfisher, 1999. Print.

Chodron, Thubten. *Buddhism for Beginners*. Ithaca: Snow Lion, 2001. Print.

Eckel, Malcolm David. *Buddhism*. Oxford: Oxford UP, 2002. Print.

Epstein, Ron. "Application of Buddhist Teachings in Modern Life." *Religion East & West* Oct. 2012: 52–61. Print.

Harding, John S. *Studying Buddhism in Practice*. Routledge, 2012. E-book. Studying Religions in Practice.

Harvey, Peter. *An Introduction to Buddhism: Teachings, History and Practices*. 2nd ed. Cambridge UP, 2013. E-book.

Heirman, Ann. "Buddhist Nuns: Between Past and Present." *International Review for the History of Religions* 58.5/6 (2011): 603–31. Print.

Langley, Myrtle. *Religion*. New York: Knopf, 1996. Print.

Low, Kim Cheng Patrick. "Three Treasures of Buddhism & Leadership Insights." *Culture & Religion Review Journal* 2012.3 (2012): 66–72. Print.

Low, Patrick Kim Cheng. "Leading Change, the Buddhist Perspective." *Culture & Religion Review Journal* 2012.1 (2012): 127–45. Print.

McMahan, David L. *Buddhism in the Modern World*. Routledge, 2012. E-book.

Meredith, Susan. *The Usborne Book of World Religions*. London: Usborne, 1995. Print.

Morgan, Diane. *Essential Buddhism: A Comprehensive Guide to Belief and Practice*. Praeger, 2010. E-book.

Wilkinson, Philip. *Buddhism*. New York: DK, 2003. Print.

Wilkinson, Philip. *Religions*. New York: DK, 2008. Print.

Christianity

General Description

Christianity is one of the world's major religions. It is based on the life and teachings of Jesus of Nazareth, called the Christ, or anointed one. It is believed that there are over thirty thousand denominations or sects of Christianity worldwide. Generally, most of these sects fall under the denominational families of Catholicism, Protestant, and Orthodox. (Anglican and Oriental Orthodox are sometimes added as separate branches.) Most denominations have developed since the seventeenth-century Protestant Reformation.

Number of Adherents Worldwide

Over 2.3 billion people around the world claim allegiance to Christianity in one of its many forms. The three major divisions are Roman Catholicism, Eastern Orthodox, and Protestant. Within each group are multiple denominations. Roman Catholics number more than 1.1 billion followers, while the Eastern Orthodox Church has between 260 and 278 million adherents. An estimated 800 million adherents follow one of the various Protestant denominations, including Anglican, Baptist, Lutheran, Presbyterian, and Methodist. Approximately 1 percent of Christians, or 28 million adherents, do not belong to one of the three major divisions

There are a number of other groups, such as the Amish, with an estimated 249,000 members, and the Quakers, numbering approximately 377,000. Both of these churches—along with Mennonites, who number 1.7 million—are in the peace tradition (their members are conscientious objectors). Pentecostals have 600 million adherents worldwide. Other groups that are not always considered Christian by more conservative groups include Jehovah's Witnesses (7.6 million) and Mormons (13 million) (Wilkinson, p. 104-121).

Basic Tenets

The summaries of the Christian faith are found in the Apostles Creed and Nicene Creed.

In addition, some churches have developed their own confessions of faith, such as Lutheranism's Augsburg Confession. Christianity is a monotheistic tradition, although most Christians believe in the Trinity, defined as one God in three separate but equal persons—Father, Son, and Holy Spirit. More modern, gender-neutral versions of the Trinitarian formula may refer to Creator, Redeemer, and Sanctifier. Many believe in the doctrine of original sin, which means that the disobedience of Adam and Eve in the Garden of Eden has been passed down through all people; because of this sin, humankind is in need of redemption. Jesus Christ was born, lived a sinless life, and then was crucified and resurrected as a substitute for humankind. Those who accept this sacrifice for sin will receive eternal life in a place of bliss after death. Many Christians believe that a Second Coming of Jesus will inaugurate a millennial kingdom and a final judgment (in which people will be judged according to their deeds and their eternal souls consigned to heaven or hell), as well as a resurrected physical body.

Sacred Text

The Bible is the sacred text of Christianity, which places more stress on the New Testament. The canon of the twenty-six books of the New Testament was finally determined in the latter half of the fourth century CE.

Major Figures

Christianity is based on the life and teachings of Jesus of Nazareth. His mother, Mary, is especially revered in Roman Catholicism and the Eastern Orthodox tradition, where she is known as Theotokos (God-bearer). Jesus spread his teachings through the twelve apostles, or disciples, who he himself chose and named. Paul (Saint Paul or Paul the Apostle), who became the first missionary to the Gentiles—and whose writings comprise a bulk of the New Testament—is a key figure for the theological treatises embedded in his letters to early churches. His conversion occurred after Jesus' crucifixion. All of these figures are biblically represented.

Under the Emperor Constantine, Christianity went from a persecuted religion to the state religion. Constantine also convened the Council of Nicea in 325 CE, which expressed the formula defining Jesus as fully God and fully human. Saint Augustine (354–430) was a key thinker of the early church who became the Bishop of Hippo in North Africa. He outlined the principles of just war and expressed the ideas of original sin. He also suggested what later became the Catholic doctrine of purgatory.

In the sixth century, Saint Benedict inscribed a rule for monks that became a basis for monastic life. Martin Luther, the monk who stood against the excesses of the Roman Catholic Church, ignited the seventeenth-century Protestant Reformation. He proclaimed that salvation came by grace alone, not through works. In the twentieth century, Pope John XXIII convened the Vatican II Council, or Second Vatican Council, which made sweeping changes to the liturgy and daily practice for Roman Catholics.

Major Holy Sites

The key events in the life of Jesus Christ occurred in the region of Palestine. Bethlehem is honored as the site of Jesus's birth; Jerusalem is especially revered as the site of Jesus's crucifixion. The capital of the empire, Rome, also became the center of Christianity until the Emperor Constantine shifted the focus to Constantinople. Rome today is the seat of the Vatican, an independent city-state that houses the government of the Roman Catholic Church. Canterbury, the site of the martyrdom of Saint Thomas Becket and seat of the archbishop of the Anglican Communion, is a pilgrimage site for Anglicans. There are also many pilgrimage sites, such as Compostela and Lourdes, for other branches of Christianity. In Ethiopia, Lalibela is the site of eleven churches carved from stone during the twelfth century. The site serves as a profound testimony to the vibrancy of the Christian faith in Africa.

Major Rites & Celebrations

The first rite of the church is baptism, a water-related ritual that is traditionally administered to infants or adults alike through some variant of sprinkling or immersion. Marriage is another rite of the church. Confession is a major part of life for Roman Catholics, although the idea is also present in other branches of Christianity.

The celebration of the Eucharist, or Holy Communion, is a key part of weekly worship for the liturgical churches such as those in the Roman Catholic or Anglican traditions. Nearly all Christians worship weekly on Sunday; services include readings of scripture, a sermon, singing of hymns, and may include Eucharist. Christians honor the birth of Jesus at Christmas and his death and resurrection at Easter. Easter is often considered the most significant liturgical feast, particularly in Orthodox branches.

Many Christians follow a calendar of liturgical seasons. Of these seasons, perhaps the best known is Lent, which is immediately preceded by Shrove Tuesday, also known as Mardi Gras. Lent is traditionally a time of fasting and self-examination in preparation for the Easter feast. Historically, Christians gave up rich foods. The day before Lent was a time for pancakes—to use up the butter and eggs—from which the term Mardi Gras (Fat Tuesday) derives. Lent begins with Ash Wednesday, when Christians are marked with the sign of the cross on their foreheads using ashes, a reminder that they are dust and will return to dust.

ORIGINS

History & Geography

Christianity was shaped in the desert and mountainous landscapes of Palestine, known as the Holy Land. Jesus was driven into the wilderness following his baptism, where he remained for forty days of fasting and temptation. The Gospels record that he often went to the mountains for solitude and prayer. The geography of the deserts and mountains also shaped early Christian spirituality, as men and women went into solitude to pray, eventually founding small communities of the so-called desert fathers and mothers.

Christianity at first was regarded as a sect within Judaism, though it differentiated itself early in the first century CE by breaking with the code of laws that defined Judaism, including the need for circumcision and ritual purity. Early Christianity then grew through the missionary work of the apostles, particularly Paul the Apostle, who traveled throughout the Mediterranean world and beyond the Roman Empire to preach the gospel (good news) of Jesus. (This is often called the Apostolic Age.)

Persecution under various Roman emperors only served to strengthen the emerging religion. In the early fourth century, the Emperor Constantine (ca. 272-337) made Christianity the official religion of the Roman Empire. He also convened the Council of Nicea in 325 CE to quell the religious controversies threatening the Pax Romana (Roman Peace), a time of stability and peace throughout the empire in the first and second centuries.

In 1054 the Great Schism, which involved differences over theology and practice, split the church into Eastern Orthodox and Roman Catholic branches. As Islam grew stronger, the Roman Catholic nations of Europe entered a period of Crusades—there were six Crusades in approximately 175 years, from 1095-1271—that attempted to take the Holy Land out of Muslim control.

A number of theologians became unhappy with the excesses of the Roman church and papal authority during the fifteenth and sixteenth centuries. The Protestant Reformation, originally an attempt to purify the church, was led by several men, most notably Martin Luther (1483-1546), whose ninety-five theses against the Catholic Church sparked the Reformation movement. Other leaders of the Protestant Reformation include John Knox (ca. 1510-1572), attributed as the founder of the Presbyterian denomination, John Calvin (1509-1564), a principle early developer of Calvinism, and Ulrich Zwingli (1484-1531), who initially spurred the Reformation in Switzerland. This period of

turmoil resulted in the founding of a number of church denominations: Lutherans, Presbyterians, and Anglicans. These groups were later joined by the Methodists and the Religious Society of Friends (Quakers).

During the sixteenth and seventeenth centuries, the Roman Catholic Church attempted to stem this wave of protest and schism with the Counter-Reformation. Concurrently, the Inquisition, an effort to root out heresy and control the rebellion, took place. There were various inquisitions, including the Spanish Inquisition, which was led by Ferdinand II of Aragon and Isabella I of Castile in mid-fifteenth century and sought to "guard" the orthodoxy of Catholicism in Spain. There was also the Portuguese Inquisition, which began in 1536 in Portugal under King John III, and the Roman Inquisition, which took place in the late fifteenth century in Rome under the Holy See.

During the modern age, some groups became concerned with the perceived conflicts between history (revealed through recent archaeological findings) and the sciences (as described by Charles Darwin and Sigmund Freud) and the literal interpretation of some biblical texts. Fundamentalist Christianity began at an 1895 meeting in Niagara Falls, New York, with an attempt to define the basics (fundamentals) of Christianity. These were given as the inerrant nature of the Bible, the divine nature of Jesus, his literal virgin birth, his substitutionary death and literal physical resurrection, and his soon return. Liberal Christians, on the other hand, focused more on what became known as the Social Gospel, an attempt to relieve human misery.

Controversies in the twenty-first century throughout Christendom focused on issues such as abortion, homosexuality, the ordination of women and gays, and the authority of the scriptures. An additional feature is the growth of Christianity in the Southern Hemisphere. In Africa, for example, the number of Christians grew from 10 million in 1900 to over 506 million a century later. Initially the result of empire-building and colonialism, the conversions in these nations have resulted in a unique blend of native religions and Christianity. Latin America has won renown for its liberation theology, which was first articulated in 1968 as God's call for justice and God's preference for the poor, demonstrated in the ministry and teachings of Jesus Christ. Africa, Asia, and South America are regions that are considered more morally and theologically conservative. Some suggest that by 2050, non-Latino white persons will comprise only 20 percent of Christians.

Founder or Major Prophet

Jesus of Nazareth was born into a peasant family. The date of his birth, determined by accounts in the Gospels of Matthew and Luke, could be as early as 4 or 5 BCE or as late as 6 CE. Mary, his mother, was regarded as a virgin; thus, Jesus' birth was a miracle, engendered by the Holy Spirit. His earthly father, Joseph, was a carpenter.

At about age thirty, Jesus began an itinerant ministry of preaching and healing following his baptism in the Jordan River by his cousin, John the Baptist. He selected twelve followers, known as apostles (sent-ones), and a larger circle of disciples (followers). Within a short time, Jesus' ministry and popularity attracted the negative attention of both the Jewish and Roman rulers. He offended the Jewish leaders with his emphasis on personal relationship with God rather than obedience to rules, as well as his claim to be coequal with God the Father.

For a period of one to three years (Gospel accounts vary in the chronology), Jesus taught and worked miracles, as recorded in the first four books of the New Testament, the Gospels of Matthew, Mark, Luke, and John. On what has become known as Palm Sunday, he rode triumphantly into Jerusalem on the back of a donkey while crowds threw palm branches at his feet. Knowing that his end was near, at a final meal with his disciples, known now to Christians as the Last Supper, Jesus gave final instructions to his followers.

He was subsequently captured, having been betrayed by Judas Iscariot, one of his own twelve apostles. A trial before the Jewish legislative body, the Sanhedrin, led to his being condemned for blasphemy. However, under Roman law, the Jews did not have the power to put anyone to death. A later trial under the Roman governor, Pontius Pilate, resulted in Jesus being crucified, although Pilate tried to prevent this action, declaring Jesus innocent.

According to Christian doctrine, following the crucifixion, Jesus rose from the dead three days later. He appeared before many over a span of forty days and instructed the remaining eleven apostles to continue spreading his teachings. He then ascended into heaven. Ultimately, his followers believed that he was the Messiah, the savior who was to come to the Jewish people and deliver them. Rather than offering political salvation, however, Jesus offered spiritual liberty.

Philosophical Basis

Jesus was a Jew who observed the rituals and festivals of his religion. The Gospels reveal that he attended synagogue worship and went to Jerusalem for celebrations such as Passover. His teachings both grew out of and challenged the religion of his birth.

The Jews of Jesus' time, ruled by the Roman Empire, hoped for a return to political power. This power would be concentrated in a Messiah, whose coming had been prophesied centuries before. There were frequent insurrections in Judea, led in Jesus' time by a group called the Zealots. Indeed, it is believed that one of the twelve apostles was part of this movement. Jesus, with his message of a kingdom of heaven, was viewed as perhaps the one who would usher in a return to political ascendancy.

When challenged to name the greatest commandment, Jesus answered that it was to love God with all the heart, soul, mind, and strength. He added that the second was to love one's neighbor as one's self, saying that these two commands summarized all the laws that the Jewish religion outlined.

Jewish society was concerned with ritual purity and with following the law. Jesus repeatedly flouted those laws by eating with prostitutes and tax collectors, by touching those deemed unclean, such as lepers, and by including

Gentiles in his mission. Women were part of his ministry, with some of them providing for him and his disciples from their own purses, others offering him a home and a meal, and still others among those listening to him teach.

Jesus's most famous sermon is called the Sermon on the Mount. In it, he offers blessings on those on the outskirts of power, such as the poor, the meek, and those who hunger and thirst for righteousness. While not abolishing the law that the Jews followed, he pointed out its inadequacies and the folly of parading one's faith publicly. Embedded in the sermon is what has become known as the Lord's Prayer, the repetition of which is often part of regular Sunday worship. Much of Jesus' teaching was offered in the form of parables, or short stories involving vignettes of everyday life: a woman adding yeast to dough or a farmer planting seeds. Many of these parables were attempts to explain the kingdom of heaven, a quality of life that was both present and to come.

Holy Places

The Christian church has many pilgrimage sites, some of them dating back to the Middle Ages. Saint James is thought to have been buried in Compostela, Spain, which was a destination for those who could not make the trip to the Holy Land. Lourdes, France, is one of the spots associated with healing miracles. Celtic Christians revere places such as the small Scottish isle of Iona, an early Christian mission. Assisi, Italy, is a destination for those who are attracted to Saint Francis (1181-1226), founder of the Franciscans. The Chartres Cathedral in France is another pilgrimage destination from the medieval period.

Jerusalem, Rome, and Canterbury are considered holy for their associations with the early church and Catholicism, as well as with Anglicanism. Within the Old City of Jerusalem is the Church of the Holy Sepulchre, an important pilgrimage site believed to house the burial place of Jesus. Another important pilgrimage site is the Church of the Nativity in Bethlehem. It is built on a cave believed to be the birthplace of Jesus, and is one of the oldest operating churches in existence.

CHRISTIANITY IN DEPTH

Sacred Symbols

The central symbol of Christianity is the cross, of which there are many variant designs. Some of them, such as Celtic crosses, are related to regions of the world. Others, such as the Crusader's cross, honor historic events. The dove is the symbol for the Holy Spirit, which descended in that shape on the gathered disciples at Pentecost after Jesus's ascension.

Various symbols represent Jesus. Candles allude to his reference to himself as the Light of the World, while the lamb stands for his being the perfect sacrifice, the Lamb of God. The fish symbol that is associated with Christianity has a number of meanings, both historic and symbolic. A fish shape stands for the Greek letters beginning the words Jesus Christ, Son of God, Savior; these letters form the word *ichthus*, the Greek word for "fish." Fish also featured prominently in the scriptures, and the early apostles were known as "fishers of man." The crucifixion symbol is also a popular Catholic Christian symbol.

All of these symbols may be expressed in stained glass. Used in medieval times, stained glass often depicted stories from the Bible as an aid to those who were illiterate.

Sacred Practices & Gestures

Roman Catholics honor seven sacraments, defined as outward signs of inward grace. These include the Eucharist, baptism, confirmation, marriage, ordination of priests, anointing the sick or dying with oil, and penance. The Eastern Orthodox Church refers to these seven as mysteries rather than sacraments.

Priests in the Roman Catholic Church must remain unmarried. In the Eastern Orthodox, Anglican, and Protestant denominations, they may marry. Both Roman Catholic and Eastern Orthodox refuse to ordain women to the priesthood.

The Orthodox Church practices a rite known as chrismation, anointing a child with oil following its baptism. The "oil of gladness," as it is known, is placed on the infant's head, eyes, ears, and mouth. This is similar to the practice of confirmation in some other denominations. Many Christian denominations practice anointing the sick or dying with oil, as well as using the oil to seal those who have been baptized.

Many Christians, especially Roman Catholics, use a rosary, or prayer beads, when praying. Orthodox believers may have icons, such as small paintings of God, saints or biblical events, as part of their worship. There may be a font of water that has been blessed as one enters some churches, which the worshippers use to make the sign of the cross, touching fingers to their forehead, heart, right chest, and left chest. Some Christians make the sign of the cross on the forehead, mouth, and heart to signify their desire for God to be in their minds, on their lips, and in their hearts.

Christians may genuflect, or kneel, as they enter or leave a pew in church. In some churches, particularly the Catholic and Orthodox, incense is burned during the service as a sweet smell to God.

In some traditions, praying to or for the dead is encouraged. The rationale for this is known as the communion of saints—the recognition that those who are gone are still a part of the community of faith.

Catholic, Orthodox, and some branches of other churches have monastic orders for both men and women. Monks and nuns may live in a cloister or be engaged in work in the wider world. They generally commit to a rule of life and to the work of prayer. Even those Christians who are not part of religious orders sometimes go on retreats, seeking quiet and perhaps some spiritual guidance from those associated with the monastery or convent.

Food Restrictions

Historically, Christians fasted during Lent as preparation for the Easter celebration. Prior to the Second Vatican Council in 1962,

Roman Catholics did not eat meat on Fridays. Conservative Christians in the Evangelical tradition tend to eliminate the use of alcohol, tobacco, and drugs.

Rites, Celebrations & Services

For churches in the liturgical tradition, the weekly celebration of the Eucharist is paramount. While many churches celebrate this ritual feast with wine and a wafer, many Protestant churches prefer to use grape juice and crackers or bread.

Church services vary widely. Quakers sit silently waiting for a word from God, while in many African American churches, hymns are sung for perhaps an hour before the lengthy sermon is delivered. Some churches have a prescribed order of worship that varies little from week to week. Most services, however, include prayer, a sermon, and singing, with or without musical accompaniment.

A church's architecture often gives clues as to the type of worship one will experience. A church with the pulpit in the center at the front generally is a Protestant church with an emphasis on the Word of God being preached. If the center of the front area is an altar, the worship's focus will be on the Eucharist.

Christmas and Easter are the two major Christian celebrations. In liturgical churches, Christmas is preceded by Advent, a time of preparation and quiet to ready the heart for the coming of Christ. Christmas has twelve days, from the birth date of December 25 to the Epiphany on January 6. Epiphany (to show) is the celebration of the arrival of the Magi (wise men) from the East who came to worship the young Jesus after having seen his star. Their arrival is believed to have been foretold by the Old Testament prophet Isaiah, who said "And the Gentiles shall come to thy light, and kings to the brightness of thy rising" (Isaiah 60:3). Epiphany is the revealing of the Messiah to the Gentiles.

In the early church, Easter was preceded by a solemn period of fasting and examination, especially for candidates for baptism and penitent sinners wishing to be reconciled. In Western churches, Lent begins with Ash Wednesday, which is six and half weeks prior to Easter. By excluding Sundays from the fast, Lent thus gives a forty-day fast, imitating that of Jesus in the wilderness. Historically forbidden foods during the fast included eggs, butter, meat, and fish. In the Eastern Church, dairy products, oil, and wine are also forbidden.

The week before Easter is known as Holy Week. It may include extra services such as Maundy Thursday, a time to remember Jesus's new commandment (*maundy* is etymologically related to *mandate*) to love one another. In some Catholic areas, the crucifixion is reenacted in a Passion play (depicting the passion—trial, suffering, and death—of Christ). Some churches will have an Easter vigil the Saturday night before or a sunrise service on Easter morning.

Judy A. Johnson, MTS

Bibliography

Bakker, Janel Kragt. "The Sister Church Phenomenon: A Case Study of the Restructuring of American Christianity against the Backdrop of Globalization." *International Bulletin of Missionary Research* 36.3 (2012): 129–34. Print.

Bandak, Andreas and Jonas Adelin Jørgensen. "Foregrounds and Backgrounds—Ventures in the Anthropology of Christianity." *Ethos: Journal of Anthropology* 77.4 (2012): 447–58. Print.

Barnes, Trevor. *The Kingfisher Book of Religions*. New York: Kingfisher, 1999. Print.

Chandler, Daniel Ross. "Christianity in Cross-Cultural Perspective: A Review of Recent Literature." *Asia Journal of Theology* 26.2 (2012): 44–57. Print.

Daughrity, Dyron B. "Christianity Is Moving from North to South—So What about the East?" *International Bulletin of Missionary Research* 35.1 (2011): 18–22. Print.

Kaatz, Kevin. *Voices of Early Christianity: Documents from the Origins of Christianity*. Santa Barbara: Greenwood, 2013. E-book.

Langley, Myrtle. *Religion*. New York: Alfred A. Knopf, 1996.

Lewis, Clive Staples. *Mere Christianity*. New York: Harper, 2001. Print.

McGrath, Alistair. *Christianity: An Introduction*. Hoboken, New Jersey: Wiley, 2006. Print.

Meredith, Susan. *The Usborne Book of World Religions*. London: Usborne, 1995. Print.

Ripley, Jennifer S. "Integration of Psychology and Christianity: 2022." *Journal of Psychology & Theology* 40.2 (2012): 150–54. Print.

Stefon, Matt. *Christianity: History, Belief, and Practice*. New York: Britannica Educational, 2012. E-book.

Wilkinson, Philip. *Christianity*. New York: DK, 2003. Print.

Wilkinson, Philip. *Religions*. New York: DK, 2008. Print.

Zoba, Wendy Murray. *The Beliefnet Guide to Evangelical Christianity*. New York: Three Leaves, 2005. Print.

East Asian Religions

General Description

East Asian religious and philosophical traditions include, among others, Confucianism, Taoism, and Shintoism. Confucianism is a philosophy introduced by the Chinese philosopher Confucius (Kongzi; 551–479 BCE) in the sixth century BCE, during the Zhou dynasty. Taoism, which centers on Tao, or "the way," is a religious and philosophical tradition that originated in China about two thousand years ago. Shinto, "the way of the spirits," is a Japanese tradition of devotion to spirits and rituals.

Number of Adherents Worldwide

Between 5 and 6 million people, the majority of them in China, practice Confucianism, once the state religion of China. About 20 million people identify as Taoists. Most of the Taoist practitioners are in China as well. In Japan, approximately 107 million people practice Shintoism, though many practitioners also practice Buddhism. Sects of Shinto include Tenrikyo (heavenly truth), founded in 1838, with nearly 2 million devotees. Shukyo Mahikari (divine light) is another, smaller sect founded in the 1960s. Like other sects, it is a blend of different religious traditions (Wilkinson 332–34).

Basic Tenets

Confucianism is a philosophy of life and does concerns itself not with theology but with life conduct. Chief among the aspects of life that must be tended are five key relationships, with particular focus on honoring ancestors and showing filial piety. Confucianism does not take a stand on the existence of God, though the founder, Confucius, referred to "heaven." Except for this reference, Confucianism does not address the question of life after death.

Taoists believe that Tao (the way or the flow) is in everything. Taoism teaches that qi, or life energy, needs to be balanced between yin and yang, which are the female and male principles

of life, respectively. With its doctrine of the evil of violence, Taoism borders on pacifism, and it also preaches simplicity and naturalness. Taoists believe in five elements—wood, earth, air, fire and water—that need to be in harmony. The five elements lie at the heart of Chinese medicine, particularly acupuncture. In Taoism, it is believed that the soul returns to a state of nonbeing after death.

Shinto emphasizes nature and harmony, with a focus on lived experience rather than doctrine. Shinto, which means "the way of the gods," is a polytheistic religion; Amaterasu, the sun goddess, is the chief god. At one point in Japan's history, the emperor was believed to be a descendant of Amaterasu and therefore divine. In Tenrikyo Shinto, God is manifested most often as Oyakami, meaning "God the parent."

Shinto teaches that some souls can become kami, a spirit, following death. Each traditional home has a god-shelf, which honors family members believed to have become kami. An older family member tends to the god-shelf, placing a bit of food and some sake (rice wine) on the shelf. To do their work, kami must be nourished. The Tenrikyo sect includes concepts from Pure Land Buddhism, such as an afterlife and the idea of salvation.

Sacred Texts

Five classic texts are sacred to the Confucians. These include the I Ching, or Book of Changes; the Book of Odes; the Book of History; the Book of Rites; and the Annals of Spring and Autumn. The Analects, a collection of Confucius's sayings, is another revered classic. The Tao Te Ching (The Way of Power) is the most sacred book of the Taoists. Those who practice Shinto hold sacred two works: the Kojiki (Record of Ancient Matters) and the Nihon-gi (Chronicles of Japan). Both texts, which contain legends and creation myths, were written during the eighth century.

Major Figures

Confucius, who lived during the sixth century, was the first great philosopher of China. Mengzi (Meng-tzu; 371–289 BCE), known in the West as Mencius, developed Confucius's teachings about the higher power guiding human life. Another ancient Chinese philosopher, Laozi(or Lao-tzu), is the founder of Taoism. He is believed to have been a contemporary of Confucius's in the central region of China. Modern scholars are not certain he ever existed, though one account includes the story of Confucius visiting Laozi. Chuang Tzu wrote of Laozi and his ideas during the fourth and third centuries BCE. Shinto's major figures include Ō no Yasumaro (d. 723), the compiler of the Kokiji who acted under the orders of Empress Gemmei and consulted a bard known to have an infallible memory; the scholar Motoori Norinaga (1730–1800), whose work led to a revived interest in ancient Shinto texts; and Nakayama Miki (1798–1887), the farmer's wife who founded Tenrikyo.

Major Holy Sites

Most Confucian sacred places are located within private homes, where an ancestral shrine and an altar to gods and spirits are maintained. In China's Shandong Province is Qufu, the site of Confucius's family mansion, temple, and cemetery. The temple was built in 478 BCE, only a year after Confucius's death, and has been maintained and enlarged. In addition to its status as a holy site, the United Nations Educational, Scientific, and Cultural Organization (UNESCO) has placed it on their World Heritage List.

Taoists regard mountains as a way to communicate with Earth's primeval powers and with those who are immortal. Five of the nine sacred mountains in China are associated with Taoism: Hengshan in both the north and the south, Songshan in the south, Taishan in the east, and Huashan in the west. The holiest of the five is Taishan, which symbolizes stability, prevents natural disasters, and ensures fertility.

Shintoism has a high regard for natural beauty. As such, Shinto shrines are everywhere, particularly in mountains or near waterfalls.

Mountains in particular are regarded as homes of the gods. Mount Fuji is the holiest Shinto mountain, and climbing it to reach the shrine on its peak is an act of worship. More than forty thousand shrines are dedicated to Inari, the rice god.

Shinto was formalized during the Yamato period (the name for ancient Japan), and because the emperor of the imperial dynasty was from the Yamato area and was considered divine, the whole region is revered. At Ise, located near the coast in Mie Prefecture, southeast of Nara, the shrine has been rebuilt every twenty years for at least fourteen centuries. This rebuilding ensures that Toyouke-Ōmikami (the harvest goddess) and Amaterasu (the sun goddess) are renewed in vigor, which in turn invigorates both the rice crop and the imperial line. Those who have died in war are revered as kami in Japan. In Tokyo, a shrine called Yasukuni is dedicated to them. However, there is controversy surrounding the place because of its association with Japan's extreme nationalism prior to World War II.

Sacred Texts

Five classic texts are sacred to the Confucians. These include the I Ching, or Book of Changes; the Book of Odes; the Book of History; the Book of Rites; and the Annals of Spring and Autumn. The Analects, a collection of Confucius's sayings, is another revered classic. The Tao te Ching (The Way of Power) is the most sacred book of the Taoists. Those who practice Shinto hold sacred two works: the Kojiki (Record of Ancient Matters) and the Nihon-gi (Chronicles of Japan). Both texts, which contain legends and creation myths, were written during the eighth century.

Major Figures

Confucius, who lived during the sixth century, was the first great philosopher of China. Mengzi (Meng-tzu; 371–289 BCE), known in the West as Mencius, developed Confucius's teachings about the higher power guiding human life. Another ancient Chinese philosopher, Laozi,(or Lao-tzu) is the founder of Taoism. He is believed to have been a contemporary of Confucius in the central region of China. Modern scholars are not certain he ever existed, though one account includes the story of Confucius visiting Laozi. Chuang Tzu wrote of Laozi and his ideas during the fourth and third centuries BCE. Shinto's major figures include Ō no Yasumaro, the compiler of the Kokiji who acted under the orders of Empress Gemmei and consulted a bard known to have an infallible memory; the scholar Motoori Norinaga (1730–1800), whose work led to a revived interest in ancient Shinto texts; and Nakayama Miki (1798–1887), the farmer's wife who founded Tenrikyo.

Major Holy Sites

Most Confucian sacred places are located within private homes, where an ancestral shrine and an altar to gods and spirits are maintained. In China's Shandong Province is Qufu, the site of Confucius's family mansion, temple and cemetery. The temple was built in 478 BCE, only a year after Confucius's death, and has been maintained and enlarged. In addition to being a holy site, the United Nations Educational, Scientific, and Cultural Organization (UNESCO) has placed it on their World Heritage List.

Taoists consider mountains as a way to communicate with Earth's primeval powers and with those who are immortal. Five of the nine sacred mountains in China are associated with Taoism. They are Hengshan in both the north and south, Songshan in the south, Taishan in the east, and Huashan in the west. The holiest of the five is Taishan, which symbolizes stability, prevents natural disasters, and ensures fertility.

Shintoism has a high regard for natural beauty. As such, Shinto shrines are everywhere, particularly in mountains or near waterfalls. Mountains in particular are regarded as homes of the gods. Mount Fuji is the holiest Shinto mountain, and climbing it to reach the shrine on its peak is an act of worship. More than forty thousand shrines are dedicated to Inari, the rice god.

Shinto was formalized during the Yamato period (the name for ancient Japan), and because the emperor of the imperial dynasty is from the Yamato area, and was considered divine, the whole region is revered. At Ise, located near the coast in the Mie prefecture southeast of Nara, the shrine has been rebuilt every twenty years for at least fourteen centuries. This rebuilding ensures that Toyouke-Ōmikami (the harvest goddess) and Amaterasu (the sun goddess) are renewed in vigor, which in turn invigorates both the rice crop and the imperial line. Those who have died in war are revered as kami in Japan. In Tokyo, a shrine called Yasukuni is dedicated to them. However, there is controversy surrounding the place because of its association with Japan's extreme nationalism prior to World War II.

Major Rites & Celebrations

Confucian celebrations have to do with honoring people rather than gods. At Confucian temples, the philosopher's birthday is celebrated each September. In Taiwan, this day is called "Teacher's Day." Sacrifices, music and dance are part of the event.

Taoism has a jiao (offering) festival near the winter solstice. It celebrates the renewal of the yang force at this turning of the year. During the festival priests, who have been ritually purified, wear lavish clothing. The festival includes music and dancing, along with large effigies of the gods which are designed to frighten away the evil spirits. Yang's renewal is also the focus of New Year celebrations, which is a time for settling debts and cleaning house. Decorations in the yang warm colors of gold, orange and red abound.

Many of the Shinto festivals overlap with Buddhist ones. There are many local festivals and rituals, and each community has an annual festival at the shrine dedicated to the kami of the region. Japanese New Year, which is celebrated for three days, is a major feast. Since the sixteenth century, the Gion Festival has taken place in Kyoto, Japan. Decorated floats are part of the celebration of the shrine.

ORIGINS

History & Geography

During the Zhou dynasty (1050–256 BCE) in China, the idea of heaven as a force that controlled events came to the fore. Zhou rulers believed that they ruled as a result of the "Mandate of Heaven," viewing themselves as morally superior to those of the previous dynasty, the Shang dynasty (1600-1046 BCE). They linked virtue and power as the root of the state.

By the sixth century the Zhou rulers had lost much of their authority. Many schools of thought developed to restore harmony, and were collectively known as the "Hundred Schools." Confucius set forth his ideas within this historical context. He traveled China for thirteen years, urging rulers to put his ideas into practice and failing to achieve his goals. He returned home to teach for the rest of his life and his ideas were not adopted until the Han dynasty (206 BCE–220 CE). During the Han period, a university for the nation was established, as well as the bureaucratic civil service that continued until the twentieth century. When the Chinese Empire fell in 1911, the Confucian way became less important.

Confucianism had influenced not only early Chinese culture, but also the cultures of Japan, Korea, and Vietnam. The latter two nations also adopted the bureaucratic system. In Japan, Confucianism reached its height during the Tokugawa age (1600–1868 CE). Confucian scholars continue to interpret the philosophy for the modern period. Some regard the ideas of Confucius as key to the recent economic booms in the so-called "tiger" economies of East Asia (Hong Kong, Singapore, South Korea, Taiwan, and Thailand). Confucianism continues to be a major influence on East Asian nations and culture.

Taoism's power (te) manifests itself as a philosophy, a way of life, and a religion. Philosophically, Taoism is a sort of self-help regimen, concerned with expending power efficiently by avoiding conflicts and friction, rather than fighting against the flow of life. In China, it is known as School Taoism. As a way of life, Taoism is concerned with increasing the amount of qi available through what is eaten and through meditation, yoga, and tai chi (an ancient Chinese martial art form). Acupuncture and the use of medicinal herbs are outgrowths of this way of

life. Church Taoism, influenced by Buddhism and Tao Chiao (religious Taoism), developed during the second century. This church looked for ways to use power for societal and individual benefit.

By the time of the Han dynasty (206–220 CE), Laozi had been elevated to the status of divine. Taoism found favor at court during the Tang dynasty (618–917 CE), during which the state underwrote temples. By adapting and encouraging people to study the writings of all three major faiths in China, Taoism remained relevant into the early twentieth century. During the 1960s and 1970s, Taoist books were burned and their temples were destroyed in the name of the Cultural Revolution (the Great Proletarian Cultural Revolution). Taoism remains popular and vital in Taiwan.

Shinto is an ancient religion, and some of its characteristics appeared during the Yayoi culture (ca. 300 BCE–300 CE). The focus was on local geographic features and the ancestry of local clan leaders. At first, women were permitted to be priests, but that equality was lost due to the influence of Confucian paternalism. The religion declined, but was revived in 1871 following the Meiji Restoration of the emperor. Shoguns (warlords) had ruled Japan for more than 250 years, and Shinto was the state religion until 1945. It was associated with the emperor cult and contributed to Japan's militarism. After the nation's defeat in World War II, the 1947 constitution forbade government involvement in any religion. In contemporary Shinto, women are permitted to become priests and girls, in some places, are allowed to carry the portable shrines during festivals.

Founder or Major Prophet

Confucius, or Kongzi ("Master Kong"), was a teacher whose early life may have included service in the government. He began traveling throughout the country around age fifty, attempting and failing to interest rulers in his ideas for creating a harmonious state. He returned to his home state after thirteen years, teaching a group of disciples who spread his ideas posthumously.

According to legend, Taoism's founder, Laozi, lived during the sixth century. Laozi may be translated as "Grand Old Master," and may be simply a term of endearment. He maintained the archives and lived simply in a western state of China. Weary of people who were uninterested in natural goodness and perhaps wanting greater solitude in his advanced years, he determined to leave China, heading for Tibet on a water buffalo. At the border, a gatekeeper wanted to persuade him to stay, but could not do so. He asked Laozi to leave behind his teachings. For three days Laozi transcribed his teachings, producing the five-thousand-word Tao Te Ching. He then rode off and was never heard of again. Unlike most founders of religions, he neither preached nor promoted his beliefs. Still, he was held with such regard that some emperors claimed descent from him.

No one is certain of the origin of Shinto, which did not have a founder or major prophet. Shinto—derived from two Chinese words, *shen* (spirit) and *dao* (way)—has been influenced by other religions, notably Confucianism and Buddhism.

Philosophical Basis

Confucianism sought to bring harmony to the state and society as a whole. This harmony was to be rooted in the Five Constant Relationships: between parents and children; husbands and wives; older and younger siblings; older and younger friends; and rulers and subjects. Each of these societal relationships existed to demonstrate mutual respect, service, honor, and love, resulting in a healthy society. The fact that three of the five relationships exist within the family highlights the importance of honoring family. Ritual maintains the li, or rightness, of everything, and is a way to guarantee that a person performed the correct action in any situation in life.

Taoism teaches that two basic components—yin and yang—are in all things, including health, the state, and relationships. Yin is the feminine principle, associated with soft, cold, dark, and moist things. Yang is the masculine principle,

and is associated with hard, warm, light, and dry things. By keeping these two aspects of life balanced, harmony will be achieved. Another concept is that of wu-wei, action that is in harmony with nature, while qi is the life force in all beings. The Tao is always in harmony with the universe. Conflict is to be avoided, and soldiers are to go as if attending a funeral, solemnly and with compassion. Taoism also teaches the virtues of humility and selflessness.

Shinto is rooted in reverence for ancestors and for the spirits known as kami, which may be good or evil. By correctly worshipping the kami, Shintoists believe that they are assisting in purifying the world and aiding in its functioning.

Holy Places

Confucianism does not always distinguish between sacred and profane space. So much of nature is considered a holy place, as is each home's private shrine. In addition, some Confucian temples have decayed while others have been restored. Temples do not have statues or images. Instead, the names of Confucius and his noted followers are written on tablets. Like the emperor's palace, temples have the most important halls placed on the north-south axis of the building. Temples are also internally symmetrical, as might be expected of a system that honors order. In Beijing, the Temple of Heaven, just south of the emperor's palace, was one of the holiest places in imperial China.

Taoism's holy places are often in nature, particularly mountains. The holiest of the five sacred mountains in China is Taishan, located in the east. Taoism also reveres grottoes, which are caves thought to be illuminated by the light of heaven.

In the Shinto religion, nature is often the focus of holy sites. Mount Fuji is the most sacred mountain. Near Kyoto the largest shrine of Inari, the rice god, is located. The Grand Shrines at Ise are dedicated to two divinities, and for more than one thousand years, pilgrims have come to it. The Inner Shrine (Naiku) is dedicated to Amaterasu, the sun goddess, and is Shinto's most holy location. The Outer Shrine (Geku) is dedicated to

Toyouke, the goddess of the harvest. Every twenty years, Ise is torn down and rebuilt, thus renewing the gods. Shinto shrines all have torii, the sacred gateway. The most famous of these is built in the sea near the island of Miyajima. Those going to the shrine on this island go by boat through the torii.

EAST ASIAN RELIGIONS IN DEPTH

Sacred Symbols

Water is regarded as the source of life in Confucianism. The water symbol has thus become an unofficial symbol of Confucianism, represented by the Japanese ideogram or character for water, the Mizu, which somewhat resembles a stick figure with an extra leg. Other sacred symbols include the ancestor tablets in shrines of private homes, which are symbolic of the presence of the ancestor to whom offerings are made in hopes of aid.

While not a sacred symbol as the term is generally used, the black and white symbol of yin and yang is a common Taoist emblem. Peaches are also of a symbolic nature in Taoism, and often appear in Asian art. They are based on the four peaches that grew every three thousand years and which the mother of the fairies gave to the Han emperor Wu Ti (140–87 BCE). They are often symbolic of the Immortals.

The Shinto stylized sun, which appears on the Japanese flag, is associated with Amaterasu, the sun goddess. The torii, the gateway forming an entrance to sacred space, is another symbol associated with Shinto.

Sacred Practices & Gestures

Confucian rulers traditionally offered sacrifices honoring Confucius at the spring and autumnal equinoxes. Most of the Confucian practices take place at home shrines honoring the ancestors.

Taoists believe that one can reach Tao (the way) through physical movements, chanting, or meditation. Because mountains, caves, and springs are often regarded as sacred sites, pilgrimages are important to Taoists. At a Taoist funeral, a paper fairy crane is part of the procession. After the funeral, the crane, which symbolizes a heavenly messenger, is burned. The soul of the deceased person is then thought to ride to heaven on the back of the crane.

Many Shinto shrines exist throughout Japan. Most of them have a sacred arch, known as a torii. At the shrine's entrance, worshippers rinse their mouths and wash their hands to be purified before entering the prayer hall. Before praying, a worshipper will clap twice and ring a bell to let the kami know they are there. Only priests may enter the inner hall, which is where the kami live. During a festival, however, the image of the kami is placed in a portable shrine and carried in a procession through town, so that all may receive a blessing.

Rites, Celebrations & Services

Early Confucianism had no priests, and bureaucrats performed any rituals that were necessary. When the Chinese Empire fell in 1911, imperial ceremonies ended as well. Rituals have become less important in modern times. In contemporary times the most important rite is marriage, the beginning of a new family for creating harmony. There is a correct protocol for each aspect of marriage, from the proposal and engagement to exchanging vows. During the ceremony, the groom takes the bride to his family's ancestor tablets to "introduce" her to them and receive a blessing. The couple bows to the ancestors during the ceremony.

After a death occurs, mourners wear coarse material and bring gifts of incense and money to help defray the costs. Added to the coffin holding are food offerings and significant possessions. A willow branch symbolizing the deceased's soul is carried with the coffin to the place of burial. After the burial, family members take the willow branch to their home altar and perform a ritual to add the deceased to the souls at the family's shrine.

Confucians and Taoists celebrate many of the same Chinese festivals, some of which originated before either Confucianism or Taoism began and reflect aspects of both traditions. While some festivals are not necessarily Taoist, they may be led by Taoist priests. During the Lantern Festival, which occurs on the first full moon of the New Year, offerings are made to the gods. Many of the festivals are tied to calendar events. Qingming (Clear and Bright) celebrates the coming of spring and is a time to remember the dead. During this time, families often go to the family gravesite for a picnic. The Double Fifth is the midsummer festival that occurs on the fifth day of the fifth month, and coincides with the peak of yang power. To protect themselves from too much of the male force, people don garments of the five colors—black, blue, red, white, and yellow—and with the five "poisons"—centipede, lizard, scorpion, snake, and toad—in the pattern of their clothes and on amulets. The gates of hell open at the Feast of the Hungry Ghosts. Priests have ceremonies that encourage the escaped evil spirits to repent or return to hell.

Marriage is an important rite in China, and thus in Taoism as well. Astrologers look at horoscopes to ensure that the bride and groom are well matched and to find the best day for the ceremony. The groom's family is always placed at the east (yang) and the bride's family to the west (yin) to bring harmony. When a person dies, the mourners again sit in the correct locations, while the head of the deceased points south. White is the color of mourning and of yin. At the home of the deceased, white cloths cover the family altar. Mourners may ease the soul's journey with symbolic artifacts or money. They may also go after the funeral to underground chambers beneath the temples to offer a sacrifice on behalf of the dead.

In the Shinto religion, rites exist for many life events. For example, pregnant women ask at a shrine for their children to be born safely, and the mother or grandmother brings a child who is thirty-two or thirty-three-days-old to a shrine for the first visit and blessing. A special festival also exists for children aged three, five or seven, who go to the shrine for purifying. In addition, a bride and groom are purified before the wedding, usually conducted by Shinto priests. Shinto priests may also offer blessings for a new car or building. The New Year and the Spring Festival are among the most important festivals, and shrine virgins, known as miko girls, may dance to celebrate life's renewal. Other festivals include the Feast of the Puppets, Boys' Day, the Water Kami Festival, the Star Feast, the Festival of the Dead, and the autumnal equinox.

Judy A. Johnson, MTS

Bibliography

Barnes, Trevor. *The Kingfisher Book of Religions*. New York: Kingfisher, 1999. Print.

Bell, Daniel A. "Reconciling Socialism and Confucianism? Reviving Tradition in China." *Dissent* 57.1 (2010): 91–99. Print.

Chang, Chung-yuan. *Creativity and Taoism: A Study of Chinese Philosophy, Art and Poetry*. London: Kingsley, 2011. E-book.

Coogan, Michael D., ed. *Eastern Religions*. New York: Oxford UP, 2005. Print.

Eliade, Mircea, and Ioan P. Couliano. *The Eliade Guide to World Religions*. New York: Harper, 1991. Print.

Lao Tzu. *Tao Te Ching*. Trans. Stephen Mitchell. New York: Harper, 1999. Print.

Li, Yingzhang. *Lao-tzu's Treatise on the Response of the Tao*. Trans. Eva Wong. New Haven: Yale UP, 2011. Print.

Littlejohn, Ronnie. *Confucianism: An Introduction*. New York: Tauris, 2011. E-book.

Littleton, C. Scott. *Shinto*. Oxford: Oxford UP, 2002. Print.

Mcvay, Kera. *All about Shinto*. Delhi: University, 2012. Ebook.

Merton, Thomas. *The Way of Chuang Tzu*. New York: New Directions, 1965. Print.

Oldstone-Moore, Jennifer. *Confucianism*. Oxford: Oxford UP, 2002. Print.

Poceski, Mario. *Chinese Religions: The EBook*. Providence, UT: Journal of Buddhist Ethics Online Books, 2009. E-book.

Van Norden, Bryan W. *Introduction to Classical Chinese Philosophy*. Indianapolis: Hackett, 2011. Print.

Wilkinson, Philip. *Religions*. New York: DK, 2008. Print.

Hinduism

General Description

Hinduism; modern Hinduism is comprised of the devotional sects of Vaishnavism, Shaivism, and Shaktism (though Smartism is sometimes listed as the fourth division). Hinduism is often used as umbrella term, since many point to Hinduism as a family of different religions.

Number of Adherents Worldwide

Between 13.8 and 15 percent of the world's population, or about one billion people, are adherents of Hinduism, making it the world's third largest religion after Christianity and Islam. The predominant sect is the Vaishnavite sect (Wilkinson, p. 333).

Basic Tenets

Hinduism is a way of life rather than a body of beliefs. Hindus believe in karma, the cosmic law of cause and effect that determines one's state in the next life. Additional beliefs include dharma, one's religious duty.

Hinduism has no true belief in an afterlife. Rather, it teaches a belief in reincarnation, known as samsara, and in moksha, the end of the cycle of rebirths. Different sects have different paths to moksha.

Hinduism is considered a polytheist religion. However, it is also accurate to say that Hinduism professes a belief in one God or Supreme Truth that is beyond comprehension (an absolute reality, called Brahman) and which manifests itself in many forms and names. These include Brahma, the creator; Vishnu, the protector; and Shiva, the re-creator or destroyer. Many sects are defined by their belief in multiple gods, but also by their worship of one ultimate manifestation. For example, Shaivism and Vaishnavism are based upon the recognition of Shiva and Vishnu, respectively, as the manifestation. In comparison, Shaktism recognizes the Divine Mother (Shakti) as the Supreme Being, while followers of Smartism worship a particular deity of their own choosing.

Major Deities

The Hindu trinity (Trimurti) is comprised of Brahma, the impersonal and absolute creator; Vishnu, the great preserver; and Shiva, the destroyer and re-creator. The goddesses corresponding to each god are Sarasvati, Lakshimi, and Parvati. Thousands of other gods (devas) and goddesses (devis) are worshipped, including Ganesha, Surya, and Kali. Each is believed to represent another aspect of the Supreme Being.

Sacred Texts

Hindus revere ancient texts such as the four Vedas, the 108 Upanishads, and others. No single text has the binding authority of the Qur'an (Islam's holy book) or Bible. Hindu literature is also defined by Sruti (revealed truth), which is heard, and Smriti (realized truth), which is remembered. The former is canonical, while the latter can be changing. For example, the Vedas and the Upanishads constitute Sruti texts, while epics, history, and law books constitute the latter. The Bhagavad Gita (The Song of God) is also considered a sacred scripture of Hinduism, and consists of a philosophical dialogue.

Major Figures

Major figures include: Shankara (788–820 CE), who defined the unity of the soul (atman) and absolute reality (Brahman); Ramanuja (1077–1157 CE), who emphasized bhakti, or love of God; Madhva (1199–1278 CE), scholar and writer, a proponent of dualism; Ramprahsad Sen (1718–1775 CE), composer of Hindu songs of devotion, poet, and mystic who influenced goddess worship in the; Raja Rammohun Roy (1772–1833 CE), abolished the custom of suttee, in which widows were burned on the funeral pyres of their dead husbands, and decried polygamy, rigid caste systems, and dowries; Rabindranath Tagore (1861–1941 CE), first Asian to win the Nobel Prize in Literature; Dr. Babasaheb R. Ambedkar (1891–1956 CE), writer of India's constitution and leader of a mass conversion to Buddhism; Mohandas K. Gandhi (1869–1948 CE), the "great soul" who left a legacy of effective use of nonviolence.

Major Holy Sites

The major holy sites of Hinduism are located within India. They include the Ganges River, in whose waters pilgrims come to bathe away their sins, as well as thousands of tirthas (places of pilgrimage), many of which are associated with particular deities. For example, the Char Dham pilgrimage centers, of which there are four—Badrinath (north), Puri (east), Dwarka (west) and Rameshwaram (south)—are considered the holy abodes or sacred temples of Vishnu. There are also seven ancient holy cities in India, including Ayodhya, believed to be the birthplace of Rama; Varanasi (Benares), known as the City of Light; Dwarka; Ujjian; Kanchipuram; Mathura; and Hardwar.

Major Rites & Celebrations

Diwali, the Festival of Lights, is a five-day festival that is considered a national holiday in India. Holi, the Festival of Colors, is the spring festival. Krishna Janmashtmi is Krishna's birthday. Shivaratri is Shiva's main festival. Navaratri, also known as the Durga festival or Dasserah, celebrates one of the stories of the gods and the victory of good over evil. Ganesh Chaturthi is the elephant-headed god Ganesha's birthday. Rathayatra, celebrated at Puri, India, is a festival for Jagannath, another word for Vishnu.

ORIGINS

History & Geography

Hinduism, which many people consider to be the oldest world religion, is unique in that it has no recorded origin or founder. Generally, it developed in the Indus Valley civilization several thousand years before the Common Era. The faith blends the Vedic traditions of the Indus Valley civilization and the invading nomadic tribes of the Aryans (prehistoric Indo-Europeans). Most of what is known of the Indus Valley civilization comes from archaeological excavations at Mohenjo-Daro (Mound of the Dead) and Harappa. (Because Harappa was a chief city of the period, the Indus Valley civilization is also referred to as the Harappan civilization.) The Vedas, a collection of ancient hymns, provides information about the Aryan culture.

The ancient Persian word *hind* means Indian, and for centuries, to be Indian was to be Hindu. Even now, about 80 percent of India's people consider themselves Hindu. The root word alludes to flowing, as a river flows. It is also etymologically related to the Indus River. At first, the term Hindu was used as an ethnic or cultural term, and travelers from Persia and Greece in the sixteenth century referred to those in the Indus Valley by that name. British writers coined the term *Hinduism* during the early part of the nineteenth century to describe the culture of India. The Hindus themselves often use the term Sanatana Dharma, meaning eternal law.

The Rigveda, a collection of hymns to various gods and goddesses written around 1500 BCE, is the first literary source for understanding Hinduism's history. The Vedas were chanted aloud for centuries before being written down around 1400 CE. The Rigveda is one of four major collections of Vedas, or wisdom: Rigveda, Yajurveda, Samaveda, and Atharvaveda. Together these four are called Samhitas.

Additionally, Hinduism relies on three other Vedic works: the Aranyakas, the Brahamans, and the Upanishads. The Upanishads is a philosophical work, possibly written down between 800 and 450 BCE, that attempts to answer life's big questions. Written in the form of a dialogue between a teacher (guru) and student (chela), the text's name means "to sit near," which describes the relationship between the two. Along with the Samhitas, these four are called Sruti (heard), a reference to their nature as revealed truth. The words in these texts cannot be altered.

Remaining works are called Smriti, meaning "remembered," to indicate that they were composed by human writers. The longer of the Smriti epics is the Mahabharata, the Great Story of the Bharatas. Written between 300 and 100 BCE, the epic is a classic tale of two rival, related families, including teaching as well as story. It is considered the longest single poem in existence, with about 200,000 lines. (A film made of it lasts for twelve hours.)

The Bhagavad Gita, or Song of the Lord, is the sixth section of the Mahabharata, but is often read as a stand-alone narrative of battle and acceptance of one's dharma. The Ramayana is the second, shorter epic of the Mahabharata, with about fifty thousand lines. Rama was the seventh incarnation, or avatar, of Vishnu. The narrative relates the abduction of his wife, Sita, and her rescue, accomplished with the help of the monkey god, Hanuman. Some have regarded the Mahabharata as an encyclopedia, and the Bhagavad Gita as the Bible within it.

Although many of the practices in the Vedas have been modified or discontinued, sections of it are memorized and repeated. Some of the hymns are recited at traditional ceremonies for the dead and at weddings.

Hinduism has affected American life and culture for many years. For example, the nineteenth-century transcendental writers Margaret Fuller and Ralph Waldo Emerson were both influenced by Hindu and Buddhist literature, while musician George Harrison, a member of the Beatles, adopted Hinduism and explored his new faith through his music, both with and without the Beatles. In 1965, the International Society for Krishna Consciousness (ISKCON), or the Hare Krishna movement, came to the Western world. In addition, many people have been drawn to yoga, which is associated with Hinduism's meditative practices.

Founder or Major Prophet

Hinduism has no founder or major prophet. It is a religion that has developed over many centuries and from many sources, many of which are unknown in their origins.

Philosophical Basis

Hinduism recognizes multiple ways to achieve salvation and escape the endless cycle of rebirth. The way of devotion is the most popular.

Through worship of a single deity, the worshipper hopes to attain union with the divine. A second path is the way of knowledge, involving the use of meditation and reason. The third way is via action, or correctly performing religious observances in hope of receiving a blessing from the gods by accomplishing these duties.

Hinduism is considered the world's oldest religion, but Hindus maintain that it is also a way of living, not just a religion. There is great diversity as well as great tolerance in Hinduism. While Hinduism does not have a set of dogmatic formulations, it does blend the elements of devotion, doctrine, practice, society, and story as separate strands in a braid.

During the second century BCE, a sage named Patanjali outlined four life stages, and the fulfilled responsibilities inherent in each one placed one in harmony with dharma, or right conduct. Although these life stages are no longer observed strictly, their ideas still carry weight. Traditionally, these codes applied to men, and only to those in the Brahman caste; members of the warrior and merchant classes could follow them, but were not obligated. The Shudra and Dalit castes, along with women, were not part of the system. Historically, women were thought of as protected by fathers in their childhood, by husbands in their youth and adulthood, and by sons in old age. Only recently have women in India been educated beyond the skills of domestic responsibility and child rearing.

The earliest life stage is the student stage, or brahmacharya, a word that means "to conduct oneself in accord with Brahman." From ages twelve to twenty-four, young men were expected to undertake learning with a guru, or guide. During these twelve years of studying the Veda they were also expected to remain celibate.

The second stage, grihastha, is that of householder. A Hindu man married the bride that his parents had chosen, sired children, and created a livelihood on which the other three stages depended.

Vanaprastha is the third stage, involving retirement to solitude. Historically, this involved leaving the house and entering a forest dwelling.

A man's wife had the option to go with him or to remain. This stage also involved giving counsel to others and further study.

At the final stage of life, sannyasis, the Hindu renounces material goods, including a home of any sort. He may live in a forest or join an ashram, or community. He renounces even making a fire, and lives on fruit and roots that can be foraged. Many contemporary Hindus do not move to this stage, but remain at vanaprastha.

Yoga is another Hindu practice, more than three millennia old, which Patanjali codified. The four forms of yoga corresponded to the Hindu avenues of salvation. Hatha yoga is the posture yoga seeking union with god through action. Jnana yoga is the path to god through knowledge. Bhakti yoga is the way of love to god. Karma yoga is the method of finding god through work. By uniting the self, the practitioner unites with God. Yoga is related etymologically to the English word *yoke*—it attempts to yoke the individual with Brahman. All forms of yoga include meditation and the acceptance of other moral disciplines, such as self-discipline, truthfulness, nonviolence, and contentment.

Aryan society was stratified, and at the top of the social scale were the priests. This system was the basis for the caste system that had long dominated Hinduism. Caste, which was determined by birth, affected a person's occupation, diet, neighborhood, and marriage partner. Vedic hymns allude to four varnas, or occupations: Brahmins (priests), Kshatriyas (warriors), Vaishyas (merchants and common people), and Shudras (servants). A fifth class, the Untouchables, later known as Dalit (oppressed), referred to those who were regarded as a polluting force because they handled waste and dead bodies. The belief was that society would function properly if each group carried out its duties. These varnas later became wrongly blended with castes, or jatis, which were smaller groups also concerned with a person's place in society.

The practice of Hinduism concerns itself with ritual purity; even household chores can be done in a ritualistic way. Some traditions demand ritual purity before one can worship. Brahmin priests, for example, may not accept water or food from non-Brahmins. Refusal to do so is not viewed as classism, but an attempt to please the gods in maintaining ritual purity.

Mohandas Gandhi was one of those who refused to use the term *Untouchable*, using the term *harijan*(children of God), instead. Dr. Babasaheb R. Ambedkar, who wrote India's constitution, was a member of this class. Ambedkar and many of his supporters became Buddhists in an attempt to dispel the power of caste. In 1947, following India's independence from Britain, the caste system was officially banned, though it has continued to influence Indian society.

Ahimsa, or dynamic harmlessness, is another deeply rooted principle of Hinduism. It involves six pillars: refraining from eating all animal products; revering all of life; having integrity in thoughts, words, and deeds; exercising self-control; serving creation, nature, and humanity; and advancing truth and understanding.

Holy Places

In Hinduism, all water is considered holy, symbolizing the flow of life. For a Hindu, the Ganges River is perhaps the most holy of all bodies of water. It was named for the goddess of purification, Ganga. The waters of the Ganges are said to flow through Shiva's hair and have the ability to cleanse sin. Devout Hindus make pilgrimages to bathe in the Ganges. They may also visit fords in the rivers to symbolize the journey from one life to another.

Pilgrimages are also made to sites associated with the life of a god. For example, Lord Rama was said to have been born in Ayodhya, one of the seven holy cities in India. Other holy sites are Dwarka, Ujjian, Kanchipuram, Mathura, Hardwar, and Varanasi, the City of Light.

After leaving his mountain home, Lord Shiva was thought to have lived in Varanasi, or Benares, considered the holiest city. Before the sixth century, it became a center of education for Hindus. It has four miles of palaces and temples along the river. One of the many pilgrimage circuits covers thirty-five miles, lasts for five days, and includes prayer at 108 different shrines. Because of the river's sacred nature, Hindus come to bathe from its many stone steps, called ghats, and to drink the water. It is also the place where Hindus desire to be at their death or to have their ashes scattered. Because Varanasi is regarded as a place of crossing between earth and heaven, dying there is thought to free one from the cycle of rebirth.

The thirty-four Ellora Caves at Maharashtra, India, are known for their sculptures. Built between 600 and 1000 CE, they were cut into a tufa rock hillside on a curve shaped like a horseshoe, so that the caves go deeply into the rock face. Although the one-mile site includes temples for Buddhist, Jain, and Hindu faiths, the major figure of the caves is Shiva, and the largest temple is dedicated to Shiva.

Lastly, Hindu temples, or mandirs, are regarded as the gods' earthly homes. The buildings themselves are therefore holy, and Hindus remove their shoes before entering.

HINDUISM IN DEPTH

Sacred Symbols

The wheel of life represents samsara, the cycle of life, death and rebirth. Karma is what keeps the wheel spinning. Another circle is the hoop of flames in which Shiva, also known as the Lord of the Dance, or Natraja, is shown dancing creation into being. The flames signify the universe's energy and Shiva's power of both destruction and creation. Shiva balances on his right foot, which rests on a defeated demon that stands for ignorance.

The lotus is the symbol of creation, fertility, and purity. This flower is associated with Vishnu because as he slept, a lotus flower bloomed from his navel. From this lotus Brahma came forth to create the world. Yoga practitioners commonly assume the lotus position for meditation.

Murtis are the statues of gods that are found in both temples and private homes. They are often washed with milk and water, anointed with oil, dressed, and offered gifts of food or flowers. Incense may also be burned to make the air around the murti sweet and pure.

One of Krishna's symbols is the conch shell, a symbol of a demon he defeated. A conch shell is blown at temples to announce the beginning of the worship service. It is a visual reminder for followers of Krishna to overcome ignorance and evil in their lives.

For many years, the Hindus used the swastika as a holy symbol. (*Swastika* is a Sanskrit word for good fortune and well-being.) The four arms meet at a central point, demonstrating that the universe comes from one source. Each arm of the symbol represents a path to God and is bent to show that all paths are difficult. It is used at a time of new beginnings, such as at a wedding, where it is traditionally painted on a coconut using a red paste called kum kum. The symbol appears as a vertical gash across the horizontal layers on the southern face of Mount Kailas, one of the Himalayas's highest peaks, thought to have been the home of Shiva. The mountain is also near the source of the Ganges and the Indus Rivers. The use of the swastika as a symbol for Nazi Germany is abhorrent to Hindus.

Some Hindus use a mala, or rosary, of 108 wooden beads when they pray. As they worship, they repeat the names of God.

Sacred Practices & Gestures

Many homes have private altars or shrines to favorite gods. Statues or pictures of these deities are offered incense, flowers and food, as well as prayers. This daily devotion, known as puja, is generally the responsibility of women, many of whom are devoted to goddesses such as Kali or Sita. A rich family may devote an entire room of their house to the shrine.

Om, or Aum, a sacred syllable recorded first in the Upanishads, is made up of three Sanskrit letters. Writing the letter involves a symbol resembling the Arabic number three. Thus, it is a visual reminder of the Trimurti, the three major Hindu gods. The word is repeated at the beginning of all mantras or prayers.

Each day the Gayatri, which is perhaps the world's oldest recorded prayer, is chanted during the fire ritual. The prayer expresses gratitude to the sun for its shining and invokes blessings of prosperity on all. The ritual, typically done at large consecrated fire pits, may be done using burning candles instead.

Holy Hindu men are known as sadhus. They lead ascetic lives, wandering, begging, and living in caves in the mountains. Regarded as having greater spiritual power and wisdom, they are often consulted for advice.

Food Restrictions

Many Hindus are vegetarians because they embrace ahimsa (reverence for and protection of all life) and oppose killing. In fact, Hindus comprise about 70 percent of the world's vegetarians. They are generally lacto-vegetarians, meaning that they include dairy products in their diets. However, Hindus residing in the cold climate of Nepal and Tibet consume meat to increase their caloric intake.

Whether a culture practices vegetarianism or not, cows are thought to be sacred because Krishna acted as a cowherd as a young god. Thus cows are never eaten. Pigs are also forbidden, as are red foods, such as tomatoes or red lentils. In addition, garlic and onions are also not permitted. Alcohol is strictly forbidden.

Purity rituals before eating include cleaning the area where the food is to be eaten and reciting mantras or praying while sprinkling water around the food. Other rituals include Annaprasana, which celebrates a child's eating of solid food—traditionally rice—for the first time. In addition, at funerals departed souls are offered food, which Hindus believe will strengthen the soul for the journey to the ancestors' world.

Serving food to those in need also generates good karma. Food is offered during religious ceremonies and may later be shared with visiting devotees of the god.

To show their devotion to Shiva, many Hindus fast on Mondays. There is also a regular fast, known as agiaras, which occurs on the eleventh day of each two-week period. On that day, only one meal is eaten. During the month of Shravan, which many consider a holy month, people may eat only one meal, generally following sunset.

Rites, Celebrations & Services

Many Hindu celebrations are connected to the annual cycle of nature and can last for many days. In addition, celebrations that honor the gods are common. Shiva, one of the three major gods, is honored at Shivaratri in February or March. In August or September, Lord Krishna is honored at Krishnajanmashtmi. Prayer and fasting are part of this holiday.

During the spring equinox and just prior to the Hindu New Year, Holi is celebrated. It is a time to resolve disputes and forgive or pay debts. During this festival, people often have bonfires and throw objects that represent past impurity or disease into the fire.

Another festival occurs in July or August, marking the beginning of the agricultural year in northern India. Raksha Bandhan (the bond of protection) is a festival which celebrates sibling relationships. During the festivities, Hindus bind a bauble with silk thread to the wrists of family members and friends.

To reenact Rama's defeat of the demon Ravana, as narrated in the Ramayana, people make and burn effigies. This festival is called Navaratri in western India, also known as the Durgapuja in Bengal, and Dasserah in northern India. It occurs in September or October each year as a festival celebrating the victory of good over evil. September is also time to celebrate the elephant-headed god Ganesha's birthday at the festival of Ganesh Chaturthi.

Diwali, a five-day festival honoring Lakshmi (the goddess of good fortune and wealth), occurs in October or November. This Festival of Lights is the time when people light oil lamps and set off fireworks to help Rama find his way home after exile. Homes are cleaned in hopes that Lakshmi will come in the night to bless it. People may use colored rice flour to make patterns on their doorstep. Competitions for designs of these patterns, which are meant to welcome God to the house, frequently take place.

Jagannath, or Vishnu, is celebrated during the festival Rathayatra. A large image of Jagannath rides in a chariot pulled through the city of Puri.

The temple for Hindus is the home of the god. Only Brahmin priests may supervise worship there. The inner sanctuary of the building is called the garbhagriha, or womb-house; there the god resides. Worshippers must be ritually pure before the worship starts. The priest recites the mantras and reads sacred texts. Small lamps are lit, and everyone shares specially prepared and blessed food after the service ends.

Judy A. Johnson, MTS

Bibliography

Barnes, Trevor. *The Kingfisher Book of Religions*. New York: Kingfisher, 1999. Print.

Harley, Gail M. *Hindu and Sikh Faiths in America*. New York: Facts on File, 2003. Print.

Iyengar, B. K. S. and Noelle Perez-Christiaens. *Sparks of Divinity: The Teachings of B. K. S. Iyengar from 1959 to 1975*. Berkeley: Rodmell, 2012. E-book.

"The Joys of Hinduism." *Hinduism Today* Oct./Dec. 2006: 40–53. Print.

Langley, Myrtle. *Religion*. New York: Knopf, 1996. Print.

Meredith, Susan. *The Usborne Book of World Religions*. London: Usborne, 1995. Print.

Rajan, Rajewswari. "The Politics of Hindu 'Tolerance.'" *Boundary 2* 38.3 (2011): 67–86. Print.

Raman, Varadaraja V. "Hinduism and Science: Some Reflections." *Journal of Religion & Science* 47.3 (2012): 549–74. Print.

Renard, John. *Responses to 101 Questions on Hinduism*. Mahwah: Paulist, 1999. Print.

Siddhartha. "Open-Source Hinduism." *Religion & the Arts* 12.1–3 (2008): 34–41. Print.

Shouler, Kenneth and Susai Anthony. *The Everything Hinduism Book*. Avon: Adams, 2009. Print.

Soherwordi, Syed Hussain Shaheed. "'Hinduism'—A Western Construction or an Influence?" *South Asian Studies* 26.1 (2011): 203–14. Print.

Theodor, Ithamar. *Exploring the Bhagavad Gita: Philosophy, Structure, and Meaning*. Farnham and Burlington: Ashgate, 2010. E-book.

Whaling, Frank. *Understanding Hinduism*. Edinburgh: Dunedin, 2010. E-book.

Wilkinson, Philip. *Religions*. New York: DK, 2008. Print.

Islam

General Description

The word *Islam* derives from a word meaning "submission," particularly submission to the will of Allah. Muslims, those who practice Islam, fall into two major groups, Sunni and Shia (or Shi'i,) based on political rather than theological differences. Sunni Muslims follow the four Rightly Guided Caliphs, or Rashidun and believe that caliphs should be elected. Shia Muslims believe that the Prophet's nearest male relative, Ali ibn Abi Talib, should have ruled following Muhammad's death, and venerate the imams (prayer leaders) who are directly descended from Ali and the Prophet's daughter Fatima.

Number of Adherents Worldwide

Approximately 1.6 billion people, or 23 percent of the world's population, are Muslims. Of that total, between 87 and 90 percent of all Muslims are Sunni Muslims and between 10 and 13 percent of all Muslims are Shia. Followers of the Sufi sect, noted for its experiential, ecstatic focus, may be either Sunni or Shia.

Basic Tenets

Islam is a monotheistic faith; Muslims worship only one God, Allah. They also believe in an afterlife and that people are consigned to heaven or hell following the last judgment.

The Islamic faith rests on Five Pillars. The first pillar, Shahadah is the declaration of faith in the original Arabic, translated as: "I bear witness that there is no god but God and Muhammad is his Messenger." The second pillar, Salah, are prayers adherents say while facing Mecca five times daily at regular hours and also at the main service held each Friday at a mosque. Zakat, "the giving of a tax," is the third pillar and entails giving an income-based percentage of one's wealth to help the poor without attracting notice. The fourth pillar is fasting, or Sawm, during Ramadan, the ninth month of the Islamic calendar. Certain groups of people are excused from the fast, however. The final pillar is the Hajj, the pilgrimage to Mecca required of every able-bodied Muslim at least once in his or her lifetime.

Sacred Text

The Qur'an (Koran), meaning "recitation," is the holy book of Islam.

Major Figures

Muhammad, regarded as the Prophet to the Arabs—as Moses was to the Jews—is considered the exemplar of what it means to be a Muslim. His successors—Abu Bakr, Umar, Uthman, and Ali—were known as the four Rightly Guided Caliphs.

Major Holy Sites

Islam recognizes three major holy sites: Mecca, home of the Prophet; Medina, the city to which Muslims relocated when forced from Mecca due to persecution; and the Dome of the Rock in Jerusalem, believed to be the oldest Islamic building in existence. Muslims believe that in 621 CE Muhammad ascended to heaven (called the Night Journey) from a sacred stone upon which the Dome was constructed. Once in heaven, God instructed Muhammad concerning the need to pray at regular times daily...

There are also several mosques which are considered primary holy sites. These include the al-Aqsa Mosque in the Old City of Jerusalem, believed by many to be the third holiest site in Islam. The mosque, along with the Dome of the Rock, is located on Judaism's holiest site, the Temple Mount, where the Temple of Jerusalem is believed to have stood. Muslims also revere the Mosque of the Prophet (Al-Masjid al-Nabawi) in Medina, considered the resting place of the Prophet Muhammad and the second largest mosque in the world; and the Mosque of the Haram (Masjid al-Haram or the Sacred or Grand Mosque) in Mecca, thought to be the largest mosque in the world and site of the Ka'bah, "the sacred house," also known as "the Noble Cube," Islam's holiest structure.

Major Rites & Celebrations

Two major celebrations mark the Islamic calendar. 'Id al-Adha, the feast of sacrifice—including animal sacrifice—held communally at the close of the Hajj (annual pilgrimage), commemorates the account of God providing a ram instead of the son Abraham had been asked to sacrifice. The second festival, 'Id al-Fitr, denotes the end of Ramadan and is a time of feasting and gift giving.

ORIGINS

History & Geography

In 610 CE, a forty-year-old businessman from Mecca named Muhammad ibn Abdullah, from the powerful Arab tribe Quraysh, went to Mount Hira to meditate, as he regularly did for the month of Ramadan. During that month, an entire group of men, the hanif, retreated to caves. The pagan worship practiced in the region, as well as the cruelty and lack of care for the poor, distressed Muhammad. As the tribe to which he belonged had become wealthy through trade, it had begun disregarding traditions prescribed by the nomadic code.

The archangel Jibra'il (Gabriel) appeared in Muhammad's cave and commanded him to read the words of God contained in the scroll that the angel showed him. Like most people of his time, Muhammad was illiterate, but repeated the words Jibra'il said. Some followers of Islam believe that this cave at Jebel Nur, in what is now Saudi Arabia, is where Adam, the first human Allah created, lived.

A frightened Muhammad told only his wife, Khadija, about his experience. For two years, Muhammad received further revelations, sharing them only with family and close friends. Like other prophets, he was reluctant about his calling, fearing that he was—or would be accused of being—possessed by evil spirits or insane. At one point, he tried to commit suicide, but was stopped by the voice of Jibra'il affirming his status as God's messenger.

Muhammad recalled the words spoken to him, which were eventually written down. The Qur'an is noted for being a book of beautiful language, and Muhammad's message reached many. The Prophet thus broke the old pattern of allegiance to tribe and forged a new community based on shared practice.

Muhammad considered himself one who was to warn the others of a coming judgment. His call for social justice and denunciation of the wealthy disturbed the powerful Arab tribe members in Mecca. These men stood to lose the status and income derived from the annual festival to the Ka'bah. The Prophet and his followers were persecuted and were the subject of boycotts and death threats. In 622 CE, Muslim families began a migration (hijrah) to Yathrib, later known as Medina. Two years earlier, the city had sent envoys seeking Muhammad's leadership for their own troubled society. The hijrah marks the beginning of the Islamic calendar.

The persecutions eventually led to outright tribal warfare, linking Islam with political prowess through the victories of the faithful. The Muslims moved from being an oppressed minority to being a political force. In 630 CE, Muhammad and ten thousand of his followers marched to Mecca, taking the city without bloodshed. He destroyed the pagan idols that were housed and worshipped at the Ka'bah, instead associating the hajj with the story of Abraham sending his concubine Hagar and their son Ishmael (Ismail in Arabic) out into the wilderness. With this victory, Muhammad ended centuries of intertribal warfare.

Muhammad died in 632, without designating a successor. Some of the Muslims believed that his nearest male relative should rule, following the custom of the tribes. Ali ibn Abi Talib, although a pious Muslim, was still young. Therefore, Abu Bakr, the Prophet's father-in-law, took the title khalifah, or caliph, which means successor or deputy. Within two years Abu Bakr had stabilized Islam. He was followed by three additional men whom Muhammad had known. Collectively, the four are known as the Four Rightly Guided Caliphs, or the Rashidun. Their rule extended from 632 until 661. Each of the final three met a violent death.

Umar, the second caliph, increased the number of raids on adjacent lands during his ten-year rule, which began in 634. This not only increased wealth, but also gave Umar the authority he needed, since Arabs objected to the idea of a monarchy. Umar was known as the commander of the faithful. Under his leadership, the Islamic community marched into present-day Iraq, Syria, and Egypt and achieved victory over the Persians in 637.

Muslims elected Uthman ibn Affan as the third caliph after Umar was stabbed by a Persian prisoner of war. He extended Muslim conquests into North Africa as well as into Iran, Afghanistan, and parts of India. A group of soldiers mutinied in 656, assassinating Uthman.

Ali, Muhammad's son-in-law, was elected caliph of a greatly enlarged empire. Conflict developed between Ali and the ruler in Damascus whom Uthman had appointed governor of Syria. The fact that the governor came from a rival tribe led to further tensions. Increasingly, Damascus rather than Medina was viewed as the key Muslim locale. Ali was murdered in 661 during the internal struggles.

Within a century after Muhammad's death, Muslims had created an empire that stretched from Spain across Asia to India and facilitated the spread of Islam. The conquerors followed a policy of relative, though not perfect, tolerance toward adherents of other religions. Christians and Jews received special status as fellow "People of the Book," though they were still required to pay a special poll tax in exchange for military protection. Pagans, however, were required to convert to Islam or face death. Later, Hindus, Zoroastrians, and other peoples were also permitted to pay the tax rather than submit to conversion. Following the twelfth century, Sufi mystics made further converts in Central Asia, India, sub-Saharan Africa, and Turkey. Muslim traders also were responsible for the growth of Islam, particularly in China, Indonesia, and Malaya.

The Muslim empire continued to grow until it weakened in the fourteenth century, when it was replaced as a major world power by European states. The age of Muslim domination ended with the 1683 failure of the Ottoman Empire to capture Vienna, Austria.

Although lacking in political power until recent years, a majority of nations in Indonesia, the Middle East, and East and North Africa are predominately Islamic. The rise of Islamic fundamentalists who interpret the Qur'an literally and seek victory through acts of terrorism began in the late twentieth century. Such extremists do not represent the majority of the Muslim community, however.

Like Judaism and Christianity, Islam has been influenced by its development in a desert climate. Arabia, a region three times the size of France, is a land of steppe and desert whose unwelcoming climate kept it from being mapped with any precision until the 1950s. Because Yemen received monsoon rains, it could sustain agriculture and became a center for civilization as early as the second millennium BCE. In the seventh century CE, nomads roamed the area, guarding precious wells and oases. Raiding caravans and other tribes were common ways to obtain necessities.

Mecca was a pagan center of worship, but it was located not far from a Christian kingdom, Ethiopia, across the Red Sea. Further north, followers of both Judaism and Christianity had influenced members of Arab tribes. Jewish tribes inhabited Yathrib, the city later known as Medina. Neither Judaism nor Christianity was especially kind to those they considered pagans. According to an Arabian tradition, in 570 the Ethiopians attacked Yemen and attempted an attack on Mecca. Mecca was caught between two enemy empires—Christian Byzantine and Zoroastrian Persia—that fought a lengthy war during Muhammad's lifetime.

The contemporary clashes between Jews and Muslims are in part a result of the dispersion of Muslims who had lived in Palestine for centuries. More Jews began moving into the area under the British Mandate; in 1948, the state of Israel was proclaimed. Historically, Jews had been respected as a People of the Book.

Founder or Major Prophet

Muslims hold Allah to be the founder of their religion and Abraham to have been the first Muslim. Muhammad is God's prophet to the Arabs. The instructions that God gave Muhammad through the archangel Jibra'il and through direct revelation are the basis for the Islamic religion. These revelations were given over a period of twenty-one years. Because Muhammad and most of the Muslims were illiterate, the teachings were read publicly in chapters, or suras.

Muhammad did not believe he was founding a new religion. Rather, he was considered God's final Prophet, as Moses and Jesus had been prophets. His task was to call people to repent and to return to the straight path of God's law, called Sharia. God finally was sending a direct revelation to the Arab peoples, who had sometimes been taunted by the other civilizations as being left out of God's plan.

Muhammad, who had been orphaned by age six, was raised by an uncle. He became a successful businessman of an important tribe and married Khadija, for whom he worked. His integrity was such that he was known as al-Amin, the trusted one. He and Khadija had six children; four daughters survived. After Khadija's death, Muhammad married several women, as was the custom for a great chief. Several of the marriages were political in nature.

Muhammad is regarded as the living Qur'an. He is sometimes referred to as the perfect man, one who is an example of how a Muslim should live. He was ahead of his time in his attitudes toward women, listening to their counsel and granting them rights not enjoyed by women in other societies, including the right to inherit property and to divorce. (It should be noted that the Qur'an does not require the seclusion or veiling of all women.)

Islam has no religious leaders, especially those comparable to other religions. Each mosque has an imam to preach and preside over prayer at the Friday services. Although granted a moral authority, the imam is not a religious leader with a role comparable to that of rabbis or priests.

Philosophical Basis

Prior to Muhammad's receiving the Qur'an, the polytheistic tribes believed in Allah, "the god." Allah was far away and not part of worship rituals, although he had created the world and sustained it. He had three daughters who were goddesses.

Islam began pragmatically—the old tribal ways were not working—as a call for social justice, rooted in Muhammad's dissatisfaction with the increasing emphasis on accumulating wealth and an accompanying neglect of those in need. The struggle (jihad) to live according to God's desire for humans was to take place within the community, or the ummah. This effort was more important than dogmatic statements or beliefs about God. When the community prospered, this was a sign of God's blessing.

In addition, the revelation of the Qur'an gave Arab nations an official religion. The Persians around them had Zoroastrianism, the Romans and Byzantines had Christianity, and the Jews of the Diaspora had Judaism. With the establishment of Islam, Arabs finally could believe that they were part of God's plan for the world.

Four principles direct Islam's practice and doctrine. These include the Qur'an; the traditions, or sunnah; consensus, or ijma'; and individual thought, or ijtihad. The term sunnah, "well-trodden path," had been used by Arabs before Islam to refer to their tribal law.

A fifth important source for Islam is the Hadith, or report, a collection of the Prophet's words and actions, intended to serve as an example. Sunni Muslims refer to six collections made in the ninth century, while Shia Muslims have a separate Hadith of four collections.

Holy Places

Mecca was located just west of the Incense Road, a major trade route from southern Arabia to Palestine and Syria. Mecca was the Prophet's home and the site where he received his revelations. It is also the city where Islam's holiest structure, the Ka'bah, "the sacred house," was located. The Ka'bah was regarded as having been built by Abraham and his son Ishmael. This forty-three-foot gray stone cube was a center for pagan idols in the time of Muhammad. In 628 the Prophet removed 360 pagan idols—one for each day of the Arabic lunar year—from inside the Ka'bah.

When the followers of Muhammad experienced persecution for their beliefs, they fled to the city of Medina, formerly called Yathrib. When his uncle Abu Talib died, Muhammad lost the protection from persecution that his uncle had provided. He left for Ta'if in the mountains, but it was also a center for pagan cults, and he was driven out. After a group of men from Yathrib promised him protection, Muhammad sent seventy of his followers to the city, built around an oasis about 215 miles north. This migration, called the hijra, occurred in 622, the first year of the Muslim calendar. From this point on, Islam became an organized religion rather than a persecuted and minority cult. The Prophet was buried in Medina in 632, and his mosque in that city is deeply revered.

Islam's third holiest site is the Dome of the Rock in Jerusalem. Muslims believe that the Prophet Muhammad ascended to heaven in 621 from the rock located at the center of this mosque. During this so-called night journey, Allah gave him instructions about prayer. In the shrine at the Dome of the Rock is a strand of hair that Muslims believe was Muhammad's.

Shia Muslims also revere the place in present-day Iraq where Ali's son, Husayn, was martyred. They regard the burial place of Imam Ali ar-Rida in Meshed, Iran, as a site of pilgrimage as well.

ISLAM IN DEPTH

Sacred Symbols

Muslims revere the Black Stone, a possible meteorite that is considered a link to heaven. It is set inside the Ka'bah shrine's eastern corner. The Ka'bah is kept covered by the kiswa, a black velvet cloth decorated with embroidered calligraphy in gold. At the hajj, Muslims walk around it counterclockwise seven times as they recite prayers to Allah.

Muslim nations have long used the crescent moon and a star on their flags. The crescent moon, which the Ottomans first adopted as a symbol during the fifteenth century, is often placed on the dome of a mosque, pointing toward Mecca. For Muhammad, the waxing and waning of the moon signified the unchanging and eternal purpose of God. Upon seeing a new moon, the Prophet confessed his faith in God. Muslims rely on a lunar calendar and the Qur'an states that God created the stars to guide people to their destinations.

Islam forbids the making of graven images of animals or people, although not all Islamic cultures follow this rule strictly. The decorative arts of Islam have placed great emphasis on architecture and calligraphy to beautify mosques and other buildings. In addition, calligraphy, floral motifs, and geometric forms decorate some editions of the Qur'an's pages, much as Christian monks once decorated hand-copied scrolls of the Bible. These elaborate designs can also be seen on some prayer rugs, and are characteristic of Islamic art in general.

Sacred Practices & Gestures

When Muslims pray, they must do so facing Mecca, a decision Muhammad made in January 624 CE. Prior to that time, Jerusalem—a holy city for both Jews and Christians—had been the geographic focus. Prayer involves a series of movements that embody submission to Allah.

Muslims sometimes use a strand of prayer beads, known as subhah, to pray the names of God. The beads can be made of bone, precious stones, or wood. Strings may have twenty-five, thirty-three or 100 beads.

Food Restrictions

Those who are physically able to do so fast from both food and drink during the daylight hours of the month Ramadan. Although fasting is not required of the sick, the aged, menstruating or pregnant women, or children, some children attempt to fast, imitating their parents' devotion. Those who cannot fast are encouraged to do so the following Ramadan. This fast is intended to concentrate the mind on Allah. Muslims recite from the Qur'an during the month.

All meat must be prepared in a particular way so that it is halal, or permitted. While slaughtering the animal, the person must mention the name of Allah. Blood, considered unclean, must be allowed to drain. Because pigs were fed garbage, their meat was considered unclean. Thus Muslims eat no pork, even though in modern times, pigs are often raised on grain.

In three different revelations, Muslims are also forbidden to consume fermented beverages. Losing self-control because of drunkenness violates the Islamic desire for self-mastery.

Rites, Celebrations, and Services

The **mosque** is the spiritual center of the Muslim community. From the minaret (a tower outside the mosque), the call to worship occurs five times daily—at dawn, just past noon, at midafternoon, at sunset, and in the evening. In earliest times, a muezzin, the official responsible for this duty, gave the cry. In many modern countries, the call now comes over a speaker system. Also located outside are fountains to provide the necessary water for ritual washing before prayer. Muslims wash their face, hands, forearms, and feet, as well as remove their shoes before beginning their prayers. In the absence of water, ritual cleansing may occur using sand or a stone.

Praying involves a series of movements known as rak'ah. From a standing position, the worshipper recites the opening sura of the Qur'an, as well as a second sura. After bowing to demonstrate respect, the person again stands, then prostrates himself or herself to signal humility. Next, the person assumes a sitting posture in silent prayer before again prostrating. The last movement is a greeting of "Peace be with you and the mercy of Allah." The worshipper looks both left and right before saying these words, which are intended for all persons, present and not.

Although Muslims stop to pray during each day when the call is given, Friday is the time for communal prayer and worship at the mosque. The prayer hall is the largest space within the mosque. At one end is a niche known as the mihrab, indicating the direction of Mecca, toward which Muslims face when they pray. At first, Muhammad instructed his followers to pray facing Jerusalem, as the Jewish people did. This early orientation was also a way to renounce the pagan associations of Mecca. Some mosques serve as community centers, with additional rooms for study.

The hajj, an important annual celebration, was a custom before the founding of Islam. Pagan worship centered in Mecca at the Ka'bah, where devotees circled the cube and kissed the Black Stone that was embedded in it. All warfare was forbidden during the hajj, as was argument, speaking crossly, or killing even an insect.

Muslims celebrate the lives of saints and their death anniversaries, a time when the saints are thought to reach the height of their spiritual life. Mawlid an-Nabi refers to "the birth of the Prophet." Although it is cultural and not rooted in the Qur'an, in some Muslim countries this is a public holiday on which people recite the Burdah, a poem that praises Muhammad. Muslims also celebrate the night that the Prophet ascended to heaven, Lailat ul-Miraj. The Night of Power is held to be the night on which Allah decides the destiny of people individually and the world at large.

Like Jews, Muslims practice circumcision, a ceremony known as khitan. Unlike Jews, however, Muslims do not remove the foreskin when the male is a baby. This is often done when a boy is about seven, and must be done before the boy reaches the age of twelve.

Healthy adult Muslims fast between sunrise and sunset during the month of Ramadan. This commemorates the first of Muhammad's revelations. In some Muslim countries, cannons are fired before the beginning of the month, as well as at the beginning and end of each day of the month. Some Muslims read a portion of the Qur'an each day during the month.

Judy A. Johnson, MTS

Bibliography

Al-Saud, Laith, Scott W. Hibbard, and Aminah Beverly. *An Introduction to Islam in the 21st Century*. Wiley, 2013. E-book.

Armstrong, Lyall. "The Rise of Islam: Traditional and Revisionist Theories." *Theological Review* 33.2 (2012): 87–106. Print.

Armstrong, Karen. *Islam: A Short History*. New York: Mod. Lib., 2000. Print.

Aslan, Reza. *No god but God: The Origins, Evolution, and Future of Islam*. New York: Random, 2005. Print.

Badawi, Emran El-. "'For All Times and Places': A Humanistic Reception of the Qur'an." *English Language Notes* 50.2 (2012): 99–112. Print.

Barnes, Trevor. *The Kingfisher Book of Religions*. New York: Kingfisher, 1999. Print.

Ben Jelloun, Tahar. *Islam Explained*. Trans. Franklin Philip. New York: New, 2002. Print.

Esposito, John L. *Islam: the Straight Path*. New York: Oxford UP, 1988. Print.

Glady, Pearl. *Criticism of Islam*.Library, 2012. E-book.

Holland, Tom. "Where Mystery Meets History." *History Today* 62.5 (2012): 19–24. Print.

Langley, Myrtle. *Religion*. New York: Knopf, 1996. Print.

Lunde, Paul. *Islam: Faith, Culture, History*. London: DK, 2002. Print.

Nasr, Seyyed Hossein. *Islam: Religion, History, and Civilization*. New York: Harper, 2002. Print.

Pasha, Mustapha Kamal. "Islam and the Postsecular." *Review of International Studies* 38.5 (2012): 1041–56. Print.

Sayers, Destini and Simone Peebles. *Essence of Islam and Sufism*. College, 2012. E-book.

Schirmacher, Christine. "They Are Not All Martyrs: Islam on the Topics of Dying, Death, and Salvation in the Afterlife." *Evangelical Review of Theology* 36.3 (2012): 250–65. Print.

Wilkinson, Philip. *Islam*. New York: DK, 2002. Print.

Wilkinson, Philip. *Religions*. New York: DK, 2008. Print.

Jainism

General Description

Jainism is one of the major religions of India. The name of the religion itself is believed to be based on the Sanskrit word *ji*, which means "to conquer or triumph," or *jina*, which means "victor or conqueror." The earliest name of the group was Nirgrantha, meaning bondless, but it applied to monks and nuns only. There are two sects: the Svetambaras (the white clad), which are the more numerous and wear white clothing, and the Digambaras (the sky clad), the most stringent group; their holy men or monks do not wear clothing at all.

Number of Adherents Worldwide

Jainism has about five million adherents, most of them in India (in some estimates, the religion represents approximately 1 percent of India's population). Because the religion is demanding in nature, few beyond the Indian subcontinent have embraced it. Jainism has spread to Africa, the United States, and nations in the Commonwealth (nations once under British rule) by virtue of Indian migration to these countries.

Basic Tenets

The principle of nonviolence (ahimsa) is a defining feature of Jainism. This results in a pacifist religion that influenced Mohandas Gandhi's ideas on nonviolent resistance. Jains believe that because all living creatures have souls, harming any of those creatures is wrong. They therefore follow a strict vegetarian diet, and often wear masks so as to not inhale living organisms. The most important aspect of Jainism is perhaps the five abstinences: ahimsa, satya (truthfulness), asteya (refrain from stealing), brahmacarya (chaste living), and aparigraha (refrain from greed).

A religion without priests, Jainism emphasizes the importance of the adherents' actions. Like Buddhists and Hindus, Jainists believe in karma and reincarnation. Unlike the Buddhist and Hindu idea of karma, Jainists regard karma as tiny particles that cling to the soul as mud clings to shoes, gradually weighing down the soul. Good deeds wash away these particles. Jainists also believe in moksha, the possibility of being freed from the cycle of death and rebirth. Like many Indian religions, Jainism does not believe in an afterlife, but in a cycle of death and rebirth. Once freed from this cycle, the soul will remain in infinite bliss.

While Jains do not necessarily believe in and worship God or gods, they believe in divine beings. Those who have achieved moksha are often regarded by Jains in the same manner in which other religions regard deities. These include the twenty-four Tirthankaras (ford makers) or jinas (victors), those who have escaped the cycle of death and rebirth, and the Siddhas, the liberated souls without physical form. The idea of a judging, ruling, or creator God is not present in Jainism.

Jainists believe that happiness is not found in material possessions and seek to have few of them. They also stress the importance of environmentalism. Jainists follow the Three Jewels: Right Belief, Right Knowledge, and Right Conduct. To be completely achieved, these three must be practiced together. Jainists also agree to six daily obligations (avashyaka), which include confession, praising the twenty-four Tirthankaras (the spiritual leaders), and calm meditation.

Sacred Text

The words of Mahavira were passed down orally, but lost over a few centuries. During a famine in the mid-fourth century BCE, many monks died. The texts were finally written down, although the Jain sects do not agree as to whether they are Mahavira's actual words. There are forty-five sacred texts (Agamas), which make up the Agam Sutras, Jainism's canonical literature. They were probably written down no earlier than 300 BCE. Two of the primary texts are the Akaranga

Sutra, which outlines the rule of conduct for Jain monks, and the Kalpa Sutra, which contains biographies of the last two Tirthankara. The Digambaras, who believe that the Agamas were lost around 350 BCE, have two main texts and four compendia written between 100 and 800 CE by various scholars.

Major Figures

Jainism has no single founder. However, Mahavira (Great Hero) is one of the Tirthankaras or jinas (pathfinders). He is considered the most recent spiritual teacher in a line of twenty-four. Modern-day Jainism derives from Mahavira, and his words are the foundation of Jain scriptures. He was a contemporary of Siddhartha Gautama, who was revered as the Buddha. Both Mahavira and Rishabha (or Adinatha), the first of the twenty-four Tirthankaras, are attributed as the founder of Jainism, though each Tirthankara maintains founding attributes.

Major Holy Sites

The Jain temple at Ranakpur is located in the village of Rajasthan. Carved from amber stone with marble interiors, the temple was constructed in the fifteenth century CE. It is dedicated to the first Tirthankara. The temple has twenty-nine large halls and each of the temple's 1,444 columns has a unique design with carvings.

Sravanabegola in Karnataka state is the site of Gomateshwara, Lord Bahubali's fifty-seven-foot statue. It was constructed in 981 CE from a single chunk of gneiss. Bahubali is considered the son of the first Tirthankara. The Digambara sect believes him to have been the first human to be free from the world.

Other pilgrimage sites include the Palitana temples in Gujarat and the Dilwara temples in Rajasthan. Sometimes regarded as the most sacred of the many Jain temples, the Palitana temples include 863 marble-engraved temples. The Jain temples at Dilwara were constructed of marble during the eleventh and thirteenth centuries CE. These five temples are often considered the most beautiful Jain temples in existence.

Major Rites & Celebrations

Every twelve years, the festival of Mahamastak-abhisheka (anointing of the head) occurs at a statue of one of Jain's holy men, Bahubali, the second son of the first Tirthankara. The statue is anointed with milk, curd, and ghee, a clarified butter. Nearly a million people attend this rite. Jainists also observe Diwali, the Hindu festival of lights, as it symbolizes Mahavira's enlightenment.

The solemn festival of Paryusana marks the end of the Jain year for the Svetambaras (also spelled Shvetambaras). During this eight-day festival, all Jains are asked to live as an ascetic (monk or nun) would for one day. Das Laxana, a ten-day festival similar to that of Paryusana, immediately follows for the Digambara sect. During these special religious holidays, worshippers are involved in praying, meditating, fasting, forgiveness, and acts of penance. These holy days are celebrated during August and September, which is monsoon season in India. During the monsoons, monks prefer to remain in one place so as to avoid killing the smallest insects that appear during the rainy season. The Kalpa Sutra, one of the Jain scriptures, is read in the morning during Paryusana.

The feast of Kartaki Purnima follows the four months of the rainy season. It is held in the first month (Kartik) according to one calendar, and marked by a pilgrimage to the Palitana temples. Doing so with a pure heart is said to remove all sins of both the present and past life. Those who do so are thought to receive the final salvation in the third or fifth birth.

ORIGINS

History & Geography

In the eastern basin of the Ganges River during the seventh century BCE, a teacher named Parshvanatha (or Parshva) gathered a community founded on abandoning earthly concerns. He is considered to be the twenty-third Tirthankara (ford-maker), the one who makes a path for salvation. During the following century, Vardhamana, called Mahavira (Great Hero), who was considered the twenty-fourth and final spiritual teacher of the age, formulated most Jain doctrine and practice. By the time of Mahavira's death, Jains numbered around 36,000 nuns and 14,000 monks.

A division occurred within Jainism during the fourth century CE. The most extreme ascetics, the Digambaras (the sky-clad), argued that even clothing showed too great an attachment to the world, and that laundering them in the river risked harming creatures. This argument applied only to men, as the Digambaras denied that a soul could be freed from a woman's body. The other group, the Svetambaras (the white-clad), believed that purity resided in the mind.

In 453 or 456 CE, a council of the Svetambara sect at Saurashtra in western India codified the canon still used. The split between the Digambaras, who did not take part in the meeting, and Svetambaras thus became permanent. Despite the split, Jainism's greatest flowering occurred during the early medieval age. After that time, Hindu sects devoted to the Hindu gods of Vishnu and Shiva flourished under the Gupta Empire (often referred to as India's golden age), slowing the spread of Jainism. Followers migrated to western and central India and the community became stronger.

The Digambaras were involved in politics through several medieval dynasties, and some Jain monks served as spiritual advisers. Royalty and high-ranking officials contributed to the building and maintenance of temples. Both branches of Jainism contributed a substantial literature. In the late medieval age, Jain monks ceased to live as ascetic wanders. They chose instead to don orange robes and to live at temples and other holy places.

The Muslims invaded India in the twelfth century. The Jains lost power and fractured over the next centuries into subgroups, some of which repudiated the worship of images. The poet and Digambara layman Banarsidas (1586-1643) played a significant role in a reform movement during the early 1600s. These reforms focused on the mystical side of Jainism, such as spiritual exploration of the inner self (meditation), and denounced the formalized temple ritual. The movement, known as the Adhyatma movement, resulted in the Digambara Terapanth, a small Digambara sect.

The Jainists were well positioned in society following the departure of the British from India. Having long been associated with the artisan and merchant classes, they found new opportunities. As traditional Indian studies grew, spurred by Western interest, proponents of Jainism began to found publications and places of study (In fact, Jain libraries are believed to be the oldest in India.) The first Jain temple outside India was consecrated in Britain during the 1960s after Jains had gone there in the wake of political turmoil.

The Jains follow their typical profession as merchants. They publish English-language periodicals to spread their ideas on vegetarianism, environmentalism, and nonviolence (ahimsa). The ideas of ahimsa were formative for Mohandas Gandhi, born a Hindu. Gandhi used nonviolence as a wedge against the British Empire in India. Eventually, the British granted independence to India in 1947.

Virchand Gandhi (1864–1901) is believed to be the first Jain to arrive in America when he came over in 1893. He attended the first Parliament of World Religions, held in Chicago. Today North America has more than ninety Jain temples and centers. Jains in the West often follow professions such as banking and business to avoid destroying animal or plant life.

Founder or Major Prophet

Mahavira was born in India's Ganges Basin region. By tradition, he was born around 599 BCE, although some scholars think he may have lived a century later. His story bears a resemblance to that of the Buddha, with whom he was believed to have been a contemporary. His family was also of the Kshatriya (warrior) caste, and his father was a ruler of his clan. One tradition states that Mahavira's mother was of the Brahman (priestly) caste, although another places her in the Kshatriya.

Because he was not the eldest son, Mahavira was not in line for leadership of the clan.

He married a woman of his own caste and they had a daughter. Mahavira chose the life of a monk, with one garment. Later, he gave up wearing even that. He became a wandering ascetic around age thirty, with some legends stating that he tore out his hair before leaving home. He sought shelter in burial grounds and cremation sites, as well as at the base of trees. During the rainy season, however, he lived in towns and villages.

He followed a path of preaching and self-denial, after which he was enlightened (kevala). He spent the next thirty years teaching. Eleven disciples, all of whom were of the Brahman caste, gathered around him. At the end of his life, Mahavira committed Santhara, or ritual suicide through fasting.

Philosophical Basis

Like Buddhists and the Brahmin priests, the Jains believe in human incarnations of God, known as avatars. These avatars appear at the end of a time of decline to reinstate proper thinking and acting. Such a person was Mahavira. At the time of Mahavira's birth, India was experiencing great societal upheaval. Members of the warrior caste opposed the priestly caste, which exercised authority based on its supposed greater moral purity. Many people also opposed the slaughter of animals for the Vedic sacrifices.

Jainists share some beliefs with both Hinduism and Buddhism. The Hindu hero Rama, for example, is co-opted as a nonviolent Jain, while the deity Krishna is considered a cousin of Arishtanemi, the twenty-second Tirthankara. Like Buddhism, Jainism uses a wheel with twelve spokes; however, Jainism uses the wheel to explain time. The first half of the circle is the ascending stage, in which human happiness, prosperity, and life span increase. The latter half of the circle is the descending stage, involving a decrease of life span, prosperity, and happiness. The wheel of time is always in motion.

For Jainists, the universe is without beginning or ending, and contains layers of both heaven and hell. These layers include space beyond, which is without time, matter, or soul. The cosmos is depicted in art as a large human. The cloud layers surrounding the upper world are called universe space. Above them is the base, Nigoda, where lowest life forms live. The netherworld contains seven hells, each with a different stage of punishment and misery. The middle world contains the earth and remainder of the universe—mankind is located near the waist. There are thirty heavens in the upper world, where heavenly beings reside. In the supreme abode at the apex of the universe, liberated souls (siddha) live.

Jainism teaches that there are six universal entities. Only consciousness or soul is a living substance, while the remaining five are non-living. They include matter, medium of rest, medium of motion, time, and space. Jainism also does not believe in a God who can create, destroy, or protect. Worshipping goddesses and gods to achieve personal gain or material benefit is deemed useless.

Mahavira outlined five basic principles (often referred to as abstinences) for Jainist life, based on the teachings of the previous Tirthankara. They are detachment (aparigraha); the conduct of soul, primarily in sexual morality (brahmacharya); abstinence from stealing (asteya); abstinence from lying (satya); and non-violence in every realm of the person (ahimsa).

Like other Indian religions, Jainism perceives life as four stages. The life of a student is brahmacharya-ashrama; the stage of family life is gruhasth-ashrama; in vanaprasth-ashrama, the Jainist concentrates on both family and aiding others through social services; and the final stage is sanyast-ashrama, a time of renouncing the world and becoming a monk.

Like many religions, Jainism has a bias toward males and toward the rigorous life of monks and nuns. A layperson cannot work off bad karma, but merely keeps new bad karma from accruing. By following a path of asceticism, however, monks and nuns can destroy karma. Even members of the laity follow eight rules of behavior and take twelve vows. Physical austerity is a key concept in Jainism, as a saint's highest ideal is to starve to death.

Holy Places

There are four major Jain pilgrimage sites: the Dilwara temples near Rajasthan; the Palitana temples; the Ranakpur temple; and Shravan Begola, the site of the statue of Lord Bahubali. In addition, Jains may make pilgrimages to the caves of Khandagiri and Udayagiri, which were cells for Jain monks carved from rock. The spaces carved are too short for a man to stand upright. They were essentially designed for prayer and meditation. Udayagiri has eighteen caves and Khandagiri has fifteen. The caves are decorated with elaborate carvings.

JAINISM IN DEPTH

Sacred Symbols

The open palm (Jain Hand) with a centered wheel, sometimes with the word *ahimsa* written on it, is a prominent Jain symbol. Seen as an icon of peace, the open palm symbol can be interpreted as a call to stop violence, and also means "assurance." It appears on the walls of Jain temples and in their publications. Jainism also employs a simple swastika symbol, considered to be the holiest symbol. It represents the four forms of worldly existence, and three dots above the swastika represent the Three Jewels. The Jain emblem, adopted in 1975, features both the Jain Hand (the open palm symbol with an inset wheel) and a swastika. This year was regarded as the 2,500th anniversary of Mahavira being enlightened.

Sacred Practices & Gestures

Jains may worship daily in their homes at private shrines. The Five Supreme Beings stand for stages in the path to enlightenment. Rising before daybreak, worshippers invoke these five. In addition, devout Jainists set aside forty-eight minutes daily to meditate.

To demonstrate faithfulness to the five vows that Jains undertake, there are four virtuous qualities that must be cultivated. They are compassion (karuna), respect and joy (pramoda), love and friendship (maitri), and indifference toward and noninvolvement with those who are arrogant (madhyastha). Mahavira stressed that Jains must be friends to all living beings. Compassion goes beyond mere feeling; it involves offering both material and spiritual aid. Pramoda carries with it the idea of rejoicing enthusiastically over the virtues of others. There are contemplations associated with these virtues, and daily practice is suggested to attain mastery.

Some Jainists, both men and women, wear a dot on the forehead. This practice comes from Hinduism. During festivals, Jains may pray, chant, fast, or keep silent. These actions are seen as removing bad karma from the soul and moving the person toward ultimate happiness.

Food Restrictions

Jainists practice a strict vegetarian way of life (called Jain vegetarianism) to avoid harming any creature. They refuse to eat root vegetables, because by uprooting them, the entire plant dies. They prefer to wait for fruit to drop from trees rather than taking it from the branches. Starving to death, when ready, is seen as an ideal.

Rites, Celebrations & Services

Some festivals are held annually and their observances are based on a lunar calendar. Mahavir Jayanti is an example, as it celebrates Mahavira's birthday.

Jains may worship, bathe, and make offerings to images of the Tirthankaras in their home or in a temple. Svetambaras Jains also clothe and decorate the images. Because the Tirthankaras have been liberated, they cannot respond as a deity granting favors might. Although Jainism rejects belief in gods in favor of worshipping Tirthankaras, in actual practice, some Jainists pray to Hindu gods.

When Svetambara monks are initiated, they are given three pieces of clothing, including a small piece of white cloth to place over the mouth. The cloth, called a mukhavastrika, is designed to prevent the monk from accidentally eating insects.

Monks take great vows (mahavratas) at initiation. These include abstaining from lying, stealing, sexual activity, injury to any living thing, and personal possessions. Monks own a broom to sweep in front of where they are going to walk so that no small creatures are injured, along with an alms bowl and a robe. The Digambara monks practice a more stringent lifestyle, eating one meal a day, for which they beg.

Nuns in the Svetambaras are three times more common than are monks, even though they receive less honor, and are required to defer to the monks. In Digambara Jainism, the nuns wear robes and accept that they must be reborn as men before progressing upward.

The observance of Santhara, which is religious fasting until death, is a voluntary fasting undertaken with full knowledge. The ritual is also known as Sallekhana, and is not perceived as suicide by Jains, particularly as the prolonged nature of the ritual provides ample time for reflection. It is believed that at least one hundred people die every year from observing Santhara.

Judy A. Johnson, MTS

Bibliography

Aristarkhova, Irina. "Thou Shall Not Harm All Living Beings: Feminism, Jainism, and Animals." *Hypatia* 27.3 (2012): 636–50. Print.

Aukland, Knut. "Understanding Possession in Jainism: A Study of Oracular Possession in Nakoda." *Modern Asian Studies* 47.1 (2013): 103–34. Print.

Barnes, Trevor. *The Kingfisher Book of Religions*. New York: Kingfisher, 1999. Print.

Langley, Myrtle. *Religion*. New York: Knopf, 1996. Print.

Long, Jeffery. *Jainism: An Introduction*. London: I. B. Tauris, 2009. Print.

Long, Jeffrey. "Jainism: Key Themes." *Religion Compass* 5.9 (2011): 501–10. Print.

Rankin, Aidan. *The Jain Path*. Berkeley: O Books, 2006. Print.

Shah, Bharat S. *An Introduction to Jainism*. Great Neck: Setubandh, 2002. Print.

Titze, Kurt. *Jainism: A Pictorial Guide to the Religion of Non-Violence*. Delhi: Motilal Banarsidass, 2001. Print.

Tobias, Michael. *Life Force: the World of Jainism*. Berkeley:Asian Humanities, 1991. E-book, print.

Wiley, Kristi L. *The A to Z of Jainism*. Lanham: Scarecrow, 2009. Print.

Wiley, Kristi L. *Historical Dictionary of Jainism*. Lanham: Scarecrow, 2004. Print.

Wilkinson, Philip. *Religions*. New York: DK, 2008. Print.

Judaism

General Description

In modern Judaism, the main denominations (referred to as movements) are Orthodox Judaism (including Haredi and Hasidic Judaism); Conservative Judaism; Reform (Liberal) Judaism; Reconstructionist Judaism; and to a lesser extent, Humanistic Judaism. In addition, the Jewry of Ethiopia and Yemen are known for having distinct or alternative traditions. Classical Judaism is often organized by two branches: Ashkenazic (Northern Europe) and Sephardic Jews (Spain, Portugal, and North Africa).

Number of Adherents Worldwide

Judaism has an estimated 15 million adherents worldwide, with roughly 41 percent living in Israel and about 41 percent living in the United States. Ashkenazi Jews represent roughly 75 percent, while Sephardic Jews represent roughly 25 percent, with the remaining 5 percent split among alternative communities. Within the United States, a 2000-01 survey stated that 10 percent of American Jews identified as Orthodox (with that number increasing), 35 percent as Reform, 26 percent as Conservative, leaving the remainder with an alternative or no affiliation. [Source: Wilkinson, 2008]

Orthodox Judaism, which was founded around the thirteenth century BCE, has 3 million followers. Members of Reform Judaism, with roots in nineteenth-century Germany, wanted to live peacefully with non-Jews. Therefore, they left the laws that prevented this vision of peace and downplayed the idea of a Jewish state. Reform Judaism, also known as Progressive or Liberal Judaism, allows women rabbis and does not require its adherents to keep kosher. About 1.1 million Jews are Reform; they live primarily in the United States. When nonkosher food was served at the first graduation ceremony for Hebrew Union College, some felt that the Reform movement had gone too far. Thus the Conservative movement began in 1887. A group

of rabbis founded the Jewish Theological Seminary in New York City, wanting to emphasize biblical authority above moral choice, as the Reform tradition stressed. Currently about 900,000 Jews practice this type of Judaism, which is theologically midway between Orthodox and Reform. The Hasidim, an ultra-conservative group, began in present-day Ukraine around 1740. There are 4.5 million Hasidic Jews.

Basic Tenets

Though there is no formal creed (statement of faith or belief), Jews value all life, social justice, education, generous giving, and the importance of living based on the principles and values espoused in the Torah (Jewish holy book). They believe in one all-powerful and creator God, Jehovah or Yaweh, a word derived from the Hebrew letters "YHWH," the unpronounceable name of God. The word is held to be sacred; copyists were required to bathe both before and after writing the word. Jews also believe in a coming Messiah who will initiate a Kingdom of Righteousness. They follow a complex law, composed of 613 commandments or mitzvot. Jews believe that they are God's Chosen People with a unique covenant relationship. They have a responsibility to practice hospitality and to improve the world.

The belief in the afterlife is a part of the Jewish faith. Similar to Christianity, this spiritual world is granted to those who abide by the Jewish faith and live a good life. Righteous Jews are rewarded in the afterlife by being able to discuss the Torah with Moses, who first received the law from God. Furthermore, certain Orthodox sects believe that wicked souls are destroyed or tormented after death.

Sacred Text

The complete Hebrew Bible is called the Tanakh. It includes the prophetic texts, called the Navi'im, the poetic writings, the Ketubim, and the Torah, meaning teaching, law, or guidance. Torah may refer to the entire body of Jewish law or to the first five books of the Hebrew Bible, known as the Pentateuch (it is the Old Testament in the Christian Bible). Also esteemed is the Talmud, made up of the Mishnah, a written collection of oral traditions, and Gemara, a commentary on the Mishnah. The Talmud covers many different subjects, such as law, stories and legends, medicine, and rituals.

Major Figures

The patriarchs are held to be the fathers of the faith. Abraham, the first patriarch, was called to leave his home in the Fertile Crescent for a land God would give him, and promised descendents as numerous as the stars. His son Isaac was followed by Jacob, whom God renamed Israel, and whose twelve sons became the heads of the twelve tribes of Israel. Moses was the man who, along with his brother Aaron, the founder of a priestly line, and their sister Miriam led the chosen people out of slavery in Egypt, where they had gone to escape famine. The Hebrew Bible also details the careers of a group of men and women known as judges, who were really tribal rulers, as well as of the prophets, who called the people to holy lives. Chief among the prophets was Elijah, who confronted wicked kings and performed many miracles. Several kings were key to the biblical narrative, among them David, who killed the giant Goliath, and Solomon, known for his wisdom and for the construction of a beautiful temple.

Major Holy Sites

Most of Judaism's holy sites are within Israel, the Holy Land, including Jerusalem, which was the capital of the United Kingdom of Israel under kings David and Solomon; David captured it from a Canaanite tribe around 1000 BCE. Within the Old City of Jerusalem is the Temple Mount (where the Temple of Jerusalem was built), often considered the religion's holiest site, the Foundation Stone (from which Judaism claims the world was created), and the Western (or Wailing) Wall. Other sites include Mount Sinai

in Egypt, the mountain upon which God gave Moses his laws.

Major Rites & Celebrations

The Jewish calendar recognizes several important holidays. Rosh Hashanah, literally "first of the year," is known as the Jewish New Year and inaugurates a season of self-examination and repentance that culminates in Yom Kippur, the Day of Atonement. Each spring, Passover commemorates the deliverance of the Hebrew people from Egypt. Shavuot celebrates the giving of the Torah to Moses, while Sukkot is the harvest festival. Festivals celebrating deliverance from enemies include Purim and Hanukkah. Young adolescents become members of the community at a bar or bat mitzvah, held near the twelfth or thirteenth birthday. The Sabbath, a cessation from work from Friday at sundown until Saturday when the first star appears, gives each week a rhythm.

ORIGINS

History & Geography

Called by God perhaps four thousand years ago, Abraham left from Ur of the Chaldees, or the Fertile Crescent in Mesopotamia in present-day Iraq, to go the eastern Mediterranean, the land of Canaan. Several generations later, the tribe went to Egypt to escape famine. They were later enslaved by a pharaoh, sometimes believed to have been Ramses II (ca. 1279–1213 BCE), who was noted for his many building projects. The Israelites returned to Canaan under Moses several hundred years after their arrival in Egypt. He was given the law, the Ten Commandments, plus the rest of the laws governing all aspects of life, on Mount Sinai about the thirteenth century BCE. This marked the beginning of a special covenant relationship between the new nation, known as Israel, and God.

Following a period of rule by judges, kings governed the nation. Major kings included David, son-in-law to the first king, Saul, and David's son, Solomon. The kingdom split at the beginning of the reign of Solomon's son

Rehoboam, who began ruling about 930 BCE. Rehoboam retained the ten northern tribes, while the two southern tribes followed a military commander rather than the Davidic line.

Rehoboam's kingdom was known as Israel, after the name Jehovah gave to Jacob. Judah was the name of the southern kingdom—one of Jacob's sons was named Judah. Prophets to both nations warned of coming judgment unless the people repented of mistreating the poor and other sins, such as idolatry. Unheeding, Israel was taken into captivity by the Assyrians in 722 BCE. and the Israelites assimilated into the nations around them.

The Babylonians captured Judah in 586 BCE. After Babylon had been captured in turn by Persians, the Jewish people were allowed to return to the land in 538 BCE. There they began reconstructing the temple and the walls of the city. In the second century BCE, Judas Maccabeus led a rebellion against the heavy taxes and oppression of the Greek conquerors, after they had levied high taxes and appointed priests who were not Jewish. Judas Maccabeus founded a new ruling dynasty, the Hasmoneans, which existed briefly before the region came under the control of Rome.

The Jewish people revolted against Roman rule in 70 CE, leading to the destruction of the second temple. The final destruction of Jerusalem occurred in 135 under the Roman Emperor Hadrian. He changed the city's name to Aelia Capitolina and the name of the country to Palaestina. With the cultic center of their religion gone, the religious leaders developed new methods of worship that centered in religious academies and in synagogues.

After Christianity became the official state religion of the Roman Empire in the early fourth century, Jews experienced persecution. They became known for their scholarship, trade, and banking over the next centuries, with periods of brutal persecution in Europe. Christians held Jews responsible for the death of Jesus, based on a passage in the New Testament. The Blood Libel, begun in England in 1144, falsely accused Jews of killing a Christian child to bake unleavened bread for Passover. This rumor persisted for centuries, and was repeated by Martin Luther during the Protestant Reformation. England expelled all Jews in 1290; they were not readmitted until 1656 under Oliver Cromwell, and not given citizenship until 1829. Jews were also held responsible for other catastrophes—namely poisoning wells and rivers to cause the Black Death in 1348—and were often made to wear special clothing, such as pointed hats, or badges with the Star of David or stone tablets on them.

The relationship between Muslims and Jews was more harmonious. During the Muslim Arab dominance, there was a "golden age" in Spain due to the contributions of Jews and Muslims, known as Moors in Spain. This ideal and harmonious period ended in 1492, when both Moors and Jews were expelled from Spain or forced to convert to Christianity.

Jews in Russia suffered as well. An estimated two million Jews fled the country to escape the pogroms (a Russian word meaning devastation) between 1881 and 1917. The twentieth-century Holocaust, in which an estimated six million Jews perished at the hands of Nazi Germany, was but the culmination of these centuries of persecution. The Nazis also destroyed more than six hundred synagogues.

The Holocaust gave impetus to the creation of the independent state of Israel. The Zionist movement, which called for the founding or reestablishment of a Jewish homeland, was started by Austrian Jew Theodor Herzl in the late nineteenth century, and succeeded in 1948. The British government, which had ruled the region under a mandate, left the area, and Israel was thus established. This ended the Diaspora, or dispersion, of the Jewish people that had begun nearly two millennia before when the Romans forced the Jews to leave their homeland.

Arab neighbors, some of whom had been removed forcibly from the land to create the nation of Israel, were displeased with the new political reality. Several wars have been fought, including the War of Independence in 1948, the Six-Day War in 1967, and the Yom Kippur War in 1973. In addition, tension between Israel and its neighboring Arab states is almost constant.

When the Jewish people were dispersed from Israel, two traditions began. The Ashkenazi Jews settled in Germany and central Europe. They spoke a mixture of the Hebrew dialect and German called Yiddish. Sephardic Jews lived in the Mediterranean countries, including Spain; their language, Ladino, mixed Hebrew and old Spanish.

Founder or Major Prophet

Judaism refers to three major patriarchs: Abraham, his son Isaac, and Isaac's son Jacob. Abraham is considered the first Jew and worshipper in Judaism, as the religion began through his covenant with God. As the forefather of the religion, he is often associated as the founder, though the founder technically is God, or Yahweh (YHWH). Additionally, the twelve sons of Jacob, who was also named Israel, became the founders of the twelve tribes of Israel.

Moses is regarded as a major prophet and as the Lawgiver. God revealed to Moses the complete law during the forty days that the Jewish leader spent on Mount Sinai during the wilderness journey from Egypt to Canaan. Thus, many attribute Moses as the founder of Judaism as a religion.

Philosophical Basis

Judaism began with Abraham's dissatisfaction with the polytheistic worship of his culture. Hearing the command of God to go to a land that would be shown to him, Abraham and his household obeyed. Abraham practiced circumcision and hospitality, cornerstones of the Jewish faith to this day. He and his descendents practiced a nomadic life, much like that of contemporary Bedouins. They migrated from one oasis or well to another, seeking pasture and water for the sheep and goats they herded.

The further development of Judaism came under the leadership of Moses. A Jewish child adopted by Pharaoh's daughter, he was raised and educated in the palace. As a man, he identified with the Jewish people, killing one of the Egyptians who was oppressing a Jew. He subsequently fled for his life, becoming a shepherd in the wilderness, where he remained for forty years. Called by God from a bush that burned but was not destroyed, he was commissioned to lead the people out of slavery in Egypt back to the Promised Land. That forty-year pilgrimage in the wilderness and desert of Arabia shaped the new nation.

Holy Places

The city of Jerusalem was first known as Salem. When King David overcame the Jebusites who lived there, the city, already some two thousand years old, became the capital of Israel. It is built on Mount Zion, which is still considered a sacred place. David's son Solomon built the First Temple in Jerusalem, centering the nation's spiritual as well as political life in the city. The Babylonians captured the city in 597 BCE and destroyed the Temple. For the next sixty years, the Jews remained in exile, until Cyrus the Persian conqueror of Babylon allowed them to return. They rebuilt the temple, but it was desecrated by Antiochus IV of Syria in 167 BCE. In 18 BCE, during a period of Roman occupation, Herod the Great began rebuilding and expanding the Temple. The Romans under the general Titus destroyed the Temple in 70 CE, just seven years after its completion.

The city eventually came under the rule of Persia, the Muslim Empire, and the Crusaders before coming under control of Britain. In 1948 an independent state of Israel was created. The following year, Jerusalem was divided between Israel, which made the western part the national capital, and Jordan, which ruled the eastern part of the city. The Western or Wailing Wall, a retaining wall built during Herod's time, is all that remains of the Second Temple. Devout Jews still come to the Wailing Wall to pray, sometimes placing their petitions on paper and folding the paper into the Wall's crevices. The Wall is known as a place where prayers are answered and a reminder of the perseverance of the Jewish people and faith. According to tradition, the Temple will be rebuilt when Messiah comes to inaugurate God's Kingdom.

The Temple Mount, located just outside Jerusalem on a natural acropolis, includes the Dome of the Rock. This shrine houses a rock held sacred by both Judaism and Islam. Jewish tradition states that it is the spot from which the world was created and the spot on which Abraham was asked to sacrifice his son Isaac. Muslims believe that from this rock Muhammad ascended for his night journey to heaven. Much of Jerusalem, including this holy site, has been and continues to be fought over by people of three faiths: Judaism, Islam, and Christianity.

Moses received the law from God on Mount Sinai. It is still regarded as a holy place.

JUDAISM IN DEPTH

Sacred Symbols

Observant Jewish men pray three times daily at home or in a synagogue, a center of worship, from the word meaning "meeting place." They wear a tallis, or a prayer shawl with tassles, during their morning prayer and on Yom Kippur, the Day of Atonement. They may also cover their heads as a sign of respect during prayer, wearing a skullcap known as a kippah or yarmulka. They find their prayers and blessings in a siddur, which literally means "order," because the prayers appear in the order in which they are recited for services. Jewish daily life also includes blessings for many things, including food.

Tefillin or phylacteries are the small black boxes made of leather from kosher animals that Jewish men wear on their foreheads and their left upper arms during prayer. They contain passages from the Torah. Placing the tefillin on the head reminds them to think about the Torah, while placing the box on the arm puts the Torah close to the heart.

The Law of Moses commands the people to remember the words of the law and to teach them to the children. A mezuzah helps to fulfill that command. A small box with some of the words of the law written on a scroll inside, a mezuzah is hung on the doorframes of every door in the house. Most often, the words of the Shema,

the Jewish recitation of faith, are written on the scroll. The Shema is repeated daily. "Hear, O Israel: the Lord your God, the Lord is one. . . . Love the Lord your God with all your heart, and with all your soul, and with all your might."

Jews adopted the Star of David, composed of two intersecting triangles, during the eighteenth century. There are several interpretations of the design. One is that it is the shape of King David's shield. Another idea is that it stands for daleth, the first letter of David's name. A third interpretation is that the six points refer to the days of the work week, and the inner, larger space represented the day of rest, the Sabbath, or Shabot. The Star of David appears on the flag of Israel. The flag itself is white, symbolizing peace and purity, and blue, symbolizing heaven and reminding all of God's activity.

The menorah is a seven-branch candlestick representing the light of the Torah. For Hanukkah, however, an eight-branched menorah is used. The extra candle is the servant candle, and is the one from which all others are lit.

Because the Torah is the crowning glory of life for Jewish people, a crown is sometimes used on coverings for the Torah. The scrolls of Torah are stored in a container, called an ark, which generally is covered with an ornate cloth called a mantle. The ark and mantle are often elaborately decorated with symbols, such as the lion of Judah. Because the Torah scroll, made of parchment from a kosher animal, is sacred and its pages are not to be touched, readers use a pointed stick called a yad. Even today, Torahs are written by hand in specially prepared ink and using a quill from a kosher bird. Scribes are trained for seven years.

A shofar is a ram's horn, blown as a call to repentance on Rosh Hashanah, the Jewish New Year. This holiday is the beginning of a ten-day preparation for the Day of Atonement, which is the most holy day in the Jewish calendar and a time of both fasting and repentance.

Sacred Practices & Gestures

Sacred practices can apply daily, weekly, annually, or over a lifetime's events. Reciting the Shema, the monotheistic creed taken from the

Torah, is a daily event. Keeping the Sabbath occurs weekly. Each year the festivals described above take place. Circumcision and bar or bat mitzvah are once-in-a-lifetime events. Each time someone dies, the mourners recite the Kaddish for seven days following death, and grieve for a year.

Food Restrictions

Kosher foods are those that can be eaten based on Jewish law. Animals that chew the cud and have cloven hooves, such as cows and lamb, and domestic poultry are considered kosher. Shellfish, pork, and birds of prey are forbidden. Keeping kosher also includes the method of preparing and storing the food. This includes animals which are slaughtered in a way to bring the least amount of pain and from which all blood is drained. In addition, dairy and meat products are to be kept separate, requiring separate refrigerators in the homes of the Orthodox.

Rites, Celebrations & Services

Sabbath is the weekly celebration honoring one of the Ten Commandments, which commands the people to honor the Sabbath by doing no work that day. The practice is rooted in the Genesis account that God rested on the seventh day after creating the world in six days. Because the Jewish day begins at sundown, the Sabbath lasts from Friday night to Saturday night. Special candles are lit and special food—included the braided egg bread called challah—for the evening meal is served. This day is filled with feasting, visiting, and worship.

Boys are circumcised at eight days of age. This rite, B'rit Milah, meaning "seal of the covenant," was first given to Abraham as a sign of the covenant. A trained circumciser, or mohel, may be a doctor or rabbi. The boy's name is officially announced at the ceremony. A girl's name is given at a special baby-naming ceremony or in the synagogue on the first Sabbath after she is born.

A boy becomes a "son of the commandment," or bar mitzvah, at age thirteen. At a special ceremony, the young man reads a portion of

Torah that he has prepared ahead of time. Most boys also give a speech at the service. Girls become bat mitzvah at age twelve. This ceremony developed in the twentieth century. Not all Orthodox communities will allow this rite. Girls may also read from the Torah and give a sermon in the synagogue, just as boys do.

When a Jewish person dies, mourners begin shiva, a seven-day mourning period. People usually gather at the home of the deceased, where mirrors are covered. In the home, the Kaddish, a collection of prayers that praise God and celebrate life, is recited. Traditionally, family members mourn for a full year, avoiding parties and festive occasions.

The Jewish calendar offers a series of feasts and festivals, beginning with Rosh Hashanah, the Jewish New Year. At this time, Jews recall the creation. They may also eat apples that have been dipped into honey and offer each other wishes for a sweet New Year. The next ten days are a time of reflection on the past year, preparing for Yom Kippur.

This Day of Atonement once included animal sacrifice at the Temple. Now it includes an all-day service at the synagogue and a twenty-five-hour fast. A ram's horn, called a shofar, is blown as a call to awaken to lead a holier life. The shofar reminds Jewish people of the ram that Abraham sacrificed in the place of his son, Isaac.

Passover, or Pesach, is the spring remembrance of God's deliverance of the people from slavery in Egypt. In the night that the Jewish people left Egypt, they were commanded to sacrifice a lamb for each household and sprinkle the blood on the lintels and doorposts. A destroying angel from God would "pass over" the homes with blood sprinkled. During the first two nights of Passover, a special meal is served known as a Seder, meaning order. The foods symbolize different aspects of the story of deliverance, which is told during the meal by the head of the family.

Shavuot has its origins as a harvest festival. This celebration of Moses receiving the Torah on Mount Sinai occurs fifty days after the second day of Passover. To welcome the first fruits of the season, the synagogue may be decorated with fruit and flowers. Traditionally, the Ten Commandments are read aloud in the synagogue.

Purim, which occurs in February or March, celebrates the deliverance of the Jews during their captivity in Persia in the fifth century BCE. The events of that experience are recorded in the Book of Esther in the Hebrew Bible (Tanakh). The book is read aloud during Purim.

Sukkot, the feast celebrating the end of the harvest, occurs in September or October. Jews recall God's provision for them in the wilderness when they left Egypt to return to Canaan. Traditionally, huts are made and decorated with flowers and fruits. The conclusion of Sukkot is marked by a synagogue service known as Simchat Torah, or Rejoicing in the Law. People sing and dance as the Torah scrolls are carried and passed from person to person.

Hanukkah, known as the Festival of Lights, takes place over eight days in December. It celebrates the rededicating of the Temple under the leader Judas Maccabeus, who led the people in recapturing the structure from Syria in 164 BCE. According to the story, the Jews had only enough oil in the Temple lamp to last one day, but the oil miraculously lasted for eight days, after which Judas Maccabeus re-dedicated the Temple. On each day of Hanukkah, one of the eight candles is lit until all are burning. The gift-giving custom associated with Hanukkah is relatively new, and may derive from traditional small gifts of candy or money. The practice may also have been encouraged among those integrated with communities that exchange gifts during the Christmas season.

Judy A. Johnson, MTS

Bibliography

Barnes, Trevor. *The Kingfisher Book of Religions*. New York: Kingfisher, 1999. Print.

"A Buffet to Suit All Tastes." *Economist* 28 Jul. 2012: Spec. section 4–6. Print.

Charing, Douglas. *Judaism*. London: DK, 2003. Print.

Coenen Snyder, Saskia. *Building a Public Judaism: Synagogues and Jewish Identity in Nineteenth-Century Europe*. Cambridge: Harvard UP, 2013. E-book.

Diamant, Anita. *Living a Jewish Life*. New York: Collins, 1996. Print.

Exler, Lisa and Rabbi Jill Jacobs. "A Judaism That Matters." *Journal of Jewish Communal Service* 87.1/2 (2012): 66–76. Print.

Gelernter, David Hillel. *Judaism: A Way of Being*. New Haven: Yale UP, 2009. E-book.

Kessler, Edward. *What Do Jews Believe?* New York: Walker, 2007. Print.

Krieger, Aliza Y. "The Role of Judaism in Family Relationships." *Journal of Multicultural Counseling & Development* 38.3 (2010): 154–65. Print.

Langley, Myrtle. *Religion*. New York: Knopf, 1996. Print.

Madsen, Catherine. "A Heart of Flesh: Beyond 'Creative Liturgy.'" *Cross Currents* 62.1 (2012): 11–20. Print.

Meredith, Susan. *The Usborne Book of World Religions*. London: Usborne, 1995. Print.

Schoen, Robert. *What I Wish My Christian Friends Knew About Judaism*. Chicago: Loyola, 2004. Print.

Stefnon, Matt. *Judaism: History, Belief, and Practice*. New York: Britannica Educational, 2012. E-book.

Wertheimer, Jack. "The Perplexities of Conservative Judaism." *Commentary* Sept. 2007: 38–44. Print.

Wilkinson, Philip. *Religions*. New York: DK, 2008. Print.

Sikhism

General Description

The youngest of the world religions, Sikhism has existed for only about five hundred years. Sikhism derives from the Sanskrit word *sishyas*, which means "disciple"; in the Punjabi language, it also means "disciple."

Number of Adherents Worldwide

An estimated 24.5 million people follow the Sikh religion. Most of the devotees live in Asia, particularly in the Punjab region of India (Wilkinson, p. 335).

Basic Tenets

Sikhism is a monotheistic religion. The deity is God, known as Nam, or Name. Other synonyms include the Divine, Ultimate, Ultimate Reality, Infinity, the Formless, Truth, and other attributes of God.

Sikhs adhere to three basic principles. These are hard work (kirt kao), worshipping the Divine Name (nam japo), and sharing what one has (vand cauko). Meditating on the Divine Name is seen as a method of moving toward a life totally devoted to God. In addition, Sikhs believe in karma, or moral cause and effect. They value hospitality to all, regardless of religion, and oppose caste distinctions. Sikhs delineate a series of five stages that move upward to gurmukh, total devotion to God. This service is called Seva. Sahaj, or tranquility, is practiced as a means of being united with God as well as of generating external good will. Sikhs are not in favor of external routines of religion; they may stop in their temple whenever it is convenient during the day.

Sikhism does not include a belief in the afterlife. Instead, the soul is believed to be reincarnated in successive lives and deaths, a belief borrowed from Hinduism. The goal is then to break this karmic cycle, and to merge the human spirit with that of God.

Sacred Text

The Guru Granth Sahib (also referred to as the Aad Guru Granth Sahib, or AGGS), composed of Adi Granth, meaning First Book, is the holy scripture of Sikhism. It is a collection of religious poetry that is meant to be sung. Called shabads, they were composed by the first five gurus, the ninth guru, and thirty-six additional holy men of northern India. Sikhs always show honor to the Guru Granth Sahib by carrying it above the head when in a procession.

A second major text is the Dasam Granth, or Tenth Book, created by followers of Guru Gobind Singh, the tenth guru. Much of it is devoted to retelling the Hindu stories of Krishna and Rama. Those who are allowed to read and care for the Granth Sahib are known as granthi. Granthi may also look after the gurdwara, or temple. In the gurdwara, the book rests on a throne with a wooden base and cushions covered in cloths placed in a prescribed order. If the book is not in use, it is covered with a cloth known as a rumala. When the book is read, a fan called a chauri is fanned over it as a sign of respect, just as followers of the gurus fanned them with chauris. At Amritsar, a city in northwestern India that houses the Golden Temple, the Guru Granth Sahib is carried on a palanquin (a covered, carried bed). If it is carried in the city, a kettle drum is struck and people welcome it by tossing rose petals.

Major Figures

Guru Nanak (1469–1539) is the founder of Sikhism. He was followed by nine other teachers, and collectively they are known as the Ten Gurus. Each of them was chosen by his predecessor and was thought to share the same spirit of that previous guru. Guru Arjan (1581–1606), the fifth guru, oversaw completion of the Golden Temple in Amritsar, India. Guru Gobind Singh (1675–1708) was the tenth and last human guru. He decreed that the True Guru henceforth would be the Granth Sahib, the scripture of the Sikhs. He also founded the Khalsa, originally a military order of male Sikhs willing to die for the faith; the term is now used to refer to all baptized Sikhs.

Major Holy Sites

Amritsar, India, is the holy city of Sikhism. Construction of the city began under Guru Ram Das (1574–1581), the fourth guru, during the 1570s. One legend says that the Muslim ruler, Emperor Akbar, gave the land to the third guru, Guru Amar Das (1552–74). Whether or not that is true, Amar Das did establish the location of Amritsar. He chose a site near a pool believed to hold healing water.

When construction of the Golden Temple began, only a small town existed. One legend says that a Muslim saint from Lahore, India, named Mian Mir laid the foundation stone of the first temple. It has been demolished and rebuilt three times. Although pilgrimage is not required of Sikhs, many come to see the shrines and the Golden Temple. They call it Harmandir Sahib, God's Temple, or Darbar Sahib, the Lord's Court. When the temple was completed during the tenure of the fifth guru, Arjan, he placed the first copy of the Guru Granth Sahib inside.

Every Sikh temple has a free kitchen attached to it, called a langar. After services, all people, regardless of caste or standing within the community, sit on the floor in a straight line and eat a simple vegetarian meal together. As a pilgrimage site, the langar serves 30,000–40,000 people daily, with more coming on Sundays and festival days. About forty volunteers work in the kitchen each day.

Major Rites & Celebrations

In addition to the community feasts at temple langars, Sikhs honor four rites of passage in a person's life: naming, marriage, initiation in Khalsa (pure) through the Amrit ceremony, and death.

There are eight major celebrations and several other minor ones in Sikhism. Half of them commemorate events in the lives of the ten gurus.

The others are Baisakhi, the new year festival; Diwali, the festival of light, which Hindus also celebrate; Hola Mahalla, which Gobind Singh created as an alternative to the Hindu festival of Holi, and which involves military parades; and the installing of the Guru Granth Sahib.

ORIGINS

History & Geography

The founder of Sikhism, Nanak, was born in 1469 CE in the Punjab region of northeast India, where both Hinduism and Islam were practiced. Both of these religions wanted control of the region. Nanak wanted the fighting between followers of these two traditions to end and looked for solutions to the violence.

Nanak blended elements of both religions and also combined the traditional apparel of both faiths to construct his clothing style. The Guru Granth Sahib further explains the division between Sikhs and the Islamic and Muslim faiths:

Nanak would become the first guru of the Sikh religion, known as Guru Nanak Dev. A Muslim musician named Bhai Mardana, considered the first follower, accompanied Nanak in his travels around India and Asia. Guru Nanak often sang, and singing remains an important part of worship for Sikhs. Before his death, Nanak renamed one of his disciples Angad, a word meaning "a part of his own self." He became Guru Angad Dev, the second guru, thus beginning the tradition of designating a successor and passing on the light to that person.

Guru Baba Ram Das, the fourth guru, who lived in the sixteenth century, began constructing Amritsar's Golden Temple. The structure was completed by his successor, Guru Arjan Dev, who also collected poems and songs written by the first four gurus and added his own. He included the work of Kabir and other Hindu and Muslim holy men as well. This became the Adi Granth, which he placed in the Golden Temple.

Guru Arjan was martyred in 1606 by Jehangir, the Muslim emperor. His son Hargobind became the sixth guru and introduced several important practices and changes. He wore two swords, representing both spiritual and worldly authority. Near the Golden Temple he had a building known as Akal Takht, or Throne of the Almighty, erected. In it was a court of justice as well as a group of administrators. Even today, orders and decisions enter the community from Akal Takht. Guru Hargobind was the last of the gurus with a direct link to Amritsar. Because of conflict with the Muslim rulers, he and all subsequent gurus moved from the city.

The tenth guru, Gobind Singh, created the Khalsa, the Community of the Pure, in 1699. The members of the Khalsa were to be known by five distinctive elements, all beginning with the letter *k*. These include kes, the refusal to cut the hair or trim the beard; kangha, the comb used to keep the long hair neatly combed in contrast to the Hindu ascetics who had matted hair; kaccha, shorts that would allow soldiers quick movement; kara, a thin steel bracelet worn to symbolize restraint; and kirpan, a short sword not to be used except in self-defense. Among other duties, members of this elite group were to defend the faith. Until the middle of the nineteenth century, when the British created an empire in India, the Khalsa remained largely undefeated.

In 1708, Guru Gobind Singh announced that he would be the final human guru. All subsequent leadership would come from the Guru Granth Sahib, now considered a living guru, the holy text Arjan had begun compiling more than a century earlier.

Muslim persecution under the Mughals led to the defeat of the Sikhs in 1716. The remaining Sikhs headed for the hills, re-emerging after decline of Mughal power. They were united under Ranjit Singh's kingdom from 1820 to 1839. They then came under the control of the British.

The British annexed the Punjab region, making it part of their Indian empire in 1849, and recruited Sikhs to serve in the army. The Sikhs remained loyal to the British during the Indian Mutiny of 1857–1858. As a result, they were given many privileges and land grants, and with

peace and prosperity, the first Singh Sabha was founded in 1873. This was an educational and religious reform movement.

During the early twentieth century, Sikhism was shaped in its more modern form. A group known as the Tat Khalsa, which was more progressive, became the dominant way of understanding the faith.

In 1897, a group of Sikh musicians within the British Army was invited to attend the Diamond Jubilee of Queen Victoria in England. They also traveled to Canada and were attracted by the nation's prairies, which were perfect for farming. The first group of Sikhs came to Canada soon after. By 1904, more than two hundred Sikhs had settled in British Columbia. Some of them later headed south to Washington, Oregon, and California in the United States. The first Sikh gurdwara in the United States was constructed in Stockton, California, in 1912. Sikhs became farmers, worked in lumber mills, and helped to construct the Western Pacific railroad. Yuba City, California, has one of the world's largest Sikh temples, built in 1968.

Sikh troops fought for Britain in World War I, achieving distinction. Following the war, in 1919, however, the British denied the Sikhs the right to gather for their New Year festival. When the Sikhs disobeyed, the British troops fired without warning on 10,000 Sikhs, 400 of whom were killed. This became known as the first Amritsar Massacre.

The British government in 1925 did give the Sikhs the right to help manage their own shrines. A fragile peace ensued between the British and the Sikhs, who again fought for the British Empire during World War II.

After the war ended, the Sikh hope for an independent state was dashed by the partition of India and Pakistan in 1947. Pakistan was in the Punjab region; thus, 2.5 million Sikhs lived in a Muslim country where they were not welcome. Many of them became part of the mass internal migration that followed Indian independence.

In 1966, a state with a Sikh majority came into existence after Punjab boundaries were redrawn. Strife continued throughout second half of twentieth century, however, as a result of continuing demands for Punjab autonomy. A second massacre at Amritsar occurred in 1984, resulting in the death of 450 Sikhs (though some estimates of the death toll are higher). Indian troops, under orders from Indian Prime Minister Indira Gandhi, fired on militant leaders of Sikhs, who had gone to the Golden Temple for refuge. This attack was considered a desecration of a sacred place, and the prime minister was later assassinated by her Sikh bodyguards in response. Restoration of the Akal Takht, the administrative headquarters, took fifteen years. The Sikh library was also burned, consuming ancient manuscripts.

In 1999, Sikhs celebrated the three-hundredth anniversary of the founding of Khalsa. There has been relative peace in India since that event. In the United States, however, Sikhs became the object of slander and physical attack following the acts of terrorism on September 11, 2001, as some Americans could not differentiate between Arab head coverings and Sikh turbans.

Founder or Major Prophet

Guru Nanak Dev was born into a Hindu family on April 15, 1469. His family belonged to the merchant caste, Khatri. His father worked as an accountant for a Muslim, who was also a local landlord. Nanak was educated in both the Hindu and Islamic traditions. According to legends, his teachers soon realized they had nothing further to teach him. After a direct revelation from Ultimate Reality that he received as a young man, Nanak proclaimed that there was neither Muslim nor Hindu. God had told Nanak "Rejoice in my Name," which became a central doctrine of Sikhism.

Nanak began to preach, leaving his wife and two sons behind. According to tradition, he traveled not only throughout India, but also eventually to Iraq, Saudi Arabia, and Mecca. This tradition and others were collected in a volume known as Janamsakhis. A Muslim servant of the family, Mardana, who also played a three-stringed musical instrument called the rebec, accompanied him, as did a Hindu poet, Bala Sandhu, who had been a friend from childhood

(though the extent of his importance or existence is often considered controversial).

Nanak traveled as an itinerant preacher for a quarter century and then founded a village, Kartarpur, on the bank of Punjab's Ravi River. Before his death he chose his successor, beginning a tradition that was followed until the tenth and final human guru.

Philosophical Basis

When Guru Nanak Dev, the first guru, began preaching in 1499 at about age thirty, he incorporated aspects of both Hinduism and Islam. From Hinduism, he took the ideas of karma and reincarnation. From Islam, he borrowed the Ultimate as the name of God. Some scholars see the influence of the religious reformer and poet Kabir, who lived from 1440 until 1518. Kabir merged the Bhakti (devotional) side of Hinduism with the Islamic Sufis, who were mystics.

Within the Hindu tradition in northern India was a branch called the Sants. The Sants believed that God was both with form and without form, unable to be represented concretely. Most of the Sants were illiterate and poor, but created poems that spoke of the divine being experienced in all things. This idea also rooted itself in Sikhism.

Guru Nanak Dev, who was raised as a Hindu, rejected the caste system in favor of equality of all persons. He also upheld the value of women, rejecting the burning of widows and female infanticide. When eating a communal meal, first begun as a protest against caste, everyone sits in a straight line and shares karah prasad (a pudding), which is provided by those of all castes. However, Sikhs are expected to marry within their caste. In some cases, especially in the United Kingdom, gurdwaras (places of worship) for a particular caste exist.

Holy Places

Amritsar, especially the Golden Temple, which was built in the sixteenth century under the supervision of the fifth guru, Guru Arjan, is the most sacred city.

Ram Das, the fourth guru, first began constructing a pool on the site in 1577. He called it

Amritsar, the pool of nectar. This sacred reflecting pool is a pilgrimage destination. Steps on the southern side of the pool allow visitors to gather water in bottles, to drink it, to bathe in it, or to sprinkle it on themselves.

SIKHISM IN DEPTH

Sacred Symbols
The khanda is the major symbol of Sikhism. It features a two-edged sword, representing justice and freedom, in the center. It is surrounded by a circle, a symbol of both balance and of the unity of God and humankind. A pair of curved swords (kirpans) surrounds the circle. One sword stands for religious concerns, the other for secular concerns. The khanda appears on Sikh flags, which are flown over every temple.

Members of the Khalsa have five symbols. They do not cut their hair, and men do not trim their beards. This symbol, kes, is to indicate a harmony with the ways of nature. To keep the long hair neat, a comb called a kangha is used. The third symbol is the kara, a bracelet usually made of steel to represent continuity and strength. When the Khalsa was first formed, soldiers wore loose-fitting shorts called kaccha. They were worn to symbolize moral restraint and purity. The final symbol is a short sword known as a kirpan, to be used only in self-defense. When bathing in sacred waters, the kirpan is tucked into the turban, which is worn to cover the long hair. The turban, which may be one of many colors, is wound from nearly five yards of cloth.

Sacred Practices & Gestures
Sikhs use Sat Sri Akal (truth is timeless) as a greeting, putting hands together and bowing toward the other person. To show respect, Sikhs keep their heads covered with a turban or veil. Before entering a temple, they remove their shoes. Some Sikhs may choose to wear a bindhi, the dot on the forehead usually associated with Hinduism.

When Guru Gobind Singh initiated the first men into the Khalsa, he put water in a steel bowl and added sugar, stirring the mixture with his sword and reciting verses from the Guru Granth as he did so. He thus created amrit (immortal), a holy water also used in baptism, or the Amrit ceremony. The water represents mental clarity, while sugar stands for sweetness. The sword invokes military courage, and the chanting of verses brings a poetic spirituality.

The Sikh ideal of bringing Ultimate Reality into every aspect of the day is expressed in prayers throughout the day. Daily morning prayer (Bani) consists of five different verses, most of them the work of one of the ten gurus; there are also two sets of evening prayers. Throughout the day, Sikhs repeat the Mul Mantra, "Ikk Oan Kar" (There is one Being). This is the first line of a brief creedal statement about Ultimate Reality.

Food Restrictions
Sikhs are not to eat halal meat, which is the Muslim equivalent of kosher. Both tobacco and alcohol are forbidden. Many Sikhs are vegetarians, although this is not commanded. Members of the Khalsa are not permitted to eat meat slaughtered according to Islamic or Hindu methods, because they believe these means cause pain to the animal.

Rites, Celebrations, & Services
The Sikhs observe four rite of passage rituals, with each emphasizing their distinction from the Hindu traditions. After a new mother is able to get up and bathe, the new baby is given a birth and naming ceremony in the gurdwara. The child is given a name based on the first letter of hymn from the Guru Granth Sahib at random. All males are additionally given the name Singh (lion); all females also receive the name Kaur (princess).

The marriage ceremony (anand karaj) is the second rite of passage. Rather than circle a sacred fire as the Hindus do, the Sikh couple walks four times around a copy of the Guru Granth Sahib, accompanied by singing. The bride often wears red, a traditional color for the Punjabi.

The amrit initiation into the Khalsa is considered the most important rite. It need not take place in a temple, but does require that five

Sikhs who are already Khalsa members conduct the ceremony. Amrit initiation may occur any time after a child is old enough to read the Guru Granth and understand the tenets of the faith. Some people, however, wait until their own children are grown before accepting this rite.

The funeral rite is the fourth and final rite of passage. A section of the Guru Granth is read. The body, dressed in the Five "K's," is cremated soon after death.

Initiation into the Khalsa is now open to both men and women. The earliest gurus opposed the Hindu custom of sati, which required a widow to be burned on her husband's funeral pyre. They were also against the Islamic custom of purdah, which required women to be veiled and covered in public. Women who are menstruating are not excluded from worship, as they are in some religions. Women as well as men can be leaders of the congregation and are permitted to read from the Guru Granth and recite sacred hymns.

The Sikh houses of worship are known as gurdwaras and include a langar, the communal dining area. People remove their shoes and cover their heads before entering. They touch their foreheads to the floor in front of the scripture to show respect. The service itself is in three parts. The first segment is Kirtan, singing hymns (kirtans) accompanied by musical instruments, which can last for several hours. It is followed by a set prayer called the Ardas, which has three parts. The first and final sections cannot be altered. In the first, the virtues of the gurus are extolled. In the last, the divine name is honored. In the center of the Ardas is a list of the Khalsa's troubles and victories, which a prayer leader recites in segments and to which the congregation responds with Vahiguru, considered a word for God. At the end of the service, members eat karah prasad, sacred food made of raw sugar, clarified butter, and coarse wheat flour. They then adjourn for a communal meal, Langar, the third section of worship.

Sikhism does not have a set day for worship similar to the Jewish Sabbath or Christian Sunday worship. However, the first day of the month on the Indian lunar calendar, sangrand,

and the darkest night of the month, masia, are considered special days. Sangrand is a time for praying for the entire month. Masia is often considered an auspicious time for bathing in the holy pool at the temple.

Four of the major festivals that Sikhs observe surround important events in the lives of the gurus. These are known as gurpurabs, or anniversaries. Guru Nanak's birthday, Guru Gobind Singh's birthday, and the martyrdoms of the Gurus Arjan and Tegh Bahadur comprise the four main gurpurabs. Sikhs congregate in the gurudwaras to hear readings of the Guru Granth and lectures by Sikh scholars.

Baisakhi is the Indian New Year, the final day before the harvest begins. On this day in 1699, Guru Gobind Singh formed the first Khalsa, adding even more importance to the day for Sikhs. Each year, a new Sikh flag is placed at all temples.

Diwali, based on a word meaning string of lights, is a Hindu festival. For Sikhs, it is a time to remember the return of the sixth guru, Hargobind, to Amritsar after the emperor had imprisoned him. It is celebrated for three days at the Golden Temple. Sikhs paint and whitewash their houses and decorate them with candles and earthenware lamps.

Hola Mohalla, meaning attack and place of attack, is the Sikh spring festival, which corresponds to the Hindu festival Holi. It is also a three-day celebration and a time for training Sikhs as soldiers. Originally, it involved military exercises and mock battles, as well as competitions in archery, horsemanship, and wrestling. In contemporary times, the festival includes athletic contests, discussion, and singing.

Judy A. Johnson, MTS

Bibliography

Barnes, Trevor. *The Kingfisher Book of Religions*. New York: Kingfisher, 1999. Print.

Dhanjal, Beryl. *Amritsar*. New York: Dillon, 1993. Print.

Dhavan, Purnima. *When Sparrows Became Hawks: The Making of the Sikh Warrior Tradition, 1699–1799*. Oxford: Oxford UP, 2011. Print.

Eraly, Abraham, et. al. *India*. New York: DK, 2008.
    Print.

Harley, Gail M. *Hindu and Sikh Faiths in America*.
    New York: Facts on File, 2003. Print.

Jakobsh, Doris R. *Sikhism and Women: History,
    Texts, and Experience*. Oxford, New York: Oxford
    UP, 2010. Print.

Jhutti-Johal, Jagbir. *Sikhism Today*. London, New
    York: Continuum, 2011. Print.

Langley, Myrtle. *Religion*. New York: Knopf, 1996.
    Print.

Mann, Gurinder Singh. *Sikhism*. Upper Saddle River:
    Prentice, 2004. Print.

Meredith, Susan. *The Usborne Book of World
    Religions*. London: Usborne, 1995. Print.

Sidhu, Dawinder S. and Neha Singh Gohil. *Civil
    Rights in Wartime: The Post-9/11 Sikh Experience*.
    Ashgate, 2009. E-book.

Singh, Nikky-Guninder Kaur. *Sikhism*. New York:
    Facts on File, 1993. Print.

Singh, Nikky-Guninder Kaur. *Sikhism: An
    Introduction*. Tauris, 2011. E-book.

Singh, Surinder. *Introduction to Sikhism and Great
    Sikhs of the World*. Gurgaon: Shubhi, 2012. Print.

Wilkinson, Philip. *Religions*. New York: DK, 2008.
    Print.

Index